Laboratory Manual to accompany

Prego!

AN INVITATION TO ITALIAN

EIGHTH EDITION

Andrea Dini
Montclair State University
Graziana Lazzarino
University of Colorado, Boulder

Mc Graw Hill
Connect Learn Succeed™

The McGraw-Hill Companies

Laboratory Manual to accompany
Prego! *An Invitation to Italian*

Published by McGraw-Hill, an imprint of The McGraw-Hill Companies, Inc., 1221 Avenue of the Americas, New York, NY 10020.

1 2 3 4 5 6 7 8 9 0 QDB QDB 0 9 8 7 6 5 4 3 2 1

ISBN: 978-0-07-738248-3
MHID: 0-07-738248-X

Vice President, Editorial: *Michael Ryan*
Editorial Director: *William R. Glass*
Publisher: *Katie Stevens*
Senior Sponsoring Editor: *Katherine K. Crouch*
Director of Development: *Susan Blatty*
Development Editor: *Sylvie L. Waskiewicz*
Executive Marketing Manager: *Héctor Alvero*
Production Editor: *Jasmin Tokatlian*
Buyer: *Louis Swaim*
Compositor: *Aptara®, Inc.*
Typeface: *Palatino*
Printer: *Quad/Graphics Dubuque*

Grateful acknowledgment is made for use of the following material:
All cartoons by permission of E'unidea s.r.l., Milan.

http://www.mhhe.com

Contents

Preface

This *Laboratory Manual* accompanies *Prego! An Invitation to Italian,* Eighth Edition.

The *Laboratory Manual* is coordinated with the *Audio Program* for the preliminary chapter and the eighteen regular chapters. A separate disc with the **In ascolto** activities is included. Each chapter has forty to fifty minutes of recorded material. The speech on the audio program represents that of many regions of Italy; the language is authentic Italian.

We suggest that students listen to the recorded material on a given vocabulary or grammar section only after that material has been covered in class. We also recommend that students spend no more than thirty minutes at a time in the laboratory. A total of sixty minutes per week should allow students time to listen to the entire chapter at least once and to repeat any material on which they feel they need additional practice.

The *Laboratory Manual* is a guide to the audio. Directions for all recorded activities are in the manual, with a model provided for most. In some cases, cues and drawings to be used with activities appear in the manual; at other times, cues are heard on the recording only.

The **Capitolo preliminare** follows the corresponding chapter in the student text point-by-point. It introduces students to the basic sounds of Italian and to a variety of useful, everyday expressions, concluding with an open-ended activity.

Changes in This Eighth Edition

- The changes to the *Laboratory Manual* reflect those made to the chapter vocabulary lists and the scope and sequence of the student text. Note that exercises have been added for the **Ancora i plurali (Capitolo 2)** and **Il gerundio (Capitolo 15)** sections, which are new to the eighth edition.
- All materials in the *Laboratory Manual* have been carefully checked to ensure that vocabulary and grammar are glossed when they are not yet active. Thus instructors will note more glossing in this edition than in previous editions, both in exercise sections (where **Parole utili** give words needed to complete a given activity) and in listening comprehension activities.
- The **Sara in Italia** dialogues have been reordered and revised to match the reorganization of the regional coverage (**L'Italia regionale**) in the student text.

Chapter Organization

Chapters 1–18 of the *Laboratory Manual* are organized as follows:

Vocabolario preliminare and **Grammatica.** These sections follow the sequence of material in the student text point-by-point. They include minidialogues and listening comprehension activities, in addition to grammar and vocabulary exercises. The **In ascolto** activities have also been integrated into each chapter at the end of the **Vocabolario** section.

Pronuncia. Capitolo 1 through **Capitolo 13** include focused practice of Italian sounds and intonation patterns.

Ed ora ascoltiamo! These short comprehension passages with simple follow-up activities help students focus on key information as they listen.

Dettato. A short dictation improves recognition of phonetic sounds and how to write them.

Dialogo. These extended passages (which include everyday conversations, a housing interview, and an oral exam given by a professor to a student) and their follow-up activities help improve students' global comprehension skills.

Sara in Italia. This light-hearted feature follows Sara, a young American woman, throughout her travels in Italy. It provides additional listening comprehension practice as well as cultural and geographical information to wrap up each chapter. Related links and keywords for this section can be found in the **Sara in rete...** feature on the ***Prego!*** website.

Answers to most activities are on the recording. A number of activities require written responses. Answers to these and to the dictations can be found at the back of this manual. The *Audioscript* is available to instructors only and can be found in the Instructor's Edition of the *Prego!* Online Learning Center (**www.mhhe.com/prego8**).

CAPITOLO
preliminare

Buon giorno, Italia!

A. Saluti e espressioni di cortesia

A. Presentazioni. You will hear two professors introduce themselves to their classes. The first time, listen carefully. Pay attention to rhythm and intonation. The second time, write the missing words. The third time, the introductions will be read with pauses for repetition. Repeat after the speakers and check what you have written. Then check your answers in the Answer Key.

1. Buon giorno. __________ __________[1] Marco Villoresi. ____________________[2] professore di italiano. Sono ____________________[3] Firenze.

2. Buon ____________________.[4] __________ __________[5] Alessandra Stefanin. Sono ____________________[6] di italiano. Sono di Venezia.

B. E io, chi (*who*) sono? Now, following the examples, introduce yourself. Use the greetings you find most appropriate. First listen. Then introduce yourself.

ESEMPI: STUDENTE 1: Buon giorno. Mi chiamo Brian Johnson. Sono studente di italiano. Sono di Knoxville.

STUDENTE 2: Salve. Mi chiamo Aliza Wong. Sono studentessa di italiano. Sono di Portland. E tu, chi sei?

Now introduce yourself, following one of the preceding models.

C. Formale o informale? You will hear three different dialogues in which people introduce themselves to each other. The first time, listen carefully. Pay attention to rhythm and intonation. The second time, write the missing words. The third time, the dialogues will be read with pauses for repetition. After repeating the dialogues, decide whether the situation presented is formal or informal, **formale o informale.** You will hear the answers at the end of the exercise. Check your written answers in the Answer Key.

DIALOGUE 1:
Professor Villoresi and Professoressa Stefanin meet for the first time at a professional meeting.

PROFESSORESSA STEFANIN: Buon giorno. Mi chiamo Alessandra Stefanin.

PROFESSOR VILLORESI: Ah, ______________[1]! Marco Villoresi. Sono di Firenze. ______________[2] Lei?

PROFESSORESSA STEFANIN: ______________[3] di Venezia! Piacere!

Now indicate whether the dialogue is formal or informal.

formale informale

DIALOGUE 2:
A student sees his professor in a restaurant.

STUDENTE: Buona sera, professor Villoresi! Come va?

PROFESSOR VILLORESI: ______________,[1] grazie. E ______________[2]?

STUDENTE: Non c'è ______________.[3]

PROFESSOR VILLORESI: Arrivederci.

STUDENTE: ______________.[4]

Now indicate whether the dialogue is formal or informal.

formale informale

DIALOGUE 3:
Laura meets her friend Roberto.

LAURA: Ciao, Roberto! Come ______________[1]?

ROBERTO: Non c'è male. E ______________[2]?

LAURA: Bene, grazie!

ROBERTO: ______________[3]!

LAURA: Ciao!

Now indicate whether the dialogue is formal or informal.

formale informale

D. Conversazioni brevi (*short*)**.** You will hear a short phrase or expression. You will hear each one twice. Listen carefully, then indicate the most appropriate response to what you have heard. Scan the choices now.

1. _____ a. Così così.
2. _____ b. Buona sera, signora Gilli.
3. _____ c. Prego!
4. _____ d. Buona notte, mamma.
5. _____ e. Mi chiamo Roberto, piacere!

In ascolto

Conversazioni. Take a moment to read over the options listed below. Then, listen to the four brief conversations and select the relationship between the speakers you consider most plausible. Check your answers in the Answer Key.

1. _____ professoressa e studente
   _____ due (*two*) studenti
   _____ madre e figlio (*mother and son*)
2. _____ colleghi di lavoro (*co-workers*)
   _____ madre e figlio
   _____ due studenti
3. _____ professoressa e studente
   _____ colleghi di lavoro
   _____ madre e figlio
4. _____ professoressa e studente
   _____ due studenti
   _____ madre e figlio

B. In classe

A. Alla (*To the*) **classe.** The instructor has asked the class to perform some actions. Match what you hear with the actions performed by the students in the drawings. Write the appropriate command from the list next to the corresponding drawing (on the next page). Then check your answers in the Answer Key. Scan the list of directions now.

Aprite il libro! Ripetete **buona notte,** per favore!
Chiudete il libro! Scrivete!

1. ______________________

2. ______________________

3. ______________________

4. ______________________

B. Come si dice? You will hear a series of brief classroom exchanges. You will hear each one twice. The first time, listen carefully. The second time, complete the dialogues with the expressions you hear. Check your answers in the Answer Key.

1. PROFESSORESSA: Paolo, ______________________[1] si ______________________[2] *alphabet* in italiano?
   STUDENTE: Alfabeto.
   PROFESSORESSA: Giusto! Benissimo!
2. STUDENTESSA: ______________________,[3] professore, come si ______________________[4] **classe?**
   PROFESSORE: C L A S S E.
   STUDENTESSA: ______________________,[5] professore.
   PROFESSORE: ______________________,[6] signorina.
3. PROFESSORESSA: ______________________[7] il libro e fate (*do*) l'esercizio.
   STUDENTE: ______________________[8]? Non ______________________.[9] Ripeta, per ______________________.[10]

C. A lezione. (*In class.*) What would you say in Italian in the following situations? Repeat the response.

ESEMPIO: *You read:* You want your instructor to repeat something.
You say: Ripeta, per favore!
You hear: Ripeta, per favore!
You repeat: Ripeta, per favore!

1. You want to know how to pronounce a word.
2. You do not understand what your instructor has said.

3. You want to know how to say *excuse me* in Italian.
4. You want to ask what something means.
5. You did not hear clearly what your instructor said.
6. You do not know how to spell a word.

D. Ecco (*Here is*) **una classe!** As you hear the word in Italian for each numbered object, find it listed in the box. Then write the word in the space provided under the corresponding drawing. Check your answers in the Answer Key.

un quaderno	una penna
	un libro
una matita	una sedia

1. ______________________

2. ______________________

3. ______________________

4. ______________________

5. ______________________

C. Alfabeto e suoni

A. «Nella vecchia fattoria... » (*"On the old farm . . . "*) You will hear a reading of «**Nella vecchia fattoria**». You will hear it twice. The first time, listen carefully. The second time, it will be read with pauses for repetition.

Nella vecchia fattoria, ia-ia-o!
Quante° bestie ha zio Tobia,° ia-ia-o! — *How many* / ha... *does uncle Tobias have*
C'è il cane (bau!) cane (bau!) ca-ca-cane,
e il gatto (miao!) gatto (miao!) ga-ga-gatto,
e la mucca (muu!) mucca (muu!) mu-mu-mucca...
nella vecchia fattoria ia-ia-o!

B. L'alfabeto italiano. You will hear the names of the letters of the Italian alphabet, along with male and female Italian names. Listen and repeat, imitating the speaker. Starting in Chapter 1, you will practice the pronunciation of most of these letters individually.

a	a	Andrea	Antonella
b	bi	Bernardo	Beatrice
c	ci	Carlo	Cecilia
d	di	Daniele	Donatella
e	e	Emanuele	Enrica
f	effe	Fabrizio	Federica
g	gi	Giacomo	Gabriella
h	acca*		
i	i	Italo	Irene
l	elle	Luca	Lorella
m	emme	Marco	Marcella
n	enne	Nicola	Nora
o	o	Osvaldo	Ombretta
p	pi	Paolo	Patrizia
q	cu	Quirino	Quirina
r	erre	Roberto	Roberta
s	esse	Sergio	Simona
t	ti	Tommaso	Teresa
u	u	Umberto	Ursola
v	vu	Vittorio	Vanessa
z	zeta	Zeno	Zita

Now listen to the pronunciation of the following five letters, which are used in Italian with words of foreign origin. Repeat each one after the speaker.

j	i lunga
k	cappa
w	doppia vu
x	ics
y	ipsilon

C. Lettere. Repeat the following abbreviations or formulas after the speaker.

1. K.O.
2. PR
3. LP
4. H_2O
5. CD
6. PC
7. S.O.S
8. P.S.
9. DVD
10. Raggi X (*X-rays*)

*There are no Italian proper names beginning with **h.**

D. Come si pronuncia? You will hear the spelling of eight words you may not know. Write them down and then try to pronounce them. Repeat the response. Then check your answers and their translations in the Answer Key.

ESEMPIO: *You hear:* a-doppia erre-e-di-a-emme-e-enne-ti-o
You write: arredamento
You say: arredamento
You hear: arredamento
You repeat: arredamento

1. ______________________
2. ______________________
3. ______________________
4. ______________________
5. ______________________
6. ______________________
7. ______________________
8. ______________________

E. Vocali. Listen to and repeat the sounds of the seven Italian vowels and some words in which they are used. Note that vowels **e** and **o** have both closed and open forms.

Vocabolario preliminare: chiusa (*closed*), aperta (*open*)

a	patata, casa, sala, banana
e chiusa	sete, e, sera, verde
e aperta	letto, è, bello, testa
i	pizza, vino, birra, timo
o chiusa	nome, dove, ora, volo
o aperta	posta, corda, porta, bosco
u	rude, luna, uno, cubo

F. Ancora (*More*) **vocali.** Repeat each word after the speaker.

1. pazzo / pezzo / pizzo / pozzo / puzzo
2. casa / case / casi / caso
3. lana / lena / Lina / luna
4. auto / aiuto / iuta / uva / uova / Europa / aiuola

G. Consonanti *c* e *g*. C and **g** each have two sounds in Italian. Their sound is hard (as in English *cat* and *get*) when followed directly by **a, o, u,** or **h.** Their sound is soft (as in English *chain* and *giraffe*) when followed directly by **e** or **i.** Repeat each word after the speaker.

1. cane / casa / gatto / gamba
2. cibo / cera / gesso / gita
3. cena / che / getta / ghetto
4. Cina / chilo / giro / ghiro
5. gotta / Giotto / cotta / cioccolato
6. custode / ciuffo / gusto / giusto

H. Consonanti doppie. In this exercise you will practice the difference between single and double consonant sounds. Repeat each word after the speaker. Note that vowels before a double consonant are shorter in length than vowels before a single consonant. Notice the differences in pronunciation in the following two pairs of words.

carro (short **a** sound) ≠ **caro** (long **a** sound)

cassa (short **a** sound) ≠ **casa** (long **a** sound)

1. pala / palla
2. moto / motto
3. fato / fatto
4. nono / nonno
5. dita / ditta
6. sete / sette
7. papa / pappa
8. sono / sonno

I. Accento tonico. Can you hear where the stress falls in an Italian word? Underline the stressed vowel in each of the following words. You will hear each word twice. Then check your answers in the Answer Key.

1. grammatica
2. importanza
3. partire
4. partirò
5. musica
6. trentatré
7. subito
8. umiltà
9. abitano
10. cantavano

J. Accento scritto. Can you tell where a written accent is used in Italian? Remember, if written accents appear in Italian, they do so only on the final syllable of a word when that syllable is stressed. Add a grave accent (`) only when necessary to the following words. You will hear each word twice. Then check your answers in the Answer Key.

1. prendere
2. prendero
3. caffe
4. universita
5. cinquanta
6. civilta
7. virtu
8. tornare

D. Numeri da uno a cento

A. Numeri. Repeat the numbers after the speaker.

0	zero	11	undici	30	trenta
1	uno	12	dodici	40	quaranta
2	due	13	tredici	50	cinquanta
3	tre	14	quattordici	60	sessanta
4	quattro	15	quindici	70	settanta
5	cinque	16	sedici	80	ottanta
6	sei	17	diciassette	90	novanta
7	sette	18	diciotto	100	cento
8	otto	19	diciannove		
9	nove	20	venti		
10	dieci	21	ventuno		

B. Prefissi e numeri di telefono. (*Area codes and telephone numbers.*) Repeat the following area codes and phone numbers after the speaker.

ESEMPIO: *You read and hear:* (0574) 46-07-87
You say: prefisso: zero-cinque-sette-quattro;
numero di telefono: quarantasei-zero sette-ottantasette

1. (0574) 46-86-30
2. (055) 66-43-27
3. (06) 36-25-81-48
4. (02) 61-11-50
5. (075) 23-97-08
6. (0573) 62-91-78

Nome ________________ Data ________ Classe ________________

In ascolto

Numeri di telefono. Take a moment to look over the telephone numbers listed below. Then, listen carefully and indicate the number you hear for each person or business. Check your answers in the Answer Key.

1. ______ Elisabetta
   a. 77-31-32
   b. 67-21-32
   c. 66-48-35
2. ______ Pasticceria Vanini
   a. 94-19-35
   b. 35-78-22
   c. 44-78-16
3. ______ signora Cecchettini
   a. 21-51-83
   b. 91-15-53
   c. 98-12-35
4. ______ Ristorante Bianchi
   a. 12-18-26
   b. 12-38-37
   c. 13-18-21

E. Calendario

A. Giorni della settimana. Write down the days of the week as you hear them. Then say them in the correct order. Check your answers in the Answer Key.

1. ____________________
2. ____________________
3. ____________________
4. ____________________
5. ____________________
6. ____________________
7. ____________________

B. I mesi. Repeat the names of the months in Italian, after the speaker.

gennaio	maggio	settembre
febbraio	giugno	ottobre
marzo	luglio	novembre
aprile	agosto	dicembre

C. In che mese? You will hear a series of questions about national holidays. Each question will be said twice. Listen carefully, then say the name of the month in which each holiday falls. Repeat the response.

ESEMPIO: *You hear:* In che mese è il giorno di Cristoforo Colombo?
You say: In ottobre.
You hear: In ottobre.
You repeat: In ottobre.

1. … 2. … 3. … 4. …

Sara in Italia

Sara, a student at the University of Wisconsin–Madison, is traveling through Italy to perfect her Italian. You will accompany her on her visit throughout the peninsula as she discovers Italian cities and meets and converses with Italians.

Now, listen as she introduces herself. Listen carefully, as many times as you need to. Then, answer the questions you hear. You will hear each question twice. Repeat the response.

Parole utili: mi piace viaggiare (*I like to travel*)

1. … 2. … 3. … 4. …

Sara in rete...

For more information about what Sara experienced during her travels, check out the links found on the *Prego!* website **(www.mhhe.com/prego8).**

CAPITOLO

Una città italiana 1

Vocabolario preliminare

A. Per cominciare. You will hear a short dialogue followed by a series of statements about the dialogue. Each statement will be read twice. Circle **vero** if the statement is true or **falso** if it is false.

STUDENTE: Scusi, Signora, un'informazione. C'è una farmacia qui vicino?
SIGNORA: Sì, in Via Marco Polo. Sempre dritto e poi a sinistra. Vicino ci sono due negozi e un cinema.
STUDENTE: Grazie e buon giorno!
SIGNORA: Prego e arrivederci!

1. vero falso
2. vero falso
3. vero falso

B. In una stazione italiana. You will hear a dialogue followed by five questions. You will hear the dialogue twice. The first time, listen carefully, paying attention to rhythm and intonation. The second time, Patrick's lines will be followed by pauses for repetition. Then answer the questions. Repeat the response.

PATRICK: Buon giorno. Due biglietti per Firenze, per favore.
IMPIEGATO: Scusi, un momento. Che destinazione?
PATRICK: Firenze.
IMPIEGATO: Bene, ecco i due biglietti per Firenze e il supplemento per l'Eurostar. Va bene?
PATRICK: Va bene. Scusi, un'informazione. C'è un ufficio postale qui in stazione?
IMPIEGATO: No, non in stazione, ma qui vicino, in Via Gramsci.
PATRICK: Grazie e arrivederci.
IMPIEGATO: Prego! Buona giornata!

1. … 2. … 3. … 4. … 5. …

C. Mezzi di trasporto. You will hear five vehicle sounds. Listen carefully to the audio, then tell which vehicle you associate with the sound you hear. Use **È...** (*It's . . .*) in your answer. Repeat the response.

ESEMPIO: *You hear:* (train sounds)
You read: un treno / un aeroplano
You say: È un treno.

1. un'auto / una moto
2. un autobus / una macchina
3. un aeroplano / un treno
4. una moto / una bicicletta
5. un treno / un autobus

D. Luoghi. You will hear six sounds of places around town. Listen carefully, then name the place you associate with the sound you hear. Use **È...** (*It's . . .*) in your answer. Repeat the response.

ESEMPIO: *You hear:* (bells ringing)
You say: È una chiesa.

1. … 2. … 3. … 4. … 5. … 6. …

E. In città. You will hear a series of statements about where things are located in the city center. You will hear each statement twice. Listen carefully, then circle **vero** if the statement is true or **falso** if it is false. First, stop the audio and look over the map.

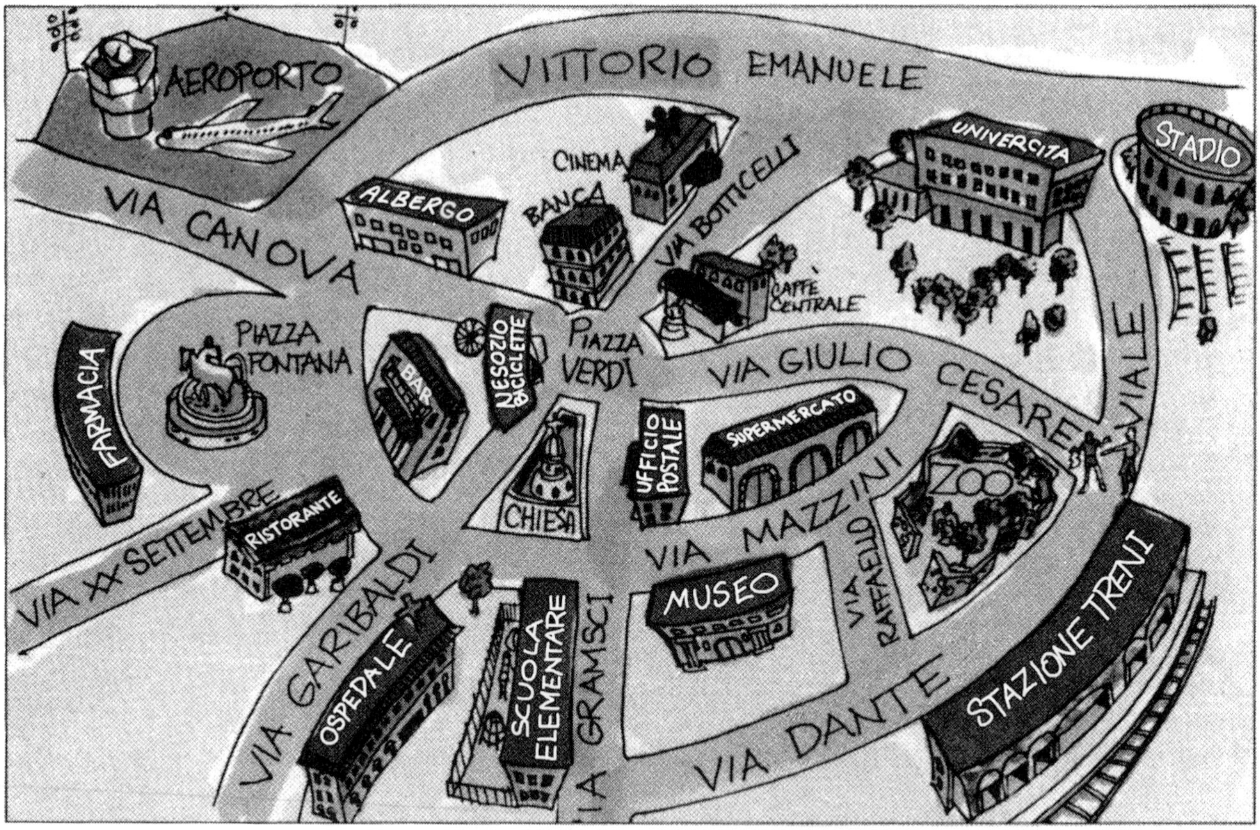

ESEMPIO: *You hear:* C'è una farmacia in Piazza Verdi.
You circle: vero / falso

1.	vero	falso	4.	vero	falso
2.	vero	falso	5.	vero	falso
3.	vero	falso	6.	vero	falso

In ascolto

In centro. (*Downtown.*) Listen carefully and refer to the map of the city on page 12. Decide whether the statements you hear are true (**vero**) or false (**falso**). Check your answers in the Answer Key.

Parole utili: tra (*in between*)

1. vero falso
2. vero falso
3. vero falso

You will hear three questions about the locations of three buildings in the city. Listen carefully, refer to the map, and write down the answers. Check your answers in the Answer Key.

4. _______________
5. _______________
6. _______________

Grammatica

A. Nomi: genere e numero

A. Per cominciare. You will hear a dialogue twice. The first time, listen carefully. The second time, the dialogue will be read with pauses for repetition. Pay careful attention to rhythm and intonation.

CAMERIERE: Buon giorno, signorine! Prego…
DANIELA: Un panino e un'aranciata, grazie.
CHIARA: Per me un cappuccino e due paste.
[…]
DANIELA: Quant'è?
CAMERIERE: Sono dieci euro.
DANIELA: Ecco quindici dollari, va bene?

B. In una stazione. Alessandra, Marco, and their son Leonardo are waiting for their train. It's past noon and they are getting hungry. You will hear their dialogue twice. Complete the chart by marking an **X** in the box corresponding to the food or drink bought for each person. Check your answers in the Answer Key. Scan the chart now.

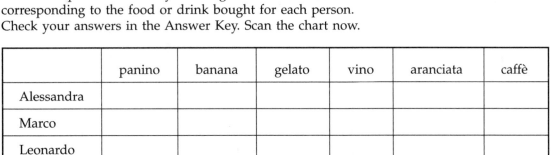

	panino	banana	gelato	vino	aranciata	caffè
Alessandra						
Marco						
Leonardo						

C. Maschile o femminile? You will hear eight words twice. Indicate their gender by circling **maschile** or **femminile** (*masculine or feminine*), as appropriate.

ESEMPIO: *You hear:* ristorante
You circle: (maschile) femminile

1. maschile femminile
2. maschile femminile
3. maschile femminile
4. maschile femminile
5. maschile femminile
6. maschile femminile
7. maschile femminile
8. maschile femminile

D. Singolare e plurale. Give the plural forms of the following words. Repeat the response.

ESEMPIO: *You hear:* macchina
You say: macchine

1. … 2. … 3. … 4. … 5. … 6. …

B. Articolo indeterminativo e *buono*

A. Per cominciare. You will hear a dialogue twice. The first time, listen carefully. The second time, the dialogue will be read with pauses for repetition.

CLIENTE: Buon giorno! Un biglietto per Venezia, per favore.
IMPIEGATO: Ecco! Sono cinquantasette euro.
CLIENTE: Ah, scusi, un'informazione. C'è un ufficio cambio qui in stazione?
IMPIEGATO: No, ma c'è una banca qui vicino, in Piazza Garibaldi.
CLIENTE: Grazie e arrivederci!
IMPIEGATO: Prego! Buona giornata!

B. Le valige. Fabio is packing his bags for a trip to the United States. He is listing all the things he will need. Listen carefully to his list and check the items that he needs to take with him. You will hear the list twice. Check your answers in the Answer Key.

un biglietto aereo
un diario
una mappa della città
una valigia grande
una carta di credito
un passaporto
uno zaino
una carta d'identità

C. Un buon caffè in aeroporto... Fabio savors his last Italian coffee at the airport bar and comments on how good all the food is. First, stop the audio and complete the following passage with the correct form of **buono.** Then start the audio and listen to Fabio's praise. Check your answers in the Answer Key. Now stop the audio and complete the passage.

FABIO: Che ____________________[1] bar è questo! Ha un ____________________[2] espresso, un ____________________[3] cappuccino e ____________________[4] panini, una ____________________[5] aranciata, una ____________________[6] bibita,[a] un ____________________[7] vino e ____________________[8] liquori.

[a]*soft drink*

D. Auguri. (*Best wishes.*) At Fabio's departure his family exclaimed, **Buon viaggio!** Now send your wishes using the following list of words, with the appropriate forms of **buono.** Say each expression in the pause after the item number. Repeat the response.

ESEMPIO: *You read:* viaggio
You say: Buon viaggio!

1. Natale (*m., Christmas*)
2. Pasqua (*Easter*)
3. Anno (*New Year*)
4. appetito
5. domenica
6. fortuna (*luck*)
7. week-end (*m.*)
8. vacanze (*vacation*)

C. Presente di *avere* e pronomi soggetto

A. Per cominciare. You will hear a dialogue twice. The first time, listen carefully. The second time, it will be read with pauses for repetition. Pay careful attention to rhythm and intonation.

MASSIMO: E Lei, signora, ha parenti in America?
SIGNORA PARODI: No, Massimo, non ho parenti, solo amici. E tu, hai qualcuno?
MASSIMO: Sì, ho uno zio in California e una zia in Florida.

B. Parenti in America. The following dialogue will be read twice. The first time, listen carefully. The second time, write the missing words. Check your answers in the Answer Key.

MASSIMO: Ecco qui, signora Parodi, in questa[a] foto ____________________[1] sono con uno zio a Disneyland e qui sono a Miami, con un cugino. ____________________[2] sono[b] di Los Angeles.

SIGNORA PARODI: ____________________[3] parenti in America?

[a]*this* [b]*they are*

MASSIMO: Sì, ________[4] uno zio in California e una zia in Virginia. E ________[5] e il signor Parodi, ________[6] parenti in America?

SIGNORA PARODI: No, Massimo, non ________[7] parenti, solo amici.

C. Cosa abbiamo? Tell what the following people have, using the oral and written cues. Repeat the response.

ESEMPIO: *You read and hear:* tu
You hear: una macchina
You say: Tu hai una macchina.

1. Roberto ed io
2. Giancarlo e Patrizia
3. tu e Elisa
4. una studentessa
5. uno studente

D. Una domanda? You will hear some phrases that can be either statements or questions. Each phrase will be read twice. Listen carefully to the intonation used and circle *statement* or *question,* as appropriate.

ESEMPIO: *You hear:* Hai fame.
You circle: (statement) question

1. statement question
2. statement question
3. statement question
4. statement question
5. statement question
6. statement question

E. Fare domande. Ask questions based on the following drawings. Use the oral and written cues. Repeat the response.

ESEMPIO: 

You hear and see: una Ferrari
You read: tu
You say: Hai una Ferrari?

1. 

Marco

2. 

Mario e Danila

3. 

tu e Valerio

4. 

io e Leslie

5. 

io

F. Persone, persone... You will hear a series of statements. Circle the pronoun that refers to the subject of each sentence. As you know, Italian doesn't need to have an expressed subject in its sentences, since the verb endings tell who is doing what. Concentrate on the verb endings and circle the corresponding subject pronoun.

1.	io	tu	4.	noi	loro
2.	noi	voi	5.	lui	voi
3.	io	lei	6.	tu	lei

D. Espressioni idiomatiche con *avere*

A. Per cominciare. You will hear a dialogue twice. The first time, listen carefully. The second time, write the missing words. Check your answers in the Answer Key.

ANGELO: Oh, che caldo. ______________________[1] proprio sete adesso.

Hai ______________________[2] di un'aranciata?

SILVIA: No, ma ho ______________________.[3] Ho voglia ______________________[4] un buon panino e di un gelato...

ANGELO: Chissà se c'è un ristorante in questa stazione...

SILVIA: Sì, c'è, ma non ______________________[5] tempo, solo cinque minuti.

ANGELO: ______________________[6] ______________________,[7] non è una buon'idea. Oh, ma c'è un bar qui vicino, che fortuna!

B. Come sta Gilda? Look at the illustrations and tell how Gilda is doing today. Respond during the pause after each item number. Repeat the response.

ESEMPIO: *You see:*

You say: Gilda ha freddo.

1.

2.

3.

C. Fame, freddo, sete, caldo, sonno. State a logical conclusion to each sentence that you hear about the following people. Write your answer in the space provided. Check your answers in the Answer Key.

ESEMPIO: *You read:* Mario
You hear: Mario ha voglia di un panino.

You say and write: Ha fame.

Parole utili: inverno (*winter*), estate (*summer*)

1. Alessandro: ________________
2. Anna: ________________
3. Sonia: ________________
4. Riccardo: ________________
5. tu: ________________

D. E tu? Answer the following questions about yourself. Answer each question in the pause provided.

1. … 2. … 3. … 4. … 5. …

Pronuncia: The sounds of the letter "c"

As you learned in the **Capitolo preliminare, c** represents two sounds: [k] as in the English word *cat,* and [č] as in the English word *cheese.* Remember that **c** *never* represents the [s] sound in Italian.

A. *C* dura. The [k] sound occurs when **c** is followed directly by **a, o, u, h,** or another consonant. Listen and repeat.

1. caldo
2. come
3. cugina
4. che
5. chi
6. clima
7. crema
8. macchina
9. fresche
10. ics

B. *C* dolce. The [č] sound occurs when **c** is followed directly by **e** or **i.** Listen and repeat.

1. cena
2. città
3. ciao
4. ciglio
5. ciuffo
6. piacere
7. ricetta
8. aranciata
9. diciotto
10. piaciuto

C. ***C* e doppia *c*.** Compare and contrast the single and double sound. Note the slight change in vowel sound when the consonant that follows is doubled. Listen and repeat.

1. aceto / accetto
2. caci / cacci
3. bacato / baccano
4. cucù / cucchiaio

D. **Parliamo** (*Let's speak*) **italiano!** You will hear each sentence twice. Listen and repeat.

1. Il cinema è vicino al supermercato.
2. Cameriere, una cioccolata ed un caffè, per piacere!
3. Come si pronuncia **bicicletta?**
4. Michelangelo è un nome, non un cognome.

Ed ora ascoltiamo!

You will hear a conversation between Dottor Ricci and Gina. Listen carefully, as many times as you need to. Pay attention to the possible location of the dialogue, and Dottor Ricci's needs and actions.

Now stop the audio and complete the sentences about Dottor Ricci.

1. Il dottor Ricci è in _____.

   a. un bar   b. una chiesa

2. Il dottor Ricci ha _____.

   a. sete   b. fame

3. Il dottor Ricci ha _____ oggi.

   a. un appuntamento   b. una lezione

4. Il dottor Ricci ha bisogno di _____.

   a. un caffè   b. un libro

Dettato

La punteggiatura. (*Punctuation.*) The following punctuation marks will be read with pauses for repetition.

punto (.) *period*
virgola (,) *comma*
punto e virgola (;) *semi-colon*
due punti (:) *colon*
punto esclamativo (!) *exclamation mark*
punto interrogativo (?) *question mark*
apostrofo (') *apostrophe*
parentesi aperta (*open parenthesis*
parentesi chiusa) *close parenthesis*
virgolette aperte « *open quote*
virgolette chiuse » *close quote*

What's in Filippo's suitcase? You will hear a brief dictation three times. The first time, listen carefully. The second time, the dictation will be read with pauses. Write what you hear. The third time, check what you have written. Pay particular attention to punctuation. Write on the lines provided. Check your dictation in the Answer Key.

Ecco che cosa ____

____

____

____

____

____

____

Dialogo

Prima parte. At the train station in Perugia, Gina and Massimo are waiting for Filippo's arrival.

Listen carefully to the dialogue.

Parole utili: è nato (*was born*)

GINA: Allora, chi è questo Filippo? Quanti anni ha? Di dov'è?
MASSIMO: È professore di italiano a Boston, ma è nato a Roma. Ha trentadue anni ed è un buon amico di famiglia....
GINA: Hai una foto?
MASSIMO: No, ma ecco Filippo! È quello lì. Finalmente!
FILIPPO: Ciao, Massimo, come va?
MASSIMO: Ciao, Filippo, bene, grazie!
GINA: Ciao, Filippo, io sono Gina, benvenuto a Perugia!
FILIPPO: Piacere, Gina e grazie!
MASSIMO: Filippo, hai sete o fame? C'è un bar qui vicino se hai voglia di un panino o di una bibita...
FILIPPO: Sì, ho fame e un panino va bene, ma ho anche bisogno di soldi.[1] C'è una banca qui in stazione?
GINA: Sì, ecco. Andiamo in banca e poi al bar. Ho caldo e ho bisogno di una bibita.

[1]*money*

Seconda parte. Listen to the dialogue again. Pay attention to places and numbers pertaining to Filippo. Try to understand what he needs as well.

Terza parte. You will hear six sentences based on the dialogue. You will hear each sentence twice. Circle **vero** if the statement is true and **falso** if false.

Parole utili: abita (*he lives*)

1. vero falso
2. vero falso
3. vero falso
4. vero falso
5. vero falso
6. vero falso

Sara in Italia

Sara is on a plane at the airport in Milan. Destination: Florence. An Italian gentleman is about to sit next to her.

Listen carefully, as many times as you need to. Then, answer the questions you hear. You will hear each question twice. Repeat the response.

Parole utili: sempre (*always*), una buona camomilla calda (*a good hot* [*cup of*] *chamomile tea*), va (*are you going,* formal), vado (*I'm going*)

1. … 2. … 3. … 4. … 5. …

Sara in rete…

For more information about what Sara experienced during her travels, check out the links found on the *Prego!* website **(www.mhhe.com/prego8).**

CAPITOLO

2

Come siamo

Vocabolario preliminare

A. Per cominciare. You will hear a dialogue twice. The first time, listen carefully. The second time it will be read with pauses for repetition.

ANDREA: Ecco la foto di una mia amica, Paola. Lei è di Palermo, in Sicilia.
VALERIA: È davvero bella…
ANDREA: Oh sì, Paola è straordinaria: è simpatica, allegra, sensibile ed è anche molto gentile…
VALERIA: Sono sicura che Paola ha una grande pazienza, perché tu sei sempre stressato e nervoso!

B. I nuovi compagni. You will hear a passage in which Angelo describes his first day of class. The passage will be read three times. The first time, listen carefully. The second time, complete the chart. The third time, check what you have written. Check your answers in the Answer Key.

Numero di studenti: ______

Descrizione di Caterina: ______

Descrizione di Enrico: ______

Descrizione di Angelo: ______

C. Nazionalità. You find yourself in a classroom full of international students. Identify the students' nationality and the language they speak. Repeat the response.

ESEMPIO: *You read and hear:* Robert è di Minneapolis.
You say: Robert è americano e parla (*speaks*) inglese.

1. Amy è di Denver.
2. Marc è di Ottawa.
3. Keiko è di Tokio.
4. Angelo è di Torino.
5. Kurt è di Berlino.
6. Héctor è di Città del Messico.
7. María è di Madrid.
8. Jean-Paul è di Aix-en-Provence.

D. Una famiglia europea. You will hear a passage about a family, followed by a series of statements. You will hear both the passage and the statements twice. Listen carefully, then indicate whether the statements you hear are **vero o falso,** true or false.

1.	vero	falso	4.	vero	falso
2.	vero	falso	5.	vero	falso
3.	vero	falso			

In ascolto

Nuovi compagni di classe. Sara attended her biology class for the first time today. Here are her notes, not about biology but about her male classmates! Listen as she reads her notes to her best friend, and fill in the missing information in the chart about the three guys she met (**i tre ragazzi**). Check your answers in the Answer Key.

	NOME	ANNI	STATURA (*HEIGHT*)	CAPELLI	OCCHI	OPINIONE DI SARA
1.	Massimo	_______	media (*average*)	_______	_______	antipatico
2.	Pietro	23	_______	biondi	_______	_______
3.	Alessandro	21	_______	_______	verdi	_______

Grammatica

A. Aggettivi

A. Per cominciare. You will hear a dialogue followed by two lists of adjectives describing Marta's new classmates and instructor. Listen carefully and complete the phrases by circling all the adjectives that describe the classmates and the instructor.

GIUSEPPE: Come sono i nuovi compagni di classe?
MARTA: Sono molto allegri e gentili.
GIUSEPPE: E l'insegnante?
MARTA: Oh, lui è molto simpatico ed energico... e l'italiano è una lingua molto interessante!

1.	I compagni sono:	allegri	gentili	simpatici	energici	interessanti
2.	L'insegnante è:	allegro	gentile	simpatico	energico	interessante

B. Dal maschile al femminile. Change each expression you hear from masculine to feminine. Repeat the response.

ESEMPIO: *You hear:* bambino buono
You say: bambina buona

1. … 2. … 3. … 4. … 5. … 6. …

C. Opinioni divergenti. You and Claudio don't see eye to eye. For each of his remarks give the opposite reaction. Repeat the response.

ESEMPIO: *You hear:* Che ragazzo simpatico!
You say: Che ragazzo antipatico!

1. … 2. … 3. … 4. … 5. … 6. …

D. Non uno, due! Point out two of the things Giovanna indicates. Repeat the response.

ESEMPIO: *You hear:* Ecco una bella casa.
You say: Ecco due belle case.

1. … 2. … 3. … 4. … 5. … 6. …

E. Un americano a Firenze. Gerry has just arrived in Florence. He is calling Francesca, who is hosting him. They have a mutual friend, Salvatore, but have never met. You will hear the phone conversation twice. The first time, listen carefully. The second time, complete the sentences describing Gerry and Francesca.

Parole utili:

Pronto?	*Hello?*
Vengo subito a prenderti.	*I'm coming to pick you up right away.*
gli occhiali	*glasses*
la barba	*beard*
un vestito	*dress, suit*

1. Gerry è _____.
   a. alto, biondo, con gli occhiali
   b. alto, con la barba e gli occhiali
   c. basso, capelli neri, barba
2. Francesca è _____.
   a. di statura media, capelli lunghi
   b. alta, bionda, capelli corti
   c. bionda, con il vestito nero
3. Gerry ha anche _____.
   a. uno zaino rosso
   b. un vestito nero
   c. gli occhiali neri

F. Identikit. You need to meet Marco, your Italian host, at the train station. Ask him questions about what he looks like, listen to his answers, and then answer the questions he asks you.

Frasi utili: Sono alto/basso.

Ho gli occhi azzurri/verdi/neri/castani.

Ho i capelli biondi/castani/rossi/neri/grigi/bianchi/lunghi/corti/ricci/lisci.

ESEMPIO: *You read and ask:* Hai gli occhi castani?
You hear: Sì, ho gli occhi castani, e tu?
You say: No, non ho gli occhi castani. Ho gli occhi blu.

1. Sei alto o basso?
2. Di che colore hai gli occhi?
3. Di che colore hai i capelli?
4. Come hai i capelli?

G. **Molto o molti?** Add the correct form of **molto** to the following sentences. Repeat the response.

ESEMPIO: *You hear and read:* Maria è timida.
You say: Maria è molto timida.

1. Pietro è curioso.
2. Roberta è sincera e sensibile (*sensitive*).
3. Luca non ha amici.
4. Luigi è triste.
5. Annalisa ha pazienza.
6. Gli spaghetti di Enrica sono buoni.

H. **Perugia, una tipica città italiana...** Stop the audio to read the following passage and complete it with the correct form of **molto.** Then start the audio and listen to the completed passage. The passage will be read twice. The second time it will be read with pauses for repetition. Check your answers in the Answer Key.

Questa[a] è Perugia, una città ___molto___[1] bella, in Umbria. Ci sono ________________[2] monumenti famosi, ________________[3] musei e ________________[4] chiese. Gli abitanti[b] sono ________________[5] orgogliosi[c] di questa città. Purtroppo[d] ci sono anche ________________[6] turisti e ________________[7] traffico. Insomma,[e] non c'è ________________[8] pace[f] (*f.*) nel centro storico.

[a]*This* [b]*inhabitants* [c]*proud* [d]*Unfortunately* [e]*In short* [f]*peace and quiet*

B. Presente di *essere*

A. **Amici di chat.** You will hear a dialogue twice. The first time, listen carefully. The second time, complete the information. Check your answers in the Answer Key. Scan the list now.

1. Nazionalità di Laura: ________________
2. Età e professione di Laura: ________________
3. Descrizione di Laura: ________________
4. Nazionalità di Pierre e Caroline: ________________
5. Professione di Pierre: ________________
6. Professione di Caroline: ________________
7. Descrizione di Pierre e Caroline: ________________

B. **Una festa** (*party*) **a casa di Sabrina.** Stop the audio to complete the dialogue with the correct form of **essere.** Then start the audio, listen to the dialogue, and answer the questions. Repeat the response. Check your written answers in the Answer Key.

Parole utili: rapporto (*relationship*)

SABRINA: Sandro, ________________[1] libero stasera[a]? C'________________[2] una festa a casa mia.

SANDRO: Ah sì, e chi c'________________[3]?

[a]*tonight*

SABRINA: Ci ______________________[4] i miei compagni di classe: Marta, Alba, Luigi e Marco.

SANDRO: Come ______________________[5]?

SABRINA: ______________________[6] ragazzi simpatici. (Noi) ______________________[7] nello stesso[b] corso di letteratura inglese. Marta e Alba ______________________[8] due sorelle gemelle[c] di diciannove anni e hanno già[d] un appartamento tutto per loro in Trastevere. Luigi e Marco ______________________[9] molto divertenti e hanno molti amici.

SANDRO: Va bene, vengo.[e] Grazie per l'invito!

1. … 2. … 3. … 4. …

[b]*same* [c]sorelle… *twin sisters* [d]*already* [e]*I'll come*

C. Nazionalità. You have friends from all over the world. Tell about them using the information you hear and the following nationalities. Repeat the response.

ESEMPIO: *You hear:* Katia e Ivan
You read: russo
You say: Katia e Ivan sono russi.

1. polacco
2. italiano
3. irlandese
4. olandese (*Dutch*)
5. messicano
6. coreano (Hint: **tu** = *f.*)
7. giapponese
8. tedesco

D. Un viaggio in Italia. You are showing Silvana a picture of the town where you stayed in Italy. Answer her questions, according to the cues. Repeat the response. First, take a moment to look at the drawing.

ESEMPIO: *You hear:* C'è una banca?
You say: No, ci sono due banche.

1. … 2. … 3. … 4. … 5. … 6. …

C. Articolo determinativo e *bello*

A. Per cominciare. You will hear a dialogue twice. The first time, listen carefully. The second time, it will be read with pauses for repetition. Pay careful attention to rhythm and intonation.

DONATELLA: Ecco la nonna e il nonno, la zia Luisa e lo zio Massimo, papà e la mamma molti anni fa... Buffi, no?
GIOVANNA: E i due in prima fila chi sono?
DONATELLA: Sono gli zii di Chicago.

B. Una lista per un cocktail party... You and your roommate are writing down a list of items to buy for a cocktail party. Confirm your roommate's choices according to the cues. Add the definite article. Repeat the response.

ESEMPIO: *You hear:* rum (*m.*)?
You say: Il rum va bene!

1. aranciata?
2. vino?
3. scotch (*m.*)?
4. grappa?
5. espresso?
6. coca-cola?

C. La nuova città. Describe your new city using the following adjectives. Repeat the response.

ESEMPIO: *You read:* grande
You hear: piazze
You say: Le piazze sono grandi.

1. nuovo
2. piccolo
3. vecchio
4. elegante
5. famoso
6. antico
7. grande

D. Che bello! You are impressed with everything in your new Italian town. Use a form of **bello** to describe each item. Repeat the response.

ESEMPIO: *You hear:* museo
You say: Che bel museo!

1. ... 2. ... 3. ... 4. ... 5. ... 6. ... 7. ... 8. ...

D. Ancora i plurali

A. Per cominciare. You will hear a dialogue twice. The first time, listen carefully. The second time, it will be read with pauses for repetition. Pay careful attention to rhythm and intonation.

LUCIANO: Questi quadri sono stupendi! Sono magnifici! Sono antichi?
VALERO: No, non sono nemmeno vecchi. Per fortuna ho molti amici e amiche che sono artisti bravissimi. Lo stile è classico ma i pittori sono contemporanei.

B. Vecchie foto. The following dialogue will be read twice. The first time, listen carefully. The second time, write the missing words. Check your answers in the Answer Key.

CHIARA: Che belle queste __________[1] fotografie, Sandra! Guarda,[a] in questo pacco[b] ci sono i __________[2] di famiglia! Ecco una con gli __________[3] Ci sono anche i figli[c] di zia Lisetta, da bambini,[d] con gli __________[4] francesi. Come sono __________[5]!

SANDRA: Ma qui, invece,[e] dove sono?

CHIARA: Alla stazione di Chamonix, in Francia. Come sono __________[6] questi treni! E guarda quante borse[f] e __________[7] hanno le __________[8]!

SANDRA: E questa foto?

CHIARA: È la casa di nonna Franca, con i vasi __________,[9] i quadri,[g] i libri e i __________[10] di musica classica di nonno Luigi!

SANDRA: Chi sono queste due signore anziane in prima fila[h]?

CHIARA: La signora Martini e la signora Barni. Loro e nonna Franca sono __________[11] __________.[12]

[a]*Look* [b]*package* [c]*sons* [d]da... *as children* [e]*on the other hand* [f]quante... *how many bags* [g]*paintings* [h]prima... *first row*

Pronuncia: The sounds of the letter "s"

The letter **s** represents two sounds in Italian: [s] as in the English word *aside,* and [z] as in the English word *reside.*

A. *S* sorda. The [s] sound occurs (1) at the beginning of a word, when **s** is followed by a vowel; (2) when **s** is followed by **ca, co, cu, ch,** or by **f, p, q,** or **t;** (3) when **s** is doubled. Listen and repeat.

1. salute
2. sete
3. simpatico
4. soldi
5. supermercato
6. scandalo
7. scolastico
8. scuola
9. schema
10. sfera
11. spaghetti
12. squadra
13. stadio
14. basso

B. *S* sonora. The [z] sound occurs (1) when **s** is followed by **b, d, g, l, m, n, r,** or **v** and (2) when **s** appears between vowels. Listen and repeat.

1. sbagliato
2. sdraio
3. sgobbare
4. slogan
5. smog
6. snob
7. sregolato
8. sveglio
9. posizione
10. uso
11. rose
12. visitare

C. ***S* e doppia *s*.** Contrast the pronunciation of single and double **s** in these pairs of words. Listen and repeat.

1. casa / cassa
2. base / basse
3. mesi / messi
4. risa / rissa
5. rose / rosse
6. illuso / lusso

D. **Parliamo italiano!** You will hear each sentence twice. Listen and repeat.

1. Sette studentesse sono snelle.
2. Non sono dei grossi sbagli di pronuncia.
3. Tommaso ha sei rose rosse.
4. Gli studenti sbadigliano spesso.
5. Non siete stanchi di sgobbare?

Ed ora ascoltiamo!

Three people will introduce themselves to you. Listen carefully as many times as you need to. Write the name of the person next to the portrait that matches the description.

Dettato

You will hear a brief dictation three times. The first time, listen carefully. The second time, the dictation will be read with pauses. Write what you hear. The third time, check what you have written. Write on the lines provided. Check your dictation in the Answer Key.

Salve! Sono Antonio ____

____

____

____

____

____

____

____

Dialogo

Prima parte. Malpensa International Airport in Milan. Dawn, an American university student of Italian, has just arrived in Italy.

Listen carefully to the dialogue.

LUCIA: Pronto?[1]
DAWN: Pronto, buon giorno, c'è Alberto, per favore? Sono l'amica di David, Dawn.
LUCIA: Ciao, Dawn, benvenuta in Italia! Sì, Alberto è qui, un momento...
ALBERTO: Ciao, Dawn, come va? Dove sei?
DAWN: Tutto bene, grazie. Sono in aeroporto.
ALBERTO: Oh bene, ho la macchina oggi, sono lì tra mezz'ora allora.
DAWN: Grazie mille, ma non c'è un autobus per il centro da questo aeroporto?
ALBERTO: Sì, c'è un autobus per la Stazione Centrale, ma no, vengo io[2] con la macchina! Piuttosto,[3] come sei? Ho una foto di te e David, ma è vecchia. Nella foto sei alta e bionda...
DAWN: Sì, con i capelli lunghi e lisci... ho anche gli occhiali.[4] E tu, come sei?
ALBERTO: Di statura media, capelli castani ricci, baffi, robusto e ho una bella macchina francese, una Peugeot blu.
DAWN: Bene. Allora, a tra poco![5] Grazie!

[1] *Hello?*
[2] vengo... *I'll come*
[3] *By the way*
[4] *glasses*
[5] allora... *See you soon then*

Seconda parte. Listen to the dialogue again. Pay particular attention to information describing Dawn and Alberto and their means of transportation.

Terza parte. You will hear six sentences based on the dialogue. You will hear each sentence twice. Circle **vero** if the statement is true and **falso** if false.

1. vero falso
2. vero falso
3. vero falso
4. vero falso
5. vero falso
6. vero falso

Sara in Italia

Sara is in Palermo, in Sicily. Today she is with her aunt Rosa Cianciotta. They are at **San Giovanni degli Eremiti,** a Norman church built in 1100.

Listen carefully, as many times as you need to. Then, answer the questions you hear. You will hear each question twice. Repeat the response.

Parole utili: come vedi (*as you can see*), visitiamo (*we'll visit*), l'architettura (*architecture*), perché (*because*), mosaici (*mosaics*), il Palazzo Reale (*Royal Palace*), il Duomo (*Cathedral*), uno stile (*style*), i templi (*temples*), molte cose da vedere (*lots of things to see*)

1. … 2. … 3. … 4. … 5. …

Sara in rete…

For more information about what Sara experienced during her travels, check out the links found on the *Prego!* website **(www.mhhe.com/prego8).**

Nome ______________________ *Data* ______________ *Classe* ______________________

CAPITOLO

Studiare in Italia 3

Vocabolario preliminare

A. Per cominciare. You will hear a dialogue followed by four questions. You will hear the dialogue twice. The first time, listen carefully. The second time, it will be read with pauses for repetition. Then answer the questions. Repeat the response.

STEFANO: Ciao, sono Stefano, e tu?
PRISCILLA: Priscilla, sono americana.
STEFANO: Sei in Italia per studiare?
PRISCILLA: Sì, la lingua e la letteratura italiana…
STEFANO: Oh, parli bene l'italiano!
PRISCILLA: Studio anche la storia dell'arte. E tu, che cosa studi?
STEFANO: Studio storia e filosofia, ma l'arte è la mia passione!

1. … 2. … 3. … 4. …

B. In che corso? You will hear five questions based on the following drawings. Answer each question and repeat the response. Scan the drawings now.

ESEMPIO: *You hear:* In che corso siamo?
You say: In un corso di antropologia.

1. 

2. 

3. 

4. 

5. 

C. Io studio... You will hear Annarita introduce herself and talk about her subjects of study. You will hear the passage twice. The first time, listen carefully. The second time, write the missing words. The first one has been done for you. Check your answers in the Answer Key.

Ciao, mi chiamo Annarita e sono una studentessa di liceo.[a] Studio ___*filosofia*___, ___________[1] e ___________.[2] Purtroppo[b] devo studiare[c] anche ___________[3] e ___________.[4] C'è anche una materia che detesto: ___________.[5] Infatti,[d] non sono brava in ___________;[6] sono brava in ___________.[7] La mia materia preferita è ___________.[8] ___________[9] è invece[e] per me una materia noiosa e anche molto difficile.

[a]*high school* [b]*Unfortunately* [c]devo... *I should study* [d]*In fact* [e]*instead*

D. Una famiglia di professori e studenti. You will hear a dialogue between two students, Alberto and Raffaella, as they are waiting to take an oral exam at the university. You will hear the dialogue twice. The first time, listen carefully. The second time, it will be read with pauses for repetition. Then complete the sentences that follow.

Parole utili:

severi	*strict*
lei mi aiuta	*she helps me*
fortunata	*lucky*

1. Raffaella ha un esame di _____.
   a. matematica b. fisica c. biologia
2. Secondo Alberto, i professori sono _____.
   a. molto severi b. bravi c. importanti
3. La sorella di Alberto studia _____.
   a. matematica b. fisica c. ingegneria
4. Il fratello di Raffaella studia _____.
   a. biologia b. chimica c. fisica
5. Il padre di Raffaella, il professor Renzi, è professore di _____.
   a. ingegneria b. fisica c. matematica

In ascolto

La vita (*life*) **degli studenti.** Fabio and Laura have a tough week ahead of them. Listen carefully to their conversation. Then stop the audio and complete the following sentences. Check your answers in the Answer Key.

Parole utili: pronto (*ready*), insieme (*together*)

1. Oggi Fabio è ______________________ perché ha gli scritti di ______________________ domani.
2. I due amici vanno (*are going*) in ______________________ stasera (*this evening*) per ______________________ insieme.
3. Fabio ha anche un esame di ______________________ mercoledì.
4. Fabio ______________________ di dimenticare (*forget*) le date importanti.
5. Laura ha un esame di ______________________.

Grammatica

A. Presente dei verbi in *-are*

A. Per cominciare. You will hear a passage twice. The first time, listen carefully. The second time, write the missing words. Check your answers in the Answer Key.

______________________[1] Sara e ______________________[2] a Roma con un'amica, Giulia. Durante la ______________________[3] io lavoro e Giulia ______________________.[4] Il sabato e la ______________________[5] incontriamo gli amici, ______________________[6] una pizza, ______________________[7] sempre la musica e ______________________[8] spesso a ballare.

B. Chi? You will hear a series of sentences. You will hear each sentence twice. Circle the subject to which the sentences refer.

ESEMPIO: *You hear:* Suonate la chitarra?
You circle: (a. voi) b. Virginia

1. a. questa ragazza b. queste ragazze
2. a. io b. lui
3. a. voi b. tu
4. a. il signor Rossi b. i signori Rossi
5. a. noi b. loro
6. a. io b. noi

C. Che confusione! You're at a party with Paolo, who has everything wrong about you and your friends. Correct him using the following information. Repeat the response.

ESEMPIO: *You read:* Voi lavorate in banca?
You hear: Sabrina e Ivan
You say: No, noi non lavoriamo in banca, Sabrina e Ivan lavorano in banca!

1. Tu parli spagnolo?
2. Michela abita a Firenze?
3. Voi studiate giapponese?
4. La professoressa Brown insegna italiano?
5. Tu suoni la chitarra?
6. Victor frequenta il corso di economia e commercio?

B. *Dare, stare, andare e fare*

A. Per cominciare. You will hear a dialogue twice. The first time, listen carefully. The second time, it will be read with pauses for repetition.

Ecco il mio segreto per studiare con successo: vado sempre a lezione, sto molto attento in classe, faccio sempre tutti i compiti e quando do gli esami non ho mai problemi!

B. Con che cosa vanno? Look at the drawings and tell how these people are getting about. Use the subjects you hear and the following places. Repeat the response.

ESEMPIO: *You see and read:*

in Italia

You hear: Giulia
You say: Giulia va in Italia in aereo.

1.

all'università

2.

a Roma

3.

a casa

4.

in centro

5.

a Firenze

C. Una persona curiosa. Rebecca is very curious about everything today. You will hear her questions twice. Answer according to the cues. Repeat the response.

Parole utili: zitto (*quiet*), una festa (*party*)

ESEMPIO: *You hear:* Fai il letto tutti i giorni?
You read: sì
You say: Sì, faccio il letto tutti i giorni.

1. no
2. sì
3. no
4. sì
5. sì
6. no

D. La vita (*life*) **degli studenti.** Fabio and Laura have a tough week ahead of them. You will hear a dialogue about their week twice. The first time, listen carefully. The second time, write the missing verbs. Check your answers in the Answer Key.

LAURA: Ciao... come ________________________[1]?

FABIO: Così così. Ho gli orali di storia dell'arte domani, è un esame terribile! ________________________[2] a casa a studiare stasera.

LAURA: ________________________[3] altri esami questa settimana?

FABIO: Sì, mercoledì ho gli scritti di latino.

LAURA: Sei pronto[a]?

FABIO: Sì, ma devo[b] ________________________[4] attento a non sbagliare[c] i verbi. E tu, ________________________[5] esami in questa sessione?

LAURA: Sì, ________________________[6] gli scritti di lingua e letteratura francese la settimana prossima.[d] ________________________[7] a casa a studiare tutto il week-end. Il mio francese è così così e gli scritti sono difficili, il dettato specialmente!

FABIO: Perché non ________________________[8] a studiare insieme[e] a casa mia? Io studio storia dell'arte e latino e tu prepari francese, va bene?

[a]*ready* [b]*I should* [c]*making mistakes with* [d]*next* [e]*together*

E. Qualche domanda anche per te (*A few questions for you too*)**...** Answer the following questions orally about your life as a student.

Parole utili: di solito (*usually*)

1. ... 2. ... 3. ... 4. ...

C. Aggettivi possessivi

A. Per cominciare. You will hear a dialogue twice. The first time, listen carefully. The second time, Roberto's lines will be read with pauses for repetition.

GIANNI: Chi è il tuo professore preferito?
ROBERTO: Beh, veramente ho due professori preferiti: il professore di biologia e la professoressa di italiano.
GIANNI: Perché?
ROBERTO: Il professore di biologia è molto famoso: i suoi libri sono usati nelle università americane. La professoressa di italiano è molto brava; apprezzo la sua pazienza e il suo senso dell'umorismo.

B. La mia professoressa preferita è... You will hear a continuation of the dialogue between Gianni and Roberto, followed by three questions. You will hear the dialogue twice. The first time, listen carefully. The second time, the part of Gianni will be read with pauses for repetition. Then, answer the questions in writing. Check your answers in the Answer Key.

Frasi utili:

anzi	*in fact*
forse	*perhaps*
la fidanzata	*girlfriend*

ROBERTO: E i tuoi professori come sono?
GIANNI: Io non sono imparziale: ho solo un professore preferito, anzi, una professoressa, l'assistente di psicologia. Le sue lezioni sono sempre super-interessanti...
ROBERTO: Mmmmmm... Non è forse la tua fidanzata questa assistente? Non insegna psicologia qui all'università?
GIANNI: Vero, vero, è proprio la mia fidanzata...

1. Chi è l'insegnante preferito di Gianni? ______________________
2. Che cosa è super-interessante? ______________________
3. Perché Gianni non è imparziale nella sua scelta (*choice*)?

____

C. Dov'è? You're very absentminded today. Ask where your things are. Repeat the response.

ESEMPIO: *You hear:* libro
You say: Dov'è il mio libro?

1. ... 2. ... 3. ... 4. ... 5. ... 6. ... 7. ... 8. ...

D. Possessivi con termini di parentela

A. Per cominciare. You will hear a passage twice. The first time, listen carefully. The second time, it will be read with pauses for repetition.

Sono Carla. Ecco la mia famiglia! Io sono la ragazza bionda, bassa e un po' cicciotta. Mio padre è dottore. Lavora all'ospedale in centro. Mia madre è infermiera e lavora con mio padre. Il mio fratellino, Tonino, è cattivo e antipatico. Non andiamo d'accordo. Noi abbiamo un cane. Il suo nome è Macchia perché è bianco e nero.

B. Un albero (*tree*) **genealogico** (*A family tree*). You will hear a passage in which Riccardo describes his family. You will hear the passage three times. The first time, listen carefully. The second time, complete the family tree with the appropriate relative term and that relative's profession (**professione**). The third time, check your answers. Check your completed information in the Answer Key. Then complete the statements, based on the passage. Scan the family tree illustration now.

Parole utili: sposata (*married*), nubile (*single*)

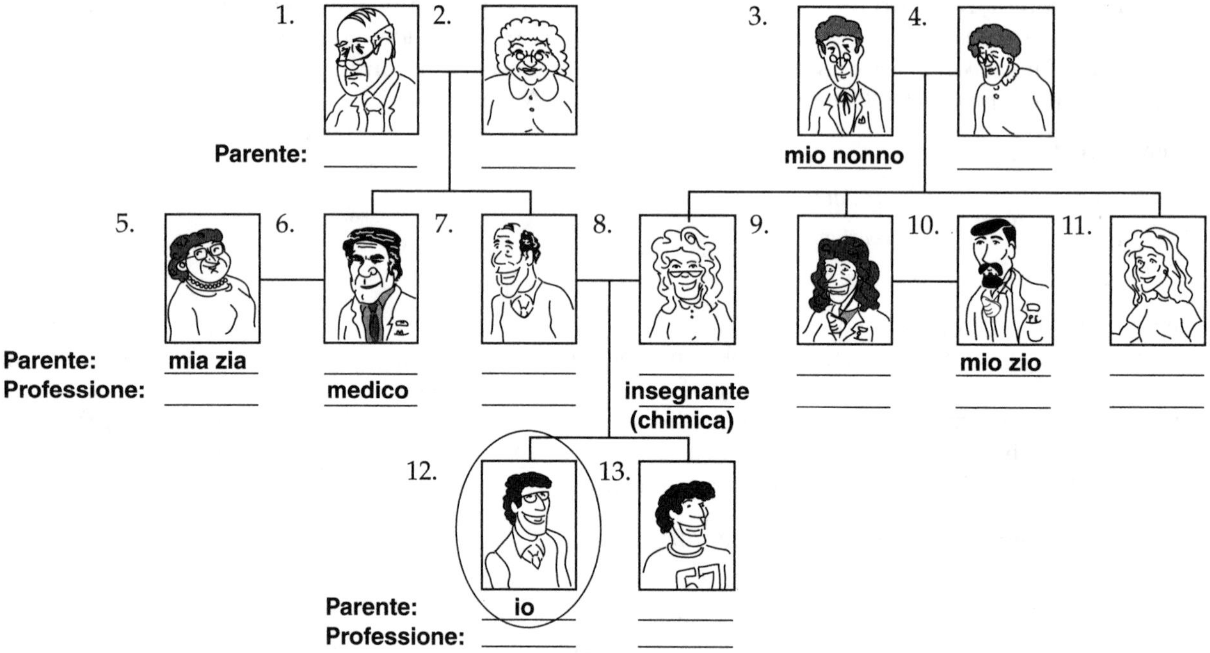

Now complete the following statements both in writing and orally. Repeat the response. Then check your written answers in the Answer Key. The first one has been done for you.

1. ___*Il*___ ___*suo*___ fratellino è studente di fisica.
2. ________ ________ insegna matematica.
3. ________ ________ insegna chimica.
4. La moglie di ________ ________ è professoressa di biologia.
5. ________ ________ ________ nubile è segretaria.
6. I ________ ________ sono dentisti.
7. ________ ________ nonni abitano a Napoli.

C. La mia famiglia. Riccardo is your guest at a family gathering. Point out your relatives to him. Repeat the response.

ESEMPIO: *You read:* lo zio Giulio, professore
You say: Ecco mio zio Giulio. Lui è professore.

1. le cugine Barbara e Daniela / studentesse di medicina
2. i nonni / in pensione (*retired*)
3. la zia Anna / dentista
4. fratello / studente
5. il cugino Emanuele / architetto

D. E il tuo albero genealogico? Answer the following six questions orally based on your own family tree.

1. … 2. … 3. … 4. … 5. … 6. …

E. *Questo e quello*

A. Per cominciare. You will hear a dialogue twice. The first time, listen carefully. The second time, the dialogue will be read with pauses for repetition.

MIRELLA: Quale compri, questo golf rosso o quella maglietta blu?

SARA: Compro quel golf rosso. E tu, cosa compri? Quel golf giallo è molto bello, ma è bella anche questa maglietta grigia.

MIRELLA: Non lo so. Tutt'e due sono belli.

B. Quale? Giacomo is unsure which people you're talking about. Answer the questions with the appropriate form of **quello.** Repeat the response.

ESEMPIO: *You hear:* Quale ragazza?
You say: Quella ragazza.

1. … 2. … 3. … 4. … 5. … 6. … 7. … 8. …

Pronuncia: The sounds of the letter "g"

As you learned in the **Capitolo preliminare,** the letter **g** represents two sounds in Italian: [g] as in the English word *go* and [ğ] as in the English word *giant.*

A. *G* dura. The [g] sound occurs when **g** is followed directly by **a, o, u, h,** or most other consonants. Listen and repeat.

1. gatto
2. gondola
3. guidare
4. ghetto
5. grasso

B. *G* dolce. The [ğ] sound occurs when **g** is followed directly by **e** or **i.** Listen and repeat.

1. gennaio
2. giapponese
3. giorno
4. giurisprudenza
5. antropologia

C. *G* e doppia *g*. Contrast the pronunciation of the single and double **g** sounds in these pairs of words. Listen and repeat.

1. fuga / fugga
2. lego / leggo
3. agio / maggio
4. pagina / paggio

D. ***Gl* e *gn*.** The clusters **gl** and **gn** have special sounds. Most of the time, **gl** is pronounced like the *ll* in the English word *million,* while **gn** is similar in sound to the first *n* in the English word *onion.* Listen and repeat.

1. gli
2. sbagliato
3. foglio
4. meglio
5. gnocchi
6. spagnolo
7. ingegneria
8. gnomo

E. **Parliamo italiano!** You will hear each sentence twice. Listen and repeat.

1. Lo spagnolo e l'inglese sono due lingue.
2. È uno sbaglio tagliare l'aglio sulla tovaglia.
3. Ecco gli insegnanti di psicologia.
4. Gli ingegneri giapponesi arrivano in agosto.
5. Giugno e luglio sono due mesi meravigliosi.
6. Giovanna e Gabriella sono giovani.

Ed ora ascoltiamo!

You will hear a description of Lisa. Listen carefully, as many times as you need to. Then you will hear six statements. Circle **vero** or **falso.**

Parole utili: subito (*right away*), di solito (*usually*)

1. vero falso
2. vero falso
3. vero falso
4. vero falso
5. vero falso
6. vero falso

Dettato

You will hear a brief dictation three times. The first time, listen carefully. The second time, the dictation will be read with pauses. Write what you hear. The third time, check what you have written. Write on the lines provided. Check your dictation in the Answer Key.

Mariella, Stefano e Patrizia, ____

____

____

____

____

____

____

____

Dialogo

Prima parte. It's June, and Mariella and Patrizia are studying for their graduation exams. They are on the phone when Stefano, Mariella's brother, arrives. Stefano is also a high school student, but he doesn't attend the same kind of high school.

Listen carefully to the dialogue.

MARIELLA: Oh, Patrizia, comincio ad avere paura di questo esame! Tra[1] due giorni cominciano gli scritti e io non sono preparata!

PATRIZIA: Anch'io non sono pronta.[2] Ho il terrore a pensare[3] a lunedì, allo scritto di italiano. Ripasso gli autori del Romanticismo, ma il mio vero problema è martedì, con lo scritto di matematica! Ho bisogno di ripassare trigonometria e di fare molti molti esercizi!

MARIELLA: Se hai voglia, stasera studiamo italiano insieme[4] qui a casa mia e facciamo un po' di esercizi di matematica. La matematica è la mia materia preferita.

PATRIZIA: Perfetto! Porto[5] i libri di italiano di mia sorella, spiegano la letteratura molto bene.

MARIELLA: Ok, allora.[6] Un momento, arriva mio fratello. Oh, com'è triste! Stefano, come va?

STEFANO: Male, va male! Preparo greco per gli scritti, ma è difficile ricordare i verbi greci!

PATRIZIA: Tuo fratello fa il Liceo Classico? Mamma mia, studia greco!

MARIELLA: Sì, è vero, ma noi allo Scientifico abbiamo matematica, non dimenticare! Abbiamo materie molto difficili anche noi! Stefano ha gli orali tra due settimane e anche latino da preparare.

PATRIZIA: Le interrogazioni orali non sono le mie favorite. Ho sempre paura di dimenticare tutto davanti[7] ai professori.

MARIELLA: Allora, Patrizia, a casa mia stasera alle otto? Porti i libri di trigonometria e italiano, ok?

PATRIZIA: Ok! Per me va benissimo!

[1] *In*
[2] *ready* / [3] *to think*
[4] *together*
[5] *I'll bring*
[6] *then*
[7] *in front of*

Seconda parte. Listen to the dialogue again. Pay particular attention to the school subjects discussed by the students and to their exam and study schedules.

Terza parte. You will hear six sentences based on the dialogue. You will hear each sentence twice. Circle **vero** if the statement is true and **falso** if false.

1. vero falso
2. vero falso
3. vero falso
4. vero falso
5. vero falso
6. vero falso

Sara in Italia

Sara is in Perugia, where her friend Priscilla (an Italian teacher in the United States) is taking a course at the Università per Stranieri during the summer. Sara calls Priscilla and invites her out.

Listen carefully, as many times as you need to. Then, answer the questions you hear. You will hear each question twice. Repeat the response.

Parole utili: tecniche didattiche (*teaching techniques*), vuol dire che (*it means that*), ripasso (*I'll review*), più (*more*), tuo aiuto (*your help*), a dopo (*until later*), felpa (*sweatshirt*)

1. … 2. … 3. … 4. … 5. …

Sara in rete…

For more information about what Sara experienced during her travels, check out the links found on the *Prego!* website **(www.mhhe.com/prego8).**

CAPITOLO

Sport e passatempi 4

Vocabolario preliminare

A. Per cominciare. You will hear a dialogue twice. The first time, listen carefully. The second time it will be read with pauses for repetition.

LORENZO: Ciao, Rita! Ciao, Alessandro! Che cosa fate oggi?
ALESSANDRO: Vado a giocare a tennis con Marcello e poi a casa: c'è un bel film alla TV.
RITA: Io invece vado a fare aerobica con Valeria, poi abbiamo un appuntamento con Vittoria per studiare. C'è un esame di matematica domani!
ALESSANDRO: E tu, Lorenzo, che programmi hai?
LORENZO: Mah, oggi non ho voglia di fare niente…
RITA: Che novità, è il tuo passatempo preferito!

B. Cosa fanno? Look at the drawings and answer the questions about what the people are doing. Repeat the response.

ESEMPIO: *You see:*

You hear: Mauro fa aerobica o ascolta i CD?
You say: Mauro ascolta i CD.

1. 

2. 

3. 

4. 

5. 

C. Cosa facciamo stasera? You will hear the following dialogue twice. The first time, listen carefully. The second time, write the missing words. Check your answers in the Answer Key.

PIERA: Romolo, cosa _______________[1] stasera?

ROMOLO: Mah, non lo so[a]... _______________[2] al cinema? O _______________[3] un film alla TV?

PIERA: No, non _______________[4] _______________[5] di andare al cinema... E alla TV non _______________[6] mai niente[b] d'interessante.

ROMOLO: E allora che _______________[7] fare? Perché non _______________[8] un giro a piedi,[c] andiamo in centro e _______________[9] le vetrine[d]...

PIERA: Ma Romolo, nevica! _______________[10] troppo freddo!

ROMOLO: Sì, nevica ma cosa vuoi fare, _______________[11] l'inverno in casa?

PIERA: Ma no...

ROMOLO: Insomma, che vuoi fare? Un caffè, allora?

PIERA: No, niente caffè... sai, piuttosto,[e] _______________[12] proprio bisogno di _______________[13] la casa...

ROMOLO: Eh, ora _______________[14]! Qui no, là no, insomma, un modo elegante per dire[f] che abbiamo bisogno di pulire la casa. E va bene, ma io _______________[15] le camere da letto e la sala da pranzo,[g] tu _______________[16] il bagno[h] e la cucina[i]!

[a]non... *I don't know* [b]*anything* [c]un... *a walk* [d]*shop window displays* [e]sai... *you know, instead* [f]un... *a nice way of saying* [g]sala... *dining room* [h]*bathroom* [i]*kitchen*

D. Che stagione? You will hear a series of months. You will hear each month twice. Listen carefully, then circle the name of the season in which the month falls.

ESEMPIO: *You hear:* febbraio
You circle: primavera estate autunno (inverno)

1. primavera estate autunno inverno
2. primavera estate autunno inverno
3. primavera estate autunno inverno
4. primavera estate autunno inverno

In ascolto

Che fai adesso (*now*)**?** What are Chiara and Stefania doing? Listen carefully and then answer the following questions. Check your answers in the Answer Key.

1. Dove va Chiara? ____________
2. Dove va invece Stefania? ____________
3. Quanti autobus deve prendere (*must take*) Chiara? ____________
4. Come sono le lezioni che prende Chiara? ____________

Grammatica

A. Presente dei verbi in *-ere* e *-ire*

A. Per cominciare. You will hear a passage followed by three completion sentences. You will hear the passage twice. The first time, listen carefully. The second time it will be read with pauses for repetition. Then indicate the best completion to each sentence.

Siamo una famiglia molto sportiva. Mio padre corre ogni giorno e poi va in ufficio; mia madre prende lezioni di tennis in estate e preferisce nuotare in piscina in inverno; mia sorella va in palestra e fa sollevamento pesi... Persino mia nonna fa aerobica!

1. a. preferisce correre.
   b. preferisce fare aerobica.
2. a. prende lezioni di tennis.
   b. fa sollevamento pesi.
3. a. fa aerobica.
   b. nuota.

B. E tu, cosa fai la sera? You will hear ten questions about your own evening activities. You will hear each question twice. Tell how often you do the given activity by checking the appropriate column: **sempre, spesso,** or **mai**.

	SEMPRE	SPESSO	MAI		SEMPRE	SPESSO	MAI
1.	☐	☐	☐	6.	☐	☐	☐
2.	☐	☐	☐	7.	☐	☐	☐
3.	☐	☐	☐	8.	☐	☐	☐
4.	☐	☐	☐	9.	☐	☐	☐
5.	☐	☐	☐	10.	☐	☐	☐

C. Una serata a casa Magnani... You will hear a passage describing the evening activities at Francesco Magnani's house. You will hear the passage read twice. The first time, listen carefully. The second time, write notes on each person's evening activity. Then complete each statement orally, when you hear the name of the person. Repeat the response.

La nonna ______________________________

La mamma ______________________________

Papà ______________________________

I fratelli ______________________________

Luigino ______________________________

Francesco ______________________________

B. *Dovere, potere* e *volere; dire, uscire* e *venire*

A. Per cominciare. You will hear a dialogue three times. The first time, listen carefully. The second time, number the script that follows from 1 to 6. Number one has been done for you. The third time, check the order. Then check your answers in the Answer Key.

_____ Domani sera allora?

_____ No, non posso. Devo studiare.

_____ Tu non hai mai tempo per me. Devo cercare un'altra ragazza!

_____ No, devo andare a una riunione...

__1__ Vuoi uscire stasera, Daniela?

_____ C'è un bel film al cinema Diana.

B. Doveri. Francesco cannot believe that people ever skip fun activities because they have to study. Answer his questions using the appropriate forms of **non potere** and **dovere studiare.** Repeat the response.

ESEMPIO: *You hear and read:* Perché non andate a ballare?
You say: Non possiamo andare a ballare. Dobbiamo studiare.

1. Perché non guardi la televisione?
2. Perché non giocano a tennis?
3. Perché non va a nuotare?
4. Perché non uscite con gli amici?

C. Desideri. Tell what everyone wants for the holidays using the oral and written cues and the correct form of **volere.** Repeat the response.

ESEMPIO: *You read:* gatto
You hear: Marta e Sara
You say: Marta e Sara vogliono un gatto.

1. bicicletta
2. cravatta (*tie*)
3. CD
4. chitarra
5. orologio
6. libro

D. **Desideri, bisogni, doveri e possibilità...** Using the information you read and the verbs you hear, say what kind of activities the following people wish to, need to, must or can perform. Repeat the response.

ESEMPIO: *You read:* Marco / suonare il piano / stasera
You hear: volere
You say: Marco vuole suonare il piano stasera.

1. io e Mirko / andare a teatro / domani
2. Luigi / prendere lezioni di arti marziali / questo semestre
3. io / usare il computer / oggi pomeriggio
4. Rosa e Amanda / correre la maratona / questo mese
5. Paola e Riccardo / pulire la casa / questo week-end
6. tu / cucinare per tutti / domani

E. **Grazie!** You are teaching little Roberto manners by pointing out to him who always says **grazie.** Answer his questions according to the cues. Repeat the response.

ESEMPIO: *You hear:* E Rossella?
You say: Rossella dice sempre «grazie!»

1. ... 2. ... 3. ... 4. ... 5. ...

F. **Quando?** Say what night of the week you and your friends go out. Repeat the response.

ESEMPIO: *You read:* il sabato
You hear: noi
You say: Noi usciamo il sabato.

1. il lunedì
2. la domenica
3. il giovedì
4. il mercoledì
5. il venerdì

G. **Anch'io!** It's a beautiful day, and everyone's coming to Marco's picnic. Answer his questions as in the example. Repeat the response.

ESEMPIO: *You hear:* E tu?
You say: Vengo anch'io!

1. ... 2. ... 3. ... 4. ... 5. ...

C. Pronomi di oggetto diretto

A. **Per cominciare.** You will hear a dialogue followed by four questions. You will hear the dialogue twice. The first time, listen carefully. The second time, Clara's lines will be read with pauses for repetition. Then answer the questions orally by selecting the appropriate response. Repeat the response.

ANNAMARIA: Mi inviti alla festa?
CLARA: Certo che ti invito!
ANNAMARIA: Inviti anche Marco?
CLARA: Certo che lo invito!
ANNAMARIA: E Maria?
CLARA: Certo che la invito!
ANNAMARIA: Compri le pizze e le bibite?
CLARA: Certo che le compro!
ANNAMARIA: Prepari panini per tutti?
CLARA: Certo che li preparo. Così mangiamo bene e passiamo una bella serata!

1. ... 2. ... 3. ... 4. ...

B. **Benny.** You will hear a dialogue followed by three questions. You will hear the dialogue twice. The first time, listen carefully. The second time, Clara's lines will be read with pauses for repetition. Then answer the questions. Repeat the response.

ANNAMARIA: Clara, in casa tua chi lava i piatti[1]?
CLARA: Che domanda! Li lava Benny!
ANNAMARIA: E chi pulisce la casa?
CLARA: La pulisce Benny!
ANNAMARIA: E chi fa il letto ogni mattina?
CLARA: Lo fa Benny!
ANNAMARIA: E la cucina[2]? E le altre faccende[3]?
CLARA: Le fa Benny! Le fa Benny!
ANNAMARIA: Che marito adorabile! Come deve amarti Benny… E tu che fai tutto il giorno?
CLARA: Lavoro con i robot. Programmo Benny con il computer!

[1]lava… *washes the dishes*
[2]*cooking* / [3]*chores*

1. … 2. … 3. …

C. **Una ricetta** (*recipe*) **facile facile… Pasta alla carbonara!** Your Italian roommate is teaching you to cook pasta carbonara. You will hear her say each line of the recipe carefully. Rephrase each sentence she says with the appropriate direct object pronoun. Repeat the response.

ESEMPIO: *You hear and read:* Prendo (*I take*) tutti gli ingredienti e metto (*I put*) gli ingredienti qui.
You say: Prendo tutti gli ingredienti e li metto qui.

1. Prendo l'acqua e metto l'acqua a bollire (*boil*).
2. Prendo il sale (*salt*) e metto il sale nell'acqua.
3. Prendo gli spaghetti e metto gli spaghetti nell'acqua.
4. Prendo le uova (*eggs*) e sbatto (*I beat*) le uova.
5. Prendo il pepe (*pepper*) e la pancetta (*bacon*) e mescolo (*I mix*) il pepe e la pancetta con le uova.
6. Quando gli spaghetti sono al dente, scolo (*I drain*) gli spaghetti.
7. Prendo la salsa e metto la salsa sugli spaghetti.
8. Servo la pasta e mangio subito la pasta.

D. L'ora

A. **Per cominciare.** You will hear a dialogue twice. The first time, listen carefully. The second time, the dialogue will be read with pauses for repetition.

MARTINA: Che ore sono?
PAOLO: Sono le 8.45.
MARTINA: È tardi, devo andare a lezione di chimica!
PAOLO: Vai a piedi?
MARTINA: No, devo correre a prendere l'autobus.

B. **La giornata di Luca.** You will hear a passage describing Luca's day. You will hear the passage twice. The first time, listen carefully. The second time, write the time that he does each activity. The first one has been done for you. Check your answers in the Answer Key.

Parole utili: piena (*full*), prima di (*before*)

Orario:

1. ___*8.00*___ studiare fisica
2. ____________ lezione di chimica
3. ____________ incontrare gli amici
4. ____________ pranzare (*to have lunch*)
5. ____________ studiare in biblioteca
6. ____________ giocare a calcio
7. ____________ cenare (*to have dinner*) con Gabriella

C. Che ore sono? Tell the time using the 12-hour clock and the appropriate time expression: **di mattina, del pomeriggio, di sera** or **di notte.** Repeat the response.

ESEMPIO: *You see:*

You say: Sono le otto meno dieci di mattina. *o* Sono le sette e cinquanta di mattina.

1. 

2. 

3. 

4. 

5. 

6. 

Pronuncia: The combination "sc"

The combination **sc** represents two sounds: [sk] as in the English word *sky,* and [š] as in the English word *shy.*

A. ***Sc* dura.** The [sk] sound occurs when **sc** is followed directly by **a, o, u, h,** or another consonant. Listen and repeat.

1. scandalo
2. sconto
3. scusa
4. schema
5. scrive
6. tedeschi

B. ***Sc* dolce.** The [š] sound occurs when **sc** is followed directly by **e** or **i.** Listen and repeat.

1. scena
2. scelta
3. scendere
4. scienza
5. sciopero
6. prosciutto

C. Parliamo italiano! Listen and repeat.

1. Cos'è il «Gianni Schicchi»? È un'opera; io ho il CD.
2. Tosca esce con uno scultore tedesco.
3. Perché non pulisci le scarpe?
4. Posso lasciare i pesci con il prosciutto?
5. Francesco preferisce sciare con questi sci.
6. «Capire fischi per fiaschi» significa capire una cosa per un'altra.

Ed ora ascoltiamo!

Vieni con me? You will hear a conversation between Patrizio and Graziella. Listen carefully as many times as you need to. Then you will hear five questions. Indicate the correct answer.

Parole utili:

l'ultimo	*the latest (film)*
rivedere	*to see again*
la vita	*life*
qualche	*some*
lo so	*I know*
una recensione	*review*
un modo	*way*
a me è piaciuto	*I liked it*
la sceneggiatura	*script*
a dire il vero	*to tell the truth*
una mostra	*exhibit*
il ladro	*thief*
io ti aiuto	*I'll help you*

1. a. Gianni Amelio b. Roberto Benigni
2. a. «La vita è bella» b. «Il ladro di bambini»
3. a. una recensione su Gianni Amelio b. una mostra fotografica
4. a. guardare un film in videocassetta b. fare fotografie
5. a. vanno al cinema b. fanno fotografie

Dettato

You will hear a brief dictation three times. The first time, listen carefully. The second time, write what you hear. The third time, check what you have written. Write on the lines provided. Check your dictation in the Answer Key.

Giovanna e Rossana ______________________________

____

____

____

____

____

____

____

____

Dialogo

Prima parte. Alessandro, Rita, and Lorenzo are talking about where to go for their winter vacation.

Listen carefully to the dialogue.

ALESSANDRO: Allora,[1] dove andiamo in montagna quest'anno? Sulle Dolomiti o in Valle d'Aosta?

RITA: Preferisco le Dolomiti,* specialmente la zona di Moena e del passo di San Pellegrino, possiamo andare a sciare sul colle[2] Margherita…

LORENZO: Io invece dico di andare in Valle d'Aosta perché ho intenzione di fare delle passeggiate nella zona del Gran Paradiso, non di sciare ogni giorno.

ALESSANDRO: Io voglio anche fare della roccia[3] se possibile.

RITA: E io lo sci di fondo[4]! Le Dolomiti hanno delle belle foreste e lo sci di fondo è eccezionale tra gli alberi[5]…

ALESSANDRO: Va bene, allora, quest'anno andiamo in Trentino. Tu che dici, Lorenzo? Dobbiamo trovare però[6] un albergo con una palestra perché, quando non sciamo, posso fare del sollevamento pesi…

RITA: …o io aerobica…

LORENZO: …e io invece penso di stare in camera a giocare con il computer! Il Trentino va bene anche per me. Mentre voi andate in palestra, io mi rilasso al caldo in albergo, dopo le mie passeggiate!

[1]*Well, then*
[2]*hill*
[3]fare… *to go rock climbing*
[4]lo… *cross-country skiing*
[5]*trees*
[6]*however*

Seconda parte. Listen to the dialogue again. Pay particular attention to information describing what the three friends want to do on vacation and where they are thinking about doing these activities.

*The Dolomites are in **Trentino.**

Terza parte. You will hear six sentences based on the dialogue. You will hear each sentence twice. Circle **vero** if the statement is true and **falso** if it is false.

1.	vero	falso	4.	vero	falso
2.	vero	falso	5.	vero	falso
3.	vero	falso	6.	vero	falso

Sara in Italia

Sara is on a skiing vacation in the Dolomites, the mountains that are part of the Alps in the Northeast and separate Italy from Austria. Today she is in Bolzano, in Trentino–Alto Adige. She overhears two people talking, a little in German, a little in Italian, and she tries to chat with them.

Listen carefully, as many times as you need to. Then, answer the questions you hear. You will hear each question twice. Repeat the response.

Parole utili: millenovecentodiciotto (*1918*), era (*was*), seconda (*second*), così (*that way*)

1. ... 2. ... 3. ... 4. ... 5. ...

Sara in rete...

For more information about what Sara experienced during her travels, check out the links found on the *Prego!* website **(www.mhhe.com/prego8).**

CAPITOLO

Caffè e cappuccino 5

Vocabolario preliminare

A. **Per cominciare.** Sentirai (*You will hear*) un dialogo due volte (*times*). La prima volta, ascolta attentamente. La seconda volta, il dialogo sarà (*will be*) ripetuto con pause per la ripetizione.

ANDREA: Silvia… cosa prendi?
SILVIA: Un cappuccino.
ANDREA: Non mangi?
SILVIA: No, di solito non faccio colazione la mattina.
ANDREA: Allora… un cappuccino, un caffè e… tre paste.
SILVIA: Tre paste? Hai proprio fame!

B. E voi, cosa prendete di solito? Sentirai tre brani in cui Bruna, Mario e Rolando dicono quello che mangiano a colazione. Sentirai i brani tre volte. La prima volta, ascolta attentamente. La seconda volta, controlla (*check*) le cose che ciascuno (*each one*) mangia a colazione. Ora guarda la lista.

Espressioni utili: di rado (*seldom*), qualche volta / certe volte (*at times*), quindi (*then*)

	BRUNA	MARIO	ROLANDO
1. un caffè (un espresso)	☐	☐	☐
2. una brioche, un cornetto	☐	☐	☐
3. un cappuccino	☐	☐	☐
4. il latte	☐	☐	☐
5. un panino	☐	☐	☐
6. una pasta	☐	☐	☐
7. una bibita	☐	☐	☐
8. i cereali	☐	☐	☐
9. un succo di frutta	☐	☐	☐
10. la spremuta d'arancia	☐	☐	☐

C. I signori desiderano... ? Sentirai Roberto e Giuditta che ordinano al cameriere. Ascolta attentamente e correggi le affermazioni false. Controlla le tue risposte con le soluzioni date in fondo al libro (*given in the Answer Key*).

1. Giuditta prende una spremuta d'arancia. vero falso

   ____

2. Roberto prende un tè freddo con ghiaccio. vero falso

   ____

3. Roberto prende un panino al prosciutto e formaggio. vero falso

   ____

4. Giuditta prende un panino al prosciutto. vero falso

   ____

In ascolto

Al tavolino o no? Valentina e Giacomo non sono d'accordo. Ascolta attentamente e decidi se ogni affermazione è vera o falsa. Poi, correggi le affermazioni false. Controlla le tue risposte con le soluzioni date in fondo al libro.

Espressioni utili: sedere a un tavolino (*to sit at a table*), al banco (*at the counter*), cartoline (*postcards*)

1. Valentina è stanca e ha sete. vero falso

   ____

2. Giacomo non vuole andare al caffè Gilli perché è lontano. vero falso

   ____

3. Valentina vuole leggere il giornale al tavolino. vero falso

____

4. Secondo Valentina, possono passare due ore al caffè. vero falso

____

5. Giacomo preferisce prendere un tè freddo al banco. vero falso

____

Grammatica

A. Preposizioni articolate

A. Per cominciare. Silvia Tarrone è una studentessa italiana. Sentirai un brano due volte. La prima volta, ascolta attentamente. La seconda volta, il brano sarà (*will be*) ripetuto con pause per la ripetizione.

Tutte le mattine vado al bar alle otto. Faccio colazione in fretta, prendo un caffè al banco e poi prendo l'autobus delle otto e un quarto per l'università. Frequento i corsi e all'una mangio alla mensa universitaria con i miei amici. Dopo pranzo, andiamo al bar a prendere un caffè e poi andiamo a studiare in biblioteca. Verso le quattro ho voglia di uno spuntino. Vado al bar e di solito prendo un tè caldo. Metto del miele nel tè e mangio un tramezzino. Verso le cinque prendo l'autobus e torno a casa.

B. La routine giornaliera di Silvia Tarrona. Sentirai un brano in cui Silvia descrive ancora la sua routine giornaliera. Prendi appunti (*Take notes*) sulla riga (*line*) che trovi dopo ogni domanda e poi rispondi oralmente alle domande. Ripeti la risposta.

1. A che ora va al bar? ______________________
2. Quale autobus prende? ______________________
3. Quando va a mangiare? ______________________
4. Dove va dopo pranzo? ______________________
5. Dove studia? ______________________
6. Come prende il tè caldo? ______________________

C. Di chi è? Aiuti a Luciano a mettere tutto a posto (*clean up*) dopo una grande festa. Aiutalo ad abbinare (*match*) le persone con gli oggetti usando i nomi che senti ed i suggerimenti. Ripeti la risposta.

ESEMPIO: *Leggi:* il CD
Senti: la studentessa
Dici: il CD della studentessa

1. la bicicletta
2. il giornale
3. la chiave (*key*)
4. la chitarra
5. i libri
6. la giacca (*jacket*)

B. Passato prossimo con *avere*

A. Per cominciare. Sentirai un discorso tra Massimo e Paolo due volte. Poi ascolta le seguenti frasi e completale con il participio passato corretto. Controlla le tue risposte con le soluzioni date in fondo al libro.

1. Massimo ha ____________ un caffè.
2. Paolo ha ____________ che la colazione è il pasto principale.
3. Massimo ha ____________ troppo.
4. Paolo ha ____________.

B. Già fatto! Spiega perché queste persone non fanno certe cose. Le hanno già fatte! Ripeti la risposta.

ESEMPIO: *Senti:* Perché non mangia Barbara?
Dici: Perché ha già mangiato.

1. … 2. … 3. … 4. … 5. … 6. …

C. Cosa hai fatto ieri? Sentirai un dialogo due volte. La prima volta, ascolta attentamente. La seconda volta, la parte di Sabrina sarà letta (*will be read*) con pause per la ripetizione.

TIZIANA: Cosa hai fatto ieri?
SABRINA: Più o meno le solite cose… Ho studiato per un esame di italiano, ho fatto una pausa per mangiare, ho letto un articolo sul giornale, ho guardato la televisione per rilassarmi, ho scritto un saggio[1] al computer, ho fatto la doccia[2] dopo aver studiato e ho giocato a tennis con Luca.

[1] *essay*
[2] ho… *I took a shower*

D. E tu, cosa hai fatto ieri? Rispondi alle seguenti domande. Prendi appunti e poi di' (*tell*) cosa hai fatto e cosa non hai fatto ieri.

1. Sì No ______________________________
2. Sì No ______________________________
3. Sì No ______________________________
4. Sì No ______________________________
5. Sì No ______________________________
6. Sì No ______________________________
7. Sì No ______________________________
8. Sì No ______________________________

Ieri ho… ____

Ieri non ho… ____

C. Passato prossimo con *essere*

A. Per cominiciare. Sentirai un dialogo due volte. La prima volta, ascolta attentamente. La seconda volta, il dialogo sarà ripetuto con pause per la ripetizione.

MARIANNA: Ciao, Carla! Siete già tornati dalle vacanze?
CARLA: Io e Antonio siamo partiti insieme la settimana scorsa e siamo andati al mare. Io sono rimasta tre giorni e sono tornata ieri per lavorare. Antonio invece è rimasto... beato lui!

B. *Avere o essere?* Di' chi ha fatto le seguenti azioni. Usa **essere** o **avere** per formare **il passato prossimo.** Ripeti la risposta.

ESEMPIO: *Senti:* Federica
Leggi: fare la spesa ieri sera
Dici: Federica ha fatto la spesa.

1. andare al mare nelle Marche
2. fare una passeggiata per Perugia
3. nascere lo stesso giorno
4. insegnare nello stesso liceo
5. uscire presto di casa
6. partire per New York
7. arrivare all'Isola d'Elba
8. scrivere una lettera a Anna

C. Un appuntamento con Giulia. Sentirai un dialogo due volte. La prima volta, ascolta attentamente. La seconda volta, scegli (*choose*) la risposta giusta. Ripeti la risposta.

CARLO: Ciao, Giulia, sei già qui! Sei venuta in macchina?
GIULIA: Ciao, Carlo, sono arrivata dieci minuti fa. Prima sono andata a comprare un giornale. E certo che ho preso l'auto. Tu hai preso l'autobus?
CARLO: Scusa il ritardo. Sono uscito di casa alle nove meno un quarto, ma l'autobus non è arrivato e allora sono venuto a piedi.
GIULIA: Allora, quando partite tu e Franca per le vacanze?
CARLO: Veramente Franca è già tornata. È partita il 7 giugno, è stata al mare per una settimana. Domani, però, parto io!
GIULIA: Non è rimasta molto al mare, perché?
CARLO: È tornata perché è nata la figlia del boss. Infatti adesso c'è il suo boss in vacanza, non lei!

1. Giulia è andata all'appuntamento _____.	a. in auto	b. in autobus
2. Carlo è uscito di casa _____.	a. alle nove	b. alle otto e quarantacinque
3. Carlo _____.	a. ha preso l'autobus	b. è andato a piedi
4. Carlo _____.	a. è già stato in vacanza	b. non è ancora partito
5. Franca è stata _____.	a. in vacanza con il boss	b. al mare
6. Franca _____.	a. non è rimasta al mare	b. ha lavorato al mare
7. Il boss di Franca _____.	a. ha avuto una figlia	b. è andato in vacanza senza la figlia

D. Cosa ha fatto Silvia ieri? Silvia ha fatto le stesse cose ieri. Di' cosa ha fatto. Comincia con **Ieri...** Ripeti la risposta.

ESEMPIO: *Senti e leggi:* Tutte le mattine vado al bar alle otto.
Dici: Ieri è andata al bar alle otto.

1. Faccio colazione: prendo un caffè.
2. Poi prendo l'autobus delle otto e un quarto per l'università.
3. Frequento i corsi e all'una mangio con i miei amici.
4. Dopo pranzo, andiamo al bar a prendere un caffè.
5. Poi andiamo a studiare in biblioteca.
6. Verso le quattro ho voglia di uno spuntino.
7. Vado al bar e prendo un tè caldo.
8. Verso le cinque prendo l'autobus e torno a casa.

D. *Conoscere e sapere*

A. Per cominciare. Sentirai un dialogo seguito da quattro frasi. Sentirai il dialogo due volte. La prima volta, ascolta attentamente. La seconda volta, la parte di Antonio sarà letta con pause per la ripetizione. Poi segna (*indicate*), per ciascuna (*each*) frase, **vero** o **falso.**

LUIGI: Conosci Marco?
ANTONIO: No, non lo conosco, ma so che suona il piano e che sa dipingere—è artista e musicista.
LUIGI: Conosci Maria?
ANTONIO: No, non la conosco, ma so che gioca bene a calcio e che sa giocare anche a football.
LUIGI: Tu non conosci molta gente, vero?
ANTONIO: No, questo è vero, ma so molte cose di molte persone!

1. vero falso
2. vero falso
3. vero falso
4. vero falso

B. Certo che li conosco! Un amico vuole sapere se conosci le seguenti persone. Rispondi che le conosci bene. Ripeti la risposta.

ESEMPIO: *Senti:* Conosci Vittoria?
Dici: Sì, la conosco bene!

1. … 2. … 3. … 4. … 5. … 6. …

C. Ma che bravi! Tu e i tuoi amici siete molto bravi. Guarda i disegni (*Look at the drawings*) e di' chi sa fare che cosa. Ripeti la risposta.

ESEMPIO: *Vedi:*

Leggi: ballare
Senti: Piero e Anna
Dici: Piero e Anna sanno ballare il tango.

1.

fare

2.

andare

3.

lavorare

4.

leggere

5.

suonare

Pronuncia: The combinations "qu" and "cu"

The combination **qu** represents the sound [kw] as in the English word *quick.* The combination **cu** followed by a vowel generally has this same sound. The pronoun **cui,** however, is one common exception to this rule.

A. ***Qu* e *cu.*** Practice the sound of **qu** and **cu.** Listen and repeat.

1. quasi
2. questo
3. qui
4. quota
5. cuore
6. cuoio
7. nacqui
8. piacque

B. **Parliamo italiano!** Listen and repeat the sentences.

1. Mia cugina ha comprato cinque quadri qui.
2. Sono quasi le quattro e un quarto.
3. La qualità di quest'acqua è cattiva.
4. Dove mangiamo di solito quelle quaglie squisite?

Ed ora ascoltiamo!

Sentirai tre conversazioni. Puoi ascoltate le conversazioni quante volte vuoi (*as many times as you need to*). Poi scegli il luogo giusto per ciascuna (*each*) conversazione.

Parole utili: non si preoccupi (*don't worry*), sbagliato (*made a mistake*)

1. a. in taxi b. in autobus
2. a. in un ristorante b. all'hotel
3. a. all'università b. in casa

Dettato

Sentirai un breve dettato tre volte. La prima volta ascolta attentamente. La seconda volta, il dettato sarà letto con pause tra le frasi. Scrivi quello che senti. La terza volta, correggi quello che hai scritto. Scrivi sulle righe date. Controlla il tuo dettato con le soluzioni date in fondo al libro.

Oggi, al bar, ______________________________

____

____

____

____

____

____

____

____

____

Dialogo

Prima parte. Daniele, Marco e Alessandra sono in un caffè.

Ascolta attentamente il dialogo.

DANIELE: Oggi pago io! Marco, che cosa prendi?
MARCO: Oh, una spremuta d'arancia, grazie. Ho già preso troppi caffè oggi.
DANIELE: E tu, Alessandra?
ALESSANDRA: Per me il solito espresso senza zucchero. E anche un'acqua naturale. Ho davvero[1] sete dopo quel panino al salame che ho mangiato. E tu, che prendi?
DANIELE: Un cappuccino.
MARCO: Un cappuccino? A quest'ora? Non hai fatto colazione? Ma via,[2] il cappuccino a mezzogiorno non puoi prenderlo!
DANIELE: Va bene, va bene, allora un caffè per me! (*Al cameriere*) Due caffè, uno senza zucchero, una spremuta d'arancia e un'acqua naturale.
IL CAMERIERE: Due caffè, una naturale e una spremuta d'arancia.

[1]*really*
[2]Ma... *Come on*

Seconda parte. Ascolta di nuovo il dialogo. Fai particolare attenzione a quello che ordinano da bere Daniele, Marco e Alessandra.

Terza parte. Sentirai due volte cinque frasi basate sul dialogo. Segna (*Indicate*), per ciascuna frase, **vero** o **falso.**

1. vero falso
2. vero falso
3. vero falso
4. vero falso
5. vero falso

Sara in Italia

Oggi Sara è a Napoli. Vuole vedere la città e il Vesuvio, il vulcano che ha distrutto (*destroyed*) le città di Pompei ed Ercolano. Ma vuole anche mangiare. Va in una vecchia pizzeria per provare la famosa pizza napoletana. Parla lì con il pizzaiolo (*pizza maker*), il signor Vincenzo Fuschino.

Ascolta attentamente il dialogo. Ascolta il dialogo quante volte vuoi. Poi, rispondi alle domande che senti. Sentirai ogni domanda due volte. Ripeti la risposta.

Parole utili: la regina (*queen*), milleottocentoottantanove (*1889*), acciughe (*anchovies*), capperi (*capers*), pomodoro (*tomato*), aglio (*garlic*), basilico (*basil*), semplice (*simple*)

1. ... 2. ... 3. ... 4. ... 5. ...

Sara in rete...

For more information about what Sara experienced during her travels, check out the links found on the *Prego!* website **(www.mhhe.com/prego8).**

CAPITOLO

Buon appetito! 6

Vocabolario preliminare

A. Per cominciare. Sentirai un dialogo due volte. La prima volta, ascolta attentamente. La seconda volta, il dialogo sarà ripetuto con pause per la ripetizione.

IRENE: Che fame, Fabio! Sono già le sette e mezzo. Cosa facciamo per cena?
FABIO: Non lo so... E poi il frigo è quasi vuoto! Perché non andiamo in una pizzeria a mangiare?
IRENE: Buon'idea! Ho proprio voglia di una pizza...
FABIO: Anch'io... o di un bel piatto di spaghetti! Invitiamo anche Marco e Alessandra?
IRENE: Se non hanno già cenato!

B. Che cosa preferisci? Sentirai un dialogo seguito da cinque domande. Sentirai il dialogo due volte. La prima volta, ascolta attentamente. La seconda volta, la parte di Irene sarà letta con pause per la ripetizione. Poi seleziona la risposta giusta.

IRENE: Allora, cosa prendiamo?
FABIO: Per me, una pizza Margherita.
IRENE: Sono indecisa: una «Quattro Stagioni» o una «Napoli»?
FABIO: Non vuoi il primo?
IRENE: No, una pizza basta.[1] No, aspetta, forse[2] anche un piatto di lasagne... Allora prendo una «Napoli»... E poi voglio uscire a prendere un gelato!
FABIO: Mmmm, forse sei indecisa anche per quello... di quale hai voglia? Tanto lo so che non sai mai quale scegliere!
IRENE: Ma che dici! Lo voglio al cioccolato e alla fragola.[3] No, aspetta, al limone e alla fragola... E tu, che gusto vuoi?
FABIO: Per me cioccolato e pistacchio. Nel cono. E tu?
IRENE: Io lo preferisco nella coppetta.[4]
FABIO: Finalmente una decisione sicura!
IRENE: Ma anche il cono non è male...

[1] *is enough* [2] *maybe*
[3] *strawberry*
[4] *cup*

1. a. una Margherita b. una Napoli
2. a. una Quattro Stagioni b. una Napoli
3. a. al cioccolato e al pistacchio b. al pistacchio e alla fragola
4. a. al cioccolato e alla fragola b. al limone e alla fragola
5. a. Fabio b. Irene

C. C'è chi è a dieta e chi a dieta non è… Sentirai un dialogo due volte. La prima volta, ascolta attentamente. La seconda volta, completa il dialogo con le parole appropriate. Controlla le tue risposte con le soluzioni date in fondo al libro.

bistecca   il dolce   gli gnocchi   un'insalata

un minestrone   patate fritte   al pomodoro   tiramisù

MARISA: Che menù impressionante! Che cosa hai voglia di mangiare?

LUCIA: Per cominciare, ______________________,[1] e tu?

MARISA: Le lasagne al forno o ______________________[2] al pesto. Ma no, prendo una cosa semplice, gli spaghetti ______________________.[3]

LUCIA: E poi?

MARISA: Una bella ______________________[4] alla griglia, con ______________________.[5]

LUCIA: Io invece prendo il pesce e ______________________.[6]

MARISA: Anche ______________________[7]?

LUCIA: No, non posso, sono a dieta.

MARISA: Davvero? Allora io prendo due porzioni di ______________________[8]… non sono a dieta e posso mangiare anche la tua parte!

In ascolto

In cucina. Lucia, Marco e Francesco, tre coinquilini, discutono della cena. Completa il menù della serata e nota chi prepara ogni piatto. Controlla le tue risposte con le soluzioni date in fondo al libro.

	ANTIPASTO	PRIMO	SECONDO	DOLCE
Lucia				
Marco				
Francesco				

Grammatica

A. Pronomi di oggetto indiretto

A. Per cominciare. Sentirai un brano due volte. La prima volta, ascolta attentamente. La seconda volta, il brano sarà letto con pause per la ripetizione.

Che cameriere sbadato! Ho ordinato un piatto di carne e lui mi ha portato un piatto di pesce. Elisabetta ha chiesto un bicchiere di vino rosso e lui le ha servito un bicchiere di vino bianco. Abbiamo chiesto il conto e lui non ci ha portato la ricevuta. Siamo andati via e… non gli abbiamo dato la mancia!

B. Quando? Di' che farai (*you will do*) le seguenti azioni domani. Sostituisci (*Substitute*) con un pronome di oggetto indiretto il nome che nella frase ha uguale (*same*) funzione. Ripeti la risposta.

ESEMPIO: *Leggi:* telefonare **alla zia**
Senti: Quando telefoni alla zia?
Dici: Le telefono domani.

1. insegnare italiano **agli studenti**
2. preparare una buona cena **per il tuo fidanzato** (*fiancé*)
3. offrire i biscotti **ai bambini**
4. preparare il risotto **per tua cugina**
5. regalare una torta **a tuo padre**
6. comprare il gelato **per tua madre**

B. Accordo del participio passato nel passato prossimo

A. Per cominciare. Sentirai un dialogo due volte. La prima volta, ascolta attentamente. La seconda volta, la parte di Gino sarà letta con pause per la ripetizione.

SARA: Stasera c'è la festa a sorpresa per Massimo. Vediamo se tutto è a posto. Hai apparecchiato la tavola?
GINO: Sì, l'ho apparecchiata.
SARA: Hai incartato i regali per Massimo?
GINO: Sì, li ho incartati.
SARA: Hai preparato gli antipasti?
GINO: Sì, li ho preparati. Sono pronti.
SARA: Hai comprato tutto?
GINO: Sì, ho comprato tutto.
SARA: Un'ultima domanda. Hai invitato Massimo?
GINO: Oh, no!

B. Di chi o di che cosa parliamo? Ascolta la frase. Seleziona la risposta appropriata. Poi, componi la frase sostituendo al pronome l'oggetto di cui si parla. (*Then, formulate the sentence using the correct object instead of the pronoun.*) Ripeti la risposta.

ESEMPIO: *Senti:* **L'ho mangiata.**
Leggi: a. la mela b. il gelato c. le pizze
Segni: (a. la mela)
Senti: a
Dici: Ho mangiato la mela.

1. a. Anna e Nora b. i film del terrore c. il Colosseo
2. a. Paolo b. il Vaticano e il Papa c. le foto
3. a. l'insalata e le patate b. il primo e il secondo c. la pasta
4. a. la doccia (*shower*) b. l'esame c. il jogging
5. a. Piera b. un messaggio c. una lettera
6. a. i film b. le bici c. le pizze e i gelati
7. a. i giornali b. le riviste c. la poesia
8. a. le moto b. le auto c. il libro

C. *Piacere*

A. Per cominciare. Sentirai un dialogo due volte. La prima volta, ascolta bene. La seconda volta, completa il dialogo con le parole che mancano. Controlla le tue risposte con le soluzioni date in fondo al libro.

ANDREA: Ragazzi, cosa vi ________________[1] sulla ________________[2]?

STEFANO: Io ________________[3] le olive, ma non mi piace il ________________.[4] A Laura le ________________[5] le acciughe, ma non le piacciono i ________________.[6] A tutti e due piace la ________________[7] e ________________[8] piacciono anche i carciofini...

ANDREA: Che confusione!! Ho io la soluzione: una ________________[9] pizza ________________[10] per tutti!

B. Gli piace? Guarda i disegni e di' se alla gente piacciono o non piacciono i cibi. Ripeti la risposta.

ESEMPIO: *Vedi:*

Senti: A Giulio piacciono le patatine?
Dici: Sì, gli piacciono.

1.

2.

3.

4.

C. Cosa vi piace? Ascolta che cosa piace fare a queste persone. Trasforma le frasi con i pronomi indiretti e il verbo **piacere,** come nell'esempio. Ripeti la risposta.

ESEMPIO: *Senti:* Giulio ama i giornali sportivi.
Dici: Gli piacciono i giornali sportivi.

1. … 2. … 3. … 4. … 5. … 6. …

D. Che gusti difficili! Queste persone ieri sono andate al ristorante ma non gli è piaciuto niente (*anything*). Leggi i piatti che hanno ordinato, ascolta i nomi delle persone che li hanno ordinati. Forma delle frasi con i pronomi indiretti come nell'esempio. Ripeti la risposta.

ESEMPIO: *Leggi:* la pasta carbonara
Senti: a Giovanna
Dici: Non le è piaciuta la pasta carbonara.

1. il pesce
2. le bruschette
3. il tiramisù
4. la bistecca alla griglia
5. le patate fritte
6. i tortellini alla bolognese

D. Interrogativi

A. Per cominciare. Sentirai un dialogo seguito da tre domande. Sentirai il dialogo due volte. La prima volta, ascolta attentamente. La seconda volta, la parte di Tiziana sarà letta con pause per la ripetizione. Poi seleziona la risposta giusta.

TIZIANA: Dove preferisci mangiare stasera, in casa o al ristorante?
CLAUDIO: Preferisco mangiare in casa.
TIZIANA: Chi cucina?
CLAUDIO: Cucino io.
TIZIANA: Cosa prepari?
CLAUDIO: Gli spaghetti e un'insalata.
TIZIANA: Quando mangiamo?
CLAUDIO: Alle otto.
TIZIANA: Perché non cucini anche un secondo?
CLAUDIO: Ma cara... questo non è un ristorante!

1. a. in casa b. al ristorante
2. a. Tiziana b. Claudio
3. a. alle sette b. alle otto

B. Roberto l'affascinante (*the charming one*). Hai tante domande da fare riguardo al (*about the*) nuovo studente, Roberto. Fai (*Ask*) le domande appropriate alle risposte che senti. Ripeti la risposta.

ESEMPIO: *Senti:* Roberto è simpatico.
Dici: Com'è Roberto?

1. ... 2. ... 3. ... 4. ... 5. ... 6. ...

C. Jeopardy culinario. Fai la domanda giusta per ogni risposta. Usa l'interrogativo dato tra parentesi. Ripeti la risposta.

ESEMPIO: *Senti e leggi:* È un formaggio dolce che è usato con la pizza. (Cos'è... ?)
Dici: Cos'è la mozzarella?

1. È una bevanda alcoolica che gli italiani bevono molto. (Cos'è... ?)
2. È della città di Parma. (Di dov'è... ?)
3. Li ha portati in Italia Cristoforo Colombo. (Chi... ?)
4. Pasta, uova, pepe, parmigiano, pancetta: questi sono gli ingredienti. (Quali sono... ?)
5. I piatti sono di solito tre: primo, secondo, dolce. (Quanti... ?)
6. Lo mangiamo prima del primo. (Quando... ?)

Pronuncia: The sounds of the letter "z"

The letter **z** represents two sounds: [ć] as in the English word *bats* and [ź] as in the English word *pads.*

A. Z sonora. At the beginning of a word, **z** is usually pronounced as [ź], although this varies from region to region. Listen and repeat.

1. zampa
2. zero
3. zitto
4. zona
5. zucchero

B. ***Z* sonora e *z* sorda.** In the middle of words, **z** can have either the [ź] or the [ć] sound. The [ć] sound occurs frequently following **l** and **n.** Listen and repeat.

1. azalea
2. pranzo
3. zanzara
4. alzare
5. differenza
6. Lazio

C. **Parliamo italiano!** Listen and repeat.

1. Sai che differenza c'è tra colazione e pranzo?
2. Alla stazione di Venezia vendono pizze senza mozzarella.
3. Conosci molte ragazze con gli occhi azzurri?
4. A mezzogiorno ho lezione di zoologia.
5. C'è un negozio di calzature in Piazza Indipendenza.

Ed ora ascoltiamo!

Che cena! Sentirai un discorso tra Laura e Danilo. Puoi ascoltare il dialogo quante volte vuoi. Poi sentirai cinque frasi due volte. Segna **vero** o **falso.**

Parole utili: alberghiera (*hotel*), almeno (*at least*)

1. vero falso
2. vero falso
3. vero falso
4. vero falso
5. vero falso

Dettato

Sentirai un breve dettato tre volte. La prima volta ascolta attentamente. La seconda volta, il dettato sarà letto con pause tra le frasi. Scrivi quello che senti. La terza volta, correggi quello che hai scritto. Scrivi sulle righe date. Controlla il tuo dettato con le soluzioni date in fondo al libro.

Danilo ha cucinato ______

Dialogo

Prima parte. Irene e Fabio aspettano Marco e Alessandra a cena e, mentre (*while*) aspettano, preparano l'ultimo piatto, il dolce.

Ascolta attentamente il dialogo.

IRENE: Allora, Fabio, hai apparecchiato la tavola?

FABIO: Sì, ho già preparato tutto, la tavola è pronta, c'è il primo nel forno, gli antipasti sono in frigorifero e la bistecca è sulla griglia, ma dobbiamo aspettare Marco e Alessandra prima di cominciare a cucinarla...

IRENE: Ma il dolce? Non hai comprato il tiramisù?

FABIO: No, ho pensato di prepararlo qui con te, è un dolce veloce da fare.

IRENE: Allora, di che cosa abbiamo bisogno?

FABIO: Prendi i biscotti savoiardi, lì, sul tavolo di cucina, poi dal frigorifero prendi otto uova, due per persona e anche il mascarpone[1]... cos'altro? Ah, lo zucchero e...

IRENE: Ho visto che c'è del caffè in cucina...

FABIO: Sì, abbiamo bisogno del caffè. Allora, prendiamo i biscotti, li bagniamo[2] nel caffè e li mettiamo, uno accanto all'altro, in un recipiente.[3] Poi mescoliamo[4] le uova, lo zucchero e il mascarpone, così per fare una crema. E mettiamo questa crema sullo strato[5] di biscotti. Bagniamo altri biscotti e...

IRENE: Ho capito, facciamo uno strato di biscotti bagnati con il caffè e poi uno strato di crema, ancora uno strato di biscotti, ancora uno di crema... e così via.[6]

FABIO: Perfetto! Poi, mettiamo il recipiente in frigorifero, per un paio d'ore, così diventa freddo. Non credo di avere dimenticato niente[7]!

[1]*type of cheese*
[2]*we soak*
[3]*container* / [4]*we mix*
[5]*layer*
[6]così... *so on*
[7]*anything*

Seconda parte. Ascolta di nuovo il dialogo. Fai particolare attenzione agli ingredienti e all'ordine della preparazione della ricetta.

Terza parte. Sentirai due volte sei frasi basate sul dialogo. Segna, per ciascuna frase, **vero** o **falso.**

1. vero falso
2. vero falso
3. vero falso
4. vero falso
5. vero falso
6. vero falso

Sara in Italia

Sara è sul treno locale che da Bologna va a Rimini, una città della costa adriatica, famosa in tutta Europa per le spiagge, il mare e i divertimenti. Sara ha visitato Parma e Bologna con il suo amico Massimiliano, uno studente universitario bolognese, ed è stata al ristorante.

Ascolta attentamente il dialogo. Ascolta il dialogo quante volte vuoi. Poi, rispondi alle domande che senti. Sentirai ogni domanda due volte. Ripeti la risposta.

Parole utili: diversissime (*very different*), besciamella (*bechamel*), cioè (*that is*), farina (*flour*), pizzico (*pinch*), noce moscata (*nutmeg*), più pregiato (*finest*)

1. … 2. … 3. … 4. … 5. …

Sara in rete…

For more information about what Sara experienced during her travels, check out the links found on the *Prego!* website **(www.mhhe.com/prego8).**

CAPITOLO 7

La vita di tutti i giorni

Vocabolario preliminare

A. Per cominciare. Sentirai un dialogo due volte. La prima volta, ascolta attentamente. La seconda volta, il dialogo sarà ripetuto con pause per la ripetizione.

LUISA: Che stress, Anna! Non so cosa mettermi per la festa di questa sera…
ANNA: Puoi metterti i pantaloni neri, la camicia bianca e le tue scarpe nuove.
LUISA: Buon'idea! Che dici, mi trucco?
ANNA: Ma no, non hai bisogno di truccarti, sei bella così!

B. Giulia e la bella figura. Giulia vuole fare bella figura quando esce stasera. Sentirai un brano due volte. La prima volta, ascolta attentamente. La seconda volta, completa il brano con le parole che mancano. Controlla le tue risposte con le soluzioni date in fondo al libro.

Giulia stasera esce e vuole farsi bella. Dopo una giornata di lavoro e studio, ha bisogno di ______________________,[1] allora decide di ______________________[2] il bagno e di ______________________ _____ ______________________.[3] Dopo il bagno, _____[4] asciuga,[a] si pettina,[b] si _____[5] allo specchio e _____ ______________________[6] un po' gli occhi. _____ ______________________[7] il rossetto[c] e infine le lenti a contatto. È quasi pronta. _____ ______________________[8] uno dei suoi vestiti da sera. _____ ______________________[9] un po' di profumo e alla fine è pronta veramente per uscire.

[a]*dries off* [b]si… *she combs her hair* [c]*lipstick*

C. **L'abbigliamento.** Identifica ogni capo (*each piece of clothing*) nel disegno. Comincia la frase con **È...** o **Sono...** . Ripeti la risposta.

ESEMPIO: *Senti:* 1
Dici: È una maglia.

2. ... 3. ... 4. ... 5. ... 6. ... 7. ... 8. ...

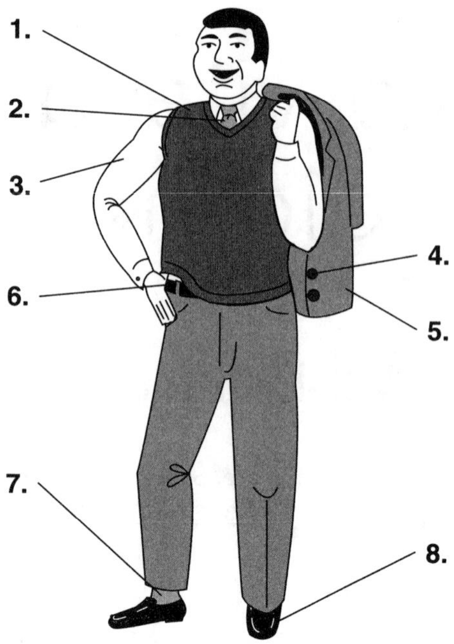

In ascolto

Che mi metto stasera? Luisa è una persona che non è mai soddisfatta. Stasera si lamenta dei suoi vestiti. Ascolta con attenzione la sua conversazione con un'amica e poi rispondi alle domande seguenti. Controlla le tue risposte con le soluzioni date in fondo al libro.

1. Perché Luisa non vuole uscire stasera?
2. Che cosa ha comprato ieri?
3. Che cosa ha comprato due giorni fa?
4. Secondo lei, di che cosa ha bisogno?

Grammatica

A. Verbi riflessivi

A. **Per cominciare.** Sentirai un dialogo due volte. La prima volta, ascolta attentamente. La seconda volta, il dialogo sarà ripetuto con pause per la ripetizione.

SIGNORA ROSSI: Nino ogni mattina si sveglia tardi e non ha tempo di lavarsi e fare colazione. Si alza presto solo la domenica per andare in palestra a giocare a pallone.

SIGNORA VERDI: Ho capito: a scuola si annoia e in palestra si diverte.

B. Abitudini. Di' che le seguenti persone hanno le stesse abitudini tue (*same habits as yours*). Ripeti la risposta.

ESEMPIO: *Leggi:* Mi lavo i denti spesso.
Senti: Cinzia
Dici: Anche lei si lava i denti spesso.

1. Mi alzo subito la mattina.
2. Mi sveglio presto.
3. Mi lavo con l'acqua fredda.
4. Mi vesto in fretta.

C. Che giornata! Sentirai un dialogo tra Franca e Gino in cui (*in which*) discutono della loro giornata stressante. Sentirai il dialogo due volte. La prima volta, ascolta attentamente. La seconda volta, prendi appunti (*take notes*) su Franca e Gino. Poi sentirai quattro domande e dovrai scegliere la risposta giusta. Leggi le risposte date prima di ascoltare il dialogo.

FRANCA ____

____

GINO ____

____

1. a. Si è solo lavata e vestita. b. Si è preparata con cura e poi ha preso l'autobus.
2. a. Gino è rilassato e riposato. b. Ha bisogno di caffè per stare bene.
3. a. Ha avuto una discussione con il direttore. b. Si è sentito molto, molto stanco.
4. a. Va al parco a rilassarsi. b. Sta a casa e dorme molto.

D. E tu, cosa hai fatto stamattina? Racconta come ti sei preparato/preparata stamattina, secondo i suggerimenti (*according to the cues*).

1. Mi sono alzato/alzata alle...
2. Mi sono lavato/lavata con l'acqua... (calda/fredda)
3. Mi sono messo/messa... (i jeans / una camicia / i calzini...)
4. (Non) Mi sono fatto la barba... / (Non) Mi sono truccata...
5. (Non) Mi sono fermato/fermata al bar a fare colazione.

B. Costruzione reciproca

A. Per cominciare. Sentirai un brano due volte. La prima volta, ascolta attentamente. La seconda volta, completa il brano con le parole che mancano. Controlla le tue risposte con le soluzioni date in fondo al libro.

Giulio e Anna ____ ____________________[1] molto bene—sono amici di infanzia. ____ ____________________[2] tutti i giorni a scuola e tutte le sere ____ ____________________[3] al telefono. Discutono sempre dei loro problemi perché ____ ____________________[4] benissimo. Secondo te, hanno intenzione di sposarsi un giorno?

B. Davide e Serena. Davide e Serena sono proprio una bella coppia. Guarda i disegni e di' cosa fanno, secondo i suggerimenti. Ripeti la risposta.

ESEMPIO: *Vedi:*

Senti: guardarsi
Dici: Davide e Serena si guardano.

1.

2.

3.

4.

5.

C. La storia di Alessia e Riccardo.

Prima parte. Il computer ha fatto confusione con la storia di Alessia e Riccardo. Ferma la registrazione (*stop the tape*) e forma delle frasi logiche con i verbi al passato prossimo. Quando hai finito di formare le frasi, continua la registrazione.

a. poi / vedersi / nel tempo libero

____

b. Alessia / andare a fare un viaggio e / scriversi lunghe lettere d'amore / ogni giorno

____

c. abbracciarsi e baciarsi / all'aeroporto / quando Alessia / tornare

____

d. il giorno dopo / telefonarsi / e parlarsi / per ore

____

e. fidanzarsi subito / e sposarsi / dopo due settimane. / E non lasciarsi mai.

____

f. Alessia e Riccardo / conoscersi / a una festa

____

Seconda parte. Ascolta le frasi formate e abbina (*match*) ogni frase della prima parte con la figura corrispondente.

1.

______

2.

______

3.

______

4.

______

5.

______

6.

______

Terza parte. La storia sarà ripetuta con le pause per la ripetizione.

D. Storie d'incontri. Marina ti fa molte domande. Ascolta le sue domande con attenzione, poi scrivi le tue risposte. Ripeti le tue risposte.

1. ____
2. ____
3. ____
4. ____
5. ____

C. Avverbi

A. Per cominciare. Sentirai un brano seguito da tre domande. Sentirai il brano due volte. La prima volta, ascolta attentamente. La seconda volta, il brano sarà ripetuto con pause per la ripetizione. Scegli poi le risposte giuste alle domande che senti.

Carla è una persona molto particolare. Si sveglia presto ogni mattina; mangia poco ma bene a colazione; si veste in fretta ma elegantemente; guida velocemente per andare in ufficio... ma arriva sempre tardi!

1. a. presto b. tardi
2. a. in fretta b. lentamente
3. a. puntuale b. in ritardo

B. Veramente. Cambia i seguenti aggettivi in avverbi. Ripeti la risposta.

ESEMPIO: *Senti:* vero
Dici: veramente

1. ... 2. ... 3. ... 4. ... 5. ... 6. ...

C. Gli italiani. Tutti i tuoi amici vogliono sapere come sono gli italiani. Rispondi alle loro domande, secondo i suggerimenti. Ripeti la risposta.

ESEMPIO: *Senti:* Come parlano gli italiani?
Leggi: veloce
Dici: Parlano velocemente.

1. elegante 2. rapido 3. abbondante 4. facile 5. gentile

D. Numeri superiori a 100

A. Per cominciare. Sentirai un dialogo due volte. La prima volta, ascolta attentamente. La seconda volta, il dialogo sarà ripetuto con pause per la ripetizione.

MONICA: Mi sono diplomata nel 2000, mi sono laureata nel 2004, mi sono sposata nel 2005, ho avuto una figlia nel 2006 e un'altra figlia nel 2007, ho accettato un posto all'università nel 2008...
SILVIA: Quando pensi di fermarti?

B. Quanto fa? Fai le addizioni dei seguenti numeri. Sentirai ogni addizione due volte. Ascolta attentamente, poi scrivi la somma dei due numeri che senti. Controlla le tue risposte con le soluzioni date in fondo al libro.

ESEMPIO: *Senti:* cento più (+) cento fa (=)...
Scrivi i numeri e fai l'addizione: 100 + 100 = 200
Scrivi: duecento

1. ______________________
2. ______________________
3. ______________________
4. ______________________
5. ______________________
6. ______________________

Pronuncia: The sounds of the letter "l"

In Italian, the letter l has a sound similar to that in the English word *love*. It is a clear sound, articulated at the front of the mouth, never at the back of the mouth, as in the English words *alter* and *will*.

A. *L.* Practice the **l** sound. Listen and repeat.

1. lavarsi
2. leggere
3. lira
4. loro
5. lunedì
6. salutare

B. ***L* doppia.** Compare and contrast the single and double sound of **l.** Note the slight change in vowel sound when the consonant that follows is doubled. Listen and repeat.

1. belo / bello
2. fola / folla
3. pala / palla
4. cela / cella

C. ***L* e *gl*.** As you learned in **Capitolo 3,** the sound of **gl** is different from the sound of **l.** Compare and contrast the sounds in the following pairs of words. Listen and repeat.

1. belli / begli
2. olio / aglio
3. male / maglia
4. filo / figlio

D. **Parliamo italiano!** Listen and repeat.

1. Come balla bene la moglie di Guglielmo! Glielo voglio dire.
2. Fa caldo a Milano in luglio?
3. Ecco il portafoglio di mio figlio.
4. Quella ragazza è alta e snella.
5. Vogliono il tè con il latte o con il limone?

Ed ora ascoltiamo!

Storiella d'amore. Sentirai un dialogo tra Romeo e Giulietta. Puoi ascoltare il dialogo quante volte vuoi. Poi sentirai cinque frasi da completare. Scegli il completamento giusto per ciascuna frase.

1. a. al bar. b. ad una festa.
2. a. quando si sono guardati. b. quando si sono salutati.
3. a. per caso (*by chance*) a Verona. b. per caso ad una festa.
4. a. a Verona. b. al Caffè Sportivo.
5. a. «Ti amo.» b. «Sì, certo.»

Dettato

Sentirai un breve dettato tre volte. La prima volta ascolta attentamente. La seconda volta, il dettato sarà letto con pause tra le frasi. Scrivi quello che senti. La terza volta, correggi quello che hai scritto. Scrivi sulle righe date. Controlla il tuo dettato con le soluzioni date in fondo al libro.

Marilena, Franca, Elena e Silvia ____

____

____

____

____

____

____

____

____

____

Dialogo

Prima parte. Gerry Milligan, uno studente di italiano in Italia, si lamenta sempre dei suoi vestiti. Adesso è a Genova, a casa di Luca e Natasha.

Ascolta attentamente il dialogo.

GERRY: Natasha, non credo di poter uscire stasera! Non ho proprio niente da mettermi!

NATASHA: Ma non hai comprato un paio di pantaloni e una camicia nuova ieri?

LUCA: Guarda, Gerry, andiamo solo al ristorante, stai benissimo, va bene così!

NATASHA: Luca, guarda che capisco benissimo questi attacchi d'ansia di Gerry. Quando sono venuta in Italia la prima volta, tutti hanno fatto dei commenti sui vestiti che mi sono messa...

GERRY: Vedi, Luca, che ho ragione? È una ragione culturale, questa. Tutti gli italiani che vedo hanno sempre vestiti che vanno bene insieme.[1] Certo che ho comprato dei vestiti nuovi ieri ma non ho le scarpe o la cintura adatte...

LUCA: Mamma mia, ma prova a metterti un paio di scarpe e andiamo, ho fame! E poi guarda me: la moda non mi interessa proprio.

NATASHA: Infatti, si vede! Luca, ma ti sei guardato allo specchio stamattina? Non ti sei fatto la barba, non ti sei pettinato[2]...

LUCA: Ma è domenica, non voglio preoccuparmi della moda, mi voglio solo rilassare!

[1] *together*

[2] non... *you didn't comb your hair*

Seconda parte. Ascolta di nuovo il dialogo. Fai particolare attenzione alle preoccupazioni di Gerry e alle obiezioni di Luca.

Terza parte. Sentirai due volte sei frasi basate sul dialogo. Segna, per ciascuna frase, **vero** o **falso.**

1. vero falso
2. vero falso
3. vero falso
4. vero falso
5. vero falso
6. vero falso

Sara in Italia

Sara è a Milano, capitale economica d'Italia e centro della moda e dell'editoria (*publishing*). Ha visitato il Duomo e il Teatro alla Scala e adesso è nella Galleria Vittorio Emanuele II a prendere un caffè. Deve incontrare il suo amico Matteo, ma Matteo non è ancora arrivato. Lo chiama allora al cellulare.

Parole utili: forse (*maybe*), firmati (*designer*), borsa di pelle (*leather purse*), aumentati (*raised*)

Ascolta attentamente il dialogo. Ascolta il dialogo quante volte vuoi. Poi, rispondi alle domande che senti. Sentirai ogni domanda due volte. Ripeti la risposta.

1. … 2. … 3. … 4. … 5. …

Sara in rete…

For more information about what Sara experienced during her travels, check out the links found on the *Prego!* website **(www.mhhe.com/prego8).**

Nome ______________________ Data ____________ Classe ______________

CAPITOLO 8

Cinema, stampa e TV

Vocabolario preliminare

A. Per cominciare. Sentirai un dialogo seguito da quattro domande. Sentirai il dialogo due volte. La prima volta, ascolta attentamente. La seconda volta, il dialogo sarà ripetuto con pause per la ripetizione. Scegli poi le risposte giuste per le domande che senti.

ROSSANA: Che programmi ci sono stasera in televisione?

FABRIZIO: C'è una partita di calcio su Rai Uno, ci sono due bei film su Rai Tre e Canale Cinque.

ROSSANA: Perché non andiamo al cinema, invece? Ho letto una recensione molto positiva sull'ultimo film di Woody Allen...

1. a. C'è una partita di calcio. b. C'è una partita di basketball.
2. a. Ci sono due film interessanti. b. C'è una partita di calcio.
3. a. Propone di vedere la partita. b. Propone di andare al cinema.

B. La stampa. Sentirai sei definizioni di parole che hanno a che fare con (*have to do with*) la stampa. Sentirai le definizioni due volte. Scegli la parola corrispondente a ciascuna definizione e scrivi la parola sulla riga data. Controlla le tue risposte con le soluzioni date in fondo al libro.

l'intervista
il quotidiano
il mensile
la recensione
la pubblicità
il settimanale

1. ______________________
2. ______________________
3. ______________________
4. ______________________
5. ______________________
6. ______________________

In ascolto

Recensioni e interviste... Sandra e Claudia discutono delle recensioni e interviste a Roberto Benigni, un famoso attore comico e regista italiano. Ascolta con attenzione la loro conversazione e rispondi alle domande seguenti. Controlla le tue risposte con le soluzioni date in fondo al libro.

1. Cosa c'è sul giornale di oggi?

   ____

2. Cosa ha letto Claudia su un settimanale?

   ____

3. Su che cosa sono le domande dell'intervista che Sandra ha letto sul giornale di oggi?

   ____

4. Cosa ha intenzione di fare Sandra stasera?

   ____

Grammatica

A. Imperfetto

A. Per cominciare. Sentirai un dialogo due volte. La prima volta, ascolta attentamente. La seconda volta, il dialogo sarà ripetuto con pause per la ripetizione.

CARLETTO: Mamma, papà, cosa vi piaceva fare quando eravate piccoli?

PAPÀ: Io leggevo i libri d'avventura e guardavo i telefilm di cow-boy alla TV.

MAMMA: Io, invece, preferivo leggere le favole e guardavo i film d'amore!

B. Come eravamo... Guardi le vecchie foto di famiglia. Di' come erano i membri della famiglia, secondo i suggerimenti. Ripeti la risposta.

ESEMPIO: *Senti:* la nonna
Leggi: essere una bella ragazza
Dici: La nonna era una bella ragazza.

1. avere la barba (*beard*) nera
2. essere grasso
3. portare vestiti buffi (*comical*)
4. andare in bicicletta
5. essere un atleta
6. portare gli occhiali
7. avere tanti (*so much*) capelli

C. Davide e Serena. Davide e Serena erano una bella coppia ma... non più. Metti le frasi di Davide all'imperfetto. Ripeti la risposta.

ESEMPIO: *Senti:* Io le porto sempre i fiori.
Dici: Io le portavo sempre i fiori.

1. ... 2. ... 3. ... 4. ... 5. ...

D. Sempre, spesso o mai? Con quale frequenza facevi le seguenti azioni da bambino o bambina? Sentirai, per due volte, otto domande. Prendi appunti sulle domande e segna nello schema con quale frequenza facevi le seguenti azioni da bambino o bambina. Poi scrivi tre frasi su cosa facevi, sempre, spesso o mai, sulle righe date (*lines given*).

	SEMPRE	SPESSO	MAI
1. ______________________	□	□	□
2. ______________________	□	□	□
3. ______________________	□	□	□
4. ______________________	□	□	□
5. ______________________	□	□	□
6. ______________________	□	□	□
7. ______________________	□	□	□
8. ______________________	□	□	□

Sempre: ______________________

Spesso: ______________________

Mai: ______________________

B. Imperfetto e passato prossimo

A. Per cominciare. Sentirai un brano due volte. La prima volta, ascolta attentamente. La seconda volta il brano sarà ripetuto con le pause per la ripetizione.

Ieri sera pioveva, così io e Marco siamo rimasti in casa. Mentre io guardavo un bel film alla TV, Marco ascoltava la radio. Ci rilassavamo... . All'improvviso è andata via la luce! Io non ho visto la fine del film e Marco non ha ascoltato la sua canzone preferita. Che rabbia!

B. Cosa indica? Quando usiamo il passato prossimo e quando usiamo l'imperfetto? Sentirai alcune frasi. Abbina le frasi con le descrizioni nella colonna in basso (*below*). Prima di iniziare, leggi le descrizioni nella colonna in basso. Puoi ascoltare le frasi quante volte vuoi. Controlla le tue risposte con le soluzioni date in fondo al libro.

1. ______ a. telling time
2. ______ b. talking about weather
3. ______ c. ongoing events in the past
4. ______ d. completed actions in the past
5. ______ e. habitual past actions
6. ______ f. interrupted actions
7. ______ g. description of physical and mental states
8. ______
9. ______
10. ______

C. **Quando? Azioni abituali e azioni puntuali.** Sentirai delle frasi. Ascolta le frasi con attenzione, dopo scegli una conclusione logica. Fai attenzione ai tempi usati. Controlla le tue risposte con le soluzioni date in fondo al libro.

1. a. sempre — b. la scorsa settimana
2. a. ogni week-end — b. ieri
3. a. domenica — b. la domenica
4. a. all'improvviso (*suddenly*) — b. tutti i giorni
5. a. ieri — b. di solito
6. a. di solito — b. ieri pomeriggio
7. a. Ogni inverno — b. Lo scorso inverno
8. a. tutti i giorni — b. una volta

D. **Ancora azioni abituali, azioni puntuali.** Leggi le espressioni di tempo in basso. Sentirai alcune frasi con l'imperfetto o il passato prossimo. Riforma ogni frase con la nuova espressione di tempo secondo l'esempio. Attenzione alla forma corretta del verbo, o all'imperfetto o al passato prossimo. Ripeti la risposta.

ESEMPIO: *Senti:* Una volta mi piaceva mangiare la bistecca al ristorante.
Leggi: lo scorso sabato
Dici: Lo scorso sabato mi è piaciuto mangiare la bistecca al ristorante.

1. spesso
2. di solito
3. ieri
4. ogni estate
5. un mese fa
6. in inverno
7. il sabato
8. domenica

E. **Anche noi!** Giancarlo ti racconta cosa ha fatto ieri. Di' che sono tutte cose che tu e i tuoi fratelli facevate da piccoli. Ripeti la risposta.

ESEMPIO: *Senti:* Ieri ho mangiato molta pizza.
Leggi: anche mia sorella
Dici: Anche mia sorella da piccola mangiava molta pizza.

1. anche mio fratello
2. anche le mie sorelle
3. anche i miei fratelli
4. anche noi
5. anch'io

F. **Che conclusioni?** Leggi le seguenti frasi incomplete. Abbina le parti delle frasi secondo le frasi complete che senti. Controlla le tue risposte con le soluzioni date in fondo al libro.

1. _____ mi sono addormentato.
2. _____ Marco e Nicola lavavano i piatti.
3. _____ tu hai usato il computer e hai scritto e-mail agli amici.
4. _____ il telefono ha suonato.
5. _____ mi sono subito sentito male.

a. Mentre ero in bagno...
b. Mentre facevo i compiti...
c. Mentre Sonia e Paola pulivano la cucina...
d. Mentre eri a fare gli esercizi...
e. Quando sei partita...

G. **Che tempo!** Completa la storia con la forma giusta del verbo che senti, o all'imperfetto o al passato prossimo. Poi, ascolta il brano e controlla le tue risposte.

ESEMPIO: *Leggi:* Ieri come tutte le mattine la sveglia _______________ alle sette.
Senti: suonare
Scrivi: Ieri come tutte le mattine la sveglia ___ha suonato___ alle sette.

Ieri come tutte le mattine la sveglia _______________[1] alle sette.

(Io) _______________[2] subito. _______________[3] in bagno a fare la doccia.

________________[4] una bella giornata. (Io) ________________[5] dalla finestra del bagno un bel sole. ________________[6] felice. ________________[7] in camera. ________________[8] con allegria.[a] ________________[9] di casa. ________________[10] l'autobus. Ma l'autobus ________________[11] in ritardo. Poi ________________[12] a piovere. (Io) Non ________________[13] l'ombrello. Allora ________________[14] un taxi. Il taxi ________________[15] subito. Ma (io) non ________________[16] i soldi per il taxi! Allora ________________[17] a aspettare l'autobus nella pioggia. Come risultato, ________________[18] un raffreddore.[b] E ________________[19] male per il resto della giornata.

[a]con... *happily* [b]*cold*

C. Trapassato

A. Per cominciare. Sentirai un brano due volte. La prima volta, ascolta attentamente. La seconda volta, completa il brano con le parole che mancano. Controlla le tue risposte con le soluzioni date in fondo al libro.

Gino aveva capito che l'appuntamento con Susanna ________________[1] alle 8.00, ma Susanna ________________ ________________[2] che era alle 7.00. Alle 7.30 Susanna ________________[3] stanca di aspettare Gino ed era molto arrabbiata. Così ________________ ________________[4] al cinema con la sua compagna di stanza. Gino ________________ ________________[5] alle 8.00 in punto, ma quando è arrivato Susanna ________________[6] già ________________.[7] Povero Gino!

B. Ma perché? Mariella vuole sapere perché sono successe certe cose. Rispondi alle sue domande, secondo i suggerimenti. Ripeti la risposta.

ESEMPIO: *Senti:* Perché eri di umore nero (*in a bad mood*)?
Leggi: lavorare troppo
Dici: Ero di umore nero perché avevo lavorato troppo.

1. studiare tutta la notte
2. alzarsi presto
3. aspettare due ore
4. mangiare solo un panino
5. dimenticare l'orologio

C. La fiaba confusa. (*Mixed-up fairy tale.*) Sentirai raccontare una fiaba piuttosto particolare. Sentirai le due parti della fiaba due volte. La prima volta, ascolta attentamente. La seconda volta, completa la prima metà con il verbo all'imperfetto e la seconda metà con il verbo al trapassato. Controlla le tue risposte con le soluzioni date in fondo al libro. Poi, inventa un finale alla fiaba. Ferma la registrazione per scrivere il finale sulle righe date.

Parole utili: Cappuccetto Rosso (*Little Red Riding Hood*), camminare (*to walk*), Cenerentola (*Cinderella*), Biancaneve (*Snow White*), la Bella Addormentata (*Sleeping Beauty*)

La prima metà

C'________________[1] una volta una bella bambina che ________________[2] sola nel bosco.[a] ________________ ________________[3] Cappuccetto Rosso perché ________________[4] un vestito con un cappuccio[b] che ________________[5] rosso come un pomodoro. Cappuccetto un giorno ________________[6] andare a fare visita alla nonna, così esce di casa e mentre ________________[7] nel bosco incontra Cenerentola.

La seconda metà

Insieme vanno dalla nonna e, quando arrivano, vedono uscire la Bella Addormentata, che ________________ ________________ appena[c] ________________[8] dal suo sonno[d] e che cercava il suo Principe. La Bella Addormentata ________________ ________________[9] invece la casa della nonna. La nonna le ________________ ________________[10] che il Principe ________________ ________________[11] a cercare Biancaneve, perché Biancaneve ________________ ________________[12] una scarpa nella foresta e il Principe ________________ ________________[13] a incontrarla. Lui aveva la scarpa che la nonna ________________ ________________.[14]

[a]*forest* [b]*hood* [c]*just* [d]*sleep, trance*

Un finale possibile:

____

____

____

____

____

____

D. Suffissi

A. Per cominciare. Sentirai un dialogo due volte. La prima volta, ascolta attentamente. La seconda volta, il dialogo sarà ripetuto con pause per la ripetizione.

VALERIA: Com'è il padre di Margherita?
ANNA: È un omone grande e grosso con due grandi baffoni e un vocione terribile.
VALERIA: E sua madre?
ANNA: Ah, sua madre è tutto il contrario: una donna piccolina con una vocina sottile sottile.
VALERIA: E il suo fratellino?
ANNA: Beh! Quello è un vero ragazzaccio!

B. Una letterona! Guarda i disegni e seleziona quello indicato nella frase che senti.

ESEMPIO: *Vedi:* a.  b. 

Senti: Ho ricevuto una letterona!

Scegli: a. ⓑ

1. a.  b. 

2. a.  b. 

3. a.  b. 

4. a.  b. 

5. a.  b. 

Pronuncia: The sounds of the letters "m" and "n"

A. ***M* e *m* doppia.** The letter **m** is pronounced as in the English word *mime.* Listen and repeat.

1. marito
2. mese
3. minuti
4. moto
5. musica

Now contrast the single and double sound of **m.** Listen and repeat.

1. m'ama / mamma
2. some / somme
3. fumo / fummo

B. ***N* e *n* doppia.** The letter **n** is pronounced as in the English word *nine.* Listen and repeat.

1. naso
2. neve
3. nipoti
4. noioso
5. numeroso

Now contrast the single and double sound of **n.** Listen and repeat.

1. la luna / l'alunna
2. noni / nonni
3. sano / sanno

C. ***Gn.*** As you learned in **Capitolo 3,** the combination **gn** has its own distinct sound. Compare and contrast the [n] and the [ny] sounds in the following pairs of words. Listen and repeat.

1. campana / campagna
2. anello / agnello
3. sono / sogno

D. **Parliamo italiano!** Listen and repeat.

1. Guglielmo Agnelli è un ingegnere di Foligno.
2. Il bambino è nato in giugno.
3. Dammi un anello, non un agnello!
4. Buon Natale, nonna Virginia!
5. Anna è la moglie di mio figlio Antonio.

Ed ora ascoltiamo!

Angela, una giovane donna italiana, è intervistata da un giornalista. Sentirai il loro dialogo. Puoi ascoltare il dialogo quante volte vuoi. Poi sentirai, due volte, cinque frasi e dovrai segnare, per ciascuna frase, **vero** o **falso.**

Parole utili: l'Italia mi manca (*I miss Italy*), ridiventa (*becomes again*), viziato (*spoiled*), in bianco (*with butter and cheese*)

1. vero falso
2. vero falso
3. vero falso
4. vero falso
5. vero falso

Dettato

Sentirai un breve dettato. La prima volta, ascolta attentamente. La seconda volta, il dettato sarà letto con pause tra le frasi. Scrivi quello che senti. La terza volta, correggi quello che hai scritto. Scrivi sulle righe date. Controlla il tuo dettato con le soluzioni date in fondo al libro.

Maurizio e Rinaldo ______________________________

____

____

____

____

____

____

____

Dialogo

Prima parte. Paola e Davide parlano di una retrospettiva dei film di Fellini che Paola ha visto recentemente a Roma.

Ascolta attentamente il dialogo.

PAOLA: È stato bello rivedere i film di Fellini nello spazio di pochi giorni; non li ho rivisti tutti ma quelli che mi sono sempre piaciuti di più…

DAVIDE: Qual è il tuo film preferito allora? Io non li conosco bene, non li ho mai visti al cinema!

PAOLA: Davvero, Davide? Mai? Io ho cominciato a vederli quando ero bambina, erano i film che piacevano di più a mio padre… E poi, anche i miei[1] sono di Rimini, la città di Fellini.

DAVIDE: Ma dimmi, allora, quale film mi consigli?

PAOLA: A me piace molto *Amarcord*. Il titolo, nel dialetto della Romagna, significa «Mi ricordo». È un film autobiografico, girato appunto[2] a Rimini con un protagonista che era come il regista quando era bambino, durante gli anni del fascismo. È un film divertente, comico e nostalgico al tempo stesso.

DAVIDE: Ma di che parla?

PAOLA: È un po' difficile dirlo. Parla di una famiglia italiana, quella del bambino, e tutto il film è visto con gli occhi del bambino che cresce,[3] osserva e interpreta la realtà di una città con il fascismo, con i contrasti con i genitori, i nonni, i primi amori e le ossessioni per le donne. Un tema comune di Fellini è l'amore per le donne, infatti, come vediamo anche in *8 1/2*!

DAVIDE: Sembra interessante.

PAOLA: Lo è! Puoi prenderlo a noleggio[4] in videocassetta o vederlo anche in DVD, credo.

[1] i… *my family*

[2] *exactly*

[3] *grows*

[4] prenderlo… *rent it*

Seconda parte. Ascolta di nuovo il dialogo. Fai particolare attenzione alle caratteristiche del film di Fellini.

Terza parte. Sentirai due volte sei frasi basate sul dialogo. Segna, per ciascuna frase, **vero** o **falso.**

1. vero falso
2. vero falso
3. vero falso
4. vero falso
5. vero falso
6. vero falso

Sara in Italia

Sara aveva comprato dei biglietti per uno spettacolo all'Arena di Verona e adesso è in Veneto, a far visita ai suoi cugini. Dopo un giro a Venezia e a Padova, adesso è tornata a Verona, la città dei suoi parenti. Per strada incontra Massimo, un amico che ha conosciuto attraverso (*through*) sua cugina Antonella.

Ascolta attentamente il dialogo. Ascolta il dialogo quante volte vuoi. Poi, rispondi alle domande che senti. Sentirai ogni domanda due volte. Ripeti la risposta.

Parole utili: uccide (*she kills*), indovinelli (*riddles*)

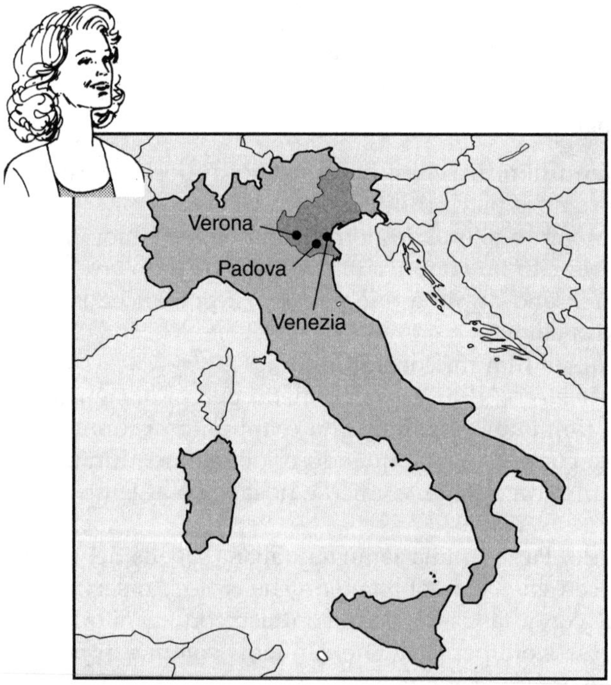

1. … 2. … 3. … 4. … 5. …

Sara in rete…

For more information about what Sara experienced during her travels, check out the links found on the *Prego!* website **(www.mhhe.com/prego8).**

Nome ______ Data ______ Classe ______

CAPITOLO

9

Sentirsi bene

Vocabolario preliminare

A. Per cominciare. Sentirai un dialogo seguito da tre frasi. Sentirai il dialogo due volte. La prima volta, ascolta attentamente. La seconda volta, il dialogo sarà ripetuto con pause per la ripetizione. Poi, ascolta le frasi e scegli, per ciascuna frase, **vero** o **falso.**

ROBERTA: Ciao, Antonella, come ti senti?
ANTONELLA: Oggi abbastanza bene, ma devo rimanere in ospedale per dieci giorni.
ROBERTA: Anch'io l'anno scorso mi sono rotta una gamba, sono rimasta a letto per un mese!
ANTONELLA: Il dottore mi ha detto che non posso scrivere per due settimane...
ROBERTA: Una bella scusa per non fare i compiti!

1. vero falso
2. vero falso
3. vero falso

B. Indovinelli. (*Riddles.*) Sentirai quattro indovinelli. Indovina la parte del corpo per ogni frase. Scrivi nella scatola (*box*) il numero corrispondente alla parola.

Parole utili: monete (*coins*), l'ossigeno (*oxygen*)

1. ... 2. ... 3. ... 4. ... 5. ...

C. **Identificazioni.** Identifica ogni parte del corpo nel disegno. Scegli le parole fra quelle suggerite. Comincia la frase con **È...** o **Sono...** Ripeti la risposta.

ESEMPIO: *Senti:* 1
Dici: Sono le dita.

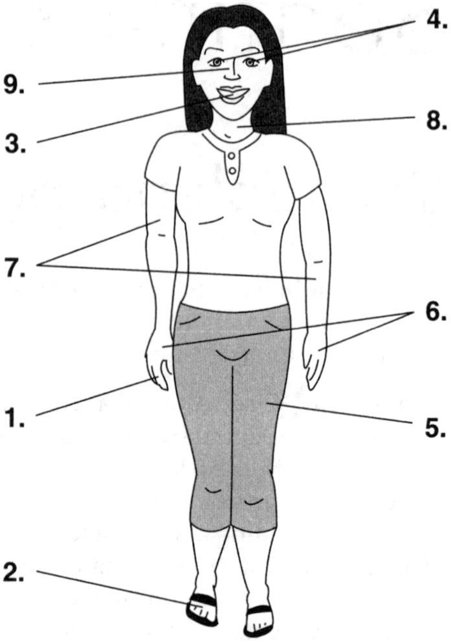

In ascolto

Un'escursione. Alessandra e Alberto fanno un programma per il week-end. Ascolta con attenzione la loro conversazione e decidi se le seguenti affermazioni sono vere o false. Poi, correggi le affermazioni false. Controlla le tue risposte con le soluzioni date in fondo al libro.

Parole utili: posti (*places*), camminare (*to walk*), speriamo (*let's hope*)

1. Alessandra ha bisogno di rilassarsi. vero falso

 ____

2. Alessandra e Alberto vogliono andare in montagna fra due settimane. vero falso

 ____

3. Alessandra conosce dei posti bellissimi sulle Dolomiti. vero falso

 ____

4. Paolo preferisce il mare perché non gli piace camminare. vero falso

 ____

5. Alberto vuole convincere Paolo ad andare in montagna. vero falso

 ____

Grammatica

A. Pronomi tonici

A. Per cominciare. Sentirai un dialogo due volte. La prima volta, ascolta attentamente. La seconda volta, il dialogo sarà ripetuto con pause per la ripetizione.

LUIGI: Nonna, hanno telefonato dall'ospedale: domani c'è la visita per te dal dottor Bianchi.
NONNA: Sei sicuro che è per me e non per tuo nonno?
LUIGI: Beh, è per tutti e due; prima visitano te e poi lui!

B. Per chi? Sentirai chiedere per chi prepari ogni specialità. Rispondi con i pronomi tonici appropriati. Ripeti la risposta.

ESEMPIO: *Senti:* Questo è per la mamma?
Dici: Sì, è per lei.

1. … 2. … 3. … 4. … 5. … 6. …

C. Curiosità. Luca ti fa tante domande oggi. Rispondi alle sue domande con i pronomi tonici appropriati. Ripeti la risposta.

ESEMPIO: *Senti:* Esci con Mario?
Dici: Sì, esco con lui.

1. … 2. … 3. … 4. … 5. …

B. Comparativi

A. Per cominciare. Sentirai un brano. Sentirai il brano due volte. La prima volta, ascolta attentamente. La seconda volta, il brano sarà ripetuto con pause per la ripetizione.

Non sono mai stata così male come in questo periodo... . Ho una brutta influenza, molto più grave di un comune raffreddore, e un mal di testa tanto fastidioso quanto doloroso. Che disastro! Forse ho bisogno di un dottore.

B. Comparazioni. Usa le informazioni che vedi ed i nomi che senti per fare confronti (*make comparisons*). Ripeti la risposta.

ESEMPIO: *Senti:* l'America, l'Italia
Leggi: grande (+)
Dici: L'America è più grande dell'Italia.

1. vecchio (−)
2. alto (+)
3. grasso (−)
4. popolare (−)
5. costoso (+)
6. violenti (+)

C. **Chi?** Guarda il disegno e rispondi alle domande. Sentirai ogni domanda due volte. Ripeti la risposta.

ESEMPIO: *Senti:* Chi è meno alto di Giorgio?
Dici: Rosa è meno alta di Giorgio.

1. … 2. … 3. … 4. … 5. …

C. Superlativi

A. **Per cominciare.** Sentirai un dialogo due volte. La prima volta, ascolta attentamente. La seconda volta, il dialogo sarà ripetuto con pause per la ripetizione.

MAMMA: Pierino, sai qual è la città più dolce d'Italia?
PIERINO: Veramente sono due: Crema e anche Cremona.
MAMMA: E qual è la città più rumorosa?
PIERINO: Napoli, credo.
MAMMA: Ma no! Chiasso! E ora sentiamo se indovini questa: qual è la città più lunga d'Italia?
PIERINO: Ventimiglia, alla frontiera con la Francia.

B. **Claudio lo straordinario!** Claudio è un giovane eccezionale. Di' quanto è bravo a confronto (*compared*) con la sua famiglia. Ripeti la risposta.

ESEMPIO: *Senti:* simpatico
Dici: È il ragazzo più simpatico della famiglia.

1. … 2. … 3. … 4. … 5. …

C. **Ma come siamo esagerati!** Noi siamo molto esagerati: ripetiamo sempre le cose che dicono le altre persone, ma parliamo con il superlativo assoluto. Ripeti la risposta.

ESEMPIO: *Senti:* Caterina è bella.
Dici: Non è bella, è bellissima!

1. … 2. … 3. … 4. … 5. … 6. …

D. **Famiglie a confronto.** Silvia ti fa molte domande. Ascolta con attenzione le sue domande e rispondi. Poi, ascolta le risposte di Silvia e ripeti le sue risposte.

1. … 2. … 3. … 4. … 5. … 6. …

D. Comparativi e superlativi irregolari

A. **Per cominciare.** Sentirai un dialogo due volte. La prima volta, ascolta attentamente. La seconda volta, il dialogo sarà ripetuto con pause per la ripetizione.

MAMMA: Ti senti meglio oggi, Carletto?
CARLETTO: No, mamma, mi sento peggio.
MAMMA: Poverino! Ora ti do una medicina che ti farà bene.
CARLETTO: È buona?
MAMMA: È buonissima, meglio dello zucchero!
…
CARLETTO: Mamma, hai detto una bugia! È peggio del veleno!

B. La medicina di Pinocchio... Pinocchio è malato o forse (*perhaps*) no. Sentirai il dialogo tra Pinocchio e la fata (*fairy*) due volte. La prima volta, ascolta attentamente. La seconda volta, completa il dialogo con le parole che mancano. Controlla le tue risposte con le soluzioni date in fondo al libro.

Parole utili: crescere (*to grow*), pericoloso (*dangerous*), allungarsi (*to get longer*)

FATA: Allora, Pinocchio, non ti senti ________________[1] oggi? Sei pronto per tornare a scuola?

PINOCCHIO: No, fatina, sto ancora male. Anzi,[a] sto ________________.[2] Questa è la ________________[3] influenza che ho mai avuto...

FATA: Mamma mia, forse è vero, anche il naso ti cresce. Dev'essere un'influenza molto pericolosa...[b] Poverino! Adesso, però,[c] ti do una medicina che ti può fare bene...

PINOCCHIO: E com'è questa medicina? È buona?

FATA: È ________________[4] dello zucchero!

PINOCCHIO: Oh, fata mia, hai detto una bugia! È ________________[5] del veleno!

FATA: Vedi il vantaggio di essere umani! Se dico una bugia, il mio naso non si allunga!

[a]*In fact* [b]*dangerous* [c]*however*

C. Secondo me... Sentirai un'opinione e dovrai esprimere l'opinione opposta. Ripeti la risposta.

ESEMPIO: *Senti:* Hanno pattinato meglio di tutti!
Dici: No, hanno pattinato peggio di tutti!

1. ... 2. ... 3. ... 4. ... 5. ...

Pronuncia: The sounds of the letter "r"

There is no parallel in English for the Italian **r** sound. The tongue is held very loosely against the alveolar ridge (right behind the upper teeth) so that the flow of air makes it vibrate.

With practice, most people can learn to roll their **r**'s. If at first you don't succeed . . . keep trying!

A. *R.* Practice the single **r** sound. Listen and repeat.

1. raccontare
2. regalare
3. riportare
4. romantico
5. russo
6. proprio

B. *Tr* e *r* finale. Pay particular attention to the combination **tr** and to the sound of **r** in final position. Listen and repeat.

1. treno
2. strada
3. centro
4. bar
5. per

C. *R* doppia. Contrast the single and double sound of **r.** Make a special effort to lengthen the sound of double **r,** and don't worry if your pronunciation seems exaggerated at first. Listen and repeat.

1. caro / carro
2. sera / serra
3. cori / corri
4. spore / porre

D. Parliamo italiano! Listen and repeat.

1. La loro sorella preferisce vestirsi di marrone.
2. Trentatré Trentini entrarono a Trento tutti e trentatré trotterellando su trentatré trattori trainati da treni.
3. Verrà stasera? Sì, ma telefonerà prima di venire.
4. Preferisce comprare le arance dal fruttivendolo? Credo di sì.
5. Corro perché sono in ritardo per le prove del coro.

Ed ora ascoltiamo!

Sentirai tre dialoghi brevi riguardo ai (*having to do with the*) problemi di salute. Puoi ascoltare i dialoghi quante volte vuoi. Dopo ognuno sentirai una domanda. Scegli la risposta giusta.

Parole utili: scocciatura (*pain, nuisance*), pronto (*hello*), la voce (*voice*)

1. a. la mano b. la gamba
2. a. l'influenza b. il raffreddore
3. a. all'ospedale b. in farmacia

Dettato

Sentirai un breve dettato tre volte. La prima volta, ascolta attentamente. La seconda volta, scrivi quello che senti. La terza volta, correggi quello che hai scritto. Scrivi sulle righe date. Controlla il tuo dettato con le soluzioni date in fondo al libro.

Il sistema nazionale ____

____

____

____

____

____

____

____

____

Dialogo

Prima parte. Sentirai un dialogo tra Valeria ed Emanuele. Valeria racconta ad Emanuele la malattia di suo fratello.

Ascolta attentamente il dialogo.

EMANUELE: Ciao, Valeria, come va?

VALERIA: Non troppo bene, anzi, male, malissimo!

EMANUELE: Che è successo?

VALERIA: A me, niente, ma ho appena saputo che mio fratello è malato di cuore.

EMANUELE: Mi dispiace davvero, è già una situazione grave?

VALERIA: Deve ancora andare a parlare con gli specialisti, ma ha già saputo che la cura migliore a questo punto è un bypass. Probabilmente deve andare a fare l'operazione nelle Marche. Là c'è un famoso Istituto cardiologico e lui deve parlare con i dottori. Ho parlato al telefono con lui mezz'ora fa.

EMANUELE: Oh, mi dispiace davvero!

VALERIA: In questi giorni sta peggio del solito. Ha problemi di respirazione, si stanca subito e non è ottimista come me. Un bypass è un'operazione difficile, però, capisco il suo pessimismo.

EMANUELE: Vero, però oggi la tecnologia e le medicine possono fare miracoli. La ricerca[1] medica è senz'altro più avanzata di qualche anno fa. E le strutture ospedaliere sono migliori. E tu, stai bene?

VALERIA: Anch'io ho qualche problema di salute in questi giorni: un'influenza fastidiosissima[2] che mi ha dato febbre, mal di testa e mal di gola. Sono andata subito dal dottore, ma mi devo curare ancora per un po'. In questi giorni le cose non potevano andare peggio per me. Prima questa mia indisposizione, poi la notizia di mio fratello!

EMANUELE: Cerca di[3] essere ottimista! Tuo fratello è molto più vecchio di te ma è anche forte come te. Sono sicuro che può vincere la sua malattia.

[1] *research*
[2] *really nasty*
[3] Cerca... *Try to*

Seconda parte. Ascolta di nuovo il dialogo. Fai particolare attenzione ai sintomi, le malattie e le cure che Valeria e Emanuele descrivono.

Terza parte. Sentirai due volte sei frasi basate sul dialogo. Segna, per ciascuna frase, **vero** o **falso.**

1. vero falso
2. vero falso
3. vero falso
4. vero falso
5. vero falso
6. vero falso

Sara in Italia

Sara è a Urbino, una piccola città delle Marche, regione centrale sulla costa adriatica. Luogo di nascita di Raffaello, Urbino è circondata (*surrounded*) dalle mura originarie (*original walls*) ed è uno dei gioielli (*jewels*) dell'architettura e dell'arte rinascimentale. Sara visita il Palazzo Ducale con un gruppo di turisti e una guida.

Ascolta attentamente il dialogo. Ascolta il dialogo quante volte vuoi. Poi, rispondi alle domande che senti. Sentirai ogni domanda due volte. Ripeti la risposta.

Parole utili: guerriero (*warrior*), dipinto (*painting*), prospettiva (*perspective*), abitanti (*inhabitants*), astratto (*abstract*)

1. ... 2. ... 3. ... 4. ... 5. ...

Sara in rete...

For more information about what Sara experienced during her travels, check out the links found on the *Prego!* website **(www.mhhe.com/prego8).**

CAPITOLO

10

Buon viaggio!

Vocabolario preliminare

A. Per cominciare. Sentirai un dialogo due volte. La prima volta, ascolta attentamente. La seconda volta, il dialogo sarà ripetuto con pause per la ripetizione.

MARIO: Allora, che programmi hai per l'estate?

DANIELE: Mah, a dire il vero non ho ancora deciso. Forse vado al mare in Sicilia… E tu, niente di speciale questa volta?

MARIO: Quest'estate non vado in vacanza. L'anno scorso ho fatto una crociera in Grecia, quest'inverno sono andato a sciare in Francia e poi ho fatto un viaggio in Olanda.

DANIELE: Ora capisco perché non vai in vacanza! O hai finito i giorni di ferie o i soldi per viaggiare all'estero!

B. Una vacanza per tutti i gusti. Sentirai un brano seguito da quattro domande. Sentirai il brano due volte. La prima volta, ascolta attentamente. La seconda volta, il brano sarà ripetuto con pause per la ripetizione. Poi sentirai le domande due volte e dovrai scegliere la risposta giusta per ogni domanda.

Finalmente progetti precisi per le nostre vacanze: chi[a] voleva affittare una casa, chi fare una crociera, chi al mare e chi in montagna… La decisione probabilmente soddisfa tutti: andiamo in campagna, in Toscana. Abbiamo trovato un piccolo albergo a due stelle,[b] con una camera singola con bagno per Roberto, una matrimoniale per Alice e Cristiano, ma solo con doccia, e per me una singola con doccia. Io, Alice e Cristiano andiamo sempre in campeggio e usare il bagno comune in albergo per noi non è un problema. Risparmiamo[c] dei soldi e siamo contenti. Non abbiamo neppure[d] dovuto lasciare un anticipo[e] con la carta di credito o mandare un assegno[f] o dei contanti. Speriamo bene![g] Degli amici comunque[h] mi hanno detto che l'albergo è carino e la zona favolosa per fare escursioni a cavallo…[i]

[a]*someone, one person* [b]*stars* [c]*We'll save* [d]*even* [e]*deposit* [f]*check* [g]speriamo… *Let's hope!* [h]*anyhow* [i]a… *on horseback*

1. a. in crociera — b. in campagna
2. a. camere in un albergo di lusso — b. camere in un albergo economico
3. a. camera matrimoniale con doccia — b. camera matrimoniale con bagno
4. a. in contanti — b. Non c'è stato anticipo.

C. Ha una camera libera?... Shannon è appena arrivata a Roma dove deve prenotare una stanza in un albergo. Cosa le chiederà l'impiegato? Ferma la registrazione e completa il dialogo con le frasi appropriate. Poi sentirai il dialogo due volte. La prima volta, controlla le tue risposte. La seconda volta, il dialogo sarà ripetuto con pause per la ripetizione.

80 euro.
Abbiamo una camera, ma senza aria condizionata.
Certo. Come si chiama?
No.
Per quante persone?
Certo, mi può dare il numero?
Per quante notti?
Una camera singola. Con bagno?

IMPIEGATO: Hotel Rex, buona sera. Desidera?

SHANNON: Ha una camera libera?

IMPIEGATO: ____ 1

SHANNON: Per due notti.

IMPIEGATO: ____ 2

SHANNON: Una.

IMPIEGATO: ____ 3

SHANNON: Con doccia va bene.

IMPIEGATO: ____ 4

SHANNON: Non importa se non c'è l'aria condizionata. Quanto costa?

IMPIEGATO: ____ 5

SHANNON: C'è pensione completa?

IMPIEGATO: ____ 6

SHANNON: Posso prenotare adesso?

IMPIEGATO: ____ 7

SHANNON: Shannon Mangiameli. Posso pagare con la carta di credito?

IMPIEGATO: ____ 8

D. Progetti di vacanze. Sentirai tre coppie che parlano dei loro progetti di vacanze. Sentirai ogni dialogo due volte. La prima volta, ascolta attentamente. La seconda volta, completa la tabella con le informazioni appropriate per ciascuna coppia. Controlla le tue risposte con le soluzioni date in fondo al libro.

Parole utili: stelle (*stars*), le comodità (*comforts*), i boschi (*woods*), sborsare (*to pay out*)

	COPPIA 1	COPPIA 2	COPPIA 3
destinazione			
mezzo di trasporto			
alloggio			
pagamento			

In ascolto

Progetti di vacanze. Renata e Enrico hanno preparato un itinerario per una vacanza in Toscana. Ascolta con attenzione la loro conversazione su una parte del viaggio, poi completa le frasi seguenti. Controlla le tue risposte con le soluzioni date in fondo al libro.

1. A Firenze in questa stagione non è facile ______________.
2. A Prato o a Pistoia la sistemazione è meno ______________ che a Firenze.
3. A Prato c'è la possibilità di una camera ______________, con ______________, in una ______________.
4. A Marina di Pietrasanta ci sono ______________.
5. A Marina di Pietrasanta è possibile fare queste attività: ______________.

Grammatica

A. Futuro semplice

A. Per cominciare. Sentirai un brano due volte. La prima volta, ascolta attentamente. La seconda volta, completa il brano con le parole che mancano. Controlla le tue risposte con le soluzioni date in fondo al libro.

Alla fine di giugno ______________[1] per l'Italia con i miei genitori e mia sorella. ______________[2] l'aereo a New York e ______________[3] a Roma. ______________[4] una settimana insieme a Roma, poi i miei genitori ______________[5] una macchina e _______________[6] il viaggio con mia sorella. Io, invece, _______________[7] a Perugia, dove _______________[8] italiano per sette settimane. Alla fine di agosto _______________[9] tutti insieme negli Stati Uniti.

B. Il matrimonio di Elsa sarà domenica... Tutti i parenti di Elsa arriveranno domenica per il suo matrimonio. Di' chi verrà e cosa farà, secondo i suggerimenti. Ripeti la risposta.

ESEMPIO: *Leggi:* arrivare per il matrimonio di Elsa
Senti: Stefania
Dici: Domenica Stefania arriverà per il matrimonio di Elsa.

1. portare il regalo per il matrimonio di Elsa
2. fare da testimoni (*to be witnesses*) al matrimonio di Elsa
3. fare le fotografie al matrimonio di Elsa
4. guidare la macchina degli sposi per il matrimonio di Elsa
5. portare i fiori per il matrimonio di Elsa
6. celebrare il matrimonio di Elsa

B. Usi speciali del futuro

A. Per cominciare. Sentirai un dialogo due volte. La prima volta, ascolta attentamente. La seconda volta, completa il dialogo con le parole che mancano. Controlla le tue risposte con le soluzioni date in fondo al libro.

CHIARA: Paola, come stai? Come va il lavoro?

PAOLA: Ciao, Chiara! Sto bene, ma sono molto stanca. Appena _______________[1] di insegnare all'università, _______________[2] a trovare i miei genitori in Italia. E tu?

CHIARA: Io _______________[3] un viaggio con mia sorella. Chissà cosa _______________[4] Marco e Tiziana.

PAOLA: Non so, loro fanno sempre viaggi straordinari. Forse questa volta _______________[5] alle Maldive.

B. Come sarà Sara? La mamma di Sara è preoccupata per sua figlia che viaggia per tutta l'Italia e si fa tante domande su quello che farà o non farà. Sentirai il brano due volte. La prima volta, ascolta attentamente. La seconda volta, completa il brano con i verbi al futuro. Controlla le tue risposte con le soluzioni date in fondo al libro.

La mia povera bambina! Dove _______________[1]? Avrà _______________[2] una camera? _______________[3] freddo? _______________[4] abbastanza? _______________[5] abbastanza? _______________[6] soldi a sufficienza[a]? _______________[7] le cartoline?

[a]a... *enough*

C. Domande personali. Di' quando farai le seguenti cose. Rispondi con il verbo al futuro.

ESEMPIO: *Senti e leggi:* Andrò al cinema se...
Dici: Andrò al cinema se avrò tempo, soldi, eccetera.

1. Studierò quando...
2. Andrò a mangiare appena...
3. Pulirò l'appartamento se...

4. Potrò riposare (*rest*) dopo che…
5. Ti scriverò un'e-mail quando…

C. *Si* impersonale

A. Per cominciare. Sentirai un brano due volte. La prima volta, ascolta attentamente. La seconda volta il brano sarà ripetuto con pause per la ripetizione.

Quando si va in Italia, si fanno molte cose interessanti: si visitano bellissime città d'arte, ci si diverte a parlare italiano e soprattutto si può mangiare l'autentica pizza napoletana!

B. Non si fa così. Rebecca fa i capricci (*is acting up*). Dovrai dirle che certe cose si fanno o non si fanno. Usa il **si** impersonale. Ripeti la risposta.

ESEMPIO: *Senti:* salutare la maestra
Dici: Si saluta la maestra.

Parole utili: ubbidire (*to obey*), rumore (*noise*)

1. … 2. … 3. … 4. … 5. …

C. Di ritorno da un viaggio in Italia. Sei stato ospite di una famiglia italiana per un mese. Un compagno vuole sapere tutto sulle tue abitudini durante il tuo viaggio in Italia. Ascolta le sue domande. Nelle tue risposte, usa il **si** impersonale e il vocabolario dato per ogni frase. Ripeti la risposta.

ESEMPIO: *Leggi:* prendere / una pasta e un caffè
Senti: Con che cosa facevate colazione?
Dici: Si prendeva una pasta e un caffè.

1. guardare / il telegiornale
2. fare la spesa (*to go shopping*) / il sabato
3. andare / al cinema con gli amici
4. cenare / alle otto
5. stare / a casa a giocare a carte con la famiglia

D. Formazione dei nomi femminili

A. Per cominciare. Sentirai un dialogo due volte. La prima volta, ascolta attentamente. La seconda volta, completa il dialogo con i nomi femminili che mancano. Controlla le tue risposte con le soluzioni date in fondo al libro.

CLAUDIO: Oggi al ricevimento dai Brambilla c'era un sacco di gente interessante.

MARINA: Ah sì? Chi c'era?

CLAUDIO: Il pittore Berardi con la moglie, ______________________[1] anche lei; dicono che è più brava del marito… La ______________________[2] di storia dell'arte Stoppato, il poeta Salimbeni con la moglie ______________________[3] e un paio di scrittori…

MARINA: Che ambiente intellettuale! Ma i Brambilla cosa fanno?

CLAUDIO: Beh, lui è un grosso industriale tessile e lei è un'ex-______________________.[4]

B. Dal mondo femminile al mondo maschile... Di' la forma al maschile di ogni nome femminile. Ripeti la risposta.

ESEMPIO: *Senti:* una regista famosa
Dici: un regista famoso

1. ... 2. ... 3. ... 4. ... 5. ... 6. ... 7. ... 8. ... 9. ... 10. ...

Pronuncia: The sounds of the letters "b" and "p"

A. *B* e doppia *b*. The letter **b** is pronounced as in the English word *boy.* Compare and contrast the single and double sounds of **b** in these pairs of words. Listen and repeat.

1. da basso / abbasso
2. abile / abbaiare
3. laboratorio / labbro
4. debole / ebbene

B. *P*. The sound of the letter **p** in Italian is similar to that in the English word *pen,* though without the aspiration or slight puff of air one hears in English. Listen carefully to these English and Italian words, then repeat the Italian word. Listen and repeat.

1. *pizza* / pizza
2. *page* / pagina
3. *palate* / palato
4. *pope* / papa
5. *pepper* / pepe

C. Doppia *p*. Compare and contrast the single and double sound of **p** in these pairs of words. Listen and repeat.

1. papa / pappa
2. capelli / cappelli
3. capi / cappi
4. rapito / rapporto

D. Parliamo italiano! Listen and repeat.

1. Paolo ha i capelli e i baffi bianchi.
2. Ho paura di guidare quando c'è la nebbia.
3. Non capisco perché ti arrabbi sempre.
4. Hai già buttato giù la pasta?
5. Giuseppe, stappa una bottiglia di vino buono!

Ed ora ascoltiamo!

Sentirai un dialogo tra Tony e Cristina in cui discutono dei soldi da portare in viaggio. Puoi ascoltare il dialogo quante volte vuoi. Poi sentirai, due volte, sei frasi e dovrai segnare, per ciascuna frase, **vero** o **falso.**

Parole utili: il bancomat (*ATM*), l'affitto (*rent*)

1. vero falso
2. vero falso
3. vero falso
4. vero falso
5. vero falso
6. vero falso

Dettato

Sentirai un breve dettato tre volte. La prima volta, ascolta attentamente. La seconda volta, il dettato sarà letto con pause tra le frasi. Scrivi quello che senti. La terza volta, correggi quello che hai scritto. Scrivi sulle righe date. Controlla il tuo dettato con le soluzioni date in fondo al libro.

Due coppie ____

Dialogo

Prima parte. Alessia e Sandra discutono dei progetti di vacanza di Alessia.

Ascolta attentamente il dialogo.

ALESSIA: Finalmente in vacanza! Adesso, quello che voglio è solo una cosa… Riposarmi, stare al sole, tornare in pensione a mangiare e fare la doccia, tornare di nuovo sulla spiaggia, abbronzarmi…

SANDRA: Non solo una cosa, allora, …hai fatto una lista!

ALESSIA: Va bene, diciamo che la mia priorità sarà di riposarmi al sole. Sono così stanca della pioggia! Questo maggio volevo cambiare casa, andare al sud. Quando mai si è visto il sole?

SANDRA: Ma come sei difficile, Alessia! A me il tempo fresco non dispiace.

ALESSIA: Tempo fresco, va bene; tempo piovoso, no, grazie.

SANDRA: Secondo le previsioni[1] del tempo, domani sarà parzialmente nuvoloso[2] e potrà anche piovere nel week-end, non è sicuro che ci sarà il sole questa settimana…

ALESSIA: Speriamo di no![3] Altrimenti,[4] questa volta il mio oroscopo ha proprio ragione. «Ci saranno problemi associati con viaggi e spostamenti[5] che causeranno insoddisfazioni.»

SANDRA: Ma Alessia! È l'oroscopo di un giornale! Mica ti fiderai?!![6] E poi è così generale… Questa vacanza non andrà male, non ti preoccupare.

ALESSIA: E chi ti ha detto che sono preoccupata? Se pioverà, pioverà, non c'è molto che posso fare… Almeno ci sono dei buoni ristoranti nella zona? Vuol dire che se pioverà o farà brutto tempo, passerò un po' di tempo al chiuso,[7] a leggere giornali…

SANDRA: Oh sì, a leggere giornali… Oroscopi, vuoi dire, la tua lettura preferita! E poi avrai altre idee come quella di oggi, che le previsioni del tempo sono scritte nel tuo destino!

[1] *forecasts*
[2] *cloudy*
[3] Speriamo… *Let's hope not!* / [4] *Otherwise*
[5] *moving*
[6] Mica… *Don't trust them?!!!*
[7] al… *indoors*

Seconda parte. Ascolta di nuovo il dialogo. Fai particolare attenzione al tempo previsto (*forecast*) e alle attività di Alessia a seconda del tempo.

Terza parte. Sentirai due volte sei frasi basate sul dialogo. Segna, per ciascuna frase, **vero** o **falso.**

1. vero falso
2. vero falso
3. vero falso
4. vero falso
5. vero falso
6. vero falso

Sara in Italia

Sara è a Porto Cervo, sulla Costa Smeralda della Sardegna, ospite dell'avvocato (*lawyer*) Corradini. I signori Corradini hanno qui la seconda casa, mentre durante l'anno abitano in provincia di Firenze. Nei mesi estivi è di moda (*fashionable*) andare in Sardegna e i signori Corradini hanno anche comprato una bella barca per navigare attorno all'isola.

Ascolta attentamente il dialogo. Ascolta il dialogo quante volte vuoi. Poi, rispondi alle domande che senti. Sentirai ogni domanda due volte. Ripeti la risposta.

Parole utili: una gita (*excursion*), al largo (*on the open sea*), folla (*crowd*)

1. … 2. … 3. … 4. … 5. …

Sara in rete...

For more information about what Sara experienced during her travels, check out the links found on the *Prego!* website **(www.mhhe.com/prego8).**

CAPITOLO

11

Spesa e spese

Vocabolario preliminare

A. Per cominciare. Sentirai un dialogo due volte. La prima volta, ascolta attentamente. La seconda volta, il dialogo sarà ripetuto con pause per la ripetizione.

SILVANA: Sono andata in centro a fare spese l'altro giorno. C'erano molti sconti nelle boutique e allora non ho resistito…
GIOVANNA: Cos'hai comprato?
SILVANA: Volevo un paio di scarpe eleganti e comode, come le tue.
GIOVANNA: Dove le hai trovate?
SILVANA: In Via Montenapoleone: un vero affare, solo 100 euro.
GIOVANNA: Io invece le ho comprate al mercato: 50 euro!

B. Dove lo comprano? Guarda i disegni e di' dove e da chi queste persone fanno la spesa. Ripeti la risposta.

ESEMPIO: *Senti:* Dove comprano le paste le ragazze?
Dici: Le comprano in una pasticceria, dalla pasticciera.

1. 

2. 

3. 

4. 

5. 

C. Dove siamo? Sentirai, per due volte, due dialoghi. Ascolta i dialoghi e di' dove hanno luogo (*they take place*).

1. a. in un negozio di alimentari — b. dal panettiere
2. a. in una gelateria — b. dal fruttivendolo

In ascolto

Un po' di spesa. Sentirai tre brevi dialoghi. Indica il negozio corrispondente ad ogni dialogo e scrivi le informazioni che mancano: che cosa compra il/la cliente e quanto costa. Controlla le tue risposte con le soluzioni date in fondo al libro.

	DIALOGO 1	DIALOGO 2	DIALOGO 3
dalla fruttivendola			
dalla lattaia			
dal macellaio			
cosa compra il/la cliente?			
quanto costa?			

Grammatica

A. Usi di *ne*

A. Per cominciare. Sentirai un dialogo seguito da tre domande. Sentirai il dialogo due volte. La prima volta, ascolta attentamente. La seconda volta, il dialogo sarà ripetuto con pause per la ripetizione. Scegli poi le risposte giuste alle domande che senti.

MAMMA: Marta, per favore mi compri il pane?
MARTA: Volentieri! Quanto ne vuoi?
MAMMA: Un chilo. Ah sì, ho bisogno anche di prosciutto cotto.
MARTA: Ne prendo due etti?
MAMMA: Puoi prenderne anche quattro: tu e papà ne mangiate sempre tanto!
MARTA: Hai bisogno d'altro?
MAMMA: No, grazie, per il resto andrò io al supermercato domani.

1. a. Ne deve prendere un chilo. — b. Ne deve prendere un chilo e mezzo.
2. a. Ne deve prendere due. — b. Ne deve prendere quattro.
3. a. Ne ha bisogno. — b. Non ne ha bisogno.

B. **Quanti?** Il tuo compagno di casa è stato via due settimane e ha tante domande da farti al suo ritorno. Rispondi alle sue domande secondo i suggerimenti. Ripeti la risposta.

ESEMPIO: *Senti:* Quanti film hai visto?
Leggi: tre
Dici: Ne ho visti tre.

Parole utili: spendere: speso (*to spend*)

1. due
2. molti
3. pochi
4. tanti
5. quattro
6. un po'

C. **Domande personali.** Rispondi alle seguenti domande. Usa **ne** nella tua risposta.

1. … 2. … 3. … 4. … 5. … 6. … 7. … 8. …

B. Usi di *ci*

A. **Per cominciare.** Sentirai un dialogo due volte. La prima volta, ascolta attentamente. La seconda volta, il dialogo sarà ripetuto con pause per la ripetizione.

MARIA: Antonio, Laura, avete fatto spese?
ANTONIO: Sì, siamo andati al nuovo centro commerciale.
MARIA: Io non ci vado mai, preferisco andare nei piccoli negozi: dal panettiere, in macelleria, nel negozio di frutta e verdura...
LAURA: Anche noi ci andiamo spesso, ma solo per comprare i prodotti freschi!

B. **Altre domande personali…** Rispondi alle domande secondo la tua esperienza personale. Usa **ne** o **ci** nella tua risposta. Poi sentirai due risposte possibili. Ripeti la risposta adatta a te.

Parole utili: voto (*grade*)

1. … 2. … 3. … 4. … 5. … 6. …

C. Pronomi doppi

A. Per cominciare. Sentirai un dialogo due volte. La prima volta, ascolta attentamente. La seconda volta, completa il dialogo con le parole che mancano. Controlla le tue risposte con le soluzioni date in fondo al libro.

COMMESSA: Allora, signora, ha provato la gonna e la camicetta? Come Le stanno?

CLIENTE: La gonna è troppo stretta, ma la camicetta va bene. La prendo.

COMMESSA: ________________________[1] incarto?

CLIENTE: No; ________________________ ________________________[2] può mettere da parte? Ora vado a fare la spesa e poi passo a prenderla quando torno a casa.

COMMESSA: Va bene, signora, ________________________[3] metto qui, dietro al banco.

B. Di che cosa parliamo? Sentirai, per due volte, sei frasi con pronomi doppi. Dovrai scegliere a quale delle tre frasi scritte si riferisce ogni frase che senti.

ESEMPIO: *Senti:* Glielo do.
Leggi: a. Do a lui i libri. b. Do a lei i libri. c. Do a lui o a lei il libro.
Scegli: c

1. a. Compriamo i giornali per loro.
   b. Compriamo le scarpe per voi.
   c. Compriamo scarpe e calzini per voi.
2. a. Regalo i profumi a lei.
   b. Regalo la penna e la matita a lei.
   c. Regalo la gonna a lei.
3. a. Diamo l'assegno a te.
   b. Diamo la carta di credito a te.
   c. Diamo i soldi a te.
4. a. Faccio la torta per lui.
   b. Faccio i compiti per lui.
   c. Faccio il compito per lei o per lui.
5. a. Presto il libro a voi.
   b. Presto la mappa e la guida turistica a voi.
   c. Presto la mappa, la guida turistica e il libro a voi.
6. a. Parlo a lui.
   b. Parlo a lei.
   c. Parlo a lui di lei.

C. Oggi no. Ti chiedono tutti dei piaceri (*favors*), ma oggi non hai tempo e rispondi di no. Ripeti la risposta.

ESEMPIO: *Senti:* Puoi comprare il pane ai vicini (*neighbors*)?
Dici: Mi dispiace; oggi non glielo posso comprare.

1. ... 2. ... 3. ... 4. ... 5. ...

D. Imperativo (*tu, noi, voi*)

A. Per cominciare. Sentirai un brano due volte. La prima volta, ascolta attentamente. La seconda volta, completa il brano con i verbi all'imperativo che mancano. Controlla le tue risposte con le soluzioni date in fondo al libro.

MAMMA: Dai, bambini, ______[1] a fare la spesa! Questa volta, ______[2] bene: tu, Lucia, ______[3] buon giorno al negoziante; e tu, Carletto, ______[4] ______[5] niente nel negozio!

B. Professore per un giorno... Immagina di fare il professore e da' istruzioni ai tuoi studenti, secondo i suggerimenti. Ripeti la risposta.

ESEMPIO: *Senti:* fare l'esercizio
Dici: Fate l'esercizio!

1. ... 2. ... 3. ... 4. ... 5. ... 6. ... 7. ... 8. ...

C. Baby-sitter autoritari... Fai la baby-sitter a Marisa e a Stefano. Dovrai dirgli cosa devono fare o non fare. Ripeti la risposta.

ESEMPIO: *Leggi:* stare zitto
Senti: Marisa e Stefano
Dici: State zitti!

1. avere pazienza
2. andare in cucina
3. non scrivere sul muro (*wall*)
4. pulire il tavolo
5. non mangiare la torta
6. essere buono

D. Ospiti. Hai due ospiti in casa. Quando ti chiedono se possono fare qualcosa, rispondi in modo affermativo. Usa **pure** e i pronomi oggetto nella tua risposta. Ripeti la risposta.

ESEMPIO: *Senti:* Possiamo leggere la rivista?
Dici: Sì, leggetela pure!

1. ... 2. ... 3. ... 4. ... 5. ...

Pronuncia: The sounds of the letters "f" and "v"

A. ***F* e *f* doppia.** The letter **f** is pronounced as in the English word *fine*. Compare and contrast the single and double sound of **f**. Listen and repeat.

1. da fare / daffare
2. tufo / tuffo
3. befana / beffare
4. difesa / piffero
5. gufo / ciuffo

B. ***V* e doppia *v*.** The letter **v** is pronounced as in the English word *vine*. Compare and contrast the single and double **v** sound in these pairs of words. Listen and repeat.

1. piove / piovve
2. bevi / bevvi
3. evidenza / evviva
4. ovest / ovvio
5. dove / ovvero

C. **Parliamo italiano!** Listen and repeat.

1. Servo il caffè all'avvocato.
2. È vero che vanno in ufficio alle nove?
3. Pioveva e faceva freddo.
4. L'imperfetto dei verbi irregolari non è difficile.
5. Vittoria aveva davvero fretta.
6. Dove vendono questo profumo?

Ed ora ascoltiamo!

Sentirai tre conversazioni ai grandi magazzini. Puoi ascoltare il dialogo quante volte vuoi. Cosa vogliono comprare queste persone? Di che colore? Di che taglia (*size*)? Inserisci nella tabella le informazioni che senti. Controlla le tue risposte con le soluzioni date in fondo al libro.

Parole utili: il maglione (*pullover*), il cappello (*hat*)

	CLIENTE A	CLIENTE B	CLIENTE C
il capo (*item*) d'abbigliamento			
il colore			
la taglia			

Dettato

Sentirai un breve dettato tre volte. La prima volta, ascolta attentamente. La seconda volta, il dettato sarà letto con pause tra le frasi. Scrivi quello che senti. La terza volta, correggi quello che hai scritto. Scrivi sulle righe date. Controlla il tuo dettato con le soluzioni date in fondo al libro.

Giovanna e Silvana _______________

Dialogo

Prima parte. Silvana e Giovanna sono a Milano, in una via con negozi molto chic.

Ascolta attentamente il dialogo.

SILVANA: Guarda che bella giacca, chissà quanto costa: è di Armani!

GIOVANNA: Beh, quanto costa puoi immaginartelo facilmente, siamo in Via Montenapoleone!

SILVANA: Dai, entriamo lo stesso! Se ci pensi bene, ci sono sempre svendite in questi negozi.

GIOVANNA: Cosa? Non siamo ai grandi magazzini! Fattelo dire dal commesso, subito, quanto costa quel vestito, così non perdi tempo a mettertelo addosso[1]... Vedi, non ci sono nemmeno[2] i prezzi in vetrina, questo è un buon segno.

SILVANA: Macchè![3] Provare un vestito è sempre meglio che vederlo in vetrina e non costa niente...

(*Silvana entra nel negozio.*)

COMMESSO: Buon giorno, in cosa posso servirLa?

SILVANA: Ha una taglia[4] quarantaquattro di quella giacca blu in vetrina?

COMMESSO: Penso di sì... Un momento, gliela porto subito. Eccola.

(*Silvana va nel camerino*[5] *a provare la giacca.*)

COMMESSO: Come va?

SILVANA: Credo bene, ha proprio una bella linea. Ma non sono sicura di questo colore...

COMMESSO: Se vuole, gliene porto un'altra di un altro colore, che ne dice del nero o del grigio scuro?

SILVANA: No, mi piaceva il blu, in vetrina, ma adesso che me la sono provata, il colore non va, ma grazie lo stesso... A proposito,[6] quanto costa?

[1] *on*
[2] *even*
[3] *of course not!*
[4] *size*
[5] *dressing room*
[6] A... *By the way*

COMMESSO: Sono solo duecento euro. Ce ne sono altre simili, in altri colori…
SILVANA: Non importa, grazie, mi interessava proprio questa. ArrivederLa.
COMMESSO: ArrivederLa.

(Silvana esce dal negozio.)

GIOVANNA: Allora, che facevi dentro? Ci sei stata quasi mezz'ora! C'erano sconti?
SILVANA: Ma di che sconti parli? Avevi ragione, gli affari si fanno solo ai grandi magazzini!

Seconda parte. Ascolta di nuovo il dialogo. Fai particolare attenzione a cosa dicono Silvana e Giovanna sugli affari, i prezzi e la giacca che Silvana vuole provare.

Terza parte. Sentirai due volte sei frasi basate sul dialogo. Segna, per ciascuna frase, **vero** o **falso.**

1. vero falso
2. vero falso
3. vero falso
4. vero falso
5. vero falso
6. vero falso

Sara in Italia

Sara è scesa a Tropea, una città della Calabria, sul Mare Tirreno, per una breve vacanza. In spiaggia, parla con una signora italiana delle cose da vedere in Basilicata e in Calabria.

Ascolta attentamente il dialogo. Ascolta il dialogo quante volte vuoi. Poi, rispondi alle domande che senti. Sentirai ogni domanda due volte. Ripeti la risposta.

Parole utili: rocce (*rocks*), rovine (*ruins*), guerrieri (*warriors*)

1. … 2. … 3. … 4. … 5. …

Sara in rete…

For more information about what Sara experienced during her travels, check out the links found on the *Prego!* website **(www.mhhe.com/prego8).**

CAPITOLO

Cercare casa 12

Vocabolario preliminare

A. Per cominciare. Sentirai un dialogo due volte. La prima volta, ascolta attentamente. La seconda volta, rispondi alle domande. Controlla le tue risposte con le soluzioni date in fondo al libro.

ANTONELLA: Ho saputo che vi sposate tra due settimane!
PATRIZIA: Eh sì, è quasi tutto pronto, ma ci manca solo la casa...
ANTONELLA: La casa!? E dove andate a abitare?
MASSIMO: Dai miei genitori... Non è la migliore soluzione ma, come sai, trovare casa oggi è quasi impossibile; costa troppo!

1. ______________
2. ______________
3. ______________

B. La casa e l'affitto... Sentirai, per due volte, un dialogo tra Carmela e Pina, seguito da tre frasi. La prima volta, ascolta attentamente. La seconda volta, il dialogo sarà ripetuto con pause per la ripetizione. Poi, sentirai le tre frasi due volte e dovrai segnare **vero** o **falso.**

CARMELA: Allora, hai trovato casa?
PINA: Sì, l'ho trovata, ma adesso devo trovare un secondo lavoro per pagare l'affitto!
CARMELA: E meno male che non abitiamo in una città come New York! Ho appena parlato con il mio amico Marco, che si è appena trasferito a New York, e che mi ha detto che gli affitti lì sono tre volte quelli di Milano, per un appartamento di due stanze!
PINA: Ma sono sicura che anche lo stipendio[1] di questo tuo amico sarà adeguato al costo degli appartamenti!

[1] *salary*

1. vero falso
2. vero falso
3. vero falso

C. Parliamo della casa. Guarda il disegno, poi scrivi le risposte alle domande che senti. Controlla le tue risposte con le soluzioni date in fondo al libro.

ESEMPIO: *Senti:* Dove lascia la bici Sara? A pianterreno o al primo piano?
Scrivi: a pianterreno

1. ______________________
2. ______________________
3. ______________________
4. ______________________
5. ______________________

D. Arrediamo (*We're furnishing*) **la nuova casa.** Sentirai sei frasi e dovrai indovinare a quale oggetto si riferisce ogni frase. Ripeti la risposta.

ESEMPIO: *Senti:* Mettiamolo nel bagno.
Dici: lo specchio

1. … 2. … 3. … 4. … 5. … 6. …

In ascolto

La prima casa. Carla cerca un appartamento per lei e per un'altra studentessa. Risponde per telefono a un annuncio (*ad*) sul giornale. Ascolta con attenzione la sua conversazione con il padrone e decidi se le seguenti affermazioni sono vere o false. Poi, correggi le affermazioni false. Controlla le tue risposte con le soluzioni date in fondo al libro.

Parole utili: disponibile (*available*), il trasloco (*move* [*of residence*]), fissare (*to set*)

1. L'appartamento è già affittato. vero falso

 ____

2. Ci sono tre stanze più bagno e cucina. vero falso

 ____

3. L'appartamento si trova al terzo piano. vero falso

 ____

4. Non c'è un balcone. vero falso

 ____

5. Il trasloco non è un problema perché c'è l'ascensore. vero falso

 ____

6. Carla e il padrone hanno appuntamento domani al numero 6, alle due del pomeriggio. vero falso

 ____

Grammatica

A. Aggettivi indefiniti

A. Per cominciare. Sentirai un dialogo due volte. La prima volta, ascolta attentamente. La seconda volta, completa il dialogo con le parole che mancano. Controlla le tue risposte con le soluzioni date in fondo al libro.

SARA: Sai, mamma, io e Carlo abbiamo visto ______________[1] appartamenti in vendita davvero carini!

MAMMA: Dove sono?

SARA: Sono in ______________,[2] vicino al parco. ______________[3] appartamento ha un bel ______________[4] con un ______________[5] di verde. Alcuni appartamenti hanno anche il camino in ______________.[6]

MAMMA: Cosa aspettate? ______________[7] uno!

B. Conformisti. Guarda i disegni e di' cosa fanno tutti i soggetti rappresentati. Segui i suggerimenti e usa **tutti** o **tutte** nelle tue risposte. Ripeti la risposta.

ESEMPIO: *Senti:* ragazzi
Leggi: correre
Dici: Tutti i ragazzi corrono.

1.  dormire

2.  cucinare

3.  cambiare casa

4.  sistemare (*to arrange*) i mobili

C. Agenzia immobiliare (*Real Estate Agency*) **Piagenti.** Sentirai la pubblicità per l'agenzia immobiliare Piagenti due volte. La prima volta, ascolta attentamente. La seconda volta, prendi appunti su quello che hai sentito. Poi ferma la registrazione e completa le frasi con gli aggettivi indefiniti appropriati. Controlla le tue risposte con le soluzioni date in fondo al libro.

Parole utili: talvolta (*sometimes*), orto (*vegetable garden*), compresa (*included*)

Aggettivi indefiniti: alcune, ogni, qualunque, tutte, tutti

1. Non vi offriamo una casa ________________________.
2. Vi offriamo una casa particolare con ________________________ precise caratteristiche.
3. ________________________ le stanze hanno l'aria condizionata.
4. ________________________ gli appartamenti hanno due bagni.
5. L'agenzia è aperta ________________________ giorno dalle 9 alle 17.

B. Pronomi indefiniti

A. Per cominciare. Sentirai un dialogo due volte. La prima volta, ascolta attentamente. La seconda volta, il dialogo sarà ripetuto con pause per la ripetizione.

MARISA: Ciao, Stefania, come va? Ho saputo che vuoi traslocare.
STEFANIA: È vero. Cerco una casa in affitto, ma sono tutte in vendita! In realtà ce ne sono alcune in affitto, ma sono troppo lontane dal centro.
MARISA: Non preoccuparti, prima o poi troverai qualcosa!

B. Che cos'è? Un tuo compagno di classe non ha studiato per l'esame di italiano e ti chiede il significato di tutti i vocaboli. Rispondi e usa **qualcuno** o **qualcosa** insieme alle informazioni date. Ripeti la risposta.

ESEMPIO: *Senti:* E il lattaio?
Leggi: vende il latte
Dici: È qualcuno che vende il latte.

1. mangiamo a colazione
2. si mangia
3. vende la frutta
4. lavora in un negozio
5. si beve
6. fa il pane

C. Problemi di casa. Sentirai cinque brevi scambi (*dialogues*) sui problemi di casa di Giulia, Marta e Cinzia, seguiti da domande. Rispondi ad ogni domanda con i pronomi indefiniti appropriati. Ripeti la risposta.

Parole utili: pieno (*full*), comode (*comfortable*)

1. … 2. … 3. … 4. … 5. …

C. Negativi

A. Per cominciare. Sentirai un dialogo due volte. La prima volta, ascolta attentamente. La seconda volta, il dialogo sarà ripetuto con pause per la ripetizione.

MARITO: Sento un rumore in cantina: ci sarà qualcuno, cara…
MOGLIE: Ma no, non c'è nessuno: saranno i topi!
MARITO: Ma che dici? Non abbiamo mai avuto topi in questa casa. Vado a vedere.
(*Alcuni minuti dopo.*)
MOGLIE: Ebbene?
MARITO: Ho guardato dappertutto ma non ho visto niente di strano.
MOGLIE: Meno male!

B. Arrivano le ragazze! Franco è contento di conoscere le tue amiche italiane che arrivano oggi. Rispondi alle sue domande negativamente. Ripeti la risposta.

ESEMPIO: *Senti:* Sono già arrivate?
Dici: No, non sono ancora arrivate.

1. … 2. … 3. … 4. … 5. …

C. Che dire? Sentirai cinque frasi due volte. Scegli, fra le seguenti coppie di frasi, quella che si collega meglio alla frase che hai sentito.

1. a. Non mi piacciono le due donne.
   b. Preferisco una delle due.
2. a. Devo ancora leggere alcune pagine del libro.
   b. È stato un bel libro.
3. a. Voglio divertirmi da solo stasera.
   b. Ho organizzato una bella cena per tutti stasera.
4. a. Ho ricevuto solo una lettera per posta.
   b. La posta non è venuta oggi.
5. a. Mi sono completamente rilassato ieri sera.
   b. Ho avuto una serata molto impegnata (*busy*).

D. Imperativo (*Lei, Loro*)

A. Per cominciare. Sentirai un dialogo due volte. La prima volta, ascolta attentamente. La seconda volta, completa il dialogo con i verbi all'imperativo che mancano. Controlla le tue risposte con le soluzioni date in fondo al libro.

SEGRETARIA: Dottoressa, il signor Biondi ha bisogno urgente di parlarLe: ha già telefonato tre volte.

DOTTORESSA MANCINI: Che seccatore! Gli ______________________[1] Lei, signorina, e gli ______________________[2] che sono già partita per Chicago.

SEGRETARIA: Pronto!… Signor Biondi?… Mi dispiace, la dottoressa è partita per un congresso a Chicago… Come dice?… L'indirizzo? Veramente, non glielo so dire: ______________________[3] pazienza e ______________________[4] tra dieci giorni!

B. Prego! Di' al tuo professore di fare le seguenti cose, se vuole. Ripeti la risposta.

ESEMPIO: *Senti:* entrare
Dici: Se vuole entrare, entri!

1. … 2. … 3. … 4. … 5. …

C. Professori. Di' a due tuoi professori di non fare le seguenti cose, se non possono. Ripeti la risposta.

ESEMPIO: *Senti:* pagare
Dici: Se non possono pagare, non paghino!

1. … 2. … 3. … 4. … 5. …

Pronuncia: The sounds of the letter "t"

The Italian sound [t] is similar to the *t* in the English word *top*, though it lacks the aspiration (the slight puff of air) that characterizes the English *t* at the beginning of a word. To pronounce **t** in Italian, place the tip of the tongue against the back of the upper teeth, but a bit lower than for the similar sound in English.

A. *T.* Compare and contrast the sounds of the English *t* and the Italian **t.** Listen to the English words, then repeat the Italian ones. Listen and repeat.

1. *tempo* / tempo
2. *type* / tipo
3. *tremble* / tremare
4. *metro* / metro
5. *mute* / muto

B. ***T* e doppia *t*.** Compare and contrast the single and double sounds of **t.** Listen and repeat.

1. tuta / tutta
2. fato / fatto
3. mete / mette
4. riti / ritti
5. moto / motto

C. Parliamo italiano! Listen and repeat.

1. Avete fatto tutto in venti minuti. Ottimo!
2. Mettete il latte nel tè?
3. Quanti tavolini all'aperto!
4. Il treno delle quattro e un quarto è partito in ritardo.
5. I salatini sono sul tavolino del salotto.

Ed ora ascoltiamo!

Luigi è veramente felice: ha trovato un appartamento ideale per lui. Sentirai una descrizione del suo appartamento. Ascolta il brano quante volte vuoi. Guarda la piantina (*floor plan*) e scrivi in ogni stanza il suo nome, secondo la descrizione. Controlla le tue risposte con le soluzioni date in fondo al libro.

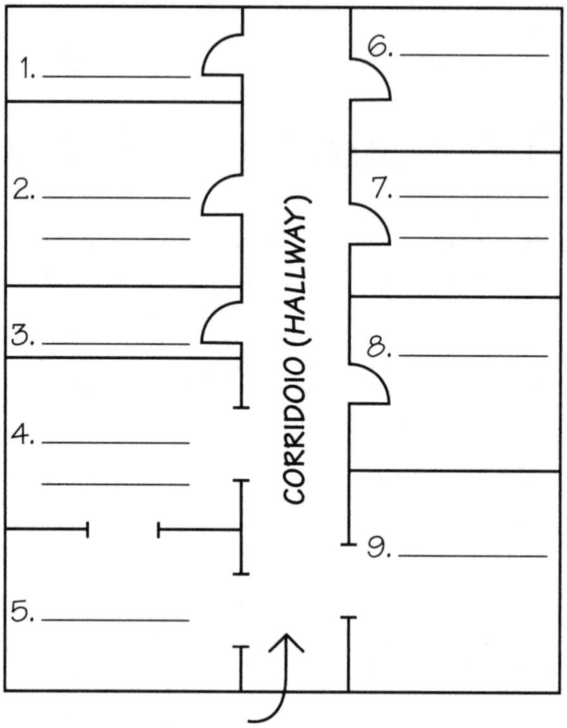

Dettato

Sentirai un breve dettato tre volte. La prima volta, ascolta attentamente. La seconda volta, il dettato sarà letto con pause tra le frasi. Scrivi quello che senti. La terza volta, correggi quello che hai scritto. Scrivi sulle righe date. Controlla il tuo dettato con le soluzioni date in fondo al libro.

Simonetta e Lucia ____________________

Dialogo

Prima parte. Carla incontra il signor Pini, il proprietario dell'appartamento che lei vuole vedere.

Ascolta attentamente il dialogo.

SIGNOR PINI: Buon giorno, signora Rossi, è pronta per vedere l'appartamento?

CARLA: Buon giorno, signor Pini. Certo che sono pronta. Se corrisponde alla Sua descrizione, credo che non avrò problemi ad affittare il Suo appartamento.

SIGNOR PINI: È un bell'appartamento e in una zona centrale, e lei sa come è difficile trovare un appartamento al prezzo che voglio io…

CARLA: A dire il vero, ero rimasta sorpresa dall'annuncio: un appartamento disponibile[1] adesso e a quel prezzo mi è sembrato[2] incredibile…

SIGNOR PINI: Se ne sono interessate molte persone, ma sono io che non ho trovato il candidato… o candidata ideale.

CARLA: Ci sono due camere da letto, vero?

SIGNOR PINI: Sì. È un appartamento con due camere da letto, una camera grande e una cameretta, che può essere lo studio… poi, come Le avevo già detto, c'è un soggiorno piuttosto grande, un bagno completo di doccia e la cucina.

CARLA: Eccoci arrivati. L'appartamento è al terzo piano, ci sono un po' di scale da fare… Peccato che non c'è l'ascensore!

SIGNOR PINI: Come vede, non è un palazzo moderno. Ma via, signorina, le scale non sono così tante… E il trasloco,[3] sa, non è un problema, le scale e le finestre sono molto larghe.

CARLA: Vedo, vedo, le scale sono molto belle, un bel marmo!

SIGNOR PINI: Sono sicuro che il problema non sarà l'appartamento, sarà l'affitto…

CARLA: Come Le ho già detto, l'affitto non è un problema.

SIGNOR PINI: Benissimo, allora. Entriamo. Ora Le mostro l'appartamento…

[1]*available* / [2]*mi… seemed to me*

[3]*move*

Seconda parte. Ascolta di nuovo il dialogo. Fai particolare attenzione a cosa dicono Carla e il signor Pini sull'affitto, l'appartamento e il palazzo.

Terza parte. Sentirai due volte sei frasi basate sul dialogo. Segna, per ciascuna frase, **vero** o **falso.**

1. vero falso
2. vero falso
3. vero falso
4. vero falso
5. vero falso
6. vero falso

Sara in Italia

Con il tempo che diventa sempre più bello, Sara decide di rimanere al sud. Oggi si trova in Puglia, a Taranto, dopo aver visitato Bari e Lecce. Parla con Elena Condoleo, una signora del posto. La signora Condoleo è tornata in Puglia, la sua regione d'origine, dopo aver vissuto tanti anni a Torino.

Ascolta attentamente il dialogo. Ascolta il dialogo quante volte vuoi. Poi, rispondi alle domande che senti. Sentirai ogni domanda due volte. Ripeti la risposta.

Parole utili: fabbrica (*factory*), da parte (*aside*), ci siamo trasferiti (*we moved*), quindi (*therefore*), albanesi (*Albanians*), muri (*walls*), rotondo (*round*), con tetti a cono (*cone-shaped roofs*)

1. … 2. … 3. … 4. … 5. …

Sara in rete…

For more information about what Sara experienced during her travels, check out the links found on the *Prego!* website **(www.mhhe.com/prego8).**

CAPITOLO 13

La difesa dell'ambiente

Vocabolario preliminare

A. Per cominciare. Sentirai il dialogo due volte. La prima volta, ascolta attentamente. La seconda volta, il dialogo sarà ripetuto con pause per la ripetizione. Poi ferma la registrazione e scegli la risposta giusta. Controlla le tue risposte con le soluzioni date in fondo al libro.

MAMMA: Giorgio, fammi un piacere: porta questi sacchetti pieni di carta, vetro e plastica giù in strada e mettili negli appositi contenitori.

GIORGIO: Ma perché non possiamo mettere tutto nella spazzatura normale?

MAMMA: Vedi, tutto può essere riciclato; così non inquineremo di più il nostro ambiente.

1. Cosa c'è nei sacchetti?

   a. rifiuti comuni   b. rifiuti riciclabili

2. Perché la mamma di Giorgio vuole riciclare?

   a. per inquinare di meno   b. per pulire la casa

B. Il traffico e l'ambiente. Sentirai, per due volte, cinque definizioni riguardo al traffico e quattro definizioni riguardo all'ambiente e dovrai identificare i termini a cui si riferiscono. Scrivi le risposte nella colonna giusta. Controlla le tue risposte con le soluzioni date in fondo al libro.

Parole utili: buttare via (*to throw away*), la raccolta (*collection*)

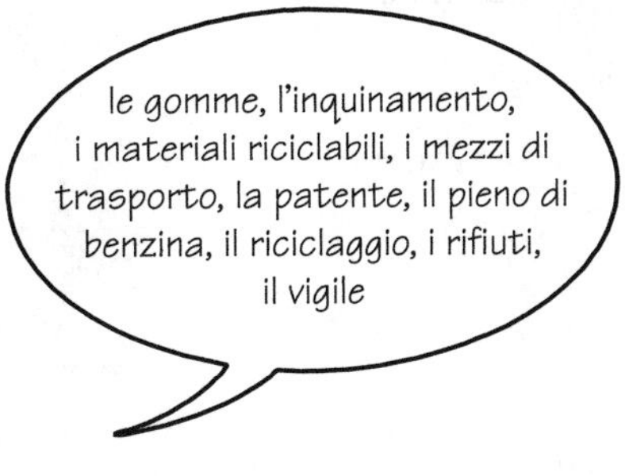
le gomme, l'inquinamento, i materiali riciclabili, i mezzi di trasporto, la patente, il pieno di benzina, il riciclaggio, i rifiuti, il vigile

IL TRAFFICO	L'AMBIENTE
1. ____________	1. ____________
2. ____________	2. ____________
3. ____________	3. ____________
4. ____________	4. ____________
5. ____________	

In ascolto

Un altro punto di vista. Saturnino e Mercurio, due extraterrestri arrivati sulla Terra in un disco volante (*flying saucer*), osservano dei ragazzi in un centro di riciclaggio. Ascolta con attenzione la loro conversazione, poi completa le seguenti frasi. Controlla le tue risposte con le soluzioni date in fondo al libro.

1. Il ragazzo biondo _____.

   a. depura l'acqua b. ricicla delle bottiglie c. scarica (*is throwing away*) rifiuti

2. Secondo Mercurio, molta gente non ricicla _____.

   a. la plastica b. i sacchetti di carta c. l'alluminio

3. I due ragazzi _____ mucchi (*piles*) di giornali.

   a. leggono b. proteggono c. riciclano

4. La macchina dei ragazzi _____ l'aria perché emette troppo fumo (*smoke*) nero.

   a. depura b. purifica c. inquina

5. Saturnino e Mercurio gli _____.

   a. offriranno un passaggio b. daranno una mano c. chiederanno un passaggio

Grammatica

A. Condizionale presente

A. Per cominciare. Sentirai un dialogo due volte. La prima volta, ascolta attentamente. La seconda volta, completa il dialogo con le parole che mancano. Controlla le tue risposte con le soluzioni date in fondo al libro.

SANDRO: Pronto, Paola? Senti, oggi sono senza macchina. È dal meccanico per un controllo. Mi ________________[1] un passaggio per andare in ufficio?

PAOLA: Ma certo! A che ora devo venire a prenderti? Va bene alle otto e un quarto?

SANDRO: Non ________________[2] possibile un po' prima: diciamo, alle otto? Mi ________________[3] un vero piacere!

PAOLA: Va bene, ci vediamo giù al portone alle otto.

B. Qualcosa da bere? Quando Paola ti offre da bere, rispondi per te e per i tuoi amici che preferireste la bibita suggerita. Ripeti la risposta.

ESEMPIO: *Senti:* Vuoi una coca-cola?
Leggi: un'aranciata
Dici: No, grazie, preferirei un'aranciata.

1. una cioccolata
2. un bicchiere di vino
3. una limonata
4. un'acqua naturale
5. un tè freddo

C. Con un milione di dollari... Cosa farebbero le seguenti persone con un milione di dollari? Rispondi secondo i suggerimenti. Ripeti la risposta.

ESEMPIO: *Senti:* i signori Colombi
Leggi: fare il giro del mondo
Dici: Farebbero il giro del mondo.

1. comprare uno yacht
2. aiutare i poveri
3. andare a vivere alle Hawaii
4. scrivere il tuo romanzo
5. dare i soldi ad un'associazione ambientalista

D. Cosa faresti? Rispondi alle seguenti domande personali.

1. ... 2. ... 3. ...

B. *Dovere, potere* e *volere* al condizionale

A. Per cominciare. Sentirai un dialogo due volte. La prima volta, ascolta attentamente. La seconda volta, il dialogo sarà ripetuto con pause per la ripetizione.

FRANCESCA: Vorrei un mondo più pulito... Tutti dovremmo fare qualcosa per proteggere l'ambiente.
PATRIZIO: Hai ragione, ma cosa... ? Siamo solo dei ragazzini!
FRANCESCA: Beh, potremmo iniziare con il riciclaggio dei rifiuti che abbiamo in casa e poi potremmo sensibilizzare i nostri compagni di classe!

B. Consigli. Daniele ti racconta delle cattive abitudini di tutti. Rispondi che dovrebbero fare o non fare le seguenti cose. Ripeti la risposta.

ESEMPIO: *Senti:* Bianca beve troppo.
Dici: Non dovrebbe bere troppo.

1. … 2. … 3. … 4. … 5. … 6. …

C. L'esperto di trasporti. Sai tutto riguardo ai viaggi in macchina. Quando i tuoi amici ti raccontano i loro problemi, proponi delle soluzioni secondo i suggerimenti. Ripeti la risposta.

ESEMPIO: *Senti:* Sono quasi rimasta senza benzina.
Leggi: fare il pieno più spesso
Dici: Potresti fare il pieno più spesso!

1. chiedere un passaggio a Laura
2. rispettare i segnali stradali
3. portarla dal meccanico
4. controllare l'olio
5. andare in bici

C. Condizionale passato

A. Per cominciare. Sentirai un dialogo due volte. La prima volta, ascolta attentamente. La seconda volta, completa il dialogo con le parole che mancano. Controlla le tue risposte con le soluzioni date in fondo al libro.

GUIDO: Guarda come guida veloce quel pazzo!

RAFFAELE: Quel vigile ______________[1] ______________[2] prendere il numero di targa e dovrebbe mandargli una multa a casa.

GUIDO: No, ______________[3] ______________[4] meglio fermarlo e fargli subito una bella multa salata! Certi automobilisti sono un pericolo pubblico!

B. Del senno di poi... (*With hindsight . . .*) Di' cosa avrebbero dovuto fare prima le seguenti persone, secondo i suggerimenti. Ripeti la risposta.

ESEMPIO: *Senti:* Laura è arrivata in ritardo.
Leggi: alzarsi
Dici: Laura avrebbe dovuto alzarsi prima.

1. prenotare
2. arrivare
3. mangiare
4. prendere
5. tornare
6. decidere

C. Tutti al mare! Tutti avevano programmato di studiare questo week-end… prima di sapere della festa al mare di Maurizio. Di' cosa hanno detto tutti, secondo i suggerimenti. Ripeti la risposta.

ESEMPIO: *Senti:* Maria
Dici: Ha detto che avrebbe studiato.

1. … 2. … 3. … 4. … 5. … 6. …

D. Pronomi possessivi

A. Per cominciare. Sentirai un dialogo due volte. La prima volta, ascolta attentamente. La seconda volta, il dialogo sarà ripetuto con pause per la ripetizione.

DANIELE: La mia macchina è una Ferrari; è velocissima. Com'è la tua?
ANTONIO: La mia è un po' vecchia, ma funziona.
DANIELE: La mia bici è una Bianchi. Che marca è la tua?
ANTONIO: Mah, non lo so. È una bici qualsiasi.
DANIELE: I miei vestiti sono tutti di Armani. E i tuoi?
ANTONIO: I miei non sono di marche famose. Di solito li compro al mercato.

B. Una macchina economica... Sentirai un dialogo tra Aldo e Carlo due volte. La prima volta, ascolta attentamente. La seconda volta, completa il dialogo con le parole che mancano. Controlla le tue risposte con le soluzioni date in fondo al libro.

ALDO: La ______________[1] macchina è una Ferrari, è velocissima, com'è la ______________[2]?

CARLO: La ______________[3] è un po' vecchia e funziona male. Ma come ti puoi permettere una Ferrari? Consuma tanta benzina!

ALDO: La prendo solo per le grandi occasioni, altrimenti uso la macchina di ______________[4] moglie.

CARLO: E cos'è la ______________[5]?

ALDO: La sua è una Fiat del 2000, viaggia bene e risparmia più della ______________...[6]

CARLO: Eh, ci credo!

C. Curiosità. Sei ad una festa dove non conosci nessuno. Dovrai cercare di fare due chiacchiere, su qualsiasi argomento (*topic*), secondo i suggerimenti. Ripeti la risposta.

ESEMPIO: *Leggi:* La mia macchina è una FIAT.
Senti: Lei
Dici: La mia è una FIAT, e la Sua?

1. Il mio lavoro è interessante.
2. Nostro zio abita con noi.
3. Le mie nonne abitano a Roma.
4. La mia lavatrice non funziona.
5. I miei figli vanno a scuola.
6. Nostra sorella è sposata.

Pronuncia: The sounds of the letter "d"

In Italian, the letter **d** is pronounced like the *d* in the English word *tide.* Unlike the English *d,* however, the Italian **d** is always clearly articulated, regardless of position.

A. ***D.*** Listen carefully to these English and Italian words, then repeat the Italian words. Listen and repeat.

1. *ditto* / dito
2. *day* / dei
3. *grandma* / grande
4. *modern* / moderno
5. *wedding* / vedi

B. ***D* e doppia *d.*** Compare and contrast the single and double sound of **d.** Listen and repeat.

1. Ada / Adda
2. cade / cadde
3. fede / Edda
4. cadi / caddi
5. idea / Iddio

C. **Parliamo italiano!** Listen and repeat.

1. Avete deciso dove andare questa domenica?
2. Fa freddo in dicembre?
3. Dammi i soldi che ti ho dato!
4. Non devi dare del tu a tutti.
5. Dieci più dodici fa ventidue.
6. Non so cosa dovrei dire al dottore.

Ed ora ascoltiamo!

Sentirai tre dialoghi seguiti da due domande. Puoi ascoltare ogni dialogo quante volte vuoi. Poi dovrai scegliere la risposta giusta a ciascuna domanda.

Parole utili: comunque (*in any case*), una folla (*crowd*), scelta (*choice*), esauriti (*sold out*)

Dialogo 1

1. a. alle sette b. alle otto
2. a. la mattina b. il pomeriggio

Dialogo 2

1. a. Massimo è andato al cinema.
   b. Massimo è uscito con la sua fidanzata.
2. a. Patrizia non è andata a sedere (*sit*) in prima fila.
   b. Patrizia avrebbe voluto sedere in prima fila.

Dialogo 3

1. a. I biglietti saranno in vendita tra un mese.
   b. I biglietti avrebbero dovuto essere comprati già da un po' di tempo.
2. a. I biglietti si potrebbero avere pagando (*paying*) di più.
   b. I biglietti non sono più sul mercato.

Dettato

Sentirai un breve dettato tre volte. La prima volta, ascolta attentamente. La seconda volta, il dettato sarà letto con pause tra le frasi. Scrivi quello che senti. La terza volta, correggi quello che hai scritto. Scrivi sulle righe date. Controlla il tuo dettato con le soluzioni date in fondo al libro.

Enrico e Paola ____

____

____

____

____

____

____

____

____

____

____

Dialogo

Prima parte. Una vigile ferma un'automobilista che ha fretta e parla con lei.

Parole utili: libretto di circolazione (*registration*), assicurazione (*insurance certificate*), una freccia (*turn signal*)

Ascolta attentamente il dialogo.

VIGILE: Patente, prego, e libretto di circolazione...

AUTOMOBILISTA: Ecco tutto qui, assicurazione compresa.[1]

VIGILE: 70 chilometri all'ora in una zona urbana con 40 di limite non sono troppi?

AUTOMOBILISTA: Lo so, lo so, Lei ha ragione! Ma devo andare da mio figlio a scuola, è caduto,[2] per questo vado in fretta...

VIGILE: Capisco la situazione, ma il limite parla chiaro! E poi, sa che ha anche una freccia[3] che non funziona?

AUTOMOBILISTA: Sì, lo so, mio marito avrebbe dovuto portare la macchina a riparare dal meccanico ieri, ma mia figlia si è fatta male mentre giocava a pallacanestro e abbiamo dovuto portarla all'ospedale. Non c'è stato tempo per la macchina... Lei che farebbe in una situazione così?

VIGILE: Non so dirLe. Non deve chiedere a me... Com'è che non ha la targa? La targa non dovrebbe dipendere da nessun problema familiare, se non mi sbaglio!

AUTOMOBILISTA: Veramente, sì... Ho comprato la macchina solo tre giorni fa e avrei anche fatto subito la targa, ma mio marito si è arrabbiato terribilmente perché l'ho pagata tutta subito; dice che avrei dovuto pagarla a rate!...[4] Non ho avuto tempo di andare a fare registrare la macchina e prendere la targa nuova!

VIGILE: Signora, mi dispiace, ma tra la velocità e la freccia deve pagare € 183,25! Riguardo alla targa, mi dispiace; ma Le dobbiamo portar via[5] la macchina*!

[1] *included*
[2] è... *he fell*
[3] *turn signal*
[4] a... *in installments*
[5] portar... *to impound*

*According to Italian law, cars without license plates are impounded by the police.

Seconda parte. Ascolta di nuovo il dialogo. Fai particolare attenzione alle giustificazioni date dalla signora alla vigile.

Terza parte. Sentirai due volte sei frasi basate sul dialogo. Segna, per ciascuna frase, **vero** o **falso.**

1. vero falso
2. vero falso
3. vero falso
4. vero falso
5. vero falso
6. vero falso

Sara in Italia

Sara è in Abruzzo, ospite dei signori Trubiano, che hanno una piccola pensione a Pescasseroli, al centro del Parco Nazionale. Sara ha già visitato Pescara, sulla costa, e L'Aquila ed è già passata in autostrada sui monti del Gran Sasso. Adesso vuole fare delle belle passeggiate nel Parco e parla con la signora Trubiano delle cose da fare e da vedere.

Ascolta attentamente il dialogo. Ascolta il dialogo quante volte vuoi. Poi, rispondi alle domande che senti. Sentirai ogni domanda due volte. Ripeti la risposta.

Parole utili: avrò nostalgia di (*I will miss*), a cavallo (*horseback riding*), purtroppo (*unfortunately*), sarebbe servito (*they would be useful*), peccato (*it's a shame*)

1. ... 2. ... 3. ... 4. ... 5. ...

Sara in rete...

For more information about what Sara experienced during her travels, check out the links found on the *Prego!* website **(www.mhhe.com/prego8).**

Nome ________________ Data ________ Classe ________________

CAPITOLO 14

La musica e il teatro

Vocabolario preliminare

A. Per cominciare. Sentirai un dialogo due volte. La prima volta, ascolta attentamente. La seconda volta, completa il dialogo con le parole che mancano. Controlla le tue risposte con le soluzioni date in fondo al libro.

GIACOMO: Che bell'________________[1] «Le nozze di Figaro»!

MARISA: Hai ragione. La ________________[2] di Mozart è davvero bella e il ________________[3] è stato eccezionale!

GIACOMO: Anche il________________[4] d'orchestra; tutti i ________________[5] e i ________________[6] sono stati molto bravi!

B. Indovinelli. Sentirai, per due volte, sette indovinelli. Indovina la parola dello spettacolo alla quale (*to which*) ogni frase si riferisce. Scrivi il numero corrispondente alla parola e di' la risposta. Ripeti la risposta.

ESEMPIO: *Senti:* È la voce femminile più alta.
Segna: 1
Dici: il soprano

C. **Musica e teatro.** Guarda i disegni e rispondi alle domande che senti. Ripeti la risposta.

ESEMPIO:

Senti: Nina e Franco guardano una commedia o una tragedia?

Dici: Guardano una tragedia.

1.

2.

3.

4.

5.

D. **Domande personali.** Rispondi alle seguenti domande personali. Scrivi sulle righe date.

1. ______________________________

____

2. ______________________________

____

3. ______________________________

____

4. ______________________________

____

In ascolto

Che bella voce! Francesca e Luca parlano di una diva del mondo lirico. Ascolta con attenzione la loro conversazione e decidi se le seguenti affermazioni sono vere o false. Poi ferma la registrazione e correggi le affermazioni false. Controlla le tue risposte con le soluzioni date in fondo al libro.

1. La diva di cui (*of whom*) parlano è un soprano. vero falso

   ____

2. La diva canta bene le arie romantiche e interpreta bene Verdi. vero falso

   ____

3. Luca ha la fortuna di ascoltarla nelle opere di Puccini. vero falso

   ____

4. Francesca l'ha vista in un'opera all'Opera di Roma. vero falso

   ____

5. Questa diva ha un grande successo anche negli Stati Uniti. vero falso

   ____

Grammatica

A. Pronomi relativi

A. Per cominciare. Sentirai un dialogo due volte. La prima volta, ascolta attentamente. La seconda volta, il dialogo sarà ripetuto con pause per la ripetizione.

ANTONIO: Conosci quel ragazzo?
BRUNO: No, non lo conosco. È il ragazzo con cui è uscita ieri Roberta?
ANTONIO: No.
BRUNO: È il ragazzo di cui è innamorata Gianna?
ANTONIO: No.
BRUNO: Allora, chi è?
ANTONIO: Tu, ovviamente, non ti intendi di musica pop. Lui è il cantautore Alex Britti di cui tutti parlano e che è conosciuto in tutto il mondo.
BRUNO: Oh! Allora, andiamo a parlargli!

B. **Benvenuta!** (*Welcome!*) È appena arrivata alla stazione una tua amica. Indica le varie cose della tua città che vedete mentre l'accompagni a casa. Segui i suggerimenti. Ripeti la risposta.

ESEMPIO: *Senti:* Vado in quella palestra.
Dici: Quella è la palestra in cui vado.

1. … 2. … 3. … 4. … 5. …

C. **Festival.** Parla del festival estivo (*summer*) dello spettacolo, secondo i suggerimenti. Usa **che** per legare le due frasi. Ripeti la risposta.

ESEMPIO: *Leggi:* Il musicista suona stasera.
Senti: È famoso.
Dici: Il musicista che suona stasera è famoso.

1. La canzone ha vinto il festival.
2. Il tenore canta l'opera.
3. La regista ha messo in scena la commedia.
4. Il soprano canta in tedesco.
5. L'attore recita nell'*Amleto.*

D. **Non lo capisco!** Simone è un tipo difficile da capire! Di' che non capisci tante cose riguardo a (*having to do with*) lui, secondo i suggerimenti. Ripeti la risposta.

ESEMPIO: *Senti:* dire
Dici: Non capisco quello che dice.

1. … 2. … 3. … 4. …

B. Chi

A. **Per cominciare.** Sentirai un dialogo due volte. La prima volta, ascolta attentamente. La seconda volta, il dialogo sarà ripetuto con pause per la ripetizione della parte di Stefania.

STEFANIA: Chi viene al balletto con me questa sera?
LUIGI: Chi non deve studiare!
STEFANIA: Chi sarebbe questa persona?
LUIGI: Chi ha già dato tutti gli esami!
STEFANIA: Ho capito, viene Paolo. Si è appena laureato!

B. **Generalità.** Trasforma le frasi che senti. Comincia la nuova frase con **Chi…** , secondo l'esempio. Ripeti la risposta.

ESEMPIO: *Senti:* Le persone che parlano troppo non sono simpatiche.
Dici: Chi parla troppo non è simpatico.

1. … 2. … 3. … 4. … 5. …

C. **Chi?** Sentirai, per due volte, cinque definizioni. Dovrai scegliere la parola che è descritta nella definizione.

ESEMPIO: *Senti:* Chi scrive e canta canzoni.
Leggi e segna: a. il basso (b. il cantautore)

1. a. il pittore b. lo scultore
2. a. l'ascensore b. le scale
3. a. l'autore b. l'attore
4. a. il regista b. il compositore
5. a. il frigo b. il forno

C. Costruzioni con l'infinito

A. **Per cominciare.** Sentirai un dialogo seguito da tre frasi da completare. Sentirai il dialogo due volte. La prima volta, ascolta attentamente. La seconda volta, sottolinea (*underline*) i verbi all'infinito. Poi dovrai fermare la registrazione e completare le frasi. Controlla le tue risposte con le soluzioni date in fondo al libro.

LUCIANO: Ieri ho incontrato la mia vecchia insegnante di canto.
MARGHERITA: Davvero? Era brava?
LUCIANO: Oh, sì! Con lei ho cominciato a prendere lezioni di canto quando avevo dieci anni. È lei che mi ha insegnato a cantare.
MARGHERITA: Beh, ora che sei in città dovresti chiederle di venire a teatro per vedere che grande tenore sei diventato!

1. Luciano ha cominciato ______________________.
2. La sua vecchia insegnante gli ha insegnato a ______________________.
3. Margherita dice che Luciano dovrebbe ______________________ di ______________________ a teatro.

B. **Propositi** (*Intentions*) **e pensieri** (*thoughts*). Quali sono i tuoi propositi? E i tuoi pensieri? Componi una frase sola, secondo i suggerimenti. Ripeti la risposta.

ESEMPIO: *Senti:* Ho paura: non voglio dimenticare l'appuntamento!
Leggi: dimenticare l'appuntamento
Dici: Ho paura di dimenticare l'appuntamento!

1. preparare la tavola
2. contare fino a (*to count up to*) cento in spagnolo
3. mangiare con noi
4. andare in vacanza
5. farmi male (*to hurt myself*) in cucina

C. **Alcune domande personali.** Rispondi alle seguenti domande secondo le tue esperienze personali. Usa la costruzione con l'infinito.

ESEMPIO: *Senti:* Che cosa hai bisogno di fare?
Dici: Ho bisogno di fare più ginnastica.

1. … 2. … 3. … 4. … 5. …

D. Nomi e aggettivi in *-a*

A. Per cominciare. Sentirai un dialogo due volte. La prima volta, ascolta attentamente. La seconda volta, il dialogo sarà ripetuto con pause per la ripetizione.

SANDRO: Finalmente il programma teatrale per la prossima stagione invernale!
EDUARDO: C'è qualcosa di interessante?
SANDRO: Oh, sì: bellissimi balletti, opere e anche un concerto del famoso pianista Marini!
EDUARDO: Fantastico! Potrebbe essere un problema trovare i biglietti però.

B. Dal plurale al singolare. Sentirai cinque frasi al plurale. Cambia le frasi al singolare. Ripeti la risposta.

ESEMPIO: *Senti:* I programmi della televisione sono ripetitivi.
Dici: Il programma della televisione è ripetitivo.

1. … 2. … 3. … 4. … 5. …

C. Chi sono? Sentirai, per due volte, quattro descrizioni di persone. Ascolta attentamente e di' chi sono le persone descritte. Ripeti la risposta.

ESEMPIO: *Senti:* È un signore che visita un paese straniero.
Dici: È un turista.

Parole utili: il capo (*head*)

1. … 2. … 3. … 4. …

D. Domande personali. Rispondi alle seguenti domande secondo le tue esperienze personali.

1. … 2. … 3. … 4. …

Ed ora ascoltiamo!

Sentirai un dialogo tra Nicoletta e Elena in cui discutono dei loro gusti musicali, seguito da quattro frasi da completare. Puoi ascoltare il dialogo quante volte vuoi. Poi dovrai fermare la registrazione e completare le frasi, secondo il dialogo. Controlla le tue risposte con le soluzioni date in fondo al libro.

Parole utili: pareti (*walls*), alberi (*trees*), insieme (*at the same time*), impegnato (*involved* [*politically*])

1. La canzone di Gino Paoli è ______________________ e ha più di ______________________ anni.
2. Gli strumenti che ci sono nelle canzoni preferite da Nicoletta sono, per esempio, ________ ______________________ e ________ ______________________.
3. Elena preferisce invece le canzoni di Dalla, De Gregori e Guccini e ________ ______________________ ______________________.
4. Nicoletta, in questa settimana, guarderà in televisione ________ ______________________ ________ ______________________.

Nome ______________________ *Data* ____________ *Classe* ______________

Dettato

Sentirai un breve dettato tre volte. La prima volta, ascolta attentamente. La seconda volta, il dettato sarà letto con pause tra le frasi. Scrivi quello che senti. La terza volta, correggi quello che hai scritto. Scrivi sulle righe date. Controlla il tuo dettato con le soluzioni date in fondo al libro.

Clark e Christie ____

Dialogo

Prima parte. Il signor Cecchi ha due figlie: Caterina, che esce con un musicista, e Valeria, che esce con un attore, regista e scrittore. Oggi conoscerà il ragazzo di Valeria, Luca.

Parole utili: sorride... ? (*are you smiling . . .* ?)

Ascolta attentamente il dialogo.

SIGNOR CECCHI: Con chi esci stasera?

VALERIA: Con Luca. Vedrai, ti piacerà, è attore, registra teatrale, scrittore...

SIGNOR CECCHI: Non vedo l'ora di incontrarlo! Lo potrei invitare a venire con me alla prima di *Sei personaggi in cerca d'autore*...

VALERIA: Beh, papà, Luca non è un tipo da vestirsi bene per andare alle prime e poi è un regista di spettacoli alternativi; Pirandello forse non gli interessa, è un autore così usato, vecchio, stanco...

SIGNOR CECCHI: E perché no, che male c'è con Pirandello? Vecchio? Stanco? Ma che dici? I suoi temi sono contemporanei… E poi, chi è questo Luca, non è forse un regista? Ogni spettacolo dovrebbe interessargli!

VALERIA: Forse hai ragione. Dovresti domandarglielo tu; se glielo chiedo io, chissà, forse mi direbbe di no. (*Suona il campanello*[1] *della porta.*) Ecco, ho sentito suonare il campanello…

LUCA: Ciao, Valeria, buona sera, signor Cecchi.

SIGNOR CECCHI: Buona sera, Luca, piacere di conoscerti, mia figlia mi ha appena detto che lavori nel teatro… Che spettacoli fai?

LUCA: Mi interessa la regia[2] di autori giovani o contemporanei, come Dario Fo, ma anche i più tradizionali, di repertorio, non mi dispiacciono…

SIGNOR CECCHI: Conosci Pirandello?

LUCA: Certo che lo conosco. Ho cominciato a collaborare proprio in questi giorni su *Così è (se vi pare)*…[3] Perché sorride,[4] signor Cecchi?

SIGNOR CECCHI: Sai, Valeria mi diceva che ero troppo vecchio perché mi piaceva Pirandello!

LUCA: Ma no, sono sicuro che Le piacerebbero anche i miei spettacoli. Mi piace rappresentare l'alienazione, le crisi d'identità, il contrasto tra l'essere e l'apparire,[5] la solitudine delle persone. Come in Pirandello!

SIGNOR CECCHI: Ho capito: la prossima settimana prendo due biglietti per il teatro e andiamo noi due, lasciamo Valeria a casa!

[1]*bell*
[2]*direction*
[3]Così... *Right You Are (If You Think So)* / [4]*are you smiling*
[5]l'essere... *being and appearing*

Seconda parte. Ascolta di nuovo il dialogo. Fai particolare attenzione ai gusti di Luca e del signor Cecchi.

Terza parte. Sentirai due volte sei frasi basate sul dialogo. Segna, per ciascuna frase, **vero** o **falso.**

1. vero falso
2. vero falso
3. vero falso
4. vero falso
5. vero falso
6. vero falso

Nome ______________________ *Data* ____________ *Classe* ______________________

Sara in Italia

Sara è a Portovenere, in Liguria, dopo avere visitato le Cinque Terre, legate (*tied*) a Eugenio Montale, poeta e premio Nobel italiano. È arrivata qui, in barca, da Lerici, per vedere il golfo amato dai poeti romantici inglesi Shelley e Byron. Sara è con Silvana, una professoressa di lettere che ama viaggiare e vedere i luoghi legati a poeti, scrittori e uomini famosi. Le loro prossime tappe saranno Genova, la città natale di Cristoforo Colombo, e poi San Remo, la città del Festival della canzone italiana ma anche di Italo Calvino, uno scrittore molto conosciuto negli Stati Uniti e in Canada.

Ascolta attentamente il dialogo. Ascolta il dialogo quante volte vuoi. Poi, rispondi alle domande che senti. Sentirai ogni domanda due volte. Ripeti la risposta.

Parole utili: scoglio (*rock, cliff*), insolite (*unusual*), non vedo l'ora di (*I can't wait to*), dipinte (*painted*), acceso (*bright*), marinai (*sailors*)

1. … 2. … 3. … 4. … 5. …

Sara in rete…

For more information about what Sara experienced during her travels, check out the links found on the *Prego!* website **(www.mhhe.com/prego8).**

CAPITOLO

Le belle arti 15

Vocabolario preliminare

A. Per cominciare. Sentirai un dialogo seguito da tre domande. Sentirai il dialogo due volte. La prima volta, ascolta attentamente. La seconda volta, il dialogo sarà ripetuto con pause per la ripetizione. Sentirai, per due volte, tre domande e dovrai scrivere le risposte giuste alle domande. Controlla le tue risposte con le soluzioni date in fondo al libro.

MARCELLO: Ornella, Raffaele, bentornati! Com'è andato il vostro viaggio in Italia?
ORNELLA: È stato meraviglioso! Abbiamo visto opere d'arte e monumenti magnifici!
RAFFAELE: Ogni museo è ricco di statue e dipinti straordinari e in molte chiese ci sono affreschi e mosaici bellissimi!
ORNELLA: Un vero sogno!

1. ________________
2. ________________
3. ________________

B. Che bella l'arte! Sentirai, per due volte, cinque frasi incomplete. Ascolta attentamente, poi dovrai scegliere la conclusione giusta.

ESEMPIO: *Senti:* Mi piace leggere, ma non mi piacciono le cose lunghe; preferisco...

Leggi e segna: a. i romanzi b. i dipinti (c. i racconti)

1. a. quadro b. scavo c. racconto
2. a. la rima b. l'archeologia c. la pittura
3. a. un capolavoro b. un affresco c. una poesia
4. a. paesaggi b. ritratti c. affreschi
5. a. pittura b. architettura c. scultura

C. **Un capolavoro della letteratura italiana: Dante e la *Divina Commedia*.** Sentirai una lettura su Dante due volte. La prima volta, ascolta attentamente. La seconda volta, completa la lettura con le parole che mancano. Controlla le tue risposte con le soluzioni date in fondo al libro. Ora ferma la registrazione, dai un'occhiata alla lettura e leggi la nota a piè di pagina (*footnote*).

Non possiamo che[a] cominciare a parlare di letteratura italiana con il nome di Dante, uno dei grandi del '300 italiano, insieme a Boccaccio e Petrarca. Il ______________________[1] di Dante è la *Divina Commedia*, un'opera in versi. L'opera narra il viaggio dell'______________________[2] nei tre regni[b] dell'Inferno, Purgatorio e Paradiso, alla ricerca di una salvezza[c] personale e collettiva. La ______________________[3] dantesca è stata molto importante per la lingua italiana. Intere generazioni hanno imparato a memoria dei versi della *Divina Commedia.* Hanno ______________________[4] dal poema, specialmente dall'inizio[d]... «Nel mezzo del cammin di nostra vita / mi ritrovai per una selva oscura / ché la diritta via era smarrita»[e]... ______________________[5] la *Divina Commedia* è difficile perché è una vera enciclopedia del sapere,[f] della poesia, della filosofia, ed è ricchissima di fatti[g] e personaggi del Medioevo. Ed è anche una storia, un ______________________[6] appassionante: Dante che passa attraverso[h] i tre regni fino alla visione finale di Dio. *L'Inferno* è la parte più famosa, nell'*Inferno* troviamo i personaggi più umani e più affascinanti. E forse noi abbiamo simpatia per queste figure perché anche noi, come Dante, ci riconosciamo in loro, anche se sono dannati...[i]

[a]Non... *We have to* [b]*realms* [c]*salvation* [d]*from the opening line* [e]*In the middle of the course of our life / I found myself in a dark wood / because I had gone astray...* [f]*knowledge* [g]*events* [h]*through* [i]*damned*

In ascolto

Una visita a Firenze. Antonella e Pasquale parlano davanti a Palazzo Vecchio, a Firenze. Ascolta con attenzione la loro conversazione, poi completa le seguenti frasi. Controlla le tue risposte con le soluzioni date in fondo al libro.

Parole utili: l'ingresso (*entrance*), bloccato (*blocked*), avvicinarsi (*to approach*), dall'alto (*from above*), prigione (*prison*)

1. Antonella voleva visitare Palazzo Vecchio ma ________________.
2. Piazza della Signoria era stata trasformata in ________________.
3. Dall'alto la gente poteva vedere ________________.
4. C'erano rovine ________________ e alcune più antiche del periodo ________________.
5. Il Bargello era una prigione ma adesso è ________________.

Grammatica

A. Passato remoto

A. Per cominciare. Sentirai un brano due volte. La prima volta, ascolta attentamente. La seconda volta, il brano sarà ripetuto con pause per la ripetizione. Poi sentirai, due volte, cinque frasi e dovrai segnare, per ciascuna frase, **vero** o **falso.**

PROFESSOR MARCENARO: Oggi vi parlerò di Michelangelo, di questo grandissimo artista che si affermò come pittore, scultore, architetto ed anche come poeta. Studiò con il Ghirlandaio e poi lavorò per principi, duchi, vescovi e papi. La sua opera più famosa sono gli affreschi della volta della Cappella Sistina. Questo immenso lavoro che Michelangelo volle eseguire senza nessun aiuto durò ben quattro anni (1508–1512). Gli affreschi illustrano episodi del Vecchio Testamento e culminano con il Giudizio Universale...

1. vero falso
2. vero falso
3. vero falso
4. vero falso
5. vero falso

B. Chi venne in America? Di' chi venne in America, secondo i suggerimenti. Ripeti la risposta.

ESEMPIO: *Senti:* mio nonno
Dici: Tuo nonno venne in America.

1. ... 2. ... 3. ... 4. ... 5. ... 6. ...

C. Dante e Beatrice. Sentirai un brano due volte. La prima volta, ascolta attentamente. La seconda volta, completa il brano con i verbi al passato remoto. Controlla le tue risposte con le soluzioni date in fondo al libro. Poi rispondi alle domande che senti. Ripeti la risposta.

Dante, il poeta più noto della letteratura italiana, ________________[1] a Firenze nel 1265. Con lui nasce, essenzialmente, la poesia in italiano (che nel Medioevo coincideva con il dialetto fiorentino). Prima di scrivere la *Divina Commedia* ________________[2] la *Vita nuova,* in cui ________________[3] il suo amore per Beatrice, che nel suo libro acquistò[a] il valore di donna-angelo, una rivelazione dell'amore di Dio per ogni essere umano, di cui lei si fa messaggera. Beatrice è una figura non solo allegorica ma storica (si chiamava Beatrice Portinari): ________________[4] giovane e la sua perdita[b] ________________[5] Dante a cantarla nella *Divina Commedia.* Nel poema Dante ________________[6] di Beatrice la sua guida per il Paradiso, colei che infatti,[c] come dal significato del nome, «porta salvezza», salute spirituale.

[a]*acquired* [b]*loss* [c]colei… *she who actually*

1. … 2. … 3. …

D. Petrarca. Il compito di tua cugina Anna sul poeta Petrarca (e su Laura, la sua ispirazione) ha molti errori. Anna ti legge alcune frasi del suo compito. Ascolta le sue frasi e correggile come nell'esempio. Usa il passato remoto dei verbi. Ripeti la risposta.

ESEMPIO: *Leggi:* incontrare Laura il 6 aprile, in primavera
Senti: Petrarca ha incontrato Laura in una calda estate.
Dici: No, Petrarca incontrò Laura il 6 aprile, in primavera.

1. scrivere 366 poesie, come per un anno bisestile (*leap year*)
2. avere capelli biondi e gli occhi azzurri
3. leggere bene la *Commedia* di Dante e la sua poesia su Beatrice
4. essere amico di Boccaccio fino alla fine della vita

B. Numeri ordinali

A. Per cominciare. Sentirai un dialogo due volte. La prima volta, ascolta attentamente. La seconda volta, il dialogo sarà ripetuto con pause per la ripetizione.

PROFESSORE: Allora, Carlo, hai letto i primi sei canti dell'*Inferno* di Dante Alighieri? Quali canti ti sono piaciuti di più?

CARLO: Mi è piaciuto il primo, quando Dante inizia il suo viaggio nell'aldilà, ed il quinto, quando parla della sfortunata storia d'amore tra Francesca e Paolo.

B. Personaggi storici. Di' il nome e il titolo di ogni personaggio. Usa i numeri ordinali. Ripeti la risposta.

ESEMPIO: *Leggi:* Giovanni Paolo II, papa
Dici: Giovanni Paolo Secondo, papa

1. Luigi XIV, re di Francia
2. Giovanni XXIII, papa
3. Enrico VIII, re d'Inghilterra
4. Carlo V, imperatore di Spagna e di Germania
5. Vittorio Emanuele II, re d'Italia
6. Elisabetta I, regina d'Inghilterra

C. In quale secolo? Di' in quale secolo successero i seguenti avvenimenti. Ripeti la risposta.

ESEMPIO: *Senti:* nell'anno 1517, la Riforma Luterana
Dici: nel sedicesimo secolo

Parole utili: la nascita (*birth*), il Giubileo (*special period in the Catholic Church*)

1. … 2. … 3. … 4. … 5. … 6. …

D. Quale periodo? Sentirai nominare un secolo e dovrai dire a quale periodo corrisponde. Ripeti la risposta.

ESEMPIO: *Senti:* il sedicesimo secolo
Dici: il Cinquecento

1. … 2. … 3. … 4. … 5. … 6. …

C. *Volerci* e *metterci*

A. Per cominciare. Sentirai un dialogo due volte. La prima volta, ascolta attentamente. La seconda volta, il dialogo sarà ripetuto con pause per la ripetizione.

AUTOMOBILISTA: Quanto ci vuole per arrivare a Cutrofiano?
PASSANTE: Dipende da quale strada sceglie. Potrebbe metterci mezz'ora o potrebbe metterci due ore.

B. Quanto ci vuole? Di' quanto ci vuole per fare le seguenti cose, secondo i suggerimenti. Ripeti la risposta.

ESEMPIO: *Senti:* Per fare la torta…
Leggi: un'ora e mezza
Dici: Per fare la torta ci vuole un'ora e mezza.

Parole utili: il bucato (*laundry*)

1. un'ora
2. tre ore e mezza
3. una mezza giornata
4. mezz'ora
5. due minuti

D. Il gerundio

A. Per cominciare. Sentirai un dialogo due volte. La prima volta, ascolta attentamente. La seconda volta, mentre ascolti il dialogo, leggi le domande e le tre possibili risposte. Sentirai poi le domande basate sul dialogo. Scegli la tua risposta e poi ascolta la risposta corretta.

1. Cosa sta facendo Marco stasera?
   a. Sta dormendo dopo aver preso le medicine.
   b. Si sta annoiando perché è a letto e non può muoversi.
   c. Sta chiacchierando con Marco per passare il tempo.
2. Come sta la sua caviglia (*cast*)?
   a. Gli sta facendo ancora male, ma solo quando cammina (*he walks*).
   b. Non gli fa più male, avendo preso le medicine.
   c. Non c'è nessuna posizione buona per evitare (*avoid*) il dolore, al momento.
3. Che cosa propone Franco?
   a. Chiacchierando per telefono, si passa meglio il tempo.
   b. Chiacchierando con gli amici durante una visita, Marco può annoiarsi di meno.
   c. Avendo chiacchierato con gli amici durante una visita, Marco può poi dormire meglio.

B. Cosa stanno facendo? Sentirai cinque frasi due volte. Usa il presente progressivo per dire cosa fanno queste persone. Ripeti la risposta.

ESEMPIO: *Senti:* Lavano l'auto in giardino.
Leggi: Rossana e Fabrizio
Dici: Rossana e Fabrizio stanno lavando l'auto in giardino.

1. Chiara
2. io e Silvana
3. tu
4. tu e Mario
5. io

C. Che cosa è successo dopo? Leggi che cosa hanno fatto queste persone e che cosa hanno fatto dopo. Poi combina le frasi, usando il gerundio. Ripeti la risposta.

ESEMPIO: *Leggi:* Rosanna e Fabrizio hanno finito di lavare l'auto. Hanno cominciato a lavare la bici.
Dici: Avendo finito di lavare l'auto, Rosanna e Fabrizio hanno cominciato a lavare la bici.

1. Chiara ha finito di studiare. È andata in giardino.
2. Io e Silvana abbiamo finito di leggere le riviste. Siamo andati in centro.
3. Tu hai bevuto un bicchiere d'aqua. Non hai avuto più sete.
4. Tu e Mario avete lavato i piatti. Siete andati a guardare la televisione.
5. Io mi sono rilassato sul divano. Sono andato fuori a giocare a tennis.

D. Cosa facevano? Di' cosa stavano facendo queste persone, secondo l'esempio. Ripeti la risposta.

ESEMPIO: *Leggi:* Io facevo la doccia.
Senti: Il telefono ha suonato.
Dici: Quando il telefono ha suonato, io stavo facendo la doccia.

1. Luca puliva l'appartamento.
2. Tu e Valeria guardavate la televisione.
3. Tu facevi la spesa al supermercato.
4. Io scrivevo una poesia.
5. Guido e io facevamo colazione.

Nome ______________________ *Data* ____________ *Classe* ______________

Ed ora ascoltiamo!

Sentirai l'inizio di una lezione su Boccaccio. Puoi ascoltare il brano quante volte vuoi. Poi sentirai, due volte, sei frasi e dovrai segnare, per ciascuna frase, **vero** o **falso.**

Parole utili: circolare (*to circulate*), i mercanti (*merchants*), il contenuto (*content*), veniva (*was*), in esse (*in them*), nonostante (*in spite of*)

1. vero falso
2. vero falso
3. vero falso
4. vero falso
5. vero falso
6. vero falso

Dettato

Sentirai un dettato tre volte. La prima volta, ascolta attentamente. La seconda volta, il dettato sarà letto con pause tra le frasi. Scrivi quello che senti. La terza volta, correggi quello che hai scritto. Scrivi sulle righe date. Controlla il tuo dettato con le soluzioni date in fondo al libro.

Petrarca scrisse le *Rime* ______________________________

Dialogo

Prima parte. Lorenzo dà un'esame sull'italiano e sull'Italia. Sentirai Lorenzo rispondere alle domande del professor Gori.

Ascolta attentamente il dialogo.

PROFESSOR GORI: Lorenzo, puoi dirmi quanti italiani parlavano davvero l'italiano nel 1861, al momento dell'unificazione della nazione?

LORENZO: Secondo il libro, solo il 2,5%. Possiamo anche spingere[1] la cifra al 7–8% dell'intera popolazione, considerando gli abitanti della Toscana, dell'Umbria, di parte del Lazio, ma il risultato non cambia molto. L'italiano, come lo chiamiamo oggi, corrispondeva al dialetto fiorentino e, nella penisola, era principalmente una lingua scritta, non parlata, e parlata solo in Toscana. L'Italia era una penisola politicamente, economicamente e culturalmente divisa. Gli italiani parlavano i dialetti delle loro regioni.

PROFESSOR GORI: Per quali ragioni il fiorentino diventò la lingua nazionale?

LORENZO: Era più prestigioso di altri dialetti in Italia perché aveva una sua letteratura, con Dante, Boccaccio, Petrarca… Al momento dell'unificazione, Firenze aveva ancora molto prestigio culturale e lo stato italiano appena formato aveva bisogno di una lingua ufficiale. Gli abitanti del resto d'Italia imparavano l'italiano a scuola, come lingua straniera.

PROFESSOR GORI: E poi che cosa successe?

LORENZO: L'italiano si trasformò molto, tutti cominciarono a parlarlo, e molte parole degli altri dialetti entrarono a far parte del patrimonio[2] comune della lingua italiana.

PROFESSOR GORI: Perché si trasformò?

LORENZO: Si trasformò perché diventò una lingua parlata, non rimase solo scritta. E poi si diffuse attraverso la televisione, la radio, i giornali e anche attraverso la scuola, perché gli italiani andarono finalmente tutti a scuola…

PROFESSOR GORI: Altre cose da aggiungere[3]?

LORENZO: Il settanta per cento delle parole che usiamo oggi sono già negli autori medievali, in Dante, per esempio. Quindi[4] vuol dire che il nucleo centrale della lingua italiana è ancora quello della lingua medievale o rinascimentale!

PROFESSOR GORI: Bravo, Lorenzo! Ci hai dato le informazioni essenziali per capire lo sviluppo[5] dell'italiano. Bene!

[1]*push*
[2]*heritage*
[3]*add*
[4]*Therefore*
[5]*development*

Seconda parte. Ascolta di nuovo il dialogo. Fai particolare attenzione alla trasformazione della lingua italiana.

Terza parte. Sentirai due volte sei frasi basate sul dialogo. Segna, per ciascuna frase, **vero** o **falso.**

1. vero falso
2. vero falso
3. vero falso
4. vero falso
5. vero falso
6. vero falso

Sara in Italia

Sara è oggi nella campagna di Siena, a San Galgano, a visitare le magnifiche rovine dell'Abbazia (*Abbey*) e del Monastero dedicati a Galgano, il guerriero che si fece monaco (*monk*) e fu poi proclamato santo. San Galgano è un luogo poco frequentato dai turisti, fuori dai centri principali. Per arrivare qui è necessaria una macchina, e Sara è venuta con suo cugino, David Lorenzetti. I signori Lorenzetti abitano a Siena, a meno di un'ora da questo luogo incantato (*enchanted*).

Ascolta attentamente il dialogo. Ascolta il dialogo quante volte vuoi. Poi, rispondi alle domande che senti. Sentirai ogni domanda due volte. Ripeti la risposta.

Parole utili: ne valeva la pena (*it was worthwhile*), pavimento di erbe (*grass floor*), tetto (*roof*), cappella (*chapel*), collina (*hill*), spada (*sword*), roccia (*stone*), rompere (*to break*), rinunciava (*he renounced*), la guerra (*war*), segno (*sign*), approvazione (*approval*), capanna (*hut*), finché (*until*)

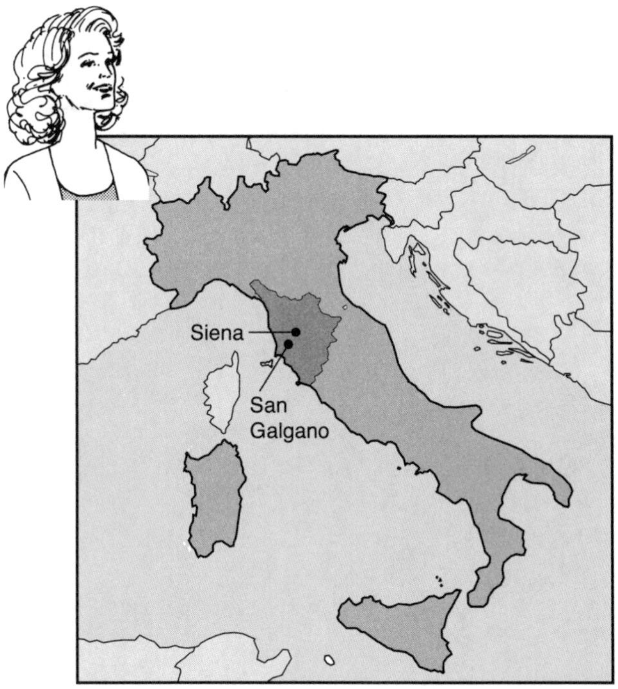

1. … 2. … 3. … 4. … 5. …

Sara in rete…

For more information about what Sara experienced during her travels, check out the links found on the *Prego!* website **(www.mhhe.com/prego8).**

Nome ____________________ Data ____________ Classe ____________________

CAPITOLO

Politica e società 16

Vocabolario preliminare

A. Per cominciare. Sentirai un dialogo seguito da tre frasi. Sentirai il dialogo due volte. La prima volta, ascolta attentamente. La seconda volta, il dialogo sarà ripetuto con pause per la ripetizione. Poi ascolta le frasi e scegli, per ciascuna frase, **vero** o **falso.**

ENRICA: Tra un paio di settimane ci saranno le elezioni. Hai già deciso per quale partito votare?

SIMONA: Non so. Durante la campagna elettorale tutti i candidati fanno belle promesse, ma poi...

ENRICA: Hai ragione, speriamo che chiunque vinca le elezioni mantenga almeno la metà delle promesse fatte!

1. vero falso
2. vero falso
3. vero falso

B. Politica e società. Sentirai, per due volte, cinque frasi da completare. Ascolta attentamente, poi scegli il completamento giusto.

ESEMPIO: *Senti:* Mia sorella è segretaria presso (*at*) l'Olivetti. È...

Segna: (a. un'impiegata.) b. un'operaia. c. una deputata.

1. a. un aumento b. una riduzione c. una coalizione
2. a. partiti politici b. ministri c. disoccupati
3. a. diminuire b. scioperare c. votare
4. a. le tasse b. gli operai c. le elezioni
5. a. in aumento b. in sciopero c. in diminuzione

C. La politica italiana e sociale... Definizioni. Sentirai, per due volte, cinque definizioni riguardo allo Stato e sei definizioni riguardo ai problemi sociali. Dovrai identificare i termini a cui si riferiscono. Scrivi le risposte nella colonna appropriata. Controlla le tue risposte con le soluzioni date in fondo al libro.

Parole utili: rami (*chambers*), esprime (*expresses*), segreta (*secret*), un assegno (*check*), un versamento (*deposit*), spesa (*expenditure*)

- la Camera dei Deputati e il Senato
- il deputato, la deputata
- la disoccupazione
- le elezioni
- l'operaio, l'operaia
- l'impiegato, l'impiegata
- il Presidente della Repubblica
- lo stipendio
- le tasse
- il voto
- uno sciopero

LO STATO	I PROBLEMI SOCIALI
1. ____________________	1. ____________________
2. ____________________	2. ____________________
3. ____________________	3. ____________________
4. ____________________	4. ____________________
5. ____________________	5. ____________________
	6. ____________________

In ascolto

Gli italiani e la politica. Laura, una studentessa americana di storia, discute con Valerio del sistema politico italiano. Ascolta con attenzione la loro conversazione, poi rispondi alle seguenti domande. Controlla le tue risposte con le soluzioni date in fondo al libro.

1. Perché Laura è confusa quando pensa al sistema politico italiano?

   ____

2. Cosa risponde Valerio a Laura?

   ____

3. Qual è la cosa che sorprende (*surprises*) Laura delle elezioni in Italia?

   ____

4. Come interpreta Valerio la situazione?

   ____

5. Cosa risponde Laura? Sei d'accordo?

   ____

Grammatica

A. Congiuntivo presente

A. Per cominciare. Sentirai un dialogo due volte. La prima volta, ascolta attentamente. La seconda volta, completa il dialogo con i verbi al congiuntivo presente che mancano. Controlla le tue risposte con le soluzioni date in fondo al libro.

SIGNOR TESTA: Ho l'impressione che i problemi del mondo ____________[1] in continuo aumento: mi pare che ____________[2] la povertà e la disoccupazione; mi sembra che ____________[3] i problemi delle minoranze e degli immigrati. Chi vuoi che ____________[4] ai pensionati?

SIGNOR MAZZOLA: Ma anche i nostri problemi sono importanti e dobbiamo farci sentire. Anzi, io penso che ____________[5] necessario che tutti ____________[6] dei problemi di tutti, non solo dei propri!

B. Candidati al Parlamento... Sentirai un dialogo tra Silvia e Marzia, seguito da tre frasi. Sentirai il dialogo due volte. La prima volta, ascolta attentamente. La seconda volta, il dialogo sarà ripetuto con pause per la ripetizione. Poi ascolta le frasi e scegli, per ciascuna frase, **vero** o **falso.**

SILVIA: E allora, cosa sai di questi candidati al Parlamento?

MARZIA: Credo siano i migliori, non mi sembra che usino alcuna demagogia: vogliono che la disoccupazione diminuisca, che i salari siano difesi,[a] che i diritti dei lavoratori[b] non siano toccati, ma sono anche coscienti[c] che tutto ha un prezzo e che tutti dovranno fare sacrifici...

SILVIA: Dipende da chi dovrà fare i sacrifici, a dire il vero: sono stanca che a pagare siano sempre le donne, le casalinghe,[d] i giovani e pensionati.

MARZIA: Sai, la mia candidata preferita ha proposto una tassa sui capitali, perché non ritiene giusto[e] che ci sia una piccola percentuale della popolazione che possiede tanta ricchezza e non paga nulla.

[a]*defended (i.e., kept the same)* [b]*workers* [c]*aware* [d]*homemakers* [e]non... *he doesn't think it's right*

1. vero falso
2. vero falso
3. vero falso

C. Le faccende di casa. (*Household tasks.*) Quando Renata ti chiede di fare le faccende di casa, rispondi che vuoi che le facciano gli altri, secondo i suggerimenti. Ripeti la risposta.

ESEMPIO: *Senti:* Pulirai il frigo?
Leggi: Paolo
Dici: No, voglio che Paolo pulisca il frigo!

1. voi
2. tu
3. gli altri
4. Claudio
5. tu e Claudio

B. Verbi e espressioni che richiedono il congiuntivo

A. Per cominciare. Sentirai un dialogo due volte. La prima volta, ascolta attentamente. La seconda volta, il dialogo sarà ripetuto con pause per la ripetizione.

CAMERIERE: Professore, vuole che Le porti il solito caffè o preferisce un cappuccino?

PROFESSORE: Fa un po' fresco... Forse è meglio che prenda un caffè corretto. Scalda di più.

CAMERIERE: Speriamo che questo sciopero finisca presto, professore!

PROFESSORE: Certo, ma bisogna che prima gli insegnanti abbiano un miglioramento del loro contratto di lavoro.

B. Opinioni. Sentirai sei domande fatte da un giornalista che ti intervista su argomenti politici. Rispondi alle sue domande con le seguenti espressioni. Ripeti la risposta.

ESEMPIO: *Senti:* Il razzismo è un problema molto grave?
Leggi: Mi pare (*It seems to me*) …
Dici: Mi pare che il razzismo sia un problema molto grave.

1. Ho l'impressione che…
2. Mi dispiace che…
3. Sono contento che…
4. Immagino che…
5. Mi dispiace che…
6. È probabile che…

C. Sfumature (*Nuances*)**.** Fai il dirigente (*director*) di un'azienda (*company*) e devi parlare in modo preciso. Esprimi le tue opinioni secondo i suggerimenti. Ripeti la risposta.

ESEMPI: *Senti:* Preferisco…
Leggi: Morelli va a Roma.
Dici: Preferisco che Morelli vada a Roma.

Senti: Sono certo…
Leggi: Avete il personale necessario.
Dici: Sono certo che avete il personale necessario.

1. Arrivate puntuali.
2. Gli operai sono in sciopero.
3. Finiamo in tempo.
4. Tutti partecipano alla riunione.
5. Dobbiamo licenziare (*fire*) qualcuno.

D. Opinioni sulla politica. Esprimi delle opinioni sulla politica, secondo i suggerimenti. Ripeti la risposta.

ESEMPIO: *Senti:* Dubito…
Leggi: il ministro / andare in Cina
Dici: Dubito che il ministro vada in Cina.

1. l'inflazione / essere ferma
2. lo sciopero / continuare
3. il mio partito / vincere le elezioni
4. il mio stipendio / aumentare
5. il governo / mettere nuove tasse
6. i politici / essere onesti

E. Cosa pensi? Sentirai quattro espressioni che richiedono il congiuntivo. Dovrai formare delle frasi complete con le espressioni che senti, utilizzando un soggetto della colonna A e un verbo della colonna B. Di' la tua frase e poi ascolta, di seguito, una risposta possibile.

ESEMPIO: *Senti:* Immagino…
Dici: Immagino che il governo aumenti le tasse.

A	B
il conflitto tra industria e operai	fermare l'inflazione
i deputati al Parlamento	essere onesto
il governo	finire prima
i ministri	aumentare le tasse
lo sciopero	avere un buon esito (*outcome*)

C. Congiuntivo passato

A. Per cominciare. Sentirai un dialogo due volte. La prima volta, ascolta attentamente. La seconda volta, il dialogo sarà ripetuto con pause per la ripetizione.

FRANCESCO: Come mai Martina non si è licenziata? Ieri mi ha detto che non le piaceva il suo lavoro e che avrebbe dato le dimissioni oggi.

LEONARDO: Penso che le abbiano aumentato lo stipendio.

FRANCESCO: Davvero?

LEONARDO: Sì, sì, e pare che lei abbia già comprato una bella macchina sportiva!

B. Speranze. Fai la parte dell'attivista politico ed esprimi la tua speranza in risposta alle domande che ti fa un giornalista. Ripeti la risposta.

ESEMPIO: *Senti:* Il governo ha aiutato i poveri?
Dici: Spero che il governo abbia aiutato i poveri.

1. … 2. … 3. … 4. …

Ed ora ascoltiamo!

Aliza, una studentessa americana di storia, discute con Valerio del sistema politico italiano. Sentirai il loro dialogo. Puoi ascoltare il dialogo quante volte vuoi. Poi sentirai, due volte, sei frasi e dovrai segnare, per ciascuna frase, **vero** o **falso.**

1. vero falso
2. vero falso
3. vero falso
4. vero falso
5. vero falso
6. vero falso

Nome ______________________ Data ______________ Classe ______________________

Dettato

Sentirai un breve dettato tre volte. La prima volta, ascolta attentamente. La seconda volta, il dettato sarà letto con pause tra le frasi. Scrivi quello che senti. La terza volta, correggi quello che hai scritto. Scrivi sulle righe date. Controlla il tuo dettato con le soluzioni date in fondo al libro.

Guido ha invitato ____

Dialogo

Prima parte. Sabrina e Davide discutono delle recenti elezioni europee e del ruolo dell'Italia in Europa.

Ascolta attentamente il dialogo.

SABRINA: Mah, che ne dici dei risultati delle elezioni europee?

DAVIDE: Guarda, non mi dire niente, non sono affatto[1] contento…

SABRINA: Io sono più neutrale, aspetto di vedere adesso quello che succederà, adesso che si discute di includere paesi dell'Est. Io sono favorevole, ma sono stata sorpresa dall'astensionismo.[2] Di solito c'è più dell'80 per cento degli italiani che vota; vedere solo il 50 per cento è stato uno choc, specialmente nel caso di elezioni europee così importanti.

DAVIDE: Sai, io non ero molto convinto ma sono andato a votare lo stesso. È stata una decisione difficile. Non credi che dobbiamo dimostrare che l'Italia vuole un'Europa più forte? Dopo tutto, più[3] la politica europea rimane unitaria, più l'Europa diventa forte economicamente.

SABRINA: Si è già dimostrato con l'euro e con il fatto che l'euro o è pari[4] al dollaro o è più forte. Speriamo solo che la situazione economica dei possibili nuovi membri non destabilizzi l'Europa.

DAVIDE: Non credo succederà. L'Italia sarà come sempre al centro delle riforme europee, siamo ormai[5] un paese profondamente europeista e non si può tornare indietro. Ma dimmi, come hai votato: per il governo o contro il governo? Per la politica europea o contro l'Italia guidata da Strasburgo?

SABRINA: È una domanda interessante perché il mio candidato alle europee non fa parte del governo, ma non è contro il governo…

DAVIDE: Va bene, non ti chiedo di più… A proposito,[6] sei andata ieri a distribuire volantini[7] alla manifestazione sulla difesa dei diritti dei lavoratori?

SABRINA: No, perché?

DAVIDE: Perché io ci sono andato ed è un peccato che tu non sia venuta. Meno male che[8] ci sono io a promuovere i lavoratori nella società…

SABRINA: Vero, vero, senza di te il mondo non andrebbe avanti…

[1] *at all*
[2] *the number of abstentions*
[3] più… *the more . . . the more*
[4] *equal*
[5] *by now*
[6] A… *By the way*
[7] *fliers*
[8] Meno… *Fortunately*

Seconda parte. Ascolta di nuovo il dialogo. Fai particolare attenzione a cosa dicono Sabrina e Davide sulle percentuali dei votanti, sulla politica europea e sull'euro.

Terza parte. Sentirai due volte sei frasi basate sul dialogo. Segna, per ciascuna frase, **vero** o **falso.**

1. vero falso
2. vero falso
3. vero falso
4. vero falso
5. vero falso
6. vero falso

Sara in Italia

Sara è oggi a Roma, capitale d'Italia e sede del governo centrale. Ha voluto evitare (*to avoid*) San Pietro e i musei Vaticani perché è domenica e i musei sono sempre affollati (*crowded*). Ha deciso invece di visitare un monumento che non aveva mai visitato nei suoi due precedenti (*previous*) soggiorni a Roma: quello dedicato a Vittorio Emanuele II, il primo re dell'Italia unita. Con lei c'è suo cugino Giovanni D'Agostino. I signori D'Agostino abitano a Roma e Sara è loro ospite.

Ascolta attentamente il dialogo. Ascolta il dialogo quante volte vuoi. Poi, rispondi alle domande che senti. Sentirai ogni domanda due volte. Ripeti la risposta.

Parole utili: assomigli (*it resembles*), una macchina da scrivere (*typewriter*), legato (*linked*), imbarazzanti (*embarrassing*), i soldati (*soldiers*), scala (*staircase*), di guardia a (*standing guard*), milite (*soldier*), ignoto (*unknown*), patria (*homeland*), Risorgimento (*unification of Italy*)

1. … 2. … 3. … 4. … 5. …

Sara in rete…

For more information about what Sara experienced during her travels, check out the links found on the *Prego!* website **(www.mhhe.com/prego8).**

CAPITOLO 17

Il mondo del lavoro

Vocabolario preliminare

A. Per cominciare. Sentirai un dialogo due volte. La prima volta, ascolta attentamente. La seconda volta, il dialogo sarà ripetuto con pause per la ripetizione.

GABRIELLA: Inflazione, disoccupazione, crisi economica... e come lo trovo un lavoro?
EMANUELE: Bisogna avere pazienza e insistere: fare domande, rispondere agli annunci, partecipare ai concorsi...
GABRIELLA: E tu, da quanto tempo insisti?
EMANUELE: A dire il vero, io un lavoro ce l'ho: e serve proprio per aiutare la gente a trovare un'occupazione. Sono impiegata al sindacato io!

B. Definizioni. Sentirai, per due volte, cinque definizioni riguardo al lavoro. Scrivi la lettera del termine a fianco del (*next to the*) numero della definizione che senti.

1. ____ a. il lavoratore
2. ____ b. il sindacato
3. ____ c. il costo della vita
4. ____ d. l'assistenza medica
5. ____ e. il colloquio di lavoro

C. **Breve storia di Alessandra.** Sentirai, per due volte, un brano seguito da cinque frasi. Ascolta attentamente. Poi dovrai scegliere, per ciascuna frase, **vero** o **falso.**

1. vero falso
2. vero falso
3. vero falso
4. vero falso
5. vero falso

In ascolto

Buon lavoro! Parlano Simone Bellini e la signora Pagani, la dirigente della ditta che l'ha assunto. Ascolta con attenzione la loro conversazione, poi completa le frasi seguenti. Controlla le tue risposte con le soluzioni date in fondo al libro.

1. La signora Pagani è molto felice di _______________ Simone Bellini.
2. Simone può incominciare (*begin*) _______________.
3. Il segretario della signora Pagani darà a Simone il modulo per _______________.
4. Secondo Simone, le sue _______________ sono molto chiare.
5. Alla fine del colloquio la dirigente presenta Simone _______________.

Grammatica

A. Congiunzioni che richiedono il congiuntivo

A. **Per cominciare.** Sentirai un dialogo due volte. Poi sentirai, due volte, tre frasi e dovrai segnare, per ciascuna frase, **vero** o **falso.**

MARCELLO: Paolo, sono disperato: benché il mio curriculum sia molto buono, non riesco a trovare un lavoro!

PAOLO: Marcello, quanta fretta, ti sei appena laureato! Prima che tu possa trovare un posto di lavoro, devi fare molte domande, anche all'estero.

MARCELLO: Forse hai ragione, cercherò lavoro anche fuori Italia, a condizione che mi paghino profumatamente!

1. vero falso
2. vero falso
3. vero falso

B. Chi si sveglia prima? La tua compagna di casa esce di casa prima di tutti la mattina. Di' prima di chi esce di casa, secondo i suggerimenti. Ripeti la risposta.

ESEMPIO: *Senti:* tu
Dici: Esce di casa prima che io mi alzi.

1. … 2. … 3. … 4. … 5. …

C. Scopi (*Goals*), **condizioni.** Parla dei tuoi programmi di carriera e anche di quelli dei tuoi amici. Completa le frasi che senti, secondo i suggerimenti. Ripeti la risposta.

ESEMPIO: *Senti:* La ditta mi assume purché…
Leggi: io / avere i requisiti
Dici: La ditta mi assume purché io abbia i requisiti.

1. tu / poter trovare lavoro facilmente
2. io / continuare a telefonare
3. lei / non avere la macchina
4. voi / accompagnarmi in agenzia
5. Beatrice / poter essere felice

D. Un vero amico. Sentirai, per due volte, un brano in cui Mauro parla a Maria di qualcosa che lei ha fatto che lo ha ferito (*hurt him*). Ascolta attentamente. Poi ferma la registrazione e completa le frasi, secondo il brano. Controlla le tue risposte con le soluzioni date in fondo al libro.

1. Ti voglio parlare affinché ____
____.
2. Anch'io sono qui benché ____.
3. Continuerò a parlarti a condizione che ______________________________.
4. …sono tuo amico, sebbene quello che tu hai fatto ______________________.
5. E sarò ancora tuo amico purché ______________________________________.
6. Ti ascolterò anche tutta la notte, a meno che ________________________.

B. Altri usi del congiuntivo

A. Per cominciare. Sentirai un dialogo due volte. La prima volta, ascolta attentamente. La seconda volta, completa il dialogo con le parole che mancano. Controlla le tue risposte con le soluzioni date in fondo al libro.

FRANCO: Ho appena risposto ad un'offerta di lavoro online. Chissà come andrà…

ANGELA: Dai, non preoccuparti! ____________________[1] cosa rispondano andrà bene. ____________________[2] tu ____________________ ____________________[3] dovrebbe essere felice di assumere una persona qualificata come te!

B. Certezze. (*Certainties.*) Di' le frasi che senti con convinzione, secondo i suggerimenti. Ripeti la risposta.

ESEMPIO: *Senti:* Le persone che cercano lavoro devono riempire questi moduli.
Leggi: Chiunque...
Dici: Chiunque cerchi lavoro deve riempire questi moduli.

1. Dovunque...
2. Qualunque cosa...
3. Comunque...
4. Chiunque...
5. Qualunque...

C. Cattivo umore. Sei di cattivo umore oggi. Lamentati di tutto, secondo i suggerimenti. Ripeti la risposta.

ESEMPIO: *Leggi:* nessuno / amarmi
Dici: Non c'è nessuno che mi ami.

1. niente / interessarmi
2. nessuno / volere studiare con me
3. niente / piacermi nel frigo
4. nessuno / farmi regali

C. Congiuntivo o infinito?

A. Per cominciare. Sentirai un dialogo due volte. La prima volta, ascolta attentamente. La seconda volta, il dialogo sarà ripetuto con pause per la ripetizione. Poi sentirai, due volte, tre frasi da completare e dovrai scegliere, per ciascuna frase, il completamento giusto.

FIORELLA: Valentina, come mai in giro a quest'ora? Non sei andata in ufficio?
VALENTINA: Non lo sapevi? Ho chiesto altri sei mesi di aspettativa per avere più tempo per mio figlio.
FIORELLA: Sei contenta di stare a casa?
VALENTINA: Per ora sì, ma tra sei mesi bisogna che io torni a lavorare e allora mio marito chiederà l'aspettativa.

1. a. in ufficio
   b. a casa
   c. in giro
2. a. licenziarsi
   b. stare di più con suo figlio
   c. tornare al lavoro subito
3. a. tre mesi
   b. sei mesi
   c. dodici mesi

B. Impressioni, pensieri (*thoughts*) **e sentimenti.** A cosa pensano tutti? Di' a cosa pensi e a cosa pensano i tuoi amici, secondo i suggerimenti. Ripeti la risposta.

ESEMPI: *Senti:* Io spero...
Leggi: Tu hai fortuna.
Dici: Io spero che tu abbia fortuna.

Senti: Lisa vuole...
Leggi: Lisa trova un lavoro.
Dici: Lisa vuole trovare un lavoro.

1. Marco è sfortunato.
2. Sonia torna presto.
3. Perdete il lavoro.
4. Sono in ritardo.
5. Herbert non dice la verità.

C. Pensieri e opinioni personali. Componi delle frasi nuove che cominciano con le espressioni suggerite. Usa **che** + indicativo, **che** + congiuntivo o l'infinito con o senza **di.** Ripeti la risposta.

ESEMPI: *Leggi:* Marco è in sciopero.
Senti: È vero...
Dici: È vero che Marco è in sciopero.

Senti: Crediamo...
Dici: Crediamo che Marco sia in sciopero.

Senti: Marco vorrebbe...
Dici: Marco vorrebbe essere in sciopero.

(Io) Voto socialista.

1. ... 2. ... 3. ... 4. ...

Hanno avuto un aumento.

1. ... 2. ... 3. ... 4. ...

Ed ora ascoltiamo!

Sentirai un'e-mail che Laura invia (*is sending*) al suo fidanzato (*fiancé*), Roberto. Puoi ascoltare il brano quante volte vuoi. Poi sentirai, due volte, cinque frasi e dovrai segnare, per ciascuna frase, **vero** o **falso.**

Parole utili: spedisco (*I'll send*), staccare (*to unplug*), mal di testa (*headache*), settore (*field*), sede (*main office*)

1. vero falso
2. vero falso
3. vero falso
4. vero falso
5. vero falso

Dettato

Sentirai un dettato tre volte. La prima volta, ascolta attentamente. La seconda volta, il dettato sarà letto con pause tra le frasi. Scrivi quello che senti. La terza volta, correggi quello che hai scritto. Scrivi sulle righe date. Controlla il tuo dettato con le soluzioni date in fondo al libro.

Stamattina Cinzia, Gabriella e Francesco ________________________________

Dialogo

Prima parte. Cinzia e Francesco parlano delle loro prospettive di lavoro.

Ascolta attentamente il dialogo.

CINZIA: Dimmi un po', Francesco, vorresti veramente cambiare professione per entrare alle Poste[1]?

FRANCESCO: Certo! Sono stanco di lavorare come portiere di notte[2] e delle mansioni associate, rispondere sempre ai telefoni, usare i computer, mandare i fax, e tutto da solo... Alle Poste almeno non devo lavorare da solo o di notte!

CINZIA: Hai tutti i requisiti necessari per fare domanda?

FRANCESCO: Sì, il mio diploma liceale è sufficiente, ho l'esperienza giusta. Ho anche mandato il mio curriculum ad altre aziende, per avere altre opportunità...

CINZIA: E gli annunci sul giornale?

FRANCESCO: Sì, anche quelli. Ho risposto a vari annunci ma per ora niente, continuo a fare il portiere di notte, come sai. Credo che al momento l'unica possibilità sia partecipare al concorso delle Poste. È un lavoro che vorrei molto, ma sai che per un posto alle Poste ci sono sempre tantissime domande. E tu, invece, che hai intenzione di fare con il tuo lavoro? Alla fine dell'aspettativa[3] torni a scuola?

CINZIA: Sì, ormai insegnare è la cosa che mi piace di più e poi, quando saremo in tre, ci sarà bisogno di uno stipendio extra. Quello solo di mio marito non sarebbe sufficiente e io non voglio andare in un appartamento meno grande di quello che abbiamo adesso. L'unico problema sarà trovare una baby-sitter per Chiara...

FRANCESCO: E tuo marito, l'aspettativa non la prende?

CINZIA: Mario? No, lui dice che non gli piace questa nuova famiglia moderna, con i padri a casa e le madri al lavoro. Ma sono sicura che gli farò cambiare idea, se ne avremo bisogno. Non è questo il momento per fare i tradizionalisti!

[1] *Postal Service*
[2] portiere... *night watchman*
[3] *maternity leave*

Seconda parte. Ascolta di nuovo il dialogo. Fai particolare attenzione a cosa dice Cinzia sulla sua situazione, su suo marito e cosa dice Francesco sulle cose che ha dovuto fare per partecipare al concorso per le Poste.

Terza parte. Sentirai due volte sei frasi basate sul dialogo. Segna, per ciascuna frase, **vero** o **falso.**

1. vero falso
2. vero falso
3. vero falso
4. vero falso
5. vero falso
6. vero falso

Sara in Italia

Sara è a Torino, in Piemonte, dove incontra Maria, un'amica di suo cugino Giovanni. Maria studia al Politecnico e sa molte cose della sua città, dove la sua famiglia, del Sud, è andata a vivere negli anni Sessanta. Dopo avere passeggiato per il centro della città e avere mangiato i gianduiotti, tipici cioccolatini torinesi, Sara e Maria vanno al parco del Valentino per rilassarsi.

Ascolta attentamente il dialogo. Ascolta il dialogo quante volte vuoi. Poi, rispondi alle domande che senti. Sentirai ogni domanda due volte. Ripeti la risposta.

Parole utili: portici (*porticoes*), a mio agio (*at ease*), chiedermi (*wonder*), pasta (*paste*), nocciola (*hazelnut*), pancia (*belly*)

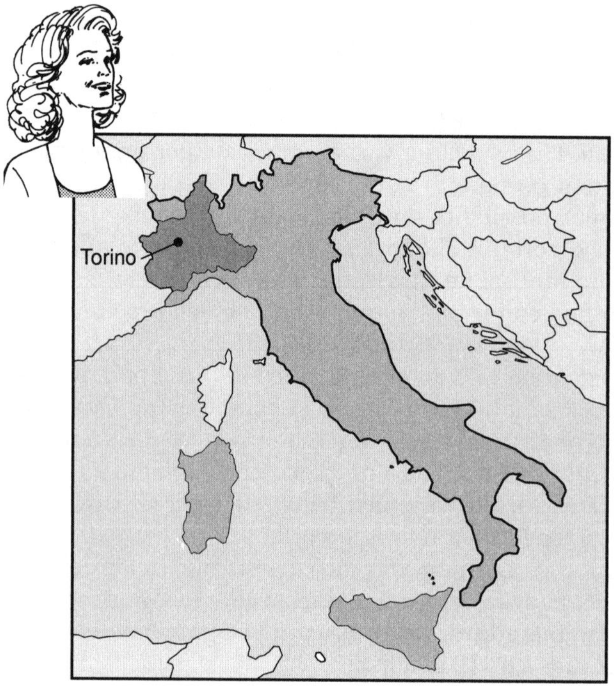

1. … 2. … 3. … 4. … 5. …

Sara in rete…

For more information about what Sara experienced during her travels, check out the links found on the *Prego!* website **(www.mhhe.com/prego8).**

CAPITOLO 18

La società multiculturale

Vocabolario preliminare

A. Per cominciare. Sentirai un dialogo due volte. La prima volta, ascolta attentamente. La seconda volta, il dialogo sarà ripetuto con pause per la ripetizione.

ANTONIO: Tu e Carla, siete andati alla manifestazione contro la violenza razzista ieri?
FABRIZIO: Sì, è stata bellissima! Con tutti quei giovani che cantavano e si tenevano per mano...
ANTONIO: Il razzismo non è genetico e non dobbiamo avere paura di chi è diverso.
FABRIZIO: È quello che dico sempre ai miei figli: che la diversità è un valore positivo e che possiamo imparare tanto dalle altre culture.

B. Definizioni. Sentirai, per due volte, cinque definizioni riguardo ai problemi sociali. Scrivi la lettera del termine a fianco del (*beside the*) numero della definizione che senti.

1. ____ a. la tossicodipendenza
2. ____ b. il razzismo
3. ____ c. l'immigrazione
4. ____ d. l'extracomunitario
5. ____ e. il consumismo

C. Per discutere dei problemi sociali... Sentirai cinque definizioni. Dovrai scegliere e dire la definizione che abbia lo stesso significato. Ripeti la risposta.

ESEMPIO: *Senti:* opporsi al razzismo
Dici: essere contro il razzismo

Parole utili: fidarsi (*to trust*)

1. ... 2. ... 3. ... 4. ... 5. ...

In ascolto

Ben arrivata! Barbara e Lorenzo parlano di amici di Lorenzo che hanno adottato una bambina etiope (*Ethiopian*). Ascolta con attenzione la loro conversazione e decidi se le seguenti affermazioni sono vere o false. Poi, correggi le affermazioni false. Controlla le tue risposte con le soluzioni date in fondo al libro.

1. Gli amici di Lorenzo non sono ancora tornati dall'Etiopia. vero falso

____

2. Il nome etiope della bambina significa «la figlia della luna». vero falso

____

3. La bambina ha già otto anni. vero falso

____

4. È stato poco complicato adottare la bambina. vero falso

____

5. La bambina, quando crescerà, sarà bilingue. vero falso

____

Grammatica

A. Imperfetto del congiuntivo

A. Per cominciare. Sentirai un dialogo due volte. La prima volta, ascolta attentamente. La seconda volta, completa il dialogo con le parole che mancano. Controlla le tue risposte con le soluzioni date in fondo al libro.

CINZIA: Così tuo padre non voleva che tu ________ ______________________[1] con Shamira?

IVAN: Assurdo! Sperava invece che ________ ______________________[2] di Daniela, così sarei diventato dirigente nell'azienda di suo padre!

CINZIA: Che materialista! E tua madre?

IVAN: Lei invece non vedeva l'ora che ________ ______________________[3] con Shamira! Non può sopportare Daniela!

B. Problemi di famiglia. Piera ti racconta dei problemi con i suoi genitori. Rispondi che sarebbe meglio che i suoi genitori non facessero quelle cose, secondo i suggerimenti. Ripeti la risposta.

ESEMPIO: *Senti:* Interferiscono sempre!
Dici: Sarebbe meglio che non interferissero.

1. … 2. … 3. … 4. …

C. Lo zio Carlo. Racconta ai tuoi amici come ha reagito (*reacted*) tuo zio, che è un tradizionalista, quando gli hai raccontato della tua vita indipendente. Ripeti la risposta.

ESEMPIO: *Leggi:* dividere un appartamento con gli amici
Dici: Non credeva che io dividessi un appartamento con gli amici.

1. guadagnarmi da vivere (*to earn a living*) a 20 anni
2. volere studiare invece di sposarsi subito
3. impegnarmi per eliminare il consumismo
4. essere felice della mia vita

B. Trapassato del congiuntivo

A. **Per cominciare.** Sentirai un dialogo due volte. La prima volta, ascolta attentamente. La seconda volta, scrivi il verbo al trapassato del congiuntivo. Controlla le tue risposte in fondo al libro.

KALEB: Allora, Laura, è tutto pronto per la nostra cena etnica?

LAURA: Credo di sì. Gli involtini egiziani sono sulla tavola...

KALEB: Hai preparato il couscous con le verdure?

LAURA: Io no, credevo che lo ______________________ ______________________ tu!

KALEB: Accidenti! E adesso che facciamo? Prepariamo dei semplici spaghetti?

LAURA: No, ci vogliono solo pochi minuti per preparare il couscous, ed è il piatto preferito di tutti.

B. **Non sapevo!** Il tuo amico ti racconta tante novità. Di' che non sapevi tali (*such*) cose, secondo i suggerimenti. Ripeti la risposta.

ESEMPIO: *Senti e leggi:* Nicoletta ha vinto il torneo di tennis.
Dici: Non sapevo che avesse vinto il torneo di tennis!

1. Nadia ha studiato tutta la notte.
2. Claudio ed io siamo andati alla riunione.
3. Fabio ed io abbiamo avuto l'aumento.
4. Mia madre è stata politicamente impegnata.
5. Ho giudicato (*judged*) male i loro amici.

C. **La zia Matilda.** Tua zia credeva nel proverbio che dice «non si è mai troppo vecchi!» Completa le frasi che elencano (*list*) le cose che ha fatto, secondo i suggerimenti. Comincia il completamento con **benché Non.** Ripeti la risposta.

ESEMPIO: *Senti e leggi:* A ottant'anni scrisse un libro...
Dici: benché non avesse mai scritto prima.

1. A settant'anni dipinse un quadro...
2. A sessant'anni scolpì una statua...
3. A cinquant'anni si sposò...
4. A settant'anni fece un lungo viaggio...

C. Correlazione dei tempi nel congiuntivo

A. Per cominciare. Sentirai un dialogo due volte. La prima volta, ascolta attentamente. La seconda volta, completa il dialogo con le parole che mancano. Controlla le tue risposte con le soluzioni date in fondo al libro.

LAURA: Mamma, ho deciso di accettare quel lavoro a New York.

MADRE: Ma non sarebbe meglio che ________ ____________________[1] qui in Italia, vicino alla famiglia, agli amici? A New York c'è il problema della violenza e della droga: non voglio che ________ ____________________[2] qualcosa di brutto...

LAURA: Mamma, il problema della violenza e della droga c'è in tutte le grandi città. E poi, vorrei che tu ____________________[3] che è importante che io ____________________[4] nuove esperienze.

MADRE: Capisco, Laura, ma è naturale che io ________ ____________________[5]...

B. Idee politiche. Completa le seguenti frasi, secondo i suggerimenti. Ripeti la risposta.

ESEMPIO: *Senti:* Vorrei che...
Leggi: il razzismo / non esistere
Dici: Vorrei che il razzismo non esistesse.

1. la gente / cercare di eliminare l'intolleranza religiosa
2. i genitori / apprezzare (*to value*) le idee dei giovani
3. la gente / prendere sul serio i problemi degli anziani
4. il governo / lavorare per eliminare la povertà

C. Acquisti. Giuseppe e Franca hanno appena acquistato una nuova macchina. Quando Giuseppe ti confida (*tells you*) i suoi pensieri sull'argomento, esprimi il tuo accordo. Ripeti la risposta.

ESEMPIO: *Senti:* Speriamo di avere fatto bene.
Dici: Anch'io spero che abbiate fatto bene.

1. ... 2. ... 3. ... 4. ... 5. ...

Ed ora ascoltiamo!

Piero ed Elio, due vecchi amici cinquantenni, discutono della società italiana di oggi e dei suoi problemi. Sentirai il loro dialogo. Puoi ascoltare il dialogo quante volte vuoi. Sentirai, per due volte, cinque frasi e dovrai segnare, per ciascuna frase, **vero** o **falso.**

Parole utili: una guerra (*war*), appartenere (*to belong*)

1. vero falso
2. vero falso
3. vero falso
4. vero falso
5. vero falso

Dettato

Sentirai un dettato tre volte. La prima volta, ascolta attentamente. La seconda volta, il dettato sarà letto con pause tra le frasi. Scrivi quello che senti. La terza volta, correggi quello che hai scritto. Scrivi sulle righe date. Controlla il tuo dettato con le soluzioni date in fondo al libro.

Laura è italoamericana ed è ______________________________

Dialogo

Prima parte. Sentirai una conversazione tra amici in un bar.

Ascolta attentamente il dialogo.

NICOLETTA: Avete sentito? Si aprirà un nuovo centro sociale vicino allo stadio!

MASSIMO: Adesso anche gli extracomunitari, mancavano solo loro qui![1] Come se non avessimo abbastanza problemi da soli, in Italia!

NICOLETTA: Ma che dici? Secondo me questa è stata la decisione più intelligente che l'amministrazione avesse potuto prendere, data la forte immigrazione dall'Albania e dalla ex-Jugoslavia. Sarebbe meglio smettessi di fare l'intollerante!

MASSIMO: Non è intolleranza, è realismo politico il mio! Siamo sessanta milioni di italiani e il dieci per cento è disoccupato: dove troviamo altro lavoro?

LORENZO: Sai una cosa, Massimo? Secondo me, la cosa che ti preoccupa tanto è la diversità.

MASSIMO: Non è affatto vero. Ma cosa possono portare gli extracomunitari al nostro paese?

LORENZO: Loro stessi, con la loro cultura, musica e letteratura. E poi, scusa, chi sei tu per decidere chi sarebbe utile alla società e chi no?

NICOLETTA: Guarda, Massimo, che anch'io pensavo come te, poi ho conosciuto degli immigrati albanesi che sono i miei vicini di casa e ho capito che la mia era solo la paura del diverso. L'Italia non ha mai avuto una popolazione immigrata così numerosa come in questi anni.

MASSIMO: Grazie di avermi dato del razzista[2]! Io ho fatto solo un discorso economico, realista…

LORENZO: Basta, ora, arrivano i panini! Comunque è bene discutere sempre apertamente. È l'unico modo di combattere i pregiudizi razziali.

[1]mancavano… *that's all we needed*

[2]avermi… *calling me a racist*

Seconda parte. Ascolta di nuovo il dialogo. Fai particolare attenzione ai discorsi riguardo agli extracomunitari in Italia.

Terza parte. Sentirai due volte, sei frasi basate sul dialogo. Segna, per ciascuna frase, **vero** o **falso.**

1. vero falso
2. vero falso
3. vero falso
4. vero falso
5. vero falso
6. vero falso

Sara in Italia

Sara è a Trieste e, dopo un giro (*tour*) della città, parla della cultura triestina con Antonella, che studia traduzione alla famosa Scuola per Interpreti e Traduttori.

Ascolta attentamente il dialogo. Ascolta il dialogo quante volte vuoi. Poi, rispondi alle domande che senti. Sentirai ogni domanda due volte. Ripeti la risposta.

Parole utili: poiché (*since*), per forza (*necessarily*), la diffusione della psicanalisi (*popularity of psychoanalysis*), legate (*linked*), combattere (*to fight*), guerra (*war*), il sacrario (*shrine*), sepolti (*buried*)

1. … 2. … 3. … 4. … 5. …

Sara in rete…

For more information about what Sara experienced during her travels, check out the links found on the *Prego!* website **(www.mhhe.com/prego8).**

Nome ______________________ Data ______________ Classe ______________

Answer Key to the Laboratory Manual

This key includes answers to the written activities not given on the audio and the text of the dictations.

CAPITOLO PRELIMINARE

A. Saluti e espressioni di cortesia

A. 1. Mi chiamo 2. Sono 3. di 4. giorno 5. Mi chiamo 6. professoressa
C. Dialogue 1: 1. piacere 2. E 3. Sono **Dialogue 2:** 1. Bene 2. Lei 3. male 4. Arrivederci
Dialogue 3: 1. va 2. tu 3. Ciao

In ascolto

1. due studenti 2. colleghi di lavoro 3. madre e figlio 4. professoressa e studente

B. In classe

A. 1. Scrivete! 2. Aprite il libro! 3. Ripetete **buona notte,** per favore! 4. Chiudete il libro!
B. 1. come 2. dice 3. Scusi 4. scrive 5. Grazie 6. Prego 7. Aprite 8. Come 9. capisco 10. favore **D.** 1. una sedia 2. un libro 3. una penna 4. una matita 5. un quaderno

C. Alfabeto e suoni

D. 1. finestra (*window*) 2. scrivania (*desk*) 3. compagno (*companion, mate*) 4. aiuole (*flower beds*) 5. lavagna (*blackboard*) 6. dizionario (*dictionary*) 7. patata (*potato*) 8. parola (*word*)
I. 1. gramm<u>a</u>tica 2. import<u>a</u>nza 3. part<u>i</u>re 4. partir<u>ò</u> 5. m<u>u</u>sica 6. trentatr<u>é</u> 7. s<u>u</u>bito 8. umilt<u>à</u> 9. <u>a</u>bitano 10. cantavano **J.** 2. prenderò 3. caffè 4. università 6. civiltà 7. virtù

In ascolto

1. b 2. c 3. b 4. a

E. Calendario

A. 1. martedì 2. giovedì 3. sabato 4. domenica 5. venerdì 6. lunedì 7. mercoledì

CAPITOLO 1

In ascolto

1. vero 2. falso 3. vero 4. in Via Dante 5. in Via Gramsci 6. in Piazza Fontana

Grammatica A. Nomi: genere e numero

B. *You should have checked the following items for each person:* ALESSANDRA: panino, caffè MARCO: panino, aranciata LEONARDO: banana

B. Articolo indeterminativo e *buono*

B. *You should have checked the following items:* un passaporto, una mappa della città, un biglietto aereo, una carta di credito, una valigia grande, uno zaino **C.** 1. buon 2. buon 3. buon 4. buoni 5. buon' 6. buona 7. buon 8. buoni

C. Presente di *avere* e pronomi soggetto

B. 1. io 2. Loro 3. Hai 4. ho 5. Lei 6. hanno 7. abbiamo

D. Espressioni idiomatiche con *avere*

A. 1. Ho 2. voglia 3. fame 4. di 5. abbiamo 6. Hai 7. ragione **C.** 1. Ha freddo. 2. Ha caldo. 3. Ha sete. 4. Ha fame. 5. Ho sonno.

Dettato

Ecco che cosa ha Filippo in una valigia: un computer, cinque libri di testo d'italiano, una carta d'Italia, quattro quaderni, tre penne e due matite.

CAPITOLO 2

Vocabolario preliminare

B. Numero di studenti: 20 nuovi compagni di classe, 13 ragazze e 7 ragazzi; Descrizione di Caterina: alta, bruna, occhi neri magnetici, simpatica; Descrizione di Enrico: robusto, sportivo, allegro, bruno, occhi verdi; Descrizione di Angelo: magro, piccolo, biondo, occhi azzurri, sportivo, energico

In ascolto

1. Massimo: *30,* media, *neri, neri,* antipatico 2. Pietro: *23, alto,* biondi, *azzurri, timido*
3. Alessandro: *21, alto, neri,* verdi, *ideale*

Grammatica A. Aggettivi

H. 2. molti 3. molti 4. molte 5. molto 6. molti 7. molto 8. molta

B. Presente di *essere*

A. 1. italiana 2. diciotto anni, studentessa di francese 3. molto sportiva 4. francesi 5. studente di inglese 6. studentessa di italiano 7. molto sportivi **B.** 1. sei 2. è 3. è 4. sono 5. sono 6. Sono 7. Siamo 8. sono 9. sono

D. Ancora i plurali

B. 1. vecchie 2. viaggi 3. zii 4. amici 5. simpatici 6. antichi 7. valige 8. zie 9. greci 10. dischi 11. vecchie 12. amiche

Dettato

Salve! Sono Antonio. Sono un ragazzo italiano. Ho diciotto anni, sono alto con i capelli corti e ricci e sono uno studente. Caroline è una ragazza francese: è alta, bionda con gli occhi castani. Lei è una ragazza molto intelligente e anche molto bella!

CAPITOLO 3

Vocabolario preliminare

C. 1. storia 2. letteratura 3. greco 4. latino 5. matematica 6. trigonometria 7. lettere 8. letteratura 9. Fisica

In ascolto

1. molto nervoso / letteratura italiana 2. biblioteca / studiare 3. storia moderna 4. ha paura 5. letteratura inglese

Grammatica A. Presente dei verbi in *-are*

A. 1. Sono 2. abito 3. settimana 4. studia 5. domenica 6. mangiamo 7. ascoltiamo 8. andiamo

B. *Dare, stare, andare* e *fare*

D. 1. va 2. Sto 3. Dai 4. stare 5. dai 6. do 7. Sto 8. andiamo

C. Aggettivi possessivi

B. 1. l'assistente di psicologia 2. le sue lezioni 3. Perché è la sua fidanzata.

D. Possessivi con termini di parentela

B. (*Answers to art*) 1. mio nonno 2. mia nonna 4. mia nonna 5. professoressa (biologia) 6. mio zio 7. mio padre: insegnante (matematica) 8. mia madre 9. mia zia: dentista 10. dentista 11. mia zia: segretaria 12. studente di fisica 13. mio fratello: studente di fisica (*Answers to exercise*) 2. Suo padre 3. Sua madre 4. suo zio 5. La sua zia 6. suoi zii 7. I suoi

Dettato

Mariella, Stefano e Patrizia, amici d'infanzia, ricordano il loro passato di studenti: quegli otto anni passati insieme, cinque alla scuola elementare e tre alla scuola media. Ed ora frequentano licei diversi. E sicuramente nel loro futuro le facoltà universitarie sono ancora diverse.

CAPITOLO 4

Vocabolario preliminare

C. 1. facciamo 2. Andiamo 3. vediamo 4. ho 5. voglia 6. danno 7. vuoi 8. facciamo 9. guardiamo 10. Fa 11. passare 12. abbiamo 13. pulire 14. capisco 15. pulisco 16. pulisci

In ascolto

1. Va in palestra. 2. Va a casa. 3. Deve prendere due autobus. 4. Sono divertenti e non molto care.

Grammatica B. *Dovere, potere* e *volere; dire, uscire* e *venire*

A. 4, 3, 6, 5, 1, 2

D. L'ora

B. 1. 8.00 2. 10.30 3. 11.45 4. 1.00 5. 2.20 6. 4.00 7. 7.30

Dettato

Giovanna e Rossana sono due ragazze di Milano. Frequentano l'Università Statale, facoltà di lettere e filosofia. Alessandra, invece, lavora: è architetto in uno studio del centro. La domenica le tre amiche stanno insieme: fanno gli esercizi di yoga, danno delle feste oppure vanno in campagna.

CAPITOLO 5

Vocabolario preliminare

C. 1. falso, Giuditta prende un'aranciata. 2. vero 3. falso, Roberto prende un panino al prosciutto. 4. falso, Giuditta prende un panino al prosciutto e formaggio.

In ascolto

1. vero 2. falso; Giacomo non vuole andare al caffè Gilli perché costa troppo. 3. falso; Valentina vuole scrivere cartoline al tavolino. 4. falso; Secondo Valentina, possono passare quarantacinque minuti al caffè. 5. falso; Giacomo preferisce prendere un espresso al banco.

Grammatica B. Passato prossimo con *avere*

A. 1. bevuto 2. letto 3. dormito 4. capito

Dettato

Oggi, al bar, non ho preso il solito caffè. Ho voluto solo un latte, semplice, caldo. Poi ho mangiato una brioche e ho bevuto anche una spremuta d'arancia. A dire il vero, il latte e il succo d'arancia non sono andati bene insieme e io sono stato male per il resto della mattina. Ho avuto mal di stomaco.

CAPITOLO 6

Vocabolario preliminare

C. 1. un minestrone 2. gli gnocchi 3. al pomodoro 4. bistecca 5. patate fritte 6. un'insalata 7. il dolce 8. tiramisù

In ascolto

Lucia—PRIMO: gli spaghetti al ragù Marco—ANTIPASTO: prosciutto e melone; DOLCE: una crostata di frutta fresca Francesco—SECONDO: pollo arrosto e insalata mista

Grammatica C. *Piacere*

A. 1. piace 2. pizza 3. preferisco 4. prosciutto 5. piacciono 6. funghi 7. mozzarella 8. ci 9. bella 10. Margherita

Dettato

Danilo ha cucinato la cena di compleanno per sua sorella Valentina. Danilo è l'esperto di cucina della famiglia e, naturalmente, conosce anche i vini. Per Valentina, invece, i vini sono tutti uguali. Danilo spiega a Valentina che i vini rossi devono accompagnare le carni mentre quelli bianchi sono adatti per il pesce o per le carni bianche.

CAPITOLO 7

Vocabolario preliminare

B. 1. rilassarsi 2. fare 3. lavarsi i capelli 4. si 5. guarda 6. si trucca 7. Si mette 8. Si mette 9. Si mette

In ascolto

1. Perché non ha niente da mettersi. 2. Ha comprato un vestito ieri. 3. Ha comprato le scarpe due giorni fa. 4. Ha bisogno di una camicia e una cintura.

Grammatica B. Costruzione reciproca

A. 1. si conoscono 2. Si vedono 3. si parlano 4. si capiscono

D. Numeri superiori a 100

B. 1. centocinquantotto 2. cinquecentottantuno 3. novecentoquarantatré 4. milleottocentottanta 5. duemilauno 6. un milione

Dettato

Marilena, Franca, Elena e Silvia vivono insieme in un appartamento nel centro di Roma. Marilena studia all'università, Franca insegna lettere in una scuola media, Elena, la più grande, si è laureata sei anni fa e lavora in laboratorio, Silvia si è specializzata in informatica e lavora in un ufficio. Le quattro ragazze non si annoiano mai: vivere insieme è stimolante e interessante, anche se qualche volta è difficile. Ma le ragazze, invece di arrabbiarsi, si capiscono e si aiutano tra di loro.

CAPITOLO 8

Vocabolario preliminare

B. 1. il settimanale 2. la pubblicità 3. la recensione 4. il mensile 5. l'intervista 6. il quotidiano

In ascolto

1. C'è una buona recensione del film di Benigni. 2. Ha letto una lunga intervista a Benigni. 3. Le domande sono sul film e su Benigni come regista. 4. Ha intenzione di stare a casa stasera a guardare la televisione.

Grammatica B. Imperfetto e passato prossimo

B. 1. g 2. d 3. c 4. e 5. a 6. d 7. b 8. f 9. g 10. e **C.** 1. a 2. a 3. a 4. a 5. b 6. b 7. a 8. b **F.** 1. d 2. c 3. b 4. a 5. e

C. Trapassato

A. 1. era 2. aveva capito 3. era 4. è andata 5. è arrivato 6. era 7. uscita **C.** 1. era 2. abitava 3. Si chiamava 4. aveva 5. era 6. doveva 7. camminava 8. si era... svegliata 9. aveva trovato 10. aveva detto 11. era andato 12. aveva perso 13. era andato 14. aveva trovato

Dettato

Maurizio e Rinaldo sono due vecchi amici. Si conoscono da quando erano piccoli. Rinaldo si è sposato e ha una bambina che va all'asilo. Lui e sua moglie Giuliana sono molto contenti. Maurizio, invece, è divorziato, lui e sua moglie non si capivano. Da quando Maurizio è divorziato sua madre fa tutto per il figlio: stira, lava, cucina, eccetera. Angela, la sorella di Maurizio, vive in America. È una donna indipendente che è andata in America da sola.

CAPITOLO 9

In ascolto

1. vero 2. falso; Alessandra e Alberto vogliono andare in montagna questo fine settimana. 3. falso; Alessandra conosce dei posti bellissimi sui Monti Sibillini. 4. vero 5. vero

Grammatica D. Comparativi e superlativi irregolari

B. 1. meglio 2. peggio 3. peggiore 4. meglio 5. peggio

Dettato

Il sistema nazionale sanitario in Italia, anche se ha dei problemi, è di buon livello. Il diritto alla salute e alle cure, come quello al lavoro, è garantito dalla Costituzione italiana. L'assistenza medica è certo meno costosa che negli Stati Uniti, ma i servizi a volte sono meno buoni, anche se adeguati. La maggior parte degli ospedali italiani sono pubblici, non privati.

CAPITOLO 10

Vocabolario preliminare

D. COPPIA 1: Viareggio, treno, albergo a tre stelle, carta di credito; COPPIA 2: l'Umbria (Gubbio, Assisi, Perugia), macchina, pensione, carta di credito / contanti; COPPIA 3: Grecia (Creta), crociera, albergo di lusso, carta di credito

In ascolto

1. trovare un albergo a buon prezzo 2. cara 3. doppia / doccia / pensione 4. delle belle spiagge 5. noleggiare una barca, prendere il sole, mangiare il pesce

Grammatica A. Futuro semplice

A. 1. partirò 2. Prenderemo 3. andremo 4. Passeremo 5. noleggeranno 6. continueranno 7. andrò 8. studierò 9. ritorneremo

B. Usi speciali del futuro

A. 1. finirò 2. andrò 3. farò 4. faranno 5. andranno **B.** 1. sarà 2. prenotato 3. Avrà 4. Mangerà 5. Dormirà 6. Avrà 7. Scriverà

D. Formazione dei nomi femminili

A. 1. pittrice 2. professoressa 3. scultrice 4. attrice

Dettato

Due coppie di amici hanno deciso che quest'anno passeranno le vacanze nel sud d'Italia. Desiderano un posto tranquillo, con il mare pulito e le spiagge non affollate. Hanno scelto la costa sud del Mare Adriatico, la Puglia. Per molti anni Enrico e Zara hanno passato vacanze attive: viaggi in paesi lontani, avventure ed esotismo. Renato e Laura hanno sempre preferito cercare dei posti isolati e tranquilli dove potersi rilassare, lasciarsi trasportare dalle letture preferite, contemplare le bellezze naturali. Hanno sempre voluto le piccole comodità, il buon cibo e il buon vino invece di viaggi nei paesi lontano.

CAPITOLO 11

In ascolto

DIALOGO 1 dalla lattaia: burro, latte, yogurt = € 5,80 DIALOGO 2 dal macellaio: prosciutto crudo, prosciutto cotto, salame, arrosto di vitello = € 19 DIALOGO 3 dalla fruttivendola: pomodori, mele, pere, arance = € 11,25

Grammatica C. Pronomi doppi

A. 1. Gliela 2. me la 3. gliela

D. Imperativo (*tu, noi, voi*)

A. 1. andiamo 2. comportatevi 3. di' 4. non 5. toccare

Ed ora ascoltiamo!

CLIENTE A: una giacca; bianca o grigia; 50; CLIENTE B: un maglione; rosso; 38 o 40; CLIENTE C: un cappello; marrone; 48

Dettato

Giovanna e Silvana sono in giro per la città per fare spese. Oltre alla spesa per il week-end le due amiche vogliono fare un giro per i negozi del centro e per i grandi magazzini alla ricerca di qualche affare. I negozi di abbigliamento di alta moda sono sempre molto cari ma nei grandi magazzini è possibile trovare delle svendite. Al mercato all'aperto, poi, non è difficile trovare dei buoni affari. Girare per le bancarelle di un grande mercato è piacevole e interessante. C'è di tutto: frutta, verdura, formaggi e salumi da una parte, e dall'altra, vestiti, scarpe e tutti gli oggetti utili per la casa.

CAPITOLO 12

Vocabolario preliminare

A. 1. La casa non è ancora pronto. 2. Perché costa troppo. 3. Andranno dai genitori di Massimo.
C. 1. un palazzo 2. l'ascensore 3. sulla strada 4. al secondo piano 5. a sinistra

In ascolto

1. falso; L'appartamento non è ancora affittato. 2. vero 3. vero 4. falso; C'è un balcone. 5. falso; Perché ci sono scale e finestre larghe. 6. falso; Hanno appuntamento domani al numero 102, alle sei di sera.

Grammatica A. Aggettivi indefiniti

A. 1. alcuni 2. periferia 3. Ogni 4. giardinetto 5. po' 6. salotto 7. Compratene
C. 1. qualunque 2. alcune 3. Tutte 4. Tutti 5. ogni

D. Imperativo (*Lei, Loro*)

A. 1. telefoni 2. dica 3. abbia 4. richiami

Ed ora ascoltiamo!

You should have labeled the floor plan as follows: 1. il ripostiglio grande 2. la camera da letto grande 3. il bagno piccolo 4. la sala da pranzo 5. la cucina 6. il bagno grande 7. la camera da letto piccola 8. lo studio 9. il soggiorno

Dettato

Simonetta e Lucia hanno frequentato lo stesso liceo ed ora si sono iscritte alla facoltà di sociologia dell'Università di Roma. Andare a Roma a frequentare l'università significa trovare casa, abitare da sole, sviluppare il senso dell'autodisciplina e della responsabilità. Tutto questo non preoccupa le due ragazze; al contrario, le stimola. Dei loro compagni di classe loro sono le uniche che hanno scelto Roma. Ora, però, cominciano i primi problemi: trovare la casa e poi un lavoretto, magari mezza giornata. Ma le due ragazze sono coraggiose e si meritano un colpo di fortuna!

CAPITOLO 13

Vocabolario preliminare

A. 1. b 2. a **B.** IL TRAFFICO 1. la patente 2. il pieno di benzina 3. le gomme 4. i mezzi di trasporto 5. il vigile L'AMBIENTE 1. i rifiuti 2. il riciclaggio 3. i materiali riciclabili 4. l'inquinamento

In ascolto

1. b 2. a 3. c 4. c 5. a

Grammatica A. Condizionale presente

A. 1. daresti 2. sarebbe 3. faresti

C. Condizionale passato

A. 1. avrebbe 2. dovuto 3. sarebbe 4. stato

D. Pronomi possessivi

B. 1. mia 2. tua 3. mia 4. mia 5. sua 6. mia

Dettato

Enrico e Paola si interessano di ecologia. Cercano di influenzare l'opinione pubblica riguardo ai problemi dell'ambiente. Il loro non è un lavoro facile: la gente è spesso pigra e preferisce non affrontare il problema. Naturalmente ci sono anche quelli che hanno scelto di essere attivi e partecipano ai gruppi dei Verdi. Ma la battaglia per la protezione dell'ambiente è lunga e incerta: interessi privati, giochi politici, eccetera contribuiscono a renderla difficile.

CAPITOLO 14

Vocabolario preliminare

A. 1. opera 2. musica 3. baritono 4. direttore 5. musicisti 6. cantanti

In ascolto

1. falso; La diva di cui parlano è una mezzosoprano. 2. falso; Canta bene le arie comiche e interpreta bene Rossini. 3. falso; Luca ha la fortuna di ascoltarla nelle opere di Rossini. 4. vero 5. vero

Grammatica C. Costruzioni con l'infinito

A. *You should have underlined the following verbs:* prendere, cantare, chiederle, venire, vedere
1. a prendere lezioni di canto quando aveva dieci anni 2. cantare 3. chiederle / venire

Ed ora ascoltiamo!

1. vecchia; quaranta 2. il violino; il pianoforte 3. le canzoni sociopolitiche 4. il festival di Sanremo

Dettato

Clark e Christie sono molto interessati alla musica italiana, tutta: dall'opera lirica alla musica leggera, dai cantautori, alla musica da liscio. Per molto tempo hanno associato all'immagine dell'Italia solo l'opera lirica ma ora hanno notato che la produzione musicale italiana è ricca e vasta. I ragazzi vorrebbero andare al festival del jazz che è allestito tutte le estati in Umbria. Quest'anno partecipano delle nuove cantanti jazz italiane e i ragazzi sono molto curiosi. È un po' tardi per trovare un albergo ma gli amici, per l'amore della musica, dormirebbero anche all'aperto!

CAPITOLO 15

Vocabolario preliminare

A. 1. È stato meraviglioso. 2. Hanno visto opere d'arte e monumenti magnifici. 3. Ci sono statue e dipinti straordinari. **C.** 1. capolavoro 2. autore 3. poesia 4. citato 5. Riassumere 6. romanzo

In ascolto

1. l'ingresso era bloccato 2. un enorme scavo archeologico 3. i ruderi 4. medievali / etrusco 5. un museo della scultura

Grammatica A. Passato remoto

C. 1. nacque 2. scrisse 3. raccontò 4. morì 5. ispirò 6. fece

Dettato

Petrarca scrisse le *Rime* o il *Canzoniere* per celebrare il suo amore per Laura, che era morta durante la peste del 1348. Il poeta lavorò al libro per la maggior parte della sua vita e lo finì poco prima di morire, ma sappiamo che avrebbe aggiunto altre poesie perché nel suo manoscritto ci sono spazi bianchi. Le *Rime* di Petrarca furono subito celebrate dai poeti italiani e europei come un capolavoro e diventarono il modello a cui ispirarsi. La poesia rinascimentale europea prese Petrarca come punto di partenza e imitò il suo *Canzoniere,* lo riscrisse, lo adattò. Si cercò insomma di esprimere nelle varie lingue il contrasto tra amore spirituale, amore carnale, poesia e memoria, che è centrale in Petrarca.

CAPITOLO 16

Vocabolario preliminare

C. LO STATO 1. il Presidente della Repubblica 2. il deputato, la deputata 3. le elezioni 4. la Camera dei Deputati e il Senato 5. il voto I PROBLEMI SOCIALI 1. uno sciopero 2. lo stipendio 3. l'impiegato, l'impiegata 4. l'operaio, l'operaia 5. le tasse 6. la disoccupazione

In ascolto

1. Perché ci sono così tanti partiti in Italia. 2. Negli Stati Uniti i due partiti sono molto simili mentre in Italia le posizioni politiche possono essere molto distanti. 3. La partecipazione di massa alle elezioni. 4. Il voto è importante per gli italiani perché sono stati senza diritto di voto durante il fascismo. E molte persone ancora credono che il voto possa cambiare le cose. 5. Nel suo paese molti pensano che sia inutile votare e molti sono contenti della situazione economica e dei diritti che già hanno. *Second part of answer will vary.*

Grammatica A. Congiuntivo presente

A. 1. siano 2. aumentino 3. crescano 4. pensi 5. sia 6. si occupino

Dettato

Guido ha invitato a cena i suoi amici Giulia ed Enrico. Enrico fa il giornalista ed è sempre ben informato sulle novità politiche, Guido e Giulia si interessano di politica dai tempi del liceo, quando militavano nel movimento studentesco. Ognuno ha il proprio punto di vista e le proprie idee. Guido è ottimista ed è convinto che gli italiani sappiano gestirsi politicamente senza mettere in pericolo la democrazia. Giulia pensa che la gente sia confusa e, forse, facile da manipolare. Per Enrico, invece, l'Europa intera è in un periodo di crisi con tanti problemi come il nazionalismo.

CAPITOLO 17

In ascolto

1. assumere 2. la settimana prossima 3. l'assistenza medica 4. mansioni 5. ai suoi nuovi colleghi

Grammatica A. Congiunzioni che richiedono il congiuntivo

D. 1. … tu capisca che cosa è successo, che cosa hai fatto e perché mi hai ferito 2. … sia stanco 3. … tu non ti arrabbi 4. … non mi piaccia 5. … tu ti comporti diversamente 6. … tu non mi chieda di andar via

B. Altri usi del congiuntivo

A. 1. Qualunque 2. Chiunque 3. abbia contattato

Dettato

Stamattina Cinzia, Gabriella e Francesco si sono incontrati per caso per le vie del centro. Così hanno preso un caffè e fatto una chiacchierata con gli amici al bar. Francesco racconta dei motivi che lo hanno spinto a licenziarsi, decisione coraggiosa e difficile. Cinzia è ancora sotto tensione per il colloquio di lavoro appena fatto. Gabriella, che avrà presto un bambino, parla con gli amici delle sue condizioni e delle sue paure. Per i tre ragazzi questa improvvisa mattinata libera diventa l'occasione per parlare di se stessi e condividere problemi ed esperienze.

CAPITOLO 18

In ascolto

1. falso; Gli amici di Lorenzo sono tornati dall'Etiopia la scorsa settimana. 2. vero 3. falso; La bambina ha otto mesi. 4. falso; È stato molto complicato adottare la bambina. 5. vero

Grammatica A. Imperfetto del congiuntivo

A. 1. ti fidanzassi 2. mi innamorassi 3. mi sposassi

B. Trapassato del congiuntivo

A. avessi preparato

C. Correlazione dei tempi nel congiuntivo

A. 1. tu restassi 2. ti capiti 3. capissi 4. faccia 5. mi preoccupi

Dettato

Laura è italoamericana ed è andata in Italia a visitare i luoghi d'origine della sua famiglia. Da bambina sentiva spesso parlare dell'Italia ed i nonni le parlavano in italiano, ma a scuola ha imparato l'inglese e con i genitori non ha mai parlato italiano. L'immagine dell'Italia le era rimasta vaga ed incerta, gli stereotipi ed i miti non le permettevano di averne una visione chiara. Solo un viaggio le avrebbe permesso di farsi un'opinione personale del paese e dei suoi abitanti. In Italia Laura ha riscoperto la propria identità etnica, ha capito meglio la cultura italiana e ha incontrato i parenti di cui aveva solo sentito parlare. È stata un'esperienza importante e Laura ne è molto soddisfatta.

Hiking Oregon's Eagle Cap Wilderness

A Guide to the Area's Greatest Hiking Adventures

Fourth Edition

Fred Barstad

FALCON GUIDES

GUILFORD, CONNECTICUT

FALCONGUIDES®

An imprint of The Rowman & Littlefield Publishing Group, Inc.
4501 Forbes Blvd., Ste. 200
Lanham, MD 20706
www.rowman.com
Falcon and FalconGuides are registered trademarks and Make Adventure Your Story is a trademark of The Rowman & Littlefield Publishing Group, Inc.

Distributed by NATIONAL BOOK NETWORK

Previous editions of this book were published by FalconGuides in 1996, 2002, and 2014.

Maps by The Rowman & Littlefield Publishing Group, Inc.
All interior photographs by Fred Barstad unless otherwise noted

British Library Cataloguing-in-Publication Information available

Library of Congress Control Number: 2020942021

ISBN 978-1-4930-4376-7 (paper : alk. paper)
ISBN 978-1-4930-4377-4 (electronic)

Contents

Overview

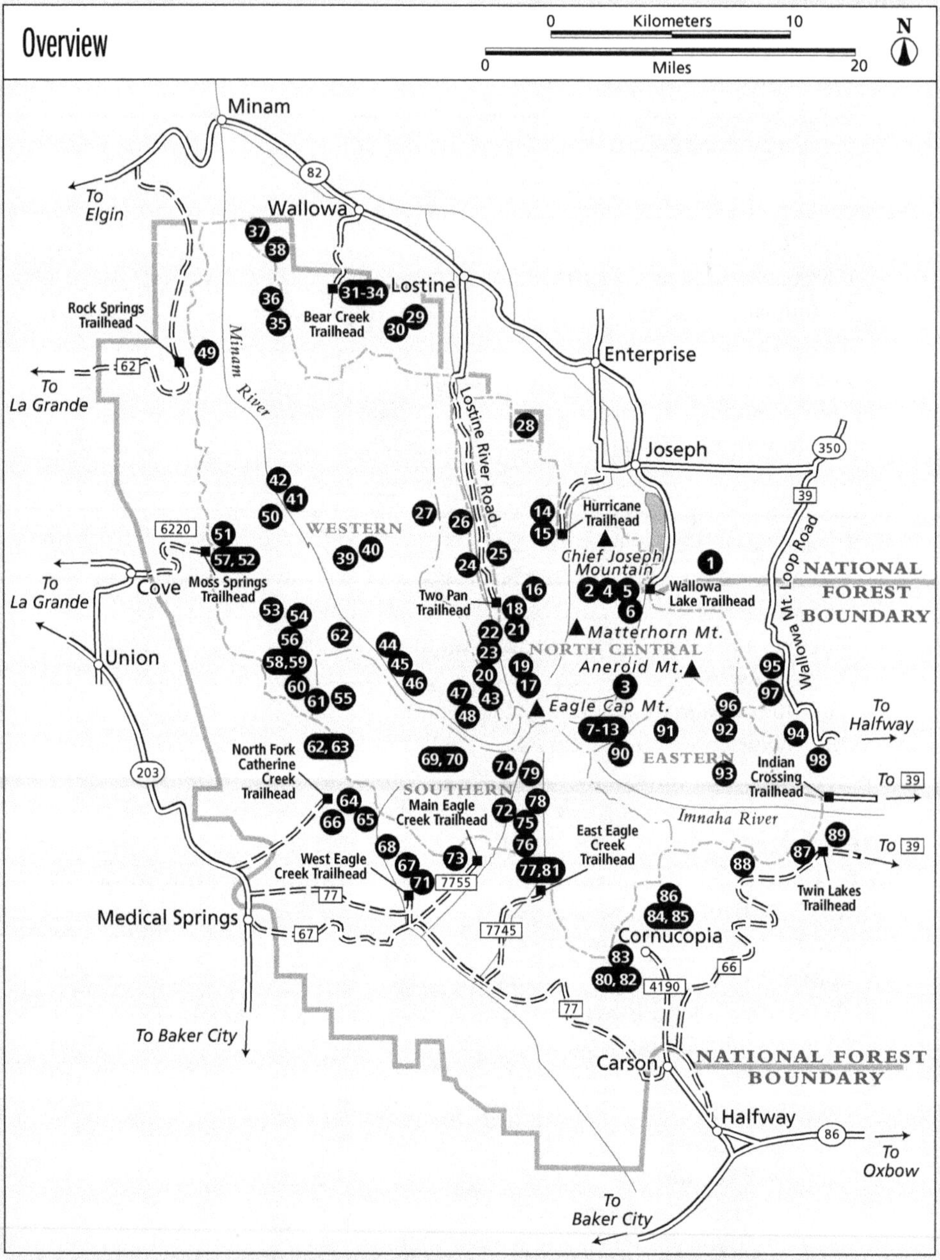

Kilometers
0
10
Miles
0
20
N
Minam
82
To Elgin
Wallowa
Lostine
Rock Springs Trailhead
Bear Creek Trailhead
31-34
62
To La Grande
Minam River
Enterprise
Lostine River Road
Joseph
350
39
6220
WESTERN
Hurricane Trailhead
Chief Joseph Mountain
Wallowa Mt. Loop Road
NATIONAL FOREST BOUNDARY
To La Grande
Cove
Moss Springs Trailhead
57, 52
Two Pan Trailhead
Wallowa Lake Trailhead
Matterhorn Mt.
NORTH CENTRAL
Union
58,59
Aneroid Mt.
Eagle Cap Mt.
To Halfway
7-13
EASTERN
North Fork Catherine Creek Trailhead
62, 63
69, 70
Indian Crossing Trailhead
To 39
203
SOUTHERN
Main Eagle Creek Trailhead
Imnaha River
East Eagle Creek Trailhead
West Eagle Creek Trailhead
7755
77,81
To 39
Twin Lakes Trailhead
77
Medical Springs
67
7745
84, 85
Cornucopia
80, 82
4190
66
77
To Baker City
Carson
NATIONAL FOREST BOUNDARY
Halfway
86
To Oxbow
To Baker City

Index to USGS 7.5 Minute Quadrangles

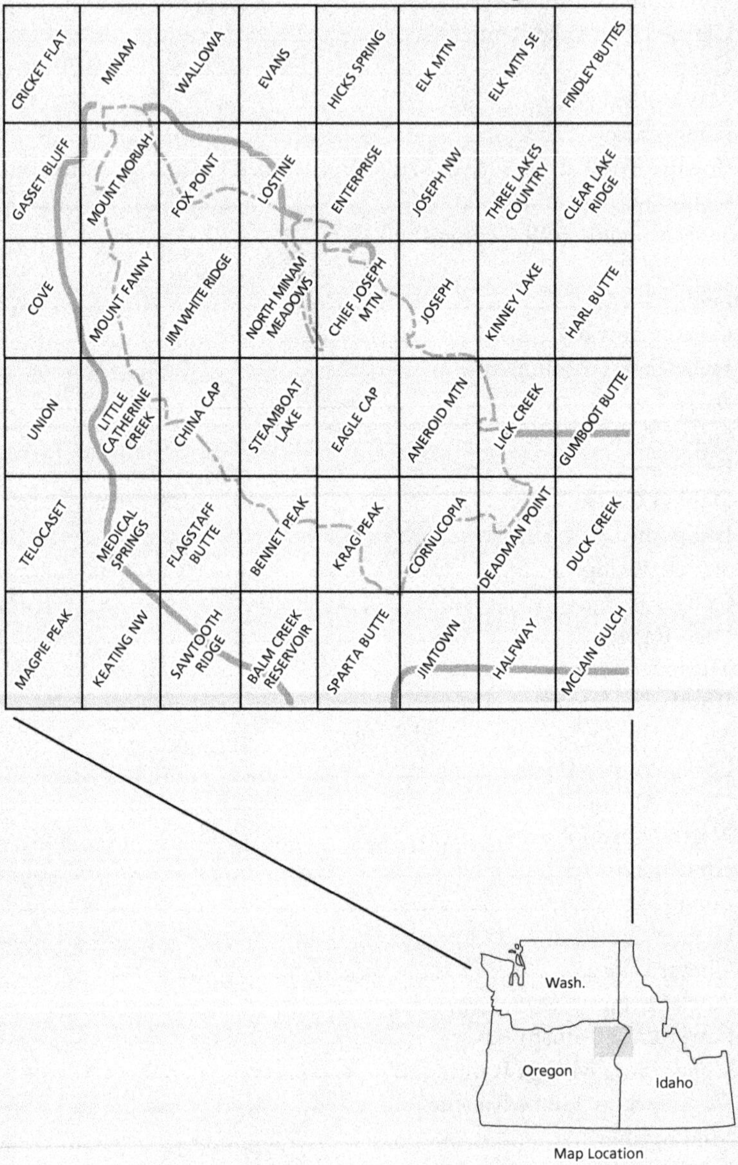

Acknowledgments

I would like to thank Gary Fletcher for hiking with me, contributing photos, and editing the text. I also want to thank Maria Forsenius, Kerry Searles, Lowell Euhus, Ettore Negri, Lance Reedy, and Jerry Lavender for hiking with me and furnishing pictures.

Thanks to Casey Barstad, Brian Barstad, Dan Knight, Doug Cracraft, Oliver Boeve, and Dave Kaufman for hiking and camping with me and keeping me company over many miles. Also of great help were Bill George, for hiking with me and sharing his knowledge of the area, and Vic Coggins, of the Oregon Department of Fish and Wildlife, for information on the bighorn sheep and mountain goats.

Thanks also to Larry Brandvold, John Hollendeak, Nancy Rudger, Sweyn Wall, and all the employees of USDA Forest Service at the Wallowa Mountains Office for much information on trail status and maintenance. Thanks to Bud Sanders for trail information. Most of all I thank my wife, Suzi Barstad, for hiking and camping with me, and for her endless hours of typing and editing to get this book ready for publication.

Introduction

Eagle Cap Wilderness is the premier backpacking country of Oregon. It covers 580 square miles of the Wallowa Mountains, in the northeast corner of Oregon. Anywhere you look in the Wallowas you will find absolutely breathtaking mountain scenery. There are fifty-two named high lakes, nearly all of which have an abundance of trout just waiting to take your bait. Many miles of rivers drain from the high alpine mountains through densely forested canyons. These rivers also have many trout, and several have received National Wild and Scenic River status for their "outstandingly remarkable" characteristics. The abundance and diversity of animal life in the Wallowa Mountains is sensational.

The trails in this book, with a couple of exceptions, are within or lead into Eagle Cap Wilderness. The wilderness encompasses nearly all of the high country of the Wallowa Mountains. It also includes much of the foothill and canyon country surrounding the Wallowa Mountains.

Much of the wilderness is used very little. Part of the purpose of this book is to encourage backpacker use of these areas, and thereby to disperse the traffic so that overused areas can recover somewhat. If you are interested in solitude, check out trails with a "light" traffic rating.

The Wallowa Mountains are steepest on the north side. On the north-central side there are almost no foothills between the Wallowa Valley and the alpine peaks. To the east, timbered ridges cut by deep canyons connect the Wallowa Mountains with Summit Ridge. Summit Ridge overlooks the Snake River in Hells Canyon National Recreation Area.

On the south side, timbered foothills lead up to the high peaks. The western and northwestern parts of the Wallowa Mountains are made up of ridges of moderate elevation. These ridges are separated by deep canyons. The average elevation of the ridges in the western part of the range is a little more than 7,000 feet. This is about 2,000 feet lower than the average ridgetop elevation in the central and north-central part of the range.

The major drainages of the Wallowas radiate from the center of the range. From the summit of Eagle Cap, most of the major drainages can be seen heading out in all directions.

The high country of the Wallowas shows much evidence of glacial carving. The larger valleys are the typical U shape of glacial valleys. There are also many cirques and hanging valleys. Most of the ice is now gone, with only a few stagnant patches left. The large moraine that holds Wallowa Lake is evidence of large glaciers that were once here.

Permits are required to enter Eagle Cap Wilderness. These self-issue permits are available at major trailheads or at USDA Forest Service offices.

Life Zones

There are four distinct life zones in the Wallowa Mountains. The transition zone reaches up to about 6,000 feet in most places. Ponderosa pine is the typical tree of this zone, with Douglas fir and true fir in wetter locations.

From approximately 6,000 to 7,500 feet is the Canadian zone. Here the typical tree is lodgepole pine. There are also fir and spruce in the Canadian zone. Mountain hemlocks also thrive in this zone on wetter slopes.

Above the Canadian zone, up to the timberline at about 8,500 feet, is the Hudsonian zone, with its subalpine fir and whitebark pine. In a few scattered locations in this zone there are stands of limber pine. The Wallowas are the only range in Oregon that have limber pine.

The highest peaks and ridges reach into the arctic alpine zone. There are almost no trees here, only scattered elfinwood, very small weather-beaten trees. At 9,700 feet, on the south side of Aneroid Mountain, a 3-foot-tall whitebark pine survives the harsh climate. This may be Oregon's highest altitude tree.

Large Animals

The Wallowa Mountains are blessed with abundant animal life. There are more deer, elk, and even bear in Wallowa County than there are humans.

Mule deer are the most common large animal. They range throughout the mountains, up to and including the alpine zone, in the summer and fall. These deer generally drop to lower elevations in winter. However, it sometimes takes a lot of snow to move them down. Big bucks usually stay high as long as they can. In years of light snow I have seen deer higher than 8,000 feet in late January. There is also a fairly large population of white-tailed deer in some canyon bottoms and around the edges of the mountains. Whitetails are common in the Wallowa Valley.

Elk inhabit the entire area. They are most common in the eastern, southern, and western parts of the Wallowas. There are some scattered herds in the higher central parts, too. Elk seem to like more moderate terrain than do mule deer. Elk are usually not seen on the rugged cliffs and ridges of the central part of the range.

Black bears live in all parts of the Wallowas. They are probably more common in the middle and upper Minam River Canyon, but they can show up anywhere. They are generally not a problem, but it always pays to keep a clean camp and hang your food anyway. They do raid the dumpsters at Wallowa Lake almost every year. Be very careful around mothers with cubs. The cubs are cute, but mamas can be dangerous. In spring watch for bears grazing in open moist areas. They eat the wild onions that grow there.

Cougars are fairly common in the Wallowas. They are not often seen by hikers, but don't be too surprised if you turn back on a trail and find large cat tracks on top of your tracks. Cougars are curious and may follow a hiker for some distance. This has happened to me at least four times. Since 1994 the use of dogs for hunting cougar has been banned, and cougars have become more common. Sightings and encounters have increased enough to become a major concern. The idea of a one-hundred-pound cat watching you makes some people very nervous.

Bighorn sheep were once native to the Wallowa Mountains but vanished about 1945, possibly from disease contracted from domestic sheep. Bighorns were reintroduced from Alberta, Canada, in 1964, but many in the Wallowa Mountains died in the late 1980s. Now they seem to be doing fine. The largest ram ever found in the United States came from the Wallowa Mountains. Bighorns normally roam the north-central part of the range, at 9,000 feet or higher during summer.

Although mountain goats may not have been native to the Wallowas, they were introduced in 1950 from northern Washington, and more were released in the 1980s from Olympic National Park, Washington, and Misty Fjords National Monument, Alaska. They can be seen on or near the tops of Hurwal and Hurricane divides or near the top of Chief Joseph Mountain. Please watch the goats and sheep from a distance. They are sensitive to human intrusion.

Smaller Animals

Coyotes are found everywhere in the Wallowas. It is common to hear them at night. Pikas can be seen or heard in most rockslides. Red diggers, a type of ground squirrel, are common in meadows at lower altitudes. Golden eagles can be seen soaring along the ridges, and grouse are quite common as well. Some of the ridgetops crawl with ladybugs in early summer.

Bighorn rams. GARY FLETCHER PHOTO

There are many other small animals in these mountains: Watch and you will see them. Rattlesnakes are not found in the higher parts of the Wallowas. However, they can be found in the canyon bottoms in the western part of the range. Rattlesnakes usually live below 4,000 feet here.

Fish

Nearly all of the rivers and lakes in the Wallowa Mountains contain a good supply of fish. The most common fish is the brightly colored and easy-to-catch brook trout. Brook trout are very prolific and tend to overpopulate their habitat; as a consequence they may be quite small. Many of the lakes, however, have larger fish, and fishing can be very good in the mornings and evenings. Some of the rivers and a few lakes also contain rainbow trout.

A few rivers have populations of the threatened bull trout, some of which are very large. If accidentally hooked, these fish should be released without removing them from the water. Because of this threatened population, and runs of Chinook salmon and steelhead, special angling regulations are in effect in the area. These regulations change from time to time, so be sure to check the current Oregon angling regulations pamphlet before fishing.

How to Use This Guide

Trail Ratings

The trails in this book are rated as easy, moderate, or strenuous, with length or time involved not considered. Only steepness of the grade, roughness of the trail, extent of erosion or rockiness, and elevation changes are considered.

Trails that are rated "easy" will generally have gentle grades and be mostly smooth; however, there may be short sections of rocky or eroded areas. Nearly anyone in reasonable condition can hike easy trails, given enough time.

Trails rated "moderate" will climb or descend more steeply than easy trails. They may climb 500 or 600 feet per mile and have fairly long stretches of rough or eroded tread. A backpacker in good physical condition can hike these trails with no problem. However, people in poor condition and small children may find them grueling.

Trails rated as "strenuous" are best done by expert backpackers and mountaineers. These trails may climb 1,000 feet or more per mile and may be very rough in spots.

All hikes are measured in one-way distances unless otherwise specified.

Climbing and Scrambling Ratings

The ratings in the climbing section of this book are not the same as the trail ratings. What is rated an easy climb is at least as difficult as a strenuous trail, and the climbs get more difficult from there. Although most of the climbing routes described are not technical (requiring ropes and protective hardware), they do require more stamina than many hikers have.

Use discretion and common sense when visiting a new area. There is an old saying that there are bold climbers and there are old climbers, but there are no old, bold climbers. With that advice, warm up on a few routes that may be well below your limit; get used to the area before pushing the limits of your ability. Mountain travel is typically classified as follows:

Class 1: Trail hiking

Class 2: Hiking over rough ground such as scree and talus; may include the use of hands for stability

Class 3: Scrambling that requires the use of hands and careful foot placement

Class 4: Scrambling over steep and exposed terrain; a rope may be used for safety on exposed areas

Class 5: Technical "free" climbing where terrain is steep and exposed, requiring the use of ropes, protection hardware, and related techniques

Some "strenuous" climbs may have considerable exposure on their scrambles. Most climbs in this book are considered Class 3, with the exception of Twin Peaks and Bonneville Mountain, which may be Class 4 and require a rope.

Parklike area along East Fork Eagle Creek.

Maintenance Ratings

Trails that have yearly maintenance will usually be cleared of obstructions by midsummer each year. If the rating is "infrequent," that means the trail is scheduled to be maintained every two to three years, but in reality it may be every five to six years. If the rating is "rare" or "seldom," it may be a very long time since the trail was cleared, and you should expect to have to climb over a few logs. Trails with no maintenance are not kept up by the forest service, but many horse riders cut logs so they can get their pack strings through. On these trails there may be long stretches with blowdowns and badly eroded sections.

A large part of the maintenance at present is being done by a volunteer group called the Wallowa Mountains Hells Canyon Trail Association (WMHCTA). WMHCTA works in partnership with the USDA Forest Service. Contact information for this association is included in appendix A.

Traffic Ratings

If the traffic rating, as described in the "Traffic and other trail users" entry, is "heavy," you should expect to meet people every few minutes to few hours, and many of the better campsites may be taken. You will probably meet one to five parties per day on trails with a "moderate" rating. On trails with a "light" traffic rating, it is unlikely you will meet more than one or two parties a day, and it may be days or even weeks before you see anyone else. These are average figures for summer and fall months; no one can say for sure how many people you will encounter on any trail on a given day.

Following a Faint Trail

Most of the trails in this book are easy to follow. Some, however, have short stretches that have become faint or nonexistent because of natural causes, such as blown-down timber or washouts, or they may have become overgrown with vegetation. Animals can also make trails difficult to follow by making their own trails that cross or fork off from the main trail. In areas where cattle graze, particularly in portions of southern Eagle Cap Wilderness, this can be a major problem. You must be able to follow a faint trail when hiking the less-used trails in the Wallowa Mountains.

The first thing to do before trying to follow one of these less-traveled trails is to carefully read its entire description in this book. The description will tell you if route-finding skills are required to follow the trail safely. Next, get a good topo map of the area. These maps are listed at the beginning of each trail description. All the United States Geological Survey (USGS) maps listed are 7.5-minute quadrangles. The Geo Graphics Wallowa Mountains Eagle Cap Wilderness map, listed on most of the trail descriptions, covers the entire area. This map is a smaller scale than the USGS maps, but it is very accurate on both the trails and the roads leading to the trailheads. The Geo Graphics map is available at most outdoor stores in the area and at major outlets in larger cities.

Be sure you have a compass and know how to use it. Remember that a compass does not actually point to true north. It points to magnetic north, which is approximately eighteen degrees east of true north in this area. Nearly all maps show an area's declination. Another helpful navigational instrument is an altimeter. Altimeters work very well if you use them correctly. However, they run on air pressure, which is always changing, so they need to be set at each known altitude point. This means several times a day, if possible.

GPS coordinates for the trailheads and some major trail junctions are given in each hike description. If you are proficient in the use of a GPS receiver, these can be very helpful. GPS signals are hard to get in some spots, especially deep in narrow canyons and sometimes in thick forests. Don't rely on your GPS as your only means of navigation. They are useful tools, but don't take the place of a map and compass. GPS batteries have a bad habit of going dead just when you need them most.

While you are hiking, watch ahead for blazes cut into the bark of trees, and rock cairns on the ground. Logs that have been sawed off may also be an indicator of the trail's route. Trees missing some branches on one side may show that the trail passes on that side of the tree. Through thick woods, look for narrow strips where the trees are much smaller or nonexistent; this could be the route once cleared for the trail. All of these things are not positive signs that you are going the right way, but taken together, with good compass and map skills, they make it much easier to follow a faint trail.

Numbered Hike Locators

On the overview maps for the Eagle Cap Wilderness and each of its regions, the numbered locators represent each of the hikes. In the opening text for each hike you will notice a number. These are forest service trail numbers that appear on forest service and most other maps. These numbers sometimes, but not always, appear on trail signs.

Create Your Own Hikes

In addition to the ninety-eight hikes described in this book, I encourage you to string together routes in the same area to make your own adventures. Look to the overview map on page vi for clusters of trailheads to suggest trails that could easily be included to add miles to your hike. And in the text, many of the trail names mentioned as intersections or nearby routes are described as hikes in their own right elsewhere—check out the table of contents or the hike index. It would be easy to spend a lifetime in Oregon's Eagle Cap Wilderness, and you'd never repeat the same hike twice.

Zero Impact

Making campfires and cutting switchbacks have probably the most negative impact on the environment where hikers are concerned. As traditional and nice as campfires are, their use should be limited. Small fires in certain areas at low elevations may be okay if regulations permit, but building fires in alpine meadows, or in any alpine area, is definitely not good practice. It takes many years for the fragile alpine environment to recover from just one small campfire. Take along a backpacking stove; it is easier to use anyway. If you must build a fire, make sure to extinguish it completely.

Cutting switchbacks is extremely hard on trails and hillsides. This practice causes much erosion and destroys plant life. Although horses can damage trails that are not designed or maintained for them, hikers do much damage also. It is always best to stay on the main trail and not take shortcuts.

Do not dismantle rock cairns, because they may be the only thing marking the route in some areas. Please leave cabins and mine sites as you found them; these are historical parts of the wilderness.

Campsite selection is also important in trying to maintain the environment. Camp in obviously used sites when available. Otherwise, camp and cook on durable surfaces such as bedrock, sand, gravel bars, or bare ground. Make camp in the timber if possible and try to avoid camping in meadows. Be careful not to trample vegetation. Camp well away from lakes and at least some distance back from streams. Check forest service regulations about campsite selection in the Eagle Cap Wilderness.

When leaving camp, or while on the trail, pack out your trash and any other trash you find.

Carry a lightweight trowel to bury human waste 6 to 8 inches deep at least 300 feet from any water source. Pack out used toilet paper.

Avoid making loud noises on the trail (unless you are in bear country) or in camp. Be courteous—remember, sound travels easily in the backcountry, especially across water.

If we all do our part, we can keep our wild areas beautiful and clean forever.

Leave no trace. Put your ear to the ground and listen carefully. Thousands of people coming behind you are thanking you for your courtesy and good sense. For more information visit LNT.org.

Making It a Safe Trip

There are a few simple things you can do that will improve your chances of staying healthy while you are in the wilderness. One of the most important is to be careful with your drinking water. All water taken from rivers, streams, lakes, or springs should be boiled, chemically treated, or filtered before drinking, washing utensils, or brushing your teeth. The water may look clean and pure—and it may be—but you can never be sure.

Check the weather report before you head into the mountains and canyons of Eagle Cap Wilderness. Cold stormy weather, with rain, snow, and high winds, is possible at all times of the year. Thunderstorms with accompanying heavy rain, hail, and wind are common during summer. Do not stay on ridges or other exposed places during a lightning storm. Very few people are struck by lightning, but you do not want to be one of them. Nighttime temperatures in the high valleys and on the ridges can drop to freezing in July and August and far below that in September. These extreme low temperatures usually occur on clear nights after the passing of a cold front.

There is at least some avalanche danger on the winter skiing routes mentioned in this book. It is a good idea to take a class in avalanche safety before venturing into the backcountry in winter. Avalanche transceivers should be carried by each member of a ski party, and everyone should know how to use them properly. Be sure that all your transceivers are on the same frequency.

Many of the glacier-carved lakes in Eagle Cap have shorelines that drop off abruptly, and children should be watched at all times when near the water. The water in most lakes is very cold, so swimming time should be limited. If you venture to any of the lakes in winter, be careful of thin ice covering the surface.

Mosquitoes can be a major annoyance in many places, so take along repellent and make sure the netting on your tent is in good shape. Ticks can also be a nuisance in early summer.

Finally, be sure to let someone know where you are going and when you plan to return.

Of all the safety tips, the most important is to take your brain with you when you go into the wilderness. Without it, no tips will help, and with it, almost any obstacle can be overcome. Think about what you are doing, be safe, and have a great time in the outdoors.

Passing Stock on the Trail

If you meet parties with pack or saddle stock on the trail, try to get as far off the trail as possible. Horse riders prefer that you stand on the downhill side of the trail, but there is some question whether this is the safest place for a hiker. If possible, I like to get well off the trail on the uphill side. It is often a good idea to talk quietly to the horses and their riders, because this seems to calm many horses. If you have the family dog with you, be sure to keep it restrained and quiet; many horse wrecks are caused by dogs.

You Might Never Know What Hit You

Thunderstorms are common in Eagle Cap Wilderness throughout the spring and summer. On the peaks and ridges it is relatively easy to see and hear a thunderstorm before it reaches your location, but in the valleys and canyons a storm can be on you with very little advance warning. If you get caught in a lightning storm, take special precautions. Remember:

- Lightning can travel far ahead of the storm, so try to take cover well before the storm hits.
- Don't try to get back to your vehicle. It isn't worth the risk. Instead seek the best shelter you can find. Lightning storms usually last only a short time, and from a safe spot you might even enjoy watching the storm.
- Stay away from anything that might attract lightning, such as metal tent poles, graphite fishing rods, and metal frame backpacks.
- Be careful not to be caught on a mountaintop or exposed ridgeline or under a solitary tree.
- If possible seek shelter in a low-lying area, ideally in a dense stand of small, uniformly sized trees.
- Get in a crouch position with both feet firmly placed on the ground; don't lean against a tree.
- If you have a pack without a metal frame or a sleeping pad, put your feet on it for extra insulation against electric shock.
- Don't walk or huddle together. Stay 50 feet apart so that if someone does get struck the others can give first aid.
- If you are in a tent, it is usually best to stay there, in your sleeping bag with your feet on your sleeping pad.

Occasionally a flash flood in one of the steep, narrow canyons can occur as a result of a thunderstorm. These floods, also known as waterspouts throughout much of the western United States, are most common when heavy rain combines with snowmelt. For this reason it is best not to camp in a narrow canyon when thunderstorms or other heavy rain is likely.

Be Cougar Alert

You're sure to see plenty of deer in the Eagle Cap Wilderness, which means mountain lions probably aren't far away. Cougars feed on deer, and the remote backcountry of northeast Oregon constitutes some of the best cougar habitat in the West. Though many people consider themselves lucky indeed to see a mountain lion in the wild, the big cats—nature's perfect predators—are potentially dangerous. Attacks on humans are extremely rare, but it's wise to educate yourself before heading into mountain lion habitat.

To stay as safe as possible when hiking in mountain lion country, follow this advice:

- Travel with a friend or group. There's safety in numbers.
- Don't let small children wander away by themselves.
- Don't let pets run unleashed.
- Avoid hiking at dawn and dusk, when mountain lions are most active.
- Know how to behave if you encounter a mountain lion.

What to Do If You Encounter a Cougar

In the majority of mountain lion encounters, these animals exhibit avoidance, indifference, or curiosity that never results in human injury, but it is natural to be alarmed if you have an encounter of any kind. Try to keep your cool and keep the following in mind:

It is important to recognize threatening cougar behavior. A few cues may gauge the risk of attack. If a mountain lion is more than 50 yards away and directs its attention to you, it may be only curious. This situation represents only a slight risk for adults, but a more serious risk to unaccompanied children. At this point, you should move away, while keeping the animal in your peripheral vision. Also, look for rocks, sticks, or something to use as a weapon, just in case.

If a mountain lion is crouched and staring at you from less than 50 yards away, it may be gauging the chances of a successful attack. If this behavior continues, your risk may be high. Do not approach the cougar. Instead, give the animal the opportunity to move on. Slowly back away, but maintain eye contact. Mountain lions are not known to attack humans to defend young or a kill, but they have been reported to "charge" in rare instances, and may want to stay in the area. It's best to choose another route.

- Do not run from a cougar. Running may stimulate a predatory response.
- Make noise. If you encounter a mountain lion, be vocal and talk or yell loudly and regularly. Try not to panic. Shout also to make others in the area aware of the situation.
- Maintain eye contact. Eye contact shows the cougar you are aware of its presence. However, if the mountain lion's behavior is not threatening (for example, it is grooming or periodically looking away), maintain visual contact through your peripheral vision and move away.
- Appear larger than you are. Raise your arms above your head and make steady waving motions. Raise your jacket or another object above your head. Do not bend over, as this will make you appear smaller and more "prey-like."

- If you are with small children, pick them up. Bring the children close to you without bending over, maintaining eye contact with the lion. If you are with other children or adults, band together.
- Defend yourself. If attacked, fight back. Try to remain standing. Do not feign death. Pick up a branch or rock; pull out a knife, pepper spray, or other deterrent. Everything is a potential weapon, and individuals have fended off mountain lions with rocks, tree limbs, and even cameras.
- Defend others. In past attacks on children, adults have successfully stopped attacks. Defend your hiking partners, but don't physically defend your pet.
- Respect any warning signs posted by agencies.
- Spread the word. Before leaving on your hike, discuss lions and teach others in your group how to behave in case of a cougar encounter.
- Report encounters. A sighting does not constitute an encounter. If you have an encounter with a mountain lion, record your location and the details of the encounter, and notify the nearest landowner or land management agency. The land management agency (federal, state, or county) may want to visit the site and, if appropriate, post education/warning signs. Fish and wildlife agencies should also be notified because they record and track such encounters.

If physical injury occurs, it is important to leave the area and not disturb the site of the attack. Cougars that have attacked people must be killed, and an undisturbed site is critical for effectively locating a dangerous cougar.

Return of the Wolf

Wolves have moved into Eagle Cap Wilderness. So far there have been no encounters between wolves and humans here, but there have been many losses of sheep and cattle in the area. There is also some danger to dogs. There is only a very small chance you will even see a wolf in Eagle Cap Wilderness. In the very unlikely event that you have an encounter, make lots of noise, don't run, and do not defend your pet.

Be Bear Aware

The first step of any hike in bear country is an attitude adjustment. Being prepared for bears means having the right information as well as the right equipment. The black bears in the Eagle Cap Wilderness rarely approach humans, but they may pose a danger if you handle your food improperly. At the very least, letting a bear get human food is like contributing—directly—to the eventual destruction of that bear. Think of proper bear etiquette as protecting the bears as much as yourself.

Camping in Bear Country

Staying overnight in bear country is not dangerous, but it adds an additional risk to your trip. The main difference is the presence of food, cooking, and garbage. Following a few basic rules greatly minimizes the risk to you and the bears.

Storing food and garbage: Be sure to finalize your food storage plans before it gets dark. It's not only difficult to store food in the dark, but it's easier to forget some juicy morsel on the ground. Also, be sure to store food in airtight, waterproof bags to prevent food odors from circulating throughout the forest. The illustrations on the following page depict three popular methods of hanging food and garbage. Try to get the bag at least 10 feet off the ground.

Take a special bag for storing food. The bag must be sturdy and waterproof. You can get dry bags at most outdoor specialty stores, but you can get by with a trash compactor bag. Regular garbage bags can break and leave your food spread on the ground.

You also need 100 feet of nylon cord. Parachute cord will usually suffice. The classic method of hanging food and gear smelling of food is to tie a rock or piece of wood to the end of your rope and toss it over the branch. Attach it to the bag and hoist it up 10 feet or more. If the load gets too heavy, wrap it around a small tree or branch for leverage.

If you can't tie the rope to the rock, put the rock in a small bag and toss it over a high branch. Use gloves so you don't get rope burns. And of course, don't let the rock or wood come down on your head. (It happens!) Also, don't let anybody stand under the bag until you're sure it is secured.

What to hang: To be as safe as possible, store everything that has any food smell. If you spilled something on your clothes, change into other clothes for sleeping, and hang clothes with food smells with the food and garbage.

What to keep in your tent: You can't be too careful in keeping food smells out of the tent. Just in case a bear has become accustomed to coming into that campsite looking for food, it's vital to keep all food smells out of the tent. This often includes your pack, which is hard to keep odor-free. Usually only take valuables (like cameras and binoculars), clothing, and sleeping gear into the tent.

Types of food: What food you have along is much less critical than how you handle it, cook it, and store it. Consider, however, the fewer dishes and/or less packaging, the better.

Hanging food at night is not the only storage issue: Also, make sure you place food correctly in your pack. Use airtight packages as much as possible. Store food in the container it came in or, when opened, in zip-locked bags. This keeps food smells out of your pack and off your other camping gear and clothes.

Don't cook too much food, so you don't have to deal with leftovers. If you do end up with extra food, you only have two choices: Carry it out or burn it. Don't bury it or throw it in a lake or leave it anywhere in bear country. A bear will most likely find and rip up any food or garbage buried in the backcountry.

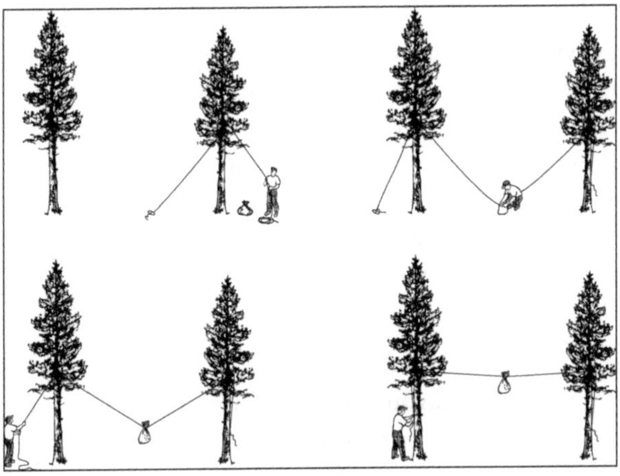

Hanging food and garbage between two trees

Hanging food and garbage over a tree branch

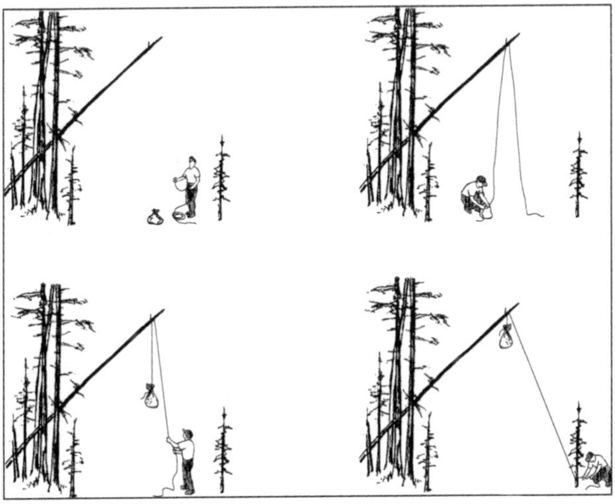

Hanging food and garbage over a leaning tree

If you end up with lots of food scraps in the dishwater, drain out the scraps and store them in zip-locked bags with other garbage, or burn them. You can bring a lightweight screen to filter out food scraps from dishwater, but be sure to store the screen with the food and garbage. If you have a campfire, pour the dishwater around the edge of the fire. If you don't have a fire, take the dishwater at least 100 yards downwind and downhill from camp and pour it on the ground or in a small hole. Don't put dishwater or food scraps in a lake or stream. Do dishes immediately after eating so a minimum of food smell lingers in the area.

The Buzz beside the Trail

Once you hear a rattlesnake buzz, it's a sound you will never forget. Forty-five of the fifty states are home to at least one species of rattlesnake. Unless you will be hiking only in Alaska, Hawaii, Rhode Island, Delaware, or Maine, you should be aware of the possibility of encountering one. Within the rattlesnake states some areas have only a very small population of these venomous reptiles, and other areas have none at all. Local inquiry is the best way to assess your chances of meeting a rattler on the trail.

Rattlesnakes are members of the "pit viper" family. Pit vipers have heat-sensing organs (pits) in their faces that are used to detect heat. This heat detection system is probably integrated with the snakes' visual senses, allowing the snake to see heat. This allows rattlers to strike easily in the dark.

Rattlesnakes inhabit a wide range of climatic zones. They are found from below sea level up to subalpine zones in the mountains of the western United States. However, they are not common above the transition (ponderosa pine) zone. Rattlers may be out at lower temperatures than is generally realized by most people. They are occasionally seen sunning themselves on warm rocks when the air temperature is only a few degrees above freezing. Conversely, the snakes seek shade and or burrows when it is very hot. For a rattlesnake, the perfect temperature is about eighty degrees.

Of the approximately 8,000 venomous snakebites in the United States each year, only ten to twenty are fatal, and in many cases these fatalities can be at least partly attributed to preexisting medical problems. Of these fatal bites, 95 percent are caused by the diamondback rattlesnake, which ranges generally south of a line from Southern California to North Carolina. This is not to say that other species of rattlers do not cause much pain and an occasional death. But your chances of being killed by a snake diminish greatly as you travel north. Of the people who are bitten, about 35 percent are not injected with venom. This "dry bite" leads some people to wrongly believe that they are immune to rattlesnake venom.

Preventing Bites

Don't count on rattlesnakes to rattle at your approach; they are generally shy creatures in their encounters with humans. In most cases they will do their best to escape or to lie quietly and let the person pass without noticing them. In my experience only about half of the snakes I've happened upon have rattled before I saw them. Rattlers will sometimes strike before rattling.

Don't place your hands or feet in places that you can't see clearly. About 65 percent of snakebites are on the hands or forearms, and another 24 percent are on the feet, ankles, and lower legs. In areas where there is a good chance of encountering a rattler, it may be advisable to wear protective clothing such as snakeproof gaiters or chaps, as well as sturdy hiking boots.

During hot weather be especially alert during the morning, evening, and night because the snakes are most active at those times.

Don't handle any snake unless you can positively identify it as being nonvenomous. Snakes that were thought to be dead have bitten many people.

Inquisitive children have a higher-than-average chance of being bitten by a rattlesnake. Because of their smaller bodies, they are also more susceptible to the toxins in the venom. Warn your children of the danger, and watch them closely when you're in snake country.

First Aid for Snakebite

The best first-aid treatment for snakebite is to get medical help as soon as possible so that an injection of antivenom can be administered. Antivenom is the only really proven treatment for snakebite. If you are within forty-five minutes of medical assistance, just get there as quickly as safety allows and don't bother with any other type of treatment.

Recommended First Aid When Medical Help Is Far Away

If you are more than forty-five minutes from medical help, first aid may be of some advantage. If there are three or more people in your party, you may want to send someone for help as you are starting the first-aid treatment. Don't leave the victim alone at this point.

A snakebite kit is necessary to adequately perform the treatment. There are two main types of snakebite kits available on the market. The most common ones include two or three rubber suction cups and a razor blade. The more advanced kits include a two-stage suction pump. The pump is capable of applying much more suction, and is the preferred kit to carry. In addition to a snakebite kit, an elastic bandage is helpful in most treatments. If there is no disinfectant already in your snakebite or general first-aid kit, you should add some to it. If there is no safety razor included in your kit, you should purchase one and add it. Before putting your snakebite kit in your pack or pocket, open it and read the instructions to familiarize yourself with its proper use.

Treatment must begin immediately after the bite occurs to be effective. If the wound is bleeding, allow it to do so for fifteen to thirty seconds. If the wound is on the hand, forearm, foot, or lower leg (which it probably will be), wrap the elastic bandage around the limb above the wound. Wrap the bandage no tighter than you would for a sprain.

If you are using the pump-type kit, place the pump, with the appropriate suction cup attached, over the wound and begin the suction procedure. If a good seal cannot be achieved over the wound because of hair, it may be necessary to shave the area with the safety razor in your kit. The suction procedure must start within five minutes of the bite to be effective and should be left in place for thirty minutes or more.

It is best not to do any cutting on the victim, but if you must use one of the kits that require it, first disinfect the wound area and the instrument that will be used to make the incisions. Make the incisions no deeper than 3 millimeters (⅛ inch) and no longer than 5 millimeters (2⁄10 inch) across the puncture marks and along the long axis of the limb. If the bite is not in a large muscle, these cuts may need to be much shallower to prevent permanent tissue damage. Making these incisions too large is where you can get into trouble by cutting muscles and tendons, so be very careful to keep them small and shallow. They just need to bleed a small amount. After making the incisions, start the suction immediately.

After getting the suction procedure going, check for a pulse below the wound. If none can be found, loosen the elastic bandage. Remember that it is better to have no constriction than it is to have too much.

If possible, try to keep the bitten extremity at approximately the victim's heart level, and try to keep him or her as calm as possible. Do not give the victim alcohol.

After completing the treatment, cover the bite as you would any other small wound. Be sure that any bandage you put on is not constrictive, as swelling will probably occur. Send someone for, or get the victim to, medical attention as soon as possible.

Northwest Forest Pass

A Northwest Forest Pass is required to park at most trailheads. Passes may be obtained at any forest service ranger station or office. These passes are valid for all national forests in Oregon and Washington.

Map Legend

Transportation

- State Road (203)
- County/Forest Road (7755)
- Local Road
- Gravel Road
- Unimproved Road

Trails

- Featured Trail
- Trail
- Climbing Route
- Cross-country Trail

Water Features

- Body of Water
- River/Creek
- Ditch
- Waterfall
- Spring

Symbols

- Bridge
- Campground
- Cliffs
- Featured Trailhead (20)
- Gate
- Point of Interest/Trailhead
- Pass
- Parking
- Peak/Elevation
- Scenic View
- Snowfield
- Town
- Trail Arrows

Land Management

- National Forest Boundary
- Wilderness Boundary
- Regional Boundary

North-Central

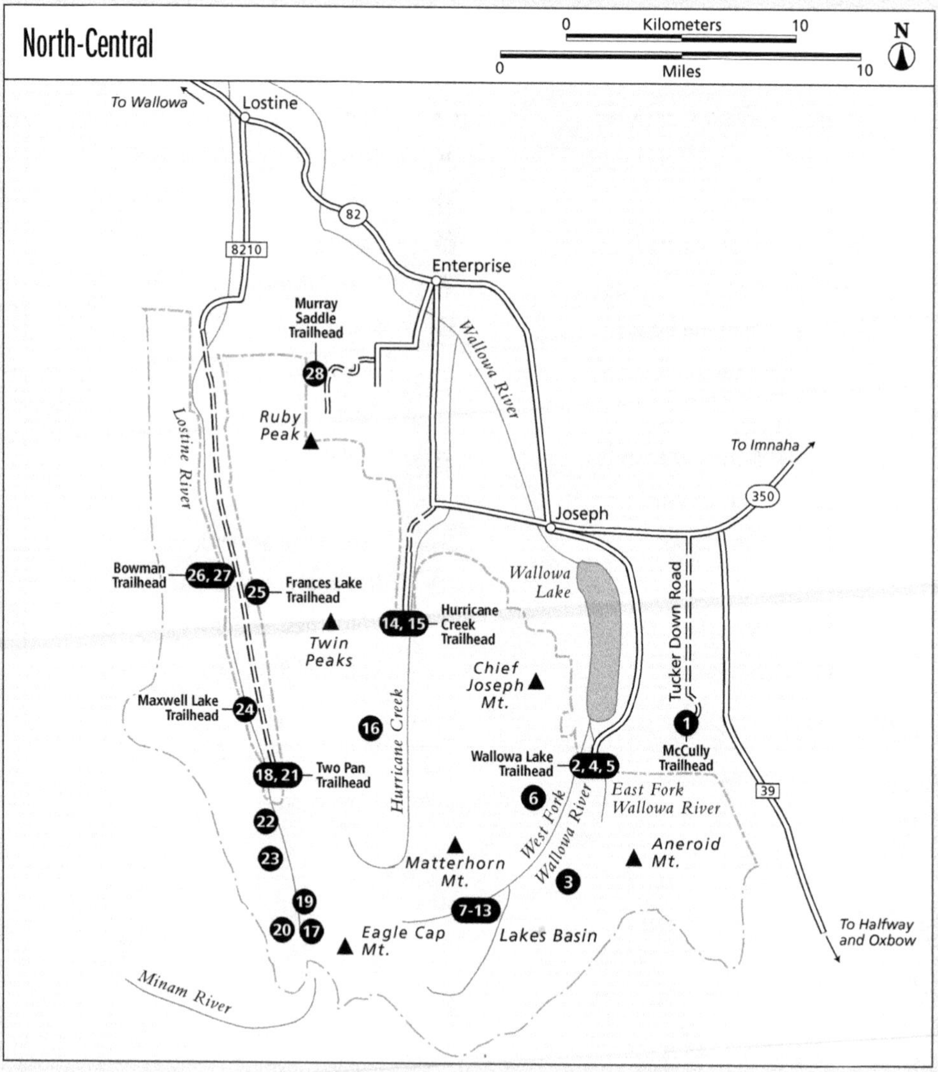

1 McCully Basin

Backpack through the subalpine country of the McCully Basin, then climb over an 8,700-foot-high pass with views in all directions before descending to a junction with the Tenderfoot Wagon Road Trail. (Trail 1812)

Distance: 10.5 miles one way to Tenderfoot Trail (1819); 11.5 miles for a shuttle hike to the Tenderfoot Trailhead
Hiking time: 4–7 hours
Difficulty: Moderate
Trail maintenance: Yearly
Best season: Mid-June through mid-Oct for hiking; Dec through Mar for skiing. Some avalanche danger in winter.
Traffic and other trail users: Light foot and horse traffic, except during Oct and Nov hunting seasons, when it may be heavier; light ski traffic in winter
Canine compatibility: Dogs permitted without leashes, but must be kept away from the stock of other parties
Fees and permits: Northwest Forest Pass and Eagle Cap Wilderness Permit
Maximum elevation: 8,700 feet
Maps: USGS Joseph OR and Aneroid Mountain OR; Geo Graphics Wallowa Mountains Eagle Cap Wilderness
Trail contact: USDA Forest Service Wallowa Mountains Office, 201 E 2nd St./ PO Box 905, Joseph, OR 97846; (541) 426-5546, (541) 426-4978; www.fs.usda.gov/wallowa-whitman

Finding the trailhead: Go east from Joseph for 5.5 miles on the Imnaha Highway and turn right on Tucker Down Road. Go 4.7 miles and turn right on FR 012. Drive 0.5 mile and turn right into McCully Trailhead parking lot. A gate blocks FR 012 next to the trailhead parking lot.
GPS: N45 16.631'/W117 08.173'

The Hike

The trail leaves the trailhead next to the restroom (5,700 ft.), but soon rejoins closed FR 012. Back on the roadbed, continue south for 0.8 mile to the Old McCully Trailhead, where the trail leaves the area that burned in 1988 in the Canal Fire. Be careful not to take the Mount Howard Trail, an unused jeep road that switches back to the right 0.5 mile after leaving the McCully Trailhead.

From the old trailhead (6,080 ft.), follow the trail south, passing the Eagle Cap Wilderness boundary (6,500 ft.) 2 miles from the trailhead. At 5.5 miles (7,600 ft.) the trail crosses McCully Creek and enters McCully Basin. At McCully Basin the character of the forest changes from the dense transition and Canadian zone forests to the more open subalpine type. This more open country affords inspiring views

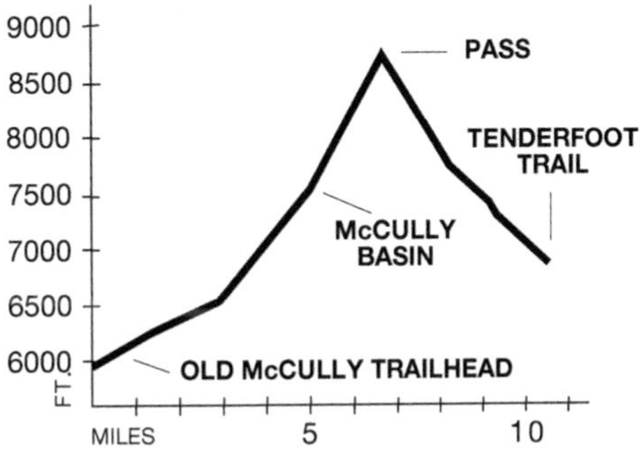

McCully Basin

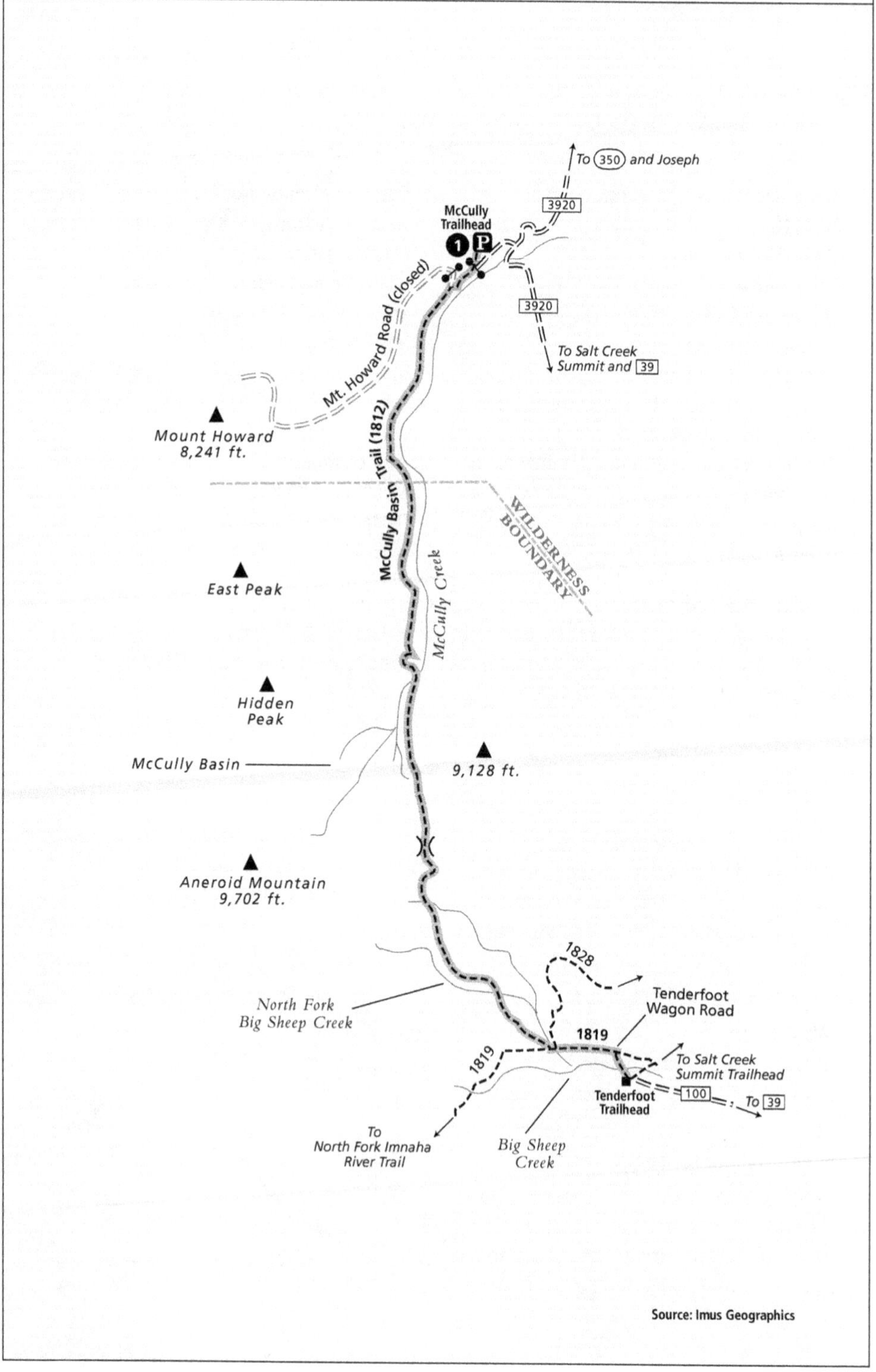

0 Kilometers 2
0 Miles 2
N
To 350 and Joseph
3920
McCully Trailhead
1
P
3920
To Salt Creek Summit and 39
Mt. Howard Road (closed)
Mount Howard 8,241 ft.
McCully Basin Trail (1812)
WILDERNESS BOUNDARY
East Peak
McCully Creek
Hidden Peak
McCully Basin
9,128 ft.
Aneroid Mountain 9,702 ft.
1828
Tenderfoot Wagon Road
North Fork Big Sheep Creek
1819
1819
To Salt Creek Summit Trailhead
Tenderfoot Trailhead
100
To 39
To North Fork Imnaha River Trail
Big Sheep Creek
Source: Imus Geographics

of the peaks that surround this lovely alpine basin. To the southwest is 9,702-foot-high Aneroid Mountain. The highest living tree in Oregon, a scruffy little whitebark pine, grows near the summit of this peak. East and Hidden Peaks are to the west of the basin, and Ferguson Ridge is to the east. McCully Basin is used as a base camp for telemark skiers in the winter.

Pass on the McCully Basin Trail.

From McCully Basin the trail continues south, climbing to the pass (8,700 ft.) dividing the McCully Creek drainage and the North Fork Big Sheep Creek drainage. South of the pass the trail switchbacks down into the basin at the head of the North Fork Big Sheep Creek. Here the trail becomes harder to see. Continue south, following the cairns. Cross a small rise and go along the left side of a meadow. At the south end of the meadow, 8.75 miles from McCully Trailhead, the trail turns left (7,770 ft.). Three-quarters of a mile farther along, the trail crosses a creek (7,240 ft.).

A short distance beyond the creek, the trail becomes difficult to see again. Go down the left side of a small open slope and find the trail again at the bottom of the opening (7,110 ft.). Descend another 0.75 mile to the southeast, to the junction with Tenderfoot Wagon Road (1819). This junction (6,770 ft.) is 10.5 miles from McCully Trailhead.

The last 3.5 miles of the McCully Basin Trail requires some route-finding skills to follow. If you want to leave the wilderness by a different route and have a car parked at Tenderfoot Trailhead, turn left at the junction with Tenderfoot Wagon Road and follow the old wagon road 1 mile to Tenderfoot Trailhead.

Miles and Directions

0.0 The trail begins at the New McCully Trailhead.

0.9 Reach the Old McCully Trailhead. (GPS: N45 16.190'/W117 08.675')

2.0 Enter the Eagle Cap Wilderness.

5.5 Cross McCully Creek.

7.0 Cross the pass into North Fork Big Sheep Creek drainage.

10.5 Arrive at the trail junction with Tenderfoot Wagon Road (1819). (GPS: N45 10.852'/W117 07.266')

2 East Fork Wallowa River

Three of the many options available on the East Fork Wallowa River Trail include a backpack to the alpine setting of the Tenderfoot Pass area, a 6-mile backpack to Aneroid Lake, with beautiful scenery and good brook trout fishing, or a long day hike to Aneroid Lake and back. (Trail 1804)

Distance: 8.5 miles one way to Tenderfoot Pass; 12 miles out and back (Aneroid Lake)
Hiking time: 4–5.5 hours to Tenderfoot Pass; 2-4 hours to Aneroid Lake, one way
Difficulty: Moderate
Trail maintenance: Yearly
Best season: July through Sept to Aneroid Lake; mid-July through Sept above Aneroid Lake; Jan through Apr for skiing. There is considerable avalanche danger on this trail in winter when snow conditions are right for it.
Traffic and other trail users: Heavy to Aneroid Lake; moderate past the lake. Heavy horse traffic to Aneroid Lake.
Canine compatibility: Dogs permitted without leashes, but must be kept away from the stock of other parties
Fees and permits: Eagle Cap Wilderness Permit. The trail crosses Pacific Power Company land at first, but soon enters Wallowa-Whitman National Forest. No special permission is necessary to cross this Pacific Power land on the trail.
Maximum elevation: 8,500 feet
Maps: USGS Joseph OR and Aneroid Mountain OR; Geo Graphics Wallowa Mountains Eagle Cap Wilderness
Trail contacts: USDA Forest Service Wallowa Mountains Office, 201 E 2nd St. / PO Box 905, Joseph, OR 97846; (541) 426-5546, (541) 426-4978; www.fs.usda.gov/wallowa-whitman. For winter use contact Wing Ridge Ski Tours, Enterprise, OR; (541) 398-1980, (888) 812-4707, ext. 3; www.facebook.com/Wing-Ridge-Ski-Tours-239313479446588/

Finding the trailhead: From Joseph take OR 351 for 7 miles south, passing Wallowa Lake, to the Wallowa Lake Trailhead (4,650 ft.).
GPS: N45 16.049' / W117 12.754'

The Hike

The trail leaves the trailhead parking area on the east side. It forks a few yards beyond the parking lot; take the left fork. A short distance up the trail a "cat road" turns off to the left. This road was built to facilitate the rebuilding of the dam, which is the intake for the powerhouse at the south end of the parking area. This road may be used as an alternate trail. If you use the cat road, be sure to turn right and cross a second bridge just below the metal gate a little more than 1 mile up the road. This will put you back on the main trail. Generally it is best to take the trail, because the road is much steeper.

The trail climbs for 2 miles to a dam (5,800 ft.). The pipe you may have noticed across the river as you were coming up the trail is the penstock that connects the dam and the powerhouse.

Meadow along the East Fork Wallowa River Trail. ▶

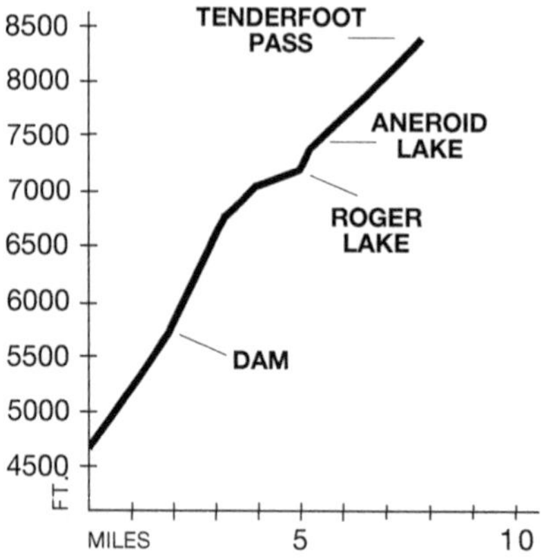

The Eagle Cap Wilderness boundary is 0.25 mile past the dam. The elevation at the wilderness boundary is 5,920 feet. Just before reaching the wilderness boundary sign, the unmarked route to Bonneville Mountain turns off to the right.

At 3.8 miles the trail crosses the East Fork Wallowa River on a bridge (6,900 ft.). A short distance above the bridge the trail divides. The trail to the right is usually used. The trail comes back together again in a short distance, at 7,120 feet. The unmarked climbing route to Aneroid Mountain turns off to the left 0.25 mile beyond the point where the trails come back together.

The trail climbs gently above this point, going through the timber on the east side of the lush meadows along the river. There are several beaver dams in the river as it flows through the meadows. The ponds behind these beaver dams have lots of small brook trout that can be easily caught on a worm or fly. The trail passes Roger Lake (7,420 ft.) at 5.5 miles. Aneroid Lake (7,500 ft.) is 0.5 mile past Roger Lake. There is a camping area at the north end of Aneroid Lake. A marked side trail leads to the campsites. Some cabins, which are not open to the public, are at the south end of the lake.

The trail passes Aneroid Lake on the left (east) side. It then climbs for 1 mile into an open meadow and to the junction with the Bonny Lakes Trail (1802; 7,820 ft.).

After passing the Bonny Lakes junction, the trail winds its way up mostly open slopes dotted with whitebark pines to Tenderfoot Pass. The pass (8,500 ft.) is 1.5 miles past the Bonny Lakes Trail junction. Jewett Lake (8,300 ft.) is to the right, about 0.5 mile off the trail a short distance below the pass.

At Tenderfoot Pass, East Fork Wallowa River Trail becomes North Fork Imnaha River Trail (1814). Return by the same trail, or use the North Fork Imnaha Trail, Polaris Pass Trail, and West Fork Wallowa River Trail for a loop trip over Polaris Pass and back to the Wallowa Lake Trailhead.

Miles and Directions

0.0 The trail begins at Wallowa Lake Trailhead.

2.0 Pass the dam on the river next to the trail. (GPS: N45 15.238'/W117 12.165')

2.2 Enter the Eagle Cap Wilderness.

3.8 Cross the East Fork Wallowa River on a bridge.

5.5 Pass Roger Lake.

6.0 Pass Aneroid Lake. This is the turnaround for a 12-mile day hike.

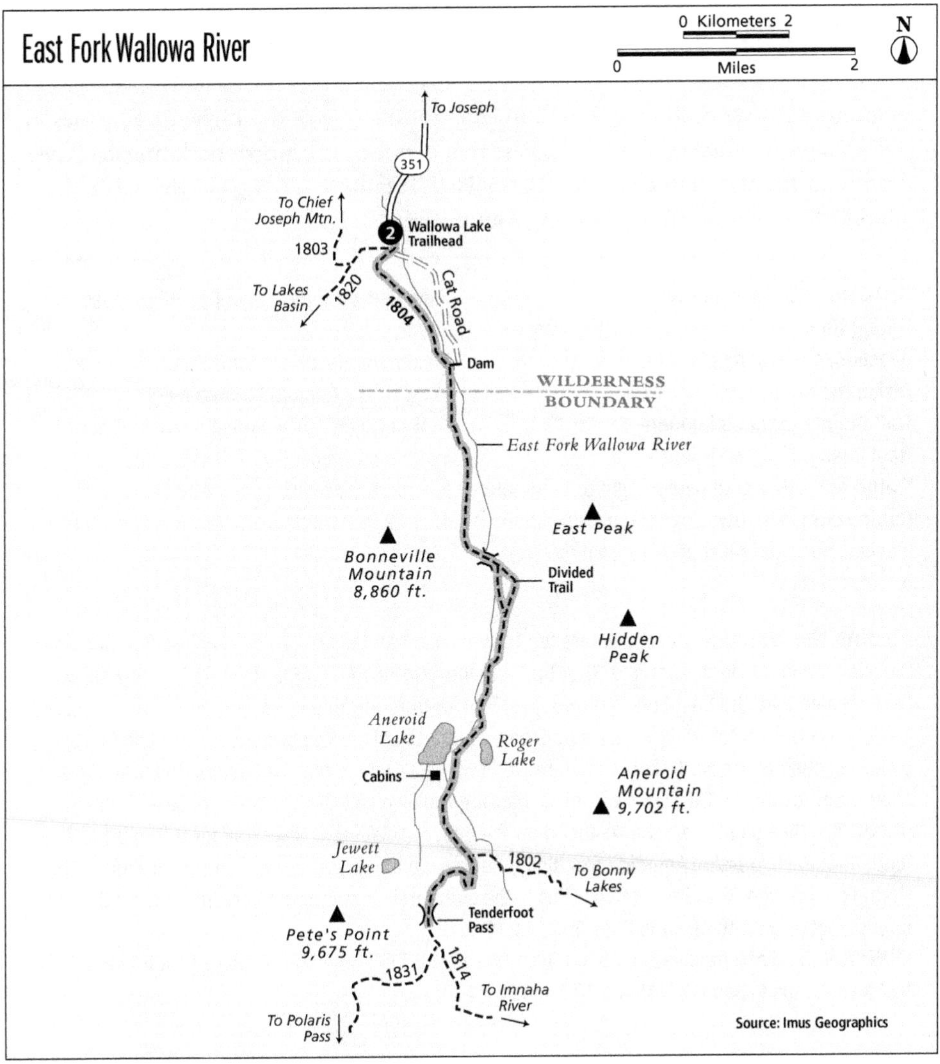

7.0 Reach the trail junction with Bonny Lakes Trail (1802). (GPS: N45 11.896'/W117 11.839')

8.5 Reach Tenderfoot Pass, where the trail becomes North Fork Imnaha River Trail (1814). (GPS: N45 11.387'/W117 12.316')

3 Polaris Pass

Beginning at over 8,000 feet elevation and crossing one of the highest trail passes in the Wallowa Mountains, the Polaris Pass Trail connects the North Fork Imnaha River Trail with the West Fork Wallowa River Trail. Fabulous views greet the hiker along almost every foot of this challenging route. (Trail 1831)

Distance: 7.5 miles one way
Hiking time: 3–4 hours in the east to west direction, more going the other way
Difficulty: Strenuous
Trail maintenance: Infrequent
Best season: Aug and Sept
Traffic and other trail users: Light to moderate
Canine compatibility: Dogs permitted without leashes, but must be kept away from the stock of other parties
Fees and permits: Eagle Cap Wilderness Permit
Maximum elevation: 8,890 feet
Map: USGS Aneroid Mountain OR
Trail contact: USDA Forest Service Wallowa Mountains Office, 201 E 2nd St./PO Box 905, Joseph, OR 97846; (541) 426-5546, (541) 426-4978; www.fs.usda.gov/wallowa-whitman

Finding the trail: The junction where the Polaris Pass Trail begins can be reached from Indian Crossing Trailhead via the Imnaha River Trail and the North Fork Imnaha River Trail, from Wallowa Lake Trailhead via the East Fork Wallowa River Trail, or from any one of several other trailheads. The easiest way is from the Wallowa Lake Trailhead via the East Fork Wallowa River Trail (1804) and a short section of the North Fork Imnaha River Trail (1814). To reach the junction this way, drive south from Joseph on OR 351 for 7 miles, passing Wallowa Lake, to the Wallowa Lake Trailhead (4,650 ft.). Hike south from the trailhead on the East Fork Wallowa River Trail for 8.5 miles to Tenderfoot Pass, passing Aneroid Lake along the way. Continue south from Tenderfoot Pass on the North Fork Imnaha River Trail (1814) (this is the same trail, just the number changes) for 0.3 mile to the junction with the Polaris Pass Trail (8,210 ft.).
GPS: Wallowa Lake Trailhead: N45 16.049'/W117 12.754'; junction of North Fork Imnaha River Trail and Polaris Pass Trail: N45 11.172'/W117 12.210'

The Hike

Polaris Pass Trail leaves North Fork Imnaha River Trail (1814) and heads southwest through open alpine terrain. It drops slightly at first, then climbs in an ascending traverse for nearly 2 miles. The trail switchbacks four times as it climbs the last 300 feet to Polaris Pass (8,890 ft.).

The view in all directions is spectacular from Polaris Pass. To the east, down the North Fork of the Imnaha River, the country is typical of the eastern Wallowas. The rock is dark brown and gray, not the lighter-colored granite and limestone you see looking west into the central part of the range. The country to the east is also far less rugged. A wide range of alpine flowers blooms in August above timberline near Polaris Pass. Some mountain goats can also be found in this area.

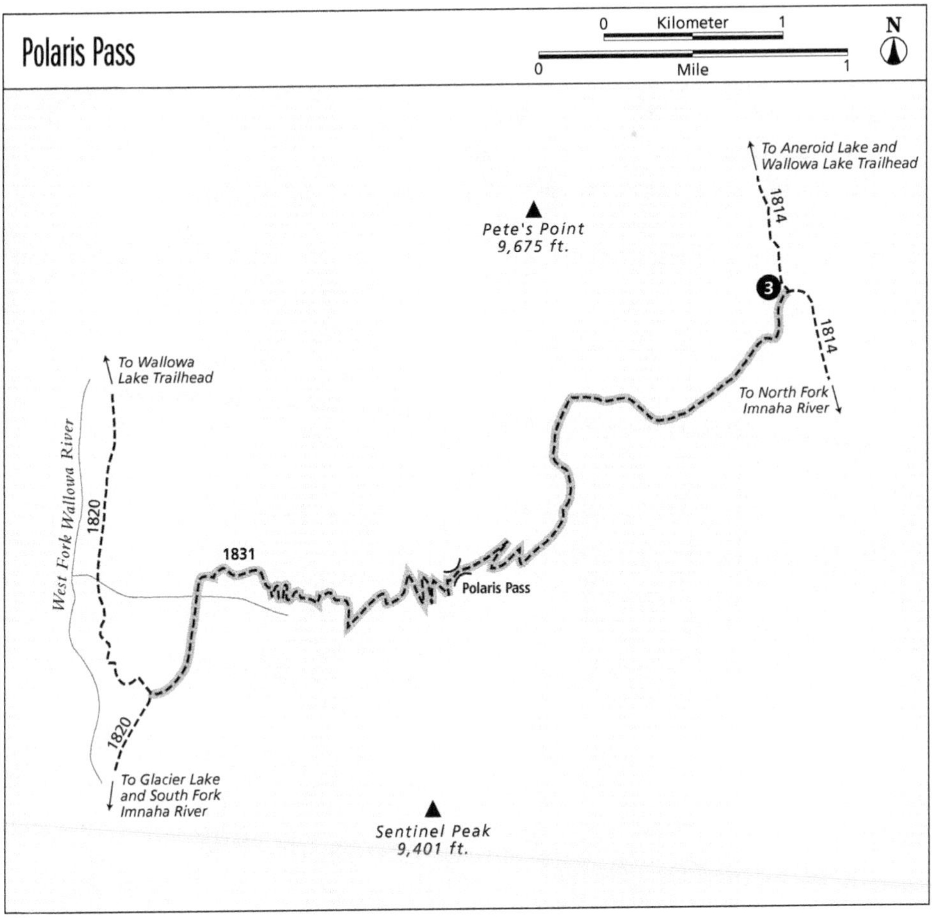

After crossing Polaris Pass the trail switchbacks continuously, first through open scree slopes, then through thickening timber. The trail drops steadily, losing more than 2,000 vertical feet in the 4.5 miles between Polaris Pass and the first creek crossing (6,810 ft.). Beyond the creek crossing the trail makes a descending traverse for 1 more mile to the junction with the West Fork Wallowa River Trail (1820). This junction, at 6,590 feet, is 7.5 miles from the North Fork Imnaha River Trail junction.

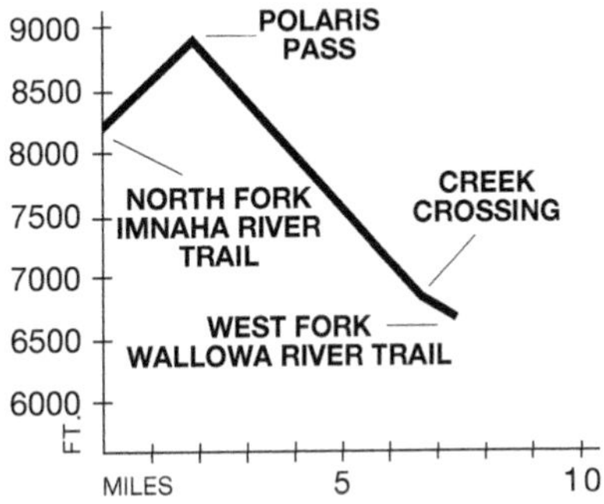

The upper part of Polaris Pass Trail is very dry in late summer. Water should be carried because it is hard to come by. Use caution on this trail in questionable weather; it can be very stormy near the top.

Miles and Directions

0.0 Begin at the junction with the North Fork Imnaha River Trail (1814).

2.0 Cross Polaris Pass. (GPS: N45 10.370'/W117 13.450')

6.5 Cross a creek.

7.5 The trail ends at the junction with the West Fork Wallowa River Trail (1820). (GPS: N45 10.093'/W117 14.625')

4 West Fork Wallowa River

Hike from Wallowa Lake Trailhead up the deep canyon that contains the West Fork of the Wallowa River, passing beneath spectacular cliffs before reaching the alpine setting of Glacier Lake. Glacier Lake is one of the most photographed lakes in the Wallowa Mountains. The first part of this trail may be used to reach Ice Lake, Lakes Basin, and Polaris Pass. (Trails 1820 and 1806)

Distance: 11.9 miles one way
Hiking time: 4.5–7 hours to Glacier Lake
Difficulty: Easy to Six Mile Meadow, moderate from there to Glacier Lake
Trail maintenance: Yearly
Best season: June through Oct to Six Mile Meadow; July through Sept to Glacier Lake
Traffic and other trail users: Very heavy foot traffic to Six Mile Meadow; heavy from there to Glacier Lake. Heavy horse traffic to Six Mile Meadow.
Canine compatibility: Dogs permitted without leashes, but must be kept away from the stock of other parties
Fees and permits: Eagle Cap Wilderness Permit. This trail goes through Pacific Power Company land at first. It also goes a short distance through Wallowa Lake State Park before reaching the national forest. No special permission is needed to cross these lands on the trail.
Maximum elevation: 8,166 feet
Maps: USGS Joseph OR, Aneroid Mountain OR, and Eagle Cap OR; Geo Graphics Wallowa Mountains Eagle Cap Wilderness
Trail contact: USDA Forest Service Wallowa Mountains Office, 201 E 2nd St./PO Box 905, Joseph, OR 97846; (541) 426-5546, (541) 426-4978; www.fs.usda.gov/wallowa-whitman

Finding the trailhead: From Joseph take OR 351 for 7 miles south, passing Wallowa Lake, to the Wallowa Lake Trailhead (4,650 ft.).
GPS: N45 16.049'/W117 12.754'

The Hike

The trail begins at Wallowa Lake Trailhead. This trail goes through Pacific Power Company land at first. It also goes a short distance through Wallowa Lake State Park before reaching the national forest. No special permission is needed to cross these lands on the trail.

To begin, go around the cable gate on the left side of the parking area. A short distance up the trail is a signboard with a trail map of the area (4,650 ft.). Take the trail to the right, signed West Fork Wallowa River Trail 1820.

The junction with Chief Joseph Mountain Trail (1803; 4,790 ft.) is at 0.3 mile. Bear left at this junction and follow the West Fork Trail south, passing Wallowa-Whitman National Forest and Eagle Cap Wilderness boundary signs. At 1.25 miles the trail goes through an area that was hit by an avalanche a few years ago. This area of broken and knocked-down trees shows the power of even a fairly small avalanche. The trail continues to climb gently, crossing a bridge at 2 miles (5,260 ft.). At 2.3 miles

(5,380 ft.) there is a switchback that allows the trail to climb to a better crossing of a side creek. One-quarter mile farther the trail is elevated slightly in a couple of places to make crossing a wet area easier. At 2.6 miles, Ice Lake Trail (1808) turns off to the right (5,530 ft.).

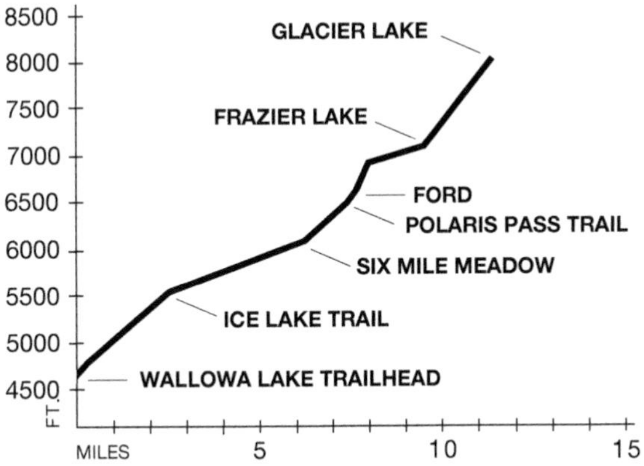

Beyond the Ice Lake junction, the trail gradually climbs for 3.3 miles to Six Mile Meadow (6,080 ft.). At Six Mile Meadow there is a trail junction with Trail 1810, which turns right and goes to the Lakes Basin. See the Lakes Basin (hike 7) entry. Six Mile Meadow used to be heavily used as a camping area, but now the meadow is closed to camping to allow it to repair itself from the damage caused by years of heavy use. Most of the West Fork Wallowa River is quite fast flowing, and hard to fish; however, here at Six Mile Meadows there are some slower areas in the river, and some good catches of brook trout can be had.

From Six Mile Meadow the West Fork Trail heads on up the West Fork Wallowa River. Soon it climbs some distance away from the river, up the east side of the canyon through thinning timber to the junction with Polaris Pass Trail (1831; 6,590 ft.). The Polaris Pass Trail junction is 7.8 miles from Wallowa Lake Trailhead.

A few feet past Polaris Pass Trail junction the trail crosses a creek. A quarter mile farther the West Fork Wallowa River flows through a short, steep canyon to the right of the trail; a waterfall is in the canyon. Hike 0.25 mile farther to where the trail fords the West Fork Wallowa River (6,900 ft.). This crossing can be hazardous during periods of high water. It is always a wet crossing.

The next 0.75 mile, from the ford to Frazier Lake, is one of the most spectacular parts of the West Fork Trail. There are huge limestone cliffs across the river to the east and south. These cliffs are overlaid with brown sedimentary rock. The trail and river canyon in this area make a curve to the right (west). When you get near Frazier Lake, a waterfall drops over the limestone cliffs.

Several good campsites are at Frazier Lake (7,127 ft.), and brook trout are here for the catching. Frazier Lake is also notorious for its mosquitoes. The trail goes around the right (north) side of the lake and climbs very slightly for 0.2 mile to the junction with South Fork Imnaha River Trail (1820; 7,140 ft.). The South Fork Imnaha River Trail turns to the left (southwest). After passing the junction, the West Fork Wallowa River Trail number changes to 1806. It climbs a couple of switchbacks, then heads northwest, staying well above the creekbed. The path continues to climb in an

◀ *West Fork Wallowa River.*

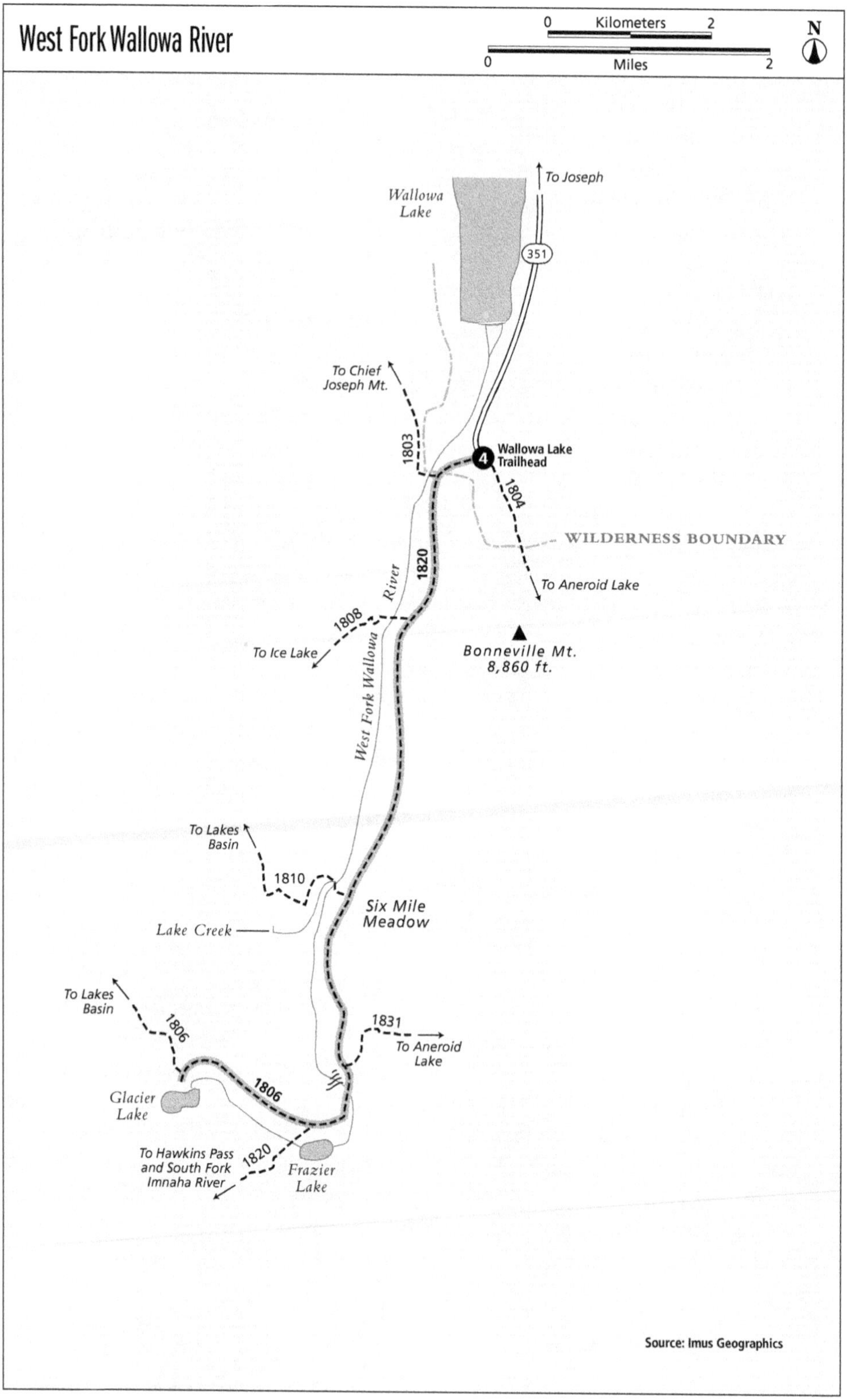
West Fork Wallowa River
0 Kilometers 2
0 Miles 2
N
To Joseph
Wallowa Lake
351
To Chief Joseph Mt.
1803
Wallowa Lake Trailhead
4
1804
WILDERNESS BOUNDARY
1820
River
To Aneroid Lake
1808
To Ice Lake
Bonneville Mt. 8,860 ft.
West Fork Wallowa
To Lakes Basin
1810
Six Mile Meadow
Lake Creek
To Lakes Basin
1806
1831
To Aneroid Lake
Glacier Lake
1806
To Hawkins Pass and South Fork Imnaha River
1820
Frazier Lake
Source: Imus Geographics

ascending traverse through thinning timber to Glacier Lake (8,166 ft.). Glacier Lake is 11.9 miles from Wallowa Lake Trailhead.

Glacier Lake is in a very picturesque alpine setting. It is one of the most photographed lakes in the Wallowas. The lake may be frozen over, at least partly, well into July. There are plenty of good campsites around the lake. Fishing for small brook trout is generally good in Glacier Lake. If you continue on past Glacier Lake, you'll reach Glacier Pass.

Miles and Directions

0.0 The trail begins at the Wallowa Lake Trailhead.

0.3 Pass the junction with Chief Joseph Mountain Trail (1803). (GPS: N45 15.972'/W117 12.988')

2.6 Pass the junction with Ice Lake Trail (1808). (GPS: N45 14.233'/W117 13.809')

6.0 Reach Six Mile Meadow and the junction with Lakes Basin Trail (1810). (GPS: N45 11.692'/W117 14.658')

7.8 Arrive at the junction with Polaris Pass Trail (1831). (GPS: N45 10.093'/W117 14.624'

8.3 The trail fords West Fork Wallowa River.

9.0 The trail passes Frazier Lake. (GPS: N45 09.300'/W117 15.310')

9.3 Pass the junction with Hawkins Pass Trail (1820). Go right on the trail to Glacier Lake (1806).

11.9 Arrive at Glacier Lake. (GPS: N45 09.795'/W117 17.030')

5 Chief Joseph Mountain

This trail leads from the Wallowa Lake Trailhead to the meadows at the base of the face of Chief Joseph Mountain. Chief Joseph Mountain Trail is used to access the First Chute climbing route on Chief Joseph Mountain. (Trail 1803)

Distance: 5 miles to the end of the fairly recently maintained portion of the trail; 7.3 to trail's end
Hiking time: 2–2.5 hours to the end of maintainance; 3–5 to the end of the trail
Difficulty: Moderate to the end of the maintained trail, strenuous past there
Trail maintenance: Yearly to B C Creek, rare past there
Best season: The first 5 miles are usually snow-free—or nearly so—from mid-Apr to mid-Nov. The upper 2.7 miles are best done July through mid-Oct.
Traffic and other trail users: Heavy foot and horse traffic up to the B C Creek crossing, 1 mile from the junction with the West Fork Wallowa River Trail, from June through Aug. Light foot traffic above that point.
Canine compatibility: Dogs permitted without leashes, but must be kept away from the stock of other parties
Fees and permits: Eagle Cap Wilderness Permit
Maximum elevation: 7,620 feet
Map: USGS Chief Joseph Mountain OR
Trail contact: USDA Forest Service Wallowa Mountains Office, 201 E 2nd St./ PO Box 905, Joseph, OR 97846; (541) 426-5546, (541) 426-4978; www.fs.usda.gov/wallowa-whitman

Finding the trailhead: From Joseph drive OR 351 for 7 miles south, passing Wallowa Lake, to the Wallowa Lake Trailhead (4,650 ft.).
GPS: Wallowa Lake Trailhead: N45 16.049'/W117 12.754'; Chief Joseph Mountain Trail junction: N45 16.005'/W117 12.988'

The Hike

Hike south from the trailhead on the West Fork Wallowa River Trail (1820) for 0.3 mile to the junction with the Chief Joseph Mountain Trail. Turn right off West Fork Wallowa River Trail onto the Chief Joseph Mountain Trail, then bear left. The trail to the extreme right goes a short distance to a viewpoint of the falls of the Wallowa River and returns to the parking area through the Pacific Power and Light campground.

Two-tenths of a mile after leaving the West Fork Wallowa River Trail, the Chief Joseph Mountain Trail crosses a bridge over the West Fork Wallowa River (4,770 ft.). Beyond the bridge the trail climbs some switchbacks, then heads north. Seven-tenths of a mile from the West Fork Trail, there is a viewpoint on the right with a good view of Wallowa Lake.

A break on Chief Joseph Mountain Trail. Ettore Negri photo

B C Creek is 0.3 mile beyond the viewpoint (5,030 ft.). The creek is a good turnaround point for less serious hikers. It forms an almost continuous waterfall as it plunges off the side of Chief Joseph Mountain.

Caution: This can be a very dangerous crossing. Don't even think of trying it before August. The water is cold and fast, the rocks in the bottom are very slippery, and there is a waterfall just below the trail. Plans to move another bridge here are in the works, but the timing—and if it will happen at all—are unsure at this time. See the optional route below to access the upper portion of the Chief Joseph Mountain Trail when this crossing is too difficult.

The trail switches back to the south 3.4 miles from the West Fork Trail junction. After a mile or so heading south, into and out of side draws, the route enters a semi-open slope of sagebrush and scattered trees. The trail crosses the open slope to another switchback at 4.7 miles (6,350 ft.). The First Chute climbing route to the summit of Chief Joseph Mountain leaves the trail at this point. These open slopes become a flower garden in late June. The principal flowers are arrowleaf balsamroot and lupine, but there are many other types.

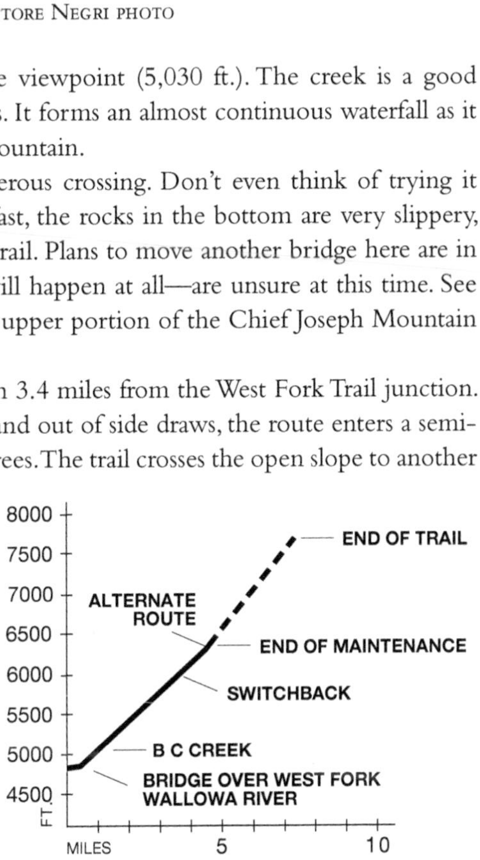

Make the switchback and climb gently, crossing the open slope again, then reenter the timber at the

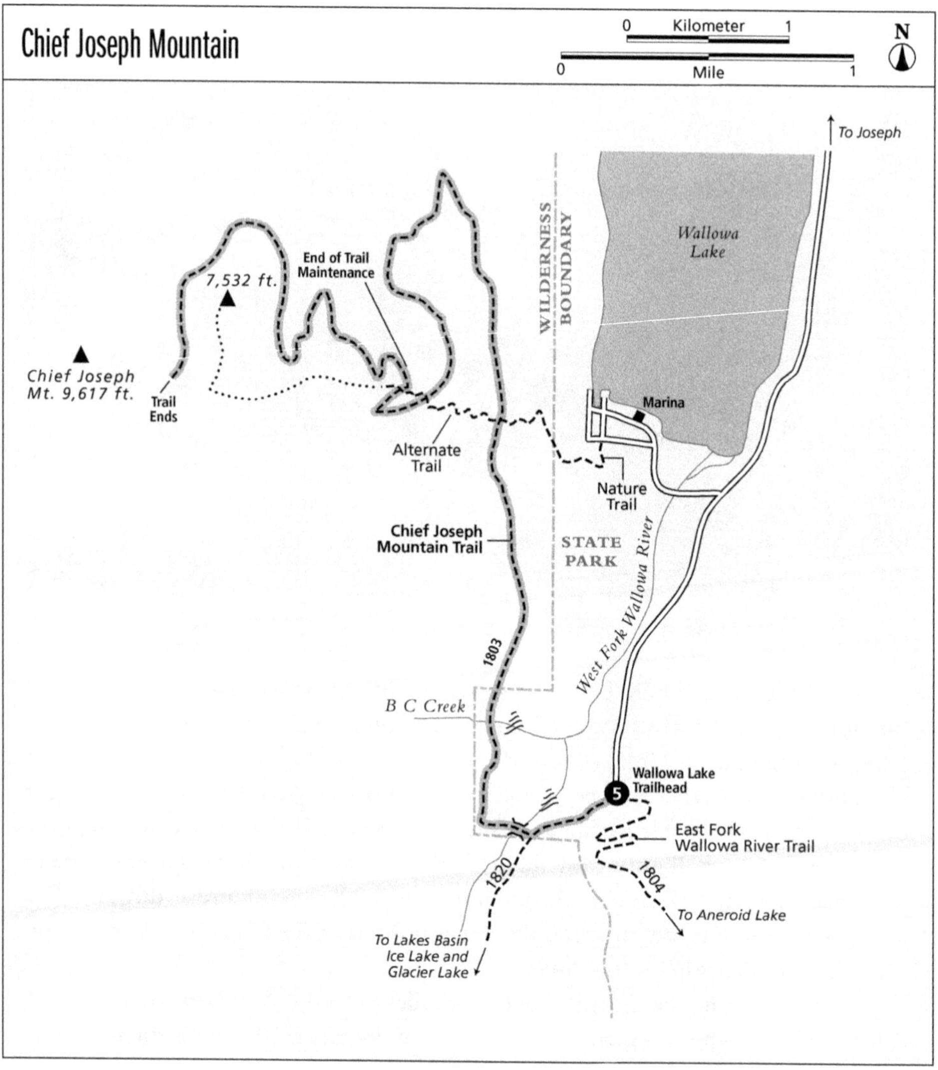

ridgetop (6,450 ft.). Trail maintenance ends a short distance into the timber. From here on the trail is choked with blown-down timber in the treed areas. In places the blowdown makes it very difficult to follow the route. If you wish to climb higher without fighting your way through the blowdowns, a cross-country route follows the ridgeline, just before you enter the timber,

Continuing through the timber, at 6 miles (6,950 ft.) the trail enters another open hillside. It continues to climb gently, reentering the timber at 7,220 feet elevation. The trail then climbs through thinning alpine timber to a point at the base of Chief Joseph Mountain. Here it ends at 7,620 feet, 7.3 miles from the Wallowa Lake Trailhead. This is a beautiful place to camp and admire the view, or to make a base camp for climbing Chief Joseph Mountain. Lack of water is a problem. If the snow is all melted, there may be no water close by. The return trip to Wallowa Lake Trailhead is made by retracing the same route; no loop trips are possible without bushwhacking.

A short climb (150 yards) to the right (west) from the end of the trail brings you to the top of a point. This point is marked with a rock pile and a wooden cross. From this point (7,650 ft.) there is an excellent view of the face of Chief Joseph Mountain, the surrounding alpine country, and the Wallowa Valley. Look for mountain goats high on the cliffs above. There are also mule deer (some very large bucks) and a few elk in this area. There is occasional rockfall off the face of Chief Joseph Mountain, so it is best not too camp to close. The view is better a little farther back, anyway.

Miles and Directions

0.0 Begin at the Wallowa Lake Trailhead.

0.3 At the junction with West Fork Wallowa River Trail (1820), turn right onto the Chief Joseph Mountain Trail.

0.5 Cross the bridge over the West Fork Wallowa River.

1.5 Ford B C Creek. (GPS: N45 16.179'/W117 13.331')

3.7 The trail switches back to the south.

4.7 The trail switches back in an open area.

5.0 Reach the end of trail maintenance.

7.3 Arrive at the end of the trail at the base of the cliffs on Chief Joseph Mountain.

Option: You can follow an alternate route to the upper portion of the Chief Joseph Mountain Trail that starts from the large parking area next to the marina at the head of Wallowa Lake. From the southwest corner of the parking area, take the Nature Trail south for slightly more than 0.1 mile (205 yards) to a junction. Get your wilderness permit at the reader board, then turn right and climb to the west (GPS: N45 16.977'/W117 12.897'). The trail climbs very steeply for about 1 mile, gaining nearly 900 feet of elevation, to meet the Chief Joseph Mountain Trail (GPS: N45 17.006'/W117 13.301'). You reach the Chief Joseph Mountain Trail approximately 1.2 miles north of (above) the B C Creek crossing. Turn right on the Chief Joseph Mountain to continue to the beautiful sloping meadows and the end of the maintained trail. This route should be used through midsummer when the crossing of B C Creek is dangerous.

6 Ice Lake

Ice Lake is the normal base camp for parties climbing the Matterhorn. Ice Lake is often seen in photographs because it is one of the most beautiful lakes in the Wallowa Mountains. The fishing can also be very good for 10- to 12-inch brook trout. (Trail 1808)

Distance: 7.7 miles one way from the Wallowa Lake Trailhead; 5.1 miles one way (backpack or day hike) from West Fork Wallowa River Trail to Ice Lake
Hiking time: 2–3 hours from the West Fork Wallowa River Trail; 3–4 hours from Wallowa Lake Trailhead
Difficulty: Moderate
Trail maintenance: Yearly
Best season: July through Sept
Traffic and other trail users: Heavy foot and horse traffic
Canine compatibility: Dogs permitted without leashes, but must be kept away from the stock of other parties
Fees and permits: Eagle Cap Wilderness Permit
Maximum elevation: 7,850 feet
Maps: USGS Aneroid Mountain OR and Eagle Cap OR; Geo Graphics Wallowa Mountains Eagle Cap Wilderness
Trail contact: USDA Forest Service Wallowa Mountains Office, 201 E 2nd St./PO Box 905, Joseph, OR 97846; (541) 426-5546, (541) 426-4978; www.fs.usda.gov/wallowa-whitman

Finding the trailhead: Drive south from Joseph on OR 351 for 7 miles, passing Wallowa Lake, to the Wallowa Lake Trailhead (4,650 ft.).
GPS: Wallowa Lake Trailhead: N45 16.049'/W117 12.754'; Ice Lake Trail junction: N45 14.224'/W117 13.809'

The Hike

The trail begins at Wallowa Lake Trailhead, first passing through Pacific Power Company land. It also goes a short distance through Wallowa Lake State Park before reaching the national forest. No special permission is needed to cross these lands on the trail.

Ice Lake Trail (1808) turns right (west) off the West Fork Wallowa River Trail (1820) 2.6 miles south of the trailhead (5,530 ft.) and soon crosses the West Fork Wallowa River. The trail then begins climbing in gentle but steady switchbacks through fairly open slopes studded with Indian paintbrush. At 1.3 miles (6,150 ft.) the trail approaches Adam Creek, which is more like a waterfall than a creek at this point. At 2.25 miles from the West Fork Trail junction (6,550 ft.), the trail overlooks a gorge with Adam Creek rushing through it. There are falls at the upper end of the gorge. From here the upper falls of Adam Creek can be seen in the distance. One-quarter mile farther (6,730 ft.), a side stream crosses the trail. The steep gray and brown slopes

Ice Lake. GARY FLETCHER PHOTO

of Hurwal Divide are above and to the right. After another 0.25 mile the trail comes into a semi-open basin with a good campsite on the right side of the trail (6,800 ft.).

A few yards past the campsite, the trail crosses a small stream and climbs another series of switchbacks to the junction with the trail that circles Ice Lake (7,844 ft.). This junction is 5.1 miles from the West Fork Trail. A bridge crosses Adam Creek a few yards to the left on the trail around the lake.

Good campsites are available at Ice Lake, but before camping here you should check forest service regulations. There may be areas closed to camping. Firewood is somewhat scarce, and fires may be prohibited. This alpine area is not the place to have campfires anyway. This is a high-use area, so please take care not to damage it further.

The view from anywhere around the lake is spectacular. Flowers start to bloom as soon as the snow leaves (late June). Mule deer are common. Mountain goats and bighorn sheep may sometimes be seen from Ice Lake, usually on the ridges to the north. Ice Lake is the normal base camp for climbing the Matterhorn, Sacajawea Peak, Hurwal Divide, and Craig Mountain. Fishing for brook trout is very good in Ice Lake.

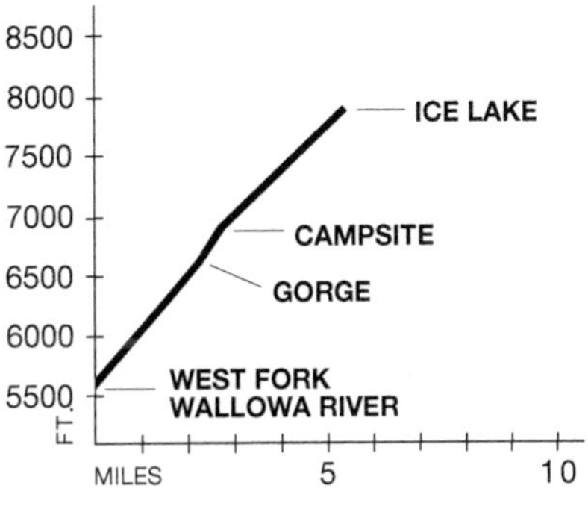

From Ice Lake, a route is possible over the high pass (8,900 ft.) to the south, via Razz

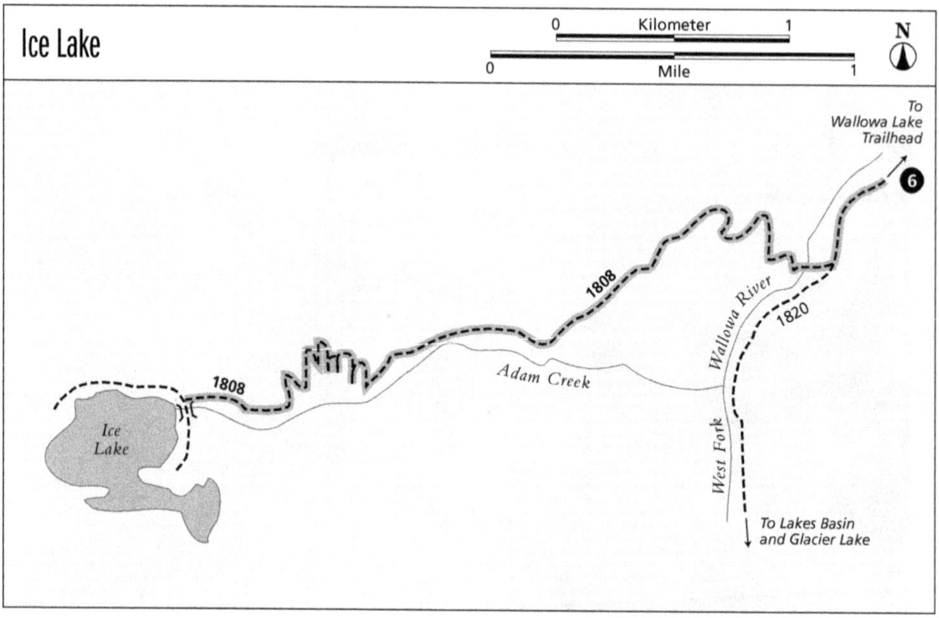

Lake, to the Lakes Basin. This route involves some skill in route-finding and some rough scrambling. It should be led only by experienced hikers or mountain climbers.

Option: By using this rough cross-country route to Razz Lake, a loop trip can be made through the Lakes Basin and back down to the West Fork Wallowa River Trail to Six Mile Meadow, then on down the West Fork Wallowa River Trail to Wallowa Lake Trailhead.

Miles and Directions

0.0 West Fork Wallowa River Trail (1820) begins at the Wallowa Lake Trailhead.

0.3 Pass the junction with Chief Joseph Mountain Trail (1803). (GPS: N45 15.972'/W117 12.988')

2.6 Turn west (right) at the junction with Ice Lake Trail (1808). (GPS: N45 14.233'/ W117 13.809')

2.7 Cross the West Fork Wallowa River.

3.9 The trail approaches Adam Creek.

4.9 The trail overlooks the Adam Creek gorge.

5.1 The trail crosses a stream.

5.3 Reach a campsite on the right of the trail.

7.7 Arrive at the junction with the around-the-lake trail at Ice Lake. (GPS: N45 13.883'/W117 16.195')

7 Lakes Basin

Backpack from Six Mile Meadow into the Lakes Basin, an area studded with subalpine lakes. This trail is one of the main access routes to the popular Lakes Basin area. Take the time to camp for a few nights and explore one or more of the side routes that start here. (Trail 1810)

Distance: 5.9 miles one way (backpack) from West Fork Wallowa River Trail (1820) to Hurricane Creek Trail (1807); 11.9 miles one way from Wallowa Lake Trailhead to the junction with Hurricane Creek Trail
Hiking time: 2–4 hours from West Fork Wallowa River Trail; 4–6 hours from Wallowa Lake Trailhead
Difficulty: Moderate
Trail maintenance: Yearly
Best season: Late June through Sept
Traffic and other trail users: Very heavy foot and horse traffic
Canine compatibility: Dogs permitted without leashes, but must be kept away from the stock of other parties
Fees and permits: Eagle Cap Wilderness Permit
Maximum elevation: 7,690 feet
Maps: USGS Aneroid Mountain OR and Eagle Cap OR; Geo Graphics Wallowa Mountains Eagle Cap Wilderness
Trail contact: USDA Forest Service Wallowa Mountains Office, 201 E 2nd St./PO Box 905, Joseph, OR 97846; (541) 426-5546, (541) 426-4978; www.fs.usda.gov/wallowa-whitman

Finding the trail: From Joseph take OR 351 for 7 miles south, passing Wallowa Lake, to the Wallowa Lake Trailhead. From Wallowa Lake Trailhead hike 6 miles south on West Fork Wallowa River Trail (1820) to Six Mile Meadow and the junction with the Lakes Basin Trail.
GPS: Wallowa Lake Trailhead: N45 16.049'/W117 12.754'; Lakes Basin Trail junction: N45 11.692'/W117 14.658'

The Hike

Lakes Basin Trail turns right (west) off the West Fork Wallowa River Trail (1820). A quarter mile from the junction it crosses the West Fork Wallowa River on a large log. There is a good campsite on the right just before crossing the river. Camping in Six Mile Meadow is prohibited, so please camp back in the trees.

After crossing the West Fork, the trail soon crosses Lake Creek. After this crossing, the trail heads up Lake Creek for a short distance. It then begins the switchbacks heading up to Horseshoe Lake. The trail climbs steadily for 2.75 miles, then flattens out on top of some huge flat rock outcroppings. One-quarter mile farther is the junction with Lee, Lily, Horseshoe Lakes Trail (1821) and Horseshoe Lake (7,133 ft.). Horseshoe Lake is 3 miles from the West Fork Trail. Fishing for small brook trout is generally excellent in Horseshoe Lake. Small flies and rooster tails attract the fish, as do regular old worms.

Crescent Lake.

At the junction, the main trail bears to the right (northwest). The unmarked route to Unit Lake heads to the right, up a small gully, 150 yards past the junction. After passing the junction, the trail climbs gradually for 0.5 mile to a creek crossing. A few feet before the crossing is the unmarked spot where the route to Razz Lake takes off to the right. See Razz Lake Route (hike 9). The elevation at this turnoff is 7,240 feet.

The trail continues to climb gradually 0.5 mile more to the junction with Lee, Lily, Horseshoe Lakes Trail. The junction with Trail 1810A (7,300 ft.) is 0.5 mile farther. Trail 1810A goes to Moccasin and Mirror Lakes. A path goes straight ahead a few yards to the east end of Douglas Lake.

At this junction, Trail 1810 turns to the right (west) and heads for Crescent Lake and Hurricane Creek Trail. Go right and climb slightly for 0.5 mile to a creek crossing at the outlet of Crescent Lake (7,350 ft.). There are good campsites on the west side of Crescent Lake. Beyond Crescent Lake the trail continues to climb, with some switchbacks, for 0.9 mile to the junction with Hurricane Creek Trail (1807; 7,690 ft.). See Hurricane Creek (hike 14). The junction with Hurricane Creek Trail is 5.9 miles from the West Fork Wallowa River Trail junction.

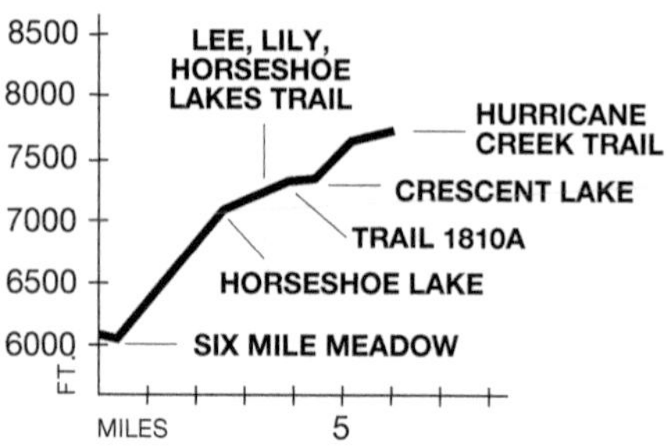

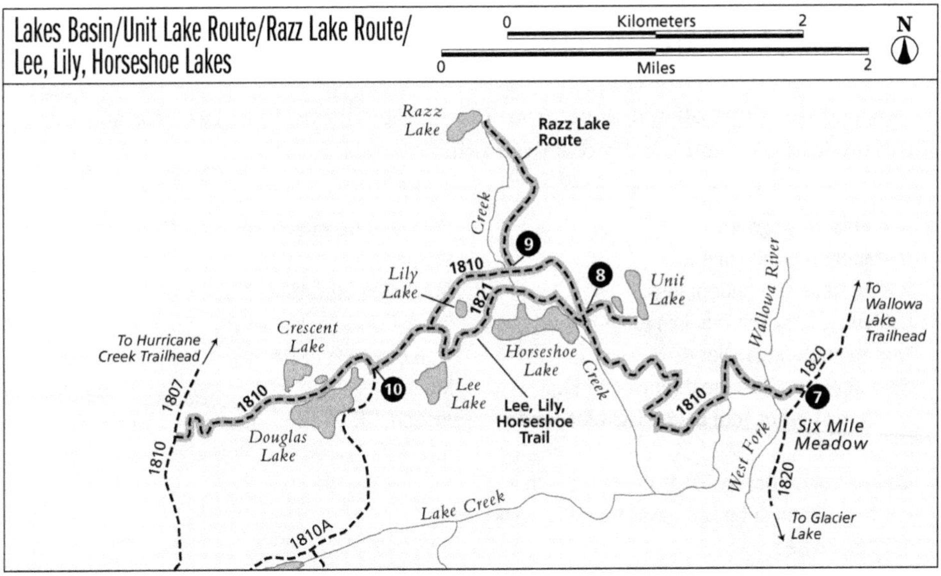

Hurwal Divide ends in spectacular cliffs to the north of Crescent Lake. Just before you reach Hurricane Creek Trail junction, the bright white limestone peak of the Matterhorn can be seen to the north.

All the lakes in the Lakes Basin have good fishing, and there are campsites scattered throughout the area. Mule deer are common, and a few bears inhabit the Lakes Basin. Usually bears are not a problem, but it doesn't hurt to hang your food and keep a clean camp. This is an extremely popular area, so you may not be alone at any of the lakes in July or August.

Miles and Directions

0.0 Start at the trail junction with the West Fork Wallowa River Trail (1820). Go right (west) on the Lakes Basin Trail (1810).

0.2 Cross the West Fork Wallowa River.

3.0 Reach Horseshoe Lake and the trail junction with Lee, Lily, Horseshoe Lakes Trail (1821).

3.5 Make a creek crossing and pass the Razz Lake route junction. (GPS: N45 12.190'/W117 16.390')

4.0 Pass the junction with the Lee, Lily, Horseshoe Lakes Trail.

4.5 Pass the trail junction with the Lakes Basin Alternate and Douglas Lake.

5.0 The trail passes Crescent Lake.

5.9 Arrive at the trail junction with Hurricane Creek Trail. (GPS: N45 11.554'/W117 18.350')

8 Unit Lake Route

Descend this short off-trail route from Horseshoe Lake to Unit Lake, for an out of the way campsite and good brook trout fishing.

See map on page 45.
Distance: 0.5 mile one way
Hiking time: 0.5 hour or less
Difficulty: Easy, but requires route-finding skills
Trail maintenance: None
Best season: Mid-June through mid-Sept
Traffic and other trail users: Light foot and horse traffic
Canine compatibility: Dogs permitted without leashes, but must be kept away from the stock of other parties
Fees and permits: Eagle Cap Wilderness Permit
Maximum elevation: 7,330 feet
Map: USGS Eagle Cap OR
Trail contact: USDA Forest Service Wallowa Mountains Office, 201 E 2nd St./PO Box 905, Joseph, OR 97846; (541) 426-5546, (541) 426-4978; www.fs.usda.gov/wallowa-whitman

Finding the trail: From Joseph take OR 351 for 7 miles south, passing Wallowa Lake, to the Wallowa Lake Trailhead. From Wallowa Lake Trailhead hike 6 miles south on West Fork Wallowa River Trail (1820) to Six Mile Meadow and the junction with the Lakes Basin Trail. Turn right and hike west on the Lakes Basin Trail for 3 miles to the junction with the Lee, Lily, Horseshoe Lakes Trail, near Horseshoe Lake. From the junction walk 150 yards north-northwest along the Lakes Basin Trail, to where the obscure route to Unit Lake leaves the trail.
GPS: Wallowa Lake Trailhead: N45 16.049'/W117 12.754'; Unit Lake route junction: N45 11.997'/W117 15.998'

The Hike

The route, which is a path up a small gully, heads to the right (northeast) from the Lakes Basin Trail (1810) and climbs for 200 yards. Here the path flattens out (7,330 ft.) and begins to drop down to the east. Do not drop down; turn left (north) off the path in the flat area. Climb over a small rocky rise and drop into the next gully to the north. Turn right (east) and do a descending traverse to the east, passing a pond. Beyond the pond, continue to descend to the east-northeast to Unit Lake (7,007 ft.). Both the pond and Unit Lake can be seen from the top of the rocky rise.

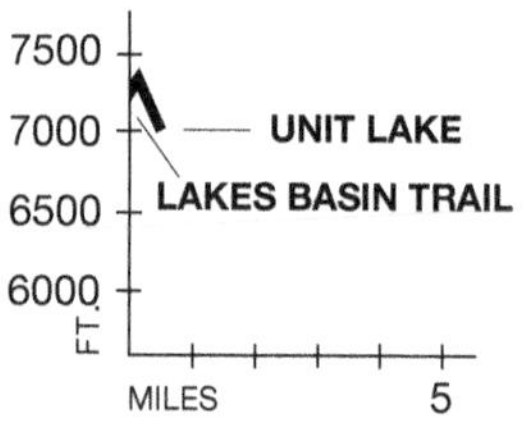

Unit Lake is the lowest lake in the Lakes Basin area. It is surrounded by thicker and larger timber than the other lakes in the area. The fishing is good for brook trout. There is plenty of firewood around Unit Lake, and it is in a more protected area than the other lakes. It is also lightly used.

Unit Lake. LOWELL EUHUS PHOTO

Unit Lake is only 0.5 mile off the main trail, and the elevation gain and loss are only a couple hundred feet; however, some route finding is required to locate it.

Miles and Directions

0.0 At the trail junction with Lakes Basin Trail (1810) near Horseshoe Lake, turn right on the path in the gully.

0.5 Arrive at Unit Lake. (GPS: N45 12.030'/W117 15.605')

9 Razz Lake Route

A steep, off-trail route climbs from the Lakes Basin to subalpine setting of Razz Lake.

See map page 45.
Distance: 1.5 miles one way
Hiking time: 1–1.5 hours
Difficulty: Strenuous
Trail maintenance: None
Best season: Late July through Sept
Traffic and other trail users: Light foot traffic
Canine compatibility: Dogs permitted without leashes, but must be kept away from the stock of other parties
Fees and permits: Eagle Cap Wilderness Permit
Maximum elevation: 8,103 feet
Map: USGS Eagle Cap OR
Trail contact: USDA Forest Service Wallowa Mountains Office, 201 E 2nd St./ PO Box 905, Joseph, OR 97846; (541) 426-5546, (541) 426-4978; www.fs.usda.gov/wallowa-whitman

Finding the trail: The Lakes Basin and Razz Lake can be reached from any one of several trailheads. The East Fork Lostine River Trail (1662) from Two Pan Trailhead and Hurricane Creek Trail (1807) from Hurricane Creek Trailhead offer fairly direct routes. The best way to reach the point in the Lakes Basin where the Razz Lake route begins is to drive south from Joseph, on OR 351 for 7 miles, passing Wallowa Lake, to the Wallowa Lake Trailhead. From Wallowa Lake Trailhead hike 6 miles south on West Fork Wallowa River Trail (1820) to Six Mile Meadow and the junction with the Lakes Basin Trail (1810). Turn right at the junction and climb west on the Lakes Basin Trail for 3.5 miles to the point where the route to Razz Lake leaves Lakes Basin Trail. This spot is 0.5 mile west of Lee, Lily, Horseshoe Lakes Trail junction (7,240 ft.). The point where the route leaves the trail is unmarked, but it can be found by going to the first main stream crossing, then backtracking (east) a few feet. At some times of the year there may be one or more very small streams, a foot or less wide, before reaching this point. The main stream is 5 to 10 feet wide.
GPS: Wallowa Lake Trailhead: N45 16.049'/W117 12.754'; Razz Lake route junction: N45 12.157'/W117 16.399'

The Hike

Turn right (north) off Lakes Basin Trail (1810) and follow a faint, steep uphill path. Stay 100 to 200 feet to the right (east) of the creek and work your way up through some rock outcroppings. At 7,500 feet, the route is the farthest away from the creek (to the east) that it gets. Continue to stay to the east of the creek, which is the outlet of Razz Lake, until you reach the lake (8,103 ft.).

The route to Razz Lake is fairly steep and requires some route finding. The total distance from the Lakes Basin Trail is 1.5 miles, and the elevation gain is 863 feet. Campsites around the lake are limited. Fishing is good most of the time, but the lake may be ice-covered until late July. Golden trout were stocked here at one time.

There is a scrambling route north from Razz Lake to Ice Lake. This route is short (1.5 miles) but is very steep and somewhat unstable. It should only be attempted by experienced mountaineers.

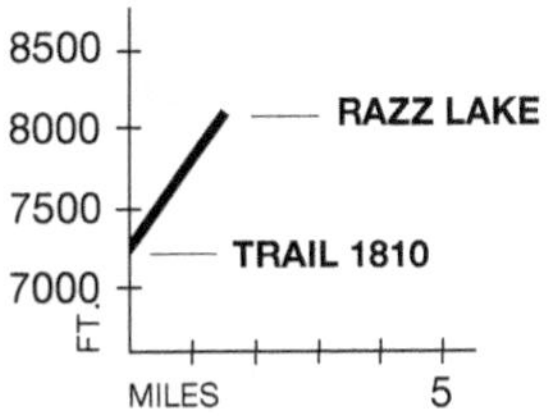

Above Razz Lake, 0.5 mile to the west, is a small, unnamed lake. To get to this higher lake, follow the stream (not the dry streambed) that flows into the west end of Razz Lake, heading up and to the west. The stream has some small ponds in it. Continue past them to the lake (8,450 ft.).

This small lake is partially surrounded by cliffs. The area around this lake is very alpine, with only a few small trees. It makes a good out-of-the-way campsite for those of us who like such places. There are probably no fish in this lake, which may be ice-covered until early August. This is big mule deer buck country, and there are mountain goats in the area, so keep your eyes open.

Miles and Directions

0.0 From the Lakes Basin Trail 1810, turn onto the Razz Lake route.

1.5 Reach Razz Lake. (GPS: N45 12.782'/W117 16.505')

10 Lee, Lily, Horseshoe Lakes

This short connecting trail links a series of lakes in the lower Lakes Basin. The Lee, Lily, Horseshoe Lakes Trail is a scenic alternate to the Lakes Basin Trail in this area and has several campsites close to it, which this section of the Lakes Basin Trail lacks. Hiking this route in the direction described below and returning on the Lakes Basin Trail makes a loop trip from Horseshoe Lake. (Trail 1821)

See map page 45.
Distance: 1.2 miles one way
Hiking time: 0.5–1 hour
Difficulty: Easy
Trail maintenance: Yearly
Best season: Late June through Sept
Traffic and other trail users: Heavy foot and horse traffic
Canine compatibility: Dogs permitted without leashes, but must be kept away from the stock of other parties
Fees and permits: Eagle Cap Wilderness Permit
Maximum elevation: 7,300 feet
Map: USGS Eagle Cap OR
Trail contact: USDA Forest Service Wallowa Mountains Office, 201 E 2nd St./ PO Box 905, Joseph, OR 97846; (541) 426-5546, (541) 426-4978; www.fs.usda.gov/wallowa-whitman

Finding the trail: Hurricane Creek Trail (1807) from Hurricane Creek Trailhead and the East Fork Lostine River Trail (1662) from Two Pan Trailhead offer fairly direct routes into the Lakes Basin and to the junction where the Lee, Lily, Horseshoe Lakes Trail begins. The best way to reach this junction is via the West Fork Wallowa River Trail (1820) from Wallowa Lake Trailhead. Drive south from Joseph on OR 351 for 7 miles, passing Wallowa Lake, to the Wallowa Lake Trailhead. From Wallowa Lake Trailhead hike 6 miles south on the West Fork Wallowa River Trail to the junction with the Lakes Basin Trail (1810) at Six Mile Meadow. Turn right and follow the Lakes Basin Trail for 4 miles to the second junction with the Lee, Lily, Horseshoe Lakes Trail. Lee, Lily, Horseshoe Lakes Trail leaves the Lakes Basin Trail 0.5 mile northeast of Douglas Lake (before reaching) and rejoins Lakes Basin Trail at Horseshoe Lake. The elevation at the trail junction is approximately 7,300 feet.
GPS: Wallowa Lake Trailhead: N45 16.049'/W117 12.754'; junction with Lakes Basin Trail, 0.5 mile from Douglas Lake: N45 11.965'/W117 16.823'

The Hike

At the western junction of Lakes Basin Trail (1810) and Lee, Lily, Horseshoe Lakes Trail (1821), turn left (southeast) off Lakes Basin Trail and descend 0.5 mile to Lee Lake (7,145 ft.).

There are several campsites at Lee Lake. The north shore of the lake drops off very abruptly. This should be a good spot to try for the many fish in Lee Lake; however, it could also be quite dangerous, especially for young children, because the bottom of the lake drops very quickly into deep water.

After leaving Lee Lake, the trail heads east-northeast. It passes a few hundred feet south of Lily Lake and reaches Horseshoe Lake in 0.5 mile. Just before Horseshoe Lake there is an excellent campsite by a stream, the outlet from Razz Lake.

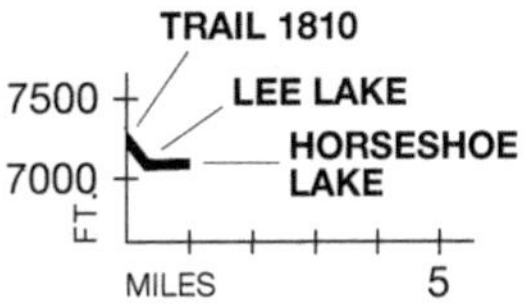

A path completely encircles Horseshoe Lake. Trail 1821 follows the north shore and rejoins Lakes Basin Trail 1810 at the east end of the lake. For more information see Lakes Basin (hike 7).

Miles and Directions

0.0 Start at the trail junction with Lakes Basin Trail (1810) near Douglas Lake.

0.5 Arrive at Lee Lake.

0.8 Pass Lily Lake a few hundred feet to the north.

1.0 Reach Horseshoe Lake.

1.2 Arrive at the trail junction with Lakes Basin Trail (1810).

11 Lakes Basin Alternate (Moccasin Lake Trail)

This trail, in the upper Lakes Basin, runs between Lakes Basin Trail at Douglas Lake and East Fork Lostine River Trail near Mirror Lake. This trail is the access to Moccasin Lake, Glacier Pass Trail, and the off-trail route to Pocket Lake. (Trail 1810A)

Distance: 1.8 miles one way
Hiking time: 1–1.5 hours
Difficulty: Easy
Trail maintenance: Yearly
Best season: July through Sept
Traffic and other trail users: Heavy foot and horse traffic
Canine compatibility: Dogs permitted without leashes, but must be kept away from the stock of other parties
Fees and permits: Eagle Cap Wilderness Permit
Maximum elevation: 7,630 feet
Map: USGS Eagle Cap OR
Trail contact: USDA Forest Service Wallowa Mountains Office, 201 E 2nd St./PO Box 905, Joseph, OR 97846; (541) 426-5546, (541) 426-4978; www.fs.usda.gov/wallowa-whitman

Finding the trail: Drive south from Joseph on OR 351 for 7 miles, passing Wallowa Lake, to the Wallowa Lake Trailhead. Hike south from Wallowa Lake Trailhead on the West Fork Wallowa River Trail (1820). Six miles from the trailhead, at Six Mile Meadow, turn right (west) on the Lakes Basin Trail (1810). Hike 4.5 miles west on the Lakes Basin Trail to the junction with the Lakes Basin Alternate (1810A). The Lakes Basin Alternate leaves Lakes Basin Trail at the east end of Douglas Lake (7,326 ft.).
GPS: Wallowa Lake Trailhead: N45 16.049' / W117 12.754'; junction with Lakes Basin Trail at Douglas Lake: N45 11.821' / W117 17.160'

The Hike

The trail heads southwest from its junction with Lakes Basin Trail (1810). It crosses the outlet of Douglas Lake and follows the lake's shoreline for a short distance.

Soon the trail leaves the lake and climbs 0.5 mile to the top of a small rise, topping out at approximately 7,600 feet. It then drops slightly for 0.25 mile to an unmarked trail junction. The route to Pocket Lake begins here. Continue straight ahead (west) 0.25 mile to Moccasin Lake and lots of fish to be caught. The trail follows the north shore of Moccasin Lake.

At the west end of Moccasin Lake is another trail junction. The trail to the left (south) goes to Glacier Pass and Glacier Lake. After passing the Glacier Pass Trail (1806) junction, the trail climbs a short distance, then flattens out for 0.5 mile to the junction with Lakes Basin Trail (1810) at Mirror Lake (7,595 ft.). If you continue another 0.25 mile, you will come to the junction with the East Fork Lostine River Trail (1662).

Moccasin Lake. ▶

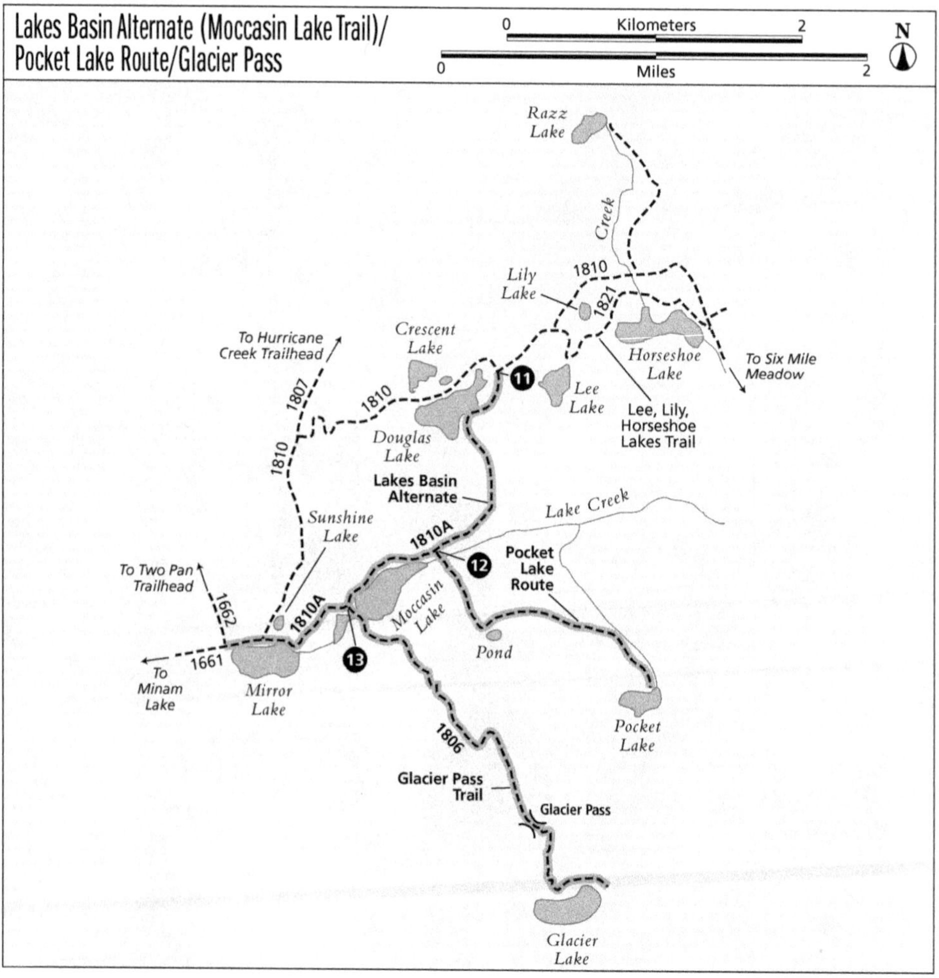

Miles and Directions

0.0 From the trail junction with Lakes Basin Trail (1810) at Douglas Lake, go southwest on the alternate route.

0.5 Reach the top of the rise.

0.8 Pass the trail junction with Pocket Lake route.

1.0 Reach Moccasin Lake and the trail junction with Glacier Pass Trail (1806). Continue on the alternate route. (GPS: N45 10.915' / W117 18.065')

1.6 Arrive at Mirror Lake and the trail junction with Lakes Basin Trail (1810).

1.8 The trail ends at the junction with East Fork Lostine River Trail (1662). (GPS: N45 10.817'/W117 18.538')

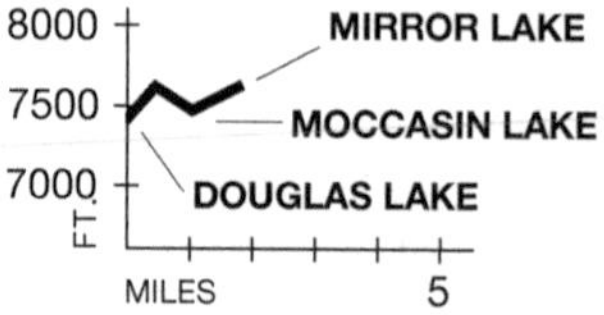

12 Pocket Lake Route

A fairly steep, off-trail route takes you from Lakes Basin Alternate Trail, near Moccasin Lake, through magnificent subalpine country to Pocket Lake. (1810A)

See map page 54.
Distance: 1.75 miles one way
Hiking time: 1.5–3 hours
Difficulty: Strenuous, with route-finding skills required
Trail maintenance: None
Best season: July through Sept
Traffic and other trail users: Light, with little or no horse traffic past the meadow
Canine compatibility: Dogs permitted without leashes, but must be kept away from the stock of other parties
Fees and permits: Northwest Forest Pass and Eagle Cap Wilderness Permit
Maximum elevation: 8,225 feet
Map: USGS Eagle Cap OR
Trail contact: USDA Forest Service Wallowa Mountains Office, 201 E 2nd St./PO Box 905, Joseph, OR 97846; (541) 426-5546, (541) 426-4978; www.fs.usda.gov/wallowa-whitman

Finding the trail: At least four trails lead directly from their respective trailheads into the Lakes Basin and to the Pocket Lake route. Hurricane Creek Trail (1807) from the Hurricane Creek Trailhead, West Fork Wallowa River Trail (1820) from Wallowa Lake Trailhead, and East Fork Eagle Creek Trail (1910) from East Eagle Creek Trailhead are all options for reaching the Lakes Basin. But the easiest way to access this route is from Two Pan Trailhead via the East Fork Lostine River Trail (1662). From Lostine drive south on Lostine River Road for 18 miles to Two Pan Trailhead. Hike south from the trailhead on the East Fork Lostine River Trail (1662) for 7.3 miles to the junction with Trail 1810 near Mirror Lake. Turn left on Trail 1810 and hike east for 0.2 mile to the junction with the Lakes Basin Alternate Trail (1810a). Bear right on the Lakes Basin Alternate and go 0.8 mile east to the point where the Pocket Lake route leaves the Lakes Basin Alternate Trail. The route to Pocket Lake begins 0.25 mile east of Moccasin Lake.
GPS: Two Pan Trailhead: N45 15.001'/W117 22.580'

The Hike

Turn south on the Pocket Lake side trail off Lakes Basin Alternate trail (1810A), and cross Lake Creek. Follow the side trail 0.5 mile to a large meadow with a stream in it. There is a campsite in a grove of trees in this meadow. Cross the stream and head east-southeast for 0.25 mile to a large pond on the north (left) side of the faint path. Then head east for 0.25 mile along the base of the cliffs. Soon a wide, steep, boulder-strewn valley will come into view to the right (southwest).

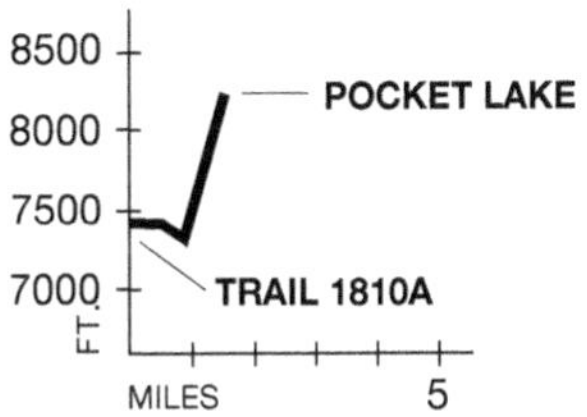

Head up the steep valley, staying to the right (west) of the small stream that flows down the center of it. Climb up the valley for 0.75 mile and 900 vertical feet to Pocket Lake (8,225 ft.).

Pocket Lake. LOWELL EUHUS PHOTO

Pocket Lake sits in a glacial cirque, with cliffs and steep mountains on three sides. It is a very alpine setting with only a few small, scattered trees. There is an excellent view of the Lakes Basin area and the West Fork Wallowa River Canyon from the rise just north of the lake. Fishing for brook trout is good at Pocket Lake. Lack of firewood and the unprotected nature of the area may be limiting factors for campsite suitability, but the beauty of the area makes the hardships worth it.

Caution: The climb to Pocket Lake is strenuous and requires considerable route finding. It should be attempted only by experienced parties in good condition.

Miles and Directions

0.0 Go south on the side trail at the unmarked junction with Lakes Basin Alternate Trail (1810A).

0.5 The route enters a meadow.

0.7 Reach the pond.

1.0 Start up a steep valley.

1.7 Arrive at Pocket Lake. (GPS: N45 10.555'/W117 16.430')

13 Glacier Pass

A fairly steep trail leads from Moccasin Lake over spectacular Glacier Pass to Glacier Lake. This trail connects the Lakes Basin with the West Fork Wallowa River and Glacier Lake. (Trail 1806)

See map page 54.
Distance: 3 miles one way from Moccasin Lake to Glacier Lake
Hiking time: 1–2 hours
Difficulty: Moderate to strenuous
Trail maintenance: Yearly
Best season: July through Sept
Traffic and other trail users: Moderate foot and horse traffic
Canine compatibility: Dogs permitted without leashes, but must be kept away from the stock of other parties
Fees and permits: Northwest Forest Pass and Eagle Cap Wilderness Permit
Maximum elevation: 8,450 feet
Map: USGS Eagle Cap OR
Trail contact: USDA Forest Service Wallowa Mountains Office, 201 E 2nd St./ PO Box 905, Joseph, OR 97846; (541) 426-5546, (541) 426-4978; www.fs.usda.gov/wallowa-whitman

Finding the trail: Although there are several trails that reach the Lakes Basin and the trail junction where this hike begins, the best way is from Two Pan Trailhead. Drive south from Lostine on the Lostine River Road for 18 miles to Two Pan Trailhead. Hike south from the trailhead on the East Fork Lostine River Trail (1662) for 7.3 miles to the junction with Trail 1810 near Mirror Lake. Turn left on Trail 1810 and hike east for 0.2 mile to the junction with the Lakes Basin Alternate Trail (1810A). Bear right on the Lakes Basin Alternate and go 0.6 mile to the junction with the Glacier Pass Trail. Glacier Pass Trail leaves Lakes Basin Alternate Trail at the west end of Moccasin Lake (7,470 ft.).
GPS: Two Pan Trailhead: N45 15.001'/W117 22.580'; Glacier Pass Trail at Moccasin Lake: N45 10.915'/W117 18.065'

The Hike

From the junction with Lakes Basin Alternate Trail (1810A), the Glacier Pass Trail heads south and crosses the inlet of Moccasin Lake. There are stepping-stones crossing the inlet stream.

After leaving Moccasin Lake, the trail goes up and down over outcroppings of glacially eroded granite. At 0.3 mile it crosses a small stream. The trail then climbs steeply in small switchbacks to another stream crossing at 7,940 feet. Beyond the second stream, the trail climbs steeply for 1 more mile, then traverses the last 0.25 mile to Glacier Pass (8,450 ft.).

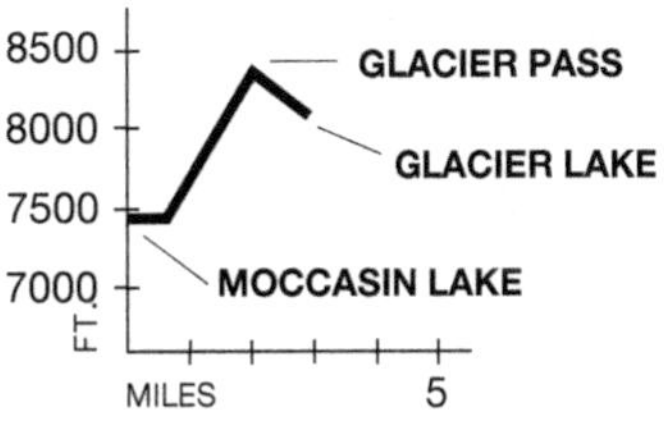

The "trees" at Glacier Pass are whitebark pine elfinwood. These small trees show the severity of the climate in this area. The view from Glacier

Glacier Lake. LOWELL EUHUS PHOTO

Pass includes Eagle Cap to the west; Lakes Basin, Hurricane Creek Canyon, and the Matterhorn to the north; Glacier Lake to the south; and West Fork Wallowa River Canyon to the southeast.

From Glacier Pass the trail switchbacks down the last mile to Glacier Lake (8,140 ft.). Here it becomes West Fork Wallowa River Trail. For more information, see West Fork Wallowa River Trail (hike 4).

Glacier Pass Trail is a rewarding day hike from a camp in the Lakes Basin. It can also be used as a connecting route to make a loop trip by continuing on down West Fork Wallowa River Trail to the Wallowa Lake Trailhead.

Miles and Directions

0.0 Take the Glacier Pass Trail (1806) southeast from the junction with Lakes Basin Alternate (1810A) at Moccasin Lake.

2.0 Cross Glacier Pass. (GPS: N45 10.030'/W117 17.080')

3.0 Arrive at Glacier Lake. (GPS: N45 09.795'/W117 17.030')

14 Hurricane Creek

A backpack route leads from Hurricane Creek Trailhead up Hurricane Creek Canyon, one of the deepest in the range, to Mirror Lake in the Lakes Basin. (Trails 1807 and 1810)

Distance: 12.1 miles one way
Hiking time: 4–6 hours
Difficulty: Moderate
Trail maintenance: Yearly
Best season: Mid-May through Oct to Echo Lake Trail junction; mid-June through Sept past the junction
Traffic and other trail users: Heavy hiking traffic to Echo Lake Trail; moderate to the trail junction with Lakes Basin Trail (1810); heavy again from the trail junction to Mirror Lake. Heavy horse traffic.
Canine compatibility: Dogs permitted without leashes, but must be kept away from the stock of other parties
Fees and permits: Northwest Forest Pass and Eagle Cap Wilderness Permit
Maximum elevation: 7,700 feet
Maps: USGS Chief Joseph Mountain OR and Eagle Cap OR; Geo Graphics Wallowa Mountains Eagle Cap Wilderness
Trail contact: USDA Forest Service Wallowa Mountains Office, 201 E 2nd St./PO Box 905, Joseph, OR 97846; (541) 426-5546, (541) 426-4978; www.fs.usda.gov/wallowa-whitman

Finding the trailhead: From Enterprise go 5 miles south on Hurricane Creek Road to Hurricane Creek Grange Hall. Turn right off the paved road and go 3 more miles south to Hurricane Creek Trailhead (5,025 ft.). There are stock loading facilities, an outhouse, and a few campsites at the trailhead.
GPS: N45 18.673'/W117 18.438'

The Hike

The trail heads south from the trailhead, passing the junction with Falls Creek Trail (1807A) at 0.1 mile (5,105 ft.). A short distance farther the trail crosses Falls Creek. There is no bridge, so crossing can be a problem during periods of high water.

At 0.75 mile the trail enters an area of knocked-down trees. This is the result of an avalanche. In the middle of the avalanche debris is the Eagle Cap Wilderness boundary sign (5,350 ft.).

The trail crosses Deadman Creek 1.5 miles from the trailhead. Legend has it that an early day miner dropped his .45 revolver on a rock near the mouth of Deadman Creek and shot himself dead. His friends buried him along Deadman Creek in the basin below the limestone cliffs west of Hurricane Creek Trail.

Just after crossing Deadman Creek, a cross-country route takes off to the west up through Deadman Basin (where the miner was buried) to Deadman Lake. The route to Deadman Lake takes lots of route-finding skills. There is a way that can be hiked by strong hikers, but if you miss this route, roped climbing may be required. Watch for

Matterhorn from upper Hurricane Creek Trail. KERRY SEARLE PHOTO

mountain goats and bighorn sheep in the higher parts of Deadman Creek drainage. They can sometimes be seen with binoculars from Hurricane Creek Trail.

One-third of a mile past Deadman Creek, the unmarked Thorp Creek Trail turns to the left. See Sacajawea Peak via Thorp Creek Basin (climb 9). At 3 miles the trail makes a switchback and climbs above a small but spectacular gorge with Hurricane Creek rushing through the bottom. Past the gorge is the Slick Rock Creek crossing. This area can be very dangerous in early or late season because of snow and ice. This is also a prime avalanche area (5,760 ft.).

At 4.25 miles the trail crosses Granite Creek and enters a moist area, where it is held in place with logs on each side. The trail crosses another creek at 5 miles and soon comes to the junction with Echo Lake Trail (1824; 6,040 ft.). See Echo Lake and Billy Jones Lake (hike 16). Just past the junction the trail crosses Billy Jones Creek, and at 5.5 miles crosses Hurricane Creek. Neither crossing has a bridge. It will probably be impossible to cross Hurricane Creek dry-footed, so take off your shoes, find a walking stick, roll up your

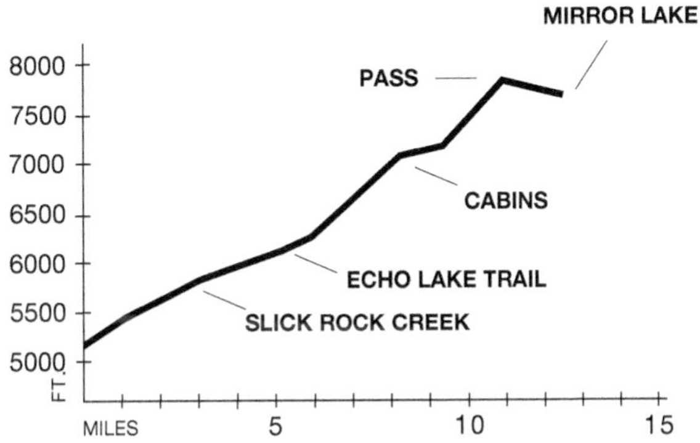

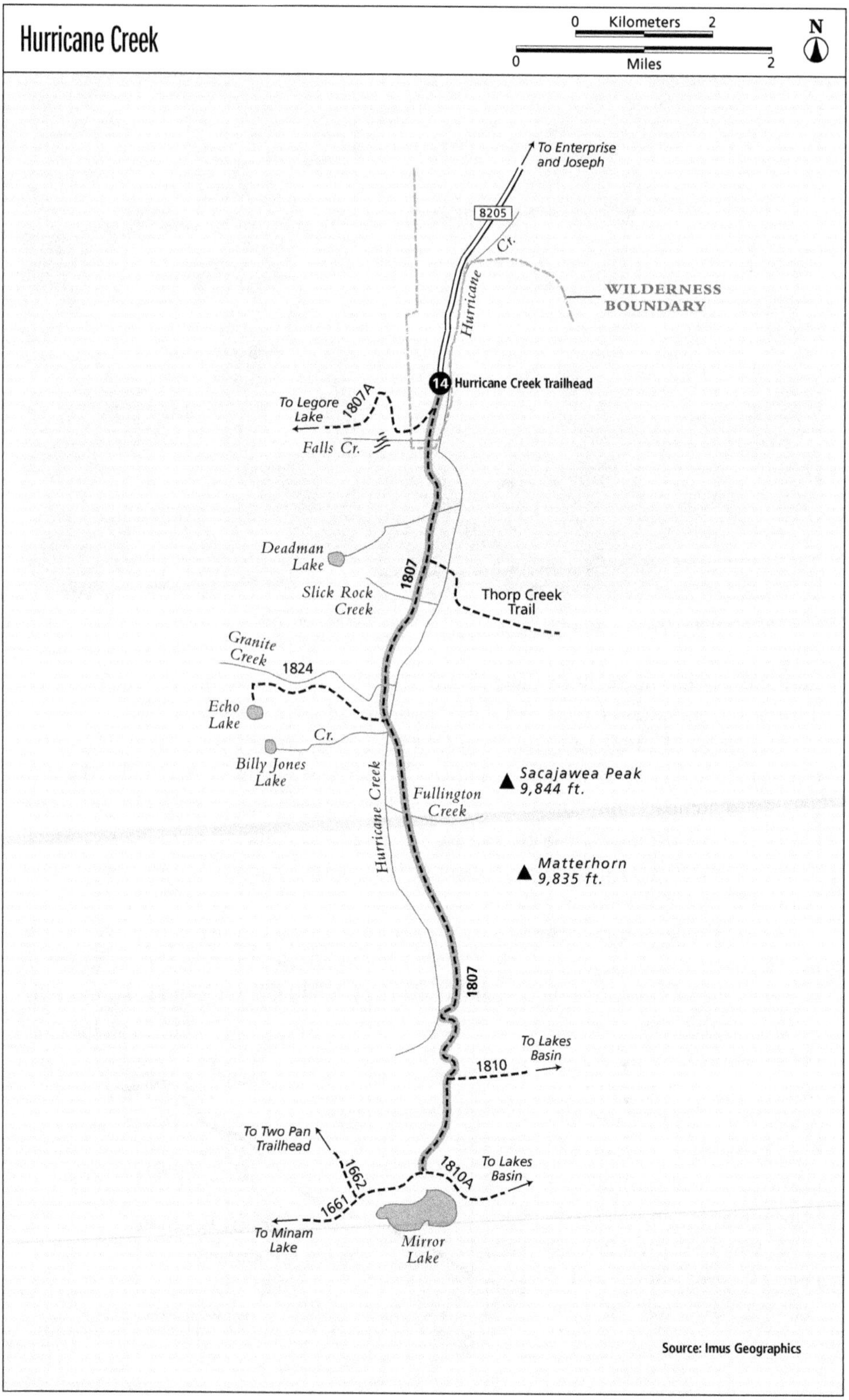

Hurricane Creek
0 Kilometers 2
0 Miles 2
N
To Enterprise and Joseph
8205
Hurricane Cr.
WILDERNESS BOUNDARY
14 Hurricane Creek Trailhead
To Legore Lake
1807A
Falls Cr.
Deadman Lake
1807
Slick Rock Creek
Thorp Creek Trail
Granite Creek
1824
Echo Lake
Cr.
Billy Jones Lake
Sacajawea Peak 9,844 ft.
Fullington Creek
Hurricane Creek
Matterhorn 9,835 ft.
1807
To Lakes Basin
1810
To Two Pan Trailhead
1662
1810A
To Lakes Basin
1661
To Minam Lake
Mirror Lake
Source: Imus Geographics

pants legs, and wade through the cold knee-deep water. There are good campsites just before the crossing, on the west side of Hurricane Creek.

At 6 miles (6,310 ft.) is Fullington Creek, with a sign to tell you its name. Just past Fullington Creek is a campsite on the right. The trail comes to an opening at 7.75 miles (6,690 ft.). Above the trail to the left is the gleaming white limestone face of the 9,834.8-foot-high Matterhorn, the second-highest peak in the Wallowa Mountains. This area abounds with pikas and other mountain rodents. Bears are also common here. Look for them on the open hillsides, digging grubs and grazing.

At 8 miles the trail makes a switchback to the left. Above the switchback at 8.3 miles (7,100 ft.), there are two old cabins to the right of the trail. The cabins are not in good enough shape to stay in, and the posted notice says to please leave them as you found them. The cabins are protected by the Antiquities Act of 1906.

Beyond the cabins the trail enters an area of beautiful meadows, with frogs croaking and extensive beaver dams on the creek, which the route crosses twice. Travel on through the meadow for a mile or so, then climb on a moderate grade over a pass (7,700 ft.). After crossing the pass the trail drops down to the junction with Lakes Basin Trail (1810), which comes in from the left. At this junction (7,660 ft.), 11 miles from the Hurricane Creek Trailhead, the trail number of the route changes to 1810. Continue 1.1 miles south, passing Sunshine Lake, to Mirror Lake (7,595 ft.) in the upper part of the Lakes Basin. Like most of the lakes in the Wallowa Mountains, Mirror Lake has good fishing for small brook trout. There are many campsites in the Lakes Basin area.

The return trip can be made over the same trail, or a one-way trip with a car shuttle can be done by using either Lakes Basin Trail or Lakes Basin Alternate and West Fork Wallowa River Trail back to the Wallowa Lake Trailhead.

Miles and Directions

0.0 Begin at the Hurricane Creek Trailhead.

0.1 Pass the trail junction with Falls Creek Trail (1807).

0.2 Cross Falls Creek.

0.8 Cross the avalanche area.

1.5 Cross Deadman Creek.

1.8 Pass the trail junction with Thorp Creek Trail. (GPS: N45 17.192'/W117 18.436')

3.0 Cross Slick Rock Creek. (GPS: N45 16.445'/W117 18.739')

4.2 Cross Granite Creek.

5.0 Pass the trail junction with Echo Lake Trail (1824). (GPS: N45 15.215'/W117 19.252')

5.5 Cross Hurricane Creek.

6.0 Cross Fullington Creek.

8.3 Pass the cabins on the right side of the trail.

10.5 Climb over the pass.

11.0 At the junction with Lakes Basin Trail (1810), continue on Trail 1810.

12.1 The route ends at the trail junction with Lakes Basin Alternate Trail (1810A) and Mirror Lake. (GPS: N45 10.817'/W117 18.538')

15 Falls Creek

A steep mine trail climbs from Hurricane Creek Trail to Legore Mine, then a faint path heads over a 9,100-foot-high pass to Legore Lake, the highest lake in the Wallowa Mountains. (Trail 1807A)

Distance: 4.1 miles one way to Legore Lake
Hiking time: 2.5-4 hours
Difficulty: Strenuous
Trail maintenance: Rare; above the falls done only by volunteers. Recently maintained by Wallowa Mountains Hells Canyon Trail Association; for info about volunteering with WMHCTA, see appendix A. This trail is not maintained for stock traffic.
Best season: June through Oct to Legore cabin; July through Sept above the cabin
Traffic and other trail users: Heavy for the first 0.25 mile to the falls; light above the falls except during late Sept and Oct hunting seasons, when traffic can be heavy
Canine compatibility: Dogs permitted without leashes, but must be kept away from the stock of other parties
Fees and permits: Northwest Forest Pass and Eagle Cap Wilderness Permit
Maximum elevation: 9,100 feet
Map: USGS Chief Joseph Mountain OR
Trail contact: USDA Forest Service Wallowa Mountains Office, 201 E 2nd St./PO Box 905, Joseph, OR 97846; (541) 426-5546, (541) 426-4978; www.fs.usda.gov/wallowa-whitman. Don't expect too much additional information from the forest service or anyone else about this trail.

Finding the trailhead: From Enterprise drive south for 5 miles on Hurricane Creek Road to Hurricane Creek Grange. Turn right at the Grange, leaving the paved road for a short distance, and go 3 more miles south to Hurricane Creek Trailhead.
GPS: Hurricane Creek Trailhead: N45 18.673'/W117 18.438'; Falls Creek Trail junction: N45 18.596'/W117 18.412'

The Hike

Hike south from Hurricane Creek Trailhead for 0.1 mile to the junction with Falls Creek Trail (1807A). Turn right (west) at the hard-to-spot sign marking Falls Creek Trail. At 0.25 mile a side trail turns to the left, leading to Falls Creek Falls. The main trail bears right. It makes a long switchback and contours up Falls Creek Canyon, parallel to, but well above, the creek. At 0.75 mile (5,520 ft.), above the point where the creek forks, the trail makes a switchback to the right. This is the point where Falls Creek Ridge route to Twin Peaks leaves the trail. This is also the first in a series of switchbacks. The trail climbs up through open areas, then through a forest of mountain mahogany. At 6,050 feet it straightens out and goes on up the canyon to the west. The trail still stays well above the creek. At 2.25 miles (6,630 ft.) the trail crosses a side creek and enters a large open area. After crossing the creek it begins another series of switchbacks and enters the timber again at the top of the clearing.

Photo time along Falls Creek Trail.

Here the trail straightens out again and continues up the canyon, high above the creek. Several waterfalls are visible from the trail in this section; the one that appears to come over the ridge to the west is the outlet from Legore Lake. At 3 miles (7,830 ft.) the trail crosses another side creek. Directly above, on the right side of the creek, are a couple of very shallow mine shafts. The trail crosses the creek and passes another mine shaft. A short climb past the mine shaft is the remains of the old Legore cabin (7,950 ft.). Please don't harm what's left of the cabin. Joe Legore, the original owner of the cabin, called this the Red Cloud Mine. The trail fades out temporarily at the cabin; head west-northwest.

A few feet above the cabin the trail becomes visible again. It climbs steeply to a saddle, then fades out. Head up the valley to the west on a talus slope of huge white boulders, and enter a beautiful timberline basin (8,620 ft.). Here the route bears left slightly. It climbs over the 9,100-foot-high pass to the south and drops to Legore Lake.

Legore Lake (8,957 ft.) is 4 miles from Hurricane Creek Trail. This is the highest lake in the Wallowa Mountains. Legore Lake has some brook trout in it, but the extreme elevation keeps them small-bodied with large heads. No firewood is available at Legore Lake. In fact, there are no trees, only some scattered whitebark pine elfinwood. There are some flat spots to camp on at this isolated lake.

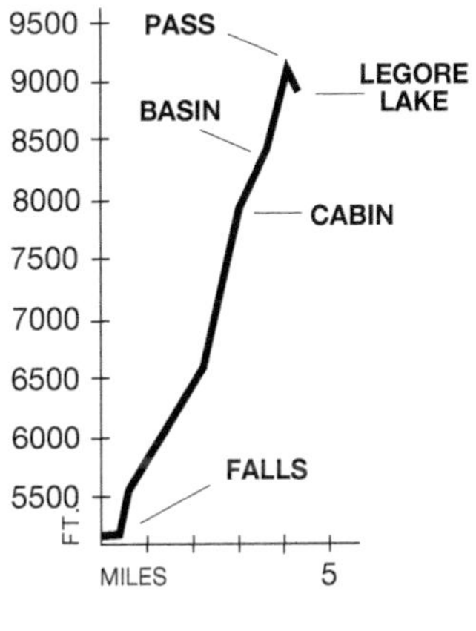

From the timberline basin, Sawtooth Peak to the north may be climbed quite easily. Sawtooth Peak (9,175 ft.) offers 360 degrees of beautiful views. A route to the summit of Twin Peaks (9,665 ft.) also leaves the trail at this point. There is a good chance

Falls Creek

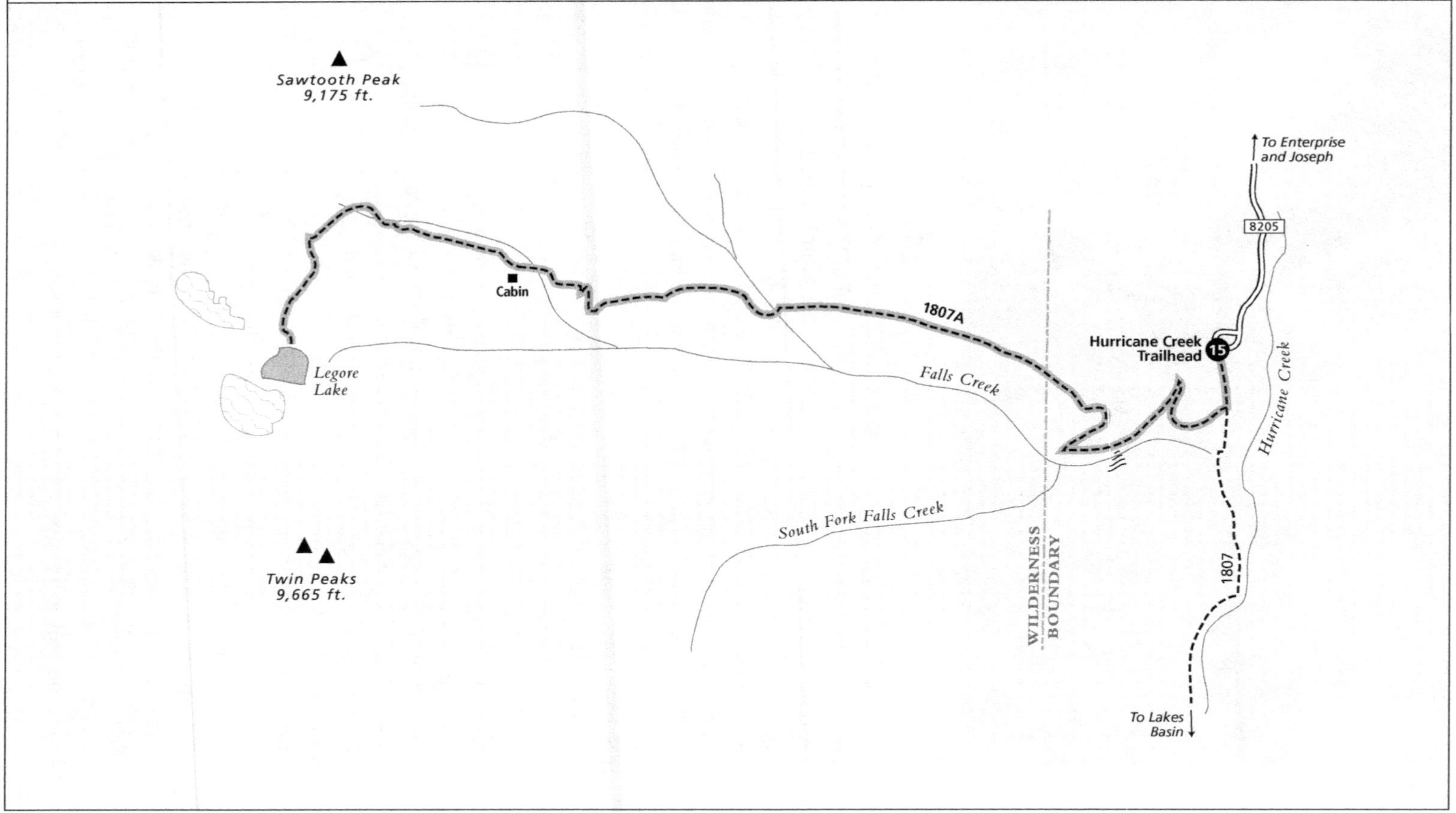

Kilometer
0
1
Mile
0
1
N
Sawtooth Peak
9,175 ft.
To Enterprise
and Joseph
8205
Cabin
1807A
Hurricane Creek
Trailhead
15
Legore
Lake
Falls Creek
Hurricane Creek
South Fork Falls Creek
WILDERNESS
BOUNDARY
1807
Twin Peaks
9,665 ft.
To Lakes
Basin

of seeing both mountain goats and bighorn sheep in and around this basin. Return by retracing the trail to Hurricane Creek Trailhead.

The Falls Creek Trail is very steep, and in some places fine sand scree on the top of a hardpan trail makes for a ball-bearing effect underfoot. It may be difficult for all but hardy hikers.

Miles and Directions

0.0 Hike south from Hurricane Creek Trailhead.

0.1 Take the Falls Creek Trail (1807A) from the junction with Hurricane Creek Trail (1807).

0.3 Pass the path to falls.

0.9 Pass the junction with the route to Twin Peaks. (GPS: N45 18.538'/W117 18.921')

2.3 Cross a side creek.

3.2 Reach the Legore cabin and mine. (GPS: N45 18.735'/W117 20.184')

3.9 Cross the pass. (GPS: N45 18.692'/W117 20.752')

4.1 Arrive at Legore Lake. (GPS: N45 18.637'/W117 20.740')

16 Echo Lake and Billy Jones Lake

This backpack leads 3 fairly steep miles from Hurricane Creek Trail (1807) to very picturesque and alpine Echo Lake. Then continue climbing through the spectacular alpine country to Billy Jones Lake. (Trail 1824)

Distance: 3 miles one way from Hurricane Creek Trail (1807) to Echo Lake; 8 miles one way from Hurricane Creek Trailhead to Echo Lake; 3.7 miles one way from Hurricane Creek Trail to Billy Jones Lake
Hiking time: 1.5–3 hours from Hurricane Creek Trail to Echo Lake; 3–6 hours from the trailhead
Difficulty: Strenuous
Trail maintenance: Infrequent; not maintained for stock
Best season: Mid-July through Sept
Traffic and other trail users: Moderate foot traffic; although this trail is not maintained for stock, they occasionally do use it.
Canine compatibility: Dogs permitted without leashes, but must be kept away from the stock of other parties
Fees and permits: Northwest Forest Pass and Eagle Cap Wilderness Permit
Maximum elevation: 8,372 feet to Echo Lake; 8,700 feet to Billy Jones Lake
Map: USGS Chief Joseph Mountain OR
Trail contact: USDA Forest Service Wallowa Mountains Office, 201 E 2nd St./ PO Box 905, Joseph, OR 97846; (541) 426-5546, (541) 426-4978; www.fs.usda.gov/wallowa-whitman

Finding the trail: From Enterprise drive south for 5 miles on Hurricane Creek Road to Hurricane Creek Grange. Turn right at the Grange, leaving the paved road for a short distance, and go 3 more miles south to Hurricane Creek Trailhead. From the trailhead, follow Hurricane Creek Trail (1807) for 5 miles south to the Echo Lake Trail junction (6,050 ft.).
GPS: Hurricane Creek Trailhead: N45 18.673'/W117 18.438'; Echo Lake Trail junction: N45 15.215'/W117 19.252'

The Hike

Echo Lake Trail turns right (west) off Hurricane Creek Trail (1807). There is a trail sign marking the junction. At first the trail climbs steeply in switchbacks, then it makes a traverse to the northwest to a creek crossing (6,800 ft.). After crossing the creek, the trail switchbacks steeply up a ridge between two small creeks, topping out at 7,680 feet. A few yards after flattening out and dropping slightly, the trail enters a small, lush meadow, then a larger one. In the larger meadow the trail crosses a stream, then heads on across the meadow in a northwesterly direction. In these swampy meadows the trail may be difficult to see for short distances.

After leaving the meadows the trail climbs steadily. Here the vegetation opens up and becomes more alpine. Whitebark pines become the dominant tree, and alpine flowers bloom along the snow line up the mountains. At 8,100 feet elevation the trail turns to the left (south) and climbs through some rock outcroppings to Echo Lake (8,372 ft.).

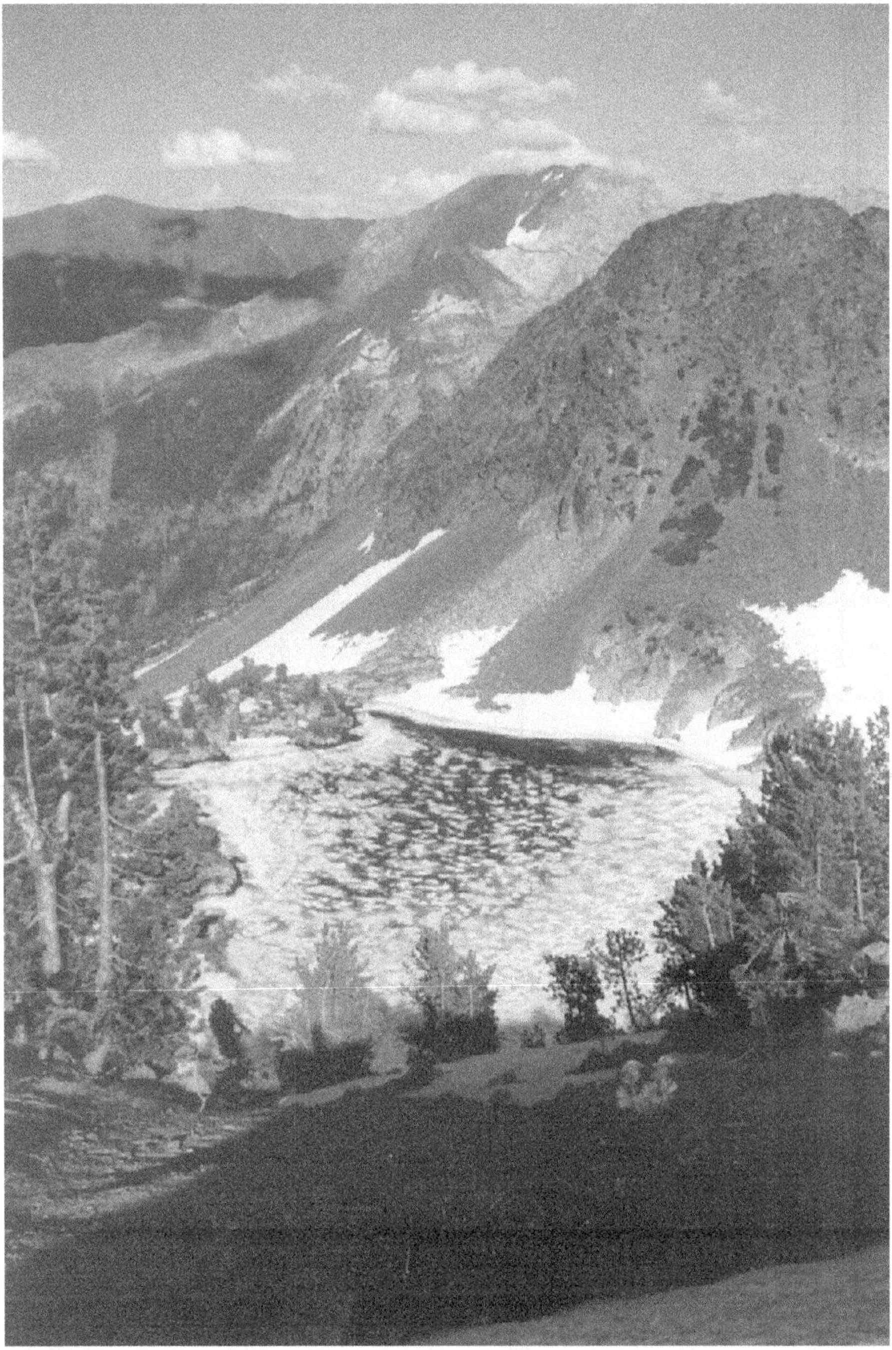

Echo Lake.

Echo Lake and Billy Jones Lake

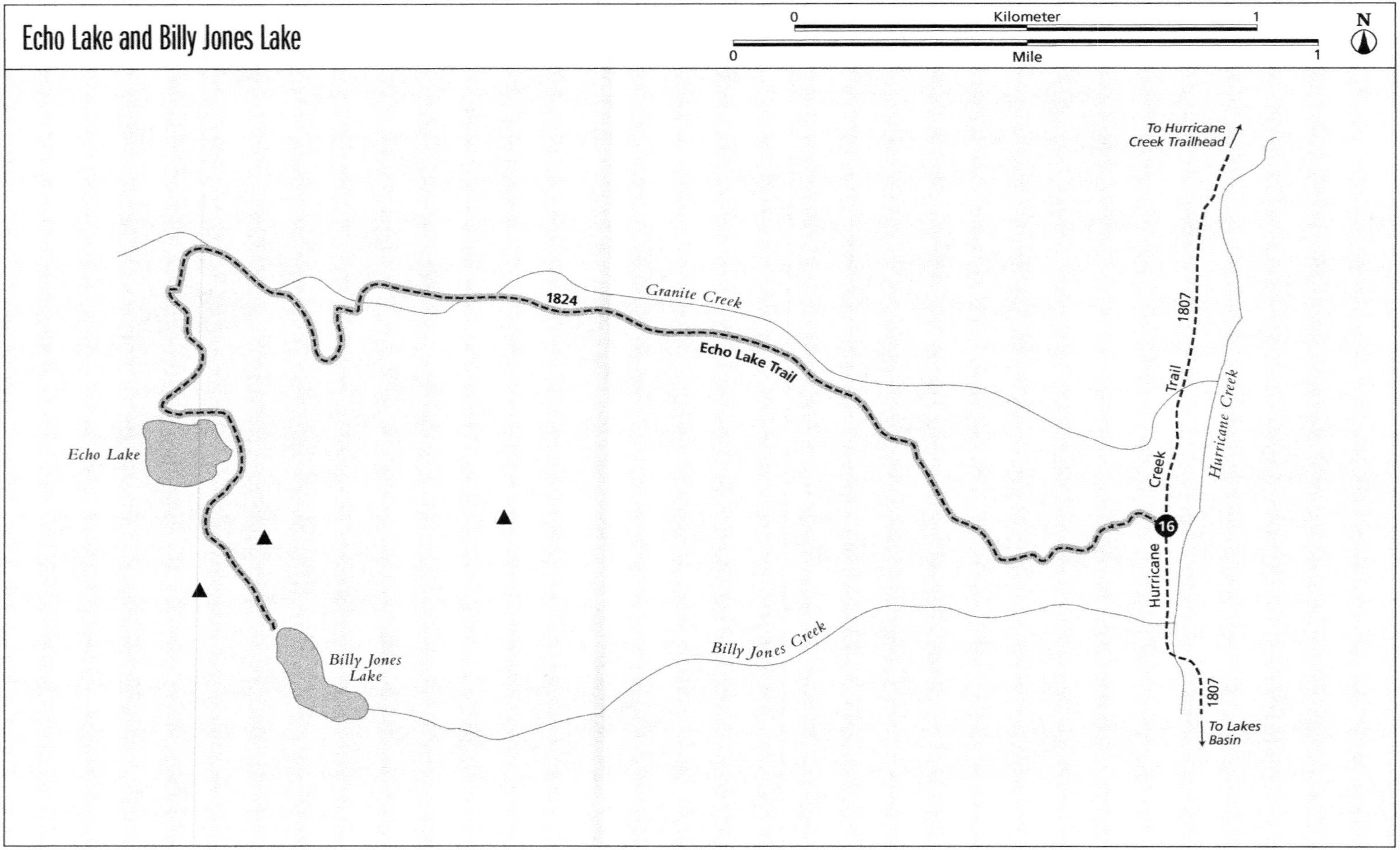

The total distance to Echo Lake from Hurricane Creek Trail is only 3 miles, but with a 2,300-foot elevation gain and an eroded, poorly maintained trail, it seems much farther. As is true with many of the steep side trails in the Wallowa Mountains, an altimeter is a better indicator of where you are than is a pedometer. The altitude gain is much more significant than the mileage.

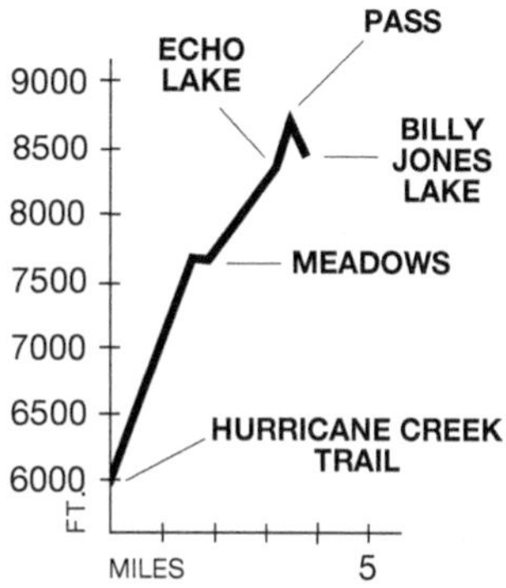

The alpine country and spectacular views around Echo Lake make the hike well worthwhile. The high ridges to the north of Echo Lake are good places to spot bighorn sheep, and large mule deer bucks abound in the area.

To go on to Billy Jones Lake, go around Echo Lake on the east side, cross the outlet, and follow a steep, rough path to the saddle south of the lake (8,700 ft.). The faint path then drops 250 vertical feet to Billy Jones Lake at 3.7 miles (8,450 ft.).

Both Echo and Billy Jones Lakes may be ice-covered well into July. Until early August there may be snow covering the trail above 8,000 feet. There are some usable campsites on the north side of Echo Lake, but camping spots are very limited at Billy Jones Lake. The return trip is made by using the same trail.

Miles and Directions

0.0 Take the Echo Lake Trail (1824) from the junction with Hurricane Creek Trail (1807).

3.0 Reach Echo Lake. (GPS: N45 15.400'/W117 21.305')

3.7 Arrive at Billy Jones Lake. (GPS: N45 15.085'/W117 21.040')

17 Eagle Cap

The trail to the summit of Eagle Cap is a fairly steep day hike from the Minam Lake/Mirror Lake Trail (1661). (Trails 1910 and 1805)

Distance: 2.7 miles one way from the Minam Lake/Mirror Lake Trail junction
Hiking time: 1–2 hours
Difficulty: Strenuous
Trail maintenance: Infrequent
Best season: Mid-July through Sept. The trail may have some snow patches into early Aug.
Traffic and other trail users: Moderate, with little or no horse traffic
Canine compatibility: Dogs permitted without leashes, but must be kept away from the stock of other parties
Fees and permits: Eagle Cap Wilderness Permit. A Northwest Forest Pass is also required to park at Two Pan Trailhead.
Maximum elevation: 9,572 feet
Map: USGS Eagle Cap OR
Trail contact: USDA Forest Service Wallowa Mountains Office, 201 E 2nd St./ PO Box 905, Joseph, OR 97846; (541) 426-5546, (541) 426-4978; www.fs.usda.gov/wallowa-whitman

Finding the trail: At least four trails lead directly from their respective trailheads into the Lakes Basin and to the Eagle Cap Trail. Hurricane Creek Trail (1807) from the Hurricane Creek Trailhead, West Fork Wallowa River Trail (1820) from Wallowa Lake Trailhead, and East Fork Eagle Creek Trail (1910) from East Eagle Creek Trailhead are all options for reaching the Lakes Basin. The East Eagle Creek Trail may be your best bet if you are on the south (Baker City) side of the Wallowas. But the easiest way to access the Eagle Cap trail is from Two Pan Trailhead via the East Fork Lostine River Trail (1662). From Lostine drive south on Lostine River Road for 18 miles to Two Pan Trailhead. Hike south from the trailhead on the East Fork Lostine River Trail (1662) for 7.3 miles to the junction with the Minam/Mirror Lake Trail (1661). Turn right (west) on the Minam Lake /Mirror Lake Trail and go a short distance to the junction with the East Fork Eagle Creek Trail (1910; 7,610 ft.).
GPS: Two Pan Trailhead: N45 15.001'/W117 22.580'; Minam Lake/Mirror Lake trail junction: N45 10.746'/W117 18.954'

The Hike

At the trail junction 0.25 mile west of Mirror Lake, turn left (south) off Minam Lake/Mirror Lake Trail (1661). Head around the east side of Upper Lake through the open alpine country on Trail 1910 toward Horton Pass. After following Trail 1910 for 1.2 miles to a junction at 8,350 feet, turn left (southwest) on Trail 1805 toward Eagle Cap. Horton Pass is straight ahead (if you don't turn left).

Above this junction the trail switchbacks and climbs out to the ridge crest (8,730 ft.). At the ridge crest a rough path turns right and drops down the ridgeline to Horton Pass. Keep on the main trail, which turns left and climbs the ridge to the

Eagle Cap Mountain. ▶

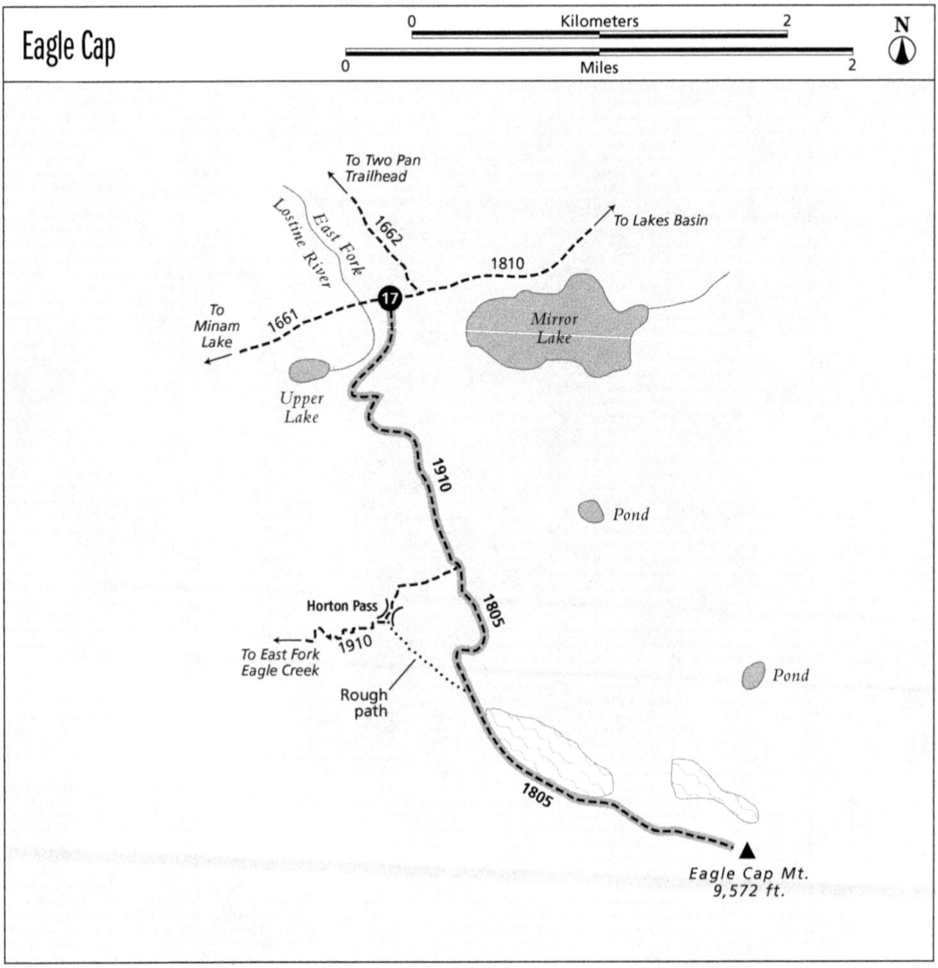

southeast, passing a viewpoint (8,950 ft.). Above the viewpoint the trail switchbacks up to the summit. The summit (9,572 ft.) is 2.7 miles from the Minam Lake/Mirror Lake Trail.

From the summit there is an unobstructed panoramic view of nearly all of the Wallowa Mountains. Whitebark pine elfinwood reaches nearly to the top, and there are usually some golden-mantled ground squirrels begging for food at the summit. Eagle Cap is the only high peak in the Wallowas with an actual trail leading to its summit. Eagle Cap is more or less the center point of the Wallowa Mountains, with canyons radiating in all directions. From the summit you can see Hurricane Creek and East Fork Lostine River flowing north, the West Fork Wallowa River flowing east and north, and East Fork Eagle Creek flowing south. A couple of miles to the northwest is Minam Lake, where both the West Fork Lostine and Minam Rivers begin. Minam Lake is not visible from the summit. Three miles to the southeast are the headwaters of the Imnaha River.

Eagle Cap was originally thought to be the highest peak in the Eagle Mountains, which the Wallowa Mountains were once called. Surveys have since shown several peaks in the range to be higher than Eagle Cap.

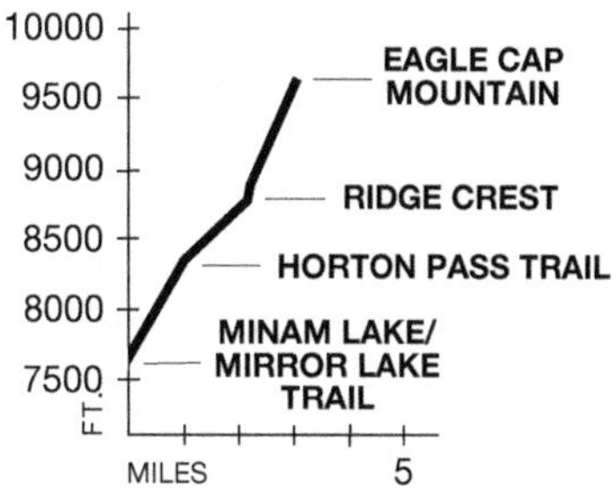

For parties wishing to make a loop hike, the rough path you passed when the Eagle Cap summit trail reached the ridgeline can be used for the descent. This path is in poorer condition than the main Eagle Cap Trail, but provides a shortcut to Horton Pass (8,470 ft.). From the junction on the ridgeline the path descends directly to Horton Pass, 0.3 mile down the northwest ridge of Eagle Cap. From Horton Pass, head north on Trail 1910 to return to Mirror Lake.

The Floyd Vernon (Jack) Horton Memorial Plaque is at Horton Pass. The plaque was placed here in remembrance of an assistant forester who began working for the forest service on May 10, 1913.

The mile of trail from Horton Pass down (north) to the junction with Eagle Cap summit trail may be covered with snow until late in the summer, but this is open country, and the route is not difficult to find, except in bad weather with low visibility.

Miles and Directions

0.0 At the junction with Minam Lake/Mirror Lake Trail (1661), take Trail 1910 toward Eagle Cap.

1.2 At the junction with Horton Pass Trail, the trail number changes to 1805 (East Fork Eagle Creek Trail).

2.0 Reach the ridge crest and the trail junction with the ridge path to Horton Pass. Stay to the left (southeast).

2.7 Reach the summit of Eagle Cap. (GPS: N45 09.822'/W17 18.090')

18 East Fork Lostine River

This trail, suitable for a day hike or backpack, leads from Two Pan Trailhead to Mirror Lake. The East Fork Lostine River Trail is one of the most scenic hikes in the Wallowas. The route climbs into a textbook perfect example of a U-shaped glacial valley, with light colored cliffs on both sides and meadows traversed by a stream in the bottom. (Trail 1662)

Distance: 7.3 miles one way
Hiking time: 2.5–4 hours
Difficulty: Moderate
Trail maintenance: Yearly
Best season: Late June through Sept
Traffic and other trail users: Heavy foot and horse traffic
Canine compatibility: Dogs permitted without leashes, but must be kept away from the stock of other parties
Fees and permits: Northwest Forest Pass and Eagle Cap Wilderness Permit
Maximum elevation: 7,619 feet
Maps: USGS Lostine OR and Eagle Cap OR; Geo Graphics Wallowa Mountains Eagle Cap Wilderness
Trail contact: USDA Forest Service Wallowa Mountains Office, 201 E 2nd St./ PO Box 905, Joseph, OR 97846; (541) 426-5546, (541) 426-4978; www.fs.usda.gov/wallowa-whitman

Finding the trailhead: From Lostine go 18 miles south on Lostine River Road to Two Pan Campground and Trailhead (5,585 ft.). There is a large parking area with a stock-loading ramp on the left side of the road across from the campground, just before the trailhead.
GPS: N45 15.001'/W117 22.580'

The Hike

Head south from the parking area. Follow the trail 200 yards south to the wilderness boundary and the junction with the West Fork Lostine River Trail. Another trail from the south side of the large parking area connects with the main trail just before the junction. Bear left at the junction. From here the trail climbs for 1 mile to a single log bridge crossing the East Fork of the Lostine River.

The trail continues to climb, making a couple of switchbacks on an open boulder-strewn hillside, then makes a couple more switchbacks and comes out in a level area 2 miles from the trailhead (6,850 ft.). You get a good view of Hurricane Divide to the east from the switchbacks on the open hillside. Watch for pikas in the rocks of the switchback area, as they are common here.

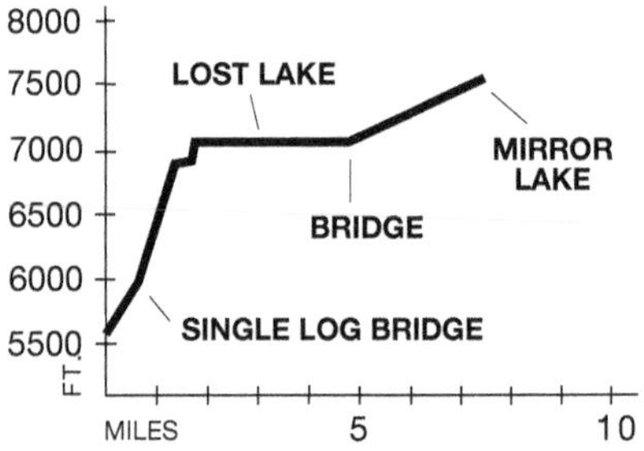

The trail is level for a short distance but soon climbs again. It enters the beautiful U-shaped upper Lostine Canyon 2.5 miles from the trailhead. The U shape is indicative of glacier-carved valleys. The elevation where

Eagle Cap from East Fork Lostine River Trail.

the trail enters the upper valley is 7,040 feet. At this point the river forms a large pool with excellent fishing for small brook trout. The trail passes Lost Lake 0.75 mile farther along. The lake is to the east (left) of the trail. After going 1.5 miles past Lost Lake, the trail crosses a bridge over the East Fork Lostine River.

After crossing the river the trail stays on the east side. It makes a couple of switchbacks and climbs above the canyon floor. Above the switchbacks the trail makes a gentle ascending traverse to the junction with Trail 1661 (7,619 ft.). Mirror Lake (7,590 ft.), in the upper part of the Lakes Basin, is to the left. There are many good campsites among the granite outcroppings along the north side of Mirror Lake. Be

East Fork Lostine River/West Fork Lostine River

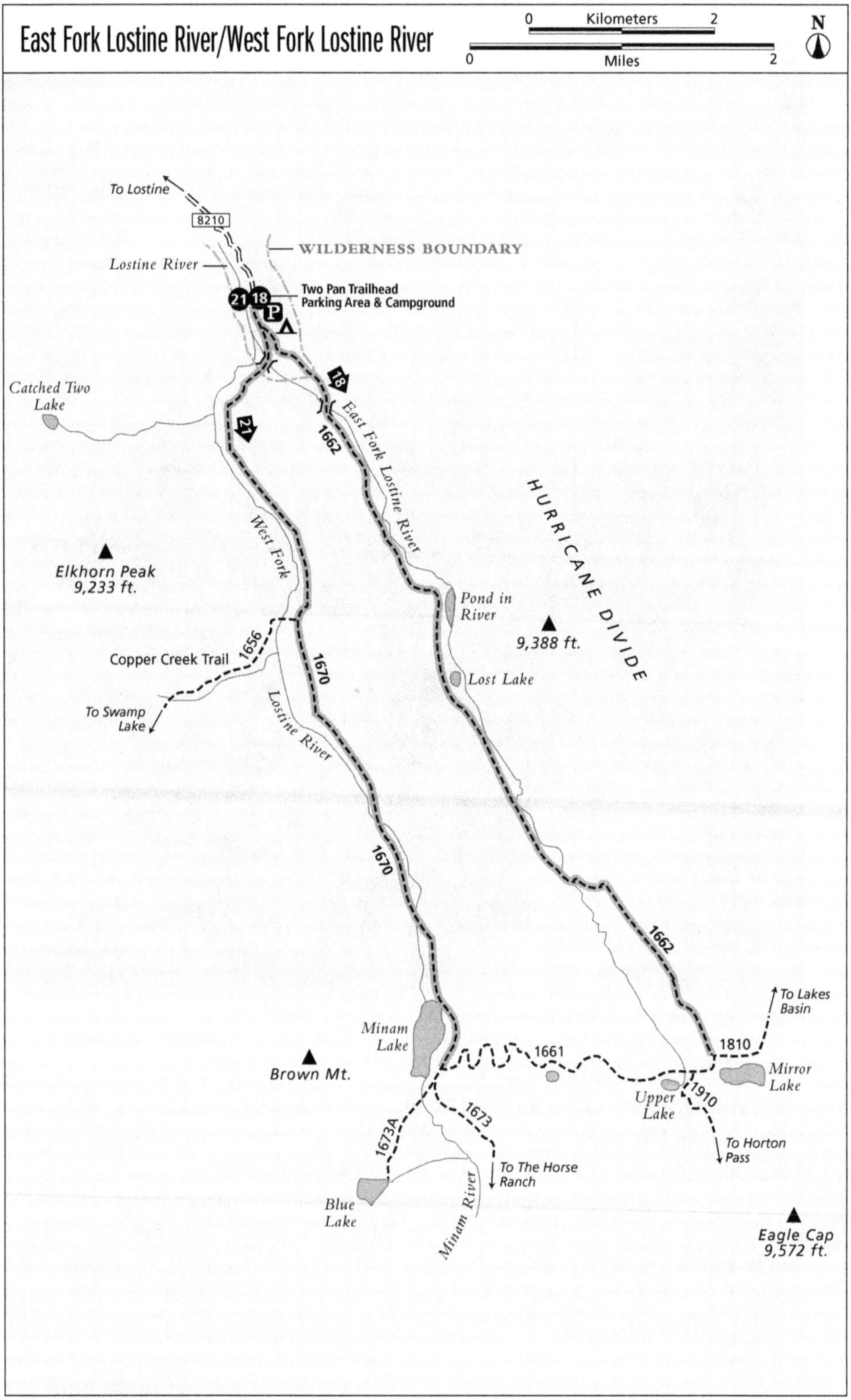

0 Kilometers 2
0 Miles 2
N
To Lostine
8210
WILDERNESS BOUNDARY
Lostine River
21
18
Two Pan Trailhead
Parking Area & Campground
P
18
21
Catched Two
Lake
1662
East Fork Lostine River
HURRICANE DIVIDE
West Fork
Elkhorn Peak
9,233 ft.
Pond in
River
9,388 ft.
1656
Copper Creek Trail
1670
Lost Lake
To Swamp
Lake
Lostine River
1670
1662
To Lakes
Basin
Minam
Lake
1810
1661
Mirror
Lake
Brown Mt.
Upper
Lake
1910
1673A
1673
To Horton
Pass
To The Horse
Ranch
Blue
Lake
Minam River
Eagle Cap
9,572 ft.

sure to camp at least 200 feet from the lake. Fishing for small brook trout is generally very good in Mirror Lake. This trail is heavily used by horse parties and may be dusty.

Option: A loop trip can be made by combining this trail with Minam Lake/Mirror Lake Trail to Minam Lake, then heading back north on West Fork Lostine River Trail.

Miles and Directions

0.0 The trail begins at Two Pan Campground and Trailhead.

0.1 Pass the junction with West Fork Lostine River Trail (1670).

1.0 Cross the river on single log bridge.

3.2 Reach Lost Lake. (GPS: N45 12.907'/W117 21.033')

4.7 Cross East Fork Lostine River again on a bridge.

7.3 Reach the junction with Minam Lake/Mirror Lake Trail (1661). (GPS: N45 10.771'/W117 18.917')

19 Minam Lake to Mirror Lake

This connecting trail climbs from Minam Lake, over Ivan Carper Pass, then descends, passing Upper Lake to Mirror Lake. The Minam Lake/Mirror Lake Trail is sometimes called Ivan Carper Trail. (Trail 1661)

Distance: 3.4 miles one way
Hiking time: 1.5-2.5 hours
Difficulty: Moderate
Trail maintenance: Infrequent
Best season: Mid-July through Sept
Traffic and other trail users: Moderate foot and horse traffic
Canine compatibility: Dogs permitted without leashes, but must be kept away from the stock of other parties
Fees and permits: Northwest Forest Pass and Eagle Cap Wilderness Permit
Maximum elevation: 8,520 feet
Map: USGS Eagle Cap OR
Trail contact: USDA Forest Service Wallowa Mountains Office, 201 E 2nd St./ PO Box 905, Joseph, OR 97846; (541) 426-5546, (541) 426-4978; www.fs.usda.gov/wallowa-whitman

Finding the trail: This trail can be accessed from either East or West Fork Lostine River Trails (Trails 1662 and 1670), from East Eagle Creek Trailhead via East Eagle Creek Trail (1910), or from Lakes Basin Trail (1810). This description starts at a junction with the West Fork Lostine Trail at Minam Lake, which is the easiest access. To reach Minam Lake drive 18 miles south on Lostine River Road from the town of Lostine to Two Pan Campground and Trailhead. The trailhead is at the end of the road (5,585 ft.). Hike south from the trailhead on the West Fork Lostine River Trail (1670) for 6.1 miles to Minam Lake and the junction with the Minam Lake/Mirror Lake Trail.
GPS: Two Pan Trailhead: N45 15.001'/W117 22.580'; Minam Lake: N45 10.667'/W117 21.098'

The Hike

The trail begins at the southeast corner of Minam Lake. It leaves West Fork Lostine River Trail (1670) at an elevation of 7,385 feet. The trail climbs steadily on meandering switchbacks and passes a couple of ponds. These ponds are below and to the right of the trail. The trail reaches Ivan Carper Pass (8,520 ft.) 1.5 miles after leaving Minam Lake. The view from the pass is quite spectacular. Minam and Blue Lakes can be seen to the west, with Upper Lake and the rest of the Lakes Basin to the east. Eagle Cap is close by to the southeast, and the Matterhorn, with its huge white limestone cliffs forming the second-highest point on Hurwal Divide and in the Wallowa Mountains, is in the distance to the northeast.

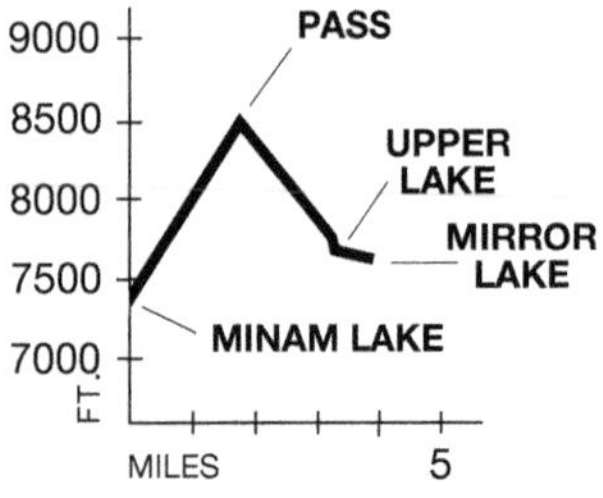

From the pass the trail meanders down 1.5 miles to Upper Lake (7,650 ft.). The trail crosses a bridge over the East Fork Lostine River 0.2 mile past Upper Lake.

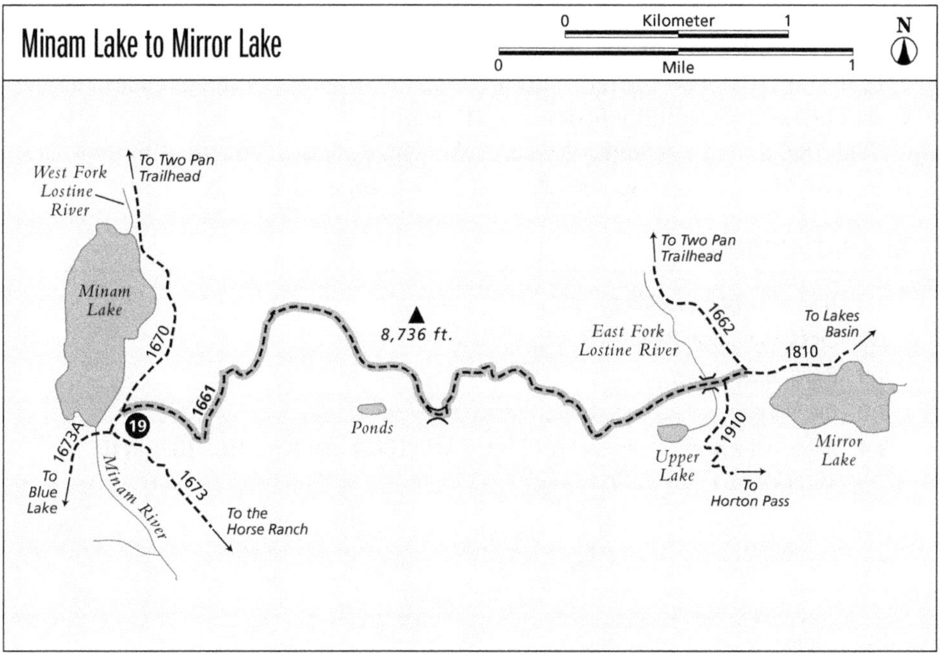

Minam Lake to Mirror Lake
0
Kilometer
1
0
Mile
1
N
To Two Pan Trailhead
West Fork Lostine River
Minam Lake
1670
1661
8,736 ft.
Ponds
19
1673A
To Blue Lake
Minam River
1673
To the Horse Ranch
To Two Pan Trailhead
1662
East Fork Lostine River
To Lakes Basin
1810
Mirror Lake
1910
Upper Lake
To Horton Pass

Mirror Lake.

Just past the bridge is the junction with Old East Fork Lostine River Trail. Mirror Lake is a short distance straight ahead. Horton Pass is to the right, and Old East Fork Trail is to the left. The East Fork Lostine River Trail (1662) is straight ahead a few yards. The elevation at this junction is 7,619 feet.

This trail is used to connect Minam Lake with the many attractions in the Lakes Basin area. Make a loop trip with the East Fork Lostine River Trail.

Miles and Directions

0.0 The trail begins near Minam Lake.

1.5 Cross Ivan Carper Pass. (GPS: N45 10.675'/ W117 19.970')

3.0 Reach Upper Lake.

3.2 The trail crosses East Fork Lostine River on a bridge.

3.4 Arrive at the junction with East Fork Lostine Trail (1662) near Mirror Lake. (GPS: N45 10.771'/W117 18.917')

20 Blue Lake

This trail connects Minam Lake and Blue Lake. Blue Lake sits in a striking subalpine bowl at the head of the Minam River. The Minam once flowed from Minam Lake, but a small earthen dam at its south end diverted its water into the Lostine drainage. This left the stream coming from Blue Lake as the source of the Minam River. (Trail 1673A)

Distance: 1 mile one way
Hiking time: About 0.5 hour
Difficulty: Easy
Trail maintenance: Infrequent
Best season: July through Sept
Traffic and other trail users: Moderate foot and horse traffic
Canine compatibility: Dogs permitted without leashes, but must be kept away from the stock of other parties
Fees and permits: Northwest Forest Pass and Eagle Cap Wilderness Permit
Maximum elevation: 7,730 feet
Map: USGS Eagle Cap OR
Trail contact: USDA Forest Service Wallowa Mountains Office, 201 E 2nd St./ PO Box 905, Joseph, OR 97846; (541) 426-5546, (541) 426-4978; www.fs.usda.gov/wallowa-whitman

Finding the trail: To reach Minam Lake drive 18 miles south on Lostine River Road from the town of Lostine to Two Pan Campground and Trailhead. The trailhead is at the end of the road (5,585 ft.). Hike south from the trailhead on the West Fork Lostine River Trail (1670) for 6.1 miles to Minam Lake and the junction with the Minam Lake/Mirror Lake Trail. The trail to Blue Lake leaves the Upper Minam River Trail (1673) just south of Minam Lake. The Blue Lake Trail junction is a few hundred feet south of the junction with Minam Lake/Mirror Lake Trail (1661).
GPS: Two Pan Trailhead: N45 15.001'/W117 22.580'; Upper Minam River Trail/Blue Lake Trail junction: N45 10.627'/W117 21.132'

The Hike

From the junction with the Upper Minam River Trail, the Blue Lake Trail heads west and crosses the Minam River creekbed. The Minam River is very small here and will probably be completely dry. The water that used to flow down the Minam River from Minam Lake was diverted many years ago. It now flows north down the West Fork Lostine River into the Wallowa Valley.

After crossing the dry creekbed, the trail turns to the southwest and begins to climb. It climbs steadily for 0.8 mile, then crosses the outlet of Blue Lake. This stream is actually now the headwaters of the Minam River, since the water from Minam Lake has been diverted. After crossing the stream, the trail turns to the right (west) and goes the last few yards to Blue Lake

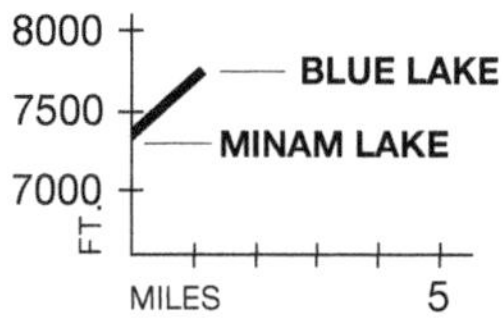

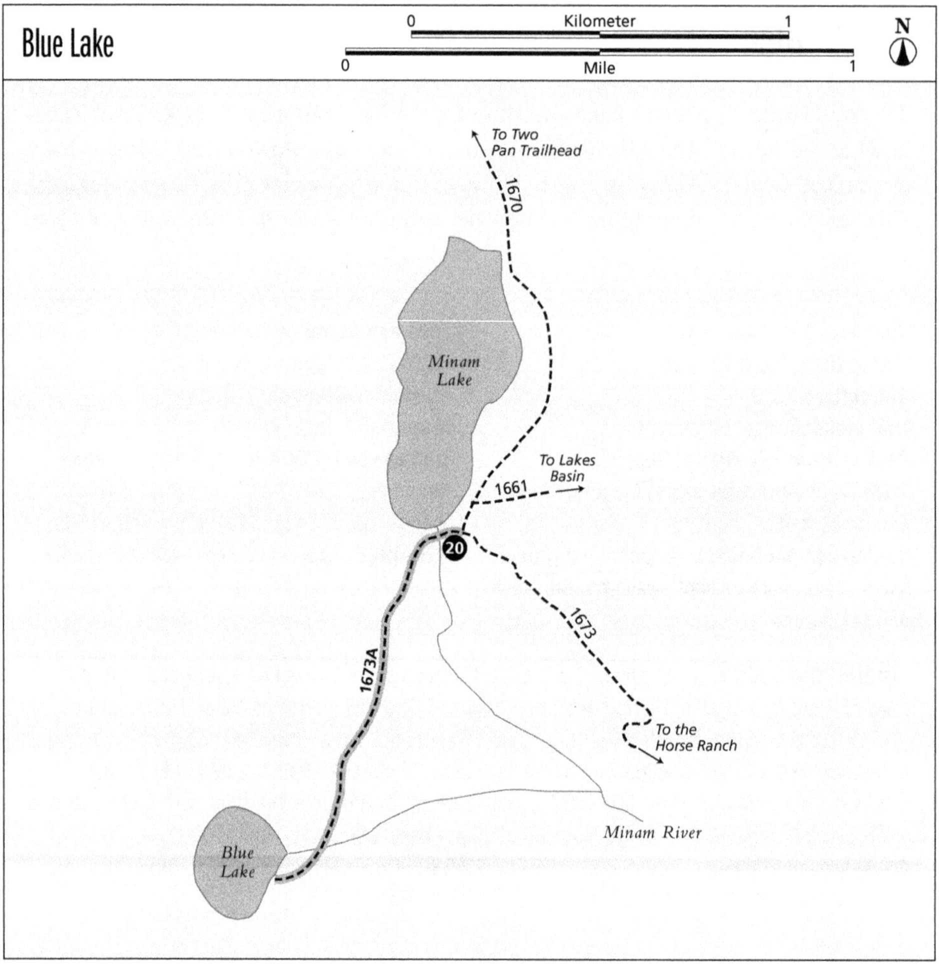

(7,703 ft.). There are several campsites around Blue Lake and trout to be caught. The return trip is made by the same trail.

Miles and Directions

0.0 Take the Blue Lake Trail (1673A) from the junction with the Upper Minam River Trail (1673).

0.8 The trail crosses outlet of Blue Lake.

1.0 Arrive at Blue Lake. (GPS: N45 10.058'/W117 21.516')

21 West Fork Lostine River

This day hike or backpack trail goes from Two Pan Trailhead to Minam Lake. This trail can be used to access Copper Creek Trail, Minam Lake/Mirror Lake Trail, and the Upper Minam River Trail. (Trail 1670)

See map page 78.
Distance: 6.1 miles one way
Hiking time: 2.5–4 hours
Difficulty: Moderate
Trail maintenance: Yearly
Best season: Mid-June through Sept
Traffic and other trail users: Heavy foot and horse traffic
Canine compatibility: Dogs permitted without leashes, but must be kept away from the stock of other parties
Fees and permits: Northwest Forest Pass and Eagle Cap Wilderness Permit
Maximum elevation: 7,430 feet
Maps: USGS Eagle Cap OR and Steamboat Lake OR; Geo Graphics Wallowa Mountains Eagle Cap Wilderness
Trail contact: USDA Forest Service Wallowa Mountains Office, 201 E 2nd St./ PO Box 905, Joseph, OR 97846; (541) 426-5546, (541) 426-4978; www.fs.usda.gov/wallowa-whitman

Finding the trailhead: Drive 18 miles south on Lostine River Road from the town of Lostine. The West Fork Lostine River Trail begins at Two Pan Campground and Trailhead, at the end of the road (5,585 ft.).
GPS: N45 15.001'/W117 22.580'

The Hike

From the trailhead follow the trail south 200 yards to the wilderness boundary and the junction with East Fork Trail (1662). Bear right at the junction. The trail crosses the East Fork of the Lostine River on a concrete bridge (5,670 ft.) 0.3 mile from the junction. The unmarked turnoff to Catched Two Lake is 0.7 mile past the bridge. See Catched Two Lake Route (hike 22). This area was hit by an avalanche some years ago, leaving it quite open. A waterfall can be seen uphill and to the right. The stream starts at Catched Two Lake. The lake is about 1 mile away and nearly 2,000 feet up. The impressive north face of Elkhorn Peak is close by to the southwest, at the Catched Two Lake turnoff.

The junction with Copper Creek Trail (1656) is 1.5 miles farther. Copper Creek Trail goes west and leads to Swamp and Steamboat Lakes. The West Fork Lostine River Trail continues straight ahead and crosses the river 1.75 miles past the Copper Creek Trail junction. It crosses the river again 1 mile farther along. Between the river crossings, the river

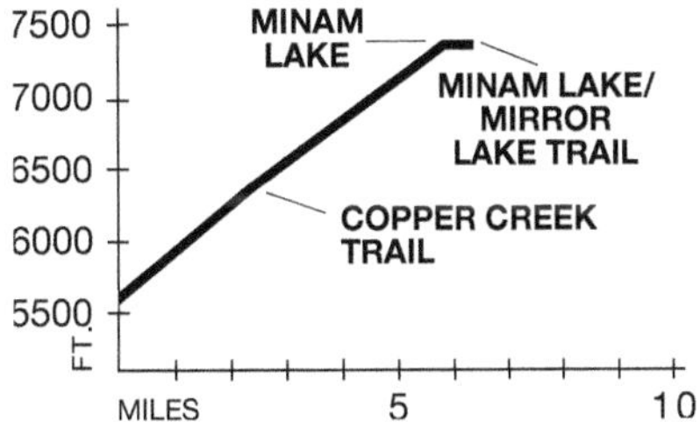

West Fork Lostine River Trail. GARY FLETCHER PHOTO

flows through open meadows. Here there are several areas of slow-flowing water that are full of small but beautiful brook trout that are just waiting to be caught. The elevation at the second crossing is 7,250 feet. Minam Lake (7,373 ft.) comes into view on the right at 5.5 miles.

The trail goes around the east (left) side of the lake and climbs 50 feet or so above the shoreline. Other access paths follow the shore in this area. At 6.1 miles the trail comes to the junction with Trail 1661, which goes to the east to Mirror Lake and the Lakes Basin. See Minam Lake to Mirror Lake (hike 19). The Upper Minam River Trail goes straight ahead at the junction. Blue Lake Trail is a short distance south on the Upper Minam River Trail. See Blue Lake (hike 20).

At the south end of Minam Lake there is an earthen dam. This dam prevents Minam Lake water from going down the Minam River. The water now drains north down the Lostine River to the Wallowa Valley, where it is used for irrigation. There are good campsites all around Minam Lake, but make sure your camp is 200 or more feet away from the water. Fishing can be good in Minam Lake. Some of the larger trout in the Wallowas live here, but you have to be there at the right time and use the right tackle, or fishing may be very slow. The timing and the bait are extremely variable, so each angler has to use his or her own ideas and take a chance.

Option: To make a loop trip, take Minam Lake/Mirror Lake Trail to Mirror Lake and return to Two Pan Trailhead via East Fork Lostine River Trail.

Miles and Directions

0.0 The trail begins at the Two Pan Trailhead and Campground.

2.6 Pass the junction with Copper Creek Trail (1656).

4.3 Cross West Fork Lostine River.

5.5 Reach the north end of Minam Lake.

6.1 Arrive at the junction with Minam Lake/Mirror Lake Trail (1661). (GPS: N45 10.667'/W117 21.098')

22 Catched Two Lake Route

A short hike along the West Fork Lostine River Trail leads to a steep off-trail climb to Catched Two Lake, cradled in a rugged alpine cirque. (Trail 1670 and off-trail)

Distance: 2 miles one way
Hiking time: 2.5–4 hours from Two Pan Trailhead
Difficulty: Strenuous
Trail maintenance: None
Best season: Mid-July through Sept
Traffic and other trail users: Light foot traffic, no stock use after leaving the West Fork Lostine River Trail
Canine compatibility: Dogs permitted without leashes, but should be kept away from the stock of other parties
Fees and permits: Northwest Forest Pass and Eagle Cap Wilderness Permit
Maximum elevation: 7,980 feet
Map: USGS Steamboat Lake OR
Trail contact: USDA Forest Service Wallowa Mountains Office, 201 E 2nd St./PO Box 905, Joseph, OR 97846; (541) 426-5546, (541) 426-4978; www.fs.usda.gov/wallowa-whitman. Further information will probably be limited.

Finding the trailhead: Drive 18 miles south from Lostine on the Lostine River Road to Two Pan Trailhead.
GPS: Two Pan Trailhead: N45 15.501'/W117 22.580'; Catched Two Lake junction: N45 14.350'/W117 22.813'

The Hike

From Two Pan Trailhead hike south on the West Fork Lostine River Trail (1670). (The West and East Fork Lostine River Trails diverge a short distance south of the trailhead.) One mile from the trailhead the route (there is no trail) leaves the trail (6,000 ft.). At the point where the route turns off the West Fork Lostine River Trail, there is a semi-open area, and a waterfall can be seen high above to the right. This waterfall is on the stream that flows out of Catched Two Lake (check your map).

The route crosses the West Fork Lostine River on a log or by wading the ice-cold waters. After crossing the river, work your way northwest to the right side of the stream coming down from Catched Two Lake. Keep to the right of the stream and climb to a point just above the falls (7,200 ft.). Above the falls follow the main fork of the stream, turn slightly to the right, and climb on up through the rock outcropping to Catched Two Lake (7,980 ft.).

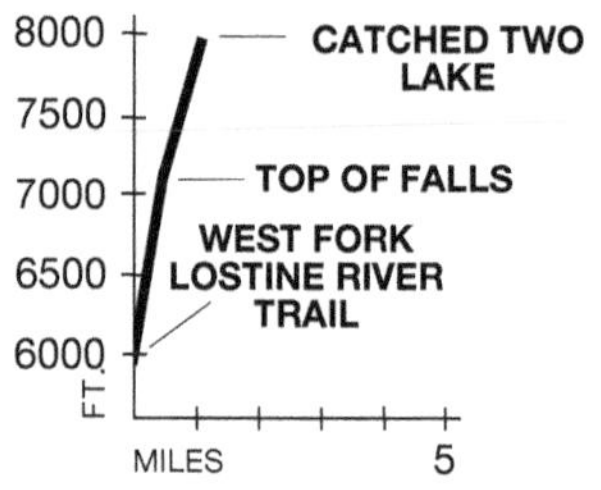

The 1,982-foot climb to Catched Two Lake takes about 2 hours under good conditions. Catched Two Lake is far enough off the trail and a steep enough climb that it is not heavily used. There are plenty of

Catched Two Lake.

brook trout to be caught, and this is a good area to see mule deer and elk. A good campsite is located next to the stream some distance below the lake, and there are some less desirable sites around the lake. The name Catched Two, as the story goes, comes from the fact that two early-day sheepherders were caught by their boss sleeping next to the lake. He said, in his broken English, "I catched two"; hence the name.

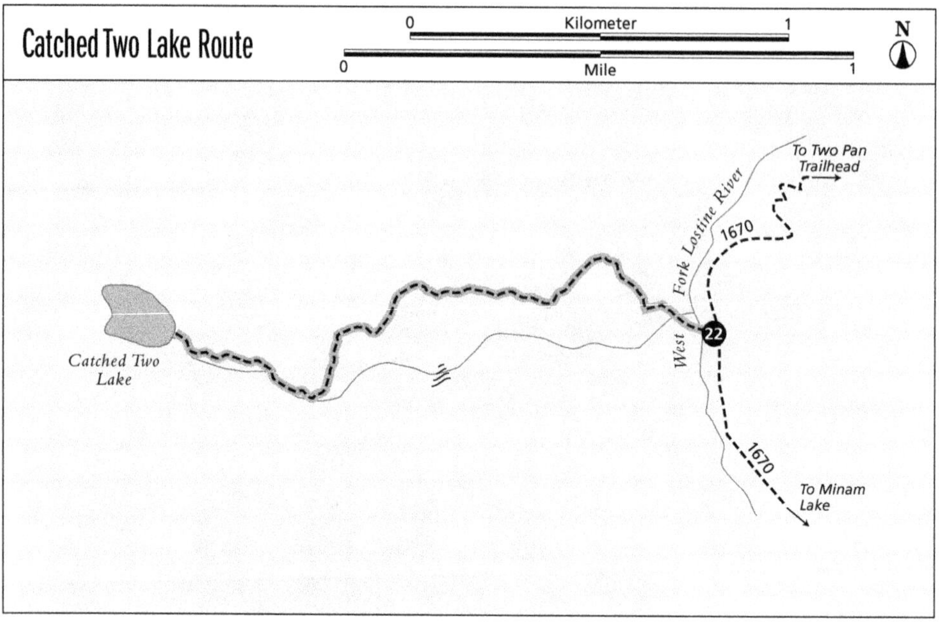

This route requires some route-finding and off-trail skills. It should not be attempted by novice hikers.

Miles and Directions

0.0 Hike south from Two Pan Trailhead.

1.0 The route leaves the West Fork Lostine River Trail (1670). (GPS: N45 14.350'/W117 22.813')

2.0 Arrive at Catched Two Lake. (GPS: N45 14.335'/W117 24.090')

23 Copper Creek

This long day hike or backpack leads from the West Fork Lostine River Trail to North Minam River Trail. This trail is also the access to Granite Creek Trail and Cheval Lake Trail. (Trail 1656)

Distance: 5 miles one way
Hiking time: 2–3.5 hours
Difficulty: Moderate to strenuous
Trail maintenance: Infrequent
Best season: July through Sept
Traffic and other trail users: Moderate foot and horse traffic
Canine compatibility: Dogs permitted without leashes, but must be kept away from the stock of other parties
Fees and permits: Northwest Forest Pass and Eagle Cap Wilderness Permit
Maximum elevation: 8,600 feet
Maps: USGS Eagle Cap OR and Steamboat Lake OR; Geo Graphics Wallowa Mountains Eagle Cap Wilderness
Trail contact: USDA Forest Service Wallowa Mountains Office, 201 E 2nd St./PO Box 905, Joseph, OR 97846; (541) 426-5546, (541) 426-4978; www.fs.usda.gov/wallowa-whitman

Finding the trail: From Lostine drive south on Lostine River Road for 18 miles to its end at Two Pan Trailhead. Hike south from the trailhead on the West Fork Lostine River Trail (1670) for 2.8 miles to the junction with Copper Creek Trail. There is a signpost at this junction (6,425 ft.).
GPS: Two Pan Trailhead: N45 15.001'/W117 22.580'; Copper Creek Trail junction: N45 13.298'/W117 22.200'

The Hike

Turn right (west) at the Copper Creek Trail junction. Copper Creek Trail crosses the West Fork Lostine River 200 yards after leaving West Fork Lostine River Trail (1670). There is no bridge at this crossing. A few yards upriver from the spot where the trail crosses is a shallower spot, which is easier to cross for people on foot. After crossing the river, the trail crosses a couple of small side streams, then begins to climb.

At 1.75 miles the trail crosses Copper Creek (6,900 ft.). After crossing Copper Creek the trail climbs steadily through thinning forest. One-half mile farther (7,320 ft.) is another crossing of Copper Creek. After crossing the creek the trail flattens out and enters the beautiful subalpine valley at the head of Copper Creek. The trail soon crosses another creek, then heads on up the valley for 0.3 mile before turning to the right and beginning to climb a series of switchbacks. There are several nice campsites in this subalpine valley.

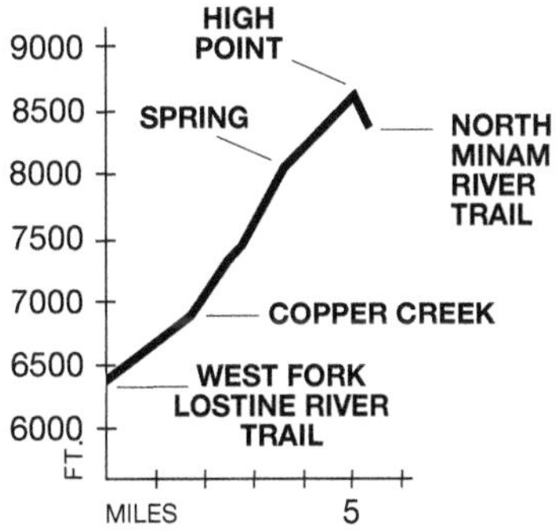

The trail climbs out of the valley and crosses Elkhorn Creek at 7,800 feet elevation and

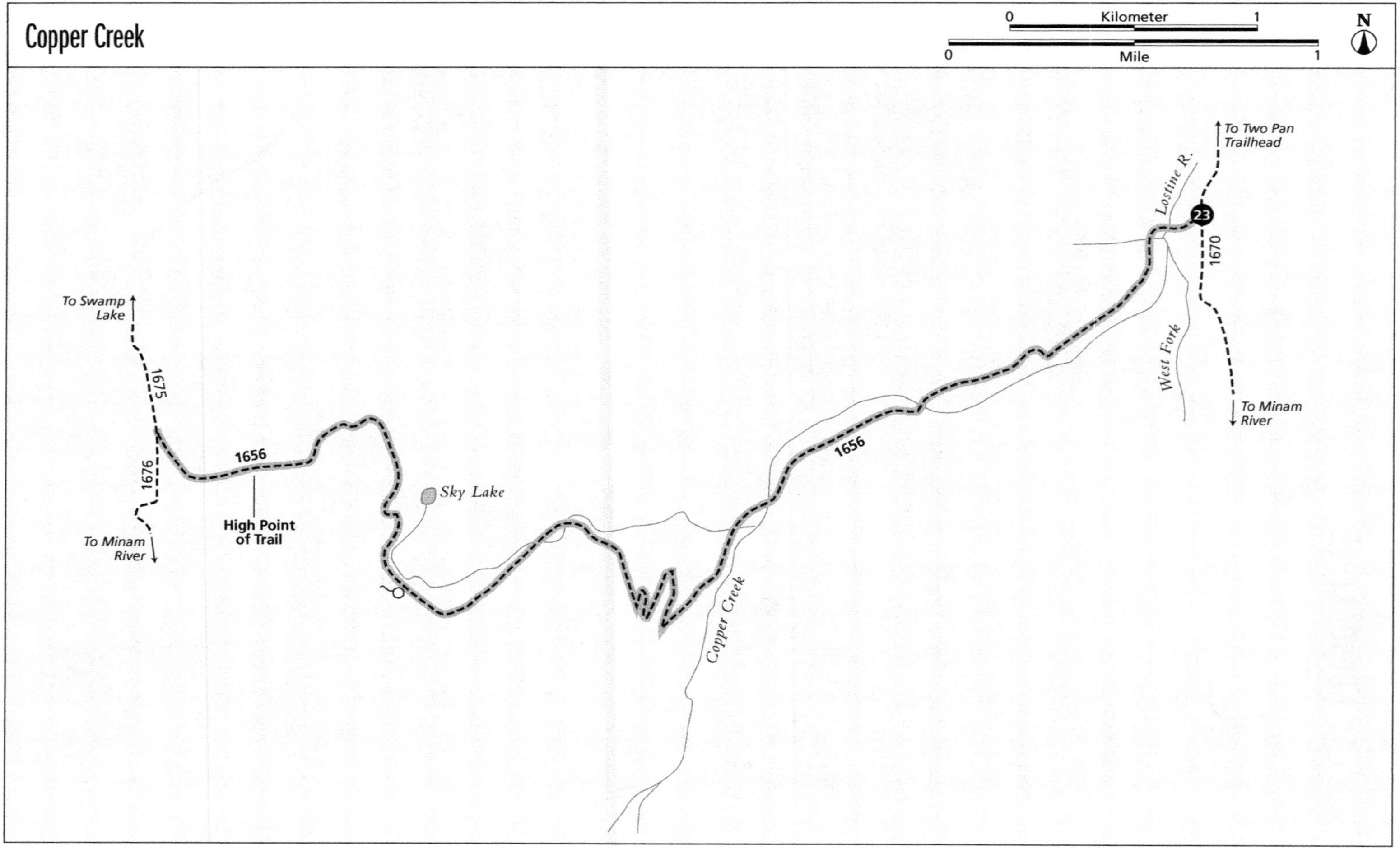
Copper Creek
Kilometer
0
1
Mile
0
1
N
To Two Pan Trailhead
Lostine R.
23
1670
West Fork
To Minam River
1656
Copper Creek
Sky Lake
1656
High Point of Trail
To Swamp Lake
1675
1676
To Minam River

enters a small alpine valley. The trail soon crosses the creek again and goes on up the valley for 0.25 mile, where it makes a couple of switchbacks. Above the switchbacks the trail makes an ascending traverse to the northwest, passing a good spring (8,110 ft.). Sky Lake is a couple hundred yards off the trail to the right (northeast), 0.25 mile after passing the spring.

After the traverse the trail works its way up through rounded granite outcroppings and small alpine meadows until it reaches the top of a rounded ridge (8,510 ft.). This ridgetop is 4.5 miles from the West Fork Lostine River Trail. After reaching the ridge the trail turns left and climbs to the southwest for 0.25 mile to its high point (8,600 ft.).

From this point Swamp Lake can be seen below to the northwest. The junction with North Minam River Trail (8,420 ft.) is 0.25 mile farther. North Minam River Trail (1675) turns right and goes down to Swamp Lake and North Minam Meadows. See North Minam River (hike 44). To the left, Granite Creek Trail (1676) heads for the Minam River. See Granite Creek (hike 47).

The area around this junction is very alpine, with only a few small trees. The country is typical of ridgetop areas in the western Wallowa Mountains. Many alpine flowers bloom in this timberline area as soon as the snow melts. This is big buck mule deer country, and it also has quite a few elk.

An extended loop trip is possible by combining Copper Creek Trail with North Minam River Trail, Upper Minam River Trail, and the West Fork Lostine River Trail.

Miles and Directions

0.0 Take the Copper Creek Trail (1656) from the junction with West Fork Lostine River Trail (1670).

0.1 Cross West Fork Lostine River.

1.7 Cross Copper Creek.

2.3 Enter the alpine valley at the head of Copper Creek.

4.7 Reach the high point overlooking Swamp Lake.

5.0 Arrive at the junction with North Minam River Trail (1675). (GPS: N45 12.730'/W117 25.630')

24 Maxwell Lake

Day hike or backpack from Maxwell Lake Trailhead on the Lostine River Road to Maxwell Lake. The alpine setting of the lake and the views along the trail make it well worth the climb. (Trail 1674)

Distance: 4 miles one way
Hiking time: 2–3.5 hours, less on the return trip
Difficulty: Moderate
Trail maintenance: Infrequent
Best season: July through Sept
Traffic and other trail users: Moderate foot and horse traffic
Canine compatibility: Dogs permitted without leashes, but must be kept away from the stock of other parties
Fees and permits: Northwest Forest Pass and Eagle Cap Wilderness Permit
Maximum elevation: 7,790 feet
Map: USGS North Minam Meadows OR
Trail contact: USDA Forest Service Wallowa Mountains Office, 201 E 2nd St./PO Box 905, Joseph, OR 97846; (541) 426-5546, (541) 426-4978; www.fs.usda.gov/wallowa-whitman

Finding the trailhead: Go 17 miles south of Lostine on Lostine River Road to the Maxwell Lake Trailhead. The trailhead (5,440 ft.) is on the east (left) side of the road. There is a small campground on the west side of the road.
GPS: N45 15.499'/W117 23.057'

The Hike

Walk across the Lostine River Road and through the campground. Then head west and cross the Lostine River on a bridge. Seventy-five feet after crossing the river is the Eagle Cap Wilderness boundary sign. At 0.2 mile there is a major creek crossing (5,470 ft.). This crossing may be difficult during periods of heavy runoff. There are boulders a few feet below the trail that can be used to aid in the crossing. After crossing the creek the trail makes several switchbacks, crossing a couple of small creeks several times. At 2.75 miles (6,600 ft.) there is a good view of Eagle Cap to the south, directly up the East Fork Lostine Canyon.

At 3 miles the trail becomes very rocky and steep. The trail below this point has been reconstructed, but above this point it has not been. The trail climbs steeply to a small meadow at 3.5 miles, where it may disappear for a short distance. The trail follows the right (north) side of the meadow and climbs slightly to a pass (7,790 ft.), then descends to Maxwell Lake (7,729 ft.).

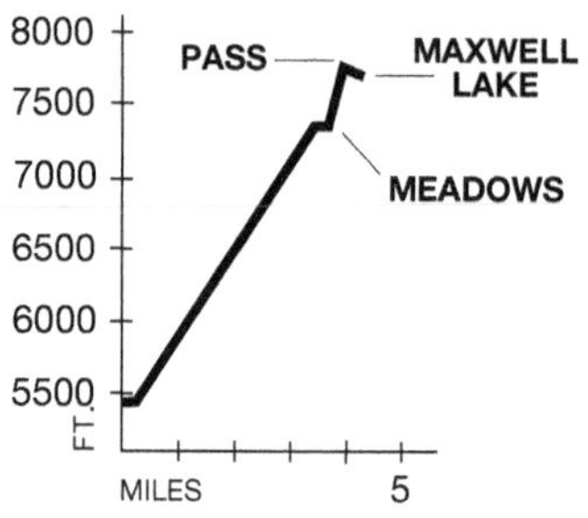

Maxwell Lake, 4 miles from the trailhead, has excellent fishing for the usual small brook trout.

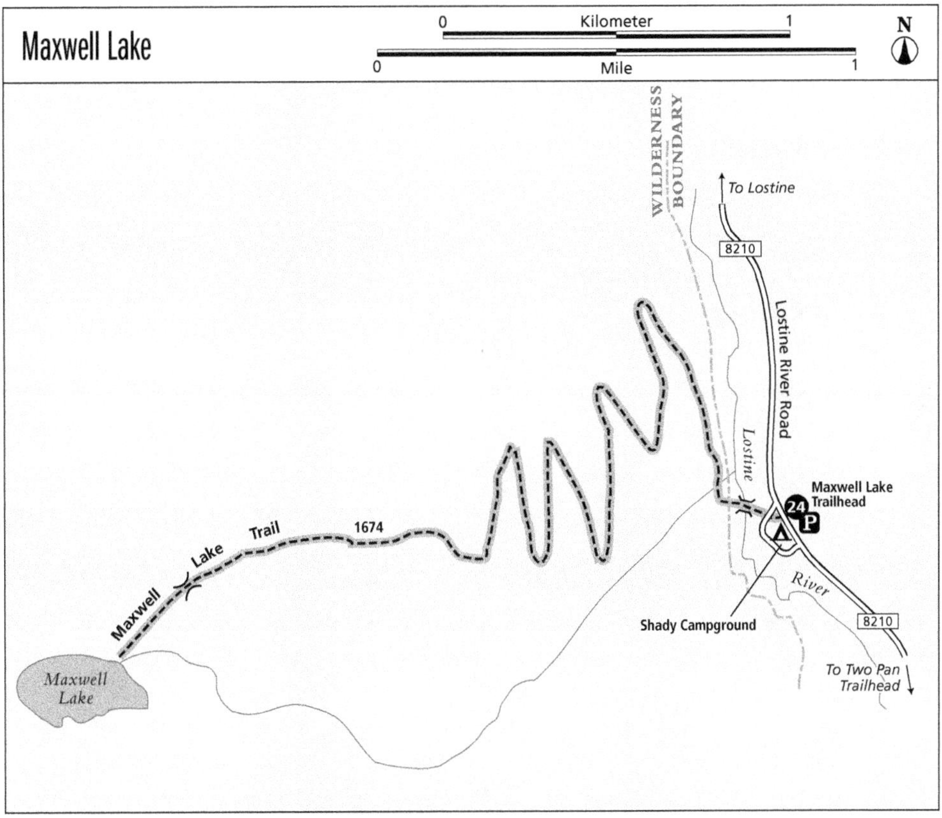
Maxwell Lake
0
Kilometer
1
0
Mile
1
N
WILDERNESS BOUNDARY
To Lostine
8210
Lostine River Road
Lostine
Maxwell Lake Trailhead
24
P
Maxwell Lake Trail 1674
River
Shady Campground
8210
To Two Pan Trailhead
Maxwell Lake

Maxwell Lake.

Campsites are not plentiful at the lake but can be found on the north side. Be sure to camp at least 200 feet from the lake. The setting of Maxwell Lake, near the top of a ridge, is well worth the hike. Return via the same trail.

Miles and Directions

0.0 Start at the Maxwell Lake Trailhead.

0.2 Cross the creek.

3.0 Reach the end of the reconstructed trail.

3.7 Cross the pass.

4.0 Arrive at Maxwell Lake. (GPS: N45 15.248'/W117 24.690')

25 Frances Lake

A long day hike or backpack leads from the Lostine River Road at the bottom of the Lostine River Canyon over one of the highest trail passes in Eagle Cap Wilderness and down to Frances Lake. (Trail 1663)

Distance: 9.2 miles one way
Hiking time: 3-5 hours
Difficulty: Moderate. This trail is never very steep, but it follows a long, 9 percent grade.
Trail maintenance: Yearly
Best season: Mid-July through Sept
Traffic and other trail users: Moderate foot and horse traffic
Canine compatibility: Dogs permitted without leashes, but must be kept away from the stock of other parties
Fees and permits: Northwest Forest Pass and Eagle Cap Wilderness Permit
Maximum elevation: 8,610 feet
Maps: USGS North Minam Meadows OR and Chief Joseph Mountain OR; Geo Graphics Wallowa Mountains Eagle Cap Wilderness
Trail contact: USDA Forest Service Wallowa Mountains Office, 201 E 2nd St./ PO Box 905, Joseph, OR 97846; (541) 426-5546, (541) 426-4978; www.fs.usda.gov/wallowa-whitman

Finding the trailhead: From Lostine go 14.7 miles south on Lostine River Road to the combined Frances Lake/Bowman Trailhead parking area. The parking area is on the east side of the road.
GPS: N45 17.606'/W117 23.675'

The Hike

Hike south from the combined trailhead for 0.2 mile. Then the trail heads east and starts the climb immediately. It passes Eagle Cap Wilderness boundary 200 feet from the trailhead. It then switches back continually at an even, easy grade. The trail crosses a creek at 1 mile (5,690 ft.). At 5.2 miles it comes to an open area and another creek crossing (7,260 ft.) below Marble Point. There are many flowers in this open area.

Above the creek crossing the trail makes a long switchback to the north. It then switches back south again, just below the ridge dividing Lake Creek drainage and the Lostine Canyon. At 7.2 miles the trail crosses the pass (8,610 ft.). From the top of the ridge the view is impressive, with the dark brown spires of 9,665-foot-high Twin Peaks to the east and Frances Lake below, to the southeast.

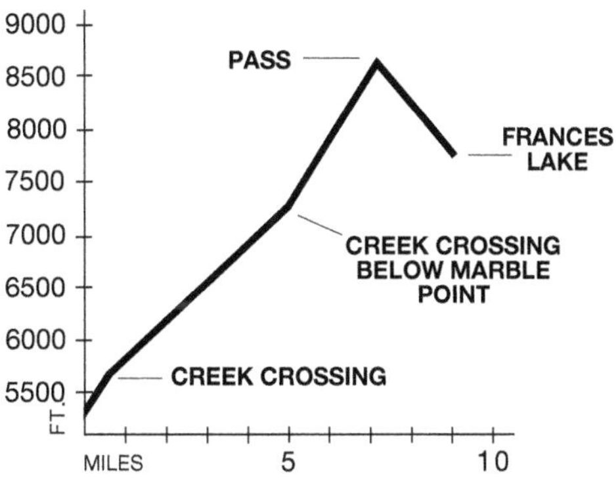

After crossing the pass, the trail descends the last 2 miles to Frances

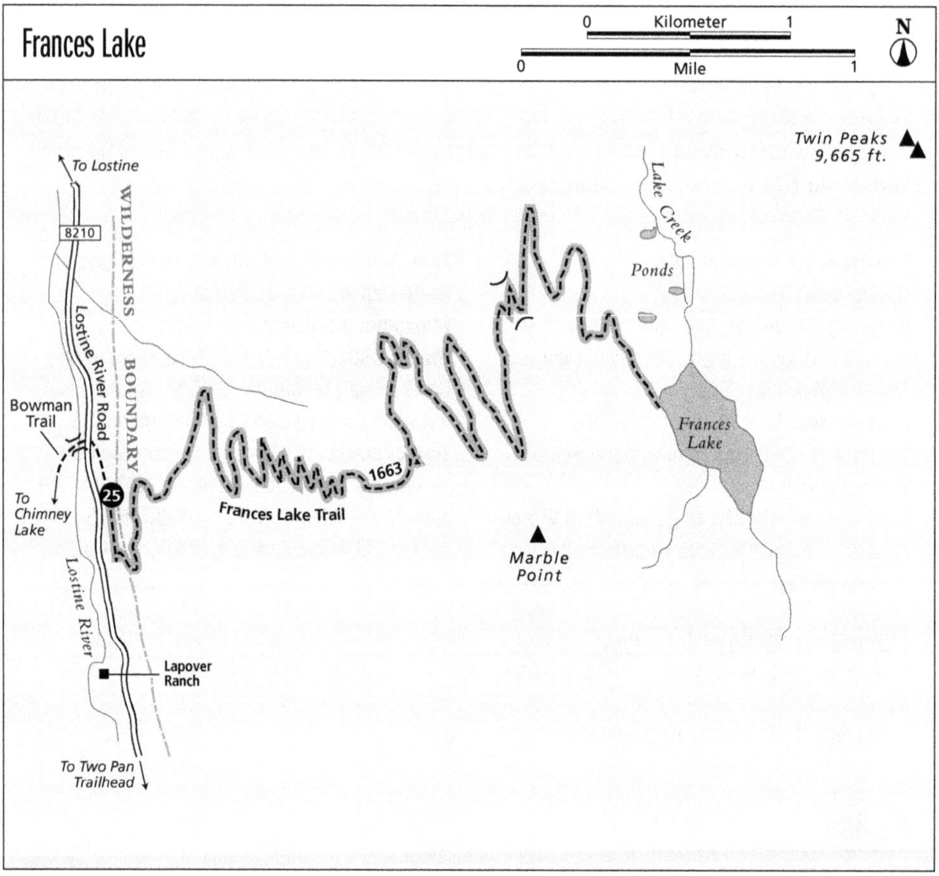

Lake (7,705 ft.). At Frances Lake the vegetation looks much like that of the mountainous areas of Alaska. There are a few stunted trees, alpine willows, and a lot of tundra and exposed rock. This is one of the best areas in the Wallowa Mountains to see mountain goats and bighorn sheep. Look for them with binoculars to the east, on Hurricane Divide.

There are many campsites around Frances Lake. The ponds in Lake Creek, below the lake, are known for their large trout, and there are lots of fish in Frances Lake itself. Return to the trailhead by going back down the same trail. The entire 9.2-mile one-way trail to Frances Lake is at an even grade. Although it is quite long, it is not difficult.

Miles and Directions

0.0 Begin at the Frances Lake/Bowman Trailhead.

0.9 Cross the creek.

5.2 Cross the creek below Marble Point.

Frances Lake.

7.2 Cross the pass. (GPS: N45 17.834'/W117 22.158')

9.2 Arrive at Frances Lake. (GPS: N45 17.632'/W117 21.607')

26 Bowman Trail

From Frances Lake/Bowman Trailhead, on the Lostine River Road, follow the trail to North Minam Meadows. The route climbs from the thickly forested bottom of the Lostine River Canyon through subalpine meadows then crosses a pass before you descend past John Henry Lake to North Minam Meadows. (Trail 1651)

Distance: 10 miles one way (backpack)
Hiking time: 4–7 hours
Difficulty: Moderate
Trail maintenance: Yearly
Best season: July through Sept
Traffic and other trail users: Heavy to Chimney Lake Trail; moderate past the junction, with moderate to heavy horse traffic
Canine compatibility: Dogs permitted without leashes, but must be kept away from the stock of other parties
Fees and permits: Northwest Forest Pass and Eagle Cap Wilderness Permit
Maximum elevation: 7,740 feet
Map: USGS North Minam Meadows OR
Trail contact: USDA Forest Service Wallowa Mountains Office, 201 E 2nd St./PO Box 905, Joseph, OR 97846; (541) 426-5546, (541) 426-4978; www.fs.usda.gov/wallowa-whitman

Finding the trailhead: From Lostine go 14.7 miles south on Lostine River Road to the combined Frances Lake/Bowman Trailhead (5,280 ft.). There is parking at the trailhead.
GPS: N45 17.606'/W117 23.685'

The Hike

From the combined trailhead, hike parallel to Lostine River Road for 0.2 mile to the north. Then cross the road and head west on the trail, crossing the Lostine River on a concrete bridge. At 0.3 mile (5,250 ft.) the Bowman Trail crosses Bowman Creek. A footbridge is located just upstream from the trail. After crossing the footbridge the trail makes a long switchback, coming back again to Bowman Creek in 0.9 mile. It then switches back south again and climbs through mixed timber and open hillsides. Near the end of this switchback, Lapover Ranch can be seen far below to the south. The mountain across the canyon to the east is Marble Point, near Frances Lake.

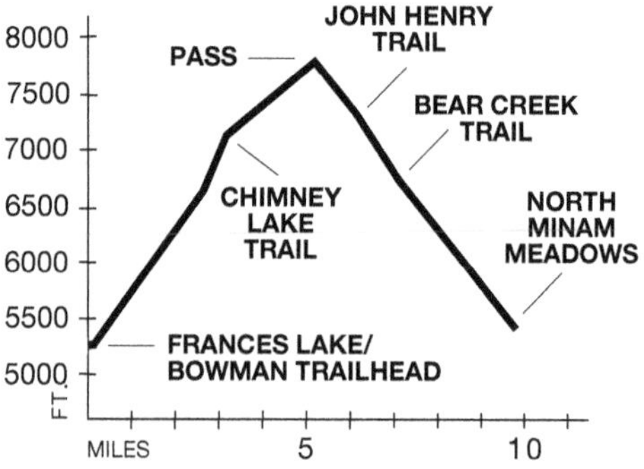

The trail crosses Bowman Creek again at slightly less than 3 miles. The creek has three channels at this point (6,670 ft.). After the crossing, the trail makes a jog to the north, then continues up Bowman Creek. Soon a meadow comes into view below the

North Minam Meadows. GARY FLETCHER PHOTO

trail to the left. This beautiful alpine meadow and the slopes around it make up Brownie Basin. There are several good campsites in Brownie Basin.

At 4 miles pass the junction with Chimney Lake Trail (1659) at 7,240 feet. At this point the trail is a couple hundred feet above the floor of Brownie Basin. Looking south from the junction, there is a good view of upper Brownie Basin and Flagstaff Point.

The trail contours along the west side of Brownie Basin, then makes two switchbacks and climbs to a pass (7,740 ft.) 1.5 miles from the Chimney Lake Trail junction. The pass is on the ridge dividing the Lostine River drainage and the North Minam River drainage. Look down to the west to see Wilson Basin, with John Henry Lake on its far (west) side.

The trail makes a hard right turn at the pass, then drops steadily for 1 mile to the unmarked junction with John Henry Lake Trail (7,200 ft.). The John Henry Lake Trail is a poor side trail that leads straight ahead to John Henry Lake from one of the switchbacks on the Bowman Trail. The junction with this side trail is just above the floor of the basin. Don't take the side trail unless you want to go to John Henry Lake. The elevation of John Henry Lake is 7,168 feet. From the junction, John Henry Lake is 0.5 mile to the southwest. There are several other side trails in Wilson Basin. Be careful to stay on the main trail, which is much more traveled than the others.

The trail continues to descend slowly through Wilson Basin to the junction with Bear Creek Trail (1653). Bear Creek Trail junction is 7.5 miles from the Bowman

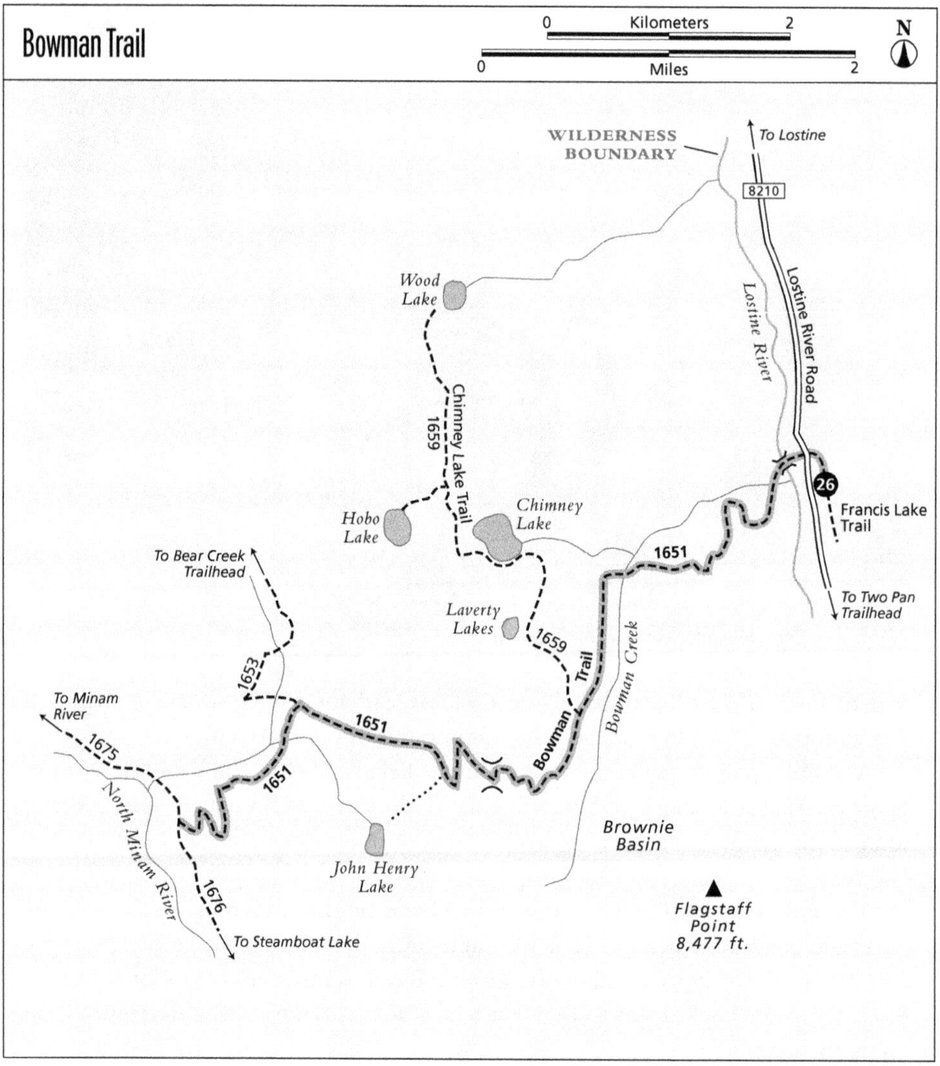

Trailhead. The altitude at the junction of Bear Creek and Bowman Trails is 6,750 feet. Bear Creek Trail heads to the north.

From the junction, the Bowman Trail winds down 2.5 miles to North Minam Meadows (5,440 ft.) and the junction with North Minam River Trail (1675). See North Minam River (hike 44). North Minam Meadows is large and lush, with the North Minam River flowing through it. It is common to see elk feeding in the meadow in the morning and late afternoon. There are many campsites around the edge of North Minam Meadows, and plenty of firewood.

A loop trip is possible by using the North Minam River, Copper Creek, and West Fork Lostine River Trails. This loop requires a short car shuttle to Two Pan Trailhead or a walk back down Lostine River Road.

Miles and Directions

0.0 The trail begins at Frances Lake/Bowman Trailhead.

4.0 Pass the junction with Chimney Lake Trail (1659). (GPS: N45 16.568'/W117 25.132')

5.5 Cross the pass.

6.5 Pass the junction with the John Henry Lake Trail.

7.5 Pass the junction with the Bear Creek Trail (1653).

10.0 Arrive at North Minam Meadows and the junction with North Minam River Trail (1675). (GPS: N45 16.125'/W117 27.645')

27 Chimney Lake

A side trail runs from Bowman Trail in Brownie Basin to Wood Lake. This trail also goes to Chimney and Hobo Lakes. Chimney Lake is a good place to camp and explore the more remote country around Wood and Hobo Lakes. (Trail 1659)

Distance: 3.6 miles one way
Hiking time: 1.5–2 hours
Difficulty: Moderate
Trail maintenance: Yearly
Best season: Mid-July through Sept
Traffic and other trail users: Heavy foot and horse traffic to Chimney Lake; moderate to Wood and Hobo Lakes
Canine compatibility: Dogs permitted without leashes, but must be kept away from the stock of other parties
Fees and permits: Northwest Forest Pass and Eagle Cap Wilderness Permit
Maximum elevation: 8,060 feet to Wood Lake; 8,380 feet to Hobo Lake
Map: USGS North Minam Meadows OR
Trail contact: USDA Forest Service Wallowa Mountains Office, 201 E 2nd St./ PO Box 905, Joseph, OR 97846; (541) 426-5546, (541) 426-4978; www.fs.usda.gov/wallowa-whitman

Finding the trail: To reach the trail junction where the Chimney Lake Trail (1659) begins, drive south from Lostine for 14.7 miles on Lostine River Road to the combined Frances Lake/Bowman Trailhead (5,280 ft.). The parking area is on the left (east) side of the road. Then hike west on the Bowman Trail (1651) for 4 miles to the junction with the Chimney Lake Trail.
GPS: Frances Lake/Bowman Trailhead: N45 17.606'/W117 23.685'; Chimney Lake Trail: N45 16.568'/W117 25.132'

The Hike

From the junction with Bowman Trail (1651; 7,240 ft.), Chimney Lake Trail turns off to the right (north). Chimney Lake Trail passes Laverty Lakes (7,450 ft.) 0.5 mile from the junction. Laverty Lakes are on the left (west) side of the trail. Chimney Lake (7,604 ft.) is another 0.75 mile past Laverty Lakes. There are good campsites to the right (north) of the trail, just before reaching Chimney Lake. There is an abundance of trout waiting to be caught in Chimney Lake.

The trail goes around the south side of Chimney Lake and leaves the lake at its southwest corner. At first the trail climbs southwest for a short distance. It then makes a sharp right turn and begins a long ascending traverse above the west side of Chimney Lake. The trail climbs to a pass (8,060 ft.) 1 mile from Chimney Lake. At the pass the faint trail to Hobo Lake turns off to the left. Up to this point the trail can be seen from Chimney Lake.

From the pass the trail drops through tundra and an avalanche area to a meadow. Go along the right side of the meadow to Wood Lake. Wood Lake (7,338 ft.) is 1.4 miles from the pass and 3.6 miles from the Bowman Trail. There are several good

Chimney Lake

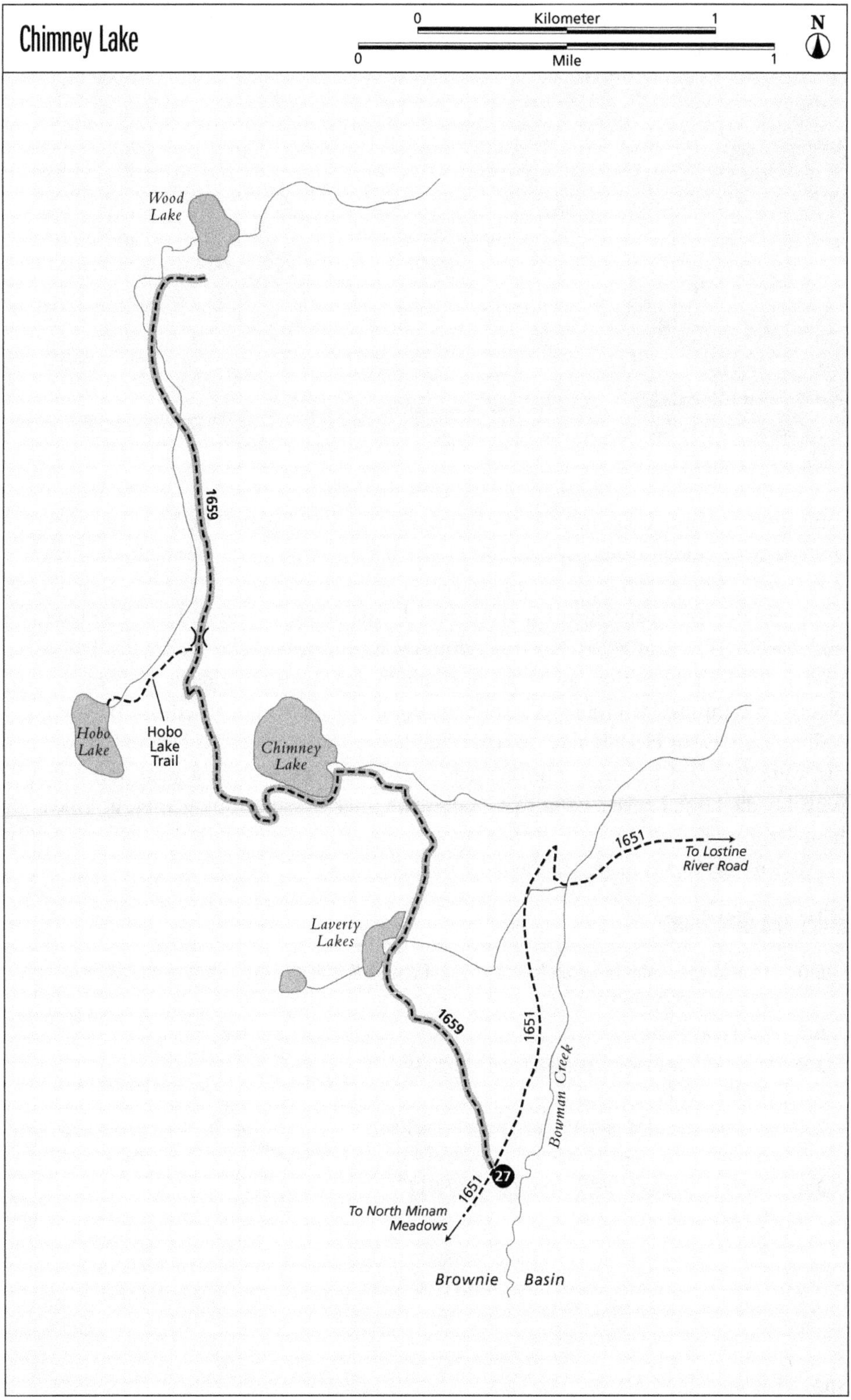

Chimney Lake.

campsites at Wood Lake. Fishing for brook trout is good here. The lake was once stocked with golden trout, as was Hobo Lake. If there are any of them left, they are very rare.

To reach Hobo Lake, turn left at the pass 1 mile above Chimney Lake. The faint trail crosses a creek at 8,180 feet, then goes on up to Hobo Lake (8,369 ft.). Hobo Lake is 0.7 mile from the pass, in an open alpine area near the ridgeline. There are plenty of campsites at Hobo Lake, but firewood is scarce and should not be used. Fishing is spotty at Hobo Lake. Golden trout, native to the Sierra Nevada in California, were once stocked here, but they have not been seen in several years and have probably died out. Legend has it that a hobo was once found camping at Hobo Lake, hence its name.

The return trip is made via the same trail.

Miles and Directions

0.0 At the junction with Bowman Trail (1651) in Brownie Basin, go right (north) on the Chimney Lake Trail (1659).

0.5 Pass Laverty Lakes.

1.3 Reach Chimney Lake (southeast end). (GPS: N45 17.350'/W117 25.637')

2.2 Cross the pass and pass the junction with the Hobo Lake Trail. (GPS: N45 17.684'/ W117 25.974')

3.6 Arrive at Wood Lake. (GPS: N45 18.450'/W117 25.937')

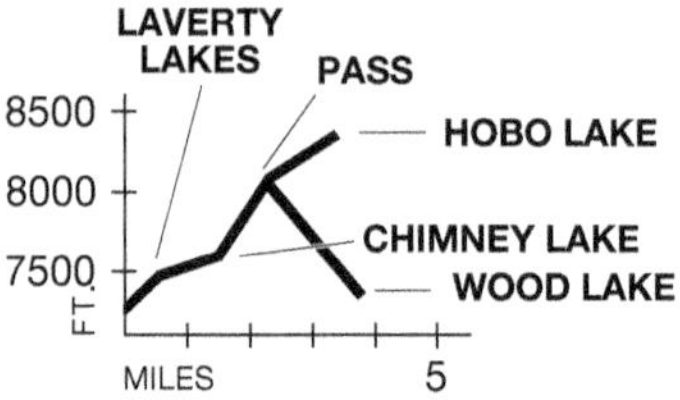

28 Murray Saddle (Bill George Trail)

This trail leads from an obscure trailhead on Lime Quarry Road to Silver Creek via Murray Saddle (aka Murray Gap or the Gap). This is not a horse trail.

Distance: 3.5 miles one way
Hiking time: 2–3 hours
Difficulty: Moderate to strenuous to Murray Saddle, easy beyond the saddle
Trail maintenance: Infrequent, as it is done by volunteers. However, the trail is usually in fairly good condition. This trail is not suited or maintained for horse traffic. If you have horses, please do not use this trail. The switchbacks are too small, and branches are not cleared more than 5 feet above the ground. Horses cause much damage to this trail. Horse traffic should use the Old Murray Saddle Trail described in the text below.
Best season: Mid-June through Oct
Other trail users: Moderate except during early Oct deer hunting season, when it can be heavy
Canine compatibility: Dogs permitted without leashes, but must be kept away from the stock of other parties
Fees and permits: Eagle Cap Wilderness Permit; you will need to get this permit at a forest service office, as they are not available at the trailhead.
Maximum elevation: 7,320 feet
Maps: USGS Enterprise OR and Chief Joseph Mountain OR cover the area, but the trail is not shown on these maps.
Trail contact: USDA Forest Service Wallowa Mountains Office, 201 E 2nd St./PO Box 905, Joseph, OR 97846; (541) 426-5546, (541) 426-4978; www.fs.usda.gov/wallowa-whitman. Further information from the forest service will probably be limited.

Finding the trailhead: From the south end of Enterprise, on OR 82, take Hurricane Creek Road. Hurricane Creek Road goes straight ahead (south) at the last 90-degree corner the highway makes in Enterprise. Go 2 blocks south on Hurricane Creek Road to Fish Hatchery Road. Turn right on Fish Hatchery Road and follow it 1.2 miles to Alder Slope Road. Turn left on Alder Slope Road and follow it 1.7 miles to Black Marble Lane. Black Marble Lane is a gravel road that goes straight ahead at a corner on Alder Slope Road. Take Black Marble Lane for 1.8 miles, then turn left on Lime Quarry Road. Follow Lime Quarry Road for 2.1 miles, passing several poor side roads, to a wide spot with room for a couple of vehicles to park. At the parking spot the number "9" is painted on a rock on the right side of the road. There is a small sign marking the trail on a tree, also on the right side of the road.
GPS: N45 22.667'/W117 21.090'

The Hike

From the trailhead (5,580 ft.), the trail, known locally as Bill George Trail, heads west up a gully. After going steeply up the gully for 100 yards, it makes a switchback to the right. The trail climbs steeply for 0.5 mile, through transition zone forest, to the top of a ridge, making twenty-one switchbacks along the way. Once it reaches the ridge, the trail heads up to the west-southwest. This ridge was once cleared for use as a stock driveway; it still remains mostly open today.

Young hiker next to Silver Creek Ditch. GARY FLETCHER PHOTO

After climbing 0.25 mile, the ridge and trail turn to the southwest (6,289 ft.). After another 0.2 mile the trail crosses a large log that has been partly chopped out by hand to make way. After crossing the log, the trail goes slightly to the left of the ridgeline as it continues to climb. It makes several small switchbacks and soon regains the top of the ridge (6,580 ft.).

There is a wet area in the trail 150 yards after reaching the top of the ridge. A hundred yards or so to the right of the trail at the wet area is a small pond. The pond cannot be seen from the trail. Just past the wet area, the ridge you have been climbing merges with the main ridge (Sheep Ridge). The trail continues to climb, making three switchbacks, then it heads southeast and drops a few feet to a creek crossing. After crossing the creek the trail climbs a short distance and enters an opening.

It makes a tiny switchback as it works along the bottom of the opening, then climbs, rounding a point (6,780 ft.). From the point the Seven Devils Mountains, across Hells Canyon, can be seen in the distance to the east.

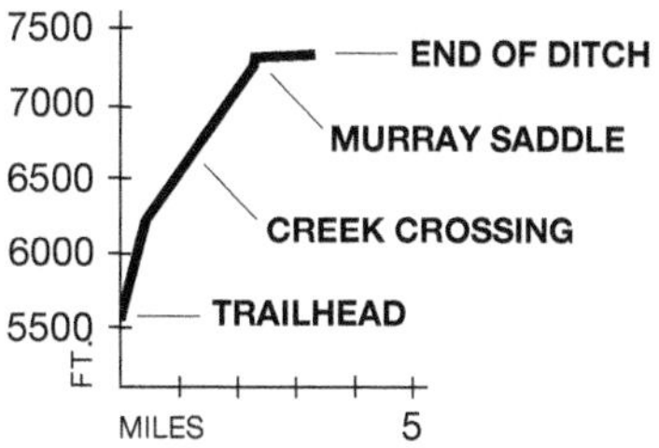

After rounding the point, the dark brown cliffs and ridges of Ruby Peak come into view to the southeast. From here on the country is more open and alpine, and the view gets better the farther you climb. Beyond the point the trail continues to climb steeply, making several more small switchbacks as it works up toward the red-brown wall of upper Sheep Ridge. About 150 yards below the cliffs, the trail traverses south to the junction with the Old Murray Saddle Trail (7,260 ft.). Murray Saddle is 100 yards past the junction.

Murray Saddle (7,290 ft.) is a beautiful spot, with the knife ridge of Ruby Peak to the southeast and the equally steep and rugged spire of Sheep Ridge to the northwest. Silver Creek Canyon and Traverse Ridge are to the southwest, and most of the Wallowa Valley can be seen to the northeast. Most of the time there is a breeze blowing through Murray Saddle; sometimes, mainly during spring, it is more like a hurricane. Watch for bighorn sheep on the ridges above the saddle.

From the saddle, a trail drops down to the southwest 100 yards to a nice campsite. This trail is the old Silver Creek pack trail. It is seldom used anymore and is very difficult to follow after about 0.5 mile. There are some springs a short distance past the campsite on the old pack trail. A climbing route for Ruby Peak leaves the trail in the saddle. See Ruby Peak from the Gap (climb 13).

At the saddle, bear left and head along the right bank of Silver Creek Ditch. This ditch was built by the Civilian Conservation Corps during the Great Depression. Please do not take horses along this ditch bank. They tear it up and cause the ditch to leak and erode. If you have horses, please take them up the bottom of the ditch in the water.

After 0.25 mile there is a wooden gate in the ditch. Cross the gate on the boards and continue on. A small stream enters the ditch on the other side 0.1 mile past the gate. After 0.2 mile pass another gate in the ditch bank, and 150 yards farther another stream enters the ditch. There is yet another gate in the ditch bank 0.1 mile past the stream, and another creekbed 150 yards farther along. Silver Creek and the beginning of Silver Creek Ditch (7,320 ft.) are 150 yards past this creek and 1 mile from the saddle. All along the ditch bank from the saddle is a lush flower garden in July.

At the upper end of the ditch, a faint trail heads up Silver Creek to the southeast. Two climbing routes to Ruby Peak take off from this path. There is a meadow with a good campsite next to it a short distance up Silver Creek from the end of the ditch. Return to the saddle along the ditch.

From the junction 100 yards north of Murray Saddle, it is possible to take the Old Murray Saddle Trail back down to the trailhead. This trail crosses private land and is

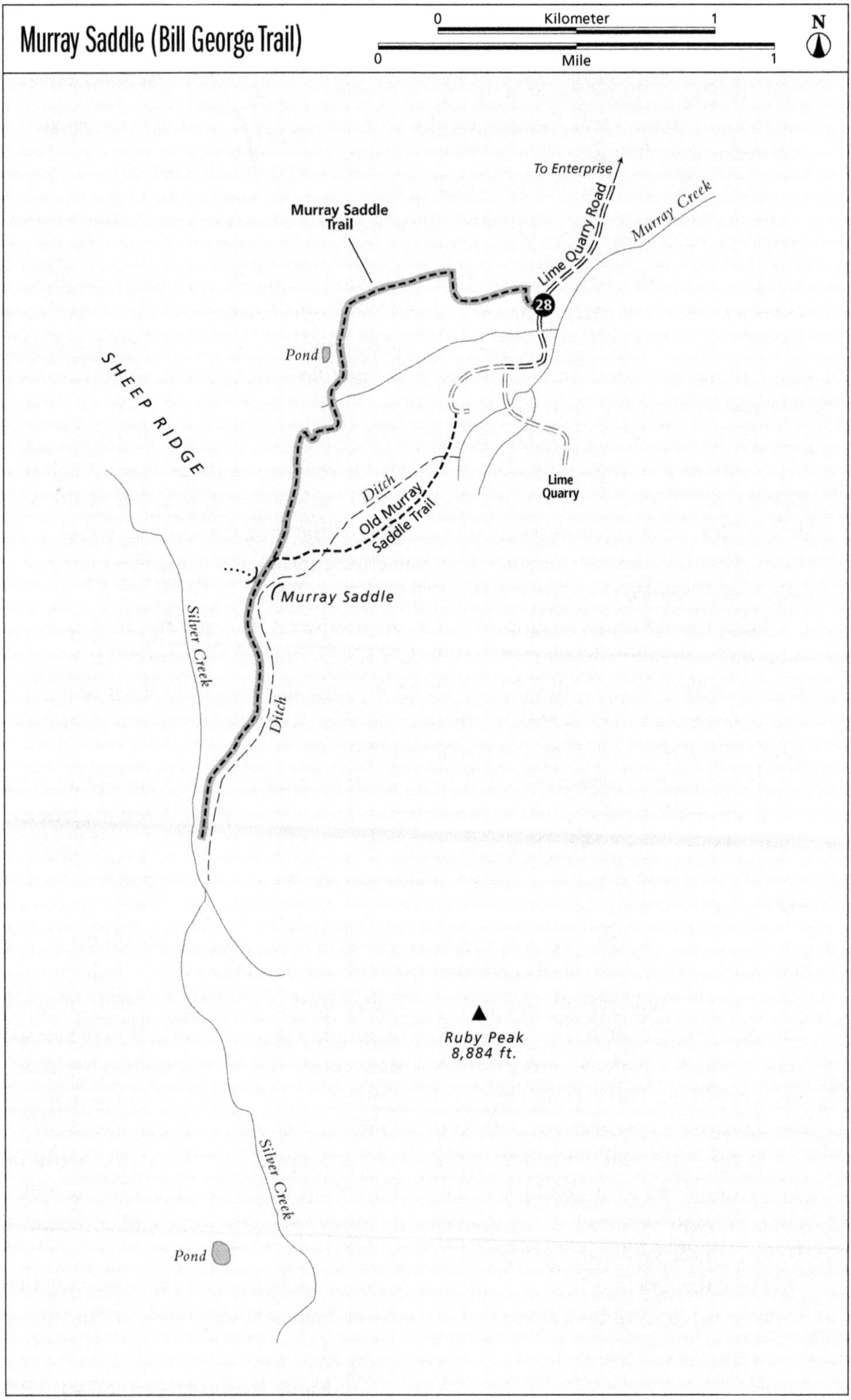

Murray Saddle (Bill George Trail)
0
Kilometer
1
0
Mile
1
N
To Enterprise
Lime Quarry Road
Murray Creek
Murray Saddle Trail
28
Pond
SHEEP RIDGE
Lime Quarry
Ditch
Old Murray Saddle Trail
Murray Saddle
Silver Creek
Ditch
Ruby Peak
8,884 ft.
Silver Creek
Pond

very steep. It gets very little maintenance. However, this is the trail to take if you have horses, as the trail described above is not suitable for stock. It is 1 mile down the old trail to a logging road, and in that distance the trail drops 1,310 vertical feet with many sharp, steep switchbacks. Turn left at the road and head down for 0.2 mile to Lime Quarry Road. The trailhead for the Bill George Trail is 0.35 mile back down Lime Quarry Road from the junction.

It is very important that horse parties use this trail.

Miles and Directions

0.0 Start at the trailhead.

0.5 Reach the top of a ridge and start to follow a stock driveway. (GPS: N45 22.744'/W117 21.451')

1.5 Cross a stream.

2.5 Reach Murray Saddle. (GPS: N45 22.094'/W117 21.963')

3.5 Reach the upper end of the ditch and Silver Creek. (GPS: N45 21.487'/ W117 22.108')

Western

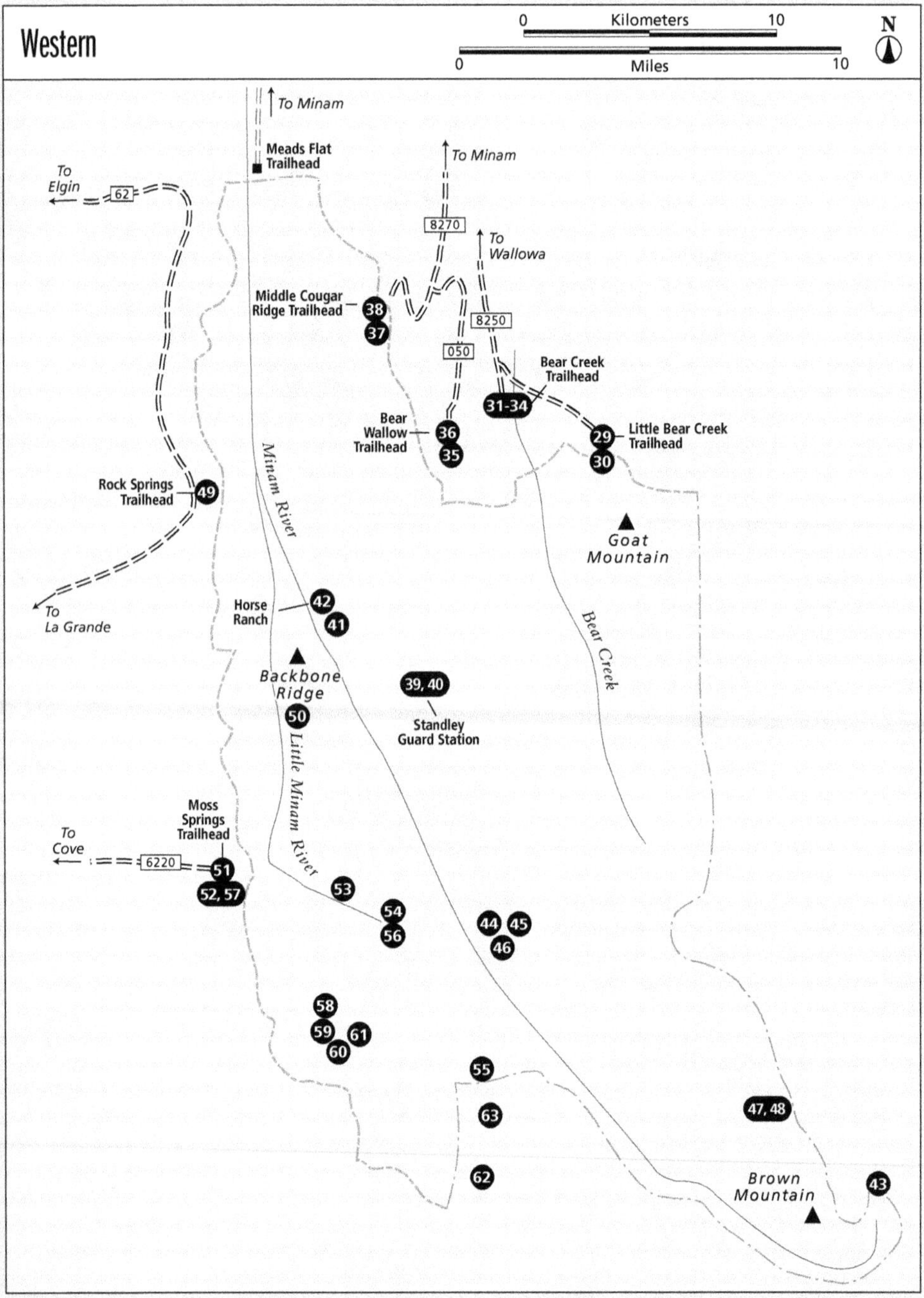

Western
0 Kilometers 10
0 Miles 10
N
To Minam
Meads Flat Trailhead
To Minam
To Elgin
62
8270
To Wallowa
Middle Cougar Ridge Trailhead
38
37
8250
050
Bear Creek Trailhead
31-34
Bear Wallow Trailhead
36
35
29
Little Bear Creek Trailhead
30
Minam River
Rock Springs Trailhead
49
Goat Mountain
To La Grande
Horse Ranch
42
41
Bear Creek
Backbone Ridge
39, 40
50
Standley Guard Station
Little Minam River
Moss Springs Trailhead
To Cove
6220
51
52, 57
53
54
56
44
45
46
58
59
61
60
55
63
47, 48
62
Brown Mountain
43

29 Green Canyon

The Green Canyon Trail is an alternate route for reaching the ridgeline of Huckleberry Mountain and the Huckleberry Mountain Trail. This trail is not an official forest service route but has been used for decades and is now more often used and in better condition than the Huckleberry Mountain Trail. There is a good campsite with a spring at the junction with the Huckleberry Mountain Trail.

Distance: 3 miles one way
Hiking time: 1.5–2 hours
Difficulty: Moderate
Trail maintenance: Seldom, done by trail users only
Best season: Mid-June through Oct
Traffic and other trail users: Light except for during fall hunting seasons, when stock traffic may be moderate
Canine compatibility: Dogs permitted without leashes, but must be kept away from the stock of other parties
Fees and permits: Eagle Cap Wilderness Permit
Maximum elevation: 7,470 feet
Maps: USGS Lostine OR; Green Trails #475sx: Wallowa Mountains Eagle Cap Wilderness. Neither of these (or any other map) shows this trail, they only show the topography. Use the map in this book.
Trail contact: USDA Forest Service Wallowa Mountains Office, 201 E 2nd St. / PO Box 905, Joseph, OR 97846; (541) 426-5546, (541) 426-4978; www.fs.usda.gov/wallowa-whitman. Further information from the forest service may be very limited.

Finding the trailhead: From Wallowa take Bear Creek Road (FR 8250) 9 miles south to Little Bear Creek Road (also FR 8250). Turn left on Little Bear Creek Road. Go east approximately 7 miles to the saddle that divides the Bear Creek drainage from the Lostine River drainage. To the right (south) of the road is the Little Bear Creek Trailhead at 5,590 feet elevation, where you can obtain your wilderness permit.
GPS: N45 26.049' / W117 28.388'

The Hike

Follow the logging road (trail) to the south for 0.4 mile from the trailhead to reach the junction with the Huckleberry Mountain Trail (GPS: N45 26.047' / W117 28.378'). If the gate on the logging road is open, it is possible, if you don't mind the brush scratching the sides of your car, to drive 0.4 mile farther along the road to reach Huckleberry Mountain Trail.

Turn left at the unmarked junction (which was once the trailhead) with the Huckleberry Mountain Trail. The junction is just after the roadbed crosses Little Bear Creek. Head south from the unmarked junction on Huckleberry Mountain Trail (1667). The track climbs through timber and a small meadow for a little less than 0.2 mile to another unmarked junction. Lady's slippers sprout beside the trail here in June.

Falls in Little Bear Creek.

This junction is the start of the Green Canyon Trail. At the junction the Huckleberry Mountain Trail goes straight ahead (southwest).

Turn left on the Green Canyon Trail, which appears to get more use than does the Huckleberry Mountain Trail, and hike south, quickly crossing a small stream. The grade soon steepens, and in a couple hundred yards the route crosses Little Bear Creek—without the benefit of a bridge. This crossing, which can be wet at times, is at approximately 5,900 feet elevation and 0.9 mile from the trailhead on FR 8250. After crossing the creek the trail climbs steeply for a short distance, then traverses a wooded slope with huckleberry bushes covering the forest floor. Hiking here in late August makes for good grazing on the sweet fruits.

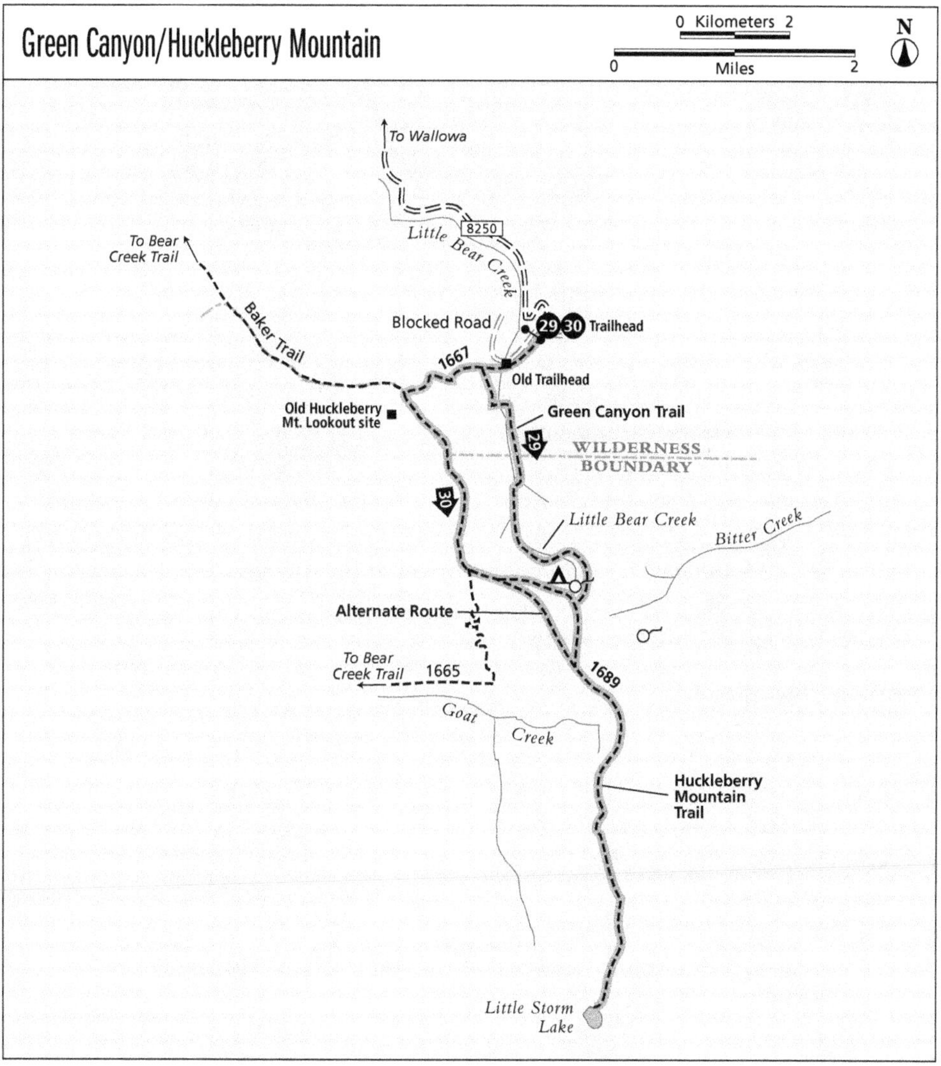

The trail crosses another fork of Little Bear Creek (Little Bear Creek has three forks in this area) about 0.9 mile farther along (at about 6,500 ft.). After this crossing the tread heads southwest, soon recrosses the middle fork, then climbs to the south along the creek's western fork. The trail is braided in places as you climb steeply between the west and middle forks of Little Bear Creek.

The route recrosses the middle fork (7,100 ft.), then quickly climbs away from the creek. Soon you make a switchback to the right and quickly pass the Eagle Cap Wilderness boundary sign. (This sign is well to the south of the actual boundary.) At the wilderness boundary sign you are 2.6 miles from the trailhead (7,200 ft.). Above the wilderness boundary sign the track soon makes a switchback to the left. The timber thins out after passing the switchback, allowing good views of the surrounding country. After climbing for a short distance, the tread makes a switchback to the right and continues to climb, heading southeast. In another 0.25 mile the course goes through a short stretch of dense woods before entering a meadow. In the meadow is the unmarked and a little hard-to-spot junction with the Huckleberry Mountain Trail (7,470 ft.).

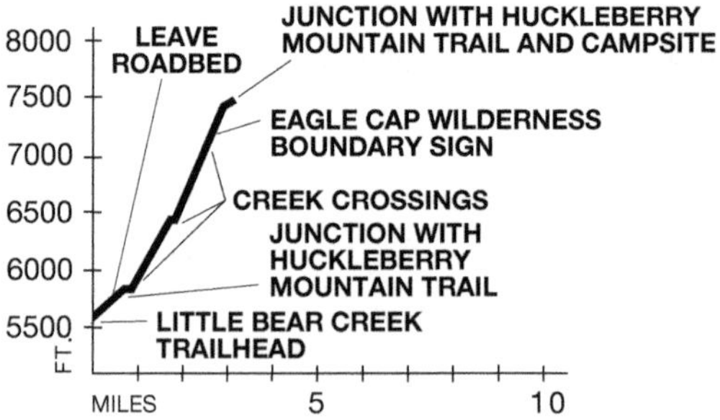

A few yards to the right (northwest) of the junction is a well-used campsite with a small pond and spring close by. This campsite makes a good base camp for exploring the ridge of Huckleberry Mountain and on to the very secluded Little Storm Lake.

Return as you came, or turn right at the junction and follow the sometimes vague Huckleberry Mountain Trail for 2.7 miles northwest along the ridgeline of Huckleberry Mountain to the unmarked junction with the Baker Trail near the old Huckleberry Mountain Lookout site. Turn right at the junction and descend the 2 miles back to the trailhead where you started. Making this loop will require some skill at route finding and following a faint trail.

Miles and Directions

0.0 Hike southwest from Little Bear Creek Trailhead. (GPS: N45 26.049'/ W117 28.388')

0.4 Unmarked junction with the Huckleberry Mountain Trail (1667); turn left, leaving roadbed. (GPS: N45 25.801'/ W117 28.786')

0.6 Unmarked junction with Green Canyon Trail; turn left. (GPS: N45 25.730'/ W117 28.795')

0.9 Cross Little Bear Creek.

2.6 Pass the Eagle Cap Wilderness boundary sign.

3.0 Unmarked junction with the Huckleberry Mountain Trail. (GPS: N45 24.302'/ W117 28.316')

30 Huckleberry Mountain

Trails 1667 and 1689 lead from Little Bear Creek Trailhead to Little Storm Lake. The track first climbs to the semi-open ridge of Huckleberry Mountain, which it follows for about 5 miles. The views are great along the ridge. Then you descend to campsites close to Little Storm Lake.

See map page 115.
Distance: 8.9 miles one way (backpack)
Hiking time: 4–7 hours
Difficulty: Moderate to strenuous; requires some route finding
Trail maintenance: Rare
Best season: Mid-June through Oct
Traffic and other trail users: Light except during Oct and Nov hunting season; may be moderate horse traffic in the fall
Canine compatibility: Dogs permitted without leashes, but must be kept away from the stock of other parties
Fees and permits: Eagle Cap Wilderness Permit
Maximum elevation: 7,860 feet
Maps: USGS Lostine OR and North Minam Meadows OR; Geo Graphics Wallowa Mountains Eagle Cap Wilderness
Trail contact: USDA Forest Service Wallowa Mountains Office, 201 E 2nd St./ PO Box 905, Joseph, OR 97846; (541) 426-5546, (541) 426-4978; www.fs.usda.gov/wallowa-whitman. Further information will probably be limited.

Finding the trailhead: From Wallowa take Bear Creek Road (FR 8250) 9 miles south to Little Bear Creek Road (also FR 8250). Turn left on Little Bear Creek Road. Go east approximately 7 miles to the saddle that divides the Bear Creek drainage from the Lostine River drainage. To the right (south) of the road is Little Bear Creek Trailhead.
GPS: N45 26.049' / W117 28.388'

The Hike

From the trailhead at 5,590 feet elevation, pass the gate and hike south along the roadbed for 0.4 mile. Then turn left at the unmarked junction with the Huckleberry Mountain Trail. The junction is just after the roadbed crosses Little Bear Creek (GPS: N45 25.801'/W117 28.786'). If the gate is open, which it usually is from July 15 to September 15, it may be possible to drive to this point. Get your water here, as there may be none for the next 4 miles.

Hike south from the unmarked junction on Huckleberry Mountain Trail (1667). The track climbs through timber and a small meadow for a little less than 0.2 mile to another unmarked junction. This junction is the beginning of the Green Canyon Trail. At the junction the Huckleberry Mountain Trail (which receives less use than the Green Canyon Trail) goes straight ahead (southwest).

At 2.4 miles the trail tops a ridge (7,330 ft.) and enters Eagle Cap Wilderness. At the ridgetop, Baker Trail (which may be hard to spot) leads to the right (northwest) down to Bear Creek. Huckleberry Mountain Trail turns left (southeast) and continues to climb a bit around the left side of a rock outcropping to the top of the ridge. Upon regaining the ridge, look to the right for a faint path that leads to the site where the Huckleberry Mountain Lookout used to be. The elevation at the old lookout site is 7,551 feet, and good cell phone service is available from here.

From the site of the Huckleberry Mountain Lookout, the trail follows the ridge of Huckleberry Mountain southeast. After another 1.5 miles, reach the junction with Goat Creek Trail (1665; 7,600 ft.). The Goat Creek Trail junction is marked only with a rock pile; no sign.

The ridgeline between the lookout and the Goat Creek Trail junction is the hydrological divide between Goat Creek and Little Bear Creek. From the lookout site up to this point, the trail has only minor ups and downs. It may be difficult to see in some spots, but when in doubt, follow the ridge. This ridgetop country is mostly open grassland. There may be many wildflowers in July along the ridge. This is also big game country: Watch for mule deer and elk grazing along the fringes of the timber. There are also a few bighorn sheep in the area, and bears are fairly common, as are cougars and coyotes.

After passing the Goat Creek Trail junction, the trail climbs slightly for 0.25 mile, then descends 0.75 mile to a spring, the upper junction with Green Canyon Trail, and a campsite. Here the trail disappears completely. Go straight ahead, across a small meadow, to pick up the trail again. Past the campsite the trail climbs slightly for 0.1 mile to the southeast, to the ridge dividing the Goat Creek and Lostine River drainages. Once on the ridge, the trail heads south. In the next 0.4 mile the trail climbs to an elevation of 7,860 feet. At this point the trail is above the head of Bitter Creek, which is a tributary of the Lostine River.

Another route can be taken from Goat Creek Trail junction to the point above Bitter Creek. The route is more direct but misses the water source at the spring. To take this route, bear to the right 0.25 mile southeast of the Goat Creek Trail junction. This is where the main trail begins to descend. Stay high, just to the left of the ridgeline. There is a large rock outcropping on the ridgeline. The route is on the left (northeast) side of the outcropping, about 50 yards downslope. Once past the outcropping, the route follows the somewhat flattened ridgetop for 0.5 mile to where it rejoins the main trail above the head of Bitter Creek.

Backpacker on Huckleberry Mountain.
GARY FLETCHER PHOTO

The trail continues south, contouring around to the right (west) side of a high point on the ridge. It then drops slightly to a saddle near the head of Goat Creek. A wilderness boundary sign was once at this saddle; now there is just a pile of rocks. Five hundred yards past the rock pile that once held the wilderness boundary sign, the faint trail bears southeast to the ridgeline. Drop over the ridgeline to the left (east) a few feet, staying just below the crest, and head south. Soon the trail will show up again.

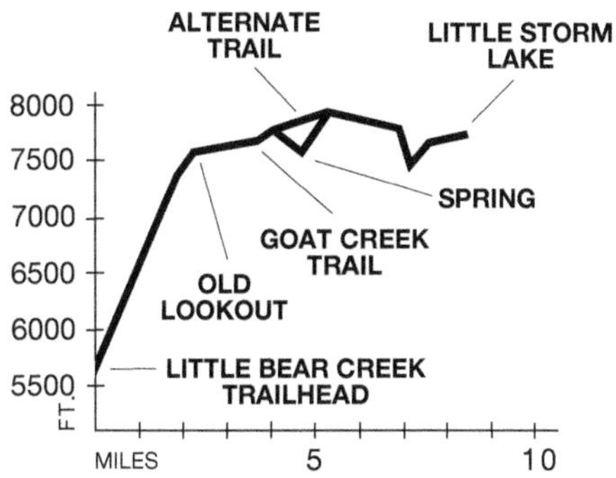

The trail drops below some cliffs, then drops some more in steep switchbacks to the bottom of a little valley (7,450 ft.). At the bottom of the valley, the trail heads south. It soon climbs to a saddle at the head of the valley (7,540 ft.), then drops down to a spring and campsite.

A few feet below the spring the trail disappears in an open, marshy area. Go straight across the open area; the trail will appear again on the other side. To the right the cliffs above have a large red rock band. From here, the trail heads south past another spring and goes through another meadow. In a few hundred yards it reaches Little Storm Lake (7,610 ft.). The total distance to Little Storm Lake is 8.9 miles. This trail requires quite a bit of route-finding ability.

The area is typical of the western Wallowa Mountains. It is mostly transition and Canadian zone forests, with a small number of Hudsonian zone plants and trees on the highest ridges. There is also much open grassland. Like much of the western Wallowas, water may be scarce in places. There are probably no fish in Little Storm Lake, but there are plenty of good campsites and lots of firewood.

The return trip can be made via the same trail.

Miles and Directions

0.0 Hike southwest from Little Bear Creek Trailhead. (GPS: N45 26.049/ W117 28.388')

0.4 Turn left at the old Little Bear Creek Trailhead. (GPS: N45 25.801'/W117 28.786')

0.6 Junction with Green Canyon Trail. Hike straight ahead (southwest). (GPS: N45 25.730'/ W117 28.795')

2.4 Bear left at the unmarked junction with the Baker Trail. (GPS: N45 25.546'/W117 29.876')

2.6 Reach the old Huckleberry Mountain Lookout site. (GPS: N45 25.459'/W117 29.726')

4.1 Pass the junction with the Goat Creek Trail (1665). (GPS: N45 24.373'/ W117 29.132')

5.1 Reach a spring and the upper junction with Green Canyon Trail. (GPS: N45 24.302'/ W117 28.316')

6.4 Cross the saddle at the head of Goat Creek.

7.6 Cross the bottom of a little valley.

7.9 Cross a saddle.

8.9 Arrive at Little Storm Lake. (GPS: N45 21.327'/W117 27.816')

31 Baker Trail

This fairly challenging trail connects the Bear Creek Trail to the Huckleberry Mountain Trail. As you climb the path, the views improve. The route traverses terrain typical of the western Wallowa Mountains: fairly level semi-open ridgetops and steep canyons with basalt cliffs. The open slopes become flower gardens in midsummer.

Distance: 6 miles one way
Hiking time: 2.5–4 hours
Difficulty: Strenuous, with some route-finding skills required
Trail maintenance: Rare to none
Best season: June through Oct
Traffic and other trail users: Very light foot and horse traffic
Canine compatibility: Dogs permitted without leashes, but must be kept away from the stock of other parties
Fees and permits: Northwest Forest Pass and Eagle Cap Wilderness Permit
Maximum elevation: 7,320 feet
Maps: USGS Fox Point OR and Lostine OR
Trail contact: USDA Forest Service Wallowa Mountains Office, 201 E 2nd St./ PO Box 905, Joseph, OR 97846; (541) 426-5546, (541) 426-4978; www.fs.usda.gov/wallowa-whitman. Further information will probably be very limited.

Finding the trail: From Wallowa drive south for 9 miles on Bear Creek Road to Boundary Campground and Bear Creek Trailhead at the end of the road. From the trailhead hike south on Bear Creek Trail. The unmarked and difficult-to-spot Baker Trail leaves Bear Creek Trail (1653) 1.75 miles south of the Bear Creek Trailhead. The trail junction (4,080 ft.) is 0.25 mile past Baker Gulch. There is a sign marking Baker Gulch.
GPS: Bear Creek Trailhead: N45 28.273'/W117 33.555'; Baker Trail junction: N45 26.770'/W117 33.229'

The Hike

Baker Trail turns to the left (east) off Bear Creek Trail (1653), but is very hard to see at the junction. At first it climbs through the open forest as a faint path, and becomes more evident after a short distance. The trail makes a long switchback to the left, then to the right, and comes to a saddle at the top of a ridge. The last 200 yards before the saddle may be overgrown with grass. Go straight ahead and look for a large ponderosa pine with a white insulator on it. This insulator was used for the old telephone line to the now nonexistent Huckleberry Mountain Lookout. The pine is at the point where the trail

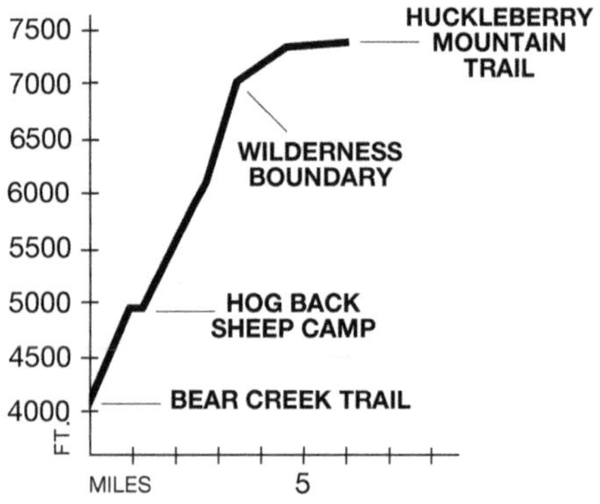

Upper section of the Baker Trail.

crosses the ridge. This saddle (4,980 ft.) is 1 mile from Bear Creek Trail. Cross the saddle and drop slightly to Hog Back Sheep Camp. There is a sign marking the camp.

At the sheep camp the trail forks; take the trail on the right. Past the sheep camp the trail climbs fairly steeply up the creekbed, then makes a switchback and comes out on a ridge at 2.75 miles (6,140 ft.). From here, the trail generally follows the ridge, sometimes going a little to the left side. There is good cell phone service above 6,000 feet along this ridge.

At 3.5 miles is the Eagle Cap Wilderness boundary sign. From here to the Huckleberry Mountain Lookout site, the wilderness boundary almost follows the trail. Past

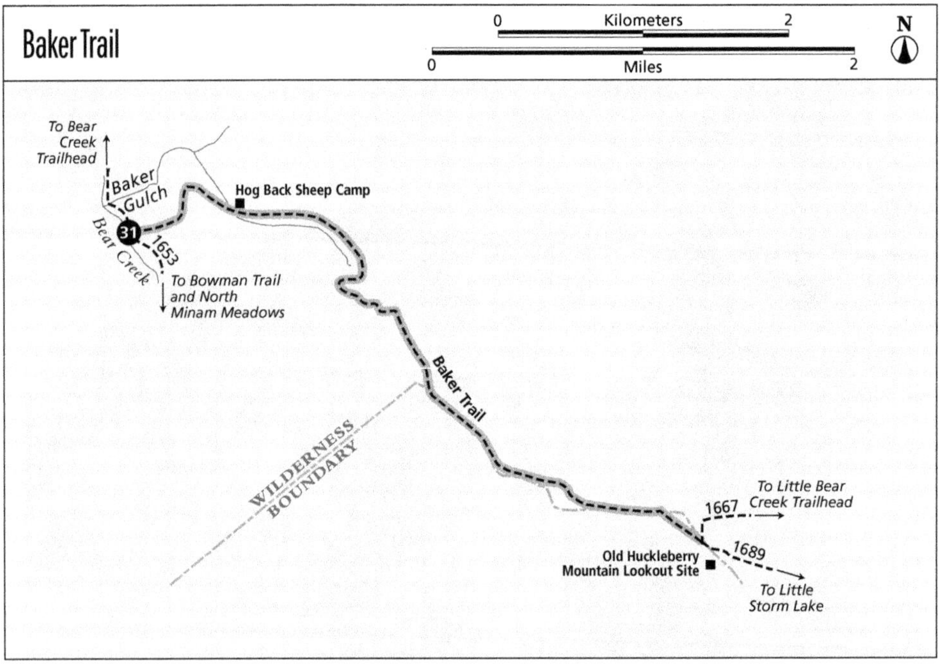

the sign, continue up the ridge to the point where it flattens out at 4.75 miles (7,250 ft.). Here the trail is faint. A few yards southeast the trail appears again, following the ridgeline. After following the ridgeline a short distance, the trail goes off to the right side to avoid climbing a high point. It soon comes back to the ridge, in a saddle. This saddle (7,320 ft.) is 6 miles from Bear Creek Trail. The Baker Trail meets the Huckleberry Mountain Trail (1667) in this saddle. See Huckleberry Mountain (hike 30) for more information.

There may be no water on this trail, so carry some along. There may be many deer, elk, and bear in the area. This trail requires some route-finding skills. An alternate return trip may be made by turning left (northeast) on Huckleberry Mountain Trail and dropping down the 2 miles to Little Bear Creek Trailhead. This loop requires an 8-mile car shuttle.

Miles and Directions

0.0 Take the Baker Trail from the junction with Bear Creek Trail (1653).

1.0 Cross a saddle and reach Hog Back Sheep Camp.

2.7 The trail reaches the ridgeline.

3.5 Pass the Eagle Cap Wilderness boundary.

6.0 Arrive at the junction with Huckleberry Mountain Trail (1667). (GPS: N45 25.546'/W117 29.876')

32 Goat Creek

This connecting trail runs between Bear Creek Trail and Huckleberry Mountain Trail. The upper part of Goat Creek Trail is very scenic. This route allows access to the top of Huckleberry Mountain a little earlier in the season than does the normal route from the north side. (Trail 1665)

Distance: 5.2 miles one way from Bear Creek Trail
Hiking time: 2–3.5 hours from Bear Creek Trail; 3.5–5 hours from Bear Creek Trailhead
Difficulty: Moderate to strenuous; some route finding may be required.
Trail maintenance: Rare, but recently worked on by WMHCTA. See appendix A to become part of this organization.
Best season: June through Oct
Other trail users: Light foot and horse traffic
Canine compatibility: Dogs permitted without leashes, but must be kept away from the stock of other parties
Fees and permits: Northwest Forest Pass and Eagle Cap Wilderness Permit
Maximum elevation: 7,600 feet
Maps: USGS Fox Point OR and Lostine OR; Geo Graphics Wallowa Mountains Eagle Cap Wilderness
Trail contact: USDA Forest Service Wallowa Mountains Office, 201 E 2nd St./ PO Box 905, Joseph, OR 97846; (541) 426-5546, (541) 426-4978; www.fs.usda.gov/wallowa-whitman. Further information will probably be very limited.

Finding the trail: From Wallowa drive south on Bear Creek Road for 9 miles to Boundary Campground and Bear Creek Trailhead. Then hike south on Bear Creek Trail (1653) for 4 miles to the junction with the Goat Creek Trail (1653) at 4,400 feet.
GPS: Bear Creek Trailhead: N45 28.273' / W117 33.555'; Goat Creek Trail junction: N45 24.909' / W117 32.168'

The Hike

Goat Creek Trail turns left (east) off Bear Creek Trail (1653). The trail climbs gently at first, then steepens and makes a switchback. Look up Goat Creek Canyon from the switchback to see Goat Creek Falls. After 1 mile the grade of the trail becomes more moderate. It continues up Goat Creek Canyon for another 2.5 miles. It then switchbacks its way to the top of Huckleberry Mountain (7,600 ft.) and the junction with the Huckleberry Mountain Trail (1689), 5.2 miles from Bear Creek Trail. Huckleberry Mountain is a nice hike

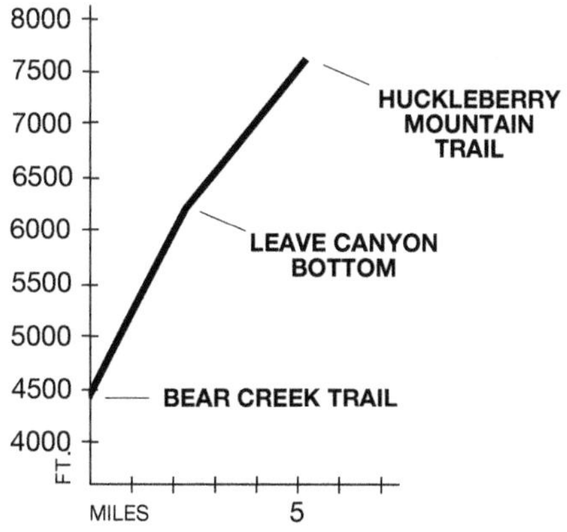

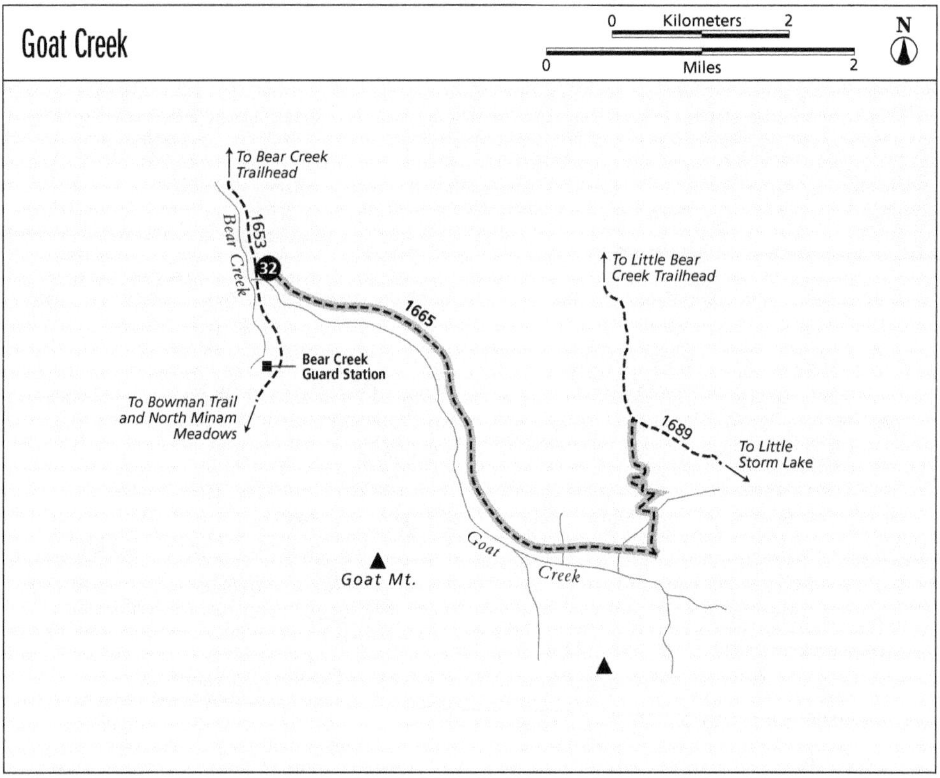

to Little Storm Lake. Watch for bighorn sheep on Goat Mountain to the south of the trail. Mule deer, elk, and bear are also common in this area.

Miles and Directions

0.0 At the junction with Bear Creek Trail (1653), go left (east) on the Goat Creek Trail (1665).

3.5 The trail starts to climb out of the canyon bottom.

5.2 Arrive at the junction with Huckleberry Mountain Trail (1689). (GPS: N45 24.373'/W117 29.132')

Option: To make a loop hike, turn left (northwest) on Huckleberry Mountain Trail and follow it 1.7 miles to the junction with Baker Trail. Take Baker Trail back to Bear Creek Trail. This loop requires considerable route-finding skills on Baker Trail. Be sure you have enough water to complete the trip, because water is scarce on this loop.

33 Bear Creek

This backpack route goes along Bear Creek from Bear Creek Trailhead to the Bowman Trail, giving access to Baker Trail, Goat Creek Trail, Dobbin Creek Trail, Washboard Trail, and Bowman Trail. It also passes a short distance from Bear Lake. (Trail 1653)

Distance: 19.2 miles one way
Hiking time: 2 days
Difficulty: Easy to moderate, but long
Best season: Apr through Nov up to Dobbin Creek Trail; mid-June through Oct for the entire route
Trail maintenance: Yearly
Traffic and other trail users: Heavy foot and horse traffic to Bear Creek Guard Station; moderate beyond the station except in Oct and Nov hunting season, when it can be heavy all the way
Canine compatibility: Dogs permitted without leashes, but must be kept away from the stock of other parties
Fees and permits: Northwest Forest Pass and Eagle Cap Wilderness Permit
Maximum elevation: 7,700 feet
Maps: USGS Fox Point OR, Jim White Ridge OR, and North Minam Meadows OR; Geo Graphics Wallowa Mountains Eagle Cap Wilderness
Trail contact: USDA Forest Service Wallowa Mountains Office, 201 E 2nd St./ PO Box 905, Joseph, OR 97846; (541) 426-5546, (541) 426-4978; www.fs.usda.gov/wallowa-whitman

Finding the trailhead: To reach Bear Creek Trailhead, take Bear Creek Road (FR 8250) south from the town of Wallowa. The road forks 8 miles south of town. Keep right (south) and go 1 mile farther to Bear Creek Trailhead (on FR 040). Boundary Campground is located near the trailhead, and there is a stock-loading ramp.
GPS: N45 28.273'/W117 33.555'

The Hike

From the trailhead (3,720 ft.) Bear Creek Trail heads south, up Bear Creek. At 0.25 mile the trail crosses a bridge over Bear Creek. There is lots of syringa (mock orange) along the lower part of this trail. An open viewpoint on the right side of the trail is 0.75 mile farther. Looking to the south, the high point is Fox Point. Fox Point is at the end of a side ridge extending northeast from Standley Ridge. There is a trail that reaches Fox Point from Standley Ridge.

At 1.5 miles the trail crosses Baker Gulch. One-quarter mile farther the unmarked—and very vague at the junction—Baker Trail turns off to the left (east) (4,080 ft.). Continue south on the main trail. At 3.3 miles (4,300 ft.) the trail enters Eagle Cap Wilderness. The junction with Goat Creek Trail 1665 is 0.7 mile past the wilderness boundary. Goat Creek Trail goes left (east). One hundred yards past Goat Creek Trail is Goat Creek bridge. There are good campsites to the right of the trail just

Bear Creek Guard Station.

past the bridge. Fishing for fairly large trout is sometimes good in this section of Bear Creek.

Bear Creek Guard Station is 0.3 mile up Bear Creek Trail from Goat Creek bridge. The old guard station is a short distance to the right (west) of the trail. To reach it turn right off the main trail and go past the outhouse, which can be seen from the main trail. The guard station is made of square-cut logs and is in quite good condition. It is locked and not available for public use. Many campsites are available in the timbered fringes of the beautiful meadows near the guard station.

Bear Creek Trail continues on to the south. Dobbin Creek Trail (1654) turns to the right (west) at a poorly marked junction 0.7 mile south of the guard station. Bear Creek Trail heads on south past Dobbin Creek Trail for another 5.6 miles to the Granite Creek crossing (5,540 ft.). The 2 miles below Granite Creek may be quite dry, as there are no major creek crossings and Bear Creek is difficult to access from the trail. Extra water should be carried in this section during dry weather.

Above Granite Creek the trail continues up Bear Creek Canyon, remaining on the east side of Bear Creek. It occasionally climbs up and away from the creekbed in switchbacks. At 6.25 miles above Granite Creek crossing, the trail has climbed nearly to the head of Bear Creek Canyon. It crosses Bear Creek for the last time (7,600 ft.). Bear Creek is a small stream at this point. The head of Bear Creek is only 0.5 mile upstream at Bear Lake. This area is much more open and alpine than the lower parts of Bear Creek Canyon. The trees are mostly subalpine firs, and the sloping meadows are teeming with alpine wildflowers.

Above the crossing the trail continues to climb for 0.25 mile to the saddle (7,700 ft.) dividing Bear Creek drainage and the North Minam drainage. At the saddle, Washboard Trail (1680) goes to the right (west). See Washboard Ridge (hike 40). The path to Bear Lake goes to the left from the saddle. Bear Lake (7,905 ft.) is 0.5 mile to the northeast on this path. The trail may not be visible for a few yards in the grassy area just below the saddle. However, it soon becomes evident again. The saddle area is subalpine in character and is typical of the ridgetops in the western part of the Wallowa Mountains.

After crossing the saddle the trail begins its descent toward Wilson Basin. Below the saddle 1.25 miles, North Minam Meadows come into view in the canyon far

Bear Creek

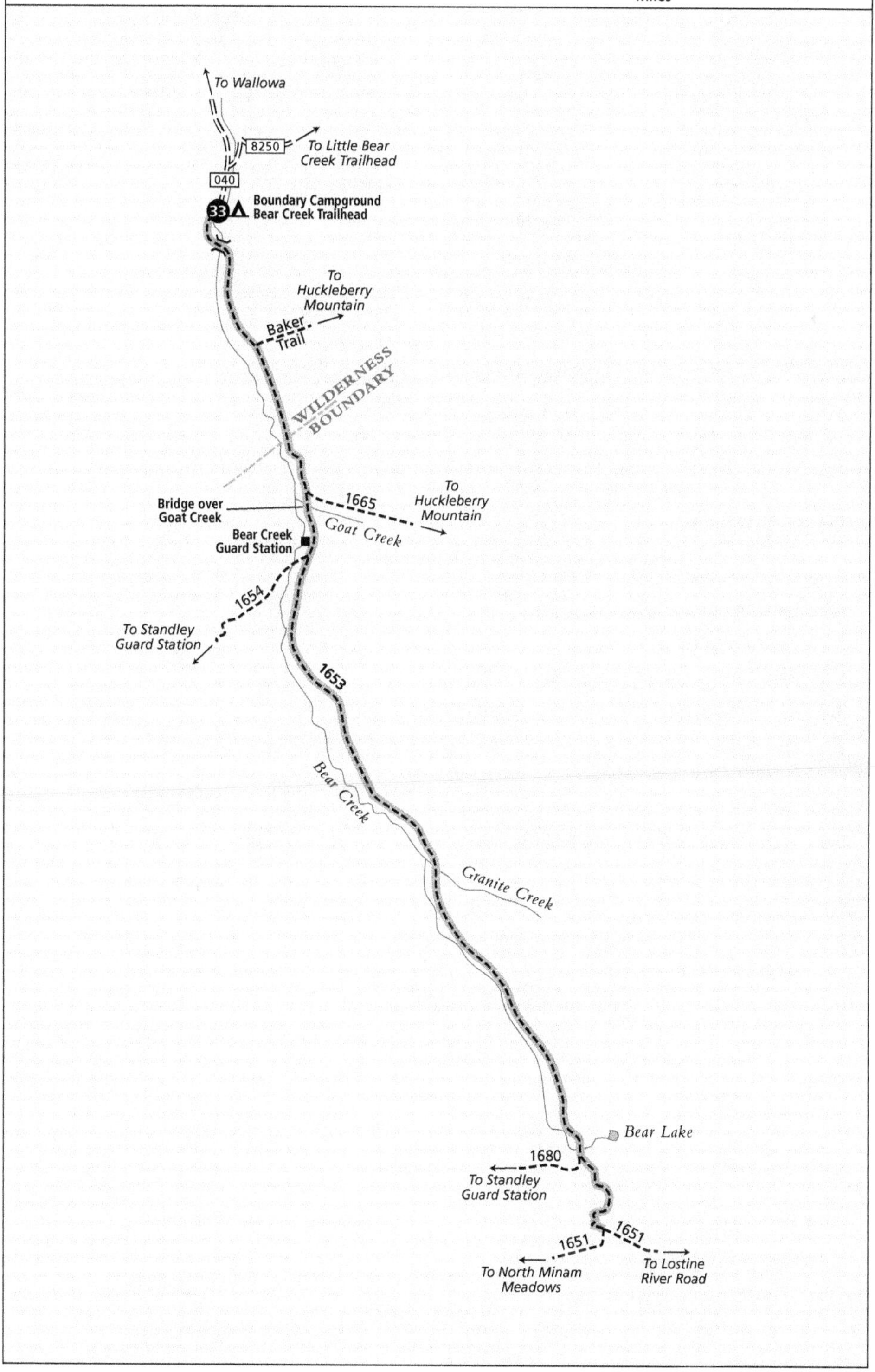

0 Kilometers 4
0 Miles 4
N
To Wallowa
8250
To Little Bear Creek Trailhead
040
33
Boundary Campground
Bear Creek Trailhead
To Huckleberry Mountain
Baker Trail
WILDERNESS BOUNDARY
Bridge over Goat Creek
1665
To Huckleberry Mountain
Goat Creek
Bear Creek Guard Station
1654
To Standley Guard Station
1653
Bear Creek
Granite Creek
Bear Lake
1680
To Standley Guard Station
1651
1651
To North Minam Meadows
To Lostine River Road

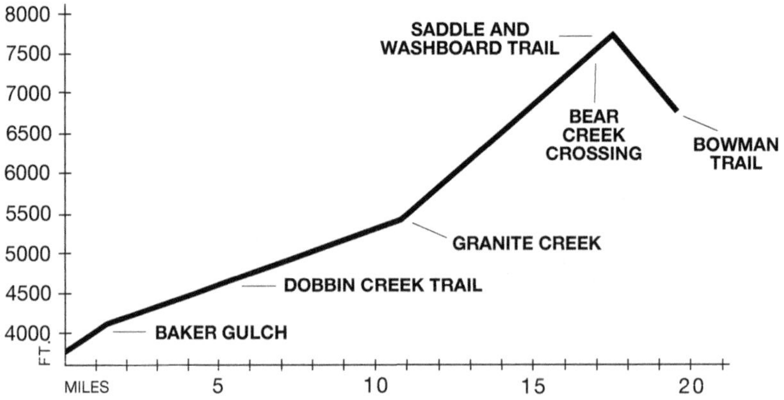

below. The junction with Bowman Trail (1651) is 0.5 mile farther at the lower end of Wilson Basin (6,750 ft.), and 19.2 miles from Bear Creek Trailhead.

Return by the same trail, or make a one-way trip via the Bowman Trail, which requires a car shuttle to the Frances Lake/Bowman Trailhead on Lostine River Road.

Miles and Directions

0.0 Begin at the Bear Creek Trailhead.

0.2 Cross the bridge over Bear Creek.

1.5 Cross Baker Gulch.

1.7 Pass the junction with the Baker Trail. (GPS: N45 26.770'/W117 33.229')

3.3 Reach the Eagle Cap Wilderness boundary.

4.0 Pass the junction with Goat Creek Trail (1665) and cross the bridge. (GPS: N45 24.909'/W117 32.168')

4.3 Pass the path to the Bear Creek Guard Station. (GPS: N45 24.612'/W117 32.041')

5.0 Pass the junction with Dobbin Creek Trail (1654). (GPS: N45 24.269'/W117 32.176')

10.6 Cross Granite Creek.

16.8 Cross Bear Creek; Bear Lake is a short distance to the left (east).

17.1 Cross the saddle and pass the trail junction with Washboard Trail (1680). (GPS: N45 17.425'/W117 27.415')

19.2 Arrive at the junction with Bowman Trail (1651).

34 Dobbin Creek

This trail connects Bear Creek Trail to Standley Ridge Trail. The area along the upper 1.5 miles was burned in the 1994 Fox Point Fire. The burned area is recovering nicely, and there are lots of flowers. (Trail 1654)

Distance: 4.1 miles one way from Bear Creek Trail
Hiking time: 1.5–3 hours from Bear Creek Trail
Difficulty: Strenuous
Trail maintenance: Rare
Best season: Mid-June through Oct
Traffic and other trail users: Light except during Oct and Nov hunting season; moderate horse traffic in the fall
Canine compatibility: Dogs permitted without leashes, but must be kept away from the stock of other parties
Fees and permits: Northwest Forest Pass and Eagle Cap Wilderness Permit
Maximum elevation: 7,060 feet
Map: USGS Fox Point OR
Trail contact: USDA Forest Service Wallowa Mountains Office, 201 E 2nd St./ PO Box 905, Joseph, OR 97846; (541) 426-5546, (541) 426-4978; www.fs.usda.gov/wallowa-whitman

Finding the trail: Drive south from Wallowa on Bear Creek Road (FR 8250 and FR 040) for 9 miles to Boundary Campground and Bear Creek Trailhead. Hike 5 miles south from the trailhead on Bear Creek Trail (1653). Dobbin Creek Trail begins 0.7 mile south of the Bear Creek Guard Station (4,470 ft.).
GPS: Bear Creek Trailhead: N45 28.273'/W117 33.555'; Dobbins Creek Trail junction: N45 24.269'/W117 32.176'

The Hike

Dobbin Creek Trail turns right off Bear Creek Trail (1653). After leaving Bear Creek Trail the path becomes faint for a short distance through a grassy area. The trail fords Bear Creek 0.1 mile from Bear Creek Trail. After crossing Bear Creek the trail becomes obvious again.

After crossing Bear Creek the trail is level for a short distance, then it climbs steeply, with many switchbacks. At 1.5 miles (5,560 ft.) the trail crosses Dobbin Creek. It continues to climb steeply to about 6,000 feet. Above 6,000 feet the trail becomes more gentle.

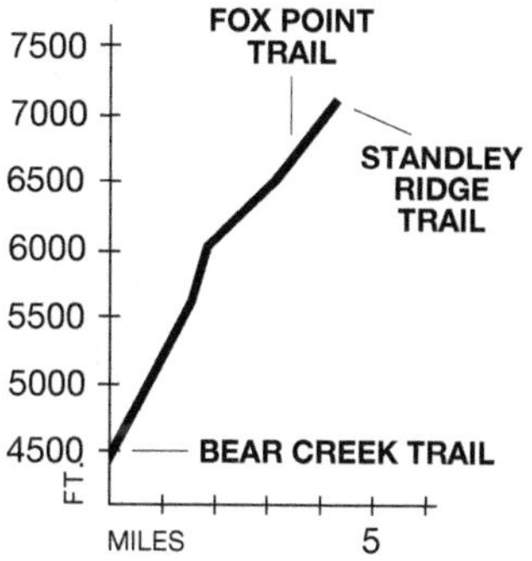

The trail enters the burn area of the Fox Point forest fire at approximately 6,300 feet. At 3.25 miles (6,600 ft.) the trail crosses another creek in a completely charred forest. It then climbs 0.4 mile farther, flattens out for 0.1 mile, then climbs again to the junction with Fox Point Trail (6,850 ft.). The

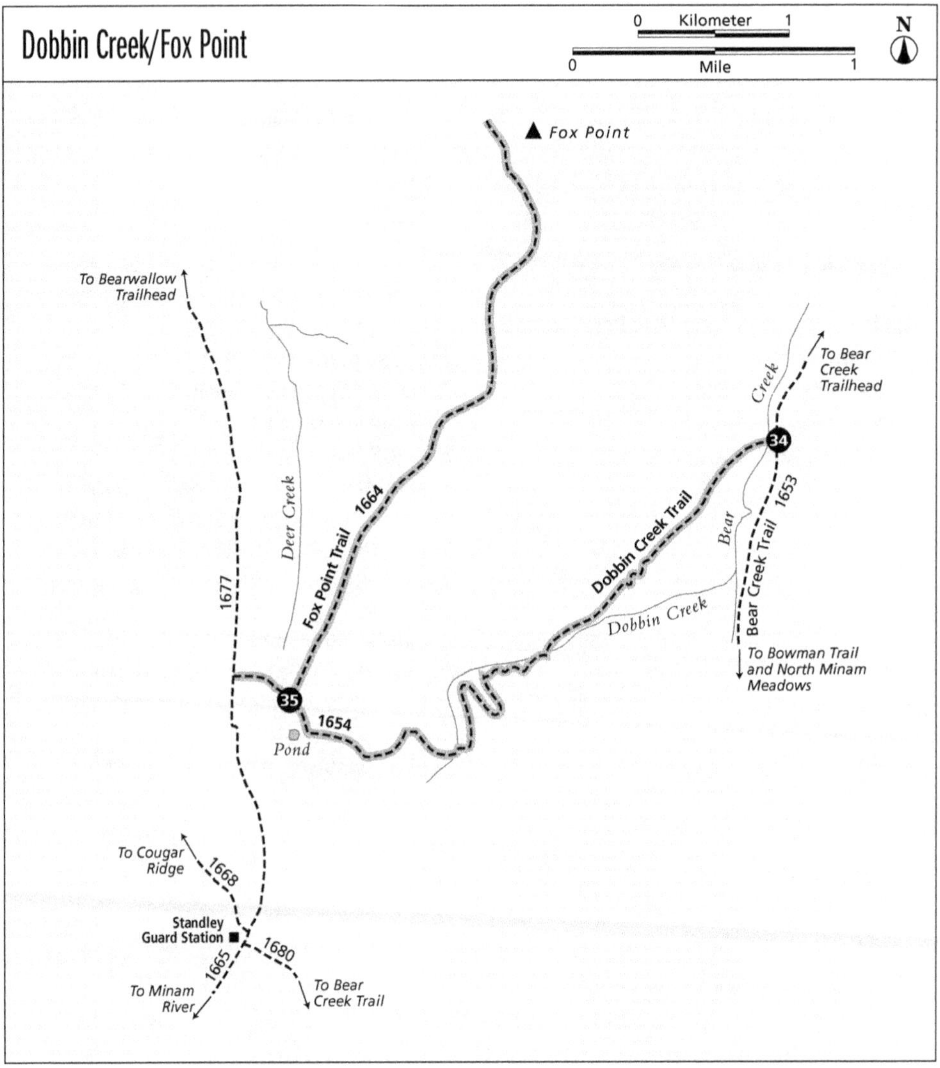

unmarked junction with Fox Point Trail can be very difficult to see. It is 50 yards up the trail to the west from the point where the trail leaves a flat area and begins its final ascent to Standley Ridge Trail junction.

Another 0.4 mile brings you to the junction with Standley Ridge Trail (1677; 7,060 ft.). See Standley Ridge (hike 36). Standley Guard Station is 1 mile to the south on Standley Ridge Trail. This may be the best way to reach Standley Guard Station early in the season, when Standley Ridge Road and Trail are still blocked with snow.

A car shuttle trip is possible by taking Standley Ridge Trail north from the junction for 3.8 miles to Bearwallow Trailhead. If you are going to make a shuttle trip, it is easier to start at Bearwallow Trailhead and end at Bear Creek Trailhead.

Miles and Directions

0.0 Take the Dobbin Creek Trail (1654) from the junction with Bear Creek Trail (1653).

0.1 Cross Bear Creek.

1.5 Cross Dobbin Creek.

3.7 Pass the junction with Fox Point Trail (1664). (GPS: N45 23.536'/W117 34.355')

4.1 Reach the junction with Standley Ridge Trail (1677). (GPS: N45 23.608'/W117 34.622')

35 Fox Point

A short hike of slightly over 2 miles leads from Dobbin Creek Trail to Fox Point. Much of the country along this route was burned some years ago. Because of the fire the views are much better than they were when this ridge was thickly forested. The flowers are also great in the burned areas. (Trail 1664)

See map page 130.
Distance: 2.3 miles one way
Hiking time: 1.5–2 hours
Difficulty: Easy, but route finding is required.
Trail maintenance: Rare. This trail is no longer maintained by the forest service.
Best season: Mid-June through mid-Nov, barring early snow
Traffic and other trail users: Light foot and horse traffic except during hunting season; moderate horse and foot traffic in Oct and early Nov
Canine compatibility: Dogs permitted without leashes, but must be kept away from the stock of other parties
Fees and permits: Northwest Forest Pass and Eagle Cap Wilderness Permit
Maximum elevation: 7,085 feet
Map: USGS Fox Point OR
Trail contact: USDA Forest Service Wallowa Mountains Office, 201 E 2nd St./PO Box 905, Joseph, OR 97846; (541) 426-5546, (541) 426-4978; www.fs.usda.gov/wallowa-whitman

Finding the trail: Bearwallow Trailhead is the closest one to the Fox Point Trail. To reach Bearwallow Trailhead turn south off OR 82, 1 mile east of Minam on Big Canyon Road (FR 8270). Follow FR 8270 for 10.4 miles to the junction with FR 050. Turn left (southeast) on FR 050 and drive 6.8 miles to Bearwallow Trailhead. Take along a national forest map to make finding this out-of-the-way trailhead easier. From Bearwallow Trailhead hike south on Standley Ridge Trail for 3.8 miles to the junction with Dobbin Creek Trail (1654). Turn left on Dobbin Creek Trail and descend 0.4 mile to the east to the point where Fox Point Trail leaves Dobbin Creek Trail.
GPS: Bearwallow Trailhead: N45 26.978'/W117 35.300'; Fox Point–Dobbin Creek junction: N45 23.536'/W117 34.355'

The Hike

A large portion of the area along this trail was burned in the Fox Point forest fire. The trail turns northeast off Dobbin Creek Trail (1654) about 50 yards above (west of) the point where Dobbin Creek Trail flattens out for the first time after leaving Standley Ridge Trail (6,860 ft.). The unmarked junction can be difficult to find in this nearly completely burned area. At first the trail crosses a small flat area through the scorched woods. Soon it begins to contour along a hillside. After traversing along, nearly level, for 0.5 mile, the trail turns uphill to the east for a short distance and climbs to the top of the ridge (7,060 ft.). From here the trail generally follows the top of the ridge, heading northeast. There is a fire line cut to the west of the trail 0.75 mile after reaching the ridgetop. This fire line may look like a trail, but it is not.

Continue along the ridge to the north for 2 miles from Dobbin Creek Trail to a place called Ranger Camp (6,880 ft.). The area around Ranger Camp is mostly burned, and the sign identifying the spot is now gone. The trail may be hard to follow when it goes through open areas, but it never disappears for long. There are good views of Bear Creek Canyon to the east in this area; also, there is a good chance of seeing wildlife.

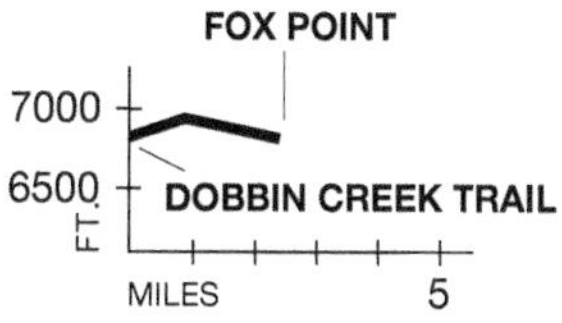

From Ranger Camp, the trail follows the open ridge heading northwest and soon leaves the burned area. It then drops slightly to Fox Point (6,850 ft.). There is an old sign here that says Fox Point Telephone, but there is no telephone. For good views of lower Bear Creek Canyon and the lower Wallowa Valley, follow the ridge another 200 yards north to an open point.

There is no water on Fox Point Trail. Fox Point Trail is like several other trails in the western Wallowas; it doesn't go to any particular place, but the scenery, wildlife, flowers, and solitude along the way make the hike well worth the effort. When I hiked this trail early one summer, I stepped over a fallen log and nearly right onto a newborn fawn. To follow this trail requires some route-finding and map-reading skills. Return via the same trail.

Miles and Directions

0.0 Take the Fox Point Trail (1664) from the junction with Dobbin Creek Trail (1654).

0.7 Reach the top of the ridge.

2.0 Arrive at Ranger Camp.

2.3 Arrive at Fox Point.

36 Standley Ridge

This can be a day hike from Bearwallow Trailhead to Standley Guard Station, or a backpack to a base camp there. Standley Guard Station is the trail hub for the area between Bear Creek and the Minam River. From here trails head out in all directions. Most of this trail follows an abandoned roadbed, which is reverting nicely to a trail. You pass through burnt forest nearly all the way to the junction with Dobbin Creek Trail, 3.8 miles from the trailhead. The area was burned in two different fires and is in varying stages of recovery. (Trail 1677)

Distance: 4.8 miles one way
Hiking time: 2-3.5 hours
Difficulty: Easy
Trail maintenance: Infrequent
Best season: June through early Nov
Traffic and other trail users: Light to moderate foot and horse traffic except in fall hunting seasons, when it is heavy
Canine compatibility: Dogs permitted without leashes, but must be kept away from the stock of other parties
Fees and permits: Eagle Cap Wilderness Permit
Maximum elevation: 7,220 feet
Map: USGS Fox Point OR
Trail contact: USDA Forest Service Wallowa Mountains Office, 201 E 2nd St./ PO Box 905, Joseph, OR 97846; (541) 426-5546, (541) 426-4978; www.fs.usda.gov/wallowa-whitman

Finding the trailhead: The trail begins at Bearwallow Trailhead. To reach Bearwallow Trailhead, turn south off OR 82, 1 mile east of Minam, on Big Canyon Road (FR 8270). Follow FR 8270 for 10.4 miles to the junction with FR 050. Turn left (southeast) and follow FR 050 for 6.8 miles to Bearwallow Trailhead. Take a national forest map along to make finding the trailhead easier. The trailhead is on top of a ridge. A few yards to the east of the trailhead parking area is an open area that allows an excellent view of Bear Creek Canyon. Big Canyon Road is also used to reach Middle Cougar Ridge Trailhead. Bearwallow Trailhead is not the same place as Bear Creek Trailhead.
GPS: N45 26.978'/W117 35.300'

The Hike

The trail begins at the southeast corner of the parking area (6,020 ft.) at Bearwallow Trailhead. The trail, which is actually an abandoned roadbed in places, goes south along the east side of a logged area. There may be a lot of blown-down trees across the trail if there has been a windstorm since the trail was last maintained.

One mile from the trailhead the trail comes into a more open area near the top of Bald Knob. The route bears right (south), going around the highest part of Bald Knob.

Past Bald Knob the trail follows the ridge south, entering the burn area at 1.9 miles. Most of the burn area is on the left (east) side of the trail, but the burn did cross over the trail in places. Pearly everlastings grow profusely in the burn area. After

Standley Guard Station.

heading south for 0.9 mile through mostly burned timber along the ridge, the trail enters Eagle Cap Wilderness (6,780 ft.). The trail continues along the ridge through mostly burned trees for 0.9 mile more, then goes for 0.1 mile through green trees to the junction with Dobbin Creek Trail (1654; 7,060 ft.). See Dobbin Creek (hike 34) for more detail. Standley Guard Station (7,220 ft.) is 1 mile past the junction, through the timber and open ridgetop meadows, 4.8 miles from Bearwallow Trailhead.

The Standley Guard Station cabin is in good condition but is not for public use. It is protected by the Antiquities Act and should be left as it was found. The Standley Guard Station area was where range studies were conducted in the early 1900s to evaluate the grazing potential, mostly for sheep, of the area. Herders grazed their sheep on these ridgetop meadows until recently. There are an outhouse and developed spring here, which are available for public use.

Standley Guard Station also is the hub for trails connecting the Minam River, North Minam River, and Bear Creek. With so many trails going in all directions from here, this is an excellent place to camp and explore the western part of the Wallowa Mountains. Good cell phone service is available on the ridge east of the guard station. Other hikes in this area include Cougar Ridge, Murphy Creek, Minam River/Standley Guard Station, and Washboard Ridge.

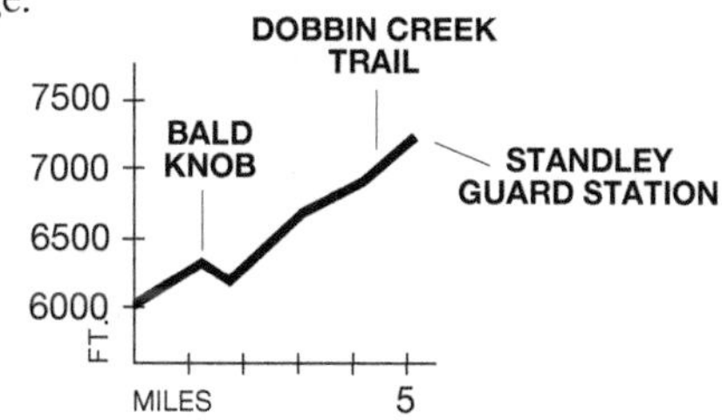

Remember that most of the ridges are dry in summer, so carry water with you. Standley Ridge has no water between Bearwallow Trailhead and Standley Guard Station. Mosquitoes can be a problem in the marshy meadows around Standley Guard

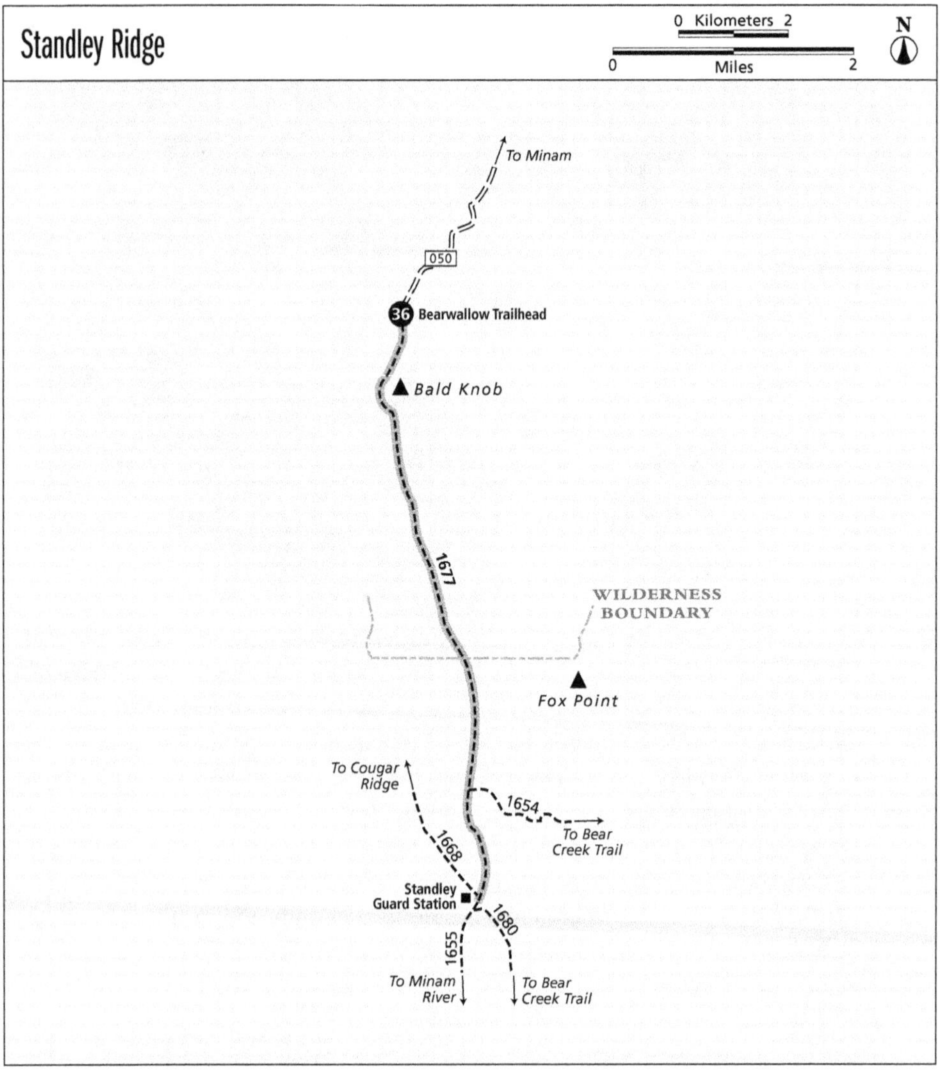

Station during the months of June and July. Return by the same trail, or use one of the trails mentioned above to make a one-way trip, requiring a car shuttle.

Miles and Directions

0.0 Start at the Bearwallow Trailhead.

1.0 Reach Bald Knob.

2.8 Cross the Eagle Cap Wilderness boundary.

3.8 Pass the junction with Dobbin Creek Trail (1654). (GPS: N45 23.608'/W117 34.622')

4.8 Arrive at the Standley Guard Station. (GPS: N45 22.924'/W117 34.503')

37 Cougar Ridge

This backpacking route leads along a ridge from the Minam River Trail, in the bottom of the Minam River Canyon to the meadowlands at Standley Guard Station. The lower 5 miles of this trail are mostly in the open, with good views of this rugged canyon country. The entire route traverses excellent elk and bear country. The upper and lower portions of this trail may be hiked separately by using Middle Cougar Ridge Trailhead. The entire Cougar Ridge Trail as described here is best done as an extention of a backpack trip along the Lower Minam River Trail. (Trails 1649 and 1668)

Distance: 13.7 miles one way
Hiking time: 6–8 hours
Difficulty: Strenuous for the lower part, but easy for the upper part; route-finding skill is required.
Trail maintenance: Rare
Best season: Late May through early Nov for the lower portion; mid-June through Oct for the upper portion
Traffic and other trail users: Very light except during fall hunting seasons; light horse traffic
Canine compatibility: Dogs permitted without leashes, but must be kept away from the stock of other parties. Keep close track of your pet on lower portion of trail; there are rattlesnakes.
Fees and permits: Eagle Cap Wilderness Permit
Maximum elevation: 7,220 feet
Maps: USGS Mount Moriah OR and Fox Point OR; Geo Graphics Wallowa Mountains Eagle Cap Wilderness
Trail contact: USDA Forest Service Wallowa Mountains Office, 201 E 2nd St./ PO Box 905, Joseph, OR 97846; (541) 426-5546, (541) 426-4978; www.fs.usda.gov/wallowa-whitman

Finding the trail: Cougar Ridge Trail leaves Lower Minam River Trail (1673) 1 mile upriver from Meads Flat Trailhead (3,020 ft.). Unfortunately the Meads Flat Trailhead can now only be reached on foot, horseback, or possibly by off-road vehicle. The Cougar Ridge Trail can also be reached at a point 5 miles from the Minam River at Middle Cougar Ridge Trailhead. To reach Middle Cougar Ridge Trailhead, take Big Canyon Road off OR 82, 1 mile east of Minam. Turn south on Big Canyon Road and go 10 miles to the junction with FR 050. This is the junction for Bearwallow Trailhead. Do not turn left, but go straight ahead, staying on FR 8270 to its end at the trailhead, approximately 6 more miles. Hike south-southwest from Middle Cougar Ridge Trailhead for 0.4 mile, over an abandoned roadbed and a broad trail, to the junction with the Cougar Ridge Trail (1668).
GPS: Lower Minam River/Cougar Ridge Trail junction: N45 30.332'/W117 41.324'; Middle Cougar Ridge Trailhead: N45 28.797'/W117 37.605'

The Hike

The Cougar Ridge Trail turns (east) off Lower Minam River Trail (1673). Initially, the trail switchbacks up onto a finger of lower Cougar Ridge. The trail reaches the top of this rounded finger 0.25 mile after leaving Lower Minam River Trail. It then heads up the finger to the east-northeast, through open timber. There may be blowdowns in this area. The trail continues up the finger for 0.5 mile. It then climbs a grassy slope with steep switchbacks for 0.25 mile more. Elevation at the top of the switchbacks is 3,990 feet.

At the top of the switchbacks the trail turns to the right (southeast). This is the beginning of a 0.5-mile-long ascending traverse. The traverse heads southeast to a saddle on Cougar Ridge (4,210 ft.).

Above the saddle the trail heads up the ridgeline to the southeast. One hundred fifty yards above the saddle the trail goes off to the left side of the ridge, slightly, for 200 yards, then gets back on top. A small switchback in open woods (4,460 ft.) is 350 yards beyond. Above the switchback the trail stays on the ridgeline for 0.9 mile, climbing to 4,920 feet. Many types of flowers bloom along this ridgeline in June. As the trail climbs higher, the horizon broadens to include sweeping views of much of the western Wallowa Mountains.

At 4,920 feet the trail goes to the right side of the ridgeline and continues to climb, staying about 50 vertical feet below the ridgeline for 0.25 mile. After 0.25 mile on the right side, the trail crosses the ridgeline (5,060 ft.) and continues up the left side for 250 yards, where it regains the ridge.

The trail passes some rock outcroppings 0.25 mile after regaining the ridge. The trail can be difficult to see in this area. Continue on up the ridge 0.5 mile more, and the trail then bears left (at 5,280 ft.) and climbs to the east for 0.3 mile to the junction with High Ridge Trail. For the last 150 yards before the junction the trail can be difficult to see. By going up to the east-northeast it will soon show up again. This junction can be especially difficult to find when descending. If you are going back down this trail, take note of where the junction is.

At the unmarked junction with High Ridge Trail (5,620 ft.), turn right (southeast). Follow the trail for 700 yards southeast to an unmarked junction with a logging "cat trail" at the upper edge of a clear-cut.

After passing the "cat trail," Cougar Ridge Trail continues along the top of the clear-cut 650 more yards to another unmarked junction. Here it meets the trail coming up from Middle Cougar Ridge Trailhead. This is the only logged area along this trail. After leaving the clear-cut area, another 250 yards of trail brings you to Division Camp (5,760 ft.). There is yet another trail here going back to Middle Cougar Ridge Trailhead.

There is a campsite (5,920 ft.) on the left side of the trail 1.8 miles past Division Camp. A rocky opening with a view to the right of Trout Creek Canyon is 0.3 mile farther. Another 0.9 mile past the viewpoint, the trail enters a grassy meadow (6,200 ft.). There is a path to the left (northeast) here, but Cougar Ridge Trail crosses the meadow and continues to head southeast. There is a red digger colony in this meadow.

Beyond the meadow the trail stays fairly close to the ridgeline. It goes through alternating areas of timber and open places. A couple of miles past the meadow, at about 6,500 feet, the timber begins to become more alpine in nature. Log Corral Camp (6,770 ft.) is 4.5 miles past the meadow. Beyond Log Corral Camp the trail

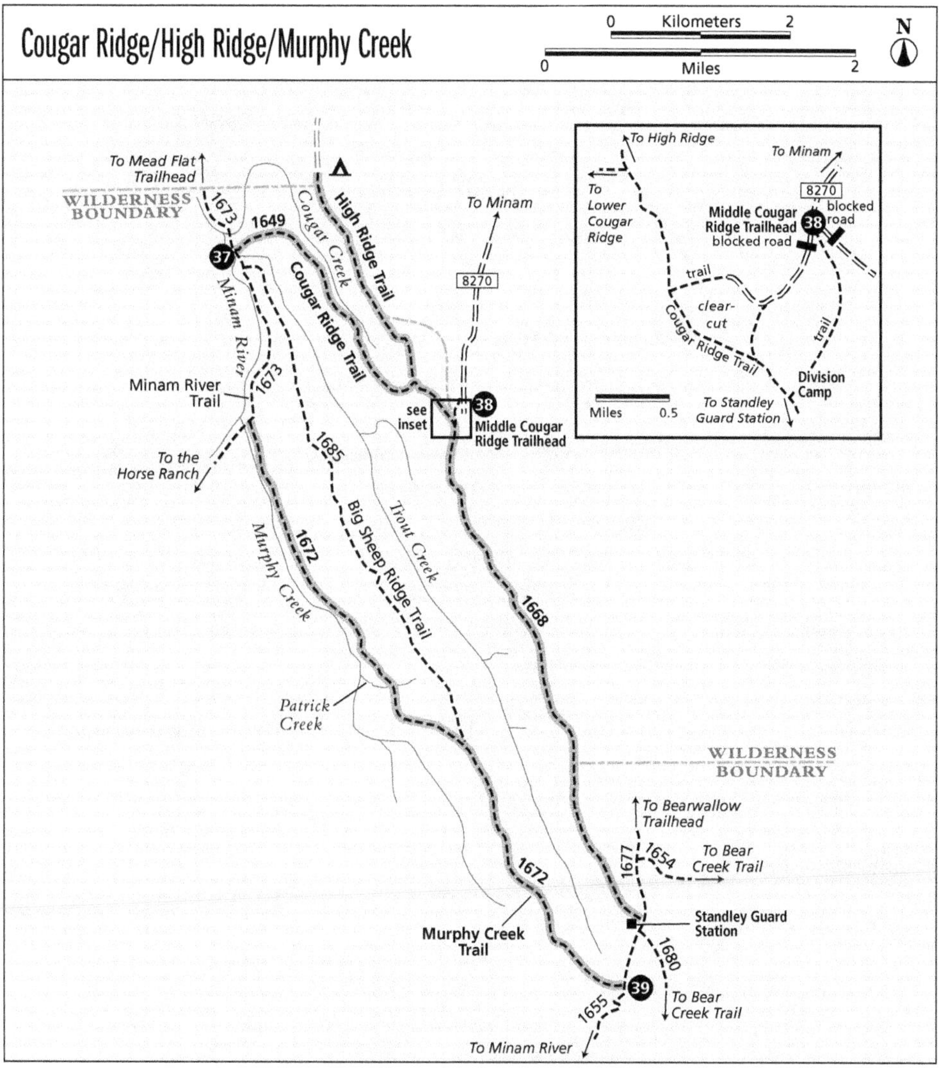

climbs steadily but gently for 1.5 miles to Standley Guard Station and Standley Spring (7,220 ft.). The junction with Trail 1677, coming from Bearwallow Trailhead, is at Standley Guard Station.

Cougar Ridge Trail, below the junction with High Ridge Trail, is quite steep in places. It is also difficult to find in spots. Above the High Ridge Trail junction it is gentle and easy to see. There is no water on lower Cougar Ridge; however, there is a spring on High Ridge Trail 0.3 mile from its junction with Cougar Ridge Trail. On upper Cougar Ridge there is no water adjacent to the trail. There is water at Standley Springs. As is true with most surface water, it should be treated, filtered, or boiled to make it safe to drink.

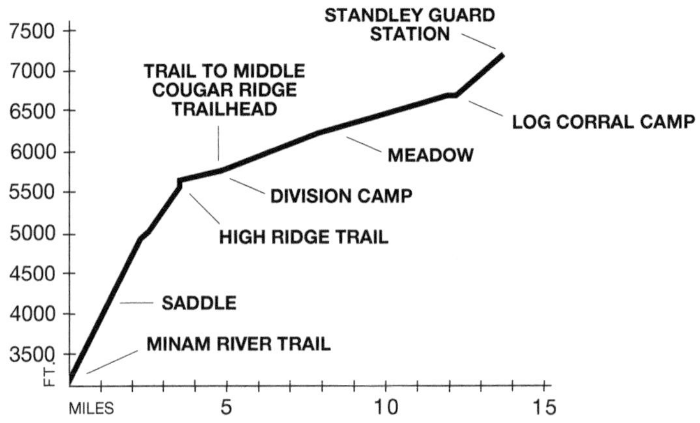

It is 13.7 miles from the Minam River Trail to Standley Springs, with 4,200 feet of elevation gain. This trail can be done in two sections, from the Middle Cougar Ridge Trailhead. Some route-finding skills may be required to follow this trail, especially the lower part. There is a lot of wildlife along Cougar Ridge. Keep your eyes open for mule deer and elk. You might also see a bear. There is the possibility of encountering a rattlesnake on the lower part of this trail. Watch where you step and especially where you place your hands when climbing.

Standley Guard Station is a good place to make camp and explore the area. The Standley Ridge, Washboard Ridge, and Minam River/Standley Guard Station Trails all meet at Standley Guard Station, and the Dobbin Creek, Fox Point, and Murphy Creek Trails are only a short distance away.

Miles and Directions

0.0 Take the Cougar Ridge Trail (1649) from the junction with Lower Minam River Trail (1673).

1.5 Reach a saddle.

4.2 Pass the junction with High Ridge Trail. (GPS: N45 28.868'/W117 38.305')

5.0 Pass the junction with the trail to the Middle Cougar Ridge Trailhead.

5.1 Pass Division Camp. (GPS: N45 28.388'/W117 37.715')

7.2 Reach the meadow with the red digger colony.

11.9 Pass Log Corral Camp.

13.7 Arrive at the Standley Guard Station. (GPS: N45 22.924'/W117 34.503')

38 High Ridge

This day hike along High Ridge leads from Middle Cougar Ridge Trailhead to a jeep road and campsite on High Ridge.

See map page 139.
Distance: 3.8 miles one way
Hiking time: 2–3 hours
Difficulty: Easy to moderate, but requires route finding
Trail maintenance: None. This trail is kept open by hunters' horse traffic.
Best season: June through Oct
Traffic and other trail users: Very light foot traffic; light horse traffic in the fall
Canine compatibility: Dogs permitted without leashes, but must be kept away from the stock of other parties
Fees and permits: Eagle Cap Wilderness Permit
Maximum elevation: 5,620 feet
Map: USGS Mount Moriah OR
Trail contact: USDA Forest Service Wallowa Mountains Office, 201 E 2nd St./ PO Box 905, Joseph, OR 97846; (541) 426-5546, (541) 426-4978; www.fs.usda.gov/wallowa-whitman. Information may be limited.

Finding the trailhead: To reach Middle Cougar Ridge Trailhead, take Big Canyon Road off OR 82, 1 mile east of Minam. Turn south on Big Canyon Road and go 10 miles to the junction with FR 050. This is the junction for Bearwallow Trailhead. Do not turn left, but go straight ahead staying on FR 8270 to its end at the trailhead, approximately 6 miles.
GPS: Middle Cougar Ridge Trailhead: N45 28.797' / W117 37.605'; High Ridge Trail junction: N45 28.868' / W117 38.305'

The Hike

Hike south-southwest from Middle Cougar Ridge Trailhead for 0.4 mile, over an abandoned roadbed and a broad trail, to the junction with the Cougar Ridge Trail (1668). Turn right on Cougar Ridge Trail and hike 0.5 mile northwest to the junction with the High Ridge Trail. At the junction the High Ridge Trail, rather than the Cougar Ridge Trail, seems to be the main route. There is no sign at the junction (5,620 ft.).

High Ridge Trail heads north-northwest from the junction with Cougar Ridge Trail. One-third mile from the junction is a spring (5,440 ft.). The trail is not always easy to see past the spring. Watch for blazes on the trees.

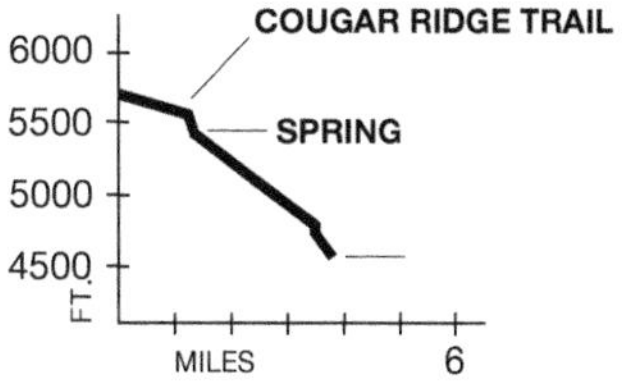

A quarter mile past the spring the trail reaches the ridgeline of High Ridge. For the next 2 miles the trail generally follows the ridgeline, dropping about 600 vertical feet in elevation. The trail goes through alternating open and wooded areas along the ridge.

There is quite a bit of both blue and yellow lupine blooming in June and July along High Ridge.

The trail begins to drop steeply and becomes braided at 2.25 miles past the spring. After dropping for 0.25 mile, the trail comes to a national forest boundary sign and a jeep road. This is the end of High Ridge Trail. There are campsites at the end of the trail but no visible water (and no water between the spring at 5,440 feet and the campsite). Elevation here is 4,570 feet. Route-finding skills may be needed to follow this trail.

Return by the same trail, and watch for mule deer and elk.

Miles and Directions

0.0 Hike south-southwest from Middle Cougar Ridge Trailhead.

0.9 Take the High Ridge Trail from the junction with Cougar Ridge Trail.

1.2 Pass the spring.

3.5 The trail begins to drop steeply.

3.8 Reach the jeep road and campsite at trail's end.

39 Murphy Creek

The Murphy Creek Trail links the Minam River/Standley Guard Station Trail, high atop Standley Ridge, with the Minam River Trail, deep in the Minam River Canyon. The route is quite scenic and passes through excellent big game country all the way. (Trail 1672, Alternate Trail 1685)

See map page 139.
Distance: 10 miles one way
Hiking time: 4–6 hours heading down as described below
Difficulty: Strenuous, with some route-finding skill required
Trail maintenance: Rare
Best season: Mid-June through Oct
Traffic and other trail users: Very light foot and horse traffic except during Oct and Nov hunting seasons, when it can be moderate
Canine compatibility: Dogs permitted without leashes, but must be kept away from the stock of other parties
Fees and permits: Eagle Cap Wilderness permit
Maximum elevation: 6,940 feet
Maps: USGS Jim White Ridge OR, Fox Point OR, and Mount Moriah OR; Green Trails #475sx: Wallowa Mountains Eagle Cap Wilderness; Geo Graphics Wallowa Mountains Eagle Cap Wilderness. The Big Sheep Ridge alternate route is shown on the Geo Graphics map but not on the USGS maps.
Trail contact: USDA Forest Service Wallowa Mountains Office, 201 E 2nd St./ PO Box 905, Joseph, OR 97846; (541) 426-5546, (541) 426-4978; www.fs.usda.gov/wallowa-whitman

Finding the trail: The closest way to reach the junction where the Murphy Creek Trail starts is via the Standley Ridge Trail (1677) from Bearwallow Trailhead. To reach Bearwallow Trailhead turn south off of OR 82, 1 mile east of Minam on Big Canyon Road (FR 8270). Drive south on Big Canyon Road for 10.4 miles to the junction with FR 050. Bear left at the junction and follow FR 050 for 6.8 miles to the trailhead. From the trailhead hike south on the Standley Ridge Trail for 4.6 miles to Standley Guard Station. From Standley Guard Station hike southwest on the Minam River/Standley Guard Station Trail (1655) for 1 mile to the junction with the Murphy Creek Trail.
GPS: Bearwallow Trailhead: N45 26.978' / W117 35.300'; Murphy Creek junction: N45 22.212' / W117 34.807'

The Hike

From the junction with Minam River/Standley Guard Station Trail (1655), Murphy Creek Trail heads to the northwest. There is a trail sign at this junction (6,930 ft.). The trail drops slightly through the timber for 0.2 mile, to the unmarked junction with the now-abandoned Trout Creek Trail. The junction is in a swampy meadow; Trout Creek Trail is difficult to spot.

After passing the junction, the trail climbs slightly. It generally follows the ridgetop for the next 0.7 mile to an unmarked junction (7,020 ft.). Just before the junction the trail goes through a burn area. The path to the left (west) is the now-abandoned Old Murphy Creek Trail. Murphy Creek Trail bears to the right (northwest) and heads

Author heading down Big Sheep Ridge. GARY FLETCHER PHOTO

down Big Sheep Ridge. Past the fork the trail gradually descends through forest and openings. For the next 2 miles it generally follows the broad ridgetop. The trail is a bit difficult to see in the open areas but never disappears for long.

After the 2 miles the ridge narrows. The trail stays close to the top of the ridge for the next mile to the junction with Big Sheep Ridge Trail (1685). This junction (6,440 ft.) is 4 miles from the junction with Minam River/Standley Guard Station Trail. The trail to the right (northwest) follows Big Sheep Ridge to the Minam River Trail (see the alternate trail description below).

At the junction Murphy Creek Trail bears left (west-northwest) and descends through thinning timber for 1.4 miles to a saddle on Mahogany Ridge (5,450 ft.). The open slopes along Mahogany Ridge may be covered with balsamroot, paintbrush, and lupine in late June and early July. At the saddle the trail turns right (north) and begins to descend steeply toward Patrick Creek. It makes eleven switchbacks as it drops the 0.5 mile to the creek crossing. The trail crosses Patrick Creek in the last switchback (4,720 ft.).

After the crossing the trail descends along Patrick Creek, crossing it a couple of times, for 0.7 mile to the lower junction with Old Murphy Creek Trail (4,160 ft.). Old Murphy Creek Trail, which is now abandoned, turns to the left and crosses Patrick Creek. There is a sign at this junction, which points up Patrick Creek to Standley.

Turn right at the junction and head down Murphy Creek Trail. There is a good campsite on the left side of the trail next to Murphy Creek 0.8 mile after passing the Old Murphy Creek Trail junction. For the next 2.6 miles, from the campsite to the

Minam River Trail junction, Murphy Creek Trail drops gently through the forested canyon bottom. The trail generally stays on the right side of Murphy Creek, but it does cross to the left side for a short time. This section of the trail is more difficult to follow because of the many blowdowns and the infrequent maintenance. At the junction with Lower Minam River Trail (1673; 3,080 ft.) there is a trail sign, and a few yards to the left (south), on Minam River Trail, there's a bridge across Murphy Creek.

Miles and Directions

0.0 Take the Murphy Creek Trail (1672) from the junction with Minam River/Standley Guard Station Trail (1655).

0.2 Pass the junction with the abandoned Trout Creek Trail.

0.9 Pass the junction with the abandoned Old Murphy Creek Trail (1685).

4.0 Pass the junction with Big Sheep Ridge Trail (1685).

5.4 The trail drops off Mahogany Ridge.

5.9 Cross Patrick Creek.

6.6 Pass the junction with the lower Old Murphy Creek Trail.

7.4 Pass a campsite.

10.0 Arrive at the trail junction with Minam River Trail (1673). (GPS: N45 28.388'/W117 41.007')

Option: From the junction with Murphy Creek Trail, Big Sheep Ridge Trail (1685) heads down Big Sheep Ridge to the northwest. The path, Big Sheep Ridge Trail, generally follows the ridgeline, keeping slightly to the left of the top and staying mostly in the open for 7 long miles. It then turns to the left and drops, making thirteen steep switchbacks in the last 0.3 mile, to the unmarked junction with Minam River Trail. Although this route is more scenic than the Murphy Creek Trail, it is a very long way, without any water at all. Also, it is next to impossible for anyone not familiar with this trail to find this junction while on the Minam River Trail (1673). See Lower Minam River (hike 42). However, finding the junction, which is 2.3 miles north of the Murphy Creek Trail junction on Minam River Trail, is no problem when coming down Big Sheep Ridge. There are several possible dry campsites in the saddles along Big Sheep Ridge.

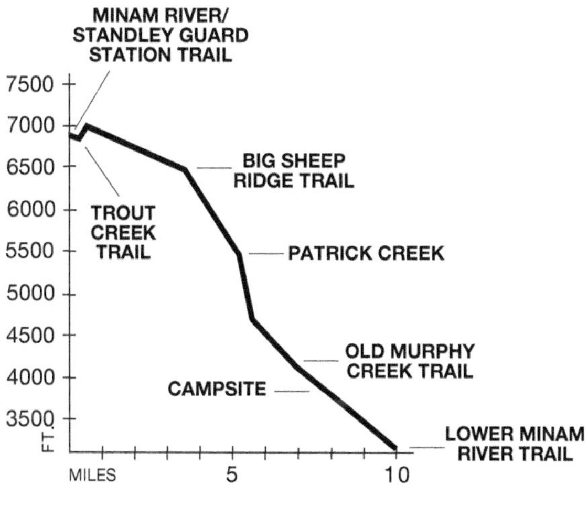

Murphy Creek Trail and the alternate route on Big Sheep Ridge require considerable route-finding skills to follow safely. Watch for mule deer, elk, and bear, common along the ridges and canyons in the western Wallowas. Along the lower parts of these trails, mostly below 4,000 feet, keep an eye on the ground ahead for an occasional rattlesnake. Carry plenty of water; there is none available along Murphy Creek Trail above Patrick Creek and none at all if you head down Big Sheep Ridge. A gallon per person may not be too much on a warm day.

For the ambitious hiker who is skilled in route finding and doesn't mind lots of elevation loss and gain, taking the alternate Big Sheep Ridge Trail down and coming back up Murphy Creek Trail makes a great hike. To do this it is best to allow two days from Standley Guard Station, and to camp at either the Minam River or the campsite 2.6 miles up Murphy Creek Trail from the Minam River.

40 Washboard Ridge

This backpack trip leads from Standley Guard Station, along the jagged crest of Washboard Ridge, to Bear Creek Trail. (Trail 1680)

Distance: 9.7 miles one way
Hiking time: 3.5–5 hours
Difficulty: Moderate to strenuous, with some route finding required
Trail maintenance: Seldom, but this trail is mostly in open country, so downed logs are not much of a problem.
Best season: Mid-July through Oct
Traffic and other trail users: Light foot and horse traffic except during fall hunting seasons, when it can be moderate to heavy. Much of the traffic is horse traffic.
Canine compatibility: Dogs permitted without leashes, but must be kept away from the stock of other parties
Fees and permits: Eagle Cap Wilderness Permit
Maximum elevation: 8,100 feet
Maps: USGS Jim White Ridge OR and North Minam Meadows OR; Geo Graphics Wallowa Mountain Eagle Cap Wilderness
Trail contact: USDA Forest Service Wallowa Mountains Office, 201 E 2nd St./ PO Box 905, Joseph, OR 97846; (541) 426-5546, (541) 426-4978; www.fs.usda.gov/wallowa-whitman

Finding the trail: The Washboard Ridge Trail can be accessed from several trailheads, including Bear Creek and Moss Springs, but the closest way to reach it is via the Standley Ridge Trail from Bearwallow Trailhead. To reach Bearwallow Trailhead turn south off OR 82, 1 mile east of Minam on Big Canyon Road (FR 8270). Drive south on Big Canyon Road for 10.4 miles to the junction with FR 050. Bear left at the junction and follow FR 050 for 6.8 miles to the trailhead. From the trailhead hike south on the Standley Ridge Trail for 4.6 miles to Standley Guard Station. The trail begins just south of Standley Guard Station and spring.
GPS: N45 22.810' / W117 34.562'

The Hike

Hike south from Standley Guard Station, quickly passing Standley Spring. Fill your water bottles at the developed spring, as there is almost no water along the trail for the first 4.6 miles. Be sure to treat, boil, or filter the water.

A short distance after passing the spring you reach the marked junction with the Washboard Ridge Trail. Bear left at the junction and continue to hike generally south on Washboard Ridge Trail. The route, which is marked with posts, may not be visible on the grass-covered ground in places here. After about 0.5 mile of traversing the semi-open slope and crossing a couple of wet-weather streams, the trail turns left (east) and climbs to the ridgeline. On the ridge the route turns right (southeasterly), next to a large rock cairn. Be sure to take note of this spot, as an abandoned trail continues to the northwest from here along the ridge. It is easy to get confused at this spot on the return trip. Along the ridge the view to the south opens up. China Cap is the prominent peak to the south across the Minam River drainage, but many other, mostly unnamed, peaks can also be seen.

As the ridge narrows, the trail drops slightly to the right of the ridgeline and heads down and southeast to a saddle. It then traverses the phlox- and lupine-covered slope on the right side of the ridgeline for 0.3 mile to another saddle. In this saddle the trail follows the ridge for a couple hundred yards, then traverses along the slope on the right side again. One-third of a mile into this traverse the trail is on a rock ledge for 100 yards or so, and 0.1 mile farther it follows another ledge for 75 yards. This is very steep and rugged country, and not well suited to inexperienced horses or riders. It could also be difficult for some novice hikers.

After leaving the second ledge, the trail comes to another saddle (7,310 ft.), with a sign pointing out Blowout Basin, which is to the left. In the saddle the trail crosses to the left side of the ridge for the first time and climbs steeply for a few yards before crossing back to the right side of the ridge. The trail reaches a rugged notch called Eagles Nest 0.2 mile after leaving Blowout Basin saddle. There is a sign at Eagles Nest. The most difficult part of the trail for horse traffic is a short distance past Eagles Nest. Here the trail is chipped out of a rock face as it climbs steeply to another saddle. Several horse wrecks have happened at this difficult spot.

After passing the difficult section, the trail makes a left turn in the saddle (7,640 ft.). After another 10 yards the trail turns right again, as it drops steeply off the left side of the ridgeline. Soon the grade moderates, as the trail descends to a meadow in a broad saddle on the ridgeline. The trail stays on the left side, but very close to the ridgeline, for 0.7 mile, then it crosses back to the right side, where it begins an ascending traverse to yet another ridgeline crossing.

The trail crosses the ridgeline at 7,800 feet, then drops slightly as it starts to traverse around the head of Miners Basin. The junction with Miners Basin Trail (1671; 7,640 ft.) is reached 0.3 mile after crossing the ridgeline. A short distance before reaching Miners Basin Trail junction, there are springs some distance below the trail to the left. Miners Basin Trail turns to the left (northeast) and descends 2.7 miles to Bear Creek Trail. At the junction, Washboard Trail heads straight ahead to the southeast and continues its traverse around the head of Miners Basin.

The trail traverses below a rocky bluff, then crosses the ridgeline again 0.25 mile after passing the junction with Miners Basin Trail. It stays close to the ridgeline for another 0.25 mile, then traverses on the right side again. The trail enters an area with no vegetation 0.5 mile after starting this traverse. In the bare area head southeast, descending slightly for about 100 yards, and the trail will soon reappear as it enters a grass-covered slope. From here to the junction with Bear Creek Trail, the trail and the country are much less rugged than they were back toward Standley Guard Station. The southeastern end of the Washboard Trail is well suited to horse traffic.

The trail traverses the grassy slope for 0.4 mile, passing below the summit of Bald Mountain, then becomes difficult to see in the grass. Head southeast, dropping slightly, and pick up the trail again as it enters some small trees. The trail rounds a small

Hiker on Washboard Ridge Trail.

sub-ridge and continues its traverse to the southeast. The lush meadow of Sturgill Basin can be seen below and to the southwest. The trail is well below the ridgeline of Washboard Ridge in this area.

After traversing above Sturgill Basin for 0.4 mile, the trail passes a good spring. The spring is a few feet below the trail to the right. At the spring the trail begins to get into thicker timber. The trail forks 0.2 mile past the spring; bear to the left to stay on the main trail. After the fork, the trail crosses a small stream and begins a 0.3-mile climb to Sturgill Saddle (7,820 ft.).

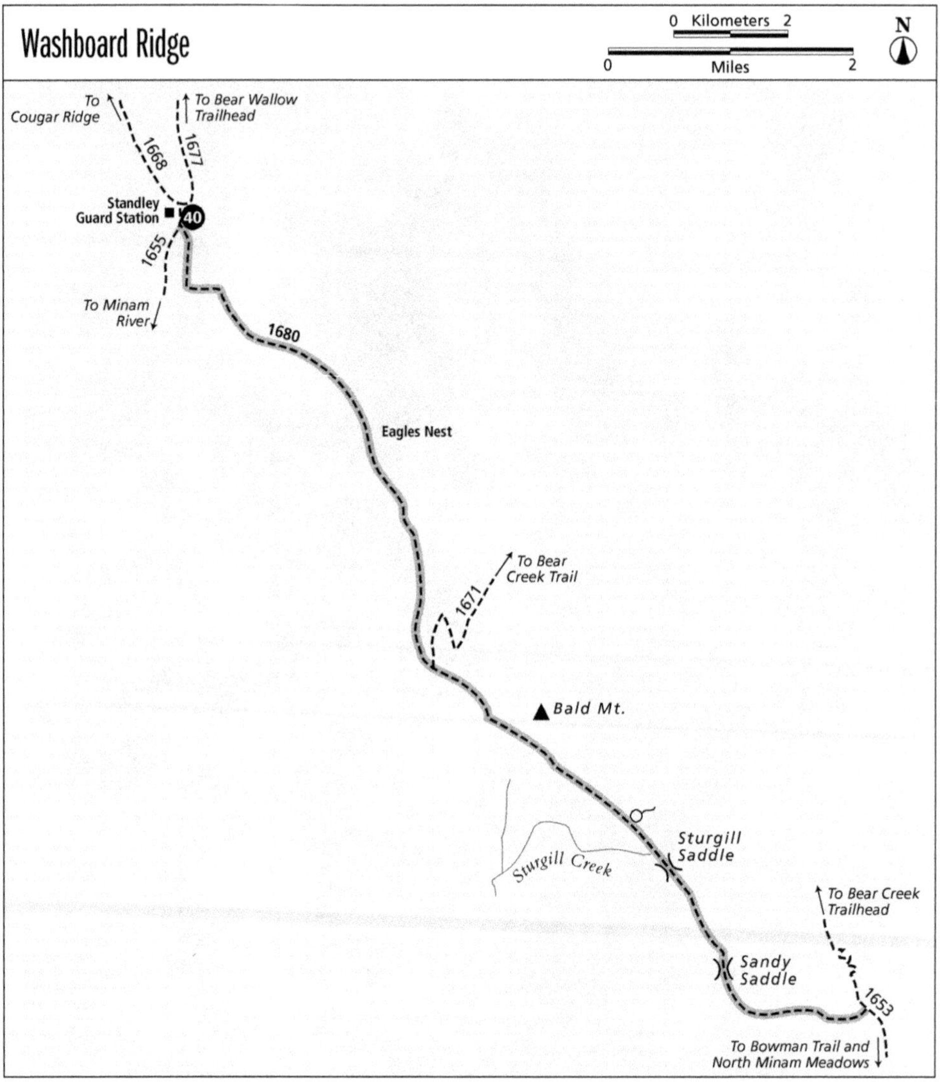

The trail crosses the saddle and drops through thin timber to a meadow, passing a campsite next to a stream along the way. The trail crosses a stream (7,590 ft.) as it enters the meadow and another stream as it is about to leave the meadow. Upon leaving the meadow the trail climbs slightly to the south-southeast, through a rocky area. Watch for cairns marking the way. The trail passes a couple of prospect holes 0.25 mile after leaving the meadow. There is lots of quartz, which was dug from these holes, lying on the ground here.

The trail crosses a smaller meadow after passing the prospect holes, then climbs a ridge made of gray-tan granite sand. At the top of the small ridge the trail turns to the left and climbs a short distance more to the main ridgeline. On the ridgeline the trail heads southeast for a short distance. This area of the ridgeline is known as Sandy Saddle, and at 8,100 feet it is the highest point reached on the Washboard Trail. The ridge is thinly timbered here, with whitebark pine and subalpine fir.

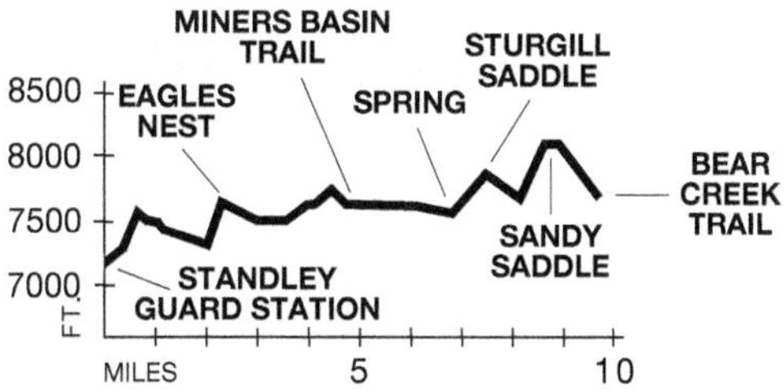

After following the nearly level ridgeline for 400 yards, the trail begins to descend. It winds its way down, sometimes steeply, through the thin but occasionally large whitebark pine for 0.7 mile to the top of the broad, open meadow in the saddle at the head of Bear Creek. As the trail enters the meadow, a rock pile with a post in it comes into view. This is the first of three such markers showing the way down to the junction with Bear Creek Trail. The trail crosses a small stream between the second and third posts. The junction with Bear Creek Trail (1653; 7,700 ft.) is on the divide between Bear Creek and the North Minam River drainages.

At the junction, Bear Creek is to the left (north), Bowman Trail and North Minam Meadows are to the right (south), and Bear Lake is straight ahead to the east. There are several campsites available near the junction.

A return trip can be made to Standley Guard Station by retracing the same trail, or you can head down Bear Creek for 13.6 miles to Dobbin Creek Trail, then climb 3.6 miles on Dobbin Creek Trail to Standley Ridge Trail, 1 mile north of Standley Guard Station. This loop is best done in two long or three short days, using the campsites along Bear Creek.

Miles and Directions

0.0 Start at the Standley Guard Station and spring.

0.7 Route reaches ridgeline. (GPS: N45 22.239'/ W117 34.062')

2.0 Pass through the saddle above Blowout Basin.

2.2 Reach Eagles Nest.

4.7 Pass the junction with Miners Basin Trail (1671).

7.3 Reach Sturgill Saddle. (GPS: N45 18.340'/W117 29.410')

8.5 Reach Sandy Saddle.

9.7 Arrive at the junction with Bear Creek Trail (1653). (GPS: N45 17.425'/W117 27.415')

41 Minam River/Standley Guard Station

This connecting trail links Upper Minam River Trail, 1.6 miles south of the Horse Ranch, to Standley Guard Station. As you climb out of the Minam River Canyon, the panorama unfolds. By the time you reach Standley Guard Station, you may have the feeling of being on the top of the world. Try to pace yourself as you climb so that you are not too tired to enjoy the country. (Trail 1655)

Distance: 4.4 miles one way
Hiking time: 2–3 hours
Difficulty: Strenuous
Trail maintenance: Infrequent
Best season: Mid-June through Oct
Traffic and other trail users: Light foot and horse traffic except during the fall hunting season, when horse traffic can be moderate
Canine compatibility: Dogs permitted without leashes, but must be kept away from the stock of other parties
Fees and permits: Eagle Cap Wilderness Permit; Northwest Forest Pass to park at Moss Springs Trailhead
Maximum elevation: 7,220 feet
Maps: USGS Jim White Ridge OR and Fox Point OR
Trail contact: USDA Forest Service Wallowa Mountains Office, 201 E 2nd St./ PO Box 905, Joseph, OR 97846; (541) 426-5546, (541) 426-4978; www.fs.usda.gov/wallowa-whitman.

To fly to the Horse Ranch, contact Spence Air Service at (541) 426-3288 in Enterprise, Oregon.

Finding the trail: There are several trailheads that can be used to access the Minam River/ Standley Guard Station Trail, including Bearwallow (closer to the Standley Guard Station end of the trail) and Bear Creek. The easiest way is to fly into the Horse Ranch from Enterprise. To reach the junction where this description for the Minam River/Standley Guard Station Trail begins by hiking, first drive 8 miles east from Cove on Mill Creek Road (FR 6220) to Moss Springs Trailhead. Then hike northeast on the Moss Springs/Horse Ranch Trail (1908) for 7.5 miles to the Horse Ranch and the junction with the Minam River Trail. Turn right on the Upper Minam River Trail (1673) and hike 1.6 miles southeast to the junction with the Minam River/Standley Guard Station Trail. Minam River/Standley Guard Station Trail (1655) leaves Upper Minam River Trail, 300 yards east-southeast of Wallowa Creek, which is marked with a sign. The elevation at the junction with Upper Minam River Trail is 3,800 feet.
GPS: Moss Springs Trailhead: N45 16.468' / W117 40.689'; Minam River/Standley Guard Station Trail junction: N45 20.565' / W117 35.850'

The Hike

At the marked junction, Minam River/Standley Guard Station Trail turns north off the Minam River Trail. It works its way up through medium-age transition zone forest and granite outcroppings to 4,500 feet, where the first basalt outcroppings appear. Basalt rock generally overlays granite in this area.

Faint Minam River/Standley Guard Station Trail below Standley Guard Station.

At 1.5 miles (5,030 ft.) a side trail leads 50 feet to the left to a creek where water may be obtained. A large ponderosa pine with an arrow cut into its side marks the spot where this side trail leaves the main trail.

The main trail continues to climb, with some switchbacks, to the top of a ridge (5,460 ft.). Here the view opens up, looking down onto the Minam River Canyon below and to Standley Ridge above. The trail climbs along the top of the ridge for a time, then traverses to the right. At 6,460 feet the trail crosses a small seasonal stream and continues to climb to the junction with Murphy Creek Trail (1672). See Murphy Creek (hike 39). The elevation at this junction is 6,930 feet; it is 3.4 miles from Minam River Trail. From the junction with Murphy Creek Trail, Standley Guard Station (7,220 ft.) is 1 mile ahead to the north.

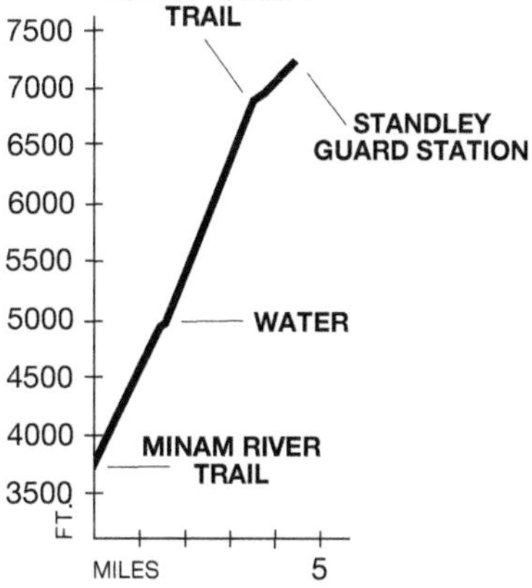

Between the seasonal stream and Murphy Creek Trail junction is a game trail that takes off to the left (west). This game trail could be mistaken for the main trail, especially when coming down. Be careful not to take it.

The ridgetop area above the Murphy Creek Trail junction is mostly open and subalpine in nature. It is typical of ridgetop areas in the

Minam River/Standley Guard Station

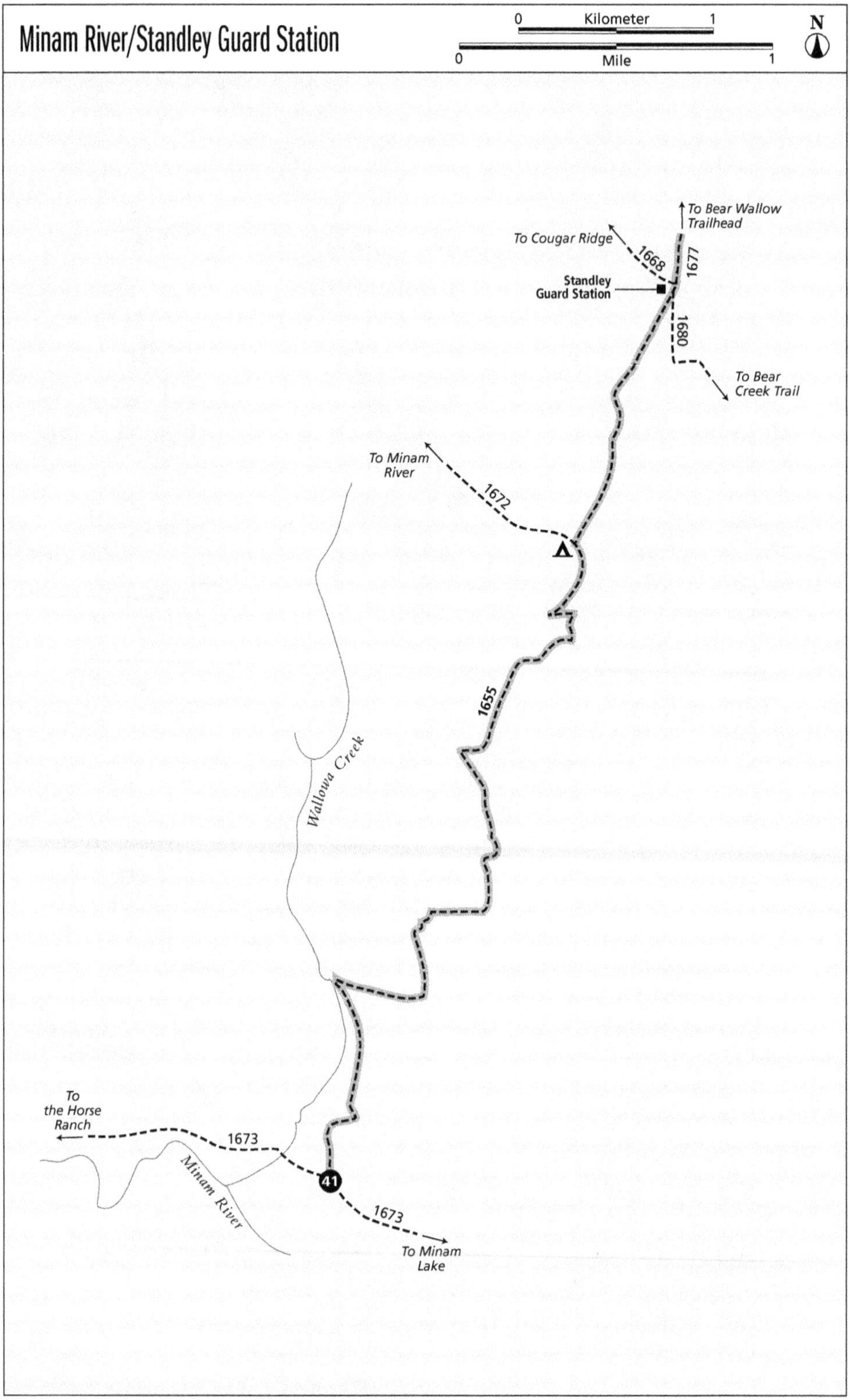

western Wallowas. There are campsites at Standley Guard Station, which is the trail hub of the area.

Miles and Directions

0.0 Take the Minam River/Standley Guard Station Trail (1655) from the junction with the Upper Minam River Trail (1673).

1.5 Pass the side trail leading to water.

3.4 Reach the trail junction with Murphy Creek Trail (1672). (GPS: N45 22.212'/W117 34.807')

4.4 Arrive at the Standley Guard Station. (GPS: N45 22.924'/W117 34.503')

42 Lower Minam River

This long, gentle backpack leads down the Minam River from the Horse Ranch to Meads Flat Trailhead and back or possibly on to the town of Minam on OR 82. (Trail 1673)

Distance: 14.5 miles one way from the Horse Ranch to Meads Flat Trailhead; 24.5 miles one way to Minam
Hiking time: 6-8 hours to Meads Flat; 13 hours to Minam
Difficulty: Easy, but long
Trail maintenance: Infrequent to Meads Flat; seldom on the trail portion downriver
Best season: Apr through Nov
Traffic and other trail users: Moderate; moderate horse traffic
Canine compatibility: Dogs permitted without leashes, but must be kept away from the stock of other parties
Fees and permits: Northwest Forest Pass if you park at Moss Springs and Eagle Cap Wilderness Permit
Maximum elevation: 3,600 feet
Maps: USGS Mount Fanny OR and Mount Moriah OR; Geo Graphics Wallowa Mountains Eagle Cap Wilderness
Trail contact: USDA Forest Service Wallowa Mountains Office, 201 E 2nd St./ PO Box 905, Joseph, OR 97846; (541) 426-5546, (541) 426-4978; www.fs.usda.gov/wallowa-whitman

For a flight to the Horse Ranch, call Spence Air Service at (541) 426-3288 in Enterprise, Oregon.

Finding the trail: Lower Minam River Trail begins at the junction of Minam River Trail (1673) and the Moss Springs/Horse Ranch Trail (1908), 100 yards east of the Horse Ranch (3,600 ft.). The easiest way, on foot, to reach the junction where the Lower Minam River Trail begins is from Moss Springs Trailhead. To get to Moss Springs Trailhead drive 8 miles east from Cove on Mill Creek Road (FR 6220). From the trailhead hike northeast on the Moss Springs/Horse Ranch Trail (1908) for 7.5 miles to the Horse Ranch and the junction with the Minam River Trail. The Horse Ranch can also be reached by flight from Enterprise.

There are several other ways to get to the Horse Ranch, but they involve longer hikes. Meads Flat may be reached by off-road vehicle from Minam. Inquire locally before trying to reach Meads Flat.

GPS: Moss Springs Trailhead: N45 16.468'/W117 40.689'; Lower Minam River Trail at the Horse Ranch: N45 20.834'/W117 37.510'

The Hike

The Horse Ranch was once a dude ranch. It has been purchased by the forest service and now has volunteer caretakers during the summer. There is an airstrip at the Horse Ranch that is open to the public. From the junction 100 yards east of the Horse Ranch the trail heads downriver to the north-northwest. The trail enters Eagle Cap Wilderness 0.5 mile from the junction. A quarter mile farther, between the river and the trail, is a good campsite. From the campsite, a small sawmill, which is part of the Minam Lodge operation, can be seen across the river to the west. There is a small

Meadow in the Minam River Canyon near the mouth of the Little Minam River.

stream just below the campsite. The trail in this area is apparently an old roadbed. There is a stream crossing at 1.5 miles (3,570 ft.).

At 1.75 miles the trail splits, with the left trail going to a beautiful riverside campsite. After passing the campsite, the side trail rejoins the main trail 0.25 mile from where it forked off. The northern, downriver end of the side trail, however, is a bit difficult to find.

After the trails join 2 miles from the Moss Springs Trail junction, the trail gets farther away from the Minam River. It stays away from the river for about 1.5 miles, crossing Horsehaven Creek. After coming closer to the river again, the trail continues on to a trail junction at 4.75 miles (3,470 ft.). The trail to the left, which is an alternate for the Little Minam River Trail, fords the river and heads west. The Lower Minam River Trail goes straight ahead.

Three hundred yards past the junction the trail passes the mouth of the Little Minam River. The Little Minam River joins the Minam River from the west—the opposite side from the trail. After another 0.4 mile the trail crosses Fawn Creek, and 0.25 mile farther is the junction with Little Minam River Trail (1901; 3,430 ft.). Crossing the Minam River here to get to Little Minam River Trail is very dangerous, and without a horse it can be difficult to impossible in the spring and early summer. There is no bridge.

At the junction with Little Minam River Trail there is an excellent campsite. The campsite is located across the flower-covered meadow to the west of the main trail, near the river. The canyon bottom in this area is mostly covered with well-diversified transition zone forest. The coniferous trees include Douglas fir, true fir, tamarack, and lodgepole and ponderosa pines. In addition to these needle-leaf trees are aspen, native hawthorn, and some cottonwood. Other plants include lots of lupine and wild strawberries.

After passing the Little Minam River Trail junction, the Lower Minam River Trail continues downriver, crossing a couple of streams in the next 2.6 miles before coming to a semi-open area. This area was logged many years ago. There is a red digger colony here; these ground squirrels can be fun to watch. This is also a nice camping area (3,240 ft.).

Eagle Creek flows into the Minam River from the southwest 1.5 miles past the open area. It flows in on the opposite side of the river from the trail.

The bridge over Murphy Creek is 1.25 miles below Eagle Creek. Just past the bridge is the junction with Murphy Creek Trail (1672; 3,040 ft.). The junction with Big Sheep Trail (1685; 2,940 ft.) is about 2.6 miles past the Murphy Creek Trail junction. This junction is unmarked and very difficult to find. It is 200 yards before Trout Creek crossing. Another 0.1 mile brings you to Trout Creek crossing (a knee-deep ford early in the season), and 0.3 mile farther is the junction with Cougar Ridge Trail (1649; 3,020 ft.).

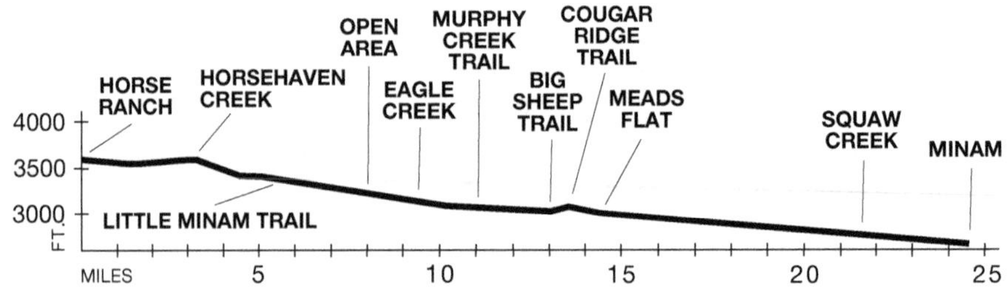

Lower Minam River

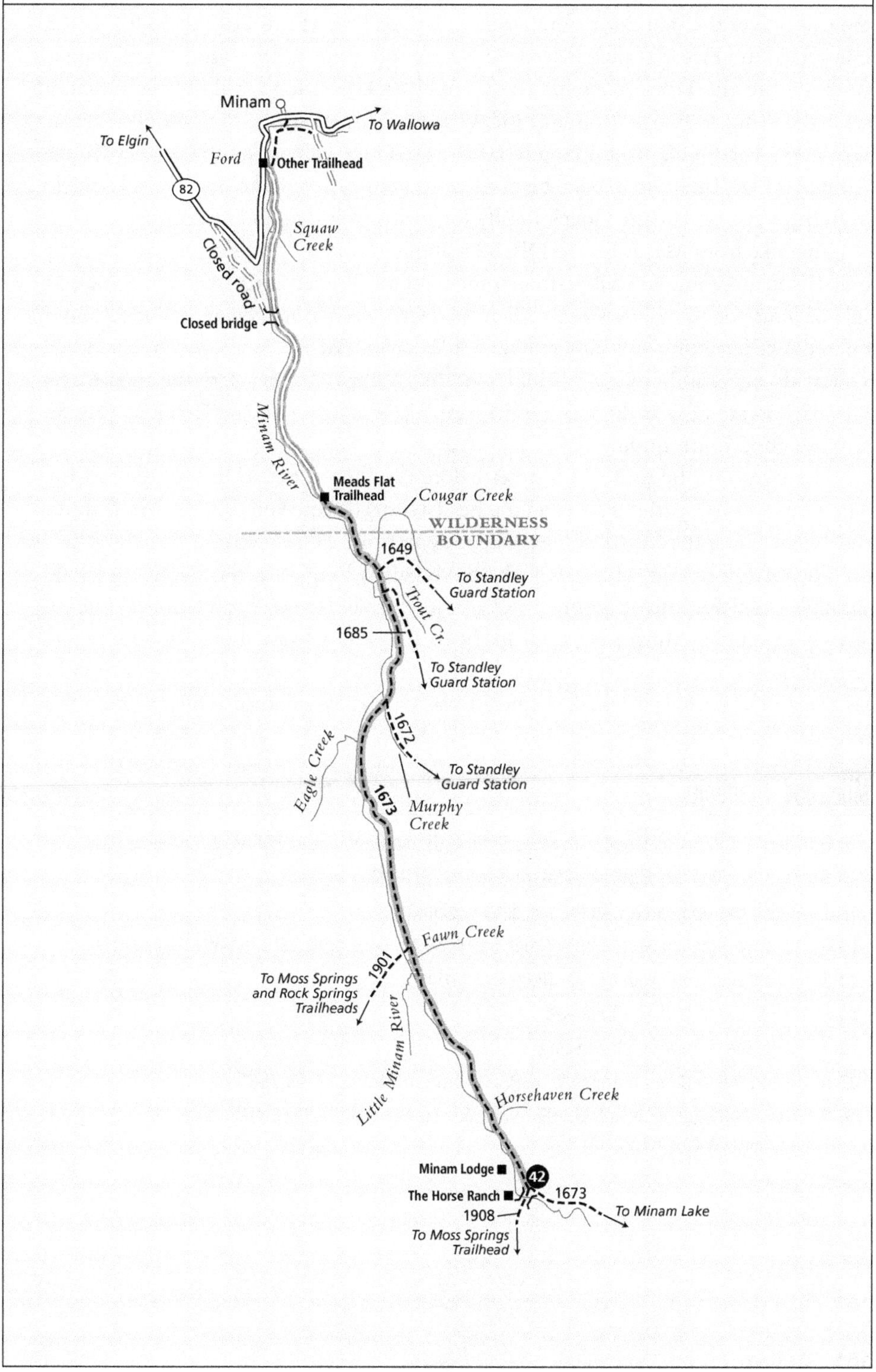
0 Kilometers 4
0 Miles 4
N
Minam
To Wallowa
To Elgin
Ford
Other Trailhead
82
Squaw Creek
Closed road
Closed bridge
Minam River
Meads Flat Trailhead
Cougar Creek
WILDERNESS BOUNDARY
1649
To Standley Guard Station
Trout Cr.
1685
To Standley Guard Station
1672
To Standley Guard Station
Eagle Creek
1673
Murphy Creek
Fawn Creek
1901
To Moss Springs and Rock Springs Trailheads
Little Minam River
Horsehaven Creek
Minam Lodge
42
The Horse Ranch
1673
To Minam Lake
1908
To Moss Springs Trailhead

One mile below the Cougar Ridge Trail junction is the national forest boundary, the Eagle Cap Wilderness boundary, and Meads Flat. There is an old foundation on the east side of the trail just before reaching Meads Flat. Meads Flat (2,930 ft.) is 14.5 miles from the Horse Ranch. Meads Flat is a good point to turn around and retrace your steps to the Horse Ranch, or you could backtrack for 1 mile to the junction with the Cougar Ridge Trail and follow it for 5 miles up to the Middle Cougar Ridge Trailhead. This would require a high-clearance vehicle shuttle to the Middle Cougar Ridge Trailhead. It may be possible to get to Meads Flat by off-road vehicle from the town of Minam. Check locally for road conditions and directions.

The hike from Meads Flat to OR 82 is about 10 miles over jeep roads and a poor trail. If you are going to walk it, follow the road for 7 miles north, staying on the east side of the river, to Squaw Creek. Then follow the sometimes vague trail for 3 more miles downriver, until you hit a road in a side canyon. Turn left on the road, go down a short distance, and cross the bridge over the Wallowa River. Here the road meets OR 82. You are now at the town of Minam. The trail from Squaw Creek to OR 82 requires good route-finding skills.

The river may be forded 1.5 miles before reaching the road in the side canyon. The ford leads to a parking area and trailhead a short distance off OR 82, 1 mile south of Minam. Cross the Minam River here only in times of low water.

The hike from the Horse Ranch to Minam is long, but it is gentle and goes through beautiful canyon country filled with forests, flowers, and animals. Fishing anywhere on the Minam River is likely to get you a trout dinner. Check www.eregulations.com/oregon/fishing for special regulations. During the warmer months keep a watch out for rattlesnakes. Once I was stalked by a cougar while walking this trail.

Miles and Directions

0.0 Start at the trail junction with Moss Springs/Horse Ranch Trail (1908) at the Horse Ranch.

5.6 Pass the junction with Little Minam River Trail (1901).

8.2 Reach the open area with the red digger colony.

10.8 Pass the junction with Murphy Creek Trail (1672). (GPS: N45 28.388'/W117 41.007')

13.5 Pass the junction with Cougar Ridge Trail (1649).

14.5 Reach the Meads Flat Trailhead.

21.5 Make the Squaw Creek crossing.

23.0 Reach the ford and a trailhead. (GPS: N45 36.446'/ W117 43.788')

24.5 Arrive at the junction with OR 82 in the side canyon near Minam. (GPS: N45 37.205'/W117 43.226')

43 Upper Minam River

A long but easy backpack drops from Minam Lake down the Minam River to the Horse Ranch. This is a main trail through the western part of Eagle Cap Wilderness. Many other trails connect with Upper Minam River Trail. (Trail 1673)

Distance: 26.4 miles one way
Hiking time: 2 or 3 days
Difficulty: Easy, but long
Trail maintenance: Infrequent; this trail recently received considerable maintenance by WMHCTA. To join the WMHCTA see appendix A.
Best season: Mid-June through Oct
Traffic and other trail users: Moderate foot and horse traffic; heavier during fall hunting seasons
Canine compatibility: Dogs permitted without leashes, but must be kept away from the stock of other parties
Fees and permits: Northwest Forest Pass and Eagle Cap Wilderness Permit
Maximum elevation: 7,380 feet
Maps: USGS Eagle Cap OR, Steamboat Lake OR, China Cap OR, and Jim White Ridge OR; Geo Graphics Wallowa Mountains Eagle Cap Wilderness
Trail contact: USDA Forest Service Wallowa Mountains Office, 201 E 2nd St./ PO Box 905, Joseph, OR 97846; (541) 426-5546, (541) 426-4978; www.fs.usda.gov/wallowa-whitman

Finding the trail: The easiest way to reach Minam Lake where this hike starts is from Two Pan Trailhead. To get to Two Pan Trailhead drive south from Lostine on Lostine River Road for 18 miles. From the trailhead hike south on the West Fork Lostine River Trail (1670) for 6 miles to Minam Lake. Upper Minam River Trail begins at the south end of Minam Lake, at the junction of Minam Lake/Mirror Lakes Trail (1661) and West Fork Lostine River Trail (7,380 ft.).
GPS: Two Pan Trailhead: N45 15.001'/W117 22.580'; Upper Minam River Trail junction: N45 10.666'/W117 21.095'

The Hike

From the junction the trail heads south a few yards to the junction with Blue Lake Trail (1673A). Blue Lake Trail turns off to the right (west). A small stream runs down the trail for a short distance 0.3 mile past Blue Lake Trail junction. There is another small creek crossing with a bridge 0.8 mile from the junction. The trail crosses another creek 325 yards after crossing the bridge.

In 0.25 mile the trail crosses the Minam River (6,880 ft.). There is no bridge here, but there is a logjam on which to cross just below the trail crossing. After crossing the Minam River, the trail heads down the right (west) side of the river 0.7 mile to the junction with Frazier Pass Trail (1947). Frazier Pass Trail turns left (east) at the junction (6,750 ft.). See Frazier Pass (hike 79). There is a large meadow to the left (east) of the trail at the junction. Around the fringes of the meadow are several campsites. This meadow and the campsites around it are often used by parties with stock, as grazing is available here. The meadow areas along the Upper Minam River are heavily used by elk as summer range.

After passing the Frazier Pass Trail junction, the trail crosses several small streams and makes a few switchbacks as it drops gently to the junction with Trail Creek Trail (1922). The Trail Creek Trail junction (5,320 ft.) is 4.1 miles from the junction with Frazier Pass Trail and 6.1 miles from Minam Lake. By the time you get to this junction, the forest has changed from Canadian zone at Minam Lake to transition zone forest. Here the trees are fir, tamarack, spruce, and some ponderosa pine. The direction in which the trail is heading has also changed. After leaving Minam Lake, the trail was heading southeast; now at Trail Creek Trail junction it has turned around and is going northwest.

There is a good campsite to the left of the trail next to the river, 4.3 miles past the Trail Creek Trail junction. The junction with Granite Creek Trail (1676; 4,920 ft.) is 250 yards past the campsite. Granite Creek Trail turns off to the right (north). After passing Granite Creek Trail, Elk Creek Trail junction is 200 yards farther down the Minam River Trail. Elk Creek Trail (1944) turns to the left (south) and crosses the Minam River. Elk Creek Trail junction is 10.5 miles from Minam Lake.

After passing Elk Creek Trail, the trail crosses four streams in the 2.6 miles to Last Chance Creek. Some of the area between Elk Creek and Last Chance Creek looks like it was logged many years ago. There are old stumps, and the trail is quite wide in places. There is no bridge at Last Chance Creek, but there are logs across it a short distance upstream.

The junction with Rock Creek Trail (1905) is 1.6 miles past Last Chance Creek. There are good campsites on Rock Creek Trail across the river from the junction, but there is no bridge. This crossing is easy during times of low water but could be dangerous during times of heavy runoff. Rock Creek Trail junction (4,590 ft.) is 14.6 miles from Minam Lake.

The trail crosses Pole Creek (4,470 ft.) 1.3 miles past Rock Creek Trail junction. There is no bridge over Pole Creek either. In the next 1.3 miles the trail crosses three small streams. After the third stream the trail goes through a stand of yew trees for about 0.25 mile. Yew is not very common in eastern Oregon; it is generally found in wetter climates. About 1 mile past the small yew stand is the bridge over North Fork Minam River (4,220 ft.). Just past the bridge is the junction with the North Minam River Trail (1675). This junction is 18.6 miles from Minam Lake.

Just past the junction are two large stream crossings without bridges. The trail climbs to a saddle 0.9 mile past the streams. This climb is to avoid the steep terrain next to the river. After crossing the saddle the trail drops down and crosses two small streams in an area called Big Burn. There are many flowers in the meadow at Big Burn. Native hawthorn trees with their white flowers or red berries, depending on the season, are common here also. There is a red digger colony here too.

One-half mile past Big Burn, the trail crosses Three Mile Creek, then crosses an unnamed creek 1.25 miles past Three Mile Creek. The Garwood Creek crossing is 0.5

Upper Minam Trail near Frazier Pass Trail junction. GARY FLETCHER PHOTO

mile farther, and another 0.25 mile farther is Whoopee Creek. Chaparral Creek is 1.25 miles past Whoopee Creek. The junction with Trail 1665 is 0.5 mile past Chaparral Creek. Trail 1665 turns to the right (north) and goes up to Standley Guard Station.

The trail crosses Wallowa Creek 300 yards past the junction. It is another 1.5 miles from Wallowa Creek to the junction with Moss Springs/Horse Ranch Trail (1908). This junction (3,600 ft.) is 26.4 miles from Minam Lake. Just before reaching the junction, there is a pond on the left side of the trail. Watch for muskrats in the pond. The Minam River Trail continues downriver from the Horse Ranch into the town of Minam.

The Horse Ranch is 100 yards west of the junction on Moss Springs/Horse Ranch Trail. There is an airstrip here, as well as a lodge and some cabins that now belong to the forest service. If you follow the trail across the airstrip and go a short distance farther, the trail to Minam Lodge turns off to the right. Minam Lodge is a short distance down the side trail. It is possible to fly in or out of the Horse Ranch. Check with Spence Air Service at (541) 426-3288 in Enterprise, Oregon. There are many possible campsites in the area around the Horse Ranch. However, there is some private land in this area. Probably the best campsites are east of the Minam River on forest service land upstream from the bridge. Do not camp on or near the airstrip.

Fishing can be good all along the Minam River. Check the current fishing regulations, as there may be some special regulations for this river. There are many more campsites than I have mentioned. The entire area abounds with wildlife, big and small, and the meadows are covered with flowers in spring and early summer, and

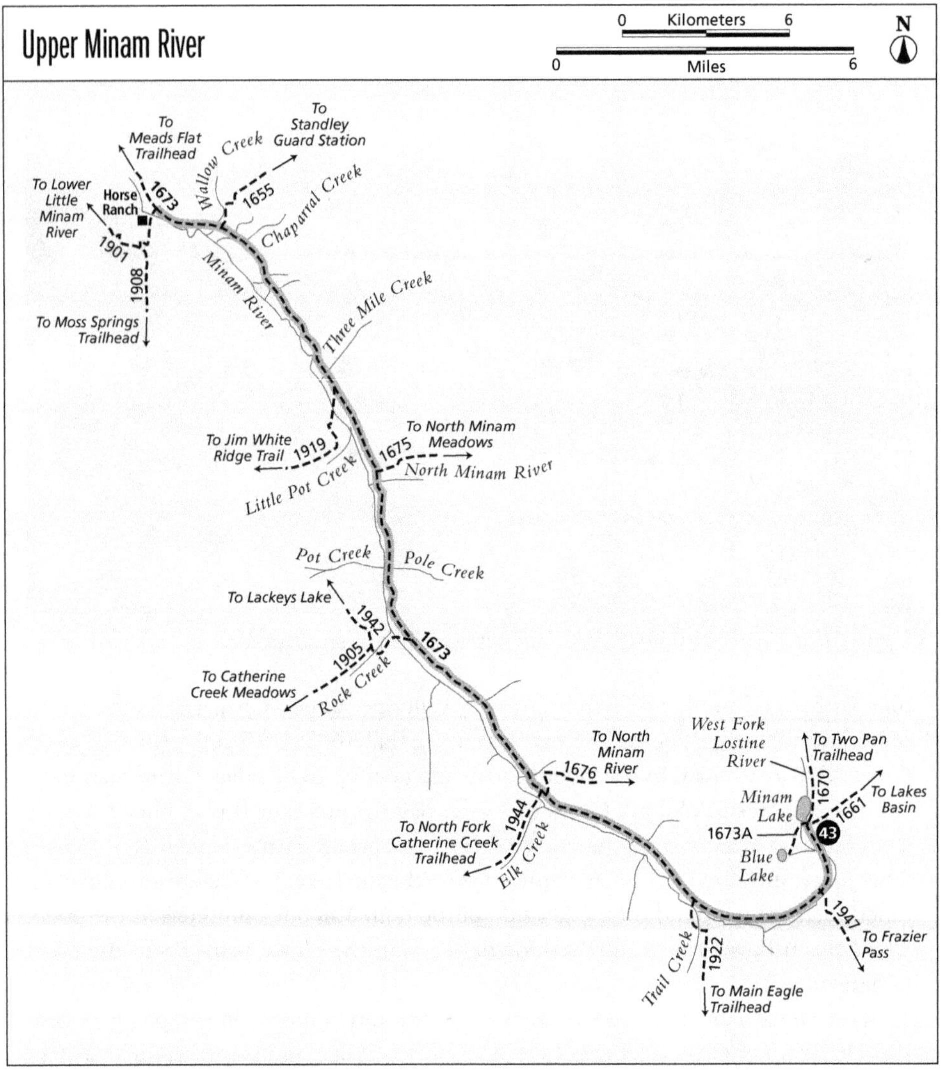

all summer near Minam Lake. The Minam River Trail is the main trunk trail in the western Wallowa Mountains. The possible side and loop trips off it are too numerous to name.

Miles and Directions

0.0 Start at Minam Lake, at the junction with West Fork Lostine River Trail (1820).

2.0 Pass the junction with Frazier Pass Trail (1947). (GPS: N45 09.616'/W117 20.360')

6.1 Pass the junction with Trail Creek Trail (1922). (GPS: N45 09.130'/W117 23.690')

10.4 Pass the junction with Granite Creek Trail (1676). (GPS: N45 10.817'/W117 27.670')

10.5 Pass the junction with Elk Creek Trail (1944). (GPS: N45 10.856'/W117 27.754')

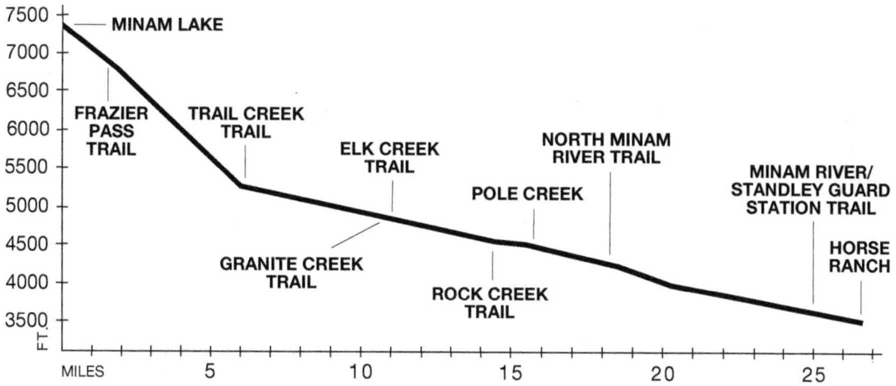

13.0 Cross Last Chance Creek.

14.6 Pass the junction with Rock Creek Trail (1905). (GPS: N45 13.365'/W117 31.250')

15.9 Cross Pole Creek.

18.6 Pass the junction with North Minam River Trail (1675). (GPS: N45 16.375'/W117 32.040')

24.9 Pass the junction with Minam River/Standley Guard Station Trail (1655). (GPS: N45 20.565'/W117 35.850')

26.4 Reach the junction with Moss Springs/Horse Ranch Trail (1908) and the Horse Ranch. (GPS: N45 20.834'/W117 37.510')

44 North Minam River

This backpack route climbs from Minam River Trail, in the depths of the Minam River Canyon, to the lush North Minam Meadows. Then the route continues its climb into the alpine country high atop the ridge that divides the Minam and Lostine River drainages and the junction with the Copper Creek Trail. (Trail 1675)

Distance: 12.8 miles one way
Hiking time: 5-7 hours
Difficulty: Moderate to strenuous
Trail maintenance: Infrequent
Best season: Mid-July through Sept
Traffic and other trail users: Moderate foot and horse traffic
Elevation gain: 4,200 feet
Canine compatibility: Dogs permitted without leashes, but must be kept away from the stock of other parties
Fees and permits: Eagle Cap Wilderness Permit; a Northwest Forest Pass is also required if you park at Moss Springs, Frances Lake/Bowman, or Two Pan Trailheads.
Maximum elevation: 8,420 feet
Maps: USGS Jim White Ridge OR, North Minam Meadows OR, and Steamboat Lake OR; Geo Graphics Wallowa Mountain Eagle Cap Wilderness
Trail contact: USDA Forest Service Wallowa Mountains Office, 201 E 2nd St./ PO Box 905, Joseph, OR 97846; (541) 426-5546, (541) 426-4978; www.fs.usda.gov/wallowa-whitman

To fly into or out of the Horse Ranch, call Spence Air Service at (541) 426-3288 in Enterprise, Oregon.

Finding the trail: This remote trail is normally done as a side trip from the Upper Minam River Trail (1673). The North Minam River Trail begins at the junction with Upper Minam River Trail. This junction is 7.8 miles upstream from the Horse Ranch and the junction with Moss Springs/Horse Ranch Trail, or 18.6 miles downriver from Minam Lake. The junction can be reached from the Moss Springs Trailhead via the Moss Springs/Horse Ranch (1908) and Upper Minam River Trails (15.3 miles one way to the junction) or from Two Pan Trailhead by way of the West Fork Lostine River Trail (1670) and the Upper Minam River Trail (24.7 miles one way). The upper end of the North Minam River Trail can also be reached from the Frances Lake/Bowman Trailhead over the Bowman Trail (1651) or Two Pan Trailhead via the West Fork Lostine River and Copper Creek Trails. The easiest way to reach the junction where this hike starts is to fly into the Horse Ranch and hike up the Upper Minam River Trail for 7.8 miles. The flight into or out of the Horse Ranch is short but spectacular.
GPS: Moss Springs/Horse Ranch Trail at the Horse Ranch: N45 20.834'/W117 37.510'; North Minam River Trail junction: N45 16.375'/W117 32.040'

The Hike

North Minam River Trail turns east off the Upper Minam River Trail (elevation at junction is 4,220 ft.). It fords a large stream, which is part of the North Minam River, 100 yards from the junction. After crossing the stream the trail climbs steeply. It crosses Sturgill Creek (4,580 ft.) 1.1 miles from the junction. There is no bridge here either.

The trail crosses seven small to very small streams in the next 2.5 miles as it climbs to the falls in the North Minam River. The falls (5,360 ft.) are a short distance to the right of the trail. The trail crosses another small stream 0.3 mile past the falls. Here there is an open area with a campsite to the right of the trail. After crossing the open area for 0.25 mile, the trail goes back into the woods. A few yards into the woods is the junction with Green Lake Trail (1666). Green Lake Trail turns to the right (southwest). This junction is 4.2 miles from the Minam River Trail. Just past the junction, the trail enters North Minam Meadows (5,440 ft.).

The trail crosses two streams in the 0.3 mile between the Green Lake junction and the junction with the Bowman Trail (1651). The Bowman Trail turns to the left (northeast). There are lots of campsites here, along the edge of North Minam Meadows. Watch for elk feeding in the meadows early and late in the day.

The trail is fairly flat for the first mile past the Bowman Trail junction, but then it begins to climb. The trail is badly eroded in places in this area. It crosses a small stream 0.6 mile after it starts to climb. Seventy-five yards after crossing the stream, the trail makes a switchback to the left. Be aware that bears have been spotted in these parts. The trail makes seven switchbacks and crosses the small streams several times in the next 2 miles. It also climbs about 1,000 feet in these switchbacks. The switchback area is mostly open slope with only scattered trees.

After going 200 yards past the last switchback, the trail crosses a very small stream (6,990 ft.). It then goes up through and around the head of a small alpine valley. It crosses the same small stream again 150 yard up the valley. In the next mile the trail crosses several small streams, then it comes to a larger one (7,140 ft.). Just past the larger stream crossing there is a view back down to North Minam Meadows.

The trail then makes a switchback to the left. There is another stream crossing 0.25 mile past the switchback. Two hundred yards past the stream crossing, there is a pond 100 yards to the right of the trail. The trail crosses nine more small streams in

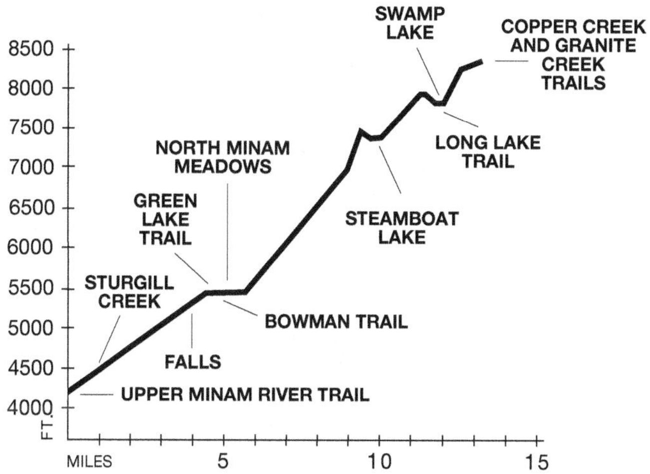

Steamboat Lake. GARY FLETCHER PHOTO

the next 0.8 mile, to where Steamboat Lake comes into view. On the way to the lake it climbs 100 vertical feet above lake level, then drops back down. Before reaching the lake the trail goes around some granite outcroppings. On these outcroppings scratch marks can be seen. These were made when the glaciers dragged rocks over exposed bedrock. Steamboat Lake (7,363 ft.) is 9.8 miles from the Minam River Trail junction.

There are several campsites and lots of fish at Steamboat Lake. The trail goes around the left (east) side of Steamboat Lake and crosses the open, lush, green, marshy meadow at its head. There are several small streams in the meadow. At the upper (south) end of the meadow the trail crosses a larger stream, then begins to climb. It crosses three more small streams. It climbs along the hillside, temporarily heading north. In the next 0.5 mile the trail makes six switchbacks as it climbs the ridge southwest of Steamboat Lake. Above these switchbacks the trail heads north-northwest for 300 yards. It then switchbacks to the left again. A few yards past this switchback the trail turns to the right and soon flattens out (7,680 ft.).

After going 125 yards on fairly flat ground there are some ponds to the right of the trail. After passing the ponds the trail heads southwest and slightly up for 250 yards to a pass (7,960 ft.). The trail crosses the pass and drops for 0.25 mile to the junction with Long Lake Trail (1669). After passing the Long Lake Trail junction, the trail goes south around the left (east) side of Swamp Lake (7,837 ft.). Swamp Lake, 11.4 miles from the Minam River Trail, sits at the head of a magnificent glacial valley. The area is very open and alpine, with snowdrifts lasting late into the summer. There are lots of fish and several campsites available here.

North Minam River

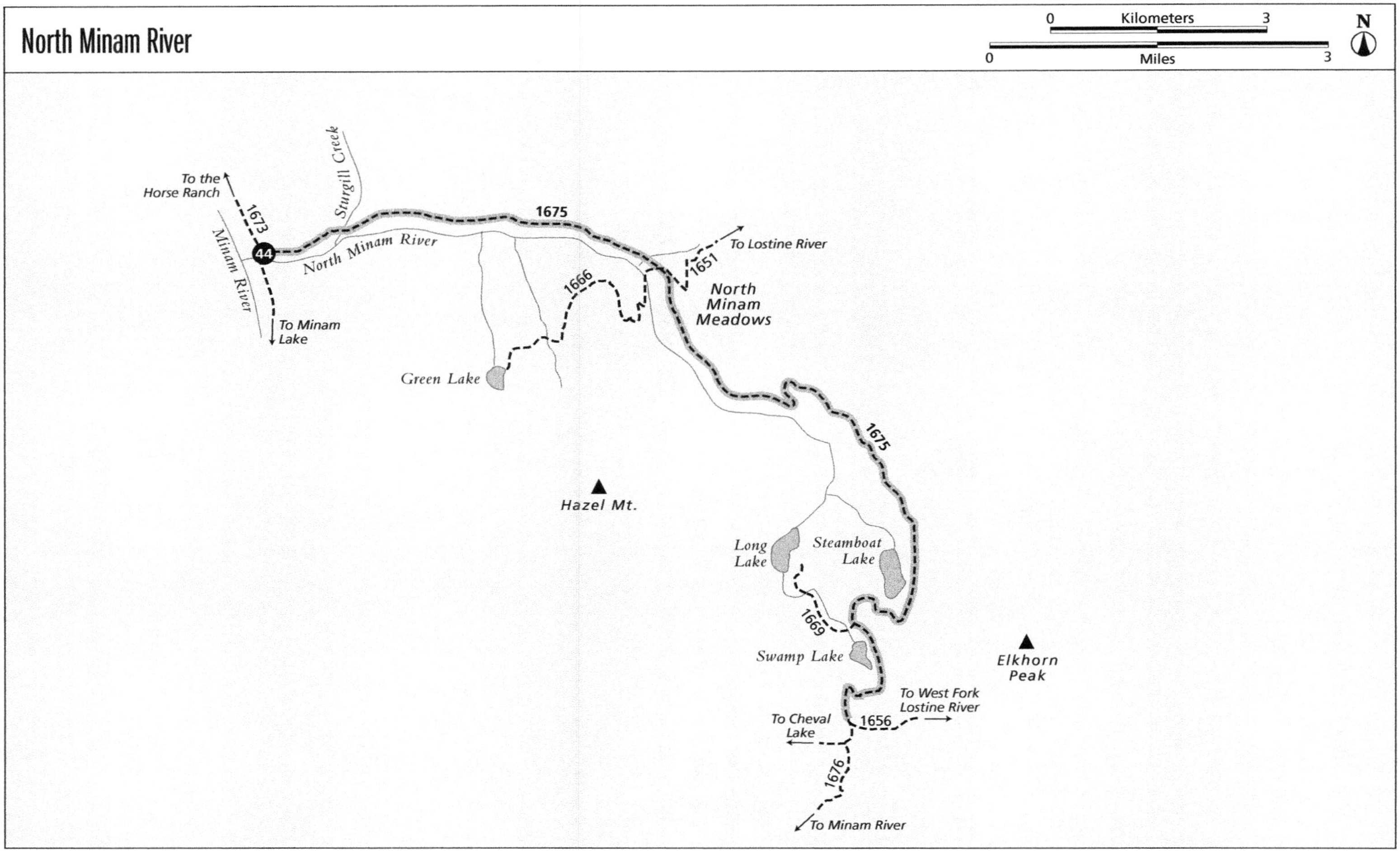

The trail crosses the meadow at the south end of Swamp Lake. It then switchbacks up the ridge to the west, nearly to the top. Here the trail levels out a bit and heads south (8,320 ft.). It then climbs slightly for 0.5 mile to the junction with Copper Creek Trail (1656) and Granite Creek Trail (1676)(8,420 ft.).

This trail may be difficult to follow above Swamp Lake before late summer because of snow. In early July, when we hiked this trail, there was still quite a bit of snow, and that was a fairly light snow year. The surrounding high alpine plateau may be covered with a variety of flowers in August. Finding your way over this open plateau area can be a problem during times of snowfall and poor visibility.

An extended loop trip can be done by combining North Minam River Trail with West Fork Lostine River Trail. From Two Pan Trailhead climb to Minam Lake, then take Upper Minam River Trail to the junction with North Minam Trail. Follow North Minam Trail as described. At the junction of North Minam Trail and Copper Creek Trail, take Copper Creek Trail back down to the east to West Fork Lostine River Trail. Follow West Fork Lostine Trail for 2.6 miles north back to Two Pan Trailhead. This makes a 47.4-mile loop, with only 2.6 miles of the trail hiked twice. Allow at least three days to make this loop, but four or five days is better.

Miles and Directions

0.0 Trail junction with Upper Minam River Trail (1673).

1.1 Cross Sturgill Creek.

3.6 Arrive at the falls in North Minam River.

4.2 Pass the junction with Green Lake Trail (1666). (GPS: N45 16.242'/W117 27.730')

4.3 Arrive at North Minam Meadows.

4.5 Pass the junction with Bowman Trail (1651). (GPS: N45 16.125'/W117 27.645')

9.8 Arrive at Steamboat Lake. (GPS: N45 13.798'/W117 25.004')

11.0 Cross the pass.

11.3 Pass the junction with Long Lake Trail (1669).

12.8 Arrive at the junction with Copper Creek (1656) and Granite Creek (1676) Trails. (GPS: N45 12.730'/W117 25.630')

45 Green Lake

This day hike or short backpack leads from a camp at North Minam Meadows to Green Lake. (Trail 1666)

Distance: 4 miles one way
Hiking time: 1.5–2 hours
Difficulty: Moderate
Trail maintenance: Rare
Best season: Mid-June through Oct
Traffic and other trail users: Moderate foot and horse traffic
Canine compatibility: Dogs permitted without leashes, but must be kept away from the stock of other parties
Fees and permits: Eagle Cap Wilderness Permit; a Northwest Forest pass is needed to park at Francis Lake/Bowman Trailhead.
Maximum elevation: 7,000 feet
Map: USGS North Minam Meadows OR
Trail contact: USDA Forest Service Wallowa Mountains Office, 201 E 2nd St./ PO Box 905, Joseph, OR 97846; (541) 426-5546, (541) 426-4978; www.fs.usda.gov/wallowa-whitman

Finding the trail: There are many ways to get to North Minam Meadows and access the Green Lake Trail. North Minam Meadows is often reached by backpackers and horse packers from the Upper Minam River Trail. The closest way to get to North Minam Meadows is via the Bowman Trail from Lostine River Road. To get to North Minam Meadows this way, first drive south from Lostine on Lostine River Road for 14.7 miles to the combined Francis Lake/Bowman Trailhead. Hike west on the Bowman Trail for 10 miles to the junction with the North Minam River Trail (1675) in North Minam Meadows. Turn right and go 0.3 mile northwest to the junction with the Green Lake Trail (5,430 ft.). This junction is 4.2 miles up the North Minam Trail from Minam River Trail.
GPS: Francis Lake/Bowman Trailhead: N45 17.606'/W117 23.675'; Green Lake Trail junction: N45 16.242'/W117 27.730'

The Hike

Green Lake Trail heads west off North Minam River Trail and crosses the North Minam River 100 yards from the junction. In the first 1.9 miles beyond the river, the trail makes seven switchbacks. In these switchbacks it crosses the same stream several times and gains 800 feet.

Above the switchbacks the trail flattens out and rounds a point. It soon begins to climb gently again. The trail crosses a creek (6,700 ft.) 0.7 mile past the last switchback. It comes to a small burn area 0.5 mile past the creek crossing. The trail makes another switchback 0.25 mile past the burn area. Green Lake is 300 yards past this switchback. The elevation of Green Lake is 6,999 feet.

There is a campsite on a small rise at the north end of the lake. The trail goes around the east side of the lake to a meadow on the south end. There is another campsite 100 yards south of the lake at the edge of this lush green meadow.

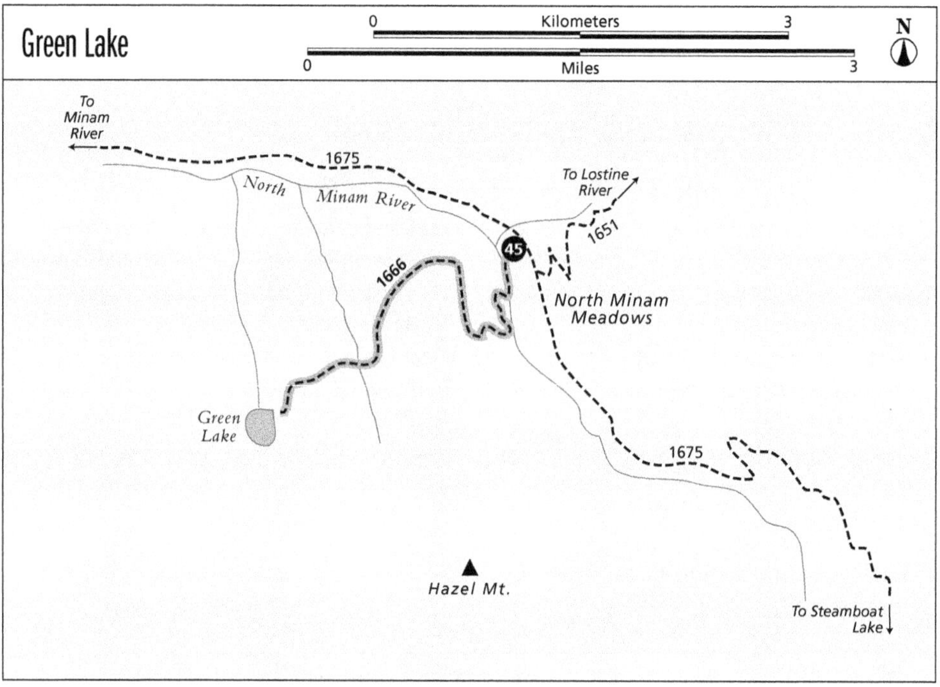

There are brook trout for the taking in Green Lake. The comparatively low elevation makes for denser forest than is found at most of the lakes in the Wallowas. As usual, watch for animals; the rockslide at the head of the lake has some pikas in it. In the summer these little "rock rabbits" will be drying hay on top of the boulders and making high-pitched calls to announce your presence. These little animals do not hibernate and need the hay to survive the long harsh winter. Once when we hiked this trail, a yearling bear ran across the trail in front of us, then quickly scrambled up the nearest tree when he became aware we were there. We also saw elk along this trail.

The return trip is made by the same trail.

Miles and Directions

0.0 Take the Green Lake Trail (1666) from North Minam Meadows and the junction with North Minam River Trail (1675).

3.2 Enter the burned area.

4.0 The trail ends at the south end of Green Lake. (GPS: N45 15.315'/W117 29.422')

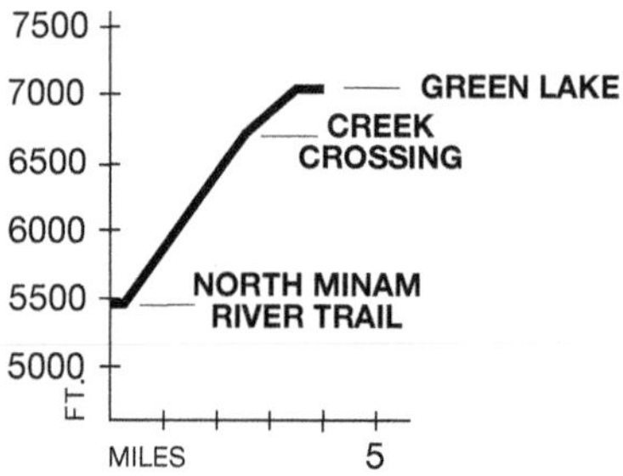

46 Long Lake

A short hike leads from the North Minam River Trail near Swamp Lake, through beautiful subalpine country, to Long Lake. (Trail 1669)

Distance: 1.3 miles one way
Hiking time: 1–1.5 hours
Difficulty: Strenuous but short, with route finding required
Trail maintenance: Seldom to none
Best season: July through Sept
Traffic and other trail users: Light foot traffic
Canine compatibility: Dogs permitted without leashes, but must be kept away from the stock of other parties
Fees and permits: Northwest Forest Pass and Eagle Cap Wilderness Permit
Maximum elevation: 7,840 feet
Map: USGS Steamboat Lake OR
Trail contact: USDA Forest Service Wallowa Mountains Office, 201 E 2nd St./ PO Box 905, Joseph, OR 97846; (541) 426-5546, (541) 426-4978; www.fs.usda.gov/wallowa-whitman

Finding the trail: From Lostine drive south on Lostine River Road for 18 miles to its end at Two Pan Trailhead. Hike south from the trailhead on the West Fork Lostine River Trail (1670) for 2.8 miles to the junction with Copper Creek Trail (1656). Turn right (west) on the Copper Creek Trail and go 5 miles to the junction with the North Minam River Trail (1675) and Granite Creek Trail (1676). Turn right (north) on the North Minam River Trail and descend 1.5 miles, passing Swamp Lake, to the junction with the Long Lake Trail (7,840 ft.).
GPS: Two Pan Trailhead: N45 15.001'/W117 22.580'; Long Lake junction: N45 13.420'/W117 25.512'

The Hike

Long Lake Trail heads west from its junction with North Minam Trail. At first it drops through small, green meadows and smooth, glacier-carved, light gray granite outcroppings. The trail crosses a couple of streams, then drops to the bottom of a pretty little glacial cirque with a stream flowing through it. The trail is very badly eroded where it drops steeply into the cirque. There are two possible paths just before the bottom: One crosses the steam and the other doesn't. From above, the trail can be seen in the grassy area in the bottom of the cirque. The elevation at the bottom of the cirque is 7,410 feet.

The trail crosses the stream at the north end of the cirque. It stays on the left side of the stream for about 0.3 mile. It then crosses the stream and heads north-northwest to Long Lake (7,117 ft.).

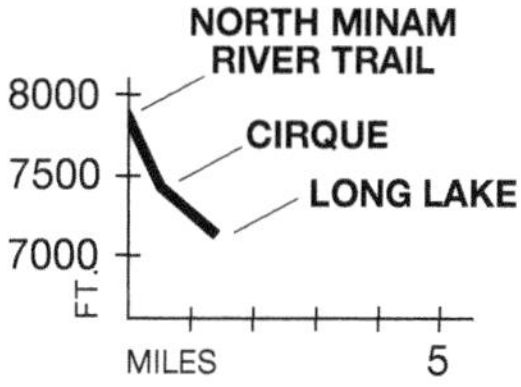

The part of the trail below the cirque is braided and not well maintained. It is difficult to tell which

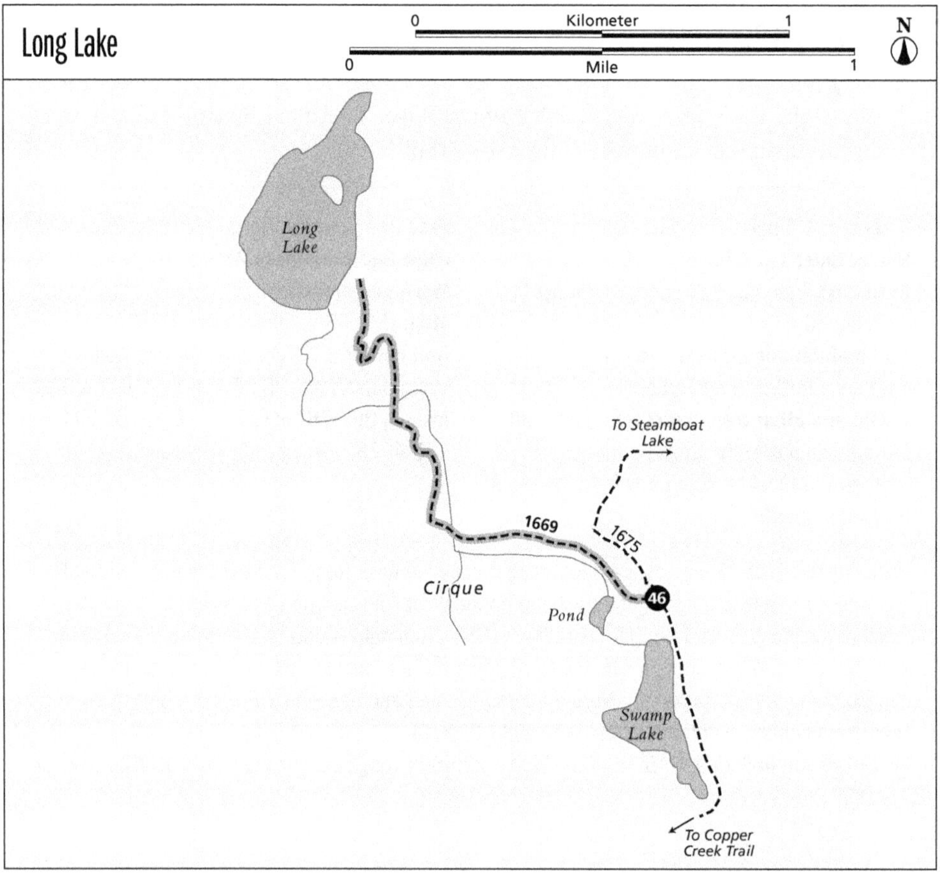

path is the right one. Remember that the stream that flows out of the cirque flows into Long Lake: You can follow it if need be.

This is a steep trail and requires some route finding. The distance to Long Lake is only a little over 1 mile, but it may seem much farther. There are campsites at the south end of Long Lake, and the fishing can be quite good. The return trip is made by the same trail.

Miles and Directions

0.0 Take the Long Lake Trail (1669) from the junction with North Minam River Trail (1675).

0.5 Reach the bottom of the cirque.

1.3 Arrive at Long Lake. (GPS: N45 13.945'/W117 26.255')

47 Granite Creek

This steep connecting trail leads south from the junction of Copper Creek and North Minam River Trails, along a windswept open ridge, then descends into the spectacular Minam River Canyon to a junction with the Upper Minam River Trail. (Trail 1676)

Distance: 5 miles one way
Hiking time: 2–3 hours
Difficulty: Strenuous
Trail maintenance: Infrequent
Best season: Mid-July through Sept
Traffic and other trail users: Light foot and horse traffic
Canine compatibility: Dogs permitted without leashes, but must be kept away from the stock of other parties
Fees and permits: Northwest Forest Pass and Eagle Cap Wilderness Permit
Maximum elevation: 8,420 feet
Map: USGS Steamboat Lake OR
Trail contact: USDA Forest Service Wallowa Mountains Office, 201 E 2nd St./PO Box 905, Joseph, OR 97846; (541) 426-5546, (541) 426-4978; www.fs.usda.gov/wallowa-whitman

Finding the trail: Drive south from Lostine on Lostine River Road for 18 miles to its end at Two Pan Trailhead. Hike south from the trailhead on the West Fork Lostine River Trail (1670) for 2.8 miles to the junction with Copper Creek Trail (1656). Turn right (west) on the Copper Creek Trail and go 5 miles to the junction with the North Minam River Trail (1675) and Granite Creek Trail. This junction (8,420 ft.) is on a plateau above and south of Swamp Lake.
GPS: Two Pan Trailhead: N45 15.001'/W117 22.580'; junction North Minam River, Copper Creek, and Granite Creek Trails: N45 12.730'/W117 25.630'

The Hike

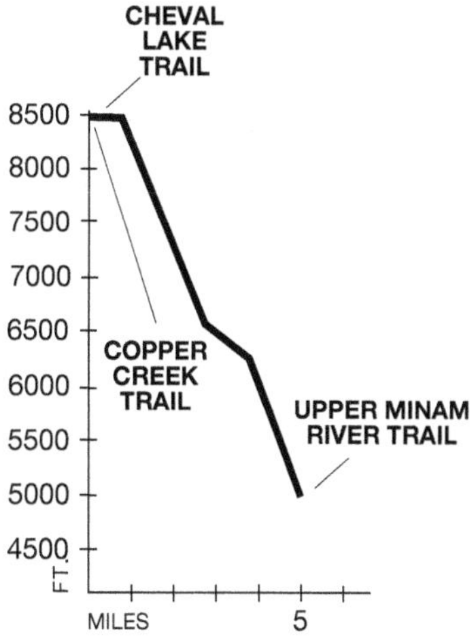

The area around the junction where Granite Creek Trail begins is open timberline country. There are granite boulders and a few groves of small alpine trees. From the junction, Granite Creek Trail heads south 0.3 mile to the unmarked junction with Cheval Lake Trail (8,420 ft.). Cheval Lake Trail turns to the right (west). After passing Cheval Lake Trail, Granite Creek Trail crosses several streambeds that were dry in September, when we walked this trail. About 250 yards past the Cheval Lake Trail junction the trail starts to drop toward the Minam River. The trail makes a switchback to the left. It then winds its way down through granite outcroppings and meadows. The area from here to the Minam River was burned

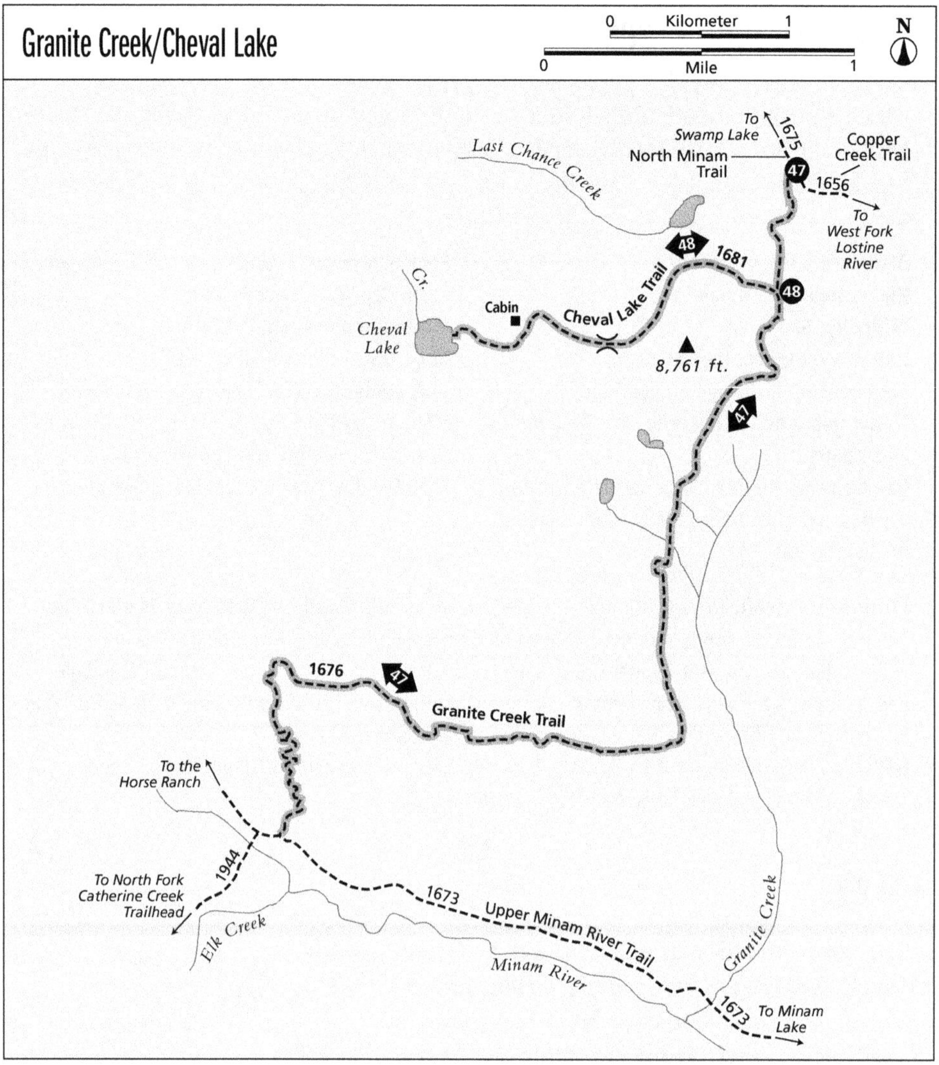

in the 2019 Granite Gulch Fire. There are some streambeds in the meadows. These were all dry by September.

After going 0.6 mile from Cheval Lake Trail junction, the trail begins to traverse the west side of Granite Creek Canyon, also known as Granite Gulch. The elevation at the beginning of the traverse is about 8,000 feet. After traversing for 0.3 mile, the trail starts to switchback again. It makes eight switchbacks in the next 0.25 mile, to where there are a couple of dry (again, in September) stream crossings. The trail winds down through open woods for 325 yards. It then makes four more switchbacks and comes to a small spring on the left side of the trail.

After going 0.3 mile past the spring, the trail begins another series of switchbacks. It makes six switchbacks in the next 0.25 mile. This area is open forest with large open areas. The first ponderosa pines on this trail start to show up at the bottom of the last switchbacks. As usual, the upper limit for ponderosa pine is about 6,500 feet.

The trail makes a long traverse after the last switchback. After traversing for 0.9 mile, there is a small stream crossing. The traverse ends with a switchback to the left 200 yards past the stream crossing. The elevation here is about 6,200 feet.

After the traverse, the trail makes twenty-three switchbacks in the 1.2 miles to the junction with Upper Minam River Trail (1673; 4,920 ft.). It also drops 1,280 feet in this distance, at a grade of about 10 percent.

This trail is easy to follow most of the way. The dry streams would likely have water in them earlier in the summer. Heading north on the route, from the Upper Minam River Trail to the junction with the Copper Creek Trail, is a steep climb.

Miles and Directions

0.0 Take the Granite Creek Trail (1676) from the junction with Copper Creek (1656) and North Minam River (1675) Trails.

0.3 Pass the junction with Cheval Lake Trail (1681). (GPS: N45 12.385'/W117 25.660')

2.9 Begin a long traverse.

3.8 End the long traverse.

5.0 Arrive at the junction with Upper Minam River Trail (1673). (GPS: N45 10.817'/W117 27.670')

48 Cheval Lake

Hike steeply downhill, from Granite Creek Trail, on a high, windswept plateau to Cheval Lake, tucked in a timbered glacial cirque. The route passes the remains of a tiny miners cabin as you descend. (Trail 1681)

See map page 176.
Distance: 1.7 miles one way from Granite Creek Trail
Hiking time: 1–1.5 hours from Granite Creek Trail
Difficulty: Strenuous
Trail maintenance: Seldom to none. This trail is no longer maintained by the forest service.
Best season: Mid-July through Sept
Traffic and other trail users: Very light foot and horse traffic
Canine compatibility: Dogs permitted without leashes, but must be kept away from the stock of other parties
Fees and permits: Northwest Forest Pass and Eagle Cap Wilderness Permit
Maximum elevation: 8,730 feet
Maps: Older Eagle Cap Wilderness maps. USGS Steamboat Lake OR covers the area, but the trail is not shown on this map.
Trail contact: USDA Forest Service Wallowa Mountains Office, 201 E 2nd St./PO Box 905, Joseph, OR 97846; (541) 426-5546, (541) 426-4978; www.fs.usda.gov/wallowa-whitman

Finding the trail: Drive south from Lostine on Lostine River Road for 18 miles to its end at Two Pan Trailhead. Hike south from the trailhead on the West Fork Lostine River Trail (1670) for 2.8 miles to the junction with Copper Creek Trail (1656). Turn right (west) on the Copper Creek Trail and go 5 miles to the junction with the North Minam River Trail (1675) and Granite Creek Trail (1676). Turn left (south) and follow Granite Creek Trail for 0.3 mile to the unmarked junction with the Cheval Lake Trail (8,420 ft.).
GPS: Two Pan Trailhead: N45 15.001'/W117 22.580'; Cheval Lake junction: N45 12.385'/W117 25.660'

The Hike

From the junction with the Granite Creek Trail, Cheval Lake Trail heads west. It drops 230 feet in the first 0.25 mile, to a meadow. Cross two streams in the meadow. There is a pond on the left at the second stream crossing. After crossing the meadow the trail climbs to the top of a spur ridge (8,320 ft.).

The trail goes southwest up the spur ridge for 0.3 mile to the top of the main ridge (8,590 ft.). This ridge divides the Last Chance Creek and Minam River drainages. Here the trail turns right and climbs for 300 yards to a pass (8,730 ft.). It makes five switchbacks before reaching the pass. From here Cheval Lake can be seen far below to the west. The peak a few yards north of this pass is a good viewpoint. From the peak, Last Chance Creek Canyon is below and to the north. You can also see the lake at the head of Last Chance Creek. This is a good place to see elk.

Cheval Lake and Ahalt cabin. LOWELL EUHUS PHOTO

The trail descends to the northwest for 0.25 mile. It then drops off to the left. After going 125 yards more, there is a cabin on the right side of the trail. This cabin was built by a miner and part-time hermit named Harold Ahalt. It is very small, only 6 by 8 feet. The cabin is in fairly good condition and has a stove inside. The elevation at the cabin is 8,360 feet. There is a mine above and east of the cabin. Please do not disturb the cabin.

Below the cabin the trail makes three switchbacks. It then drops into a small meadow about 50 yards wide. The trail is difficult to see in the meadow. Bear slightly to the left and look for blazes on the trees on the far side. Cross the meadow and streambed, which may be dry in early fall, and then begin to drop steeply down. Watch for cairns. After dropping 300 yards, the trail climbs slightly 15 feet to the right. It then drops steeply again, making four switchbacks, before reaching Cheval Lake (7,801 ft.).

There is a nice campsite on the east side of the lake. Cheval Lake is 1.7 miles from Granite Creek Trail and is a very isolated place to camp. It is possible to camp here for some time without seeing another party.

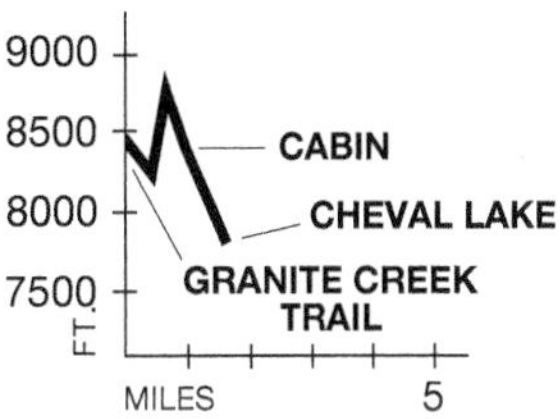

The trail is difficult to see just above the lake. There are several possible routes to take in the last 150 vertical feet. Much of the trail is steep and rocky. Some route-finding skills are required to get to Cheval Lake. Return by using the same trail.

Miles and Directions

0.0 Take the Cheval Lake Trail (1681) from the unmarked trail junction with Granite Creek Trail (1676).

0.3 Pass the meadow.

0.6 Reach the top of the main ridge.

0.7 Go over the pass.

1.0 Pass the Ahalt cabin.

1.7 Arrive at Cheval Lake. (GPS: N45 12.207'/W117 26.975')

49 Rock Springs

Hike from the Rock Springs Trailhead on the Minam Rim Road into the Little Minam River Canyon and a junction with the Little Minam River Trail. This trail reaches the Little Minam River near its confluence with the Minam River. (Trail 1928)

Distance: 3.5 miles one way
Hiking time: 1.5–3 hours
Difficulty: Moderate to strenuous
Trail maintenance: Infrequent
Best season: June through Oct
Traffic and other trail users: Light foot and horse traffic
Canine compatibility: Dogs permitted without leashes, but must be kept away from the stock of other parties
Fees and permits: Eagle Cap Wilderness Permit
Maximum elevation: 5,850 feet
Map: USGS Mount Moriah OR
Trail contact: USDA Forest Service Wallowa Mountains Office, 201 E 2nd St./PO Box 905, Joseph, OR 97846; (541) 426-5546, (541) 426-4978; www.fs.usda.gov/wallowa-whitman

Finding the trailhead: Rock Springs Trailhead can be reached from OR 82 by turning south on Hindman Road, which is 9.4 miles west of the town of Minam. Head south on Hindman Road for 7.2 miles. At this point Hindman Road becomes Minam Rim Road (FR 62). Go 11 miles more on FR 62 to Rock Springs Trailhead (5,850 ft.).
GPS: N45 24.264'/W117 42.410'

The Hike

From the parking area at Rock Springs, walk back north for 80 yards on FR 62 to where the trail heads east from the road. From this point the trail heads down into the canyon, heading east past the wilderness boundary signs. There were two signs when I hiked this trail in June 2012. The first sign was 60 yards down, and the second was in an open area (5,720 ft.) with a view of the Minam and Little Minam River Canyons. The rugged, dark brown ridge visible between the Minam and Little Minam Canyons is Backbone Ridge. From here the trail goes down a ridge another 125 yards, then drops off to the right.

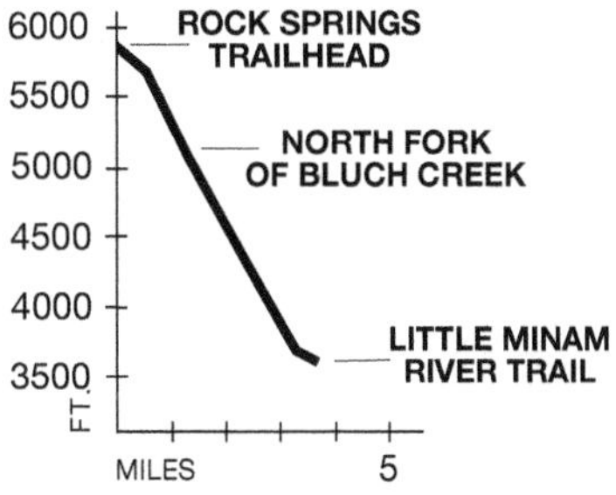

The trail crosses the North Fork of Bluch Creek (5,100 ft.) 1.1 miles from the trailhead. A switchback is 175 yards past the creek crossing. The trail crosses the North Fork of Bluch Creek again in another 120 yards.

At 1.9 miles the trail crosses a ridgeline (4,550 ft.). It crosses another stream 350 yards after the ridgeline. The trail makes a couple of switchbacks

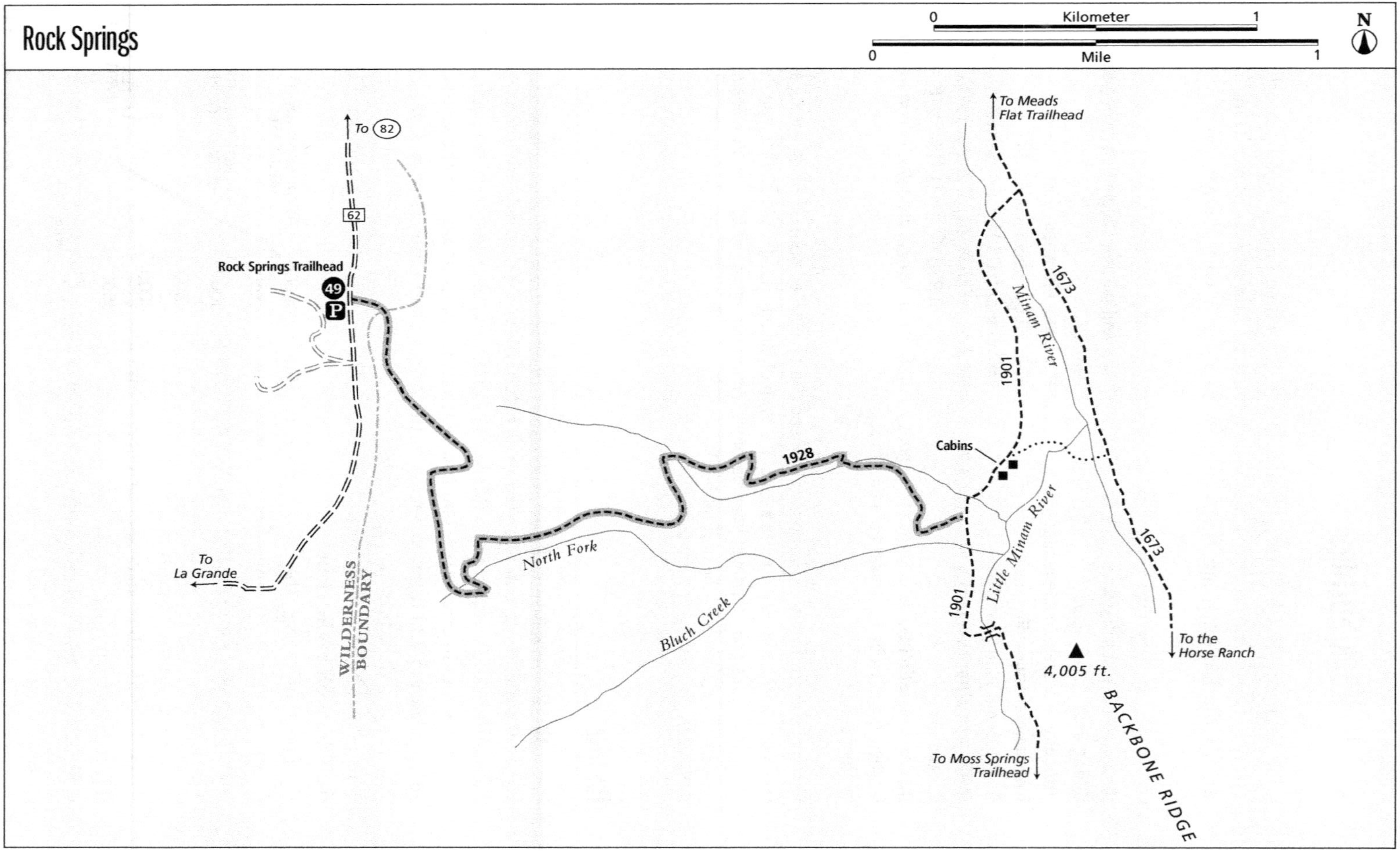

Rock Springs
0
Kilometer
1
0
Mile
1
N
To 82
62
Rock Springs Trailhead
49
P
To
La Grande
WILDERNESS
BOUNDARY
North Fork
Bluch Creek
1928
Cabins
1901
1901
Minam River
Little Minam River
1673
1673
To Meads
Flat Trailhead
To the
Horse Ranch
4,005 ft.
BACKBONE RIDGE
To Moss Springs
Trailhead

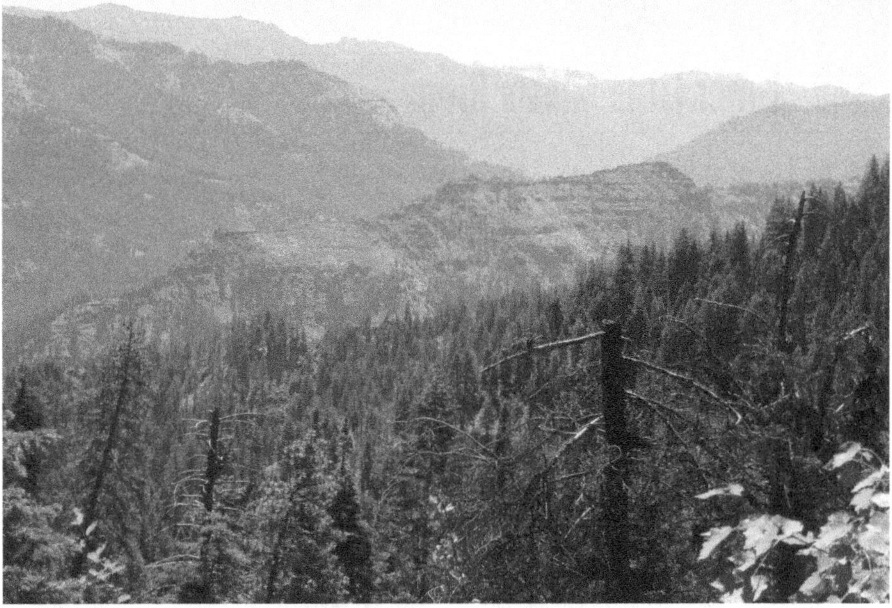

Minam Canyon from the Rock Springs Trail.

0.75 mile beyond the ridgeline. The trail crosses the same stream again 120 yards past the switchbacks. One-quarter mile past the last creek crossing, the trail makes another switchback, this one very close to, but not crossing, Bluch Creek (3,680 ft.). The junction with Little Minam River Trail (1901; 3,580 ft.) is 175 yards farther.

Trail 1928 is easy to follow; however, it does lose quite a bit of elevation. Watch for mule deer, elk, and bear along this trail. The fishing is usually pretty good in the Little Minam River.

Miles and Directions

0.0 Begin at Rock Springs Trailhead.

1.1 Cross North Fork Bluch Creek.

1.9 Cross the ridgeline.

3.5 Arrive at the trail junction with the Lower Little Minam River Trail (1901). (GPS: N45 23.870'/W117 40.607')

50 Lower Little Minam River

This backpack along the Little Minam River leads from the Moss Springs/Horse Ranch Trail to the confluence of the Little Minam and Minam Rivers and to Lower Minam River Trail. (Trail 1901)

Distance: 6.3 miles one way
Hiking time: 2–3 hours
Difficulty: Easy grade, but trail may be badly overgrown with brush in places.
Trail maintenance: Seldom. This trail recently received considerable work by the Wallowa Mountains Hells Canyon Trail Association. To join this group see appendix A.
Best season: May through Oct, although access to the trail from the Moss Springs and Rock Springs Trailheads may be blocked by snow until mid-June. For early-season trips you may have to hike up the Minam River or fly into the Horse Ranch. The best time for the flowers is June.
Traffic and other trail users: Light foot and horse traffic except during fall hunting seasons, when it may be heavier
Canine compatibility: Dogs permitted without leashes, but must be kept away from the stock of other parties
Fees and permits: Northwest Forest Pass and Eagle Cap Wilderness Permit
Maximum elevation: 4,330 feet
Maps: USGS Mount Fanny OR and Mount Moriah OR; Geo Graphics Wallowa Mountains Eagle Cap Wilderness
Trail contact: USDA Forest Service Wallowa Mountains Office, 201 E 2nd St./ PO Box 905, Joseph, OR 97846; (541) 426-5546, (541) 426-4978; www.fs.usda.gov/wallowa-whitman

To fly in, call Spence Air Service at (541) 426-3288 in Enterprise, Oregon.

Finding the trail: The easiest way, on foot, to reach the junction where the Lower Little Minam River Trail begins is from Moss Springs Trailhead. To get to Moss Springs Trailhead drive 8 miles east from Cove on Mill Creek Road (FR 6220). From the trailhead hike northeast on the Moss Springs/Horse Ranch Trail (1908) for 6.5 miles to the junction with the Lower Little Minam River Trail. Little Minam River Trail leaves Moss Springs/Horse Ranch Trail (1908) 1 mile south of (before reaching) the Horse Ranch (4,330 ft.). It is also fairly easy to reach the lower (north) end of the Lower Little Minam River Trail from the Rock Springs Trailhead on FR 62. Flying into the Horse Ranch is also an option and not as expensive as you might think.
GPS: Moss Springs Trailhead: N45 16.468'/W117 40.689'; Lower Little Minam River junction: N45 20.237'/W117 37.818'

The Hike

From the junction with Moss Springs/Horse Ranch Trail, the Lower Little Minam River Trail traverses to the northwest and drops slightly. When we walked this section in early summer, there was a bear ripping apart a log below the trail. The bear was looking for grubs in the rotten wood and left at our approach. After about 1 mile of

Bridge over the Little Minam River.

traversing along the west side of Backbone Ridge, the trail drops into Little Minam Meadows.

Little Minam Meadows is a semi-open area 1 mile long, at 3,850 feet. There are many campsites and plenty of firewood in the meadows. There are also plenty of mule deer in the area. The trail stays along the right side of the more open meadow area.

After passing Little Minam Meadows, the trail stays east of the Little Minam River along the bottom of Backbone Ridge. There is very little water along this section of trail. You can drop down to the Little Minam River, but this can be quite a climb in places.

The trail crosses the Little Minam River on a bridge 3 miles below Little Minam Meadows (3,550 ft.). The route crosses Bluch Creek 0.25 mile past the bridge. The junction with Rock Springs Trail (1928) is 175 yards past Bluch Creek (3,580 ft.). Trail 1928 comes down from Rock Springs Trailhead on the Minam Rim Road, FR 62.

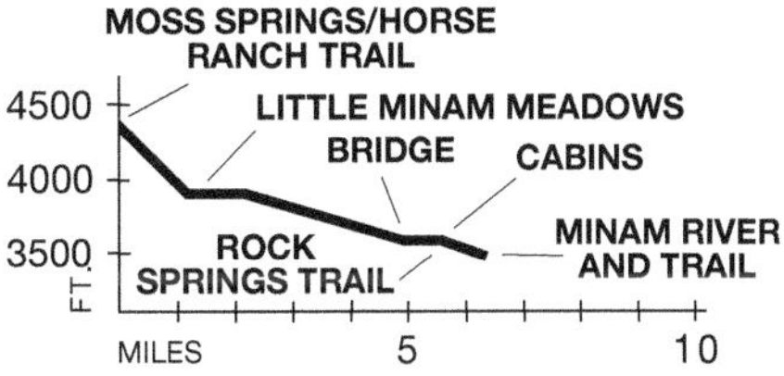

The trail enters a meadow 125 yards past the junction. Here some old cabins are a short distance to the right of the trail. The remains of some old farm machinery

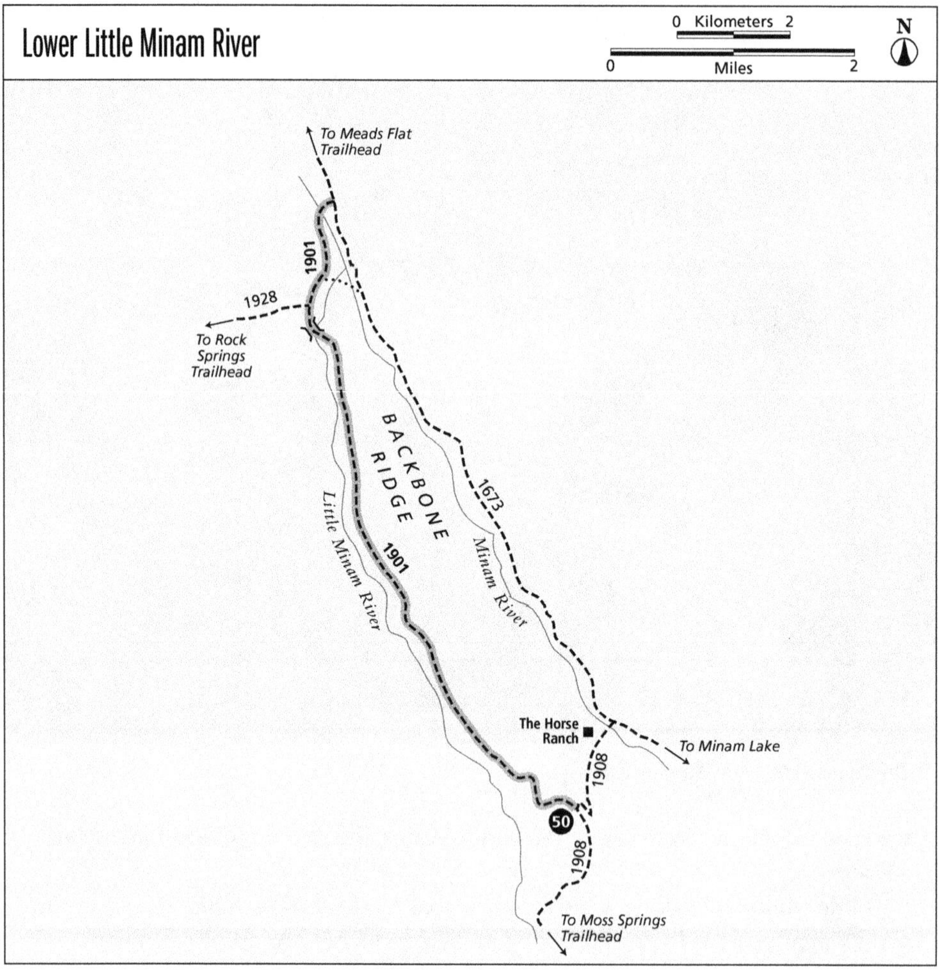

and a colony of red diggers (ground squirrels) are in the meadow. The trail forks 100 yards past the cabins. Take the left (north) fork. The right fork is a shortcut for parties that are going up the Minam River. An old wood fence is 0.3 mile past the cabins.

The trail crosses the Minam River 0.4 mile past the fence. Crossing the Minam River is very dangerous during high water. People have drowned, even on horseback. It is generally better not to try to cross the Minam River here on foot except during low water. The area between the cabins and the river crossing is a great place to camp, watch the wildlife, look at the flowers, fish in the Minam and Little Minam Rivers, and relax.

After crossing the river, the trail goes 300 yards through an open area to the junction with Lower Minam River Trail (1673; 3,430 ft.). The flowers in this area are excellent in June and July, but the rivers are high and dangerous. There is an excellent campsite on the east side of the Minam River between the river and Lower Minam River Trail.

A return trip can be made to the Horse Ranch via Lower Minam River Trail during times of low water, when crossing the Minam River is safe. From the Horse Ranch it is only 1 mile back to the start of the Lower Little Minam River Trail via Moss Springs/Horse Ranch Trail.

Miles and Directions

0.0 The trail begins at the junction with Moss Springs/Horse Ranch Trail (1908).

1.0 Reach Little Minam Meadows.

5.3 Pass the junction with Rock Springs Trail (1928). (GPS: N45 23.870'/W117 40.607')

6.3 Cross the Minam River and arrive at the junction with Lower Minam River Trail (1673).

51 Upper Little Minam River

This day hike or backpack in the Upper Little Minam River Canyon goes from Moss Springs Trailhead to the junction with Jim White Ridge, Cartwheel Ridge, and Lackeys Hole Trails. (Trail 1942)

Distance: 7.8 miles one way
Hiking time: 3–4 hours
Difficulty: Moderate
Trail maintenance: Infrequent
Best season: Mid-June through Oct
Traffic and other trail users: Moderate foot and horse traffic. Traffic is heaviest during Oct and Nov hunting seasons.
Canine compatibility: Dogs permitted without leashes, but must be kept away from the stock of other parties
Fees and permits: Northwest Forest Pass and Eagle Cap Wilderness Permit
Maximum elevation: 7,400 feet
Maps: USGS Mount Fanny OR, Jim White Ridge OR, and China Cap OR; Geo Graphics Wallowa Mountains Eagle Cap Wilderness
Trail contact: USDA Forest Service Wallowa Mountains Office, 201 E 2nd St./PO Box 905, Joseph, OR 97846; (541) 426-5546, (541) 426-4978; www.fs.usda.gov/wallowa-whitman

Finding the trailhead: To reach Moss Springs Trailhead, take Mill Creek Road east from the town of Cove. Go 8 miles on Mill Creek Road (FR 6220) to Moss Springs Trailhead.
GPS: N45 16.468'/W117 40.689'

The Hike

Upper Little Minam River Trail 1942 begins at Moss Springs Trailhead (5,800 ft.). At the start, the Moss Springs/Horse Ranch Trail and Upper Little Minam River Trail are the same trail for a short distance. The trails fork 100 yards from the trailhead. At the fork, Upper Little Minam River Trail is to the right (southeast). The wide trail descends into the Little Minam River Canyon through a forest of lodgepole pine, fir, and tamarack (western larch).

Slightly more than 0.5 mile down, the trail makes a switchback to the left (5,600 ft.). The trail makes two more switchbacks in the next 0.75 mile to where it reaches the river bottom (5,200 ft.). Bears are common along this trail, especially in the first 2 miles.

A few yards after reaching the river bottom, the trail crosses Fireline Creek, then heads up the river to the southeast 0.75 mile more to the unmarked junction with Art Garrett Trail (1913; 5,250 ft.). Art Garrett Trail heads to the right (south). Keep on the main Little Minam River Trail, which heads east.

Beyond the junction the trail drops a few feet and crosses Dobbin Creek. A few yards past the creek crossing is the junction with Crib Point Trail (1909), which heads to the right (southeast). Just past the junction with Crib Point Trail, the Upper Little Minam Trail crosses the Little Minam River (5,220 ft.). A few yards upstream is a

Crossing the Little Minam River.

log on which to cross. The distance to the river crossing is 2.1 miles from the Moss Springs Trailhead.

After crossing the Little Minam River, the trail heads east up the Little Minam Canyon. It gradually gets farther away from the river as it climbs. A path goes down

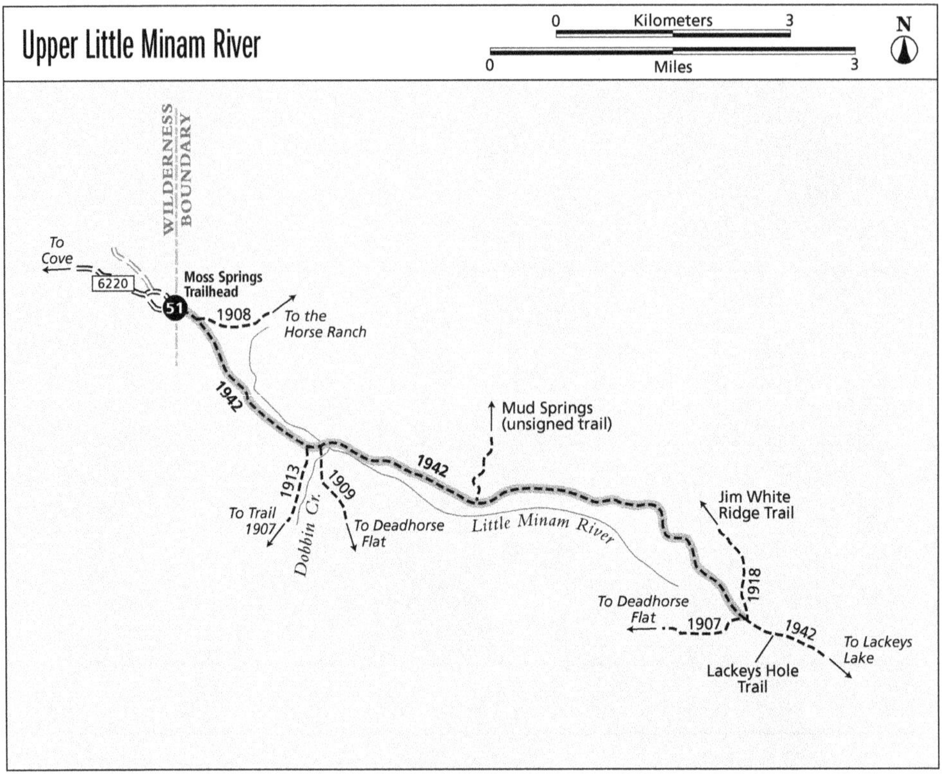

to the right to a campsite 0.6 mile above the crossing. There is another campsite 0.3 mile farther along, also below the trail to the right. Between the campsites there are a couple of stream crossings. The unmarked Mud Springs Trail heads up hill to the left (north) 0.4 mile past the second campsite. There is another path to the left 300 yards before Mud Springs Trail, but this path fades out quickly. It may be just a game trail. The Mud Springs Trail junction (5,600 ft.) is 1.3 miles from the Little Minam River crossing and 3.4 miles from Moss Springs Trailhead.

The trail enters a burn area 1.1 miles past Mud Springs Trail junction. The fire in this area, like most forest fires, did not burn all the timber. It left some patches of green trees. Watch for goldenrod in the burned area. After entering the burn area, the trail climbs, with some switchbacks, through fairly open country. There are many small streambeds in this area; however, most of them are dry in late summer. This semi-open area is excellent range for mule deer and elk.

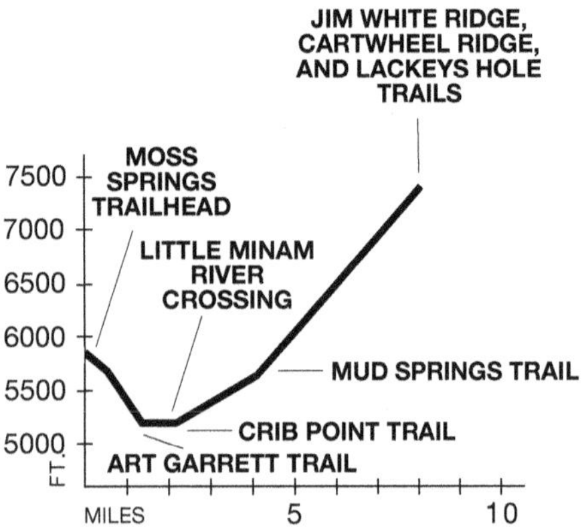

Three and eight-tenths miles after passing Mud Springs Trail, in a saddle on the ridge dividing the Minam River and Little Minam River drainages, is the junction with Jim White Ridge, Lackeys Hole, and Cartwheel Ridge Trails (7,400 ft.). None of these trails is marked; however, there is a sign pointing back to the Little Minam River and ahead to Rock Creek on Lackeys Hole Trail. This junction is 7.8 miles from Moss Springs Trailhead.

From the saddle and junction, a loop can be made by turning right (southwest) and following Cartwheel Ridge Trail to Deadhorse Flat, then taking Crib Point Trail down to Little Minam River Trail and returning to Moss Springs on Little Minam River Trail. Other, longer loops are possible. Check your map for the possibilities.

Miles and Directions

0.0 Begin at Moss Springs Trailhead.

2.0 Pass the junction with Art Garrett Trail (1913). (GPS: N45 15.478'/W117 39.250')

2.1 Cross Little Minam River.

3.4 Pass the junction with Mud Springs Trail (unmarked).

7.8 Reach the junction with Jim White Ridge (1918), Lackeys Hole (1942), and Cartwheel Ridge (1907) Trails. (GPS: N45 14.340'/W117 34.760')

52 Moss Springs/Horse Ranch

This is a day hike from Moss Springs Trailhead to the Horse Ranch, or a starter for an extended backpack in the western Wallowa Mountains. This trail accesses Jim White Ridge, Lower Little Minam River, as well as Upper and Lower Minam River Trails. It is also the main trail access to Minam Lodge, a privately owned lodge with an airstrip. Reservations are mandatory if you wish to stay at Minam Lodge. (Trail 1908)

Distance: 7.5 miles one way
Hiking time: 2.5–4 hours
Difficulty: Easy to moderate
Trail maintenance: Yearly
Best season: June through Oct
Traffic and other trail users: Moderate to heavy foot traffic; moderate to heavy horse traffic
Canine compatibility: Dogs permitted without leashes, but must be kept away from the stock of other parties
Fees and permits: Northwest Forest Pass and Eagle Cap Wilderness Permit
Maximum elevation: 5,840 feet
Map: USGS Mount Fanny OR
Trail contact: USDA Forest Service Wallowa Mountains Office, 201 E 2nd St./ PO Box 905, Joseph, OR 97846; (541) 426-5546, (541) 426-4978; www.fs.usda.gov/wallowa-whitman

Finding the trailhead: Moss Springs/Horse Ranch Trail begins at Moss Springs Trailhead. To reach Moss Springs Trailhead, take Mill Creek Road east from the town of Cove. Go 8 miles on Mill Creek Road (FR 6220) to Moss Springs Trailhead.
GPS: N45 16.468'/W117 40.689'

The Hike

From Moss Springs Trailhead (5,840 ft.), Moss Springs/Horse Ranch Trail heads east. It forks 100 yards from the trailhead at the Eagle Cap Wilderness boundary. The right fork is Upper Little Minam River Trail (1942). Take the left fork and descend to the east on mostly open, grass-covered slopes into the Little Minam Canyon. Watch for bears in this area, especially in late August and September, when they may be chowing down on the abundant huckleberries.

At 1.5 miles the trail crosses a bridge over Horseshoe Creek (5,130 ft.). Just past the bridge, the rushing Little Minam River is close to the right (east) side of the trail. One mile after crossing the bridge, there is a campsite on the right between the trail and the river (4,950 ft.). Another campsite (4,870 ft.), with a path leading down to it, is 0.5 mile from the first campsite. This campsite is also on the right side of the trail.

Travel 1.4 more miles to the ford across the Little Minam River. Between the last campsite and the ford there are several small stream crossings. There are also some groves of small yew trees, which are not common in eastern Oregon. The trail forks just before the ford. Take the right (east) fork. There is a campsite here, next to the

The Horse Ranch.

river (4,560 ft.). This ford, through the icy cold waters of the Little Minam River, can be difficult in times of heavy runoff, but it is usually not a problem.

After crossing the river the trail heads east for 100 yards to the junction with Jim White Ridge Trail (1918). Moss Springs/Horse Ranch Trail turns left (north) at the junction. For the next 2.1 miles, between the Jim White Ridge Trail junction and the Lower Little Minam River Trail (1901) junction, the trail stays nearly level, except for the last 0.25 mile, where it descends slightly. See Lower Little Minam River (hike 50). The Lower Little Minam River Trail junction (4,330 ft.) is in the saddle where Jim White Ridge and Backbone Ridge merge. Moss Springs/Horse Ranch Trail bears right (north) at the junction.

Beyond the Lower Little Minam Trail junction the trail makes a few switchbacks and drops through thick timber for 1 mile to the Horse Ranch (3,600 ft.). The trail crosses the airstrip and passes the ranch house. A short distance before crossing the airstrip, a trail to the left (northwest) leads to Minam Lodge. Past the buildings the trail goes through a gate and over a small rise. It then crosses the Minam River on a bridge. Just after crossing the river is the junction with Minam River Trail (1673). See Lower Minam River (hike 42) and Upper Minam River (hike 43) also.

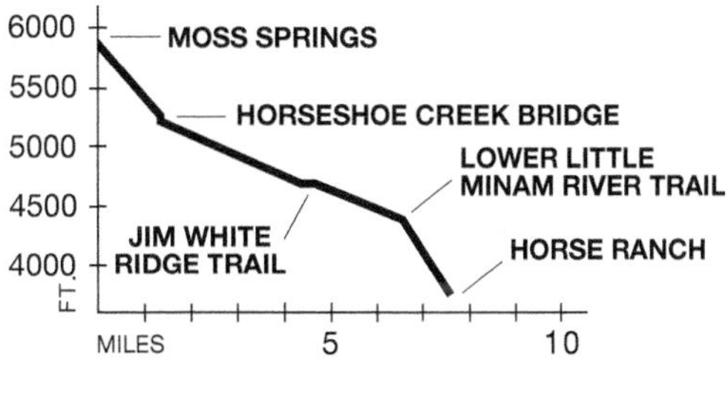

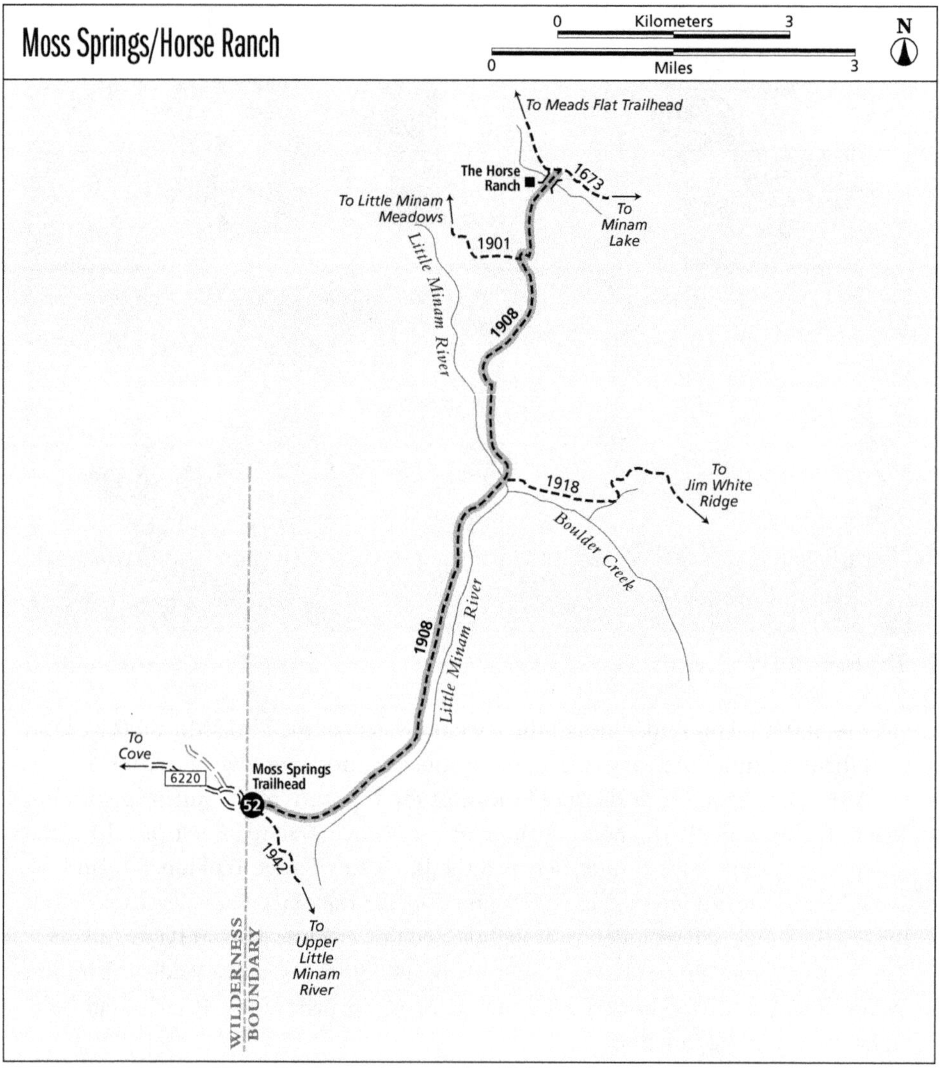

There are plenty of campsites along the Minam River near the Horse Ranch. However, there are a few sections of private land that must be respected. Please don't camp on or near the airstrip. It is best to camp on the east side of the Minam River above the bridge. This area is a great place for a base camp when exploring the many trails in the western Wallowa Mountains. Fishing is good in both the Minam and Little Minam Rivers.

Return via the same trail, or use Upper or Lower Minam River Trails to make an extended backpack. It may also be possible to fly in and out of the Horse Ranch. Call Spence Air Service at (541) 426-3288 in Enterprise.

Miles and Directions

0.0 Begin at Moss Springs Trailhead.

1.5 Cross the bridge over Horseshoe Creek.

4.4 Cross the Little Minam River and pass the junction with Jim White Ridge Trail (1918). (GPS: N45 18.719'/W117 37.873')

6.5 Pass the junction with Lower Little Minam River Trail (1901).

7.5 Arrive at the Horse Ranch and the trail junction with Minam River Trail (1673). (GPS: N45 20.834'/W117 37.510')

53 Mud Springs

The steep-in-places Mud Springs Trail connects the Upper Little Minam River Trail with the Jim White Ridge Trail, high atop Jim White Ridge. (Trail 1929)

Distance: 3.9 miles one way
Hiking time: 3-3.5 hours
Difficulty: Strenuous
Trail maintenance: Rare
Best season: June through Oct
Traffic and other trail users: Light foot and horse traffic
Canine compatibility: Dogs permitted without leashes, but must be kept away from the stock of other parties
Fees and permits: Northwest Forest Pass and Eagle Cap Wilderness Permit
Maximum elevation: 7,590 feet
Maps: USGS Jim White Ridge OR covers the area but does not show all of this trail; Green Trails #475sx: Wallowa Mountains Eagle Cap Wilderness shows the entire trail.
Trail contact: USDA Forest Service Wallowa Mountains Office, 201 E 2nd St./ PO Box 905, Joseph, OR 97846; (541) 426-5546, (541) 426-4978; www.fs.usda.gov/wallowa-whitman. Further information will probably be limited.

Finding the trail: The best way to reach the Mud Springs Trail is from the Moss Springs Trailhead. To reach Moss Springs Trailhead, take Mill Creek Road east from the town of Cove. Go 8 miles on Mill Creek Road (FR 6220) to Moss Springs Trailhead. Hike southeast from the trailhead (Moss Springs/Horse Ranch Trail and the Upper Little Minam Trail follow the same route for the first 100 yards) on the Upper Little Minam River Trail (1942) for 3.4 miles to the unsigned junction with the Mud Springs Trail. There is a large rock cairn at the junction.
GPS: Moss Springs Trailhead: N45 16.468' / W117 40.689'; Mud Springs Trail junction: N45 15.162'/ W117 37.732'

The Hike

Turn left off the Upper Little Minam River Trail at the unsigned junction (5,670 ft.) and start to climb north, making several switchbacks as you follow the remains of a long-abandoned roadbed. The route generally follows the roadbed for a bit over a mile. Leaving the roadbed the track steepens some, and in about 0.3 mile you reach a stream crossing (6,560 ft.). There is a good campsite next to the stream.

After crossing the stream the track continues north for another 0.3 mile. Then the route swings around to the right to head east. Where the route turns to the east was once the junction with the now-abandoned and nearly impossible to follow Ben Point Trail. Head easterly and reach a fork in the trail in about 0.25 mile. This fork is in a semi-open area at 6,780 feet. Take the right fork. The trail soon heads east, climbing gently through an open area. It goes through some timber for a few yards 0.4 mile past the fork. There are what appear to be a series of ditches on the hillside above the trail here.

Mount Fanny from the trail near Mud Springs.

At 0.25 mile past the timber, the trail becomes badly eroded for 0.1 mile. The trail goes up steeply in the eroded area, then flattens out and heads to the southeast. The old burn area of the Little Minam Fire can be seen several hundred yards below the trail, to the right. The trail traverses the hillside for 0.25 mile, then turns uphill again. Mud Springs is up the hill 125 yards. The spring (7,280 ft.) is to the right of the trail. There is a campsite in some trees a few yards up the trail from the spring. Mud Springs is slightly under 3.2 miles from the junction with the Upper Little Minam River Trail.

From the campsite the trail heads southeast for 120 yards in the open, then enters a dense stand of timber for 200 yards. Beyond the timber it traverses an open hillside for 0.7 mile to the junction with Jim White Ridge Trail (1918). This is an unmarked, triangle junction (7,590 ft.). See Jim White Ridge (hike 54). At the junction the Mud Springs Trail is more visible on the ground than is the Jim White Ridge Trail.

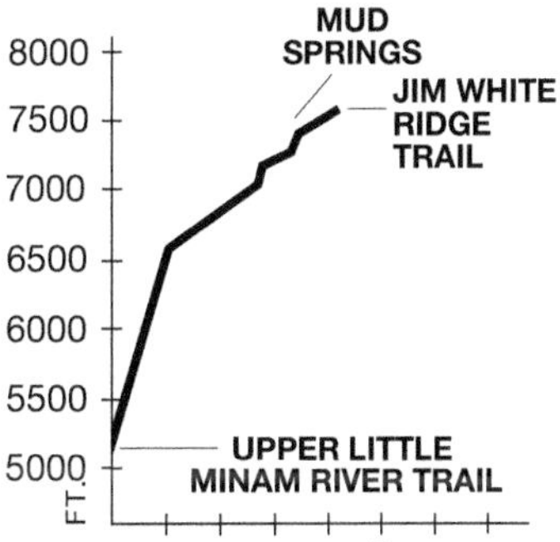

Return as you came, or make a loop by turning right at the junction on the Jim White Ridge Trail and following it to the Upper Little Minam River Trail. Turn right again on the Upper Little Minam River Trail and follow it northwest (downriver)

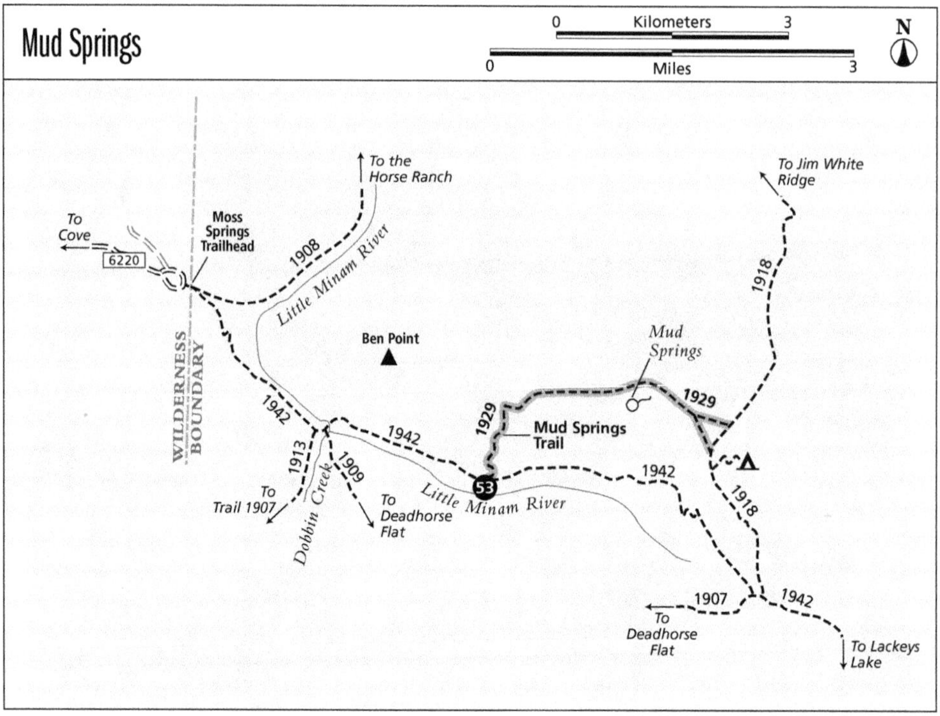

back to the junction with the Mud Springs Trail, completing the loop. From this junction follow the Upper Little Minam River Trail back to Moss Springs Trailhead.

Miles and Directions

0.0 Climb north from the junction with the Upper Little Minam River Trail (1942). (GPS: N45 15.162'/ W117 37.732')

3.2 Pass Mud Springs; continue southeast.

3.9 Reach the Jim White Ridge Trail (1918).

54 Jim White Ridge

This trail heads down Jim White Ridge from the Upper Little Minam River Trail to Moss Springs/Horse Ranch Trail. (Trail 1918)

Distance: 8.8 miles one way
Hiking time: 3.5–5 hours
Difficulty: Moderate to strenuous (heading down), with some route finding required
Trail maintenance: Rare
Best season: Mid-June through Oct
Other trail users: Light foot and horse traffic except during Oct and Nov hunting seasons, when it may be heavier.
Canine compatibility: Dogs permitted without leashes, but must be kept away from the stock of other parties
Fees and permits: Northwest Forest Pass and Eagle Cap Wilderness Permit
Maximum elevation: 7,600 feet
Maps: USGS Jim White Ridge OR and Mount Fanny OR; Geo Graphics Wallowa Mountains Eagle Cap Wilderness; Green Trails #475sx: Wallowa Mountains Eagle Cap Wilderness
Trail contact: USDA Forest Service Wallowa Mountains Office, 201 E 2nd St./PO Box 905, Joseph, OR 97846; (541) 426-5546, (541) 426-4978; www.fs.usda.gov/wallowa-whitman

Finding the trail: Jim White Ridge is most easily accessed from the North Fork Catherine Creek Trailhead or Moss Springs Trailhead. The best way is from Moss Springs, which allows for the loop hike described below. To reach Moss Springs Trailhead, take Mill Creek Road east from the town of Cove. Go 8 miles on Mill Creek Road (FR 6220) to Moss Springs Trailhead. Hike southeast from the trailhead on the Upper Little Minam River Trail (1942) for 7.8 miles to the junction with the Jim White Ridge Trail. Jim White Ridge Trail begins at the junction with Upper Little Minam River Trail (1942), Cartwheel Ridge Trail (1907), and Lackeys Hole Trail (1942). This four-way junction (7,400 ft.) is in a saddle on the ridge that divides the Little Minam and Minam River drainages.
GPS: Moss Springs Trailhead: N45 16.468'/W117 40.689'; Jim White Ridge Trail junction: N45 14.340'/W117 34.760'

The Hike

Jim White Ridge Trail heads north from the junction. At first the trail climbs a grassy slope, nearly reaching the top of the ridge. The view to the east is of the Minam River Canyon and the higher parts of the Wallowa Mountains. A short distance farther, the trail enters an old burn area. Soon it comes to the junction with Little Pot Creek Trail (1919; 7,500 ft.). The unmarked junction with Little Pot Creek Trail is 1.2 miles from the junction with Upper Little Minam River Trail. Little Pot Creek Trail descends a short distance to the right (east) to a spring and campsite; beyond that point it is nearly impossible to follow and probably should not be used.

The unmarked, triangle junction with Mud Springs Trail is a short distance past the Little Pot Creek Trail junction. Mud Springs Trail seems to get more use than Jim White Ridge Trail, and it looks like the main trail here. At the junction, take the less-used trail to the right (northwest).

After passing the Mud Springs Trail junction, the trail traverses around the right side of Lackeys Point. It then drops to the saddle northeast of the point. Between the Mud Springs Trail junction and this saddle, watch for blazes and cairns marking the trail. The elevation at the saddle is 7,420 feet, and it is 0.4 mile from the Mud Springs Trail junction.

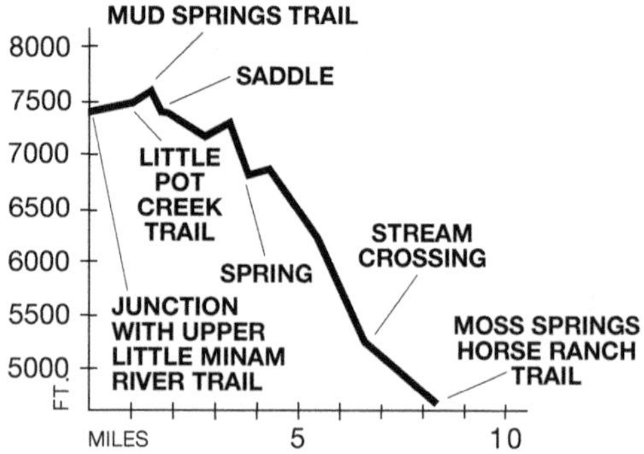

There is a faint path 0.1 mile past the saddle that drops off to the right to a campsite. Jim White Ridge Trail goes back and forth across the ridgeline a couple of times in the next 0.5 mile. Here the ridge becomes more rounded. The trail continues to descend through small timber. In another 0.3 mile it comes to a low point on the ridge (7,150 ft.).

From the low point the trail climbs for 650 yards onto the now flat-topped ridge. A couple hundred yards farther it starts to drop again for a short distance. Soon the trail becomes hard to see in a grassy area. It goes east a bit, then north on the fairly flat ridgetop. Watch for blazes. The trail is hard to see in spots for the next 0.5 mile, then it drops off the right side of the ridge into the trees, where it becomes easy to see again. In the next 0.2 mile the trail makes a switchback to the right, then a turn to the left. One-third mile after turning back to the left (north), there is a very large cairn on the right side of the trail. This cairn marks a spring, which is a few yards to the right of the trail. The spring is 4 miles from Upper Little Minam River Trail at 6,800 feet.

The trail climbs slightly after passing the spring. Soon it is back on top of the ridgeline. The trail becomes difficult to see again about 350 yards past the spring, as it goes slightly to the right of the ridgeline for 120 yards in an open area. The trail then goes back into the woods very near to the top of the ridge. Once in the woods, it is easy to see the trail again. Watch for cairns in the open area. There are many round rocks on the ridge in this area.

Another 0.75 mile and the trail begins to drop more steeply. After dropping for 0.25 mile, there is a campsite on the left side of the trail. A spring is above the campsite, but the water looks to be of poor quality. Elevation here is 6,200 feet. The trail stays fairly close to the ridgeline for the next 0.25 mile. Then it bears to the left (west) and heads down more steeply.

After going down steeply for 700 yards, the trail flattens out a bit. The view to the left (southeast) is of Boulder Creek Canyon. The trail continues down 0.5 mile more to a small stream crossing. This is a very small stream. The trees have become much larger than they were up above, and there are also lots of huckleberry bushes. These berries ripen in late August and September and can add pleasure and nourishment to the long hike down Jim White Ridge. As is usually the case in the Wallowa Mountains, watch for bears gorging themselves on the sweet purple fruit.

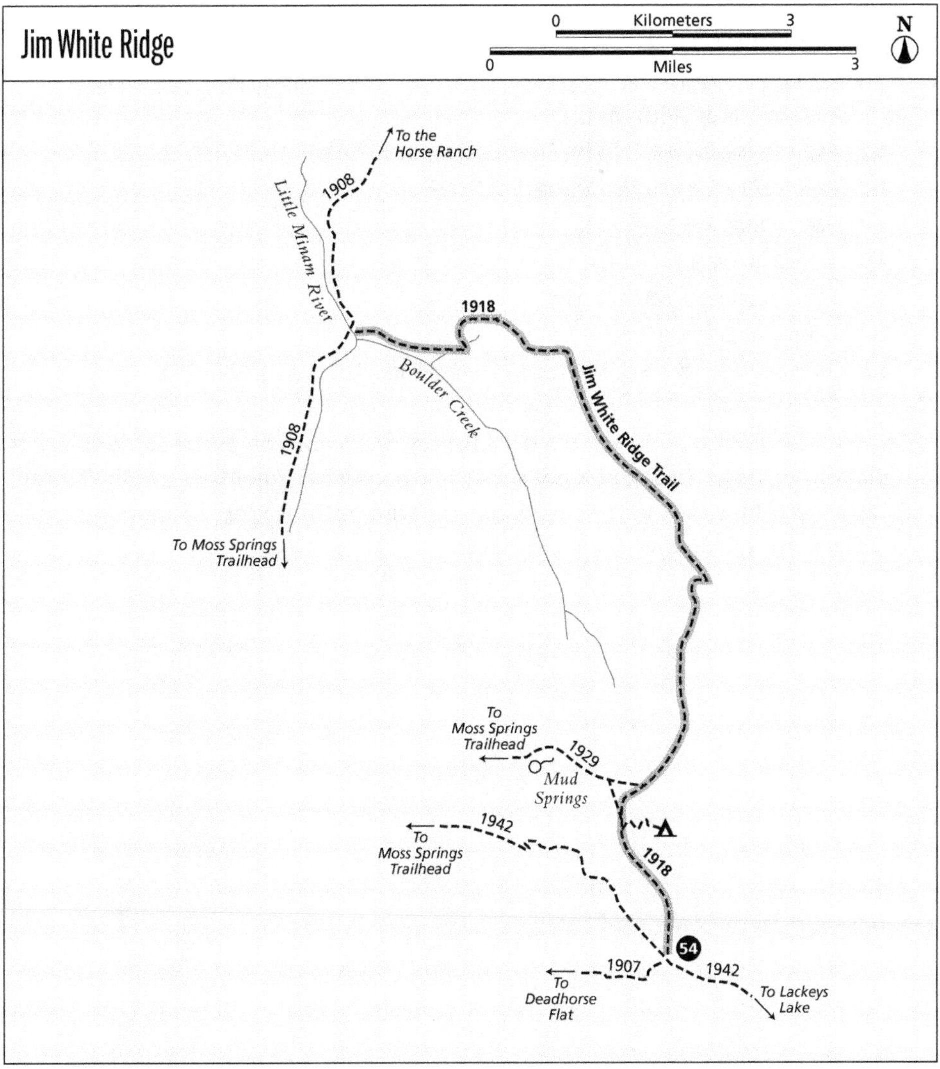

After crossing the tiny stream, the trail wanders back and forth another 700 yards to a crossing (5,260 ft.) of a much larger stream. After crossing the rushing stream, the trail turns right and crosses the same creek again. There is a campsite to the left between the crossings. A couple hundred yards after crossing the stream the second time, the trail makes a switchback to the left.

The trail meets Moss Springs/Horse Ranch Trail (1908) 1.5 miles farther. This junction (4,580 ft.) is 8.8 miles from Upper Little Minam River Trail. See Moss Springs/Horse Ranch (hike 52). There are many possible loop hikes to make from the trail; consult your map. Jim White Ridge Trail takes considerable route-finding skills.

Miles and Directions

0.0 Start at the junction with Upper Little Minam River (1942), Lackeys Hole (1942), and Cartwheel Ridge (1907) Trails.

1.2 Pass the junction with Little Pot Creek Trail (1919). (GPS: N45 15.145'/W117 35.154')

1.5 Pass the junction with Mud Springs Trail (1929).

1.8 Reach the saddle.

4.0 Arrive at the spring.

5.2 Pass the campsite next to the trail.

7.2 Cross a larger stream twice.

8.8 Arrive at the junction with Moss Springs/Horse Ranch Trail (1908). (GPS: N45 18.719'/W117 37.873')

Option: The trail can be done as a day hike (by masochists) by going up the Upper Little Minam River Trail, down Jim White Ridge, and back up Moss Springs/Horse Ranch Trail. This makes a 21-mile round-trip, with 3,620 feet of elevation gain and loss. Estimated hiking time is 8 to 11 hours.

55 Rock Creek

This backpacking and horse trail connects North Fork Catherine Creek Trail with Upper Minam River Trail in a remote area of the western Wallowa Mountains. (Trail 1905)

Distance: 4.3 miles one way
Hiking time: 1.5–3 hours
Difficulty: Moderate to strenuous
Trail maintenance: Infrequent
Best season: July through Oct
Traffic and other trail users: Light foot and horse traffic except during Oct and Nov hunting seasons, when horse traffic can be moderate to heavy
Canine compatibility: Dogs permitted without leashes, but must be kept away from the stock of other parties
Fees and permits: Northwest Forest Pass and Eagle Cap Wilderness Permit
Maximum elevation: 7,430 feet
Map: USGS China Cap OR
Trail contact: USDA Forest Service Wallowa Mountains Office, 201 E 2nd St./PO Box 905, Joseph, OR 97846; (541) 426-5546, (541) 426-4978; www.fs.usda.gov/wallowa-whitman

Finding the trail: The easiest way to reach Rock Creek Trail is from the North Fork Catherine Creek Trailhead. To reach the trailhead, take OR 203 southeast from Union for 11 miles to the junction with FR 7785. Turn left on FR 7785 and head east, then northeast, for 6 miles to North Fork Catherine Creek Trailhead (4,200 ft.). From the trailhead hike north then east then south on the North Fork Catherine Creek Trail (1905) for 9 miles to the junction with Meadow Mountain Trail (1927) and Rock Creek Trail (also 1905). There is no sign at the junction.
GPS: North Fork Catherine Creek Trailhead: N45 09.250'/W117 36.956'; Rock Creek Trail junction: N45 12.490'/W117 34.479'

The Hike

This description of Rock Creek Trail begins at the junction of North Fork Catherine Creek Trail (1905) and Meadow Mountain Trail (1927). No sign marks the junction, which is on the ridge 0.3 mile northeast of the summit of Meadow Mountain. From the junction, Rock Creek Trail descends to the east on the right (south) side of the ridge on a slope covered with lupine, buckwheat, and scattered timber. After descending for 0.25 mile the trail enters an old burn area, which it goes through for 0.2 mile. Upon leaving the burn the trail continues down through spruce and fir forest, passing a meadow in another 0.25 mile.

Just after passing the meadow, the trail crosses a small stream and soon begins to drop more steeply on an open slope covered with paintbrush, lupine, and sego lilies. The trail makes six switchbacks as it descends the slope, then makes four more as it drops through the timber below. It crosses a small stream while descending the last

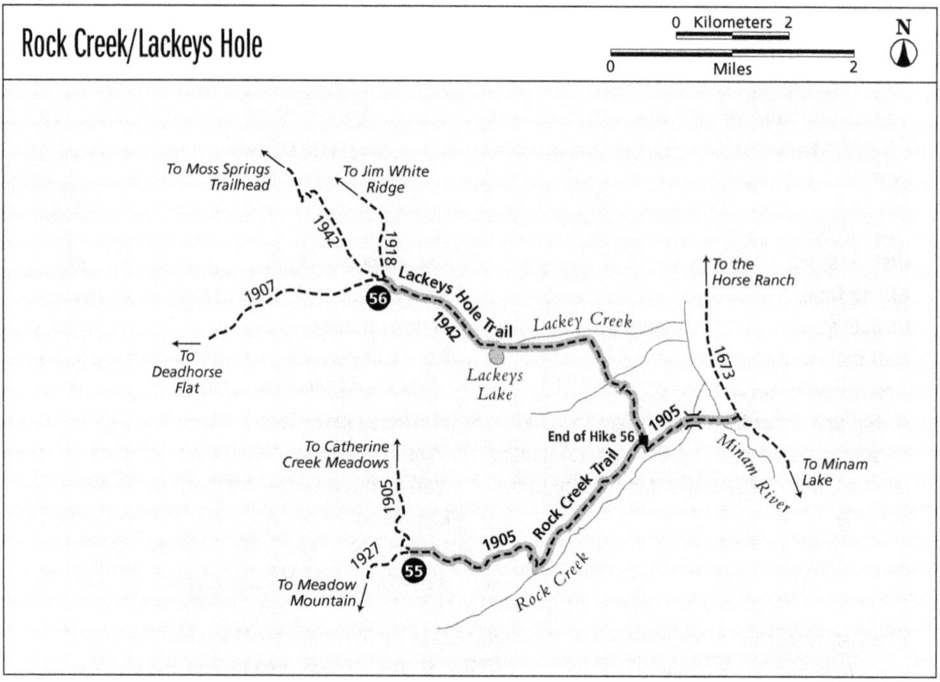

few switchbacks. At the bottom of the switchbacks (6,000 ft.), the trail comes close to Rock Creek but does not cross it.

The trail does not drop as steeply as the creek, so over the next mile it gradually gets farther away from the streambed. On the right of the trail 0.6 mile past the last switchback, there is a lodgepole pine with a large burl all the way around it.

The trail makes a switchback to the right 0.25 mile after passing the tree with the burl, then makes a switchback to the left a short distance farther along. The junction with Lackeys Hole Trail (1942) is reached 0.25 mile past this switchback. There is a sign at the junction with Lackeys Hole Trail (5,530 ft.). After passing the junction with Lackeys Hole Trail, Rock Creek Trail makes eighteen more switchbacks as it descends through a dense forest of fairly large fir, pine, and tamarack trees for 0.8 mile to a bridge over Rock Creek. The trail crosses a small stream 0.25 mile after crossing the bridge, then heads south for a short distance along a meadow. It soon turns left (east) and crosses the meadow to the Minam River. There is a campsite next to the river. The trail fords the Minam River and goes 0.1 mile more to the junction with Upper Minam River Trail.

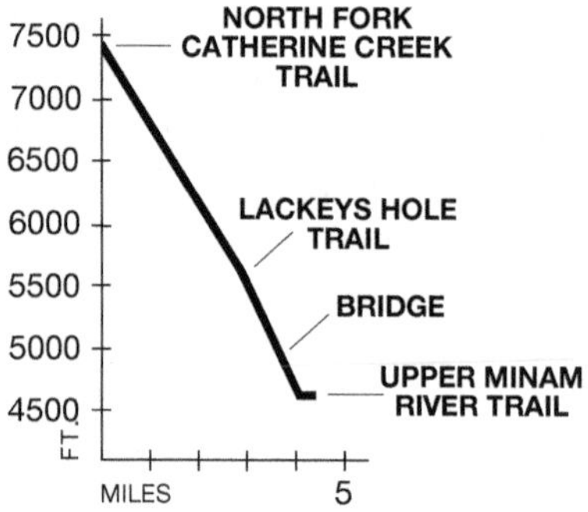

Crossing the Minam River may be dangerous during periods of high water. Be careful. The return is best done by going back on the same trail, unless a very extended trip—possibly involving a car shuttle—is desired. The most likely extended trip would be to head up the Minam River to Elk Creek Trail, then follow Elk Creek Trail back to Buck Creek Trailhead and from there to North Fork Catherine Creek Trailhead via Trail 1951 and FR 100.

Miles and Directions

0.0 Take the Rock Creek Trail from the junction with North Fork Catherine Creek (1905) and Meadow Mountain (1927) Trails.

3.0 Pass the junction with Lackeys Hole Trail (1942). (GPS: N45 13.291'/W117 32.143')

4.2 Cross the Minam River.

4.3 Arrive at the junction with Upper Minam River Trail (1673). (GPS: N45 13.365'/W117 31.250')

56 Lackeys Hole

This backpack and horse trail connects to Upper Little Minam River Trail at its junction with Jim White Ridge Trail, high on the ridgeline dividing the Little Minam and Minam River drainages. From the high ridge you descend, passing Lackeys Lake, to a junction with Rock Creek Trail. (Trail 1942)

See map page 204.
Distance: 5 miles one way
Hiking time: 2–3 hours heading down
Difficulty: Moderate
Trail maintenance: Infrequent
Best season: July through Oct
Traffic and other trail users: Generally light foot and horse traffic, but there may be moderate horse traffic during Oct and Nov hunting seasons.
Canine compatibility: Dogs permitted without leashes, but must be kept away from the stock of other parties
Fees and permits: Northwest Forest Pass and Eagle Cap Wilderness Permit
Maximum elevation: 7,510 feet
Maps: Geo Graphics Wallowa Mountains Eagle Cap Wilderness; Green Trails #475sx: Wallowa Mountains Eagle Cap Wilderness
Trail contact: USDA Forest Service Wallowa Mountains Office, 201 E 2nd St./ PO Box 905, Joseph, OR 97846; (541) 426-5546, (541) 426-4978; www.fs.usda.gov/wallowa-whitman

Finding the trail: The easiest way to reach the junction where the Lackeys Hole Trail (1942) begins is from the Moss Springs Trailhead. To reach Moss Springs Trailhead, take Mill Creek Road east from the town of Cove. Go 8 miles on Mill Creek Road (FR 6220) to Moss Springs Trailhead. Hike southeast from the trailhead on the Upper Little Minam River Trail (1942) for 7.8 miles to the four-way junction with the Jim White Ridge (1918), Upper Little Minam River (1942), Cartwheel Ridge (1907), and Lackeys Hole (also 1942) Trails. The lower (southeast) end of Lackeys Hole Trail joins Rock Creek Trail (1905) 1.3 miles from the Minam River.
GPS: Moss Springs Trailhead: N45 16.468' / W117 40.689'; Lackeys Hole Trail junction: N45 14.340' / W117 34.760'

The Hike

This trail is a continuation of Upper Little Minam River Trail (1942). Lackeys Hole Trail begins at a junction in a high, gentle saddle on the ridge dividing the Little Minam and Minam River drainages. The mostly open ridgetop country around the junction abounds with wildflowers in July, and elk are likely to be seen up here on their summer range.

From the junction (7,400 ft.) the trail heads southeast. It climbs slightly at first, through an area that was burned several years ago. This burn area is recovering nicely, as the ground is mostly covered with grass and flowers, and there are many small alpine trees growing up between the silver snags. A couple hundred yards after leaving the junction, the trail crosses a saddle and enters the North Fork Catherine

Campsite in the first saddle on Lackeys Hole Trail.

Creek drainage. Catherine Creek Meadows can be seen from the saddle, far below to the southwest.

After crossing the saddle the trail begins to traverse the steep, open slope on the right side of the ridgeline. It crosses a small stream a short distance after beginning the traverse. There are some possible campsites in the saddle, and this stream is a source of water. Late in the summer and in the fall, this stream may be dry, however.

The trail comes to another saddle 0.25 mile after crossing the stream. It follows the ridgeline for 100 yards in this saddle, then starts a slightly ascending traverse on the right side of the ridge again. This ascending traverse lasts 0.3 mile to where the trail reaches another saddle (7,510 ft.). As the trail crosses this saddle, it makes a switchback to the left and begins to descend on the left side of the ridgeline. After descending 100 yards or so, the trail makes another switchback to the right and continues to drop along a slope covered with subalpine fir and whitebark pine. The trail descends for 0.6 mile, makes a couple of switchbacks, then comes to yet another saddle on a sub-ridge (7,250 ft.). Soon after crossing the saddle, Lackeys Lake can be seen through the trees to the right. After crossing the saddle the trail drops the last 0.25 mile to a stream crossing, making one more switchback along the way. This stream is the outlet of Lackeys Lake. The lake is a few yards to the right, upstream from the trail. Lackeys Lake is more like a pond than a lake—shallow, with marshy edges and lots of mosquitoes. There is a good campsite along the east side of the lake, but there are no fish.

The trail continues to descend a mostly open hillside after crossing the outlet stream. It makes a couple of switchbacks and crosses the stream two more times, then crosses another small stream, which begins at a spring a few yards above the trail 0.6 mile after leaving Lackeys Lake. The route then winds its way down through the forest, making several switchbacks and crossing four tiny streams before rounding a ridge and leaving the Lackey Creek drainage 1.4 miles from the lake.

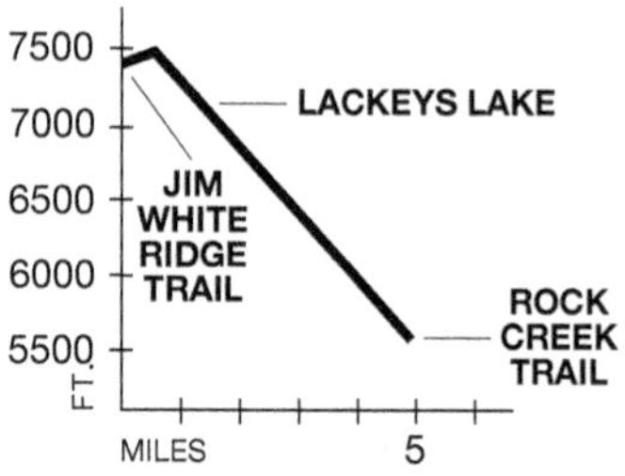

The trail crosses an unnamed creek 0.3 mile after leaving Lackey Creek drainage. It may be wise to fill your water bottles here, as there may be no water available from here to Rock Creek. After crossing the creek, the trail passes a muddy spring, then traverses a steep hillside heading southeast. It soon makes a switchback to the left. The trail makes five more switchbacks as it descends the remaining 1.3 miles to the junction with Rock Creek Trail (1905; 5,530 ft.). See Rock Creek (hike 55).

Miles and Directions

0.0 From the junction with Upper Little Minam River (1942), Jim White Ridge (1918), and Cartwheel Ridge (1907) Trails, take the Lackeys Hole Trail southeast.

1.5 Reach Lackeys Lake. (GPS: N45 13.862'/W117 33.580')

3.2 Cross an unnamed creek.

5.0 Arrive at the junction with Rock Creek Trail (1905). (GPS: N45 13.291'/W117 32.143')

57 Lodgepole Trail

This trail goes along the southwestern boundary of Eagle Cap Wilderness from Moss Springs Trailhead to the junction with Trail 1907. Parts of the trail follow old, mostly abandoned roadbeds. (Trail 1920)

Distance: 6.7 miles one way
Hiking time: 2.5–4 hours
Difficulty: Easy, but requires some route-finding and map-reading skills
Trail maintenance: Infrequent
Best season: June through Oct
Traffic and other trail users: Light to moderate foot and horse traffic; heavier during fall hunting seasons.
Canine compatibility: Dogs permitted without leashes, but must be kept away from the stock of other parties
Fees and permits: Northwest Forest Pass and Eagle Cap Wilderness Permit.
Maximum elevation: 6,580 feet
Maps: USGS Mount Fanny OR and Little Catherine Creek OR; Geo Graphics Wallowa Mountains Eagle Cap Wilderness
Trail contact: USDA Forest Service Wallowa Mountains Office, 201 E 2nd St./ PO Box 905, Joseph, OR 97846; (541) 426-5546, (541) 426-4978; www.fs.usda.gov/wallowa-whitman

Finding the trailhead: Lodgepole Trail begins at Moss Springs Trailhead (5,800 ft.). To reach Moss Springs Trailhead, take Mill Creek Road east from the town of Cove. Go 8 miles on Mill Creek Road (FR 6220) to Moss Springs Trailhead. There is a sign at the trailhead that points south along a closed dirt road (FR 410).
GPS: N45 16.468'/W117 40.689'

The Hike

From Moss Springs Trailhead walk south on closed FR 410. Forty yards from the trailhead, continue past FR 415, which turns off to the left. Another road goes off to the left 650 yards farther along. This one is unmarked. Forty yards past the unmarked road, FR 418 also heads to the left. Stay on FR 410. The junction with FR 360 is 350 yards farther. FR 360 turns to the right, FR 420 goes straight ahead, and FR 410 goes to the left. Head left (south-southeast) for 550 yards on FR 410 to the junction with Lodgepole Trail (1920). This junction is 0.6 mile from Moss Springs Trailhead.

At the junction (5,950 ft.) FR 410 turns to the right, and the Lodgepole Trail goes straight ahead. There is a sign marking this junction. The forest to this point has been almost all lodgepole pine trees. Past the junction there are more spruce, fir, and tamarack (western larch) trees.

One-half mile past the junction the trail appears to fork. This is a short section of trail realignment. Follow the main trail. The trail climbs over a small rise, then drops again to a dirt road. Turn right on the road, go 20 yards, then bear left again on the trail. The elevation here is 6,170 feet. Two hundred yards after leaving the dirt road

Hiker on the Lodgepole Trail.

the trail makes a switchback to the right. Then it climbs for 0.25 mile to a point near the top of a ridge (6,440 ft.). The trail follows the ridgetop for 0.25 mile to a rocky outcropping. The outcropping is a few yards to the left of the trail. There is a good viewpoint on the top of the outcropping. The Little Minam River Canyon is to the northeast, and the Elkhorn Mountains are to the south, on the other side of the Powder Valley.

The trail goes around and under the southeast side of the outcropping. Then it bears slightly to the right and drops to the southeast. The trail is difficult to see in this area; watch for blazes. A half mile past the outcropping, the trail becomes very difficult to see in a small opening. Head east-southeast and watch for blazes and cut logs.

The trail becomes wide, like a jeep road, which it may have been at one time, 300 yards past the opening. After another 250 yards, reach a junction with another dirt road. Turn right on the road and head south-southeast. Do not take the path that is across the opening at the junction. Soon the road becomes more of a trail again. The trail comes to the Allen Dungan Ditch (6,190 ft.) 0.4 mile past the junction, 3.4 miles from Moss Springs Trailhead.

Turn left along the ditch bank and follow it for 0.5 mile. Here the trail crosses the ditch and heads east-southeast. It climbs a small rise and comes to Dobbin Ditch Camp (6,260 ft.) 400 yards after crossing the ditch. In September 1994, when I walked this trail, there were two fires in this area. Firefighters were picking up packages that had been air-dropped to them at Dobbin Ditch Camp. The camp is in a small meadow. There is a sign marking Dobbin Ditch Camp.

After leaving Dobbin Ditch Camp, the trail climbs gently. It crosses two streambeds, then heads up along a streambed. These streambeds may have water at wetter

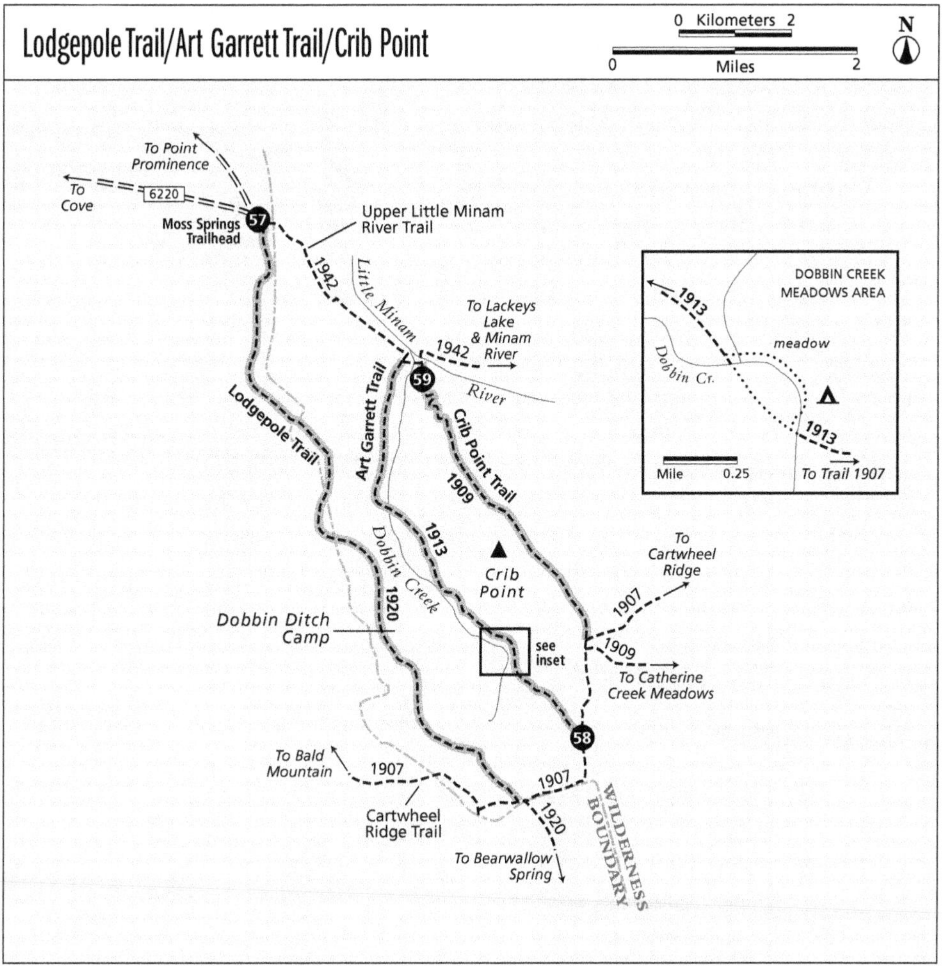

times of the year. Two-thirds of a mile past the camp the trail bears left and climbs for 200 yards to the top of a small rise (6,560 ft.). There is an old 5-mile marker on the right side of the trail at the top of the rise. Another streambed is 0.25 mile past the rise. After another 0.25 mile the trail comes into a meadow. This meadow (6,460 ft.) is 5 miles from Moss Springs Trailhead.

The trail heads east through the meadow, but is hard to see. Watch for blazes and cut limbs on the small trees in the meadow. About 250 yards into the meadow the trail crosses a small stream. The trail becomes easy to see again at the east end of the meadow; look for blazes on the trees at the east end. There are some good campsites around the edges of this meadow.

A sign that says LODGEPOLE TRAIL is on the right side of the trail 250 yards past the meadow. The junction with Cartwheel Ridge Trail (1907) is 6.7 miles from Moss Springs Trailhead and 0.5 mile past the sign. Elevation at the junction is 6,580 feet. This four-way trail junction can be hard to spot. It's in the second of two small clearings. A path turns left in the first clearing, but this path soon fades out. The Art Garrett Trail turns left (northwest) in the second clearing. There are blazes marking Art Garrett Trail, but no sign.

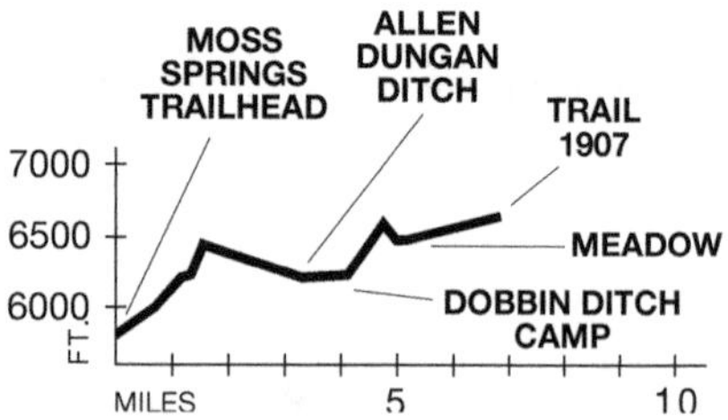

This trail requires route-finding and map-reading skills, but the hiking is easy. The Lodgepole Trail goes through forest for nearly its whole length. The views from the trail are generally not too spectacular, but it is a good place to check out the trees and flowers and to watch for wildlife.

From the junction with the Cartwheel Ridge Trail (1907), a loop trip can be made by following Trail 1907 to either Art Garrett Trail or Crib Point Trail, then taking one of these trails down to Upper Little Minam River Trail and taking Upper Little Minam River Trail back to Moss Springs Trailhead. Both of these return trails have more than 1,000 feet of elevation loss, and Upper Little Minam River Trail climbs 600 feet to get back to Moss Springs Trailhead from its junction with Crib Point or Art Garrett Trails. The distance back to Moss Springs Trailhead by either trail is 7.5 miles (including the distance to these trails on the Cartwheel Ridge Trail). Crib Point Trail is somewhat easier to find and follow. It is easier to do either of these loops in a counterclockwise direction.

Miles and Directions

0.0 Begin at Moss Springs Trailhead and follow FR 410.

0.3 Turn onto Lodgepole Trail (1920).

3.4 Reach the Allen Dungan Ditch.

4.1 Reach Dobbin Ditch Camp.

5.0 The trail enters a meadow.

6.7 Arrive at the junction with Cartwheel Ridge Trail (1907). (GPS: N45 12.415'/W117 38.144')

58 Art Garrett Trail

This trail connects Cartwheel Ridge Trail (1907) with Little Minam River Trail, descending through wooded country most of the way. Do not confuse this with the Dobbin Creek Trail, which is in the Bear Creek drainage. Both of these hikes follow a "Dobbin Creek," and this one is sometimes referred to as Dobbin Creek Trail. (Trail 1913)

See map page 211.
Distance: 4.4 miles one way
Hiking time: 1.5–2.5 hours
Difficulty: Moderate, but requires route-finding skills
Trail maintenance: Infrequent
Best season: June through Oct
Traffic and other trail users: Light foot and horse traffic; may be moderate during fall hunting seasons
Canine compatibility: Dogs permitted without leashes, but must be kept away from the stock of other parties
Fees and permits: Northwest Forest Pass and Eagle Cap Wilderness Permit
Maximum elevation: 6,420 feet
Map: Geo Graphics Wallowa Mountains Eagle Cap Wilderness. This trail is not shown on newer USGS Little Catherine Creek OR and Mount Fanny OR quads, which cover this area.
Trail contact: USDA Forest Service Wallowa Mountains Office, 201 E 2nd St./ PO Box 905, Joseph, OR 97846; (541) 426-5546, (541) 426-4978; www.fs.usda.gov/wallowa-whitman

Finding the trail: There are two good ways to access the junction where the Art Garrett Trail begins. One of them is from the Moss Springs Trailhead via the Lodgepole and Cartwheel Ridge Trails. The other, slightly closer way is from the North Fork Catherine Creek Trailhead. To reach the North Fork Catherine Creek Trailhead drive 11.5 miles southeast from Union on OR 203 to the junction with FR 7785. Turn left at the junction and follow FR 7785 for 6 miles east and northeast to the North Fork Catherine Creek Trailhead. Hike north from the trailhead on the North Fork Catherine Creek Trail (1905) for 4.8 miles to the junction with the Catherine Creek/Deadhorse Flat Trail (1909). Turn left at the junction and go 1.2 miles to the junction with the Cartwheel Ridge Trail (1907) at Deadhorse Flat. Turn left on the Cartwheel Ridge Trail and walk south for 0.7 mile to the junction with the Art Garrett Trail. The place where Art Garrett Trail leaves Cartwheel Ridge Trail is difficult to see. It turns off to the northwest in a small clearing. There are two clearings close together on Trail 1907; Art Garrett Trail turns off in the one closer to Deadhorse Flat. The elevation at this junction is 6,320 feet. There are old blazes marking the Art Garrett Trail, but no sign.
GPS: North Fork Catherine Creek Trailhead: N45 09.250'/W117 36.956'

The Hike

After you find the place where Art Garrett Trail turns northwest off Trail 1907, the Art Garrett route is easy to see in the woods. But it soon becomes hard to see again in a small opening. A few yards from the start of the opening, head northwest. Past the

Creek crossing along the Art Garrett Trail.

opening the trail climbs slightly for 0.3 mile to the top of a small rise (6,420 ft.). The trail then drops slightly and crosses Dobbin Creek in a meadow 0.6 mile past the rise.

After crossing the creek, turn right. Go downstream for 200 yards, then cross Dobbin Creek again. Turn left and follow the trail down through the meadow. Stay close to Dobbin Creek. Be careful not to go up a side stream that comes into the meadow from the other end (see map). Cross the side stream and continue down Dobbin Creek a few more yards. Soon you will pick up the trail again. This point can also be reached by going straight ahead through the trees after crossing Dobbin Creek the first time. This area can be very confusing. There is a nice campsite at the upper (southeast) end of this meadow.

After leaving the meadow area, the trail, which is now easy to see, climbs 50 yards to the right of Dobbin Creek. One-third mile past the meadow the trail becomes difficult to see in an open area. Stay level across the open area, then drop a few yards to the left at its far edge. Here the trail shows up again. It is quite wide at this point, almost like an old roadbed.

The trail crosses a very small stream (6,090 ft.) 0.3 mile past the open area. Two hundred yards farther the trail crosses another small stream. The trail is some distance above Dobbin Creek at this point. There is another stream crossing (5,990 ft.) 0.3 mile farther. Two hundred yards past this stream the trail starts to drop more steeply and crosses yet another small stream. There are lots of huckleberry bushes in this area, among the lodgepole pines.

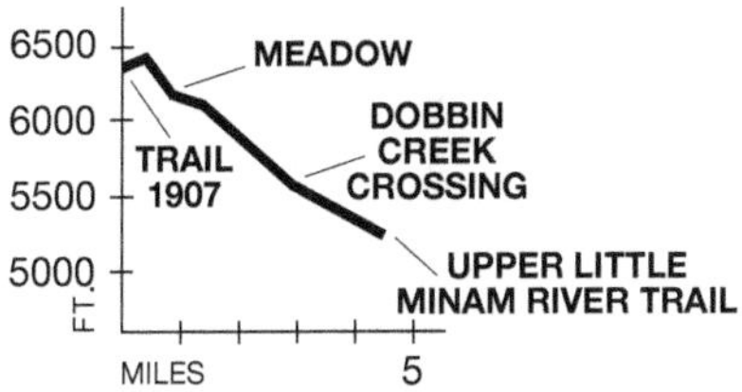

Soon the trail makes a couple of semi-switchbacks. It then heads down toward Dobbin Creek. The trail crosses Dobbin Creek (5,520 ft.) 0.25 mile past the switchbacks. The crossing is approximately 3 miles from the junction with Trail 1907.

The trail crosses a small stream 175 yards after crossing Dobbin Creek. A fence line with a gate is 75 yards past the stream. The trail goes through the gate. It crosses two more small streams on the way down to Upper Little Minam River Trail (1942), 1.4 miles past the last crossing of Dobbin Creek. The junction with Upper Little Minam River Trail (5,250 ft.) is unmarked but very easy to see when coming down Art Garrett Trail.

Most of this trail is easy to see; however, a couple of spots are very difficult to find. Route-finding skills are required. This trail can be very hard to find at the top, which is at the junction with Trail 1907. The total mileage is 4.4 miles, and the elevation loss when heading northwest is 1,170 feet. Art Garrett Trail can be done as part of a loop from Moss Springs Trailhead by using Lodgepole, Cartwheel Ridge, and Upper Little Minam River Trails.

Miles and Directions

0.0 At the junction with Cartwheel Ridge Trail (1907), take the Art Garrett Trail (1913) to the northwest.

0.6 Reach the meadow.

3.0 Cross Dobbin Creek.

4.4 Arrive at the junction with Upper Little Minam River Trail (1942). (GPS: N45 15.478'/W117 39.250')

59 Crib Point

This trail climbs a lightly forested ridgeline from the Upper Little Minam River Trail to the Cartwheel Ridge Trail (1907) at Deadhorse Flat, where there are several good campsites close to a spring. (Trail 1909)

See map page 211.
Distance: 3.6 miles one way
Hiking time: 1.5–2.5 hours
Difficulty: Strenuous
Trail maintenance: Infrequent
Best season: June through Oct
Traffic and other trail users: Light foot and horse traffic
Canine compatibility: Dogs permitted without leashes, but must be kept away from the stock of other parties
Fees and permits: Northwest Forest Pass and Eagle Cap Wilderness Permit
Maximum elevation: 6,600 feet
Maps: USGS Mount Fanny OR and Little Catherine Creek OR; Geo Graphics Wallowa Mountains Eagle Cap Wilderness
Trail contact: USDA Forest Service Wallowa Mountains Office, 201 E 2nd St./ PO Box 905, Joseph, OR 97846; (541) 426-5546, (541) 426-4978; www.fs.usda.gov/wallowa-whitman

Finding the trail: There are a couple of ways to access the Crib Point Trail. The eastern end of the route can be reached from the North Fork Catherine Creek Trailhead by using the North Fork Catherine Creek, Catherine Creek/Deadhorse Flat, and the Cartwheel Ridge Trails. To reach the junction where this hike description begins it's much easier to come in from Moss Springs Trailhead. To reach Moss Springs Trailhead, take Mill Creek Road east from the town of Cove. Go 8 miles on Mill Creek Road (FR 6220) to Moss Springs Trailhead. From the trailhead hike southeast on the Upper Little Minam River Trail (1942) for 2.1 miles to the junction with the Crib Point Trail (1909; 5,220 ft.). There are campsites at the junction, next to the Little Minam River.
GPS: Moss Springs Trailhead: N45 16.468' / W117 40.689'; Crib Point Trail junction: N45 15.510' / W117 39.183'

The Hike

The trail turns right (southwest) off Upper Little Minam River Trail. After leaving Upper Little Minam River Trail, Crib Point Trail makes seven switchbacks as it climbs through thick timber 620 vertical feet in the first mile. After 1 mile there is an opening in the woods. The trail then makes a couple more switchbacks in and out of the trees as it climbs on up the ridgeline. At 1.3 miles the trail gets on top of the ridgeline (6,070 ft.). Go another 0.3 mile and the trail flattens out a bit, following the semi-forested ridgeline through a mixed forest of lodgepole pine, subalpine fir, tamarack (western larch), and Engelmann spruce.

The trail makes a couple of semi-switchbacks 1 mile farther, then climbs to where the ridge broadens at about 6,500 feet. The trail climbs another 100 vertical feet, then drops a little. From here on the trail remains fairly flat, not gaining or losing more than about 100 feet in elevation. This area is mostly dense lodgepole pine forest. The trail is wide and appears to have been an old jeep trail. As the trail gets closer to Deadhorse Flat, the forest contains more fir and hemlock.

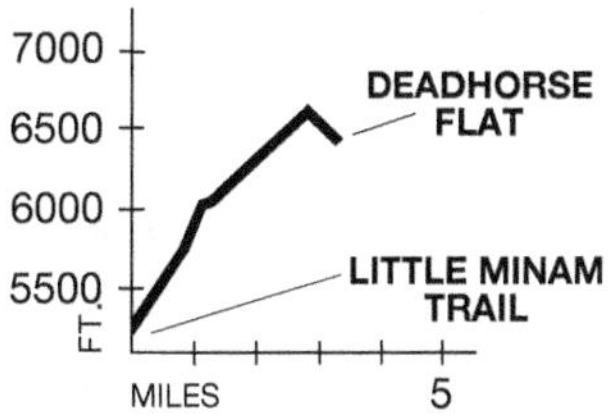

The trail enters the meadow at Deadhorse Flat (6,460 ft.) 3.6 miles from Upper Little Minam River Trail. The trail is hard to see in the large, lush Deadhorse Flat meadow. However, there is a signpost in the middle of the meadow. This is the junction with Cartwheel Ridge Trail (1907). There are several good campsites and a spring at Deadhorse Flat.

Several loop trips are possible by connecting Crib Point Trail with others described in this guide: Lodgepole Trail, Art Garrett Trail, and Cartwheel Ridge Trail.

Miles and Directions

0.0 At the junction with Upper Little Minam River Trail (1942), turn right onto the Crib Point Trail (1909).

1.3 Reach the top of the ridge.

3.6 Arrive at Deadhorse Flat and the junction with Cartwheel Ridge Trail (1907). (GPS: N45 13.499'/W117 37.453')

60 Cartwheel Ridge

This connecting trail goes from Lodgepole Trail (1920) to Upper Little Minam River Trail (1942) via Deadhorse Flat. At Deadhorse Flat the trail connects with Crib Point Trail and Catherine Creek/Deadhorse Trail. After passing Deadhorse Flat, Cartwheel Ridge Trail connects with Upper Little Minam River Trail, Jim White Ridge Trail, and Lackeys Hole Trail. (Trail 1907)

Distance: 4.3 miles one way
Hiking time: 1.5–2.5 hours
Difficulty: Easy to moderate
Trail maintenance: Infrequent
Best season: Mid-June through Oct
Traffic and other trail users: Light to moderate foot and horse Traffic; heavier in the fall
Canine compatibility: Dogs permitted without leashes, but must be kept away from the stock of other parties
Fees and permits: Northwest Forest Pass and Eagle Cap Wilderness Permit
Maximum elevation: 7,400 feet
Maps: USGS Little Catherine Creek OR and China Cap OR; Geo Graphics Wallowa Mountains Eagle Cap Wilderness
Trail contact: USDA Forest Service Wallowa Mountains Office, 201 E 2nd St./ PO Box 905, Joseph, OR 97846; (541) 426-5546, (541) 426-4978; www.fs.usda.gov/wallowa-whitman

Finding the trail: The easiest way to access the Cartwheel Ridge Trail is from the Moss Springs Trailhead. To reach Moss Springs Trailhead, take Mill Creek Road east from the town of Cove. Go 8 miles on Mill Creek Road (FR 6220) to Moss Springs Trailhead. From the trailhead hike southeast on the Lodgepole Trail (1920) for 6.7 miles to the four-way junction with Trail 1907 (6,560 ft.). **GPS:** Moss Springs Trailhead: N45 16.468'/W117 40.689'; Trail 1907 junction: N45 12.415'/W117 38.144'

The Hike

Trail 1907, which becomes Cartwheel Ridge Trail at Deadhorse Flat, heads east-northeast from the junction with the Lodgepole Trail (6,580 ft.). The other trails leaving this junction are Trail 1920, which heads southeast then south to Bearwallow Springs, and Bald Mountain Trail, which goes southwest then west to Bald Mountain.

Trail 1907 climbs gently for 0.4 mile to the top of a rise (6,620 ft.). Past the rise the trail drops through mixed forest for 0.6 mile to the unmarked junction with the Art Garrett Trail (1913; 6,320 ft.). This hard-to-spot junction is in the second of two small clearings. A path turns left in the first clearing, but this path soon fades out. The Art Garrett Trail turns left (northwest) in the second clearing. There are blazes marking Art Garrett Trail, but no sign.

After going 0.4 mile past the Art Garrett Trail junction, the trail tops another rise (6,480 ft.). It crosses a small stream in a meadow 0.25 mile past this rise. Another 50 yards farther is the junction with Crib Point Trail (1909). The meadow is Deadhorse Flat. Deadhorse Flat (6,460 ft.) is 1.8 miles from the Lodgepole Trail.

Vague spot in the trail on Cartwheel Ridge.

At Deadhorse Flat there is another four-way junction. Crib Point Trail turns left and goes northwest. Catherine Creek/Deadhorse Flat Trail (1909) turns right and heads southeast, down to Catherine Creek Meadows. Trail 1907 becomes Cartwheel Ridge Trail and heads northeast. There are good campsites all around Deadhorse Flat. There is also a spring emerging from the green meadow near its east edge. Before leaving the meadow at Deadhorse Flat, the trail crosses a stream. The crossing is just below the spring where the stream begins.

The trail is very wide where it leaves the meadow. It was a jeep road at one time. Climb at a moderate grade through forest and open areas and reach the top of a rise (6,770 ft.) 0.6 mile past Deadhorse Flat. The view to the right (southeast) is of the North Fork Catherine Creek Canyon and Catherine Creek Meadows.

Nine-tenths of a mile past the viewpoint, at the top of the rise, there are rock outcroppings on the right side of the trail. The trail steepens 700 yards past the outcroppings and climbs through thinning timber. There may be cattle in this area. The trail comes to a fence line 350 yards farther along. It crosses the fence through a gate. This is the end of the old jeep trail (7,240 ft.).

After going through the fence, the trail traverses around the right side of a high point on the ridge. After passing the high point, it drops slightly to a saddle (7,200 ft.). The trail enters an old burn area 150 yards beyond the saddle. After going 125 yards through the burn area, it begins a 300-yard-long ascending traverse around the left side of the ridge. The junction with the Upper Little Minam River Trail (1942) is 130 yards past the end of the traverse. This junction (7,400 ft.) is 4.3 miles from the Lodgepole Trail and 2.5 miles from Deadhorse Flat. This is also the junction with Jim White Ridge Trail and Lackeys Hole Trail. The timber at the junction is still partly burned, but there are patches of green trees.

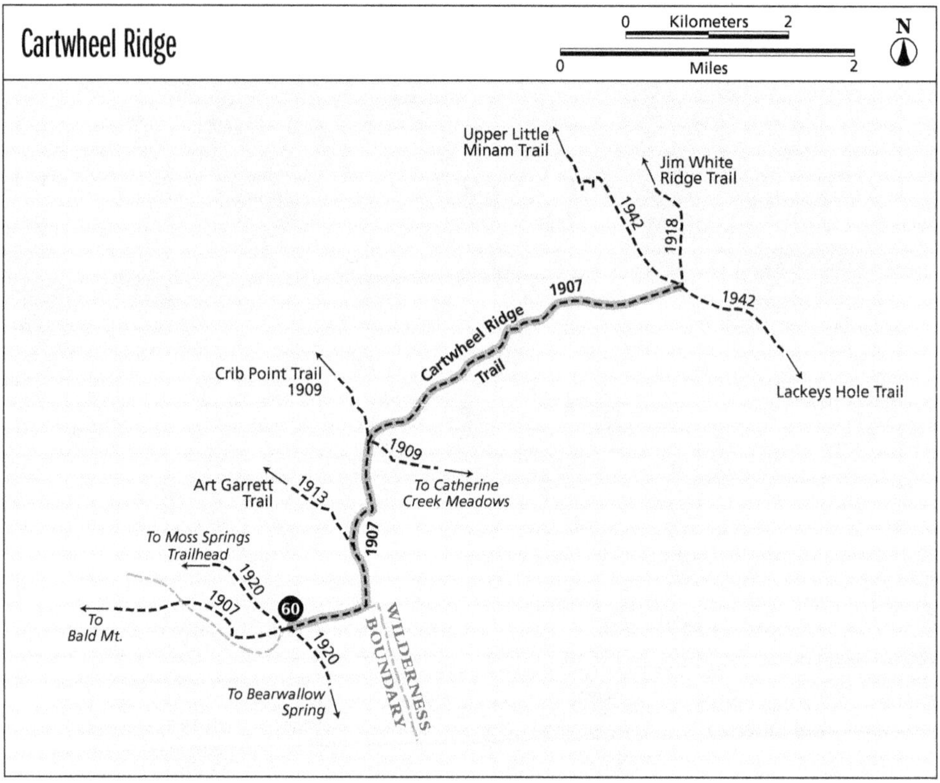

A return hike back to Moss Springs Trailhead can be made by taking the Upper Little Minam River Trail. This 18.2-mile loop, including Lodgepole, Cartwheel Ridge, and Upper Little Minam River Trails, is best done in two or more days. There is a much longer return alternative available for the hardy hiker, which is to take Jim White Ridge Trail down to Moss Springs/Horse Ranch Trail and follow that trail back up to Moss Springs Trailhead. See Jim White Ridge (hike 54) and Moss Springs/Horse Ranch (hike 52).

Miles and Directions

0.0 At the four-way junction with Lodgepole Trail (1920), take Trail 1907 east-northeast.

1.1 Pass the junction with Art Garrett Trail (1913).

1.8 Arrive at Deadhorse Flat and the junctions with Crib Point (1909) and Deadhorse Flat/Catherine Creek (1909) Trails.

4.3 Arrive at the junction with Upper Little Minam River (1942), Jim White Ridge (1918), and Lackeys Hole (1942) Trails. (GPS: N45 14.340'/W117 34.760')

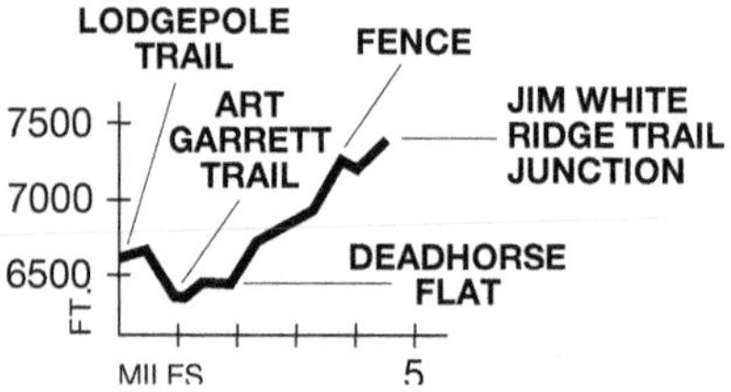

61 Catherine Creek/Deadhorse Flat

A short trail that climbs from the lush Catherine Creek Meadows to the ridgeline at Deadhorse Flat. (Trail 1909)

Distance: 1.2 miles one way
Hiking time: About 0.5 hour
Difficulty: Moderate
Trail maintenance: Infrequent
Best season: June through Oct
Traffic and other trail users: Light to moderate foot and horse traffic
Canine compatibility: Dogs permitted without leashes, but must be kept away from the stock of other parties
Fees and permits: Northwest Forest Pass and Eagle Cap Wilderness Permit
Maximum elevation: 6,460 feet
Map: USGS China Cap OR
Trail contact: USDA Forest Service Wallowa Mountains Office, 201 E 2nd St./ PO Box 905, Joseph, OR 97846; (541) 426-5546, (541) 426-4978; www.fs.usda.gov/wallowa-whitman

Finding the trail: The easiest way to get to the Catherine Creek/Deadhorse Flat Trail is from the North Fork Catherine Creek Trailhead. To reach the North Fork Catherine Creek Trailhead, drive 11.5 miles southeast from Union on OR 203 to the junction with FR 7785. Turn left at the junction and follow FR 7785 for 6 miles east and northeast to the North Fork Catherine Creek Trailhead. Hike north from the trailhead on to the North Fork Catherine Creek Trail (1905) for 4.8 miles to the junction with the Catherine Creek/Deadhorse Flat Trail (1909), on the west side of Catherine Creek Meadows (5,670 ft.).
GPS: North Fork Catherine Creek Trailhead: N45 09.250'/W117 36.956'; Catherine Creek/ Deadhorse Flat Trail: N45 13.320'/W117 36.703'

The Hike

Catherine Creek/Deadhorse Trail (1909) heads west from the junction of North Fork Catherine Creek Trail (1905). After going 150 yards the trail makes a switchback, then crosses a stream 200 yards farther along. The trail then climbs, making eight switchbacks in the next 0.6 mile. Above the switchbacks the trail flattens out at the top of a spur ridge. It crosses a small stream 275 yards after topping out. Just after crossing the stream, the trail comes into a meadow. This meadow is Deadhorse Flat. The trail heads 125 yards out into the meadow to a signpost at the junction with Cartwheel Ridge Trail (1907; 6,460 ft.).

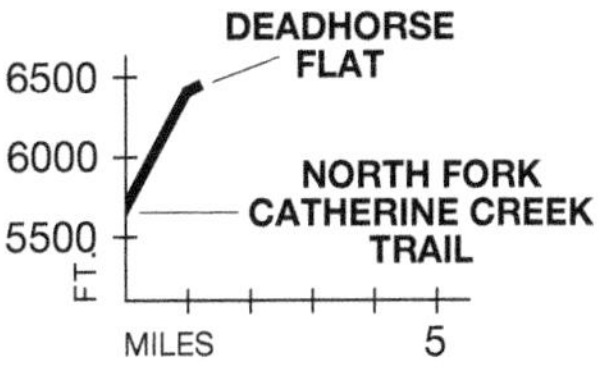

Miles and Directions

0.0 From the junction with North Fork Catherine Creek Trail (1905) in Catherine Creek Meadows, the Catherine Creek/Deadhorse Flat Trail (1909) heads west.

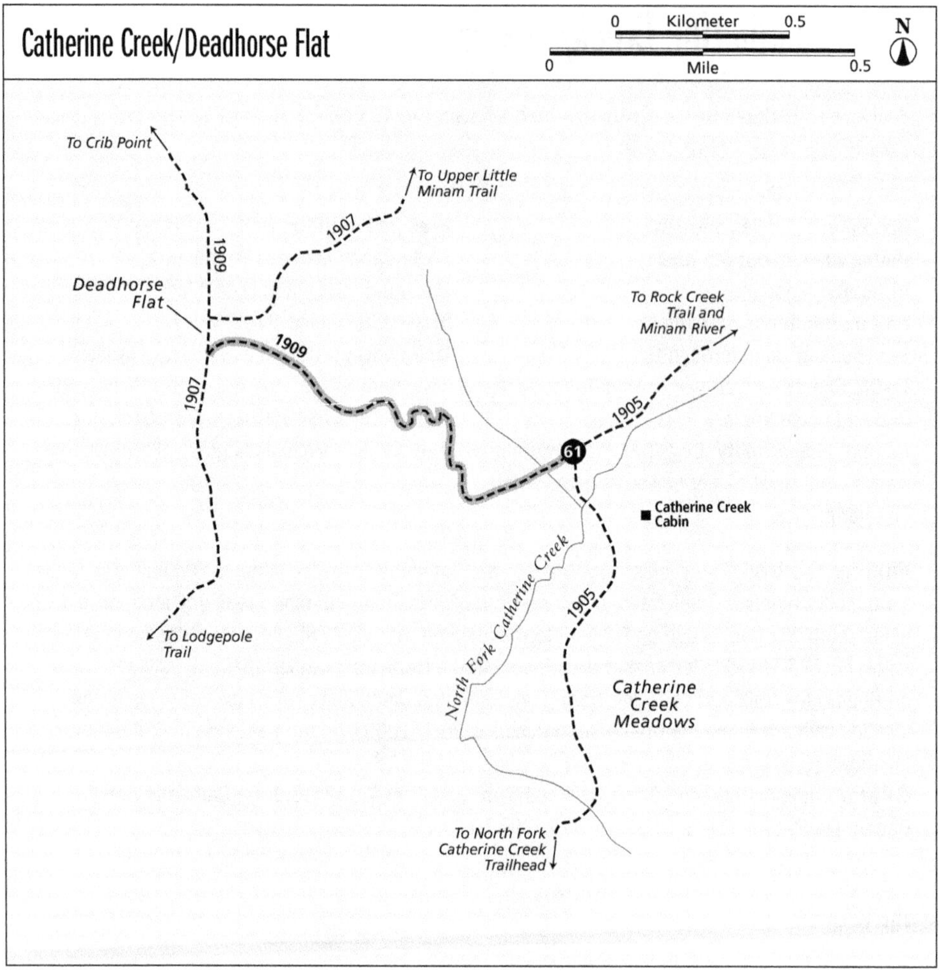

1.0 Reach the top of the spur ridge.

1.2 Arrive at Deadhorse Flat and the junction with Cartwheel Ridge Trail (1907). (GPS: N45 13.448'/W117 37.457')

62 North Fork Catherine Creek

A backpacking and stock trail goes along the North Fork Catherine Creek from North Fork Catherine Creek Trailhead to the pass where Trail 1905 becomes Rock Creek Trail. The junction with Meadow Mountain Trail is also at this pass. (Trail 1905)

Distance: 9 miles one way
Hiking time: 4–6 hours
Difficulty: Easy to moderate
Trail maintenance: Yearly
Best season: June through Oct to Catherine Creek Meadows; mid-June through Oct past the meadows
Traffic and other trail users: Moderate to heavy foot traffic; moderate horse traffic
Canine compatibility: Dogs permitted without leashes, but must be kept away from the stock of other parties
Fees and permits: Northwest Forest Pass and Eagle Cap Wilderness Permit
Maximum elevation: 7,430 feet
Map: USGS China Cap OR
Trail contact: USDA Forest Service Wallowa Mountains Office, 201 E 2nd St./PO Box 905, Joseph, OR 97846; (541) 426-5546, (541) 426-4978; www.fs.usda.gov/wallowa-whitman

Finding the trailhead: The trail starts at the North Fork Catherine Creek Trailhead (4,200 ft.). To reach the trailhead, take OR 203 southeast from Union, past Catherine Creek State Park 8 miles from town, and drive 3.5 miles more to the junction with FR 7785. Turn left on FR 7785 and head east, then northeast, for 6 miles to North Fork Catherine Creek Trailhead.
GPS: N45 09.250'/W117 36.956'

The Hike

From the trailhead, the trail heads north-northeast up the west side of the North Fork Catherine Creek. It crosses six small to very small streams in the first 1.25 miles. At 1.25 miles (4,690 ft.) the trail crosses the North Fork Catherine Creek. The forest along this creek bottom is a mix of ponderosa pine, spruce, and cottonwood. There are also some open areas and some brush.

After crossing the North Fork Catherine Creek, the trail crosses one more stream, Chop Creek, before reaching the Eagle Cap Wilderness boundary (5,090 ft.) at 2 miles. Just past the wilderness boundary the trail crosses Jim Creek. Three hundred yards past the wilderness boundary there is a meadow between the trail and the North Fork Catherine Creek. The meadow continues along the creek for about 350 yards. There are several campsites along the creek here, with paths leading down to them from the trail. At 3 miles the trail crosses Boot Hill Creek (5,320 ft.). The trail widens into what looks like an old roadbed 500 yards past Boot Hill Creek. After going 300 more yards, there is a bridge over a small creek. At 0.5 mile past the bridge, the trail has climbed above the North Fork Catherine Creek, which

Catherine Creek Meadows.

is in a steep canyon. Go through a gate in a broken-down old fence line 0.8 mile past the bridge. Another 130 yards farther the trail enters Catherine Creek Meadows (5,650 ft.).

After entering the meadows the trail crosses a small stream. A short distance past the stream is a signpost. This is the junction with China Ridge Trail (1906); the sign points to Meadow Mountain. China Ridge Trail, of which this section is now decommissioned, turns to the right (east). The North Fork Catherine Creek Trail continues up through the meadows, then goes through a strip of trees and crosses another stream on a wooden bridge.

The trail forks a little way past the bridge. Take the left fork, as the right fork goes a short distance to Catherine Creek cabin. The trail crosses the North Fork Catherine Creek 125 yards past the trail fork. Cross the creek, turn right, and go 125 yards to the junction with Catherine Creek/Deadhorse Flat Trail (1909; 5,670 ft.). This junction is 4.8 miles from the trailhead. Trail 1909 heads to the left (west) to Deadhorse Flat. See Catherine Creek/Deadhorse Flat (hike 61).

Past the junction the North Fork Catherine Creek Trail goes along the left side of the meadow through stands of trees for 400 yards. After leaving the meadow the trail follows the left side of North Fork Catherine Creek. It crosses several small side streams before reaching another meadow, which is 2.3 miles after leaving Catherine Creek Meadows. There are campsites along the sides of this 200-yard-long meadow, and a small stream at the far end of the meadow. At the southeast end of the meadow

North Fork Catherine Creek

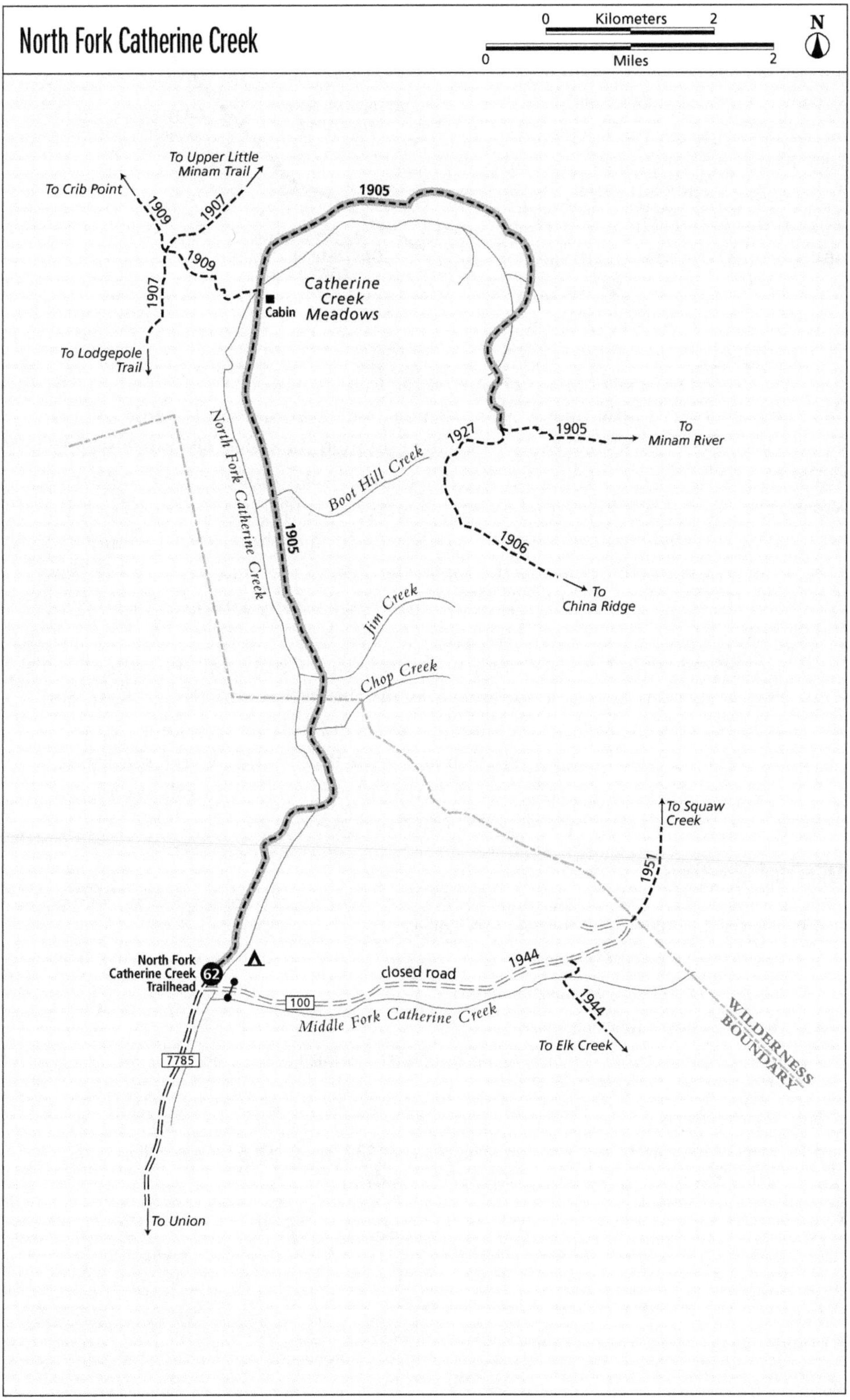

0 Kilometers 2
0 Miles 2
N
To Upper Little Minam Trail
To Crib Point
1909
1907
1905
1909
Catherine Creek Meadows
Cabin
1907
To Lodgepole Trail
North Fork Catherine Creek
1905
To Minam River
1927
Boot Hill Creek
1905
1906
To China Ridge
Jim Creek
Chop Creek
To Squaw Creek
1951
North Fork Catherine Creek Trailhead
62
1944
closed road
100
1944
Middle Fork Catherine Creek
To Elk Creek
WILDERNESS BOUNDARY
7785
To Union

the trail enters the timber and crosses a larger stream (6,550 ft.). This larger stream is a fork of Catherine Creek.

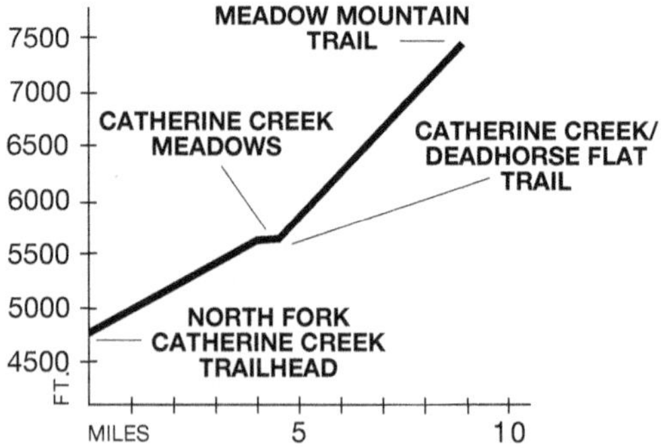

After crossing the stream the trail heads generally south and up. It is braided here from use by cattle. Follow the blazes. There is a creek and campsite on the right side of the trail 0.3 mile after crossing the stream. Another stream crossing is 125 yards past the campsite. Go 0.4 mile farther to a meadow on the left side of the trail.

The trail enters a little open valley 0.4 mile past this meadow. This little valley is about 150 yards long. A small creek runs down through the valley. The creek was dry when I hiked this trail in September. Round a switchback to the right 300 yards after leaving the little valley; 100 yards farther is another switchback. A few yards past the switchback is a fence line and a gate. The trail goes through the gate, then climbs 125 yards more to the top of a ridge. At the top of the ridge is the junction with Meadow Mountain Trail (1927; 7,430 ft.). This junction is 9 miles from North Fork Catherine Creek Trailhead.

This junction is the end of North Fork Catherine Creek Trail. From here on, Trail 1905 is Rock Creek Trail and goes straight ahead, down to Rock Creek and the Minam River. The river is 4.3 miles away and 2,860 vertical feet down. Meadow Mountain Trail turns right at the junction and heads up the ridge to the southwest.

North Fork Catherine Creek Trail is generally easy to see and follows a gentle grade except for the last couple of miles, where the grade is moderate.

Miles and Directions

0.0 Start at the North Fork Catherine Creek Trailhead.

1.3 Cross the North Fork Catherine Creek.

2.0 Pass the Eagle Cap Wilderness boundary.

4.5 Reach Catherine Creek Meadows.

4.8 Pass the junction with Catherine Creek/Deadhorse Flat Trail (1909). (GPS: N45 13.320'/W117 36.703')

7.1 Reach a meadow.

9.0 Arrive at the junction with Meadow Mountain Trail (1927). Trail 1905 becomes Rock Creek Trail at this point. (GPS: N45 12.490'/W117 34.479')

63 Meadow Mountain

This short connecting trail goes from North Fork Catherine Creek Trail over the summit of Meadow Mountain to China Ridge Trail. This trail traverses view property all the way. (Trail 1927)

Distance: 0.4 mile one way
Hiking time: 15–30 minutes
Difficulty: Moderate
Trail maintenance: Rare
Best season: July through Sept
Traffic and other trail users: Light foot and horse traffic
Canine compatibility: Dogs permitted without leashes, but must be kept away from the stock of other parties
Fees and permits: Northwest Forest Pass and Eagle Cap Wilderness Permit
Maximum elevation: 7,820 feet
Map: USGS China Cap OR
Trail contact: USDA Forest Service Wallowa Mountains Office, 201 E 2nd St./PO Box 905, Joseph, OR 97846; (541) 426-5546, (541) 426-4978; www.fs.usda.gov/wallowa-whitman

Finding the trail: This trail starts at the junction of North Fork Catherine Creek Trail and Rock Creek Trail (1905), 9 miles from North Fork Catherine Creek Trailhead. To reach the North Fork Catherine Creek Trailhead from Union, take OR 203 southeast, pass Catherine Creek State Park at 8 miles, and drive 3.5 miles more to the junction with FR 7785. Turn left on FR 7785 and head east, then northeast, for 6 miles to North Fork Catherine Creek Trailhead. From the trailhead hike north, then east, then south, for 9 miles to the junction with Rock Creek (1905) and Meadow Mountain Trails. The junction (7,430 ft.) is on top of a ridge northeast of Meadow Mountain.
GPS: North Fork Catherine Creek Trailhead: N45 09.250'/W117 36.956'; Meadow Mountain junction: N45 12.490'/W117 34.479'

The Hike

From the junction with the North Fork Catherine Creek Trail (1905), the Meadow Mountain trail heads southwest up the ridge. After a few yards it traverses around the left side of the ridge. The traverse ends a short distance farther in a saddle. At the saddle a fence runs a few feet to the right of the trail. A little farther along, the fence crosses the trail (7,450 ft.).

At about 0.1 mile from the Trail 1905 junction, a long, narrow meadow spreads to the right of the trail at the base of Meadow Mountain. Along the right (east) side of the meadow is a path. The path goes northwest for 600 yards, dropping slightly to a pond. This is a fairly large pond with meadow and campsites around it.

After passing the path and narrow meadow, Trail 1927 begins to climb Meadow Mountain. First there is an ascending traverse to the right. Up the traverse 200 yards is a switchback to the left. About the same distance farther is another switchback to the right. Past the second switchback, go 150 yards farther to the summit of Meadow

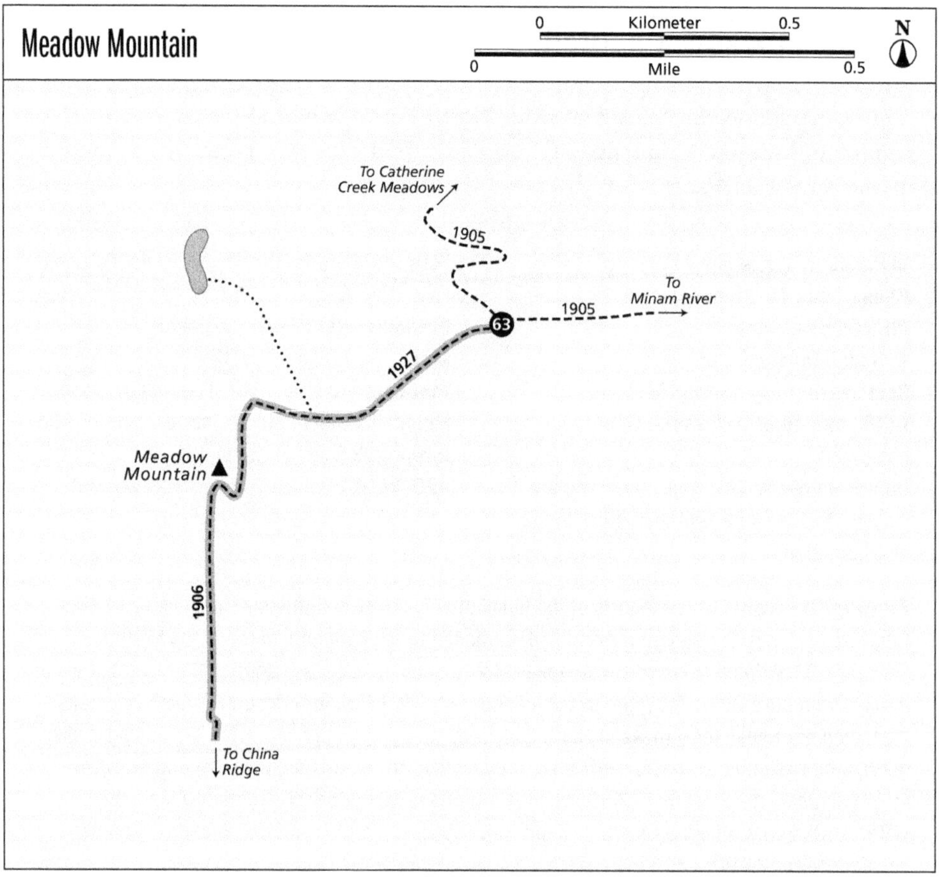

Mountain (7,820 ft.). On the summit there are the remains of what appears to be an old lookout. There are also some mining prospect holes. From the summit, Catherine Creek Meadows is far below to the west.

Beyond the summit the trail goes south along the ridge and drops slightly to the junction with China Ridge Trail (1906; 7,800 ft.). The distance from Trail 1905 to Trail 1906 is only 0.4 mile.

Miles and Directions

0.0 At the junction with North Fork Catherine Creek Trail (1905), take the Meadow Mountain Trail (1927) southwest up the ridge.

0.1 Pass the narrow meadow to the right of the trail and the path to the pond.

0.4 Reach the summit of Meadow Mountain and descend to the junction with China Ridge Trail (1906).

Southern

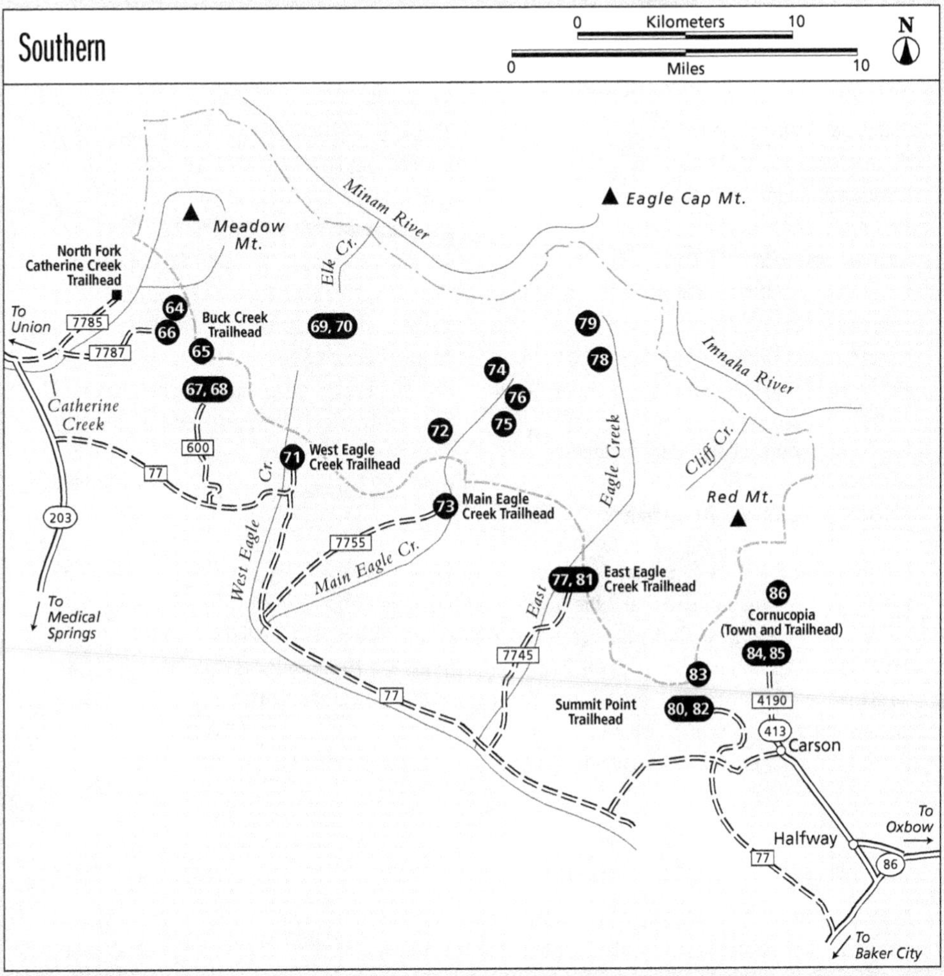
Southern
Kilometers
0
10
Miles
0
10
N
Meadow Mt.
Minam River
Eagle Cap Mt.
Elk Cr.
North Fork Catherine Creek Trailhead
To Union
7785
7787
64
66
65
Buck Creek Trailhead
69, 70
79
78
Imnaha River
74
76
75
67, 68
Catherine Creek
72
Cliff Cr.
Eagle Creek
600
71
West Eagle Creek Trailhead
77
Cr.
73
Main Eagle Creek Trailhead
Red Mt.
203
7755
West Eagle
Main Eagle Cr.
East
77, 81
East Eagle Creek Trailhead
86
Cornucopia (Town and Trailhead)
To Medical Springs
84, 85
7745
83
77
Summit Point Trailhead
80, 82
4190
413
Carson
To Oxbow
Halfway
86
77
To Baker City

64 Squaw Creek

This trail connects FR 100 to the China Ridge Trail (1906). Squaw Creek Trail is a little out of the way and not heavily used, so there is a good chance you will have it to yourself. There are good views looking south into the Powder River Valley from the upper part of the route, and at the junction with China Ridge Trail, the view opens up to the north and includes much of the Wallowa Mountains. There is also a good chance of seeing wildlife along this trail. (Trail 1951)

Distance: 3 miles one way
Hiking time: 1.5–2.5 hours
Difficulty: Moderate to strenuous
Trail maintenance: Infrequent
Best season: Mid-June through Oct
Traffic and other trail users: Generally light foot traffic, heavier in the fall; light horse traffic
Canine compatibility: Dogs permitted without leashes, but must be kept away from the stock of other parties
Fees and permits: Eagle Cap Wilderness Permit
Maximum elevation: 7,430 feet
Maps: USGS China Cap OR; Geo Graphics Wallowa Mountains Eagle Cap Wilderness. The Geo Graphics map shows this trail more accurately.
Trail contact: USDA Forest Service Wallowa Mountains Office, 201 E 2nd St./ PO Box 905, Joseph, OR 97846; (541) 426-5546, (541) 426-4978; www.fs.usda.gov/wallowa-whitman; or USDA Forest Service Pine Field Office, 38470 Pine Town Ln., Halfway, OR 97834; (541) 742-7511. Office closed Dec 21 through Apr 30; contact Baker City office at (541) 523-6391.

Finding the trailhead: Squaw Creek Trail leaves FR 100 3 miles east of the North Fork Catherine Creek Campground. To reach the North Fork Catherine Creek Campground from Union, take OR 203 southeast, pass Catherine State Park 8 miles from town, and continue another 3.5 miles along OR 203 to the junction with FR 7785. Turn left on FR 7785 and head east, then northeast, for 6 miles to North Fork Catherine Creek Campground. Turn right on FR 100 and drive 3 miles to the unsigned Squaw Creek Trailhead.
GPS: Squaw Creek Trail junction: N45 09.535'/W117 33.410'

The Hike

Squaw Creek Trail turns to the right a short distance after FR 100 makes a switchback to the left. There is no sign at the trailhead.

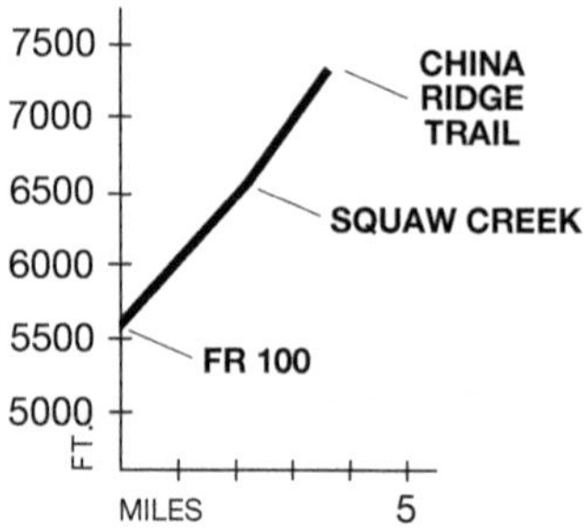

After leaving the road the trail climbs, makes a couple of switchbacks, then heads generally north. The trail here is well above and west of Squaw Creek. It crosses several very small streams as it climbs to the north. The tread crosses Squaw Creek 1.8 miles from the trailhead.

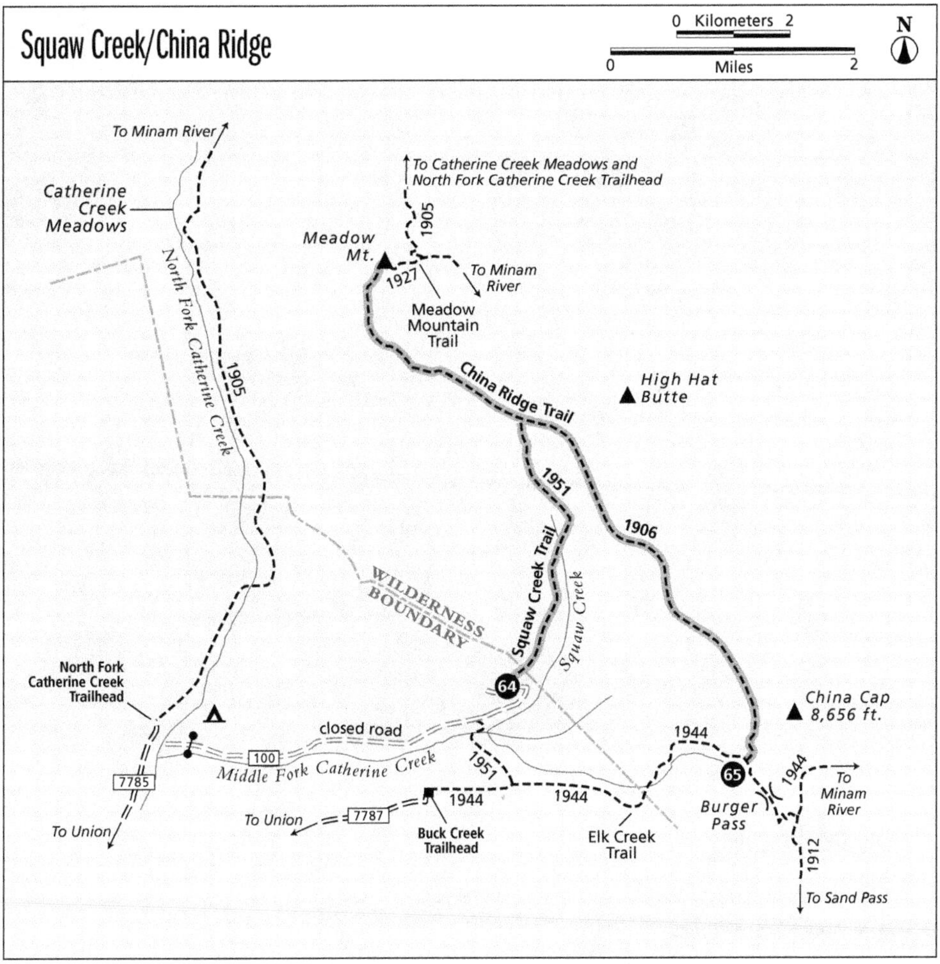

After the crossing the trail heads up on the right (east) side of Squaw Creek, going through an open sloping meadow for some distance. In this open area watch for elk grazing on the grassy slopes above. A campsite is 0.6 mile beyond the crossing on the left side of the trail near the creek. Beyond this point there is no water in late summer and fall. Beyond the campsite the trail climbs fairly steeply for the last 0.75 mile to the junction with China Ridge Trail.

The junction with China Ridge Trail is in a saddle (7,430 ft.) on the ridge dividing the Catherine Creek and Minam River drainages. The trail at the junction may be hard to see because the saddle is covered with thick grass.

Squaw Creek Trail (1951) is fairly easy to follow. However, cattle use this area, so there are some "extra" trails.

Flowers in upper Squaw Creek Canyon.

Miles and Directions

0.0 Leave FR 100 on the Squaw Creek Trail (1951).

1.8 Cross Squaw Creek.

3.0 Arrive at the junction with China Ridge Trail (1906). (GPS: N45 11.430'/W117 33.565')

65 China Ridge

This connecting trail leads from Elk Creek Trail (1944) to Meadow Mountain and Meadow Mountain Trail (1927). The trail also connects with Squaw Creek Trail (1951). This is a ridgetop trail with fantastic views. (Trail 1906)

See map page 231.
Distance: 6.4 miles one way
Hiking time: 2.5–3.5 hours
Difficulty: Strenuous
Trail maintenance: Seldom
Best season: July through mid-Oct
Traffic and other trail users: Lightfoot traffic; little or no horse traffic
Canine compatibility: Dogs permitted without leashes, but must be kept away from the stock of other parties
Fees and permits: Northwest Forest Pass and Eagle Cap Wilderness Permit
Maximum elevation: 8,010 feet
Maps: USGS China Cap OR; Green Trails 475sx: Wallowa Mountains Eagle Cap Wilderness
Trail contact: USDA Forest Service Wallowa Mountains Office, 201 E 2nd St./ PO Box 905, Joseph, OR 97846; (541) 426-5546, (541) 426-4978; www.fs.usda.gov/wallowa-whitman; or USDA Forest Service Pine Field Office, 38470 Pine Town Ln., Halfway, OR 97834; (541) 742-7511. Office closed Dec 21 through Apr 30; contact Baker City office at (541) 523-6391.

Finding the trail: China Ridge Trail (1906) begins at a junction with Elk Creek Trail (1944), southwest of China Cap Mountain. To reach Buck Creek Trailhead where Elk Creek Trail begins, drive southwest from Union on OR 203 for 11.5 miles to the junction with FR 7785. Turn left on FR 7785 and follow it 4 miles to the junction with FR 7787. Turn right on FR 7787 and go approximately 3.7 miles, then turn left and drive 0.3 mile to Buck Creek Trailhead. From Buck Creek Trailhead hike 3.8 miles east to the junction with the China Ridge Trail (7,450 ft.).
GPS: Buck Creek Trailhead: N45 08.919'/W117.34.340'; China Ridge Trail junction: N45 08.995'/W117 31.128'

The Hike

China Ridge Trail heads north from the junction with Elk Creek Trail. It climbs through open forest of lodgepole pine and subalpine fir, with China Cap to the right as it heads north. The trail crosses a very small stream 0.3 mile after leaving the junction. The first whitebark pines start showing up near this creek crossing. After the creek crossing, the trail comes to a saddle in 0.3 mile. This saddle is on the ridge that divides the Minam River and Catherine Creek drainages. The saddle is 0.5 mile west-northwest of China Cap Mountain. From the saddle it is quite easy to climb to the peak.

After crossing the saddle the trail traverses northeast on the right side of the ridgeline, offering a magnificent view of the Minam River Canyon to the northwest. The trail stays on the right side of the ridge for 0.6 mile, then crosses the ridge at 8,000 feet. Another 150 yards farther the trail crosses to the right side again, but now stays

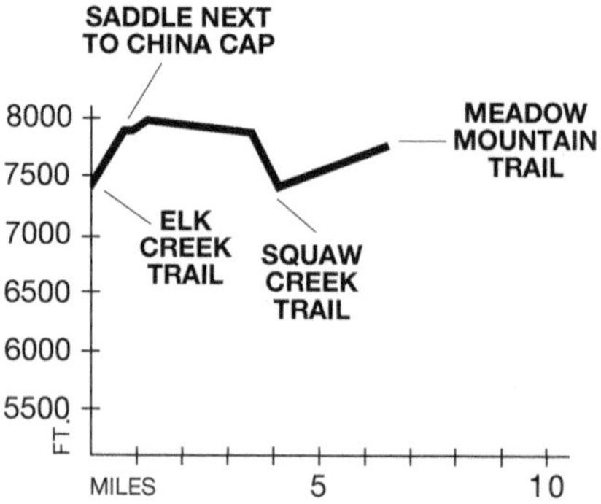

close to the top of the ridgeline. Begin a traverse along the right side of the ridgeline about 700 yards farther along. This traverse lasts 0.5 mile before the trail regains the ridgeline again. After regaining the ridgeline it goes off on the left side and passes some very old, large whitebark pine trees. After being on the left side of the ridgeline for 0.6 mile, the trail traverses a steep rocky area. It then climbs nearly back to the ridgeline.

The trail stays close to the ridgeline while continuing to traverse the rocky, steep, sidehill. After 0.4 mile the trail comes to a saddle in the ridge. Another trail turns off to the right: Be careful not to take it, as it drops off quickly the wrong way. This side trail is not marked and is not on Eagle Cap Wilderness maps or USGS quads.

From the saddle the China Ridge Trail traverses on the left side of the ridge again. It crosses a grassy slope with stands of whitebark pine and subalpine fir. After traversing for 0.7 mile, the trail gets back to the ridgeline. It then drops down the ridge 350 yards to the junction (7,430 ft.) with Squaw Creek Trail (1951). This unmarked junction is at a low spot in the ridge, 4.1 miles from Elk Creek Trail. The trails here are difficult to see because of the grass. Squaw Creek Trail turns off to the left (south-southeast) at the junction.

From the junction with Squaw Creek Trail, China Ridge Trail goes straight ahead, up the ridge to the west. It stays generally left of the ridgeline but gets very near to it in a saddle 0.7 mile from the junction (7,580 ft.). Beyond the saddle the trail climbs slightly. It stays on the left side of the ridge for just more than 0.5 mile, then gets back on top. After the trail gets back on top, the junction with Meadow Mountain Trail (1927; 7,800 ft.) is 0.2 mile farther.

There are few good campsites and very little water along this trail, but a mostly open ridge with a great view makes it well worth hiking.

Miles and Directions

0.0 From the junction with Elk Creek Trail (1944), head north on the China Ridge Trail (1906).

0.7 Reach the saddle below China Cap Mountain.

4.1 Pass the junction with Squaw Creek Trail (1951). (GPS: N45 11.430'/W117 33.565')

6.4 Arrive at the junction with Meadow Mountain Trail (1927).

66 Elk Creek

A backpack route that runs from Buck Creek Trailhead to the Minam River. This trail also gives access to Squaw Creek, China Ridge, Sand Pass, and Tombstone Lake Trails. (Trail 1944)

Distance: 11.6 miles one way
Hiking time: 4.5–7 hours, longer when returning
Difficulty: Moderate, but long
Trail maintenance: Infrequent
Best season: Mid-June through Oct
Traffic and other trail users: Light to moderate foot traffic; may be heavy during fall hunting seasons; moderate horse traffic
Canine compatibility: Dogs permitted without leashes, but must be kept away from the stock of other parties
Fees and permits: Northwest Forest Pass and Eagle Cap Wilderness Permit
Maximum elevation: 7,940 feet
Maps: USGS China Cap OR and Steamboat Lake OR; Geo Graphics Wallowa Mountains Eagle Cap Wilderness
Trail contact: USDA Forest Service Wallowa Mountains Office, 201 E 2nd St./PO Box 905, Joseph, OR 97846; (541) 426-5546, (541) 426-4978; www.fs.usda.gov/wallowa-whitman; or USDA Forest Service Pine Field Office, 38470 Pine Town Ln., Halfway, OR 97834; (541) 742-7511. Office closed Dec 21 through Apr 30; contact Baker City office at (541) 523-6391.

Finding the trailhead: From the town of Union, take OR 203 11.5 miles southeast. Turn left on FR 7785 and follow it 4 miles to the junction with FR 7787. Turn right on FR 7787 and go approximately 3.7 miles, then turn left and drive 0.3 mile to Buck Creek Trailhead.
GPS: N45 08.919'/W117.34.340'

The Hike

Hike east from the northeast corner of the Buck Creek Trailhead parking and camping area. In about 50 yards the trail crosses a roadbed. Continue east and in 0.7 mile you reach the unsigned junction with Trail 1951. Trail 1951, which was once the main Elk Creek Trail, descends to the north to join FR 100 in about 0.7 mile. Turn right at the junction and quickly reach the junction with now-abandoned Trail 1944A.

At the junction, Elk Creek Trail (1944) turns left (east) and climbs along the ridge for 0.5 mile. Then the route begins a traverse along the left side of the ridgeline. After traversing for 0.6 mile, it gets back on the ridgeline again (6,570 ft.). The trail goes up the ridgeline for 200 yards, then traverses up the right side for 600 yards, where there is a switchback to the left. The Eagle Cap Wilderness boundary (6,860 ft.) is 0.25 mile past the switchback.

After crossing the wilderness boundary, the trail rounds a point overlooking Squaw Creek and the Middle Fork Catherine Creek Canyon. It crosses a stream (7,060 ft.) 0.4 mile past the wilderness boundary. The trail crosses a rockslide area

0.4 mile after the stream crossing. From here you can see the flat-topped peak of China Cap Mountain to the northeast. A couple of hundred yards past the rockslide, the trail crosses a small stream, which may not have water in late summer. There is a meadow below the trail here.

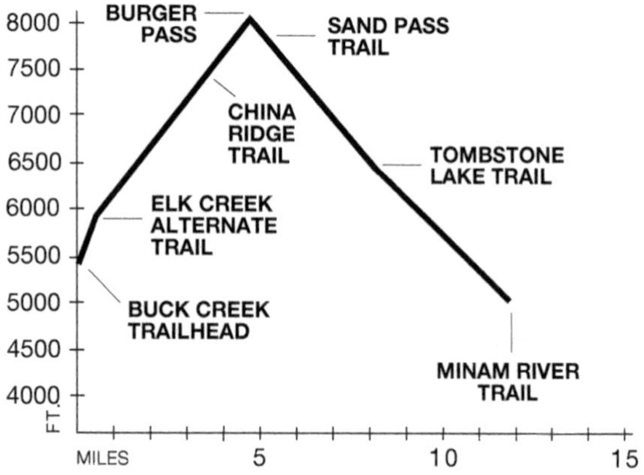

After traveling 200 yards past the meadow, a trail goes off to the right. Do not take this trail. Go 200 yards more to the junction with China Ridge Trail (1906). This junction (7,440 ft.) is 3.8 miles from Buck Creek Trailhead and is marked with a sign.

At the junction Elk Creek Trail (1944) turns to the right (south). It winds its way 0.75 mile to the top of Burger Pass (7,940 ft.). Then it makes a descending traverse for 0.3 mile to the south. After the traverse it makes several switchbacks down to the junction with Sand Pass Trail (1912; 7,620 ft.). This junction is 1.5 miles from the China Ridge Trail junction. The Sand Pass Trail junction is on the west side of Burger Meadows. From the junction Sand Pass Trail can be seen as it climbs the light tan slope below Sand Pass, to the south.

Beyond the junction Elk Creek Trail heads north and northeast for 0.3 mile to the junction with Old Elk Creek Trail. Bear left to stay on the main trail, heading northeast for another 0.7 mile, where the trail makes a switchback to the right. There is a spring above the trail 200 yards past the switchback. Watch for mule deer, which seem to be plentiful in this area. A very small stream runs down across the trail from the spring.

The trail crosses three more very small streams in the next 600 yards to where it makes another switchback. There are two more small stream crossings in the 300 yards to the next switchback. After this switchback the trail descends, crossing two more small streams to another junction with Old Elk Creek Trail. The old trail comes up from the left. Just past this junction the trail crosses a larger stream. There is a waterfall above the trail here. A few yards farther is another junction with the old trail; it bears to the right here. The newer, main trail heads to the left and makes a couple of switchbacks. It then drops down across the meadow to the east and crosses Elk Creek as it goes the last few yards to the junction with Tombstone Lake Trail (1943). This junction (6,420 ft.) is 7.8 miles from Buck Creek Trailhead. There is a good campsite just before crossing Elk Creek on the lower end of the lush, but sometimes wet, meadow. See Tombstone Lake (hike 69).

At the junction Elk Creek Trail turns to the left (north). Between here and the next place that the trail crosses Elk Creek, some maps (USGS Steamboat Lake quad)

Elk Creek

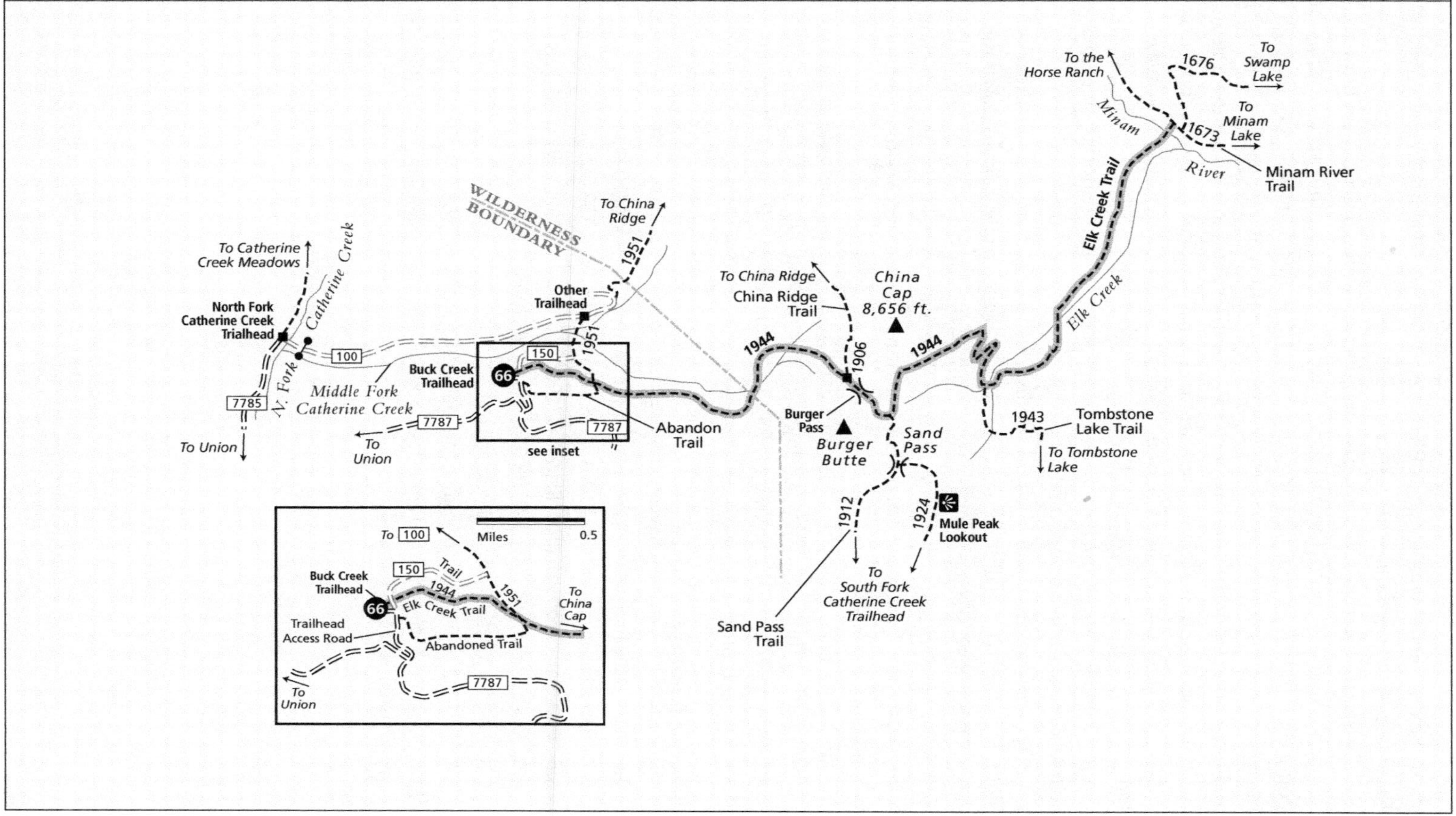

0 Kilometers 2
0 Miles 2
N
To the Horse Ranch
1676
To Swamp Lake
Minam
1673
To Minam Lake
River
Minam River Trail
Elk Creek Trail
Elk Creek
WILDERNESS BOUNDARY
To China Ridge
1951
To Catherine Creek Meadows
Catherine Creek
North Fork Catherine Creek Trialhead
Other Trailhead
100
150
1951
N. Fork
Buck Creek Trailhead
66
Middle Fork Catherine Creek
7785
7787
To Union
To Union
see inset
Abandon Trail
To China Ridge
China Ridge Trail
China Cap 8,656 ft.
1944
1906
1944
Burger Pass
Burger Butte
Sand Pass
1943
Tombstone Lake Trail
To Tombstone Lake
1912
1924
Mule Peak Lookout
To South Fork Catherine Creek Trailhead
Sand Pass Trail
To 100
Miles 0.5
150
Trail
1944
1951
Buck Creek Trailhead
66
Elk Creek Trail
To China Cap
Trailhead Access Road
Abandoned Trail
7787
To Union

show the trail on the wrong side of Elk Creek. The Geo Graphics Wallowa Mountains Eagle Cap Wilderness map shows it correctly.

The stream crossing 125 yards past the junction is the outlet of Tombstone Lake. There is a waterfall below the trail to the left, 175 yards past the creek crossing. After going 0.25 mile from the junction, there is a burn area. The trail goes through the burn for about 250 yards. Another 350 yards down the trail is a switchback to the left, and one to the right 250 yards farther along. Another 250 yards farther the trail enters the burn area again. It stays in the burn area for about 350 yards this time, making two switchbacks and crossing a stream. The trail crosses another stream as it leaves the burn. The trail makes a switchback to the left 350 yards after leaving the burn and crosses a creek a short distance later. It then drops, making another switchback to where it crosses Elk Creek (5,870 ft.).

After crossing Elk Creek the trail climbs a few feet and makes a switchback to the right. It crosses five small streams in the next 1.4 miles while it heads down the west side of Elk Creek, staying well above it most of the time. The forest here is thicker than it was up above, and the trees are larger. There are several log steps in the trail 3.3 miles below the Tombstone Lake Trail junction. The trail reaches the Minam River 0.5 mile past the steps.

There is a bridge over the Minam River here. A good campsite is located just before crossing the river. After crossing the river the trail climbs for 100 yards to the junction with Minam River Trail (1673). This junction (4,910 ft.) is 11.6 miles from Buck Creek Trailhead.

Miles and Directions

0.0 Start at the Buck Creek Trailhead and walk east on Elk Creek Trail (1944).

0.7 Reach the junction with Trail 1951. (GPS: N45 08.873'/W117 33.565')

3.8 Pass the junction with China Ridge Trail (1906). (GPS: N45 08.995'/W117 31.128')

4.9 Cross Burger Pass. (GPS: N45 08.674'/W117 30.799')

5.3 Pass the junction with Sand Pass Trail (1912).

7.8 Pass the junction with Tombstone Lake Trail (1943). (GPS: N45 08.794'/W117 29.615')

11.6 Cross the Minam River and arrive at the junction with Minam River Trail (1673). (GPS: N45 10.856'/W117 27.754')

67 Sand Pass

This steep, sometimes difficult-to-find trail connects the obscure South Fork Catherine Creek Trailhead with Elk Creek Trail (1944). This trail also allows access to Mule Peak Trail. (Trail 1912)

Distance: 6.4 miles one way
Hiking time: 3–4.5 hours
Difficulty: Strenuous
Trail maintenance: Seldom
Best season: July through Sept
Traffic and other trail users: Light foot and horse traffic
Canine compatibility: Dogs permitted without leashes, but must be kept away from the stock of other parties
Fees and permits: Eagle Cap Wilderness Permit
Maximum elevation: 8,120 feet
Maps: USGS Flagstaff Butte OR and China Cap OR; Geo Graphics Wallowa Mountains Eagle Cap Wilderness
Trail contact: USDA Forest Service Wallowa Mountains Office, 201 E 2nd St./ PO Box 905, Joseph, OR 97846; (541) 426-5546, (541) 426-4978; www.fs.usda.gov/wallowa-whitman; or USDA Forest Service Pine Field Office, 38470 Pine Town Ln., Halfway, OR 97834; (541) 742-7511. Office closed Dec 21 through Apr 30; contact Baker City office at (541) 523-6391.

Finding the trailhead: To get to the South Fork Catherine Creek Trailhead, take OR 203 for 13.5 miles southeast from the town of Union. Turn left on FR 77 and follow it for approximately 9 miles to the junction with FR 600. Turn left on FR 600 and go approximately 3 miles to the junction with FR 650. Turn right and find a parking spot. FR 650 is closed to vehicles and blocked off. This is the trailhead for Sand Pass and Mule Peak Trails (4,880 ft.). A good map is a big help in finding the trailhead.
GPS: N45 06.481'/W117 33.594'

The Hike

The trail starts out as a continuation of FR 650. First the trail (road) crosses a creek and passes a trail sign. Cross Sand Pass Creek 0.25 mile from the trailhead. There is a spring above the trail (road), 0.2 mile past Sand Pass Creek. A tiny stream originates at the spring and crosses the trail. After going 0.3 mile past the spring, the trail turns left on spur FR 660. This is a much poorer road. There is a trail sign a few yards up FR 660 (5,270 ft.). After going 0.1 mile up FR 660, the trail switchbacks to the left on yet another spur road, which becomes a trail 1 mile from the trailhead.

After leaving the road the trail climbs for 0.3 mile, nearly to the top of a rounded ridgeline. It makes a couple of switchbacks while climbing to the ridgeline. Here it turns right (northeast) and heads up, just to the right of the ridgeline. After climbing along the ridge for 1.4 miles, the trail comes to the top of a small, open, rounded hilltop (6,250 ft.). Here the trail drops a few feet, then starts to climb again. After climbing for 300 yards, it makes a switchback to the left. At 0.25 mile past the switchback, the trail crosses a small stream and enters an open area. It makes a switchback to the left 300 yards after crossing the small stream. A path goes straight ahead at this switchback. Do not take it.

At the switchback the trail starts an ascending traverse to the northwest through an open area. After climbing the ascending traverse for 500 yards, the trail comes to the junction with Mule Peak Trail (1924). This junction (6,760 ft.) is marked only with a pile of rocks. The Mule Peak Trail, which turns off to the right (northeast), is difficult to see as it has been overgrown with grass. To the northeast, Mule Peak Lookout can be seen from this open area. It is quite a distance away and a bit hard to spot.

The trail leaves the open area 150 yards past the junction. It goes along a semiopen hillside for 0.25 mile, then drops slightly to cross Sand Pass Creek (6,670 ft.). There is a campsite at the crossing, and a trail heads west-southwest past the campsite. This trail can be taken for a short distance, then turns right up a semiopen ridge to regain Sand Pass Trail, but Sand Pass Trail actually turns right just after the creek crossing. Up to this point the trail has been easy to follow, but from here on it is more of a challenge.

Turn right just after crossing Sand Pass Creek and head north. Watch for blazes marking the trail. There may be a lot of blown-down trees in this area. Head north and up for 0.25 mile and enter an open area. The trail goes along the right (east) side of this open area. It crosses a small stream at 6,950 feet, and 275 yards past the stream it bears to the left into the open area. Here it can be seen in most places.

The trail, which is deeply eroded in places, then twists its way up a small rib through country that is becoming more alpine. Continue to head up, to the north. After climbing the rib for 0.3 mile, the trail turns off to the right. It soon heads steeply up to the north again for 400 yards. The trail then crosses a small stream and heads northeast for 150 yards. It turns north again and heads up another 150 yards to another small stream. This stream comes out of the bottom of a rocky slope. Cross the stream and head northeast for 150 yards to another small stream. This stream also comes out of the rocky slope. After crossing this stream the trail winds uphill, steeply, for 0.5 mile to Sand Pass.

Sand Pass (8,120 ft.) is a light tan, sandy notch between dark rock outcroppings on the ridgeline. There is a signpost at the pass pointing to Mule Peak, which is to the right (east). It also points straight ahead and down to the Minam River. At Sand Pass the view to the north opens up. Looking down from this alpine notch you see Burger Meadow and the nearly 3,000-foot-deep Minam River

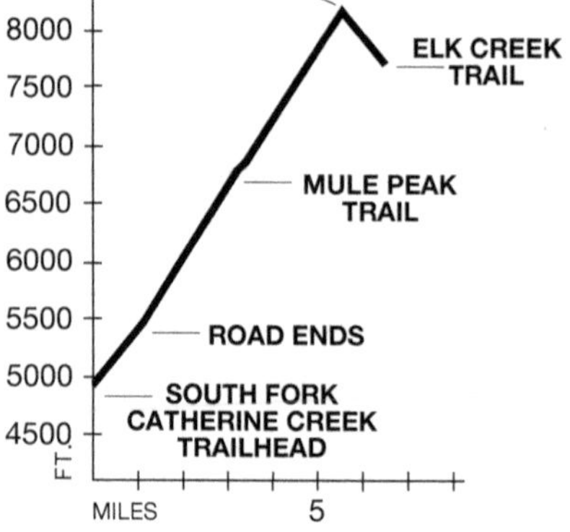

Sand Pass/Mule Peak

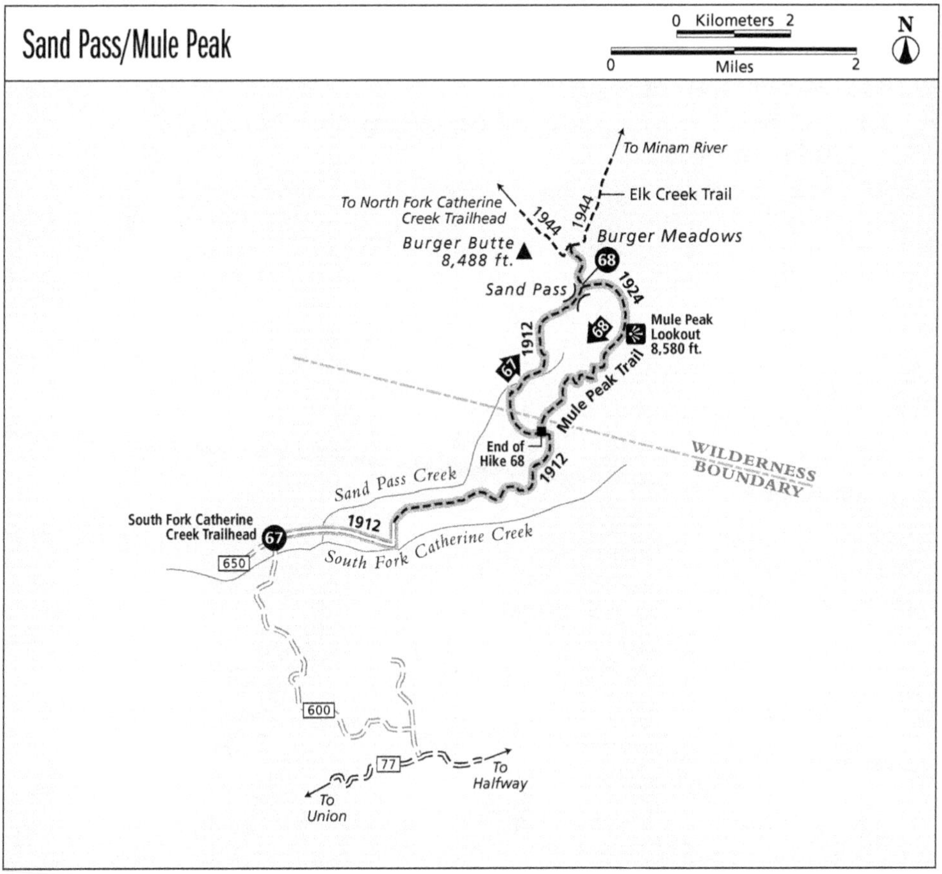

Canyon. The high peaks of the north-central Wallowa Mountains are to the northeast, in the distance, and China Cap is to the northwest.

After crossing Sand Pass the trail makes six steep downhill switchbacks. It then bears left and winds its way down along the west side of Burger Meadow to the junction with Elk Creek Trail (1944). The junction (7,620 ft.) is 1 mile from Sand Pass and 6.4 miles from the trailhead.

This trail is quite difficult to follow for 2 miles south of Sand Pass. Good route-finding skills are required for this section. The rest of the trail is in good condition and is fairly easy to follow. Sand Pass Trail climbs 3,200 vertical feet and is a fairly strenuous hike. A loop hike can be made from Sand Pass by taking Mule Peak Trail to the right and rejoining Sand Pass Trail at the lower Mule Peak Trail junction.

Miles and Directions

0.0 Start at the South Fork Catherine Creek Trailhead (1912).

0.2 Cross Sand Pass Creek.

0.4 Pass the spring.

1.0 The roadbed ends.

1.3 The trail reaches the ridgeline.

3.1 Pass the junction with the lower end of Mule Peak Trail (1924).

5.3 Reach Sand Pass and the junction with the upper end of Mule Peak Trail. (GPS: N45 08.234'/W117 30.537')

6.4 Arrive at the junction with Elk Creek Trail (1944).

68 Mule Peak

This trail runs along the ridge from Sand Pass to Mule Peak Lookout, and then down to Sand Pass Trail. There is a great view from Mule Peak Lookout. (Trail 1924)

See map page 241.
Distance: 3.1 miles one way
Hiking time: 1.5–2 hours
Difficulty: Strenuous
Trail maintenance: Rare
Best season: July through Sept
Traffic and other trail users: Light foot and very little horse traffic
Canine compatibility: Dogs permitted without leashes, but must be kept away from the stock of other parties
Fees and permits: Eagle Cap Wilderness Permit
Maximum elevation: 8,580 feet
Maps: USGS Flagstaff Butte OR and China Cap OR; Geo Graphics Wallowa Mountains Eagle Cap Wilderness
Trail contact: USDA Forest Service Wallowa Mountains Office, 201 E 2nd St./ PO Box 905, Joseph, OR 97846; (541) 426-5546, (541) 426-4978; www.fs.usda.gov/wallowa-whitman; or USDA Forest Service Pine Field Office, 38470 Pine Town Ln., Halfway, OR 97834; (541) 742-7511. Office closed Dec 21 through Apr 30; contact Baker City office at (541) 523-6391.

Finding the trail: To get to the South Fork Catherine Creek Trailhead, and Sand Pass Trail, take OR 203 for 13.5 miles southeast from the town of Union. Turn left on FR 77 and follow it for approximately 9 miles to the junction with FR 600. Turn left on FR 600 and go approximately 3 miles to the junction with FR 650. Turn right and find a parking spot. FR 650 is closed to vehicles and blocked off. This is the trailhead for Sand Pass and Mule Peak Trails (4,880 ft.). A good map is a big help in finding the trailhead. From the trailhead hike northeast on Sand Pass Trail (1912) for 5.3 miles to Sand Pass and the upper junction with the Mule Peak Trail (8,120 ft.).
GPS: South Fork Catherine Creek Trailhead: N45 06.481'/W117 33.594'; Mule Peak Trail junction: N45 08.234'/W117 30.537'

The Hike

From Sand Pass, Mule Peak Trail heads east, up along the left side of the ridgeline. This is a fairly open alpine area, with whitebark pine and subalpine fir trees. Burger Meadows can be seen below to the left. The trail is marked with cairns in this area.

After the trail climbs for 0.2 mile, there is a switchback to the right. Follow the cairns and blazes. Beyond the switchback the trail winds uphill, first northeast, then east, then southeast, for another 0.2 mile, to the ridgeline. After reaching the ridgeline, the trail heads up over light-colored granite sand to the east-northeast. It soon turns to the right and traverses on the right side of the ridgeline, heading southeast. The slope along this traverse is covered with granite boulders and small alpine trees. The trail drops slightly and comes to a saddle (8,430 ft.) after traversing 0.2 mile.

After going across this saddle, the trail heads up the ridge to the east-southeast for 0.1 mile to another saddle. It then climbs up the ridge 300 yards, passing an outhouse, to Mule Peak Lookout (8,580 ft.). The open area where Mule Peak Trail meets Sand Pass Trail can be seen below, to the south-southwest. Take a note of its location before descending.

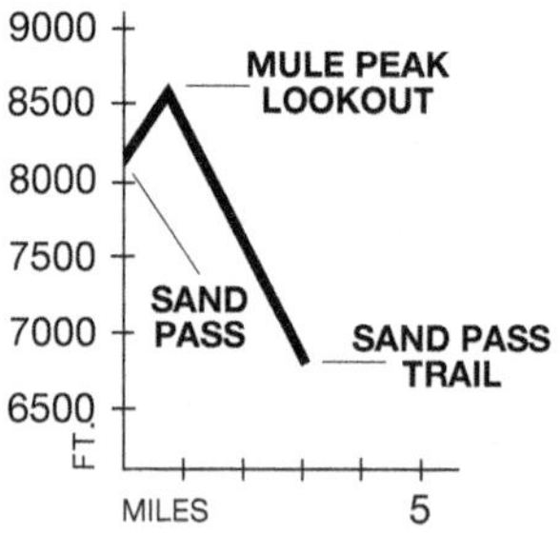

A few yards past the lookout, the trail turns down to the right (south). It makes six switchbacks in the next 600 yards, then turns down steeply for 150 yards. Watch for cairns and blazes. The trail makes six more switchbacks in the next 0.4 mile, then goes down steeply again for 50 yards. The trail is badly eroded here. It makes five more switchbacks in the next 0.1 mile to a stream crossing (7,790 ft.). This is a very small stream. In the next 0.5 mile the trail makes six more switchbacks. It then heads south on a grassy, open hillside.

The trail may be hard to see in this grassy area. After going 0.4 mile along and down this open hillside, the trail makes a switchback to the right. The Eagle Cap Wilderness boundary sign is 5 yards past the switchback on the left side of the trail. From the switchback to the junction with Sand Pass Trail, Mule Peak Trail heads southwest. It goes through a finger of timber and meets the Sand Pass Trail 350 yards from the last switchback. Elevation at the junction is 6,760 feet. There is no sign marking the junction.

This trail takes some route-finding skill to follow. It may be done as part of a loop hike with Sand Pass Trail (hike 67).

Miles and Directions

0.0 At Sand Pass and the junction with Sand Pass Trail (1912), head east on the Mule Peak Trail (1924).

0.8 Arrive at the Mule Peak Lookout. (GPS: N45 07.825'/W117 30.159')

2.9 Pass the Eagle Cap Wilderness boundary.

3.1 Arrive at the junction with Sand Pass Trail.

69 Tombstone Lake

This backpack trail from Elk Creek Trail climbs over an 8,210-foot-high pass to West Fork Eagle Creek Trail. Besides Tombstone Lake, this trail is also the access to Diamond Lake. (Trail 1943)

Distance: 8.1 miles one way
Hiking time: 3.5–5 hours
Difficulty: Moderate to strenuous
Trail maintenance: Infrequent
Best season: July through Sept
Traffic and other trail users: Moderate foot and horse traffic
Canine compatibility: Dogs permitted without leashes, but must be kept away from the stock of other parties
Fees and permits: Northwest Forest Pass and Eagle Cap Wilderness Permit
Maximum elevation: 8,210 feet
Maps: USGS Steamboat Lake OR and Bennet Peak OR
Trail contact: USDA Forest Service Wallowa Mountains Office, 201 E 2nd St./ PO Box 905, Joseph, OR 97846; (541) 426-5546, (541) 426-4978; www.fs.usda.gov/wallowa-whitman; or USDA Forest Service Pine Field Office, 38470 Pine Town Ln., Halfway, OR 97834; (541) 742-7511. Office closed Dec 21 through Apr 30; contact Baker City office at (541) 523-6391.

Finding the trail: To reach Buck Creek Trailhead where Elk Creek Trail begins, drive southwest from Union on OR 203 for 11.5 miles to the junction with FR 7785. Turn left on FR 7785 and follow it 4 miles to the junction with FR 7787. Turn right on FR 7787 and go approximately 3.7 miles, then turn left and drive 0.3 mile to Buck Creek Trailhead. From Buck Creek Trailhead hike 7.8 miles east on the Elk Creek Trail (1944) to the junction with the Tombstone Lake Trail. This junction is only 3.8 miles up Elk Creek Trail from the Minam River.
GPS: Buck Creek Trailhead: N45 08.919'/W117.34.340'; Tombstone Lake Trail junction: N45 08.794'/W117 29.615'

The Hike

From the junction with Elk Creek Trail (6,420 ft.), Tombstone Lake Trail heads southeast. It crosses a small stream 350 yards from the junction. It then makes a switchback to the left and crosses the same stream again. In the next 0.4 mile the trail makes twelve more switchbacks to where it crosses another stream, with a campsite by the crossing. Elevation at the campsite is 6,700 feet.

A path goes to the left here, but Tombstone Lake Trail goes straight ahead. In the next mile the trail makes thirteen switchbacks and climbs 600 feet. It goes over the top of a rise at 7,300 feet, then drops for 200 yards to the junction with Diamond Lake Trail (7,250 ft.). This junction is not marked with a sign, but a good path heads 0.1 mile to the left (north) to Diamond Lake.

Just past the Diamond Lake junction, the trail goes by a small meadow. It then makes an ascending traverse along a talus slope. The trail makes a switchback to the

Tombstone Lake. LOWELL EUHUS PHOTO

right 275 yards past the Diamond Lake junction. It makes four more switchbacks in the next 400 yards as it climbs to the top of the rise. A few yards farther is Tombstone Lake. Tombstone Lake (7,421 ft.) is 2.4 miles from Elk Creek Trail. There are a few campsites at the lake and, like most of the lakes in the Wallowas, the fishing is good to excellent.

The trail goes along the left (northeast) side of the lake and soon begins to climb away from it. There is a campsite between the trail and the lake as the trail climbs away. The trail makes sixteen switchbacks in the first 0.8 mile after leaving Tombstone Lake. It then makes an ascending traverse to the south for another 0.5 mile. After the traverse the trail makes three more switchbacks up to the pass (8,210 ft.). The ridge that this pass is on divides the Elk Creek and West Fork Eagle Creek drainages.

After crossing the pass the trail heads down toward West Fork Eagle Creek. A few yards below the pass the trail makes a switchback. It then winds on down through granite outcroppings and scattered small trees. The trail makes another switchback 0.3 mile below the pass. In the next 0.9 mile, to a small meadow, the trail makes sixteen more switchbacks. The trail then makes a left turn as it comes into the meadow (7,520 ft.). There is a streambed in the meadow, but it was dry in September, when we hiked this trail. The trail crosses the meadow.

The trail makes a switchback to the left 275 yards past the meadow, then one to the right. Just past the switchbacks the trail crosses a small stream, which may also be dry by September. The trail then starts a set of thirty-three switchbacks, 250 yards past the stream. There is one small stream that goes through a culvert under

Tombstone Lake/Diamond Lake

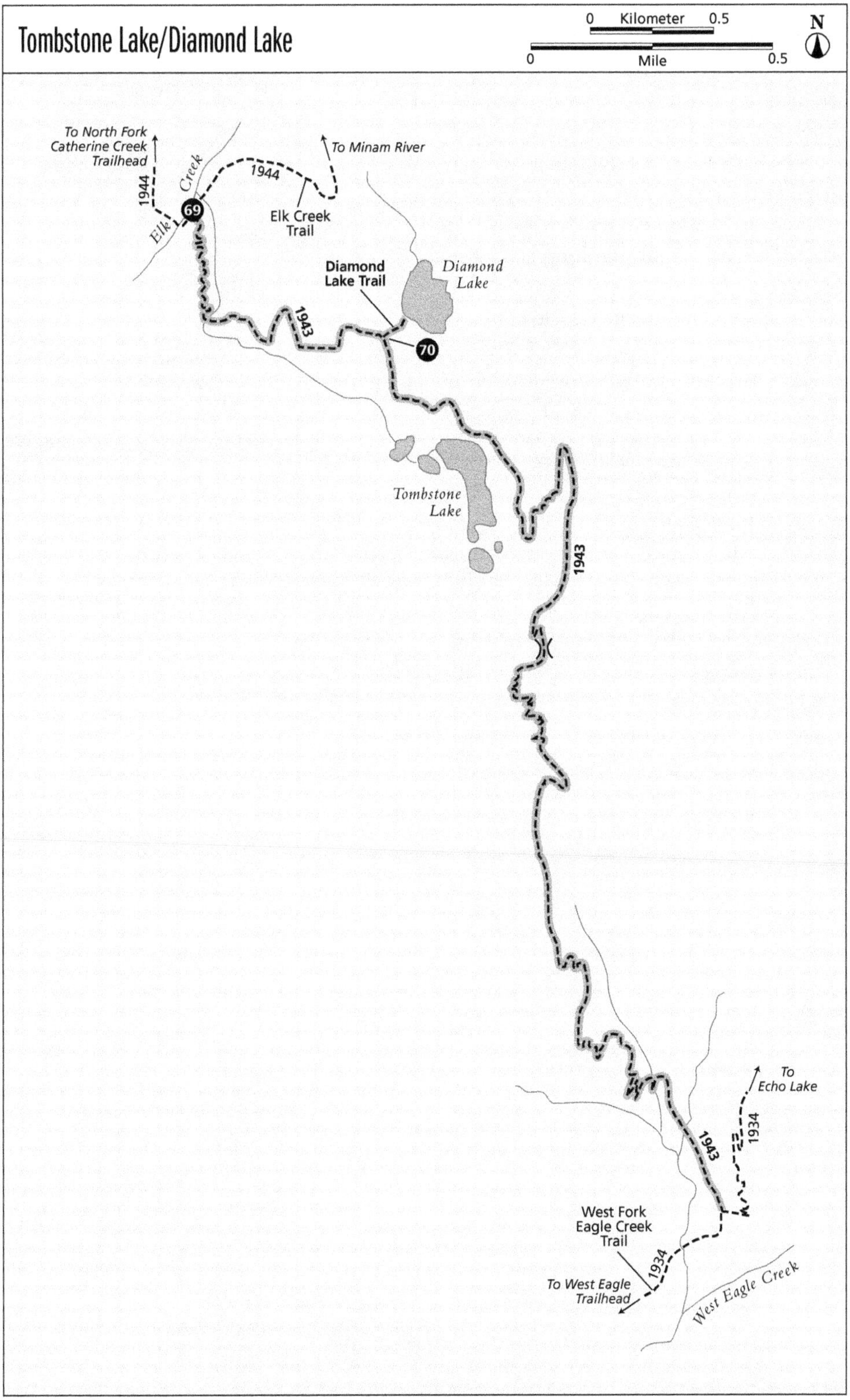

0 Kilometer 0.5
0 Mile 0.5
N
To North Fork Catherine Creek Trailhead
To Minam River
1944
1944
Elk Creek
69
Elk Creek Trail
Diamond Lake Trail
Diamond Lake
1943
70
Tombstone Lake
1943
To Echo Lake
1934
1943
West Fork Eagle Creek Trail
1934
To West Eagle Trailhead
West Eagle Creek

the trail, and a small waterfall next to the trail on the twenty-ninth switchback. This set of switchbacks is 2.4 miles long and drops 1,020 feet to a creek crossing. After the creek crossing the switchbacks begin again. There are thirteen more switchbacks on the way to another creek crossing. This set of thirteen is 0.4 mile long and drops 230 feet.

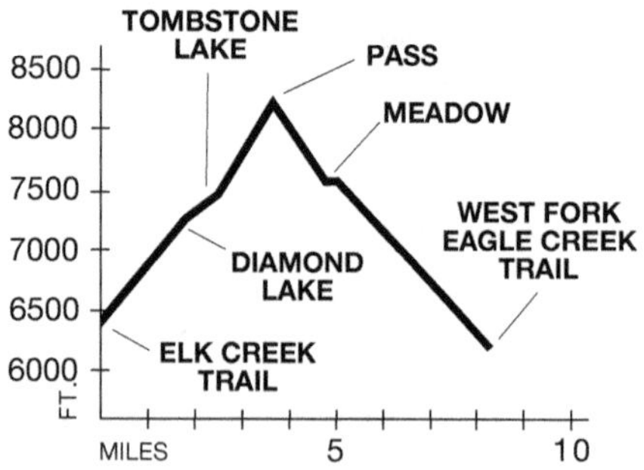

Cross West Fork Eagle Creek; the junction with West Fork Eagle Creek Trail (1934; 6,250 ft.) is 400 yards past the creek crossing. This junction is 8.1 miles from the junction with Elk Creek Trail.

A one-way trip can be made from the West Fork Eagle Creek Trail junction by heading south on West Fork Eagle Creek Trail to West Eagle Trailhead, 2.6 miles away. This trip involves a car shuttle.

Miles and Directions

0.0 From the junction with Elk Creek Trail (1944), take the Tombstone Lake Trail (1943) to the southeast.

1.8 Pass the junction with Diamond Lake Trail.

2.4 Arrive at Tombstone Lake. (GPS: N45 08.290'/W117 28.722')

3.7 Cross the pass.

4.9 Pass through a meadow.

8.1 Arrive at the junction with West Fork Eagle Creek Trail (1934).

70 Diamond Lake

This path connects Tombstone Lake Trail (1943) with Diamond Lake.

See map page 247.
Distance: 0.1 mile one way from Tombstone Lake Trail
Hiking time: About 5 minutes from Tombstone Lake Trail
Difficulty: Easy
Trail maintenance: None
Best season: Mid-June through Oct
Traffic and other trail users: Light to moderate foot and horse traffic
Canine compatibility: Dogs permitted without leashes, but must be kept away from the stock of other parties
Fees and permits: Northwest Forest Pass and Eagle Cap Wilderness Permit
Maximum elevation: 7,250 feet
Map: USGS Steamboat Lake OR
Trail contact: USDA Forest Service Wallowa Mountains Office, 201 E 2nd St./ PO Box 905, Joseph, OR 97846; (541) 426-5546, (541) 426-4978; www.fs.usda.gov/wallowa-whitman; or USDA Forest Service Pine Field Office, 38470 Pine Town Ln., Halfway, OR 97834; (541) 742-7511. Office closed Dec 21 through Apr 30; contact Baker City office at (541) 523-6391.

Finding the trail: To reach the junction with the Tombstone Lake Trail, where the path to Diamond Lake starts, first drive southwest from Union on OR 203 for 11.5 miles to the junction with FR 7785. Turn left on FR 7785 and follow it 4 miles to the junction with FR 7787. Turn right on FR 7787 and go approximately 3.7 miles, then turn left and drive 0.3 mile to Buck Creek Trailhead. From Buck Creek Trailhead hike 7.8 miles east on the Elk Creek Trail (1944) to the junction with the Tombstone Lake Trail. Turn right on the Tombstone Lake Trail (1943) and go 1.8 miles to the junction with the path to Diamond Lake (7,250 ft.). This junction may also be reached from the West Eagle Trailhead via the West Fork Eagle Creek Trail (1934) and the Tombstone Lake Trail.
GPS: Buck Creek Trailhead: N45 08.919'/W117.34.340'; Tombstone Lake Trail junction: N45 08.794'/W117 29.615'

The Hike

From the Tombstone Lake Trail, the path to Diamond Lake drops slightly to the north-northeast for 200 yards to a campsite overlooking the lake. There is a stream next to the campsite. The lake (7,041 ft.) is about 75 feet below the campsite. There are fish to be caught in the lake, but the campsites are very limited.

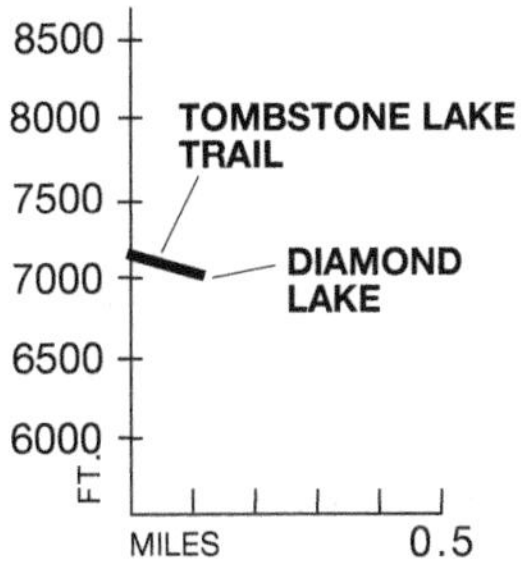

Miles and Directions

0.0 At the junction with Tombstone Lake Trail (1943), turn north-northeast on the Diamond Lake Trail.

0.1 Arrive at Diamond Lake. (GPS: N45 08.548'/W117 28.882')

71 West Fork Eagle Creek

This backpack route runs from West Eagle Creek Trailhead to the junction with Trail Creek Trail via Echo and Traverse Lakes. (Trail 1934)

Distance: 13.3 miles one way
Hiking time: 5.5–8 hours
Difficulty: Strenuous
Trail maintenance: Infrequent
Best season: Mid-July through Sept
Traffic and other trail users: Moderate foot and horse traffic
Canine compatibility: Dogs permitted without leashes, but must be kept away from the stock of other parties
Fees and permits: Northwest Forest Pass and Eagle Cap Wilderness Permit
Maximum elevation: 8,500 feet
Maps: USGS Bennet Peak OR and Steamboat Lake OR; Geo Graphics Wallowa Mountains Eagle Cap Wilderness
Trail contact: USDA Forest Service Wallowa Mountains Office, 201 E 2nd St./PO Box 905, Joseph, OR 97846; (541) 426-5546, (541) 426-4978; www.fs.usda.gov/wallowa-whitman; or USDA Forest Service Pine Field Office, 38470 Pine Town Ln., Halfway, OR 97834; (541) 742-7511. Office closed Dec 21 through Apr 30; contact Baker City office at (541) 523-6391.

Finding the trailhead: From Union take OR 203 southeast for 14.1 miles to the junction with Eagle Creek Road (FR 77). Turn left (east) on FR 77 and follow it 15.2 miles to the West Eagle Creek Trailhead junction. Turn left (north) into the parking area and campground. FR 77 is very rough in places.
GPS: N45 04.785'/W117 28.593'

The Hike

From the trailhead (5,460 ft.) the trail heads north, crossing a bridge over a small stream. It then passes through the timber along the east side of West Eagle Meadows for 0.5 mile to the unmarked junction with Fake Creek Trail. Fake Creek Trail bears right and crosses the ridge to Main Eagle Road near Boulder Park, 6 miles to the east.

At the junction West Eagle Creek Trail bears left (northwest). The trail crosses Fake Creek 0.2 mile past the junction. A few yards after crossing Fake Creek, the trail enters a lush meadow and crosses a small stream. It makes some small switchbacks 0.1 mile past the meadow, crosses a creek, and soon comes to the slightly more than knee-deep crossing of West Eagle Creek. This crossing may be much deeper and possibly dangerous during spring and early summer.

After the crossing the trail crosses a small stream on a bridge and comes to the Eagle Cap Wilderness boundary. The trail enters an open, sloping meadow covered with wildflowers 0.3 mile after entering the wilderness. It crosses a couple of small streams, then climbs three small switchbacks to the top of a granite outcropping overlooking the rushing waters of West Eagle Creek. Past the outcropping the trail makes several more switchbacks, climbing through the woods, then comes out on another open slope that is partly covered with brush. The trail crosses West Eagle Creek (5,850 ft.) again, 1.1 miles past the wilderness boundary.

Shortly after the knee-deep crossing, the trail begins to climb more steeply as it heads up in switchbacks on lightly timbered slopes toward the junction with Tombstone Lake Trail. On the climb the broad, cascading waterfall of the East Fork of the West Fork Eagle Creek can be seen to the east. The waterfall drops over a granite ledge and tumbles into a jungle of boulders and slide alder. After the trail climbs ten switchbacks, the trail junction with Tombstone Lake Trail (1943) is reached. See Tombstone Lake (hike 69).

From the junction with Tombstone Lake Trail (6,250 ft.), the trail starts the switchbacks heading up to Echo Lake. In the next 2 miles the trail makes forty switchbacks and climbs 800 vertical feet. This climb is mostly on open slopes.

After climbing the switchbacks the trail crosses the West Fork of Eagle Creek and gets off the sidehill that it has been on for the last 2 miles. Head to the east, up the high valley toward Echo Lake. There is a pond to the right of the trail 200 yards past the stream crossing. Beyond the pond the trail turns to the left, then makes a switchback to the right. There are two very small stream crossings 0.25 mile past the pond. There is a campsite on the right side of the trail 150 yards past the last stream crossing. Near the campsite two more small streams go under the trail in culverts. Echo Lake is 200 yards farther, on the right (south) side of the trail.

Echo Lake, like so many other lakes on the south side of the Wallowa Mountains, has been dammed. This damming allows the lakes to hold water for irrigation, but it makes them look a lot less beautiful than they once did. Because of the variation in water level, the lakes have areas of mud around their shorelines. The elevation at Echo Lake is 7,270 feet.

The trail goes along the left (north) side of the lake. It crosses a couple more very small streams that flow through culverts. Past the lake 0.4 mile, the trail makes four more switchbacks. The trail enters a talus slope 0.2 mile past the switchbacks. The talus slope is about 125 yards wide. Past the talus slope the trail traverses along a lightly wooded hillside for 200 yards. Then it makes two more switchbacks as it climbs the last 200 yards to Traverse Lake (7,720 ft.).

Traverse Lake is also a reservoir. There is a notch cut through the rock at its outlet. This allows water to be taken out below the lake's natural level. This notch is 5 or 6 feet deep and maybe 3 feet wide. A little dam down in the notch has a gate valve in it; this allows the outflow to be regulated. There are lots of possible campsites along the north side of Traverse Lake. When the water is low there is a sandy beach on the north side. There are also lots of brook trout in the lake.

After going along the north side of Traverse Lake, the trail begins to climb again. It makes twelve switchbacks in the first 0.8 mile above the lake, coming very close to the ridgeline. To the left of the trail and up a few feet is a viewpoint that overlooks Lowery Creek.

Falls in the East Fork of the West Fork Eagle Creek.

The trail makes a switchback to the left 300 yards past the viewpoint. This switchback is close to the base of a granite wall. Make nine more switchbacks before reaching Wonker Pass. This pass (8,500 ft.) is on the ridge dividing the West Fork Eagle Creek drainage and Trail Creek in the Minam River drainage. The view to the east-northeast is into Trail Creek Canyon. The slopes on the Trail Creek side are very alpine, having almost no trees for the first 1,000 feet down, unlike the Traverse Lake side, which has scattered whitebark pines all the way up.

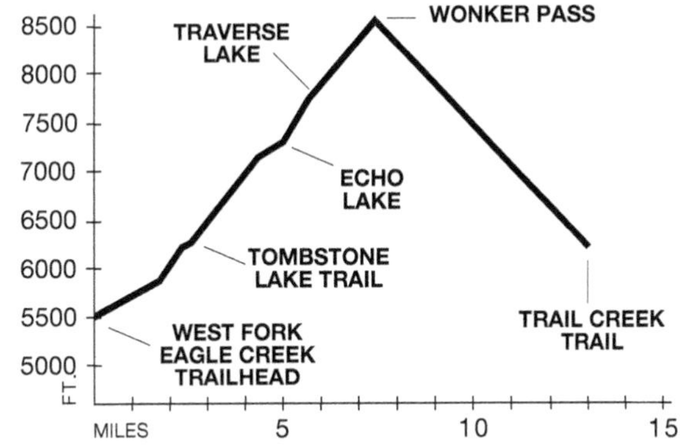

The trail heads down the Trail Creek side. It makes twenty-five switchbacks and then starts a long descending traverse. The trail crosses a very small stream 150 yards into the 0.75-mile-long traverse. By the end of the traverse the trail is in a lightly forested area again. After the traverse the trail makes eleven switchbacks in 1.5 miles, then crosses two very small streams in culverts, turns left, and goes 75 yards to a meadow (6,650 ft.). There is a finger of trees in the meadow with a campsite in it. The trail goes through the trees and crosses a creek on the far (south) side of the meadow. The trail may be difficult to see in the grass.

The trail soon begins to switchback down again, through much larger timber than there was above. It makes six switchbacks in the 0.7 mile to Trail Creek. The trail crosses the creek and climbs a few feet to the junction with Trail Creek Trail (1922; 6,240 ft.). The distance from West Eagle Trailhead to the junction with Trail Creek Trail is 13.3 miles. This is a fairly strenuous hike, but the country you go through is well worth it.

The return trip may be made by the same route, or by taking Trail Creek Trail and Main Eagle Creek Trail back to Main Eagle Trailhead. See Trail Creek (hike 74) and Main Eagle Creek (hike 73). A car shuttle can be done from Main Eagle Trailhead to West Eagle Trailhead. For the more ambitious and adventuresome hiker, the 6-mile-long Fake Creek Trail, which is not described in this book, can be taken over the ridge from Main Eagle Trailhead back to West Eagle Trailhead. This eliminates the need for a car shuttle, but it is quite strenuous and requires some route-finding skills.

Miles and Directions

0.0 Start at the West Eagle Creek Trailhead.

0.5 Pass the junction with Fake Creek Trail (1914).

1.2 Cross West Fork Eagle Creek.

2.4 Cross West Fork Eagle Creek again.

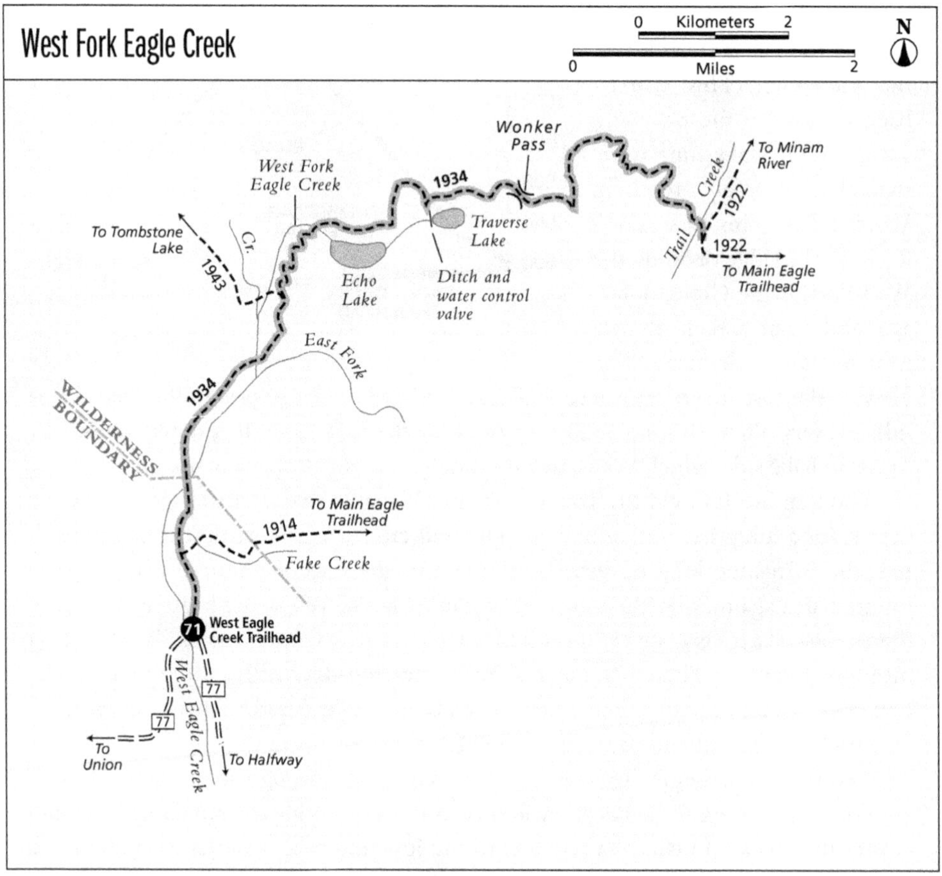

3.0 Pass the junction with Tombstone Lake Trail (1943).

5.4 Reach Echo Lake. (GPS: N45 07.070'/W117 27.135')

6.4 Reach Traverse Lake. (GPS: N45 07.290'/W117 26.400')

7.9 Top the pass. (GPS: N45 07.315'/W117 25.670')

13.3 Arrive at the junction with Trail Creek Trail (1922).

72 Bench Canyon

Climbing from Main Eagle Creek Trail to Trail Creek Trail, the Bench Canyon Trail traverses subalpine terrain with good chances for wildlife viewing. The route also provides access to Heart and Arrow Lakes. (Trail 1937)

Distance: 3.1 miles one way
Hiking time: 2–3 hours
Difficulty: Strenuous, as trail is very rough and rocky in places.
Trail maintenance: Seldom
Best season: July through Oct
Traffic and other trail users: Moderate foot traffic
Canine compatibility: Dogs permitted without leashes, but must be kept away from the stock of other parties
Fees and permits: Northwest Forest Pass and Eagle Cap Wilderness Permit
Maximum elevation: 7,840 feet
Map: USGS Bennet Peak OR
Trail contact: USDA Forest Service Wallowa Mountains Office, 201 E 2nd St./ PO Box 905, Joseph, OR 97846; (541) 426-5546, (541) 426-4978; www.fs.usda.gov/wallowa-whitman; or USDA Forest Service Pine Field Office, 38470 Pine Town Ln., Halfway, OR 97834; (541) 742-7511. Office closed Dec 21 through Apr 30; contact Baker City office at (541) 523-6391.

Finding the trail: Bench Canyon Trail leaves Main Eagle Creek Trail (1922) 2.6 miles north of Main Eagle Creek Trailhead. Main Eagle Creek Trail starts at Main Eagle Creek Trailhead. To reach the trailhead, take Big Creek Road (FR 67) east from the town of Medical Springs. Follow FR 67 approximately 16 miles to its junction with FR 77. Turn left on FR 77 and go 1 mile to the junction with FR 7755. Turn right on FR 7755 and go 6 miles to Boulder Park and Main Eagle Creek Trailhead (4,910 ft.). This is the site of the old Boulder Park Resort, which was wiped out by an avalanche some years ago. From the trailhead hike northeast on Main Eagle Creek Trail for 2.6 miles to the junction with the Bench Canyon Trail (5,750 ft.).
GPS: Main Eagle Trailhead: N45 04.089'/W117 24.391'

The Hike

At the junction with Main Eagle Creek Trail, Bench Canyon Trail turns off to the left (northwest). At first the trail winds steeply uphill, then it makes a long ascending traverse to the north. The trail crosses a small stream 0.7 mile after leaving Main Eagle Creek Trail. This crossing is at approximately 6,300 feet.

The trail makes eight switchbacks in the next 0.5 mile, to where it crosses another small stream. Here the trail gets off the sidehill and heads up Bench Canyon. It crosses another stream 500 yards farther along. The route is a little brushed in at this crossing. The trail tops a rise after another 0.4 mile.

There is a campsite on the right side of the trail 100 yards after topping the rise. The unmarked path to Heart Lake is about 300 yards past the campsite. Heart Lake is 0.25 mile to the left (south) of the trail. The path to the lake is hard to see, but the

Heart Lake.

lake can be seen from the top of the small rise just south of the trail. The elevation where the path to Heart Lake leaves the trail is 7,420 feet. The elevation of the lake is approximately 7,300 feet.

After passing the path to Heart Lake, the trail climbs steeply for 0.5 mile to Arrow Lake (7,800 ft.). Arrow Lake is the pond 100 yards to the left of the trail. There are probably no fish in the lake. After passing Arrow Lake the trail climbs gently for 250 yards to the top of a pass (7,840 ft.) on the ridge dividing the Eagle Creek and Minam River drainages.

After crossing the pass the trail drops a couple hundred yards to two small, steep switchbacks, then 500 yards more to a meadow. The swampy alpine meadow with a gray granite cliff and talus slope at its east end is on the right side of the trail. The lush meadow has several springs in its upper end. At the northwest end of the meadow the trail crosses the stream, which originates from the springs, and comes to the junction with Trail Creek Trail (7,410 ft.). This junction is 3.1 miles from the junction with Main Eagle Trail. Note that Trail Creek Trail and Main Eagle Trail

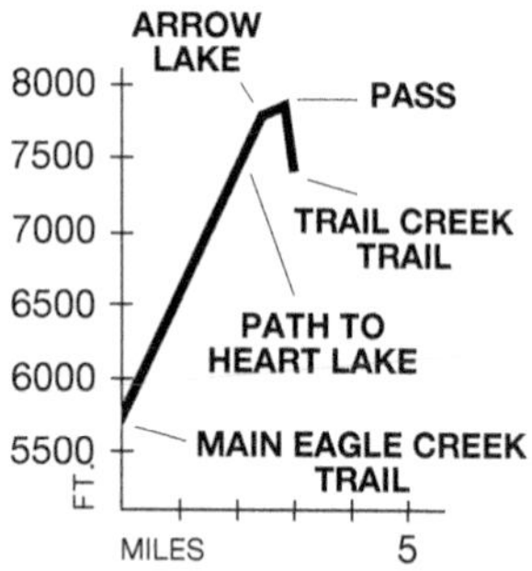

Bench Canyon

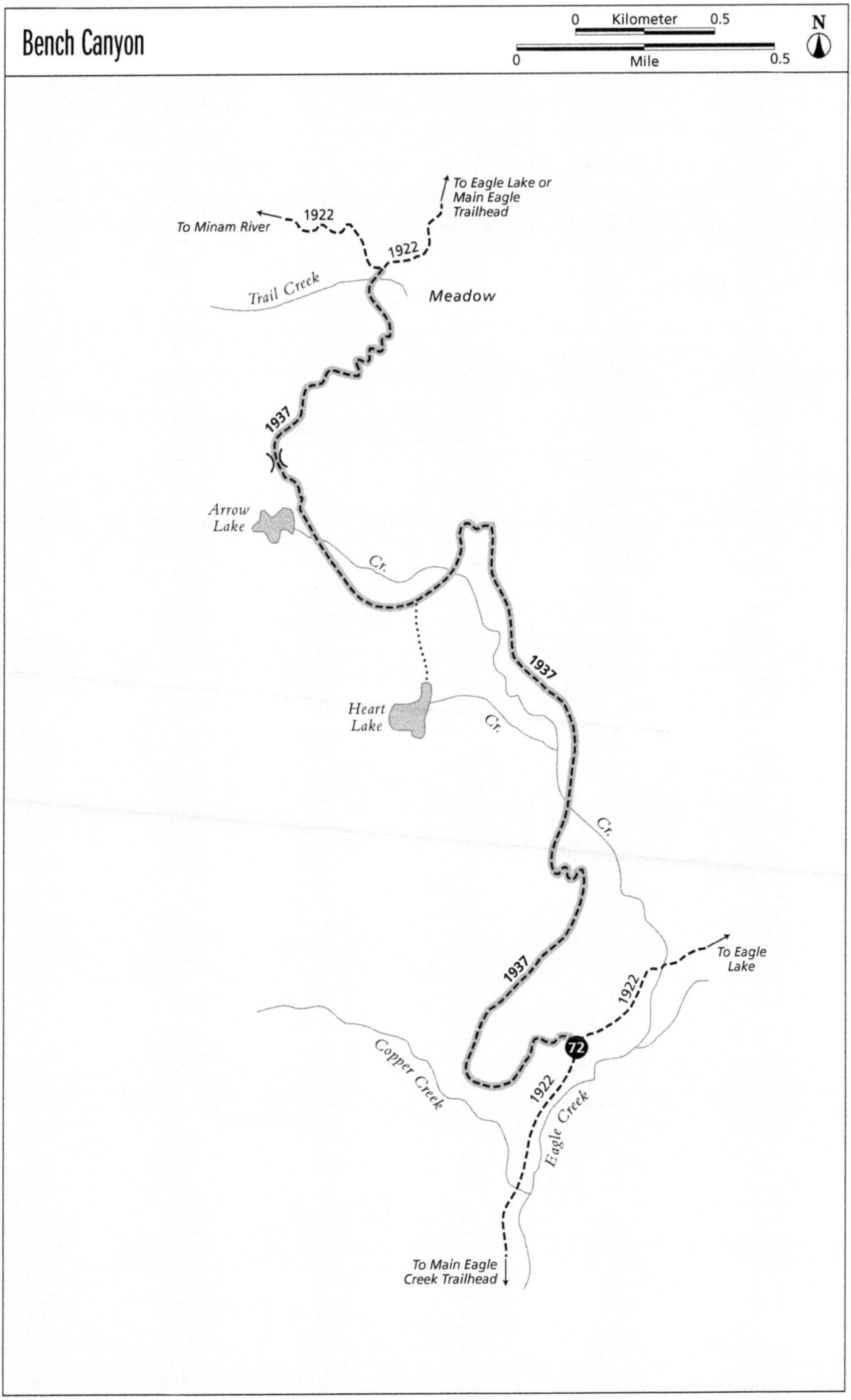

have the same trail number; Trail Creek Trail is a continuation of Main Eagle Creek Trail. See Trail Creek (hike 74).

Bench Canyon Trail is very rough and rocky, but easy to follow. It is fairly steep and gains almost 2,100 feet in the 2.75 miles up to the pass. From the junction with Trail Creek Trail, a loop hike can be made by turning right on Trail Creek Trail and following it and Main Eagle Creek Trail back to Main Eagle Creek Trailhead, also known as Boulder Park Trailhead.

Miles and Directions

0.0 At the junction with Main Eagle Creek Trail (1922), take the Bench Canyon Trail (1937) to the left. (GPS: N45 05.720' / W117 23.022')

1.5 Enter a burn area.

2.1 Pass the junction with the path to Heart Lake. (GPS: N45 06.508' / W117 23.224')

2.6 Pass Arrow Lake.

2.7 Cross the pass.

3.1 Arrive at the junction with Trail Creek Trail (1922). (GPS: N45 07.005'/W117 23.330')

73 Main Eagle Creek

This backpack or long day hike from Main Eagle Creek Trailhead to Eagle Lake accesses Bench Canyon, Lookingglass Lake, and Trail Creek Trails. (Trails 1922 and 1931)

Distance: 6.8 miles one way
Hiking time: 3.5–5 hours
Difficulty: Moderate
Trail maintenance: Infrequent
Best season: Mid-June through Sept
Traffic and other trail users: Heavy foot and horse traffic
Canine compatibility: Dogs permitted without leashes, but must be kept away from the stock of other parties
Fees and permits: Northwest Forest Pass and Eagle Cap Wilderness Permit
Maximum elevation: 7,450 feet
Maps: Bennet Peak OR, Krag Peak OR, and Eagle Cap OR; Geo Graphics Wallowa Mountains Eagle Cap Wilderness
Trail contact: USDA Forest Service Wallowa Mountains Office, 201 E 2nd St./PO Box 905, Joseph, OR 97846; (541) 426-5546, (541) 426-4978; www.fs.usda.gov/wallowa-whitman; or USDA Forest Service Pine Field Office, 38470 Pine Town Ln., Halfway, OR 97834; (541) 742-7511. Office closed Dec 21 through Apr 30; contact Baker City office at (541) 523-6391.

Finding the trailhead: Main Eagle Creek Trail starts at Main Eagle Creek Trailhead. To reach the trailhead, take Big Creek Road (FR 67) east from the town of Medical Springs. Follow FR 67 approximately 16 miles to its junction with FR 77. Turn left on FR 77 and go 1 mile to the junction with FR 7755. Turn right on FR 7755 and go 6 miles to Boulder Park and Main Eagle Creek Trailhead (4,910 ft.). This is the site of the old Boulder Park Resort, which was wiped out by an avalanche some years ago.
GPS: N45 04.089'/W117 24.391'

The Hike

The trail heads up the left (west) side of Eagle Creek and crosses Boulder Creek. It then climbs some distance away from Eagle Creek to get around slide debris. The trail crosses another creek 0.5 mile after crossing Boulder Creek, and 75 yards after crossing this creek, it crosses Eagle Creek on a bridge (5,020 ft.).

The trail makes five switchbacks in the next 0.4 mile. After passing the switchbacks the trail climbs 0.8 mile more to the Eagle Cap Wilderness boundary (5,600 ft.). The trail crosses a side stream 0.1 mile past the wilderness boundary. There is a meadow between the trail and Eagle Creek 0.3 mile after crossing the stream. The trail goes along and through the meadow for 300 yards, then crosses back over Eagle Creek on a single log footbridge (5,650 ft.).

From here the trail heads up the left side of Eagle Creek again. There is another stream crossing 0.2 mile after crossing the bridge. The junction with Bench Canyon

Eagle Lake. LOWELL EUHUS PHOTO

Trail (5,750 ft.) is another 0.2 mile past the stream crossing. This junction is 2.6 miles from Main Eagle Creek Trailhead. Bench Canyon Trail turns off to the left. See Bench Canyon (hike 72).

The trail crosses a stream and traverses out onto an open hillside 0.3 mile past the junction with Bench Canyon Trail. It traverses this open hillside for just over 1 mile to the junction with Lookingglass Lake Trail (1921; 6,150 ft.). The trail is some distance above Eagle Creek in this area. At the Lookingglass Lake Trail junction there is a meadow between the trail and Eagle Creek, with some good campsites along Eagle Creek next to this meadow. Lookingglass Lake Trail turns to the right, drops down, and crosses the meadow.

Main Eagle Creek Trail goes by some campsites and crosses a couple of small streams in the next 0.5 mile, to where it makes a switchback. After making the switchback the trail climbs, crossing two more very small streams, and then crosses Cached Creek. Cached Creek is 0.5 mile past the switchback.

After crossing Cached Creek the trail climbs on. It makes two more switchbacks, crosses a small stream, and makes two additional switchbacks to reach the junction with Trail Creek Trail (6,880 ft.). Trail Creek Trail junction is 5.7 miles from Main Eagle Creek Trailhead.

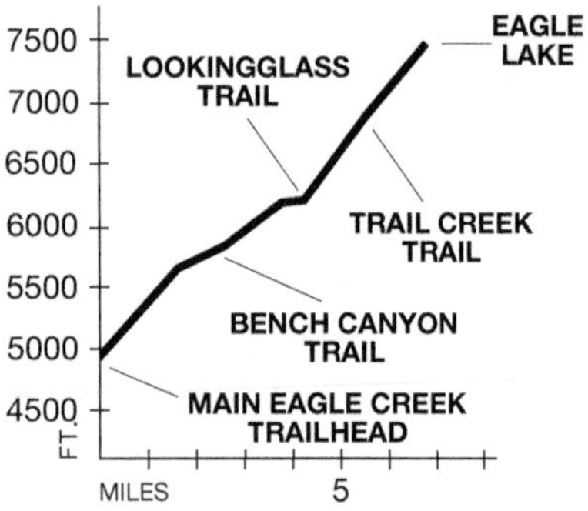

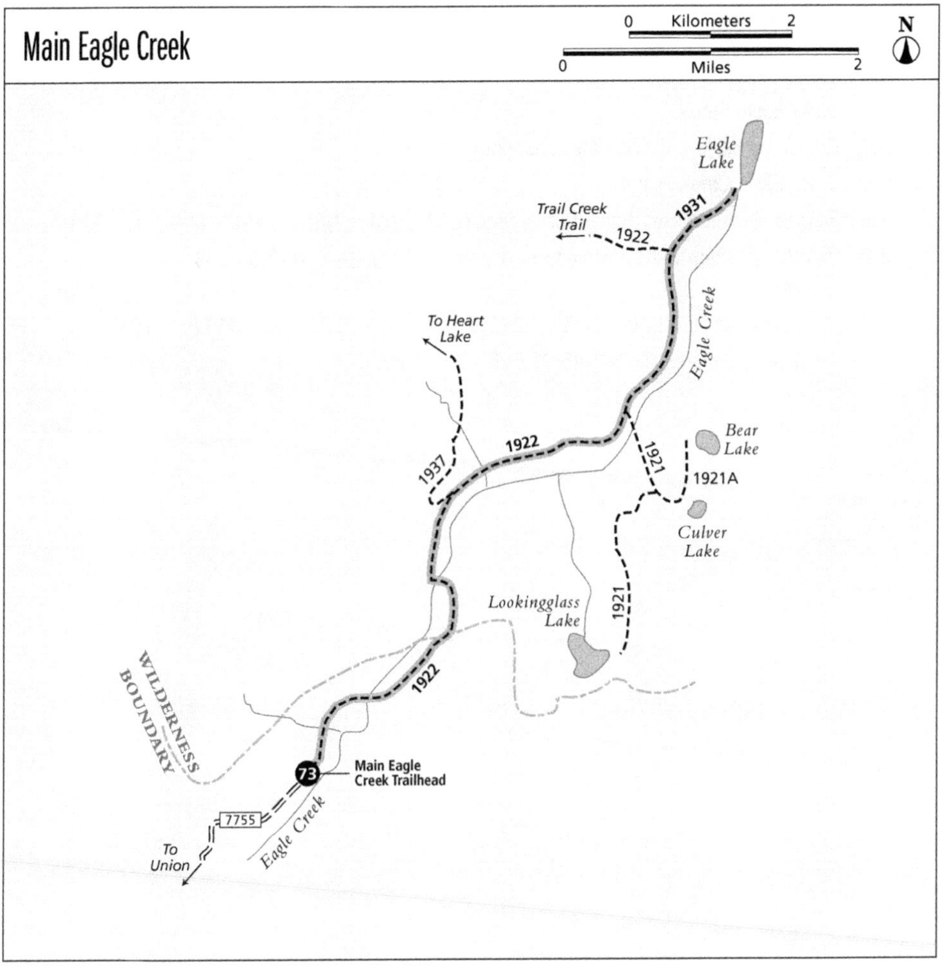

At Trail Creek Trail junction the trail number of Main Eagle Creek Trail changes to 1931, and Trail 1922 becomes Trail Creek Trail. Main Eagle Creek Trail turns right (northeast) at the junction. It crosses two small streams 0.2 mile past the junction and starts a series of six switchbacks 0.1 mile after crossing the streams. The trail comes to Eagle Lake 150 yards after the last switchback. Eagle Lake (7,448 ft.) is 1.1 miles from the Trail Creek Trail junction and 6.8 miles from Main Eagle Creek Trailhead.

Like so many other lakes on the south side of the Wallowas, Eagle Lake is dammed. This is good for storing water, but not so good for the looks of the lake. There is almost no timber around Eagle Lake and no really good campsites. The only area flat enough to camp on is just across the dam to the east. All the way around the lake the mountains drop steeply into the water. There are fish in Eagle Lake and the scenery is nice; however, it would be a good idea to camp somewhere else. The return trip is made by the same trail.

Miles and Directions

0.0 Start at the Main Eagle Creek Trailhead and Boulder Park.

0.5 Cross Eagle Creek.

1.7 Reach the Eagle Cap Wilderness boundary.

2.2 Cross Eagle Creek again.

2.6 Pass the junction with Bench Canyon Trail (1937). (GPS: N45 05.720'/W117 23.022')

4.0 Pass the junction with Lookingglass Lake Trail (1921). (GPS: N45 06.053'/W117 21.583')

5.7 Pass the junction with Trail Creek Trail (1922). (GPS: N45 07.168'/W117 21.107')

6.8 Arrive at Eagle Lake. (GPS: N45 07.515'/W117 20.520')

74 Trail Creek

This backpack route leaves the Main Eagle Creek Trail, passes Cached Lake and climbs over a pass, then descends to the bottom of the Minam River Canyon and the junction with the Upper Minam River Trail. The route connects with Bench Canyon and West Fork Eagle Creek Trails along the way. (Trail 1922)

Distance: 10.3 miles one way
Hiking time: 4–6 hours
Difficulty: Moderate
Trail maintenance: Infrequent
Best season: July through Sept
Traffic and other trail users: Moderate foot and horse traffic
Canine compatibility: Dogs permitted without leashes, but must be kept away from the stock of other parties
Fees and permits: Northwest Forest Pass and Eagle Cap Wilderness Permit
Maximum elevation: 8,160 feet
Maps: USGS Krag Peak OR, Bennet Peak OR, and Steamboat Lake OR; Geo Graphics Wallowa Mountains Eagle Cap Wilderness
Trail contact: USDA Forest Service Wallowa Mountains Office, 201 E 2nd St./PO Box 905, Joseph, OR 97846; (541) 426-5546, (541) 426-4978; www.fs.usda.gov/wallowa-whitman; or USDA Forest Service Pine Field Office, 38470 Pine Town Ln., Halfway, OR 97834; (541) 742-7511. Office closed Dec 21 through Apr 30; contact Baker City office at (541) 523-6391.

Finding the trail: Trail Creek Trail leaves Main Eagle Creek Trail 5.7 miles from Main Eagle Creek Trailhead. To reach Main Eagle Creek Trailhead, take Big Creek Road (FR 67) east from the town of Medical Springs. Follow FR 67 approximately 16 miles to its junction with FR 77. Turn left on FR 77 and go 1 mile to the junction with FR 7755. Turn right on FR 7755 and go 6 miles to Boulder Park and Main Eagle Creek Trailhead (4,910 ft.). This is the site of the old Boulder Park Resort, which was wiped out by an avalanche some years ago. From the trailhead hike north on Main Eagle Creek Trail to the junction with the Trail Creek Trail (6,880 ft.).
GPS: Main Eagle Creek Trailhead: N45 04.089'/W117 24.391'; Trail Creek Trail junction: N45 07.168'/W117 21.107'

The Hike

From the junction with Main Eagle Creek Trail, Trail Creek Trail heads northwest and crosses three very small streams in the first 0.75 mile. It makes a switchback to the right 0.2 mile past the third stream crossing. The trail then makes two more switchbacks in the next 300 yards and crosses another very small stream 300 yards past the last switchback. Cached Lake comes into view 300 yards past the last stream crossing.

Cached Lake (7,343 ft.) is 100 or so yards to the left (south) of the trail. There is a meadow on the northeast side of the lake and several good campsites in the timber next to it. Cached Lake is a popular destination in July and August, so you may not be alone if you camp here. There are fish to be caught in the lake.

Cached Lake. LOWELL EUHUS PHOTO

Leaving Cached Lake the trail crosses a stream and begins to climb again in switchbacks. It makes four switchbacks in the next 350 yards. The trail disappears in a grassy area 300 yards past the switchbacks. Head southwest for a short distance to pick it up again. After getting through the grassy area, the trail crosses another stream. It then makes thirteen switchbacks in 1.2 miles to the top of a pass. The trail climbs 820 feet from Cached Lake to the top of the pass. The area near the pass (8,160 ft.) is mostly open alpine country. The pass area is definitely view property.

From the pass the trail heads north along the ridgeline. After 0.25 mile it switchbacks to the left. Here the trail begins a 0.5-mile-long series of nine switchbacks as it drops down off the pass. There is a meadow with a wet weather pond to the right of the trail 0.9 mile after the switchbacks. The junction with Bench Canyon Trail is 0.3 mile past the meadow. This junction (7,410 ft.) is at the northwest end of a fairly large meadow with several springs in it. Bench Canyon Trail turns to the left (south).

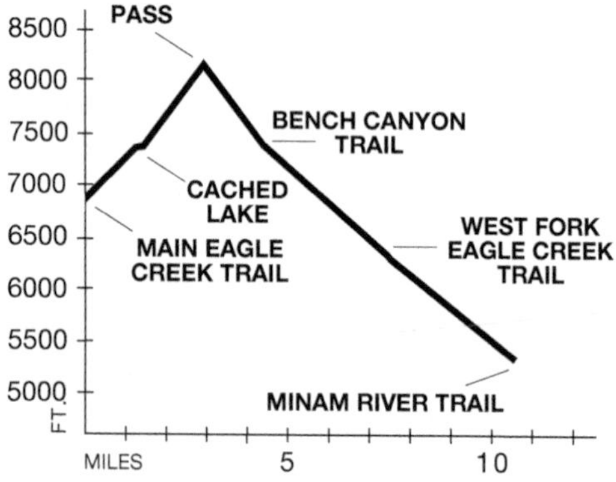

A loop hike can be done from here back to Main Eagle Creek Trailhead. To hike this loop, turn left on Bench Canyon Trail and follow it 3.1

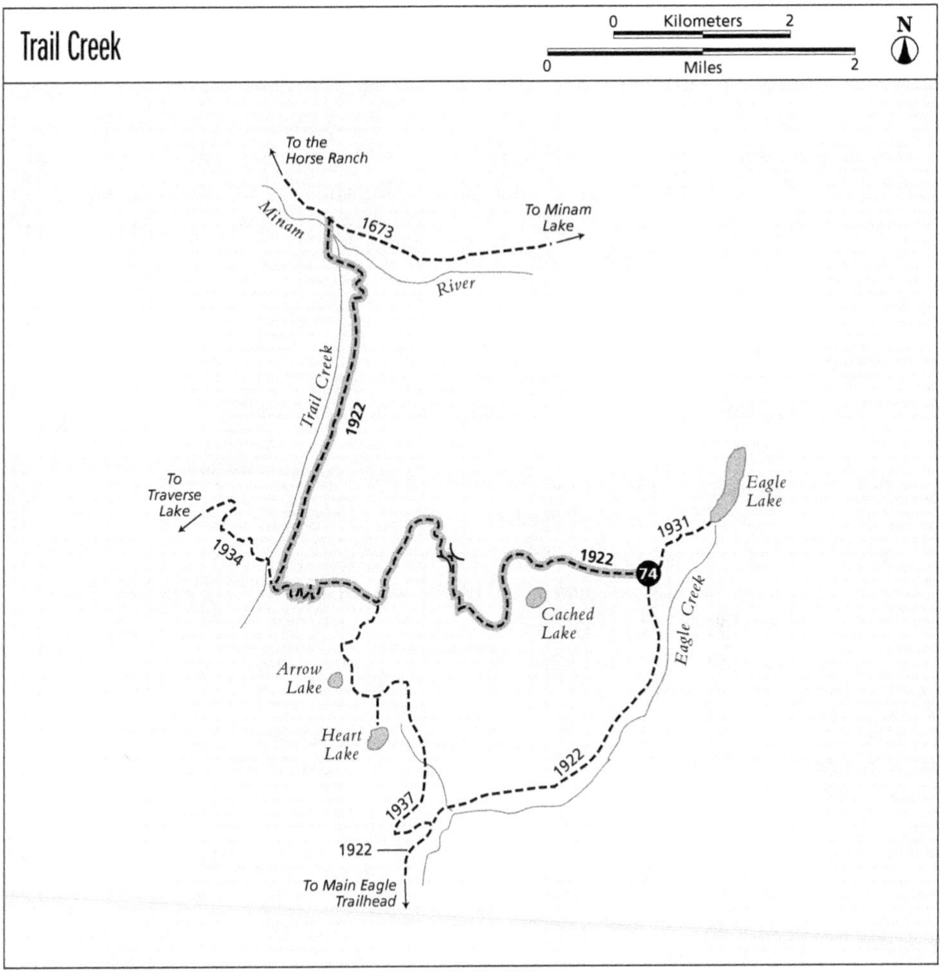

miles to the junction with Main Eagle Creek Trail. Then turn right on Main Eagle Creek Trail and head south the 2.6 miles to Main Eagle Creek Trailhead. See Main Eagle Creek (hike 73).

After passing Bench Canyon Trail junction, Trail Creek Trail starts its descent into Trail Creek Canyon. It makes many switchbacks as it drops 1,170 feet in 2.7 miles to the junction with West Eagle Creek Trail (1934; 6,240 ft.). See West Fork Eagle Creek (hike 71). By the time the trail reaches the junction with West Fork Eagle Creek Trail, the woods have changed from the open alpine setting near timberline at the top of the pass to dense transition forest along lower Trail Creek.

Just below the junction the trail crosses a small stream in a culvert. It goes down along the right (east) side of Trail Creek for 2 miles, crossing five streambeds and going through several meadows. These streambeds may have water in them earlier in the summer but were dry by September, when we hiked this trail.

After going the 2 miles along Trail Creek, the trail turns to the right and gets away from the creek. The trail switchbacks down for the next 0.5 mile, then returns to and crosses Trail Creek. After crossing Trail Creek the trail goes through a sloping meadow with a lot of avalanche debris in it. Soon it drops out of the meadow, switchbacks to the right, and crosses the Minam River (5,320 ft.). This crossing could be difficult or impossible during times of high water. After crossing the river the trail winds its way up 300 yards to the Minam River Trail. This junction is 10.3 miles from the junction with Main Eagle Creek Trail. From this junction, Minam Lake is to the right (east), upriver 6.1 miles.

Miles and Directions

0.0 At the junction with Main Eagle Creek Trail (1931), go west (left) on Trail Creek Trail (1922).

1.5 Pass Cached Lake.

3.1 Cross the pass.

4.6 Pass the junction with Bench Canyon Trail (1937). (GPS: N45 07.005'/W117 23.330')

7.3 Pass the junction with West Fork Eagle Creek Trail (1934).

10.3 Cross the Minam River and arrive at the junction with Upper Minam River Trail (1673). (GPS: N45 09.150'/W117 23.743')

75 Lookingglass Lake

This side trail connects Main Eagle Creek Trail (1922) with Lookingglass Lake and is also the access route to Bear Lake Trail. (Trail 1921)

Distance: 2.6 miles one way
Hiking time: 1–1.5 hours
Difficulty: Moderate
Trail maintenance: Infrequent
Best season: Mid-June through Oct
Traffic and other trail users: Moderate foot and horse traffic
Canine compatibility: Dogs permitted without leashes, but must be kept away from the stock of other parties
Fees and permits: Northwest Forest Pass and Eagle Cap Wilderness Permit
Maximum elevation: 7,530 feet
Map: USGS Krag Peak OR
Trail contact: USDA Forest Service Wallowa Mountains Office, 201 E 2nd St./ PO Box 905, Joseph, OR 97846; (541) 426-5546, (541) 426-4978; www.fs.usda.gov/wallowa-whitman; or USDA Forest Service Pine Field Office, 38470 Pine Town Ln., Halfway, OR 97834; (541) 742-7511. Office closed Dec 21 through Apr 30; contact Baker City office at (541) 523-6391.

Finding the trail: Lookingglass Lake Trail leaves Main Eagle Creek Trail 4 miles from Main Eagle Creek Trailhead. To reach Main Eagle Creek Trailhead, take Big Creek Road (FR 67) east from the town of Medical Springs. Follow FR 67 approximately 16 miles to its junction with FR 77. Turn left on FR 77 and go 1 mile to the junction with FR 7755. Turn right on FR 7755 and go 6 miles to Boulder Park and Main Eagle Creek Trailhead (4,910 ft.). This is the site of the old Boulder Park Resort, which was wiped out by an avalanche some years ago. Hike north then northeast for 4 miles on the Main Eagle Creek Trail (1922) to the junction with the Lookingglass Lake Trail (6,150 ft.).
GPS: Main Eagle Creek Trailhead: N45 04.089'/W117 24.391'; Lookingglass Lake junction: N45 06.053'/W117 21.583'

The Hike

Lookingglass Lake Trail turns to the right (east) off Main Eagle Creek Trail. It drops slightly, crosses a meadow, then crosses Eagle Creek. After crossing Eagle Creek the trail starts to climb. It makes a switchback to the right 0.7 mile after crossing Eagle Creek. The junction with Bear Lake Trail (6,830 ft.) is 0.3 mile past the switchback. See Bear Lake (hike 76). The 680-foot climb in this first mile makes this section of trail quite steep.

The trail crosses the outlet of Culver Lake 175 yards past the Bear Lake Trail junction. Soon after crossing the stream the trail starts to climb steeply. It makes two switchbacks while climbing 0.4 mile to the top of the ridgeline. After reaching the ridgeline the trail goes around to the other (southwest) side of the ridge and does an ascending traverse. From here the falls in the creek below Lookingglass Lake can be seen across the canyon to the south.

Lookingglass Lake/Bear Lake

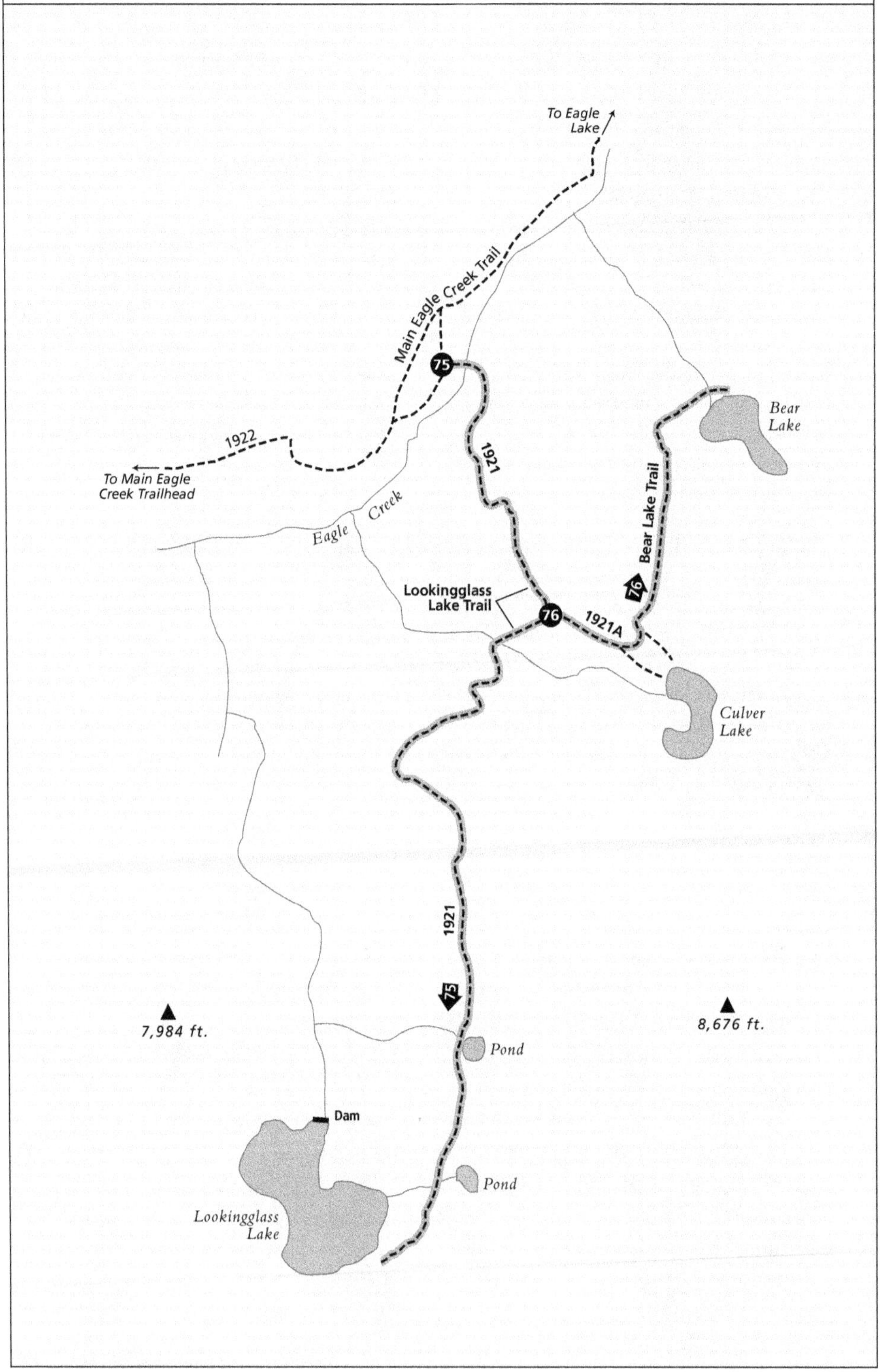

Lookingglass Lake. LOWELL EUHUS PHOTO

After climbing for 0.1 mile, the trail flattens out a bit. It crosses three small streams, then climbs fairly steeply for another 100 yards and flattens out again. Soon Lookingglass Lake can be seen to the right (south), across the canyon. There is a pond on the left side of the trail 350 yards past the top of the last steep climb. The trail starts to drop and crosses a small stream 350 yards past the pond. Just before crossing the stream, the trail reached its highest point (7,530 ft.). After the stream crossing the trail drops for 0.25 mile to Lookingglass Lake (7,302 ft.), 2.6 miles from Main Eagle Creek Trail.

Lookingglass Lake is a reservoir, like most of the lakes on this side of the mountains. It is held up 15 feet or so by a dam. This makes the shoreline at low water mostly mud. The area around the lake is mostly timbered with subalpine fir and some whitebark pine. There are fish in the lake and a few campsites. The return is made via the same trail.

Miles and Directions

0.0 At the junction with Main Eagle Creek Trail (1922), turn right on Lookingglass Lake Trail (1921).

1.0 Pass the junction with Bear Lake Trail (1921A). (GPS: N45 05.768'/W117 21.220')

2.6 Arrive at Lookingglass Lake. (GPS: N45 04.729'/W117 21.653')

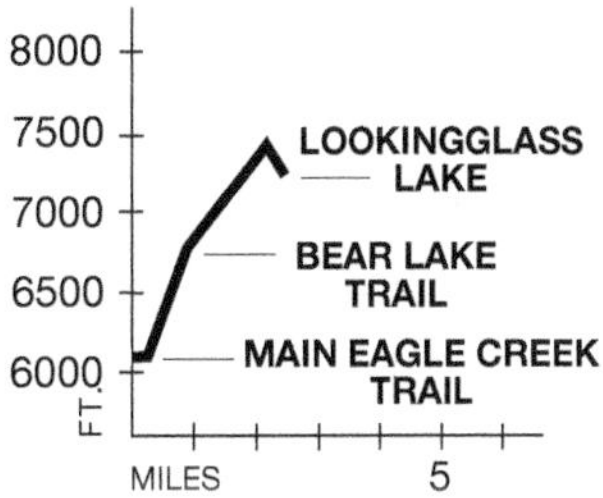

76 Bear Lake

Hike this short trail, in the very scenic Main Eagle Creek Canyon, from the Lookingglass Lake Trail (1921) to small but pristine Bear Lake, where you can camp, fish, or just relax. (Trail 1921A)

See map page 268.
Distance: 1 mile one way
Hiking time: About 0.5 hour
Difficulty: Easy
Trail maintenance: Infrequent
Best season: Mid-June through Oct
Traffic and other trail users: Light to moderate foot traffic; light horse traffic
Canine compatibility: Dogs permitted without leashes, but must be kept away from the stock of other parties
Fees and permits: Northwest Forest Pass and Eagle Cap Wilderness Permit
Maximum elevation: 7,230 feet
Map: USGS Krag Peak OR
Trail contact: USDA Forest Service Wallowa Mountains Office, 201 E 2nd St./ PO Box 905, Joseph, OR 97846; (541) 426-5546, (541) 426-4978; www.fs.usda.gov/wallowa-whitman; or USDA Forest Service Pine Field Office, 38470 Pine Town Ln., Halfway, OR 97834; (541) 742-7511. Office closed Dec 21 through Apr 30; contact Baker City office at (541) 523-6391.

Finding the trail: Access to the Bear Lake Trail is from the Main Eagle Creek Trailhead. To reach Main Eagle Creek Trailhead, take Big Creek Road (FR 67) east from the town of Medical Springs. Follow FR 67 approximately 16 miles to its junction with FR 77. Turn left on FR 77 and go 1 mile to the junction with FR 7755. Turn right on FR 7755 and go 6 miles to Boulder Park and Main Eagle Creek Trailhead (4,910 ft.). This is the site of the old Boulder Park Resort, which was wiped out by an avalanche some years ago. Hike north and northeast on the Main Eagle Creek Trail for 4 miles to the junction with the Lookingglass Lake Trail (1921). Turn right at the junction and go southeast for 1 mile to the junction with the Bear Lake Trail (1921A; 6,830 ft.).
GPS: Main Eagle Creek Trailhead: N45 04.089'/W117 24.391'; Bear Lake Trail junction: N45 05.768'/W117 21.220'

The Hike

Bear Lake Trail turns to the left (southeast, but soon north) off the Lookingglass Lake Trail. After leaving the Lookingglass Lake Trail, it climbs for 0.3 mile to the unmarked junction with the Culver Lake path.

There are actually two paths that lead to Culver Lake, which are about 125 yards apart. Both of the paths turn to the right (southeast) off Bear Lake Trail. The elevation at this junction is approximately 7,000 feet. Culver Lake (7,030 ft.) is about 200 yards off Bear Creek Trail.

After passing the Culver Lake paths, Bear Lake Trail continues to climb 0.5 mile more to the top of a ridge (7,230 ft.). From the ridgeline the trail drops for 250 yards

Bear Lake. LOWELL EUHUS PHOTO

to Bear Lake. The trail goes on around to the north side of the lake, crossing the outlet stream.

Bear Lake (7,030 ft.) is 1 mile from Lookingglass Lake Trail. The lake area is heavily timbered with mostly subalpine fir and spruce and some whitebark pine. There are campsites on the north side of the lake and trout to be caught in it. Unlike many lakes in this area, neither Culver Lake nor Bear Lake has a dam. The return trip is via the same trail.

Miles and Directions

0.0 From the junction with Lookingglass Lake Trail (1921), go left onto the Bear Lake Trail (1921A).

0.3 Pass the junctions with the Culver Lake paths.

0.9 Cross the ridgeline.

1.0 Arrive at Bear Lake. (GPS: N45 06.066'/W117 20.870')

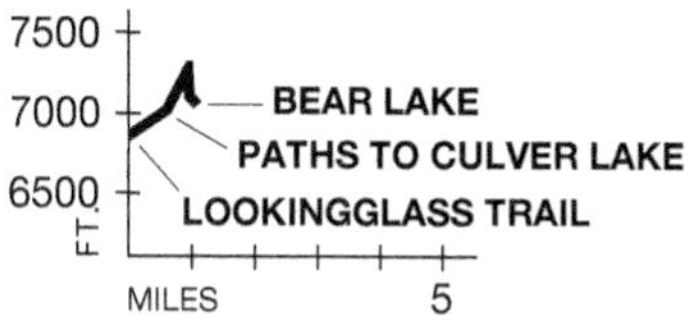

77 East Fork Eagle Creek

This trail (backpack) runs from East Eagle Creek Trailhead to Mirror Lake, providing the easiest access to the popular Lakes Basin area from the south. The route also accesses Hidden Lake, Frazier Pass, and Minam Lake/Mirror Lake Trails. The route climbs the East Eagle Creek Canyon, which is probably the most scenic in the southern part of the Wallowa Mountains. The canyon is really a deep glacial valley with mostly light gray cliffs rising above. At the head of the valley the track forces its way over Horton Pass, very close to 9,572-foot-high Eagle Cap. (Trail 1910)

Distance: 13.6 miles one way
Hiking time: 5–9 hours
Difficulty: Moderate to strenuous, depending on snow cover over Horton Pass
Trail maintenance: Infrequent
Best season: Mid-July through Sept
Traffic and other trail users: Moderate to heavy
Canine compatibility: Dogs permitted without leashes, but must be kept away from the stock of other parties
Fees and permits: Northwest Forest Pass and Eagle Cap Wilderness Permit
Maximum elevation: 8,470 feet
Maps: USGS Krag Peak OR and Eagle Cap OR; Geo Graphics Wallowa Mountains Eagle Cap Wilderness
Trail contact: USDA Forest Service Wallowa Mountains Office, 201 E 2nd St./ PO Box 905, Joseph, OR 97846; (541) 426-5546, (541) 426-4978; www.fs.usda.gov/wallowa-whitman; or USDA Forest Service Pine Field Office, 38470 Pine Town Ln., Halfway, OR 97834; (541) 742-7511. Office closed Dec 21 through Apr 30; contact Baker City office at (541) 523-6391.

Finding the trailhead: From Union take OR 203 and go 20 miles southeast to Medical Springs. At Medical Springs, turn left (southeast) on Big Creek Road and stay on it; it soon becomes FR 67. Follow FR 67 for 14.2 miles to the junction with FR 77. Turn right (east) on FR 77 and go 6.6 miles to the junction with East Eagle Creek Road (FR 7745). Turn left (north) on FR 7745 and follow it 6.5 miles to the Old East Eagle Creek Trailhead. There is parking at the trailhead. A separate parking area and trailhead have been built 0.8 mile south of (before) the Old East Eagle Creek Trailhead. For stock users, a trail connects this new trailhead with the old one.
GPS: N45 03.401'/W117 19.335'

The Hike

From the trailhead (4,580 ft.), East Eagle Creek Trail begins as a jeep road heading north. After going 0.25 mile the trail bears to the right, off the jeep road. A sign here marks the trail. The trail enters the Eagle Cap Wilderness after climbing a rocky grade for 300 yards. At the wilderness boundary there is a melt pond on the right side of the trail. The gray cliffs across East Eagle Creek to the west are called Granite Cliffs on the USGS map. This is strange, as they appear to be limestone.

The trail crosses a creek and enters a brushy area 0.5 mile after entering the wilderness. As in so many areas along East Eagle Creek, the lack of large trees is caused

Upper basin and Horton Pass.

by the regular scouring done by avalanches. On the far side of the brushy area the trail crosses another creek. The trail fords Curtis Creek (5,150 ft.) 1.8 miles from the trailhead. Just after crossing Curtis Creek, a falls in East Eagle Creek can be seen below the trail to the left. Soon the forest opens up for a view of the higher mountains ahead.

There is another falls in East Eagle Creek a short distance farther along. The trail crosses a side stream with a waterfall a few feet above the trail and soon goes back into large timber again. The big timber lasts only a couple hundred yards before the trail comes back out into another large opening and crosses a stream. The trail crosses the 300-yard-wide opening, then climbs through a finger of timber to another opening. There are alternating open and lightly timbered areas and a couple of small stream crossings in the next 0.7 mile, to where the trail crosses Coon Creek (5,350 ft.). Just after crossing Coon Creek the trail enters a flat, parklike area with large cottonwood trees and a colony of red diggers (ground squirrels). The trail crosses the parklike area, then crosses another stream as it begins to climb gently.

French Creek enters East Eagle Creek from the west 0.1 mile after leaving the park area. In another 0.4 mile, after three small stream crossings, the trail comes to a finger of larger spruce and fir timber. A few feet into the trees the trail makes a switchback to the right and climbs back into the open area. It then makes a switchback to the left and traverses the finger of timber. At the first switchback there is a campsite in the trees a few feet off the trail.

The trail leaves the big timber and soon passes another waterfall in East Eagle Creek (5,570 ft.). The trail stays away from the creek and crosses several small streams

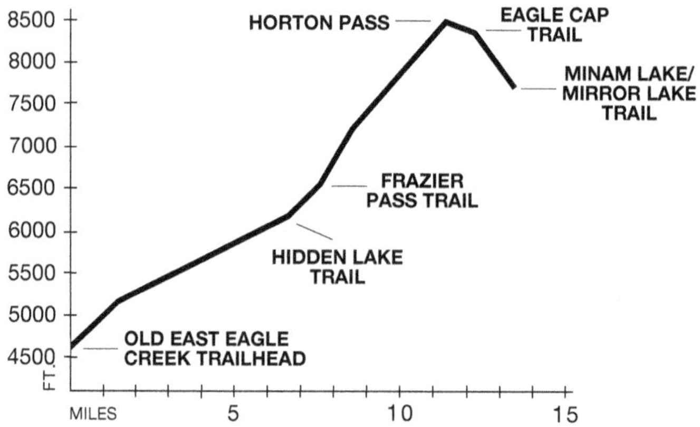

in the next 0.5 mile, then comes back close to East Eagle Creek again. Here East Eagle Creek foams and boils through a gorge below the trail. The trail crosses Dodge Creek (5,850 ft.) 0.1 mile after passing the gorge. Watch for elk, which abound in this area.

One mile and several small stream crossings after crossing Dodge Creek, the trail crosses Dennis Creek (5,970 ft.). After another 0.5 mile and a small stream crossing, the trail comes to the junction with Hidden Lake Trail (1915; 6,170 ft.). The country is becoming much more open and alpine. After passing the Hidden Lake Trail junction, the trail climbs, crosses a small stream, and makes a couple of switchbacks before crossing Knight Creek (6,310 ft.). The trail then climbs gently through a magnificent alpine valley and crosses several small streams in the mile to the junction with Frazier Pass Trail (6,520 ft.). There is a good campsite between the trail and East Fork Eagle Creek next to the junction.

At the junction East Fork Eagle Creek Trail turns to the right and heads east for a short distance before resuming its northerly course up the valley, staying some distance away from East Eagle Creek. It crosses several small streams as it makes its way up the east side of the valley 1.3 miles to the first switchback (7,150 ft.), at the beginning of the climb up to Horton Pass. The trail makes four switchbacks as it climbs a mostly open slope strewn with granite boulders, crossing some of the same streams again. It enters the lower of two small glacial basins 0.3 mile after making the last switchback. The trail crosses East Fork Eagle Creek as it enters the basin, then makes an ascending traverse along the west side of the basin to another stream crossing and the gully leading to the upper basin. The trail goes up the gully on the right side of the streambed, into the upper basin that is the head of East Fork Eagle Creek Valley (8,000 ft.). Much of the granite in the upper basin was smoothed by glacial action, and some of it has a pink tinge.

In the upper basin the trail turns to the east and switchbacks its way up the last 450 vertical feet to Horton Pass (8,470 ft.). Parts of the trail in and above the upper basin may be snow-covered until August. Horton Pass is the most easterly notch in the ridge above the upper basin, so even if snow covers most of the trail here, it is

East Fork Eagle Creek

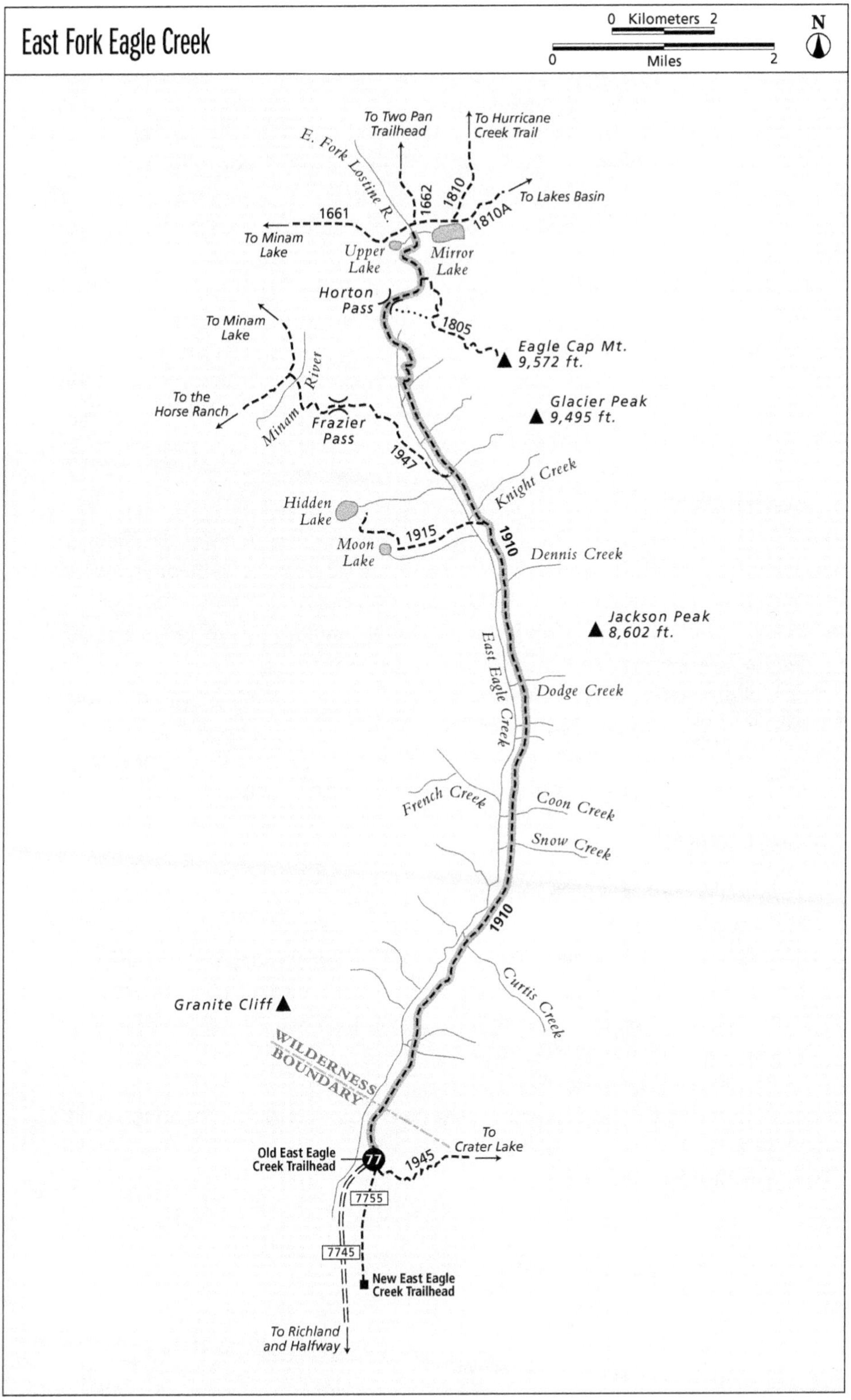
0 Kilometers 2
0 Miles 2
N
To Two Pan Trailhead
To Hurricane Creek Trail
E. Fork Lostine R.
1662
1810
To Lakes Basin
1810A
1661
To Minam Lake
Upper Lake
Mirror Lake
Horton Pass
1805
Eagle Cap Mt. 9,572 ft.
To Minam Lake
Minam River
To the Horse Ranch
Frazier Pass
Glacier Peak 9,495 ft.
1947
Knight Creek
Hidden Lake
1915
Moon Lake
1910
Dennis Creek
Jackson Peak 8,602 ft.
East Eagle Creek
Dodge Creek
French Creek
Coon Creek
Snow Creek
1910
Curtis Creek
Granite Cliff
WILDERNESS BOUNDARY
To Crater Lake
Old East Eagle Creek Trailhead
77
1945
7755
7745
New East Eagle Creek Trailhead
To Richland and Halfway

not difficult to find. This is a fairly steep ascent; if this trip is done when the trail is snow-covered, an ice ax should be taken along for each person, and all members of the party should know how to use one.

Take some time to rest and take in the view at Horton Pass. The U-shaped valley to the north is the upper East Fork Lostine Canyon, to the north-northeast is the limestone face of the Matterhorn, and to the northeast is the Lakes Basin. As with all higher passes in the Wallowa Mountains, watch the weather when you are making the crossing.

At Horton Pass a rough path to the summit of Eagle Cap turns off to the right (southeast). After crossing the pass, East Fork Eagle Creek Trail (1910) descends, making several small switchbacks 0.9 mile to the junction with Eagle Cap Trail. The area between Horton Pass and the Eagle Cap Trail junction will likely be covered with snow until August, and it may be hard to find the junction, but this is open country and the route on down is not difficult to find. Ice axes may be needed on this descent when the trail is covered with snow.

After passing the junction the trail winds down 1.1 miles to Upper Lake, at the west end of the Lakes Basin. The junction with Minam Lake/Mirror Lake Trail is 0.2 mile after passing Upper Lake. Mirror Lake (7,595 ft.) is 0.2 mile to the right (east) on the Minam Lake/Mirror Lake Trail. There are lots of campsites around Mirror Lake. Be sure to camp at least 200 feet from the lake, as forest service regulations require. Fishing for brook trout is usually excellent in the lake.

One of the best trips in the Wallowa Mountains can be made by combining East Fork Eagle Creek Trail and Hurricane Creek Trail. This 25.6-mile trip goes through what are unquestionably two of the most spectacular canyons in the range. A car shuttle of about 120 miles is required to make this one-way trip.

Miles and Directions

0.0 Start at Old East Eagle Creek Trailhead.

1.8 Ford Curtis Creek.

6.5 Pass the junction with Hidden Lake Trail (1915). (GPS: N45 08.335'/W117 18.132')

7.5 Pass the junction with Frazier Pass Trail (1947). (GPS: N45 08.830'/W117 18.625')

11.3 Top Horton Pass and pass the junction with the path leading up the ridge to the summit of Eagle Cap. (GPS: N45 10.205'/W117 18.990')

12.1 Pass the junction with Eagle Cap Trail (1805).

13.4 Reach the junction with Minam Lake/Mirror Lake Trail (1661). (GPS: N45 10.746'/W117 18.954')

13.6 Arrive at Mirror Lake.

78 Hidden Lake

This side trail climbs from the East Fork Eagle Creek Trail in the spectacular East Fork Eagle Creek Canyon to Hidden Lake, passing Moon Lake along the way. (Trail 1915)

Distance: 1.8 miles one way
Hiking time: About 1 hour heading up
Difficulty: Moderate
Trail maintenance: Infrequent
Best season: July through Oct
Traffic and other trail users: Moderate foot and horse traffic
Canine compatibility: Dogs permitted without leashes, but must be kept away from the stock of other parties
Fees and permits: Northwest Forest Pass and Eagle Cap Wilderness Permit
Maximum elevation: 7,280 feet
Map: USGS Eagle Cap OR
Trail contact: USDA Forest Service Wallowa Mountains Office, 201 E 2nd St./ PO Box 905, Joseph, OR 97846; (541) 426-5546, (541) 426-4978; www.fs.usda.gov/wallowa-whitman; or USDA Forest Service Pine Field Office, 38470 Pine Town Ln., Halfway, OR 97834; (541) 742-7511. Office closed Dec 21 through Apr 30; contact Baker City office at (541) 523-6391.

Finding the trail: The trail begins at the junction with East Fork Eagle Creek Trail (1910) 6.5 miles north of East Eagle Creek Trailhead. To reach East Eagle Creek Trailhead from Union, take OR 203 and go 20 miles southeast to Medical Springs. At Medical Springs, turn left (southeast) on Big Creek Road and stay on it; it soon becomes FR 67. Follow FR 67 for 14.2 miles to the junction with FR 77. Turn right (east) on FR 77 and go 6.6 miles to the junction with East Eagle Creek Road (FR 7745). Turn left (north) on FR 7745 and follow it 6.5 miles to the Old East Eagle Creek Trailhead. There is parking at the trailhead. A separate parking area and trailhead have been built 0.8 mile south of (before) the Old East Eagle Creek Trailhead. For stock users, a trail connects this new trailhead with the old one. From the trailhead hike north on the East Fork Eagle Creek Trail (1910) to the junction with the Hidden Lake Trail.
GPS: Old East Eagle Creek Trailhead: N45 03.401'/W117 19.335'; Hidden Lake junction: N45 08.335'/W117 18.132'

The Hike

The Hidden Lake Trail turns left (west) off the East Fork Eagle Creek Trail (6,170 ft.). It drops slightly for 50 yards, then crosses East Fork Eagle Creek. After crossing the creek it heads northwest for 0.2 mile, then makes a switchback to the left at the edge of the timber. There is a campsite in the timber, next to the switchback. After making the switchback the trail works its way up, staying on the north side of the outlet stream of Moon Lake. At first it goes through some timber, then it climbs on mostly open slopes and crosses several small streams to reach Moon Lake (7,060 ft.). There are several camping spots in the trees around Moon Lake.

Hidden Lake in early June.

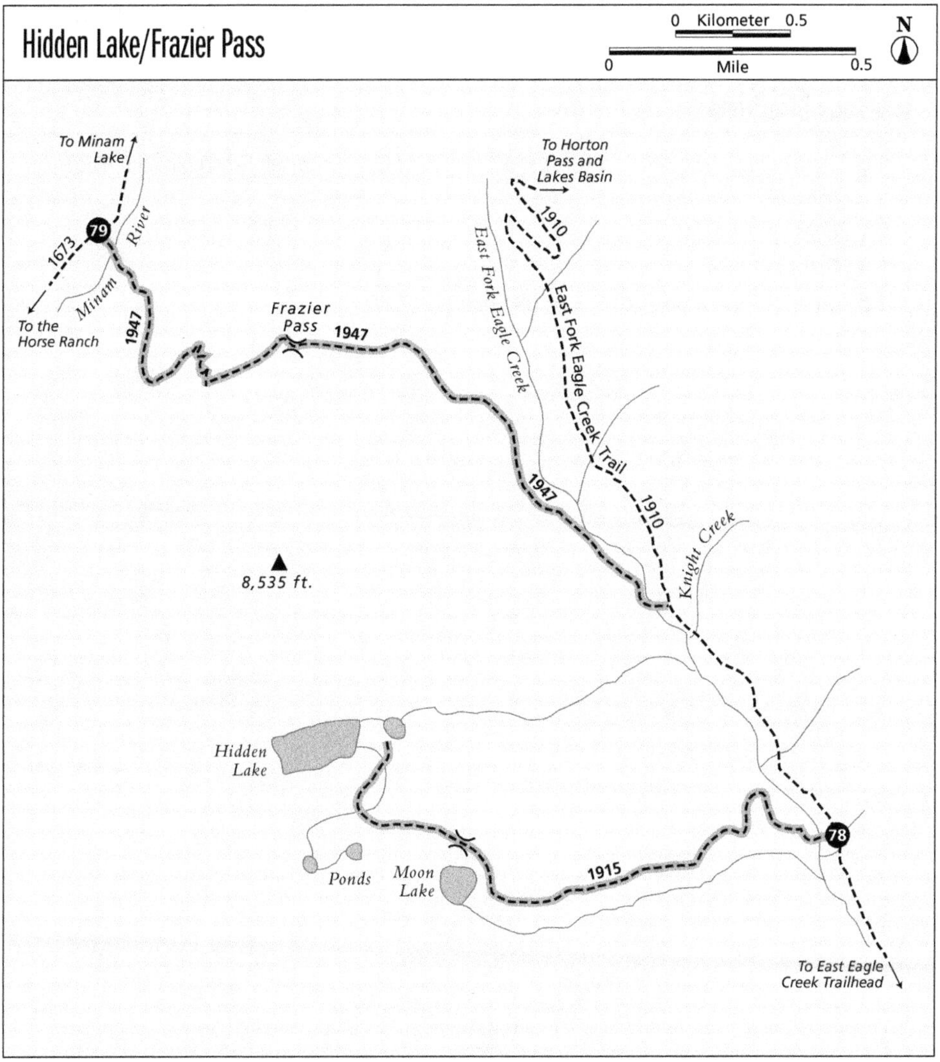

The trail goes around Moon Lake on the east and north sides, then climbs to a pass (7,280 ft.) northwest of the lake. A very large bear crossed this pass just ahead of me when I hiked this trail. After crossing the pass the trail passes a pond, which is on the left side of the trail. The trail continues northwest a short distance, then turns northeast, crosses a stream, and comes to the east end of Hidden Lake (7,173 ft.). There is a pond just to the east of Hidden Lake to the right of the trail.

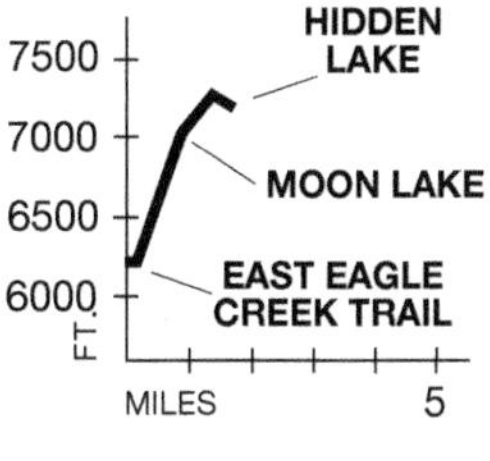

There are nice campsites at Hidden Lake and fish to be caught. There is a good view of Eagle Cap when looking northeast from Hidden Lake; however, Eagle

Cap is not as spectacular from this side as it is from the Mirror Lake side. The return trip is made by the same trail.

Miles and Directions

0.0 From the junction with East Fork Eagle Creek Trail (1910), turn left (west) onto the Hidden Lake Trail (1915).

1.1 Reach Moon Lake.

1.4 Cross the pass.

1.8 Arrive at Hidden Lake. (GPS: N45 08.565'/W117 19.553')

79 Frazier Pass

Climb from Upper Minam River Trail to Frazier Pass on the ridgeline between East Fork Eagle Creek and the Minam River, then descend into the fantastic East Fork Eagle Creek Canyon and the East Fork Eagle Creek Trail. (Trail 1947)

See map page 279.
Distance: 2.7 miles one way
Hiking time: 1–1.5 hours
Difficulty: Moderate
Trail maintenance: Infrequent
Best season: Mid-June through Oct
Traffic and other trail users: Moderate foot and horse traffic
Canine compatibility: Dogs permitted without leashes, but must be kept away from the stock of other parties
Fees and permits: Northwest Forest Pass and Eagle Cap Wilderness Permit
Maximum elevation: 7,560 feet
Map: USGS Eagle Cap OR
Trail contact: USDA Forest Service Wallowa Mountains Office, 201 E 2nd St./PO Box 905, Joseph, OR 97846; (541) 426-5546, (541) 426-4978; www.fs.usda.gov/wallowa-whitman; or USDA Forest Service Pine Field Office, 38470 Pine Town Ln., Halfway, OR 97834; (541) 742-7511. Office closed Dec 21 through Apr 30; contact Baker City office at (541) 523-6391.

Finding the trail: Frazier Pass Trail can be accessed from several trailheads, including East Fork Eagle Creek, East Fork Lostine River, Hurricane Creek, and even from the Wallowa Lake Trailhead. This trail is a connector in the center of the wilderness. The closest way to reach the trail junction where this description starts is from the Two Pan Trailhead via the West Fork Lostine River Trail. To come in this way drive south from Lostine on Lostine River Road for 18 miles to Two Pan Trailhead. Hike south from the trailhead on the West Fork Lostine River Trail (1670) for 6.1 miles to Minam Lake and the junction with the Upper Minam River Trail (1673) and the Minam/Mirror Lake Trail (1661). From the junction follow the Upper Minam River Trail for 2 miles south to the junction with the Frazier Pass Trail (6,750 ft.).
GPS: Two Pan Trailhead: N45 15.001'/W117 22.580'; Frazier Pass junction: N45 09.616'/W117 20.360'

The Hike

Frazier Pass Trail heads east off the Minam River Trail. Many good campsites are available along the Minam River close to this junction. It drops slightly, crosses a meadow, then crosses the Minam River. Watch for blazes on the trees near the river. The trail becomes easier to see on the east side of the river. Cross a stream 125 yards after crossing the river. A short distance beyond the stream, the trail becomes difficult to see in a swampy area. Watch for the blazes on the far side of the swampy area.

The trail crosses a small stream after leaving the swampy area. Beyond the stream the trail starts to climb. It makes a switchback to the left 0.2 mile after crossing the small stream. In the next 0.4 mile the trail makes four more switchbacks. Above the

East Eagle Creek Canyon from Frazier Pass Trail. GARY FLETCHER PHOTO

switchbacks the trail climbs for 0.5 mile to Frazier Pass (7,560 ft.). Frazier Pass is 1.3 miles from Upper Minam River Trail.

After crossing Frazier Pass the trail starts to drop fairly steeply. It makes four small switchbacks 125 yards below the pass. Beyond the switchbacks the trail twists its way down a couple hundred yards, then flattens out for 50 yards or so. The trail starts to drop again, making five more switchbacks in the next 0.3 mile, then crosses three small streams. There is a large spring on the left side of the trail 0.4 mile after crossing the small streams.

The trail crosses East Fork Eagle Creek (6,530 ft.) 0.25 mile past the spring. A short distance past the crossing the Frazier Pass Trail meets East Fork Eagle Creek Trail (1910). This junction is 2.7 miles from Upper Minam River Trail.

Miles and Directions

0.0 At the junction with Upper Minam River Trail (1673), go east on the Frazier Pass Trail (1947).

1.3 Cross Frazier Pass.

2.6 Cross East Fork Eagle Creek.

2.7 Arrive at the junction with East Fork Eagle Creek Trail (1910). (GPS: N45 08.830'/W117 18.625')

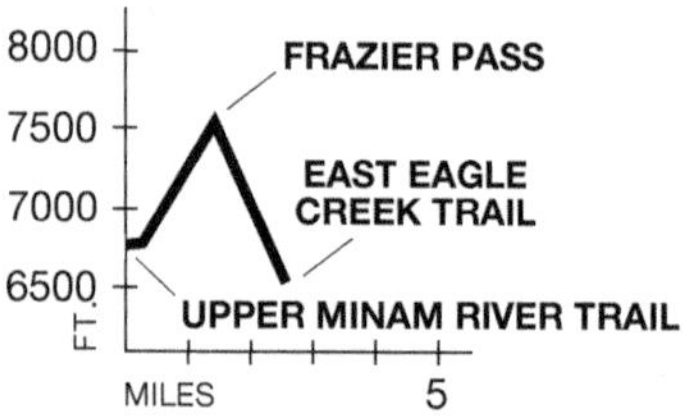

80 Cliff Creek

This backpack route leads from Summit Point Trailhead to the South Fork Imnaha River. You traverse ridgetop meadows covered with flowers and pass Crater Lake before descending into the South Fork Imnaha River Canyon. This trail also accesses Cornucopia Trail, Pine Lakes Trail, and Little Kettle Creek Trail. (Trail 1885)

Distance: 11.8 miles one way
Hiking time: 4.5–7 hours
Difficulty: Moderate
Trail maintenance: Infrequent
Best season: Mid-July through Sept
Traffic and other trail users: Foot traffic is moderate to Little Kettle Creek Trail junction near Crater Lake, light beyond Crater Lake; light to moderate horse traffic.
Canine compatibility: Dogs permitted without leashes, but must be kept away from the stock of other parties
Fees and permits: Eagle Cap Wilderness Permit
Maximum elevation: 8,040 feet
Maps: USGS Cornucopia OR and Krag Peak OR; Geo Graphics Wallowa Mountains Eagle Cap Wilderness
Trail contact: USDA Forest Service Wallowa Mountains Office, 201 E 2nd St./PO Box 905, Joseph, OR 97846; (541) 426-5546, (541) 426-4978; www.fs.usda.gov/wallowa-whitman; or USDA Forest Service Pine Field Office, 38470 Pine Town Ln., Halfway, OR 97834; (541) 742-7511. Office closed Dec 21 through Apr 30; contact Baker City office at (541) 523-6391.

Finding the trailhead: From Halfway take Cornucopia Road (OR 413) and go 5.4 miles northwest to the poorly marked Carson Grade junction. The junction is marked with a sign pointing to West Carson Lane. Turn left (west) at the junction and head up West Carson Lane (aka West Carson Grade), which soon becomes FR 7710. Follow FR 7710 for 3.3 miles to the junction with FR 77. Turn right on FR 77 and go 0.8 mile to the junction with FR 7715. This junction is directly across the road from McBride Campground. Turn right (north) on FR 7715 and follow it 4.8 miles to Summit Point Trailhead. There is a parking area at the trailhead. The Geo Graphics map shows this trailhead correctly, but forest service maps do not. There is good cell phone service at the trailhead.
GPS: N44 58.604'/W117 14.348'

The Hike

The trail begins as the old road to Summit Point Lookout. From the trailhead (6,450 ft.), head up to the north-northwest, climbing fairly steeply. After climbing for 0.6 mile the trail leaves the road, which makes a switchback to the right and climbs a short distance more to Summit Point Lookout. There is a sign marking the trail, which goes straight ahead, to the north-northwest, from the junction. The trail still follows the remains of an old road for some distance.

After leaving the Summit Point Road, the trail traverses along the left (west) side of the ridgeline for 0.4 mile to a saddle. A few feet before reaching the saddle the trail

Cornucopia Peak from Cliff Creek Trail.

bears to the left and leaves the old road. The old road goes through the saddle. The trail continues to traverse on the left side of the ridge through sage-covered slopes and groves of alpine trees. It reaches the now-rounded ridgeline 0.4 mile from the saddle. Here, on the grass- and flower-covered ridgetop, the view of the mountains to the north opens up. Lupine nearly covers parts of this ridgetop meadow; it blooms here about July 1.

Along the ridgetop the trail drops gently to the Eagle Cap Wilderness boundary and a small pond (7,200 ft.). The trail reaches the junction with Cornucopia Trail 0.5 mile after entering the wilderness. There are many campsites in this area around the fingers of timber, some distance away from the trail.

Upon entering the scattered timber just past the junction, the trail may become difficult to see for a few yards. It climbs slightly to the north through a small opening and soon becomes obvious again. From here to the junction with unmarked Trail 1946 at Nip Pass, the trail traverses the steep, lightly timbered west side of Cornucopia Peak. Nip Pass and the junction are 1.6 miles from the junction with Cornucopia Trail. At the pass, Cliff Creek Trail turns to the right (northeast) and continues to traverse another 0.5 mile to the junction with Pine Lakes Trail (1880), which is in the small notch called Tuck Pass. See Pine Lakes (hike 83). Tuck Pass (8,040 ft.) is the highest point on Cliff Creek Trail. From the pass, Crater Lake can be seen in the distance to the north.

From Tuck Pass, Cliff Creek Trail continues its traverse on a steep, granite boulder-strewn slope dotted with subalpine fir and whitebark pine. The trail rounds a point 0.6 mile into the traverse, then continues to traverse 0.3 mile farther. After the traverse the trail makes a turn to the right, then one to the left, climbs slightly, and rounds another point. It then heads east for 150 yards and crosses a small, lush meadow surrounded by granite boulders. The trail soon enters thicker timber and drops slightly.

Half a mile after crossing the meadow, the trail crosses a stream as it makes its way through the alpine timber and granite outcroppings. This stream crosses the trail in two channels. There is a waterfall in the stream a short distance above the trail, but it cannot be seen from the crossing.

After crossing the stream the trail climbs gently for 0.4 mile to the junction with Little Kettle Creek Trail (1945; 7,550 ft.). Crater Lake is 0.2 mile to the left (west) from the junction. At the junction Cliff Creek Trail turns to the right (north), crosses 75 yards of flat ground, then begins a descent through a forest of small subalpine fir. As the trail starts down, the ground is blanketed with mountain heather, which may be covered with pink blooms. The trail descends gently but steadily through the woods; the trees quickly get larger with the loss of altitude.

The trail crosses a stream and enters an open slope 0.4 mile after leaving the Crater Lake junction. From here the 9,555-foot-high summit of Red Mountain dominates the view to the right (east). The open slope is covered with grass and lupine; there are also a few sego lilies. The trail heads on down the left side of Cliff Creek Valley, crossing mostly open slopes that are occasionally dissected with fingers of timber, for 0.9 mile to another stream crossing. It crosses several very small streams as it goes across the slopes covered with paintbrush, sego lilies, and many other flowers. At the stream crossings, look for Lewis' monkeyflower.

The trail crosses another stream 0.5 mile farther along, then another 0.7 mile after that. At 0.1 mile after the second stream crossing, the trail makes a couple of switchbacks before crossing another small stream. It crosses several more small streams in the next 1.4 miles, where it reaches the junction with Cliff Creek Alternate Trail (1885A). There are very few good campsites along this trail, between the Little Kettle Creek Trail junction and the Imnaha River. However, there are some possible sites in the openings next to Cliff Creek a few hundred yards east of the trail.

At the junction (6,090 ft.) Cliff Creek Trail turns to the left (northwest). The trail climbs slightly over a small rise, then descends gently through the timber to the Imnaha River 0.6 mile from the junction with Trail 1885A. The trail fords the river and meets the South Fork Imnaha River Trail a few yards after the crossing (6,100 ft.). See South Fork Imnaha River (hike 90).

If you intend to go downriver (east) on South Fork Imnaha River Trail, bear right at the junction with Trail 1885A and take it 0.6 mile to a crossing of the Imnaha River and junction with South Fork Imnaha River Trail. This junction (5,910 ft.) is 0.8 mile below the junction with Cliff Creek Trail.

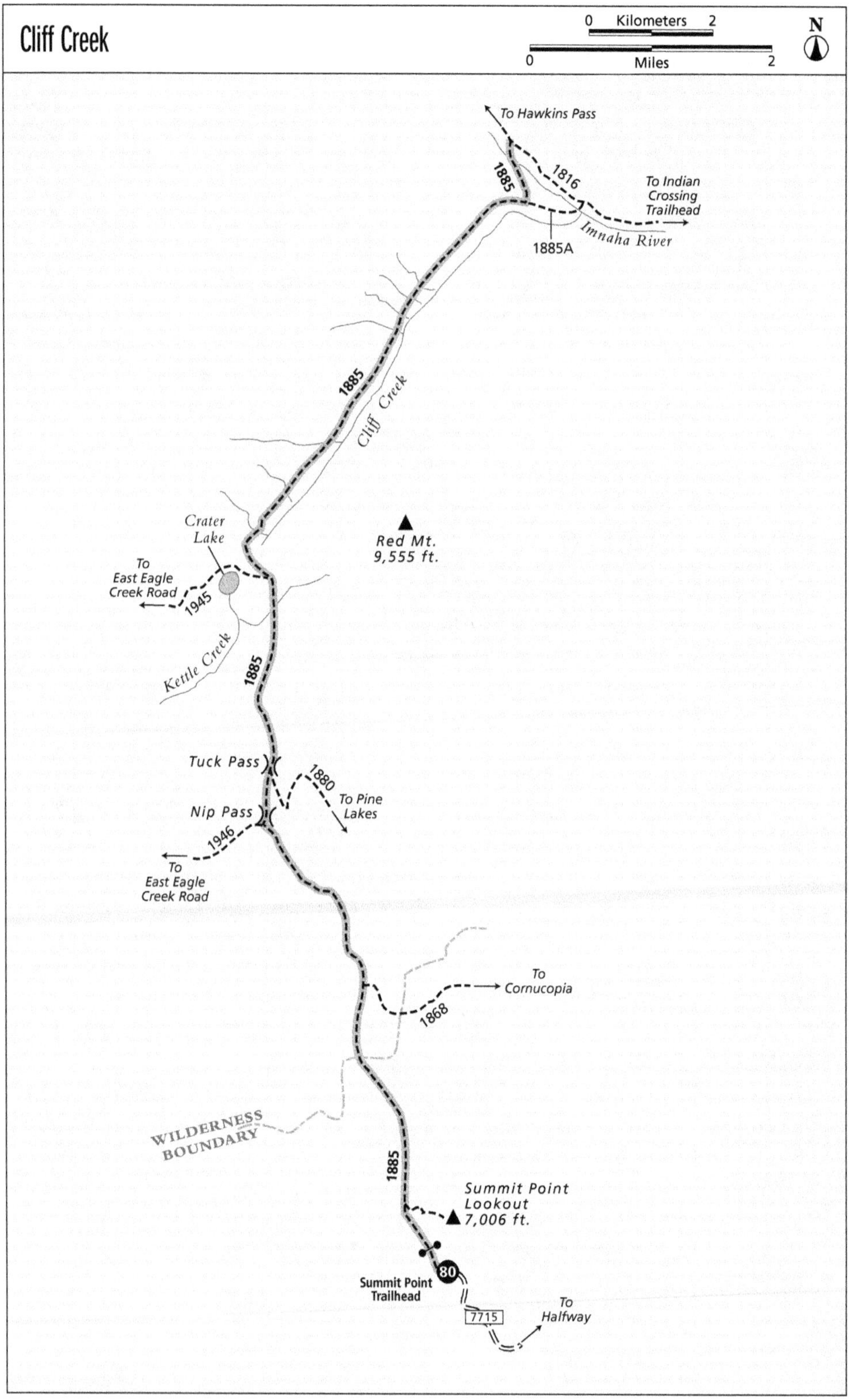
Cliff Creek
0 Kilometers 2
0 Miles 2
N
To Hawkins Pass
1885
1816
To Indian Crossing Trailhead
1885A
Imnaha River
1885
Cliff Creek
Red Mt. 9,555 ft.
Crater Lake
To East Eagle Creek Road
1945
Kettle Creek
1885
Tuck Pass
1880
To Pine Lakes
Nip Pass
1946
To East Eagle Creek Road
To Cornucopia
1868
WILDERNESS BOUNDARY
1885
Summit Point Lookout 7,006 ft.
80
Summit Point Trailhead
7715
To Halfway

The return trip can be made by the same trail, or you can hike on down the Imnaha River to Indian Crossing Trailhead. There are many campsites along the Imnaha River. A car shuttle is required if you end your hike at Indian Crossing Trailhead.

Miles and Directions

0.0 Start at the Summit Point Trailhead.

0.6 Reach the junction with the trail to Summit Point Lookout (road).

2.3 Pass the Eagle Cap Wilderness boundary.

2.8 Pass the junction with Cornucopia Trail (1868). (GPS: N45 00.432'/W117 15.140')

4.4 Cross Nip Pass and pass the junction with unmarked Trail 1946.

4.9 Cross Tuck Pass and pass junction with Pine Lakes Trail (1880). (GPS: N45 02.148'/W117 16.075')

7.0 Pass the junction with Little Kettle Creek Trail (1945). (GPS: N45 03.485'/W117 16.115')

11.2 Pass the junction with alternate Trail 1885A.

11.8 Reach the Imnaha River and the junction with South Fork Imnaha River Trail (1816). (GPS: N45 06.555'/W117 13.651')

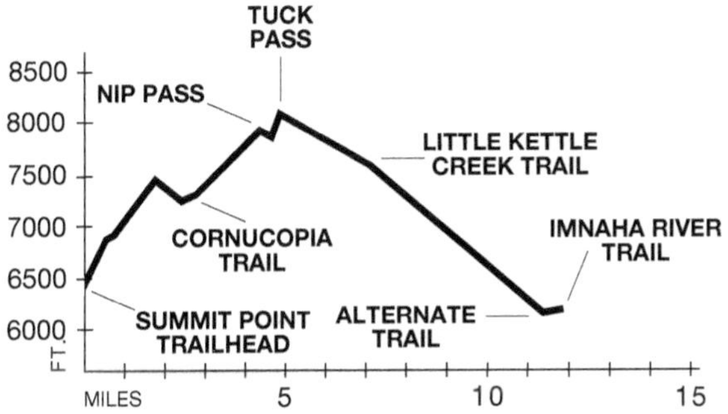

81 Little Kettle Creek

This backpack trip or day hike climbs from Old East Eagle Creek Trailhead to Crater Lake and the junction with Cliff Creek Trail. (Trail 1945)

Distance: 6.5 miles one way
Hiking time: 2.5–4 hours
Difficulty: Moderate
Trail maintenance: Infrequent, but this trail only passes short distances through woods, so downed logs are not much of a problem.
Best season: Mid-July through Sept
Traffic and other trail users: Moderate foot and horse traffic
Canine compatibility: Dogs permitted without leashes, but must be kept away from the stock of other parties
Fees and permits: Northwest Forest Pass and Eagle Cap Wilderness Permit
Maximum elevation: 7,620 feet
Map: USGS Krag Peak OR
Trail contact: USDA Forest Service Wallowa Mountains Office, 201 E 2nd St./ PO Box 905, Joseph, OR 97846; (541) 426-5546, (541) 426-4978; www.fs.usda.gov/wallowa-whitman; or USDA Forest Service Pine Field Office, 38470 Pine Town Ln., Halfway, OR 97834; (541) 742-7511. Office closed Dec 21 through Apr 30; contact Baker City office at (541) 523-6391.

Finding the trailhead: Little Kettle Creek Trail begins at Old East Eagle Creek Trailhead. From Union take OR 203 and go 20 miles southeast to Medical Springs. At Medical Springs turn left (southeast) on Big Creek Road and stay on it; it soon becomes FR 67. Follow FR 67 for 14.2 miles to the junction with FR 77. Turn right (east), on FR 77 and go 6.6 miles to the junction with East Eagle Creek Road (FR 7745). Turn left (north) on FR 7745 and follow it 6.5 miles to the Old East Eagle Creek Trailhead. There is parking at the trailhead. A separate parking area and trailhead have been built 0.8 mile south of (before) the Old East Eagle Creek Trailhead. For stock users, a trail connects this new trailhead with the old one.
GPS: N45 03.401'/W117 19.335'

The Hike

Little Kettle Creek Trail starts on the east side of the turnaround parking area at Old East Eagle Creek Trailhead (4,580 ft.). At first the trail climbs gently through a forest of large spruce and fir on the remains of an old roadbed. After 150 yards the trail bears to the right, off the roadbed. The trail makes a switchback to the right 0.1 mile after leaving the roadbed. It soon makes another switchback and climbs out of the dense forest, entering a semi-open, brush-covered slope. The trail continues to climb, making twenty-six switchbacks in the next 2.3 miles. The trail passes the Eagle Cap Wilderness boundary, which is 1.6 miles from the trailhead, as it climbs these switchbacks.

At the top of the switchbacks the trail begins an ascending traverse to the east along the mostly open but brushy mountainside. About 0.25 mile into the traverse, the trail crosses a shallow gully filled with paintbrush, fireweed, asters, and many other wildflowers. After crossing the flower-filled gully, the trail goes up steeply for 50 yards

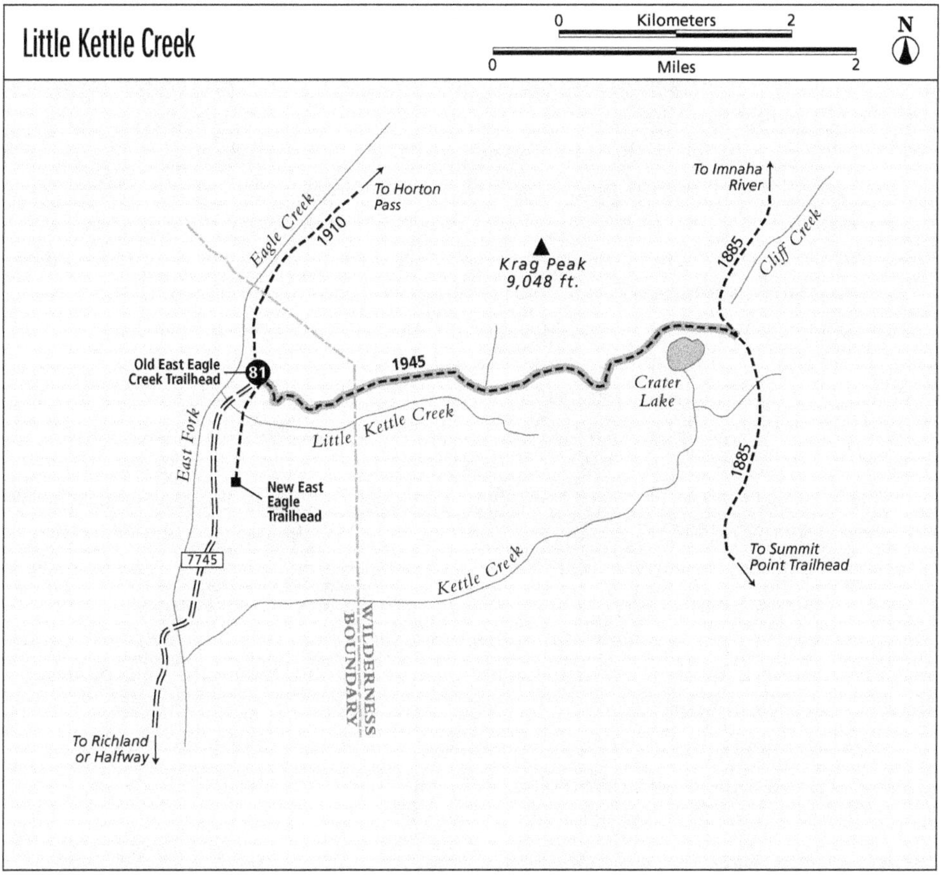

and soon crosses another gully. This one is strewn with boulders but still has room for lots of flowers.

The trail enters a stand of fairly large fir trees a short distance after crossing the boulder-strewn gully. It goes through the timber for 150 yards before coming out into the open again. In the open the trail makes a couple of switchbacks, then climbs steeply for 100 yards to a creek crossing. After crossing the creek the trail climbs steeply again for 200 more yards on a slope covered with sage and flowers. It soon bears to the right and crosses the slope, then begins a series of switchbacks. Watch the ground for sego lilies in this area.

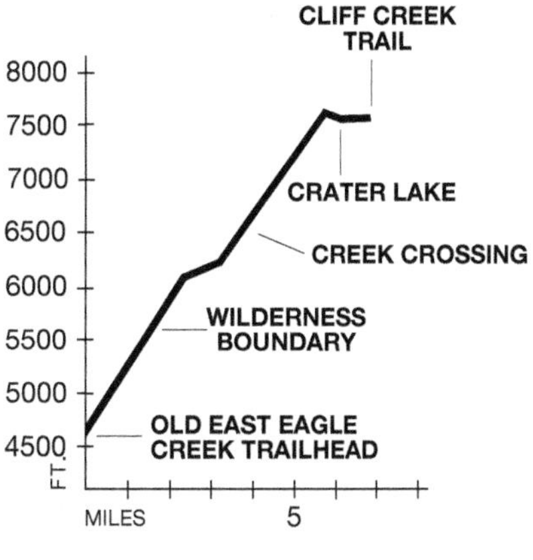

The trail climbs the series of four switchbacks, then enters some timber. In the timber there is a very small stream along the right side of the trail for a few yards. The trail comes out of the timber after a short distance and climbs a semi-open slope, making several more switchbacks. It then enters a talus slope dotted with small groves of scrubby subalpine fir. The trail makes eight switchbacks as it climbs the talus slope.

Above the talus slope the trail crosses a small stream, which flows through a culvert under the trail, then passes a pond. The pond, which is to the right of the trail, has a lush meadow around it. There is another, smaller pond just to the east of the first one. The trail makes a couple more switchbacks in the next 0.25 mile, passing through scattered small alpine trees, granite outcroppings, and mountain heather, to the top of a rise. The top of this rise is the highest elevation reached on this trail at 7,620 feet.

From the top of the rise, the trail drops for the 0.1 mile to Crater Lake (7,560 ft.), making a switchback to the left just before reaching it. The trail works its way for 0.25 mile around the north shore of the lake to the dam on its northeast corner. It crosses the dam and heads east for 300 yards, over the top of a couple of small rises, to the junction with Cliff Creek Trail (7,550 ft.). See Cliff Creek (hike 80).

From the dam to the junction is the roughest part of the entire trail. This section is easy to follow but is not graded. There are few reasonably good campsites around Crater Lake, but with a little looking, a place to pitch a tent can be found. Lots of fish are available for the catching in the lake. The lake level fluctuates because of the dam, but the muddy shorelines present at some of the lakes on this side of the mountains are not a problem here.

From Crater Lake the return trip is best made by the same trail, unless an extended trip involving a car shuttle is desired. If you want to make an extended trip, the Cliff Creek hike entry lists just some of the possibilities.

Miles and Directions

0.0 Start at the Old East Eagle Creek Trailhead.

1.6 Pass the Eagle Cap Wilderness boundary.

3.7 Make a creek crossing.

6.0 Reach Crater Lake.

6.5 Arrive at the junction with Cliff Creek Trail (1885). (GPS: N45 03.485'/W117 16.115')

82 Cornucopia

This downhill day hike goes from Summit Point Trailhead to Cornucopia. The trail is mostly on old mine trails and roads. To hike this one way, as described here, a car shuttle is required. (Trails 1885 and 1868)

Distance: 6.5 miles one way
Hiking time: 3–4 hours
Difficulty: Moderate as described, strenuous if hiked in the other direction. Much of this trail is rough and rocky.
Trail maintenance: Rare
Best season: Mid-June through Oct
Traffic and other trail users: Moderate foot and horse traffic
Canine compatibility: Dogs permitted without leashes, but must be kept away from the stock of other parties
Fees and permits: Eagle Cap Wilderness Permit
Maximum elevation: 7,420 feet
Maps: USGS Jim Town OR, Sparta Butte OR, Krag Peak OR, and Cornucopia OR; Geo Graphics Wallowa Mountain Eagle Cap Wilderness. This trail is in the corner of four quad maps. Cornucopia quad covers most of it.
Trail contact: USDA Forest Service Wallowa Mountains Office, 201 E 2nd St./PO Box 905, Joseph, OR 97846; (541) 426-5546, (541) 426-4978; www.fs.usda.gov/wallowa-whitman; or USDA Forest Service Pine Field Office, 38470 Pine Town Ln., Halfway, OR 97834; (541) 742-7511. Office closed Dec 21 through Apr 30; contact Baker City office at (541) 523-6391.

Finding the trailhead: From Halfway take Cornucopia Road (OR 413) and go 5.4 miles northwest to the poorly marked Carson Grade junction. The junction is marked with a sign pointing to West Carson Lane. Turn left (west) at the junction and head up West Carson Lane (aka West Carson Grade), which soon becomes FR 7710. Follow FR 7710 for 3.3 miles to the junction with FR 77. Turn right on FR 77 and go 0.8 mile to the junction with FR 7715. This junction is directly across the road from McBride Campground. Turn right (north) on FR 7715 and follow it 4.8 miles to Summit Point Trailhead. There is a parking area at the trailhead. The Geo Graphics map shows this trailhead correctly, but forest service maps do not. There is good cell phone service at the trailhead.
GPS: Summit Point Trailhead: N44 58.604'/W117 14.348'; Cornucopia Trail junction: N45 00.432'/W117 15.140'

The Hike

From Summit Point Trailhead hike 2.5 miles north along the ridgetop on the Cliff Creek Trail (1885), passing below (west of) Summit Point Lookout, to the junction with the Cornucopia Trail (7,280 ft.). The area around the Cornucopia junction is mostly ridgetop meadows. It is a likely place to see mule deer, especially big bucks. There are ponds and streams here, which make it a good place to camp.

Cornucopia Trail heads southeast from the junction. At first it follows old road ruts east-southeast to where the trail shows up. In about 300 yards the trail bends

Schneider cabin. LOWELL EUHUS PHOTO

around to the east-northeast and crosses two small streams. The trail comes to Schneider cabin (7,320 ft.) 0.1 mile after crossing the streams. This cabin, with a pole fence around it, is well kept up and is being used. Please do not bother the cabin.

The trail heads slightly uphill to the east and a little north from the cabin. It crosses a small gully. After about 250 yards it begins a traverse on an open slope. The trail traverses for 0.25 mile before turning to the right and heading down. The elevation at the end of the traverse is 7,420 feet.

From the end of the traverse, the trail drops 700 feet in the next 0.9 mile, making eight switchbacks. Below the switchbacks the trail follows a steep, rough old roadbed down a ridge. There is a saddle in the ridgeline, 0.5 mile and 600 vertical feet below the last switchback.

The trail makes a switchback to the right 250 yards past the saddle. Another 250 yards down, the trail turns nearly straight uphill for a couple hundred yards. It soon heads down again and becomes a much wider roadbed. At a fork in the road, head down. There are many signs of old mining operations in this area.

The trail (road) crosses Jim Fiske Creek 500 yards below the fork. This crossing (5,430 ft.) is 3.25 miles from the junction with Trail 1885. The trail comes to a road that is in use 200 yards past the crossing. Follow this road down 0.7 mile to the old mining town of Cornucopia. The distance from Trail 1885 to Cornucopia is 4 miles. In Cornucopia the trail's end is some distance south and across Pine Creek from the main Cornucopia Trailhead.

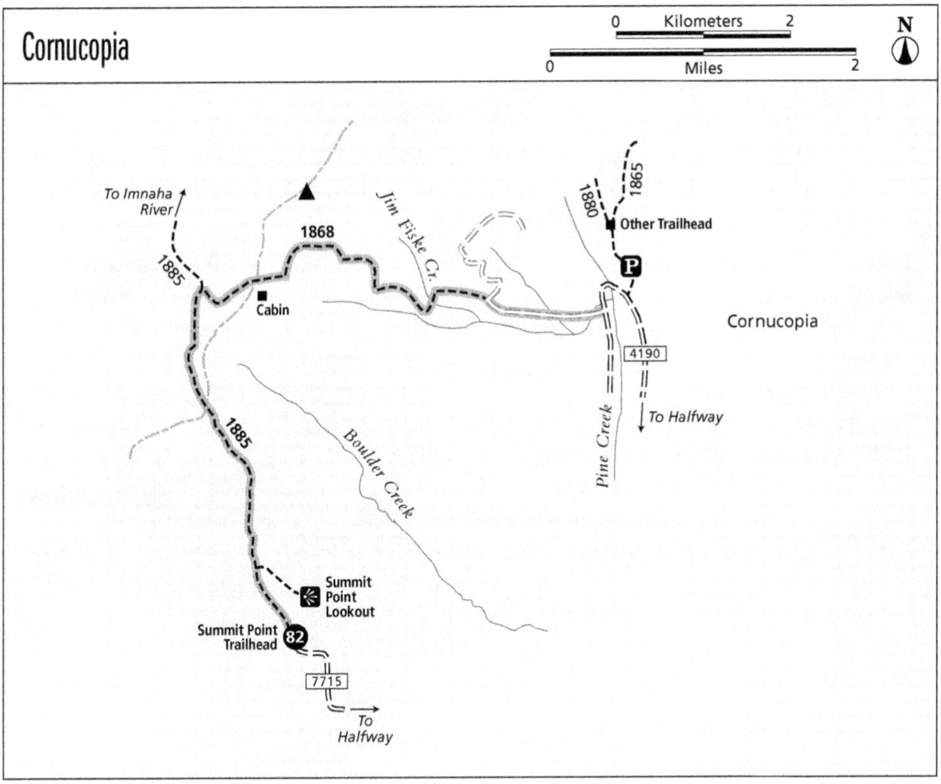

This trail is best hiked one way from the Summit Point Trailhead. It is not only mostly downhill in this direction, but it is also easier to follow. There is some private land in Cornucopia, but if you stay on the road, which is also the trail, no special permission is necessary.

Miles and Directions

0.0 Hike north from the Summit Point Trailhead.

2.5 At the junction with Cliff Creek Trail (1885), head southwest on the Cornucopia Trail (1868).

3.0 Reach the Schneider cabin. (GPS: N45 00.689'/W117 14.511')

5.7 Cross Jim Fiske Creek.

6.5 Arrive in Cornucopia. (GPS: N45 00.373'/W117 11.799')

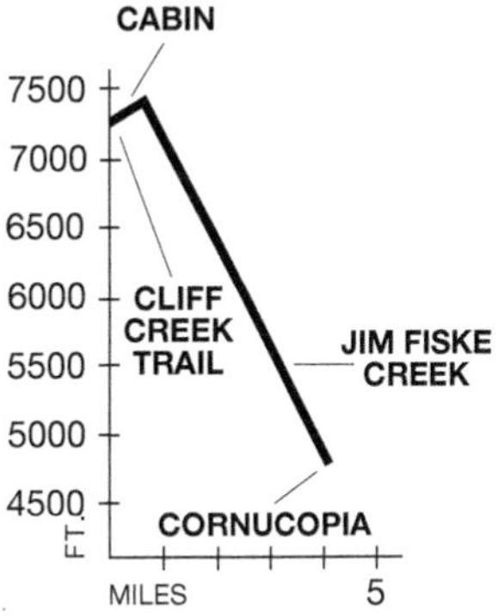

83 Pine Lakes

Hike from Tuck Pass on the Cliff Creek Trail, descending into the subalpine cirque that contains Pine Lakes. Allow time to camp and/or fish for a while before descending the rest of the way down to the old mining town of Cornucopia. (Trail 1880)

Distance: 10.6 miles one way
Hiking time: 4–6 hours
Difficulty: Moderate in the direction described, strenuous if coming up from Cornucopia
Trail maintenance: Yearly
Best season: July through Sept
Traffic and other trail users: Moderate to heavy foot traffic; moderate horse traffic
Canine compatibility: Dogs permitted without leashes, but must be kept away from the stock of other parties
Fees and permits: Eagle Cap Wilderness Permit
Maximum elevation: 8,380 feet
Maps: USGS Krag Peak OR and Cornucopia OR (Jim Town OR, if coming from Summit Point Trailhead); Geo Graphics Wallowa Mountains Eagle Cap Wilderness covers the entire trip.
Trail contact: USDA Forest Service Wallowa Mountains Office, 201 E 2nd St./PO Box 905, Joseph, OR 97846; (541) 426-5546, (541) 426-4978; www.fs.usda.gov/wallowa-whitman; or USDA Forest Service Pine Field Office, 38470 Pine Town Ln., Halfway, OR 97834; (541) 742-7511. Office closed Dec 21 through Apr 30; contact Baker City office at (541) 523-6391.

Finding the trail: Pine Lakes Trail starts at the junction with Cliff Creek Trail (8,020 ft.), 4.9 miles north of Summit Point Trailhead. To reach Summit Point Trailhead drive northwest from Halfway on Cornucopia Road (OR 413) for 5.4 miles to the poorly marked Carson Grade junction. The junction is marked with a sign pointing to West Carson Lane. Turn left (west) at the junction and head up West Carson Lane (aka West Carson Grade), which soon becomes FR 7710. Follow FR 7710 for 3.3 miles to the junction with FR 77. Turn right on FR 77 and go 0.8 mile to the junction with FR 7715. This junction is directly across the road from McBride Campground. Turn right (north) on FR 7715 and follow it 4.8 miles to Summit Point Trailhead. There is a parking area at the trailhead. The Geo Graphics map shows this trailhead correctly, but forest service maps do not. Hike north from the Summit Point Trailhead on the Cliff Creek Trail to Tuck Pass and the junction with the Pine Lakes Trail. There is good cell phone service at the trailhead and along the ridge north of it.

The Cornucopia Trailhead, where this hike description ends, can be reached by following Cornucopia Road north from the town of Halfway 10 miles to Cornucopia. The trailhead is at the north end of town.

GPS: Summit Point Trailhead: N44 58.604'/W117 14.348'; Pine Lakes Trail junction: N45 02.148'/W117 16.075'; Cornucopia Trailhead: N45 00.936'/W117 11.709'

The Hike

Pine Creek Trail is a 10.6-mile day hike or a two-day backpack. I describe the route from its junction with Cliff Creek Trail (1885) to Cornucopia. This may seem

Pine Lakes. LOWELL EUHUS PHOTO

backward, but it is a much easier hike in this direction. Even including the 4.9-mile hike from Summit Point Trailhead to the beginning of Pine Lakes Trail at the junction with Cliff Creek Trail, it is no farther than the round-trip to Pine Lakes from Cornucopia. The elevation gain going in the direction I describe is much less, and you do not have to cover the same ground twice. However, it does require a car shuttle.

From the junction with Cliff Creek Trail, Pine Lakes Trail climbs to the south-southeast for 0.5 mile. It then makes a switchback to the left. The trail reaches a pass (8,380 ft.) 0.25 mile past the switchback. Pine Lakes can be seen from the pass.

The trail makes ten switchbacks in the next 0.5 mile, down the steep, open slope to the first lake. This lake is little more than a pond. It is to the right (south) of the trail 50 or so yards. The elevation at this first lake is approximately 8,100 feet. After passing the first lake, the trail makes a couple more switchbacks, then winds down through granite outcroppings to a stream crossing (7,840 ft.). There is a small rock bridge over this stream.

After crossing the stream the trail goes along the right side of a meadow. A little less than 0.5 mile past the stream crossing, the trail starts down another series of switchbacks. There are eight switchbacks in the next 0.5 mile. Upper Pine Lake (7,540 ft.) is at the bottom of the switchbacks. A short distance farther is Lower Pine Lake. Pine Lakes are 3.5 miles from the junction with Cliff Creek Trail, and there are 7.1 miles to go to Cornucopia. A few good campsites can be had at Pine Lakes, and there seem to be plenty of fish. A short, steep stream runs between the lakes. The trail goes around the left side of Lower Pine Lake, then crosses the outlet stream just below the dam.

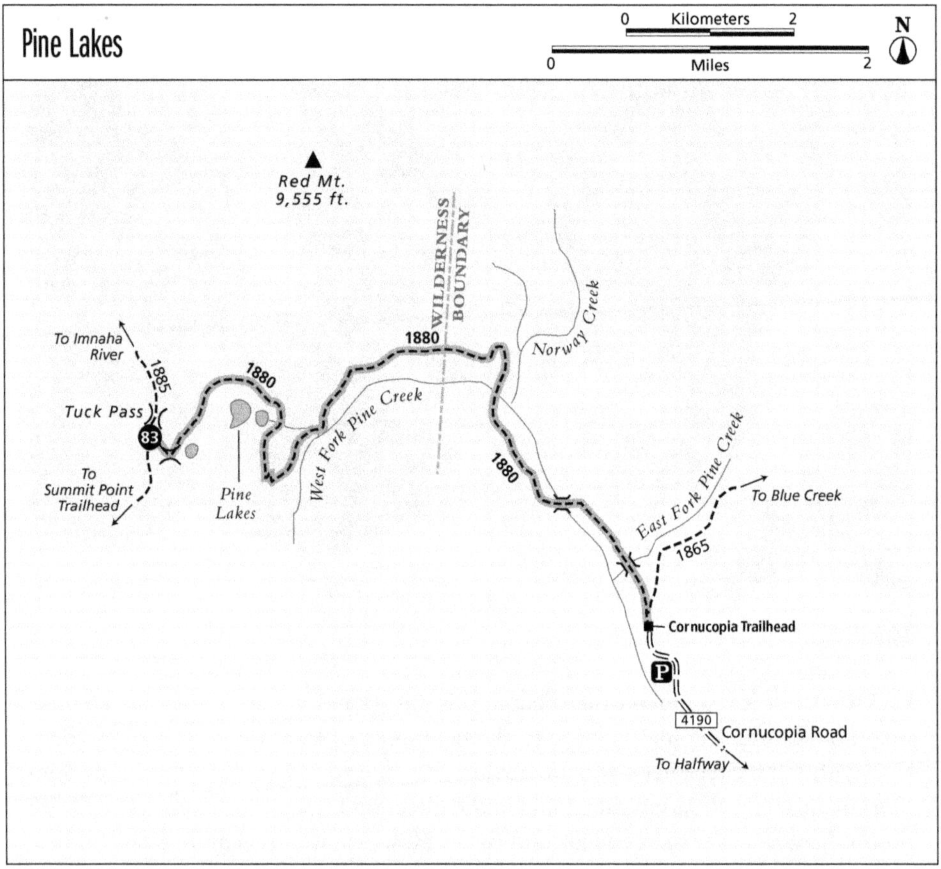

Below Pine Lakes the trail makes eighteen switchbacks and crosses several small streams while descending into a lush alpine valley. This valley faces northeast, which is probably why it has more lush vegetation than the country just over the ridge to the west. The trail heads down the valley for a short distance. It then makes four more little switchbacks and crosses a meadow on an elevated trail. After crossing the meadow the trail crosses the outlet stream of Pine Lakes. A waterfall is to the left of the trail.

The trail begins to descend more steeply again 0.25 mile after the creek crossing. It makes four switchbacks, crosses a couple of small streams, then makes another switchback. This area was burned many years ago. There are many silver snags. The burned area is about 600 yards across. Beyond the burn is a set of four more switchbacks. These switchbacks take the trail down a granite talus slope. There is a small stream crossing 0.3 mile past the last switchback. The Eagle Cap Wilderness boundary (6,070 ft.) is just less than 0.5 mile past the small stream crossing.

The trail crosses a ridgeline 0.25 mile past the wilderness boundary. It starts another series of nine switchbacks that bring it down to the bridge over the West Fork Pine Creek (5,260 ft.). The trail becomes an old roadbed after crossing the bridge. The trail crosses a small stream 0.7 mile after crossing the West Fork Pine Creek. A couple hundred yards after crossing the stream, the trail crosses Pine Creek on a bridge (4,980 ft.). This bridge is in very poor condition.

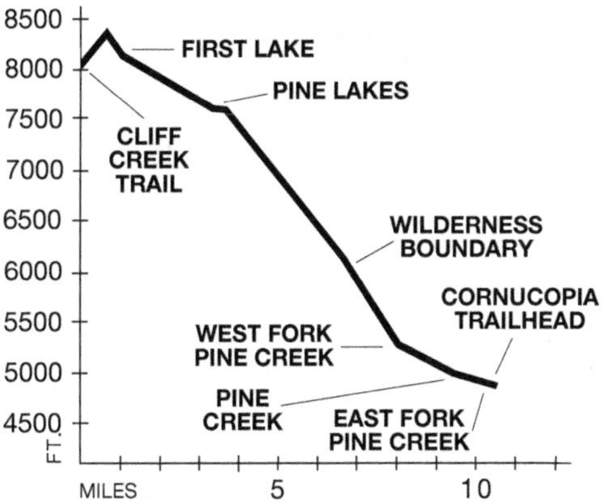

After crossing Pine Creek the trail goes 0.25 mile to the crossing of another very small stream. There is a footbridge over another stream 300 yards past the small stream crossing. In another 150 yards a footbridge goes over the East Fork Pine Creek. Just after crossing the East Fork, the trail crosses another small stream. The pack station is 500 yards farther, as is the Cornucopia Trailhead sign. The elevation at the trailhead is 4,830 feet.

The Cornucopia Trailhead is 10.6 miles from the junction with Cliff Creek Trail. Cornucopia is an interesting old mining town. There is a fairly large parking area 0.25 mile south of the trailhead on the main road.

Miles and Directions

0.0 At the junction of Cliff Creek Trail (1885) and Pine Lakes Trail (1880), go right (south-southeast) on the Pine Lakes Trail.

0.7 Cross the pass.

1.0 Pass the first lake (pond).

3.5 Reach Pine Lakes. (GPS: N45 02.278'/W117 15.130')

6.7 Pass the Eagle Cap Wilderness boundary.

8.2 Cross West Fork Pine Creek.

9.5 Cross Pine Creek.

10.3 Cross East Fork Pine Creek.

10.6 Arrive at the Cornucopia Trailhead.

84 Norway Basin

An alternate route for a section of East Fork Pine Creek/Blue Creek Trail (1865), this trail is generally more scenic than East Pine Creek Trail but is somewhat steeper and rougher. It follows old mine roads part of the way. Most of the country along this trail has burned at least once since 2000, and the flowers are wonderful. (Trail 1896)

Distance: 4.8 miles one way
Hiking time: 2–3 hours
Difficulty: Moderate to strenuous
Trail maintenance: Frequent on road section; infrequent beyond
Best season: July through Oct
Traffic and other trail users: Light foot and horse traffic, motor vehicle traffic is possible, but very unlikely, before reaching Norway Basin.
Canine compatibility: Dogs permitted without leashes, but must be kept away from the stock of other parties
Fees and permits: Eagle Cap Wilderness Permit
Maximum elevation: 7,630 feet
Map: USGS Cornucopia OR
Trail contact: USDA Forest Service Wallowa Mountains Office, 201 E 2nd St./ PO Box 905, Joseph, OR 97846; (541) 426-5546, (541) 426-4978; www.fs.usda.gov/wallowa-whitman; or USDA Forest Service Pine Field Office, 38470 Pine Town Ln., Halfway, OR 97834; (541) 742-7511. Office closed Dec 21 through Apr 30; contact Baker City office at (541) 523-6391.

Finding the trail: Norway Basin Trail begins at its junction with East Pine Creek Trail (1865), 1.2 miles north of the Cornucopia Trailhead. To reach the trailhead go 10 miles north from Halfway on Cornucopia Road (OR 413) to Cornucopia. The trailhead is at the north end of the old town, next to the pack station. There is a large open area for parking 0.25 mile before the trailhead. A signboard at the trailhead points out the trails. Hike northeast from the trailhead on the East Fork Pine Creek/Blue Creek Trail (1865) for 1.2 miles to the junction with the Norway Basin Trail (5,640 ft.). The trail is actually an old road here, as are many trails, or parts of trails, in the Cornucopia area.
GPS: Cornucopia Trailhead: N45 00.936'/W117 11.709'; Norway Basin Trail junction: N45 01.858'/W117 11.000'

The Hike

Norway Basin Trail leaves East Fork Pine Creek Trail just after that trail crosses the East Fork Pine Creek, 1.2 miles from Cornucopia Trailhead. Norway Basin Trail turns to the left. There is a sign marking this junction. The trail heads southwest, crosses a creek, and soon climbs around the end of a ridge. After rounding the ridge it heads to the north and climbs steeply.

The trail flattens out some 0.5 mile after leaving East Fork Pine Creek Trail. After climbing at a gentler grade for 275 yards, it crosses one of the forks of Simmons Creek. This crossing (6,000 ft.) is just above a fork in the creek. After crossing the creek the trail steepens again and heads up a ridgeline to the northwest. The forest

Flowers along the Norway Basin Trail.

opens up along this ridge, which makes it a good area to see elk, as I have several times when I've hiked this trail.

The trail climbs up the ridgeline for 0.7 mile, then turns off to the left. There is an old roadbed going straight up the ridge here, but the trail sign points to the left. Another old roadbed crosses the trail 0.3 mile farther along. The trail sign here points straight ahead. After going 350 yards past the roadbed crossing, Norway Basin Trail finally bears right off the roadbed it has followed all the way from East Fork Pine Creek Trail. A trail sign here points to the right (north).

An old mine can be seen far below the trail 0.25 mile after leaving the roadbed. This mine is across Norway Creek on the other side of the canyon. The roadbed you turned off leads to the mine. The Eagle Cap Wilderness boundary is another 0.3 mile up the trail. The elevation at the boundary is 7,120 feet.

The trail crosses Norway Creek 1.1 miles past the wilderness boundary. The trail comes to the junction with Sugarloaf Trail (1887; 7,630 ft.) 350 yards after crossing Norway Creek. This junction is in a saddle on the ridge dividing the Pine Creek and Imnaha River drainages. There is a ditch coming through the saddle that takes water from the Imnaha side and puts it on the Pine Creek side. A fairly good campsite is located to the right (east) of the trail at the saddle.

Norway Basin Trail goes across the saddle and starts to drop down the Imnaha River and Blue Creek side of the ridge. Just below the saddle it goes through an area of springs. After crossing the wet area the trail continues to drop, crossing four small

Norway Basin/East Fork Pine Creek/Blue Creek/East Lakes Reservoir

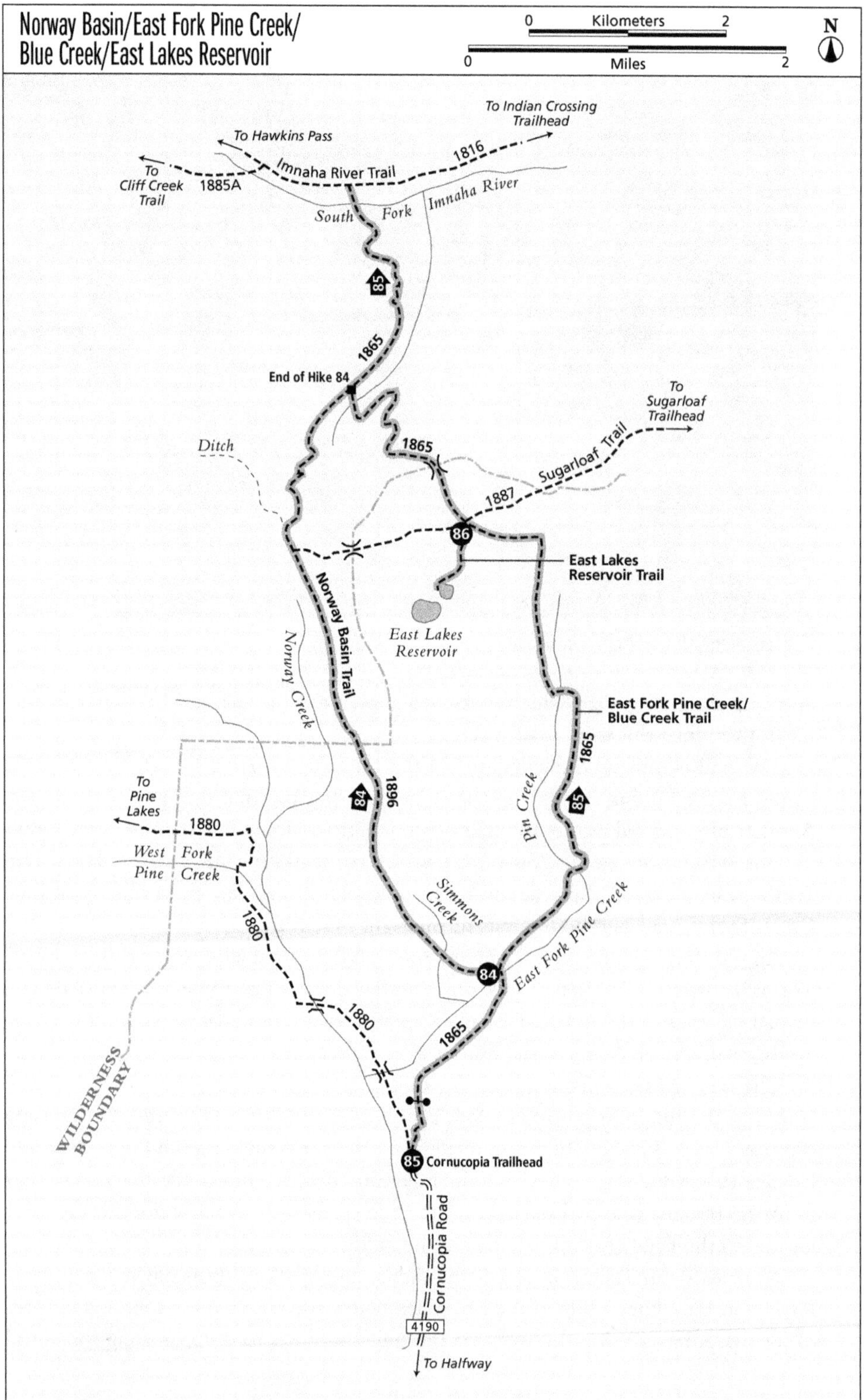

streams in the mile to the junction with East Fork Pine Creek/Blue Creek Trail, which is 2.8 miles above the Imnaha River. This is the end of Norway Basin Trail (6,800 ft.). The return trip can be made on East Fork Pine Creek/Blue Creek Trail back to Cornucopia Trailhead.

Miles and Directions

0.0 At the junction with East Fork Pine Creek Trail (1865), go left on the Norway Basin Trail (1896).

3.6 Pass the junction with Sugarloaf Trail (1887). (GPS: N45 04.240' / W117 12.610')

4.8 Arrive at the junction with Blue Creek Trail (1865). (GPS: N45 04.944'/W117 12.145')

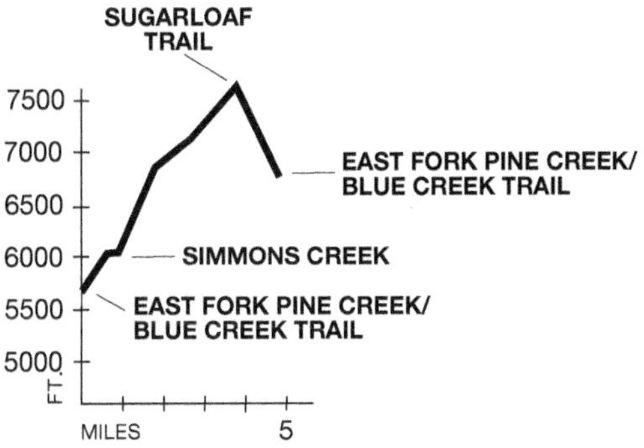

85 East Fork Pine Creek/Blue Creek

This backpack trip or long day hike leads from Cornucopia Trailhead to the Imnaha River and provides access to Norway Basin and Sugarloaf Trails. The route climbs steadly for the first 5.8 miles, much of the way through fairly open country, some of it burned in the last few years. In summer there are lots of flowers along this route. Elk are common here, especially in the burned areas; watch for them morning and evening. Once past the pass the route descends steadily to the Imnaha River. (Trail 1865)

See map page 300.
Distance: 9.7 miles one way
Hiking time: 5–7 hours
Difficulty: Moderate to strenuous
Trail maintenance: Infrequent
Best season: July through Oct
Traffic and other trail users: Moderate foot and horse traffic to Norway Basin Trail; light from there to the Imnaha River. There may be occasional motor vehicle traffic up to the first Norway Basin Trail junction.
Canine compatibility: Dogs permitted without leashes, but must be kept away from the stock of other parties
Fees and permits: Eagle Cap Wilderness Permit
Maximum elevation: 7,540 feet
Map: USGS Cornucopia OR
Trail contact: USDA Forest Service Wallowa Mountains Office, 201 E 2nd St./ PO Box 905, Joseph, OR 97846; (541) 426-5546, (541) 426-4978; www.fs.usda.gov/wallowa-whitman; or USDA Forest Service Pine Field Office, 38470 Pine Town Ln., Halfway, OR 97834; (541) 742-7511. Office closed Dec 21 through Apr 30; contact Baker City office at (541) 523-6391.

Finding the trailhead: The trail begins at Cornucopia Trailhead. To reach the trailhead, go 10 miles north from Halfway to Cornucopia, on Cornucopia Road (OR 413). The trailhead is at the north end of the old town, next to the pack station. There is a large open area for parking 0.25 mile before the trailhead. A signboard at the trailhead points out the trails, which begin from here on old mining roads.
GPS: N45 00.936'/W117 11.709'

The Hike

Trail 1865 begins at Cornucopia Trailhead (4,830 ft.). Like several other trails in the Cornucopia area, this trail starts out as an old roadbed. The trail, or road, heads north from the trailhead. After going 200 yards there is a stream crossing and a junction. Bear to the right (north-northeast). There is another junction 200 yards farther up the trail; bear right (north-northeast) again. A few yards past this junction is an iron gate blocking the road to vehicles. The elevation at the gate is 4,950 feet.

The trail continues to climb and crosses a small stream 0.7 mile past the gate. It crosses the East Fork Pine Creek 0.3 mile after crossing the small stream. The junction with Norway Basin Trail is reached a few yards after crossing the East Fork Pine Creek (5,640 ft.). Norway Basin Trail turns to the left (southwest).

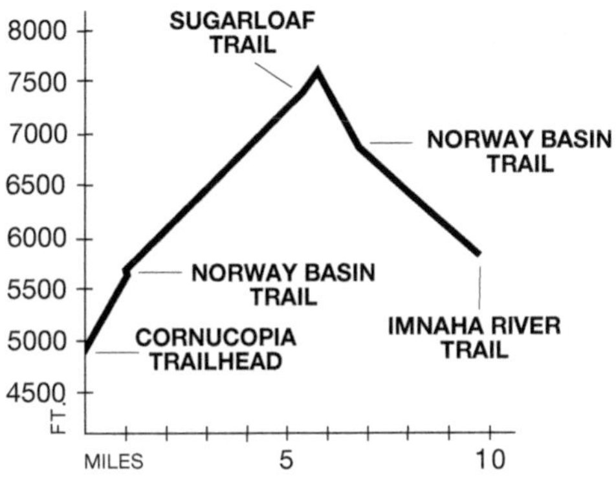

In the next 0.9 mile, three cattle trails turn off the main trail. Stay on the main trail, heading up the left side of the creek. After going 0.9 mile up the left side of the creek, the trail turns to the right and crosses the East Fork Pine Creek again. There is a waterfall just above the crossing.

After the crossing, the trail climbs, making some switchbacks, then heads up through mostly open meadows to another creek crossing 0.9 mile after crossing the East Fork. The trail crosses three more streams as it climbs through alternating timber and sloping meadows, in 1.7 more miles, to the junction with Sugarloaf Trail and East Lakes Reservoir Trail. This junction (7,320 ft.) is 5.4 miles from Cornucopia Trailhead. Follow the signs at the junction. This is where East Fork Pine Creek Trail becomes Blue Creek Trail.

From the junction, Blue Creek Trail heads up and to the northwest. It climbs for 0.4 mile to a saddle (7,540 ft.). In the saddle the trail enters Eagle Cap Wilderness. There is a sign at the boundary. After going through the meadow in the saddle, the trail makes five switchbacks as it drops the first mile toward the Imnaha River. In the 0.5 mile to the junction with Norway Basin Trail, the trail crosses two small streams on bridges as it descends through the forest. It then crosses Blue Creek and comes to the junction (6,800 ft.).

Bear right (northeast) at the junction, cross a small muddy stream, and head on down Blue Creek. The trail crosses a wooden bridge over a small stream 150 yards from the junction and soon enters an area of sloping meadows bisected by strips of timber. A bit over a mile beyond the junction, the trail begins to descend more steeply. It makes eight switchbacks as it drops through thick forest for 1.6 miles to a wooden bridge over a small stream. On the way down, much of the forest floor is covered with huckleberry bushes.

After crossing the bridge, the trail heads northwest through the woods on nearly flat ground for 0.2 mile to the Imnaha River. The trail fords the Imnaha River, angling upstream, then goes the last few yards to the junction with Imnaha River Trail (5,832 ft.). This crossing could be dangerous during periods of high water.

There are no really good campsites along this trail, but several can be found near the junction with the Imnaha River Trail on the north side of the Imnaha River. An excellent one-way trip can be made by combining this trail with part of the Imnaha River Trail. To do this trip, head down the Imnaha River to Indian Crossing Trailhead. This combination trip requires a car shuttle.

Miles and Directions

0.0 Start at the Cornucopia Trailhead.

1.2 Pass the junction with Norway Basin Trail (1896). (GPS: N45 01.858'/W117 11.000')

5.4 Pass the junction with Sugarloaf Trail (1887). (GPS: N45 04.274'/W117 11.189')

5.8 Cross the pass.

6.9 Pass the second junction with Norway Basin Trail. (GPS: N45 04.944'/W117 12.145')

9.7 Arrive at the Imnaha River and the junction with Imnaha River Trail (1816). (GPS: N45 06.010'/W117 12.197')

86 East Lakes Reservoir

This side trip leads from the junction of Sugarloaf and East Fork Pine Creek Trails to East Lakes Reservoir. Elk are common along this route.

See map page 300.
Distance: 0.5 mile one way
Hiking time: About 0.25 hour
Difficulty: Easy
Trail maintenance: None
Best season: Mid-June through Oct
Traffic and other trail users: Light traffic, except for cows
Canine compatibility: Dogs permitted without leashes, but must be kept away from the stock of other parties
Fees and permits: Eagle Cap Wilderness Permit
Maximum elevation: 7,320 feet
Map: USGS Cornucopia OR covers the area, but this trail is not shown on the map.
Trail contact: USDA Forest Service Wallowa Mountains Office, 201 E 2nd St./ PO Box 905, Joseph, OR 97846; (541) 426-5546, (541) 426-4978; www.fs.usda.gov/wallowa-whitman; or USDA Forest Service Pine Field Office, 38470 Pine Town Ln., Halfway, OR 97834; (541) 742-7511. Office closed Dec 21 through Apr 30; contact Baker City office at (541) 523-6391.

Finding the trail: To reach the junction where the East Lakes Reservior Trail starts, drive 10 miles north from Halfway to Cornucopia, on Cornucopia Road (OR 413). The trailhead is at the north end of the old town, next to the pack station. There is a large open area for parking 0.25 mile before the trailhead. A signboard at the trailhead points out the trails, which begin from here on old mining roads. Hike northeast from the trailhead on the East Fork Pine Creek/Blue Creek Trail (1865) for 5.4 miles to the junction with the Sugarloaf Trail (1887), where the path to East Lakes Reservoir begins.
GPS: Cornucopia Trailhead: N45 00.936'/W117 11.709'; East Lakes Reservoir Trail junction: N45 04.274'/W117 11.250'

The Hike

From the junction with Sugarloaf Trail, East Lakes Reservoir Trail heads southwest. After going about 500 yards, the trail becomes difficult to see in some woods. Keep going southwest. Stay nearly level, then go over a small rise to where the trail shows up again and the lakes come into view. The trail then drops down slightly to the lakes (7,272 feet).

East Lakes Reservoir is two lakes that have been dammed to hold more water for irrigation. This damming was a common practice with the lakes on the south side of the Wallowa Mountains in past years. Damming does hold water for summer use, but it makes a real mess out of lakeshores. To compound the mess at East Lakes Reservoir, the muddy shorelines are further degraded by cattle tromping in the mud.

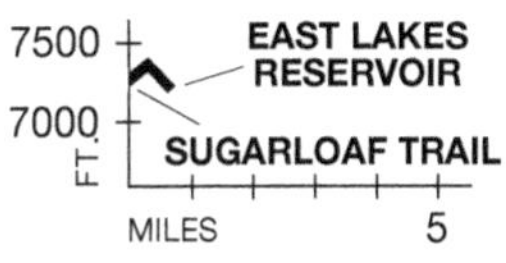

The area around the reservoir is a high, ridgetop plateau. There is much open grassland and groves of subalpine trees. This is prime summer range for elk. Return to the junction via the same trail.

Miles and Directions

0.0 At the junction with Sugarloaf Trail (1887), head southwest on the East Lakes Reservoir Trail.

0.5 Arrive at East Lakes Reservoir. (GPS: N45 03.902'/W117 11.460')

Eastern

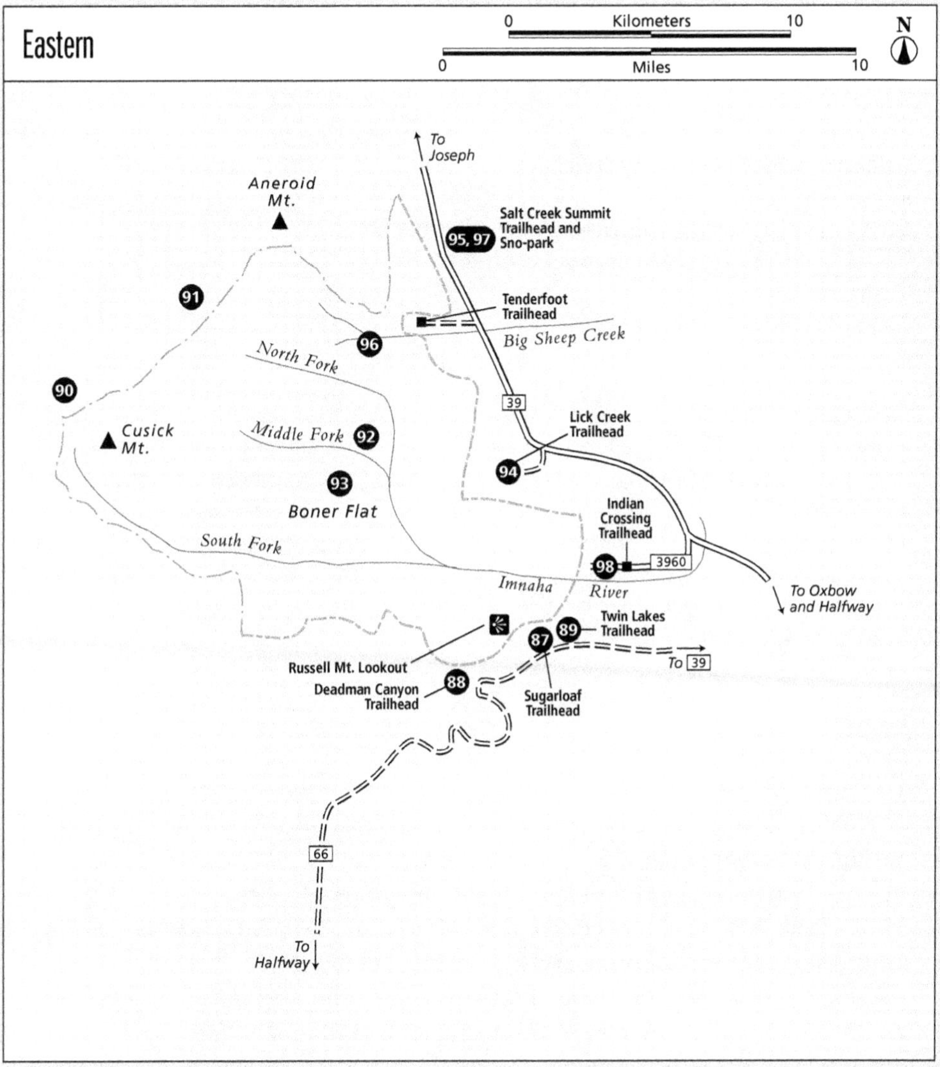
Eastern
0
Kilometers
10
0
Miles
10
N
To Joseph
Aneroid Mt.
Salt Creek Summit Trailhead and Sno-park
95, 97
91
Tenderfoot Trailhead
96
Big Sheep Creek
North Fork
90
39
Lick Creek Trailhead
Cusick Mt.
Middle Fork
92
94
93
Boner Flat
Indian Crossing Trailhead
South Fork
98
3960
Imnaha
River
To Oxbow and Halfway
Twin Lakes Trailhead
89
87
To 39
Russell Mt. Lookout
88
Deadman Canyon Trailhead
Sugarloaf Trailhead
66
To Halfway

87 Sugarloaf

This backpack route from Twin Lakes to Norway Basin Trail runs along the south rim of the Imnaha River Canyon. Several parts of this trail are very vague. The Sugarloaf Trail traverses some of the best elk country in the west. (Trail 1887)

Distance: 9.9 miles one way
Hiking time: 4–6 hours
Difficulty: Easy, but good route-finding skills are required.
Trail maintenance: Rare
Best season: July through Oct
Traffic and other trail users: Moderate foot and horse traffic
Canine compatibility: Dogs permitted without leashes, but must be kept away from the stock of other parties
Fees and permits: Eagle Cap Wilderness Permit
Maximum elevation: 7,930 feet
Maps: USGS Deadman Point OR and Cornucopia OR; Geo Graphics Wallowa Mountains Eagle Cap Wilderness
Trail contact: USDA Forest Service Wallowa Mountains Office, 201 E 2nd St./ PO Box 905, Joseph, OR 97846; (541) 426-5546, (541) 426-4978; www.fs.usda.gov/wallowa-whitman; or USDA Forest Service Pine Field Office, 38470 Pine Town Ln., Halfway, OR 97834; (541) 742-7511. Office closed Dec 21 through Apr 30; contact Baker City office at (541) 523-6391.

Finding the trailhead: To reach the Twin Lakes Campground from Halfway, take OR 86 east for 9 miles. Turn left (north) on FR 39 and go 14 miles to FR 66. Turn left (west) and follow FR 66 12 miles to Twin Lakes Campground. FR 39 can also be reached from Joseph. From Joseph take the Imnaha Highway east for 8 miles to the junction with the Wallowa Mountain Loop Road (FR 39). Turn right and follow FR 39 for 40 miles to the junction with FR 66. Turn right (west) on FR 66 and follow it to Twin Lakes Campground. Don't turn into the campground but continue west for 0.2 mile to the trailhead on the right side of the road.
GPS: N45 04.518'/W117 03.400'

The Hike

The Sugarloaf Trail heads west-southwest from the rough parking lot at the trailhead (6,490 ft.). The trail, which is an abandoned roadbed for the first mile, climbs through the burned timber of the 1994 Twin Lakes forest fire. The trail heads southwest and climbs in a narrow sloping meadow 0.3 mile after leaving the parking lot. At the top of the meadow the trail turns to the right. Watch for blazes and sawed logs marking the trail. It soon turns left again and goes up another meadow.

About 1 mile from the parking lot, the trail climbs up through an open area. It is difficult to see the trail here. The trail goes back into the woods at the north-northwest corner of the open area and soon enters another open area. After going 300 yards, a creek flows a few yards to the left of the trail.

The trail soon enters yet another open area. There is a large lodgepole pine in the middle of this open area, with a blaze on it. Head west-southwest past the lodgepole

Russel Mountain Lookout.

pine. Turn left slightly at the upper end of the opening, then climb to the top of a low, rounded ridge. At the top of the ridge the trail turns left and heads south-southwest.

The trail soon enters another meadow. Go up the middle of this meadow, then left, slightly, at the top. The trail hits another meadow 0.25 mile farther along. Head west-northwest and look for the cut logs that make an opening for the trail on the other side of the meadow. Go through a line of trees and head west-southwest across a wet meadow for 200 yards. At the upper end of the wet area, another cut log marks an opening for the trail.

The trail comes to the Russel Mountain Lookout Road (FR 450) 0.25 mile past the wet area. The trail from Twin Lakes to Russel Mountain Lookout Road takes some route-finding skills. Most of this section was at least partly burned in the fire, so some of the best trail markers are the logs that were sawed off to reopen the trail.

The trail turns right (northwest) on the Russel Mountain Lookout Road and climbs 250 yards to Russel Mountain Lookout (7,508 ft.). This is also a trailhead, but the road to it is very rough. Good cell phone service is available.

From the lookout the trail begins to drop slightly to the west. The trail enters a meadow 0.7 mile past the lookout and goes along the left side of this long meadow. It stays on the edge of the trees and heads to the west. The meadow is nearly 0.5 mile long.

The junction with Deadman Canyon Trail (1869) is 0.3 mile past the end of the meadow through another patch of burnt forest. The trail leaves the burned area at this point. The junction (7,230 ft.) is 1.6 miles from Russel Mountain Lookout. Deadman Canyon Trailhead is to the left (south) at the junction. The trail that goes to the right dead-ends. The Sugarloaf Trail goes straight ahead, to the west-southwest, but is very difficult to see here. Head west-southwest and cross two streams. Deadman Canyon Trail and Sugarloaf Trail follow the same route for about 500 yards. Then Deadman Canyon Trail turns off to the right (northwest) and heads for the Imnaha River. There is a signpost at this junction.

From the second Deadman Canyon Trail junction, Sugarloaf Trail heads west-southwest. At first it climbs toward Sugarloaf Mountain, and then bears slightly to the left and begins a traverse around the south side of the mountain. It may be difficult to see in spots here. There is a trail marker sign 0.3 mile from the junction. The signpost is on the left side of the trail. Beyond the marker the trail becomes a two-track, unused jeep road. Another trail comes in from the left (south) 0.2 mile past the trail sign. There is another trail marker sign on the right side of the trail here. The trail goes through a saddle 0.3 mile past the second trail sign. Red Mountain comes into view, straight ahead at the saddle.

After passing the saddle the trail drops slightly, then continues its traverse. The trail goes between two posts 1.1 miles past the saddle. A panoramic view of the upper Imnaha drainage opens up about 300 yards after going between the posts. The trail traverses around the slope, then descends west for 0.25 mile to a saddle. There is a pond in this saddle. The saddle (7,380 ft.) is one of the better campsites along Sugarloaf Trail. The trail is difficult to see near the pond.

Pick up the trail on the west side of the pond. There is a broken-down corral just past the pond, on the left side of the trail. The trail comes to a burned area 0.3 mile past the saddle. It climbs 0.1 mile through the lightly burned area to another saddle (7,550 ft.). The trail goes around the north side of a low hill and comes to a spring 0.5 mile past the saddle. The small spring is right in the trail.

After passing the spring the trail drops steeply west for 0.3 mile to another saddle. The junction with Blue Creek Trail (1865) is 0.6 mile past the saddle on the left

Sugarloaf

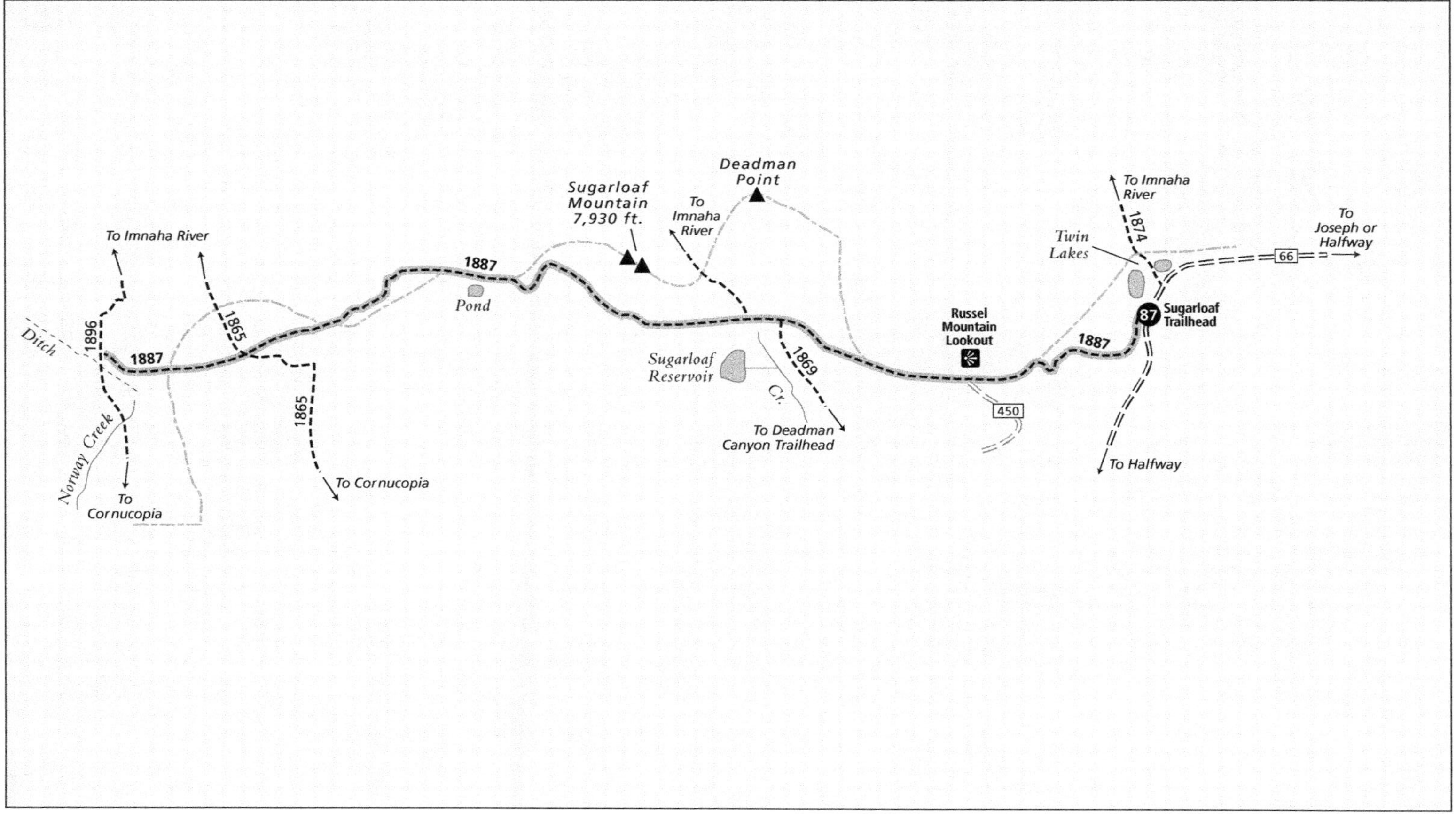

0 Kilometers 2
0 Miles 2
N
Deadman Point
Sugarloaf Mountain 7,930 ft.
To Imnaha River
To Imnaha River
To Imnaha River
To Joseph or Halfway
Twin Lakes
1874
66
87 Sugarloaf Trailhead
1887
1887
1887
Pond
Russel Mountain Lookout
Sugarloaf Reservoir
Cr.
1869
450
To Deadman Canyon Trailhead
To Halfway
Ditch
1896
1865
1865
Norway Creek
To Cornucopia
To Cornucopia

(south) side of the ridgeline. The area between the saddle and the trail junction may be nearly covered with phlox in early summer. This junction (7,320 ft.) is 8.7 miles from Twin Lakes.

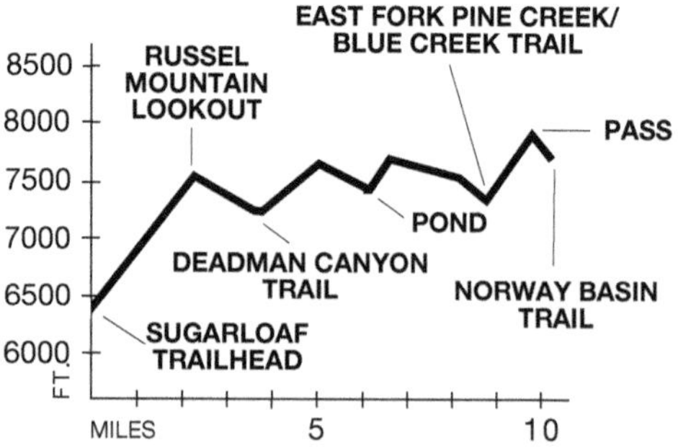

Beyond the junction the trail soon becomes difficult to see. It goes west, then southwest, and crosses a very small stream, which may be dry, 150 yards from the junction. There is a post marking the trail 100 yards past the stream. Here the trail becomes easy to see again. There are also some rock cairns marking it. The trail gradually turns to the west 250 yards past the post. In about 100 yards more, it fades out again in an open area. The trail goes up the right (north) side of a little valley to the west, then climbs over a small rise and bears slightly to the left. Here the trail can be seen ahead as it heads up to a pass. There are also blazes on the scattered trees. The trail climbs to the pass (7,930 ft.), the high point of this trail.

Looking west from the pass, there is a good view of Red Mountain. To the northwest, across the South Fork Imnaha River Canyon, is Cusick Mountain.

From the pass the trail heads down steeply, first to the west-southwest, then to the west. It is difficult to see in spots, but is never gone too long. It drops for 0.4 mile to the junction with Norway Basin Trail (1896). The Norway Basin Trail junction (7,630 ft.) is 9.9 miles from the Sugarloaf Trailhead.

Sugarloaf Trail generally follows the rim of the Imnaha River Canyon and parallels the Eagle Cap Wilderness boundary from Twin Lakes to Norway Basin Trail. After climbing the first mile from Twin Lakes, the trail stays above 7,000 feet all the rest of the way. All of this trail goes through excellent elk summer range, and there is a good chance of seeing these large animals.

A one-way trip can be made by combining Sugarloaf Trail with the south 3.6 miles of Norway Basin Trail and the south 1.2 miles of East Fork Pine Creek/Blue Creek Trail. Doing this trip involves a car shuttle to Cornucopia.

Miles and Directions

0.0 Start at the Sugarloaf Trailhead.

2.2 Pass Russel Mountain Lookout. (GPS: N45 04.100'/W117 05.213')

3.8 Pass the junction with Deadman Canyon Trail (1869; to trailhead).

4.0 Pass the junction with Deadman Canyon Trail (to Imnaha River). (GPS: N45 04.560'/W117 06.970')

6.2 Pass the pond.

8.7 Pass the junction with East Fork Pine Creek/Blue Creek Trail (1865) and East Lakes Reservoir Trail. (GPS: N45 04.274'/W117 11.250')

9.9 Arrive at the junction with Norway Basin Trail (1896). (GPS: N45 04.240'/W117 12.610')

88 Deadman Canyon

This backpack or long day hike runs from the Deadman Canyon Trailhead near Fish Lake to the Imnaha River. The route first climbs gently through meadowlands, where bands of elk can often be seen. Then you descend to the bank of the scenic Imnaha River. Much of the area along this route has burned in recent years; this opens up the ground to more sunlight, making for better elk forage and more flowers. (Trail 1869)

Distance: 6.1 miles one way
Hiking time: 3–5 hours
Difficulty: Moderate to strenuous, with some route-finding skills required
Trail maintenance: Infrequent
Best season: July through Oct
Traffic and other trail users: Light to moderate foot and horse traffic
Canine compatibility: Dogs permitted without leashes, but must be kept away from the stock of other parties
Fees and permits: Eagle Cap Wilderness Permit
Maximum elevation: 7,460 feet
Maps: USGS Deadman Point OR and Cornucopia OR; Geo Graphics Wallowa Mountains Eagle Cap Wilderness
Trail contact: USDA Forest Service Wallowa Mountains Office, 201 E 2nd St./PO Box 905, Joseph, OR 97846; (541) 426-5546, (541) 426-4978; www.fs.usda.gov/wallowa-whitman; or USDA Forest Service Pine Field Office, 38470 Pine Town Ln., Halfway, OR 97834; (541) 742-7511. Office closed Dec 21 through Apr 30; contact Baker City office at (541) 523-6391.

Finding the trailhead: Deadman Canyon Trail begins at Deadman Canyon Trailhead, just north of Fish Lake. To reach the trailhead from Halfway, take OR 86 east for 9 miles. Turn left (north) on FR 39 and go 14 miles to FR 66. Turn left (west) and follow FR 66 for 12 miles to Twin Lakes Campground and the trailhead. FR 39 can also be reached from Joseph. From Joseph take the Imnaha Highway for 8 miles east to the junction with the Wallowa Mountain Loop Road (FR 39). Once on FR 39, continue south for 40 miles to the junction with FR 66. Turn west on FR 66 and drive 16 miles to the junction with FR 410. Turn right (west) on FR 410 and go 0.4 mile to Deadman Canyon Trailhead. The junction of FR 66 and FR 410 is just north of Fish Lake.

Fish Lake can also be reached from Halfway by taking East Pine Creek Road north from town. East Pine Creek Road becomes FR 66 and leads to Fish Lake and the junction with FR 410. The Geo Graphics map is a big help for finding your way around the roads in this area.
GPS: N45 03.062'/W117 06.092'

The Hike

From Deadman Canyon Trailhead (6,760 ft.), Deadman Canyon Trail starts out as a road that is closed to motor vehicles. A sign at the trailhead points to the Imnaha River. The trail, or road, heads west to start. About 150 yards from the trailhead, the trail crosses a creek as it climbs gently through the timber. In another 300 yards a creek flows down the trail for a short distance. The junction with the trail to Clear

Meadow along Deadman Canyon Trail.

Creek Reservoir Trail (1867) is reached 0.4 mile from the trailhead. The map below also shows an alternate route for the first 0.5 mile of this hike. The alternate route may be used if desired.

The trail to Clear Creek Reservoir turns to the left (northwest). A short distance past the junction, the Deadman Canyon Trail bears to the north and leaves the closed road. The trail crosses a creek 0.3 mile after leaving the old roadbed and crosses another one 0.2 mile farther along. The trail comes to the junction with Sugarloaf Reservoir Trail 0.8 mile after the last creek crossing. The reservoir is 0.25 mile to the left (west), across the meadow.

Deadman Canyon Trail goes straight ahead (north) 0.2 mile more to the second junction with Sugarloaf Trail (1887). The junction (7,230 ft.) is 2.1 miles from the trailhead. This junction area is where this description disagrees with both the Geo Graphics and USGS maps. A short section of alternate trail, shown on the map below, bypasses the first junction with the Sugarloaf Trail. Either route may be used here. At this junction Deadman Canyon Trail turns to the left and follows Sugarloaf Trail to the west-southwest. A sign here points out Sugarloaf Trail. The path that goes straight ahead (north) dead-ends. Turn left and follow the Sugarloaf Trail.

After following Sugarloaf Trail for 500 yards and crossing a couple of small streams, there is another junction with a signpost. The signs can be confusing here. The Deadman Canyon Trail turns to the right (northwest) and climbs gently through mostly

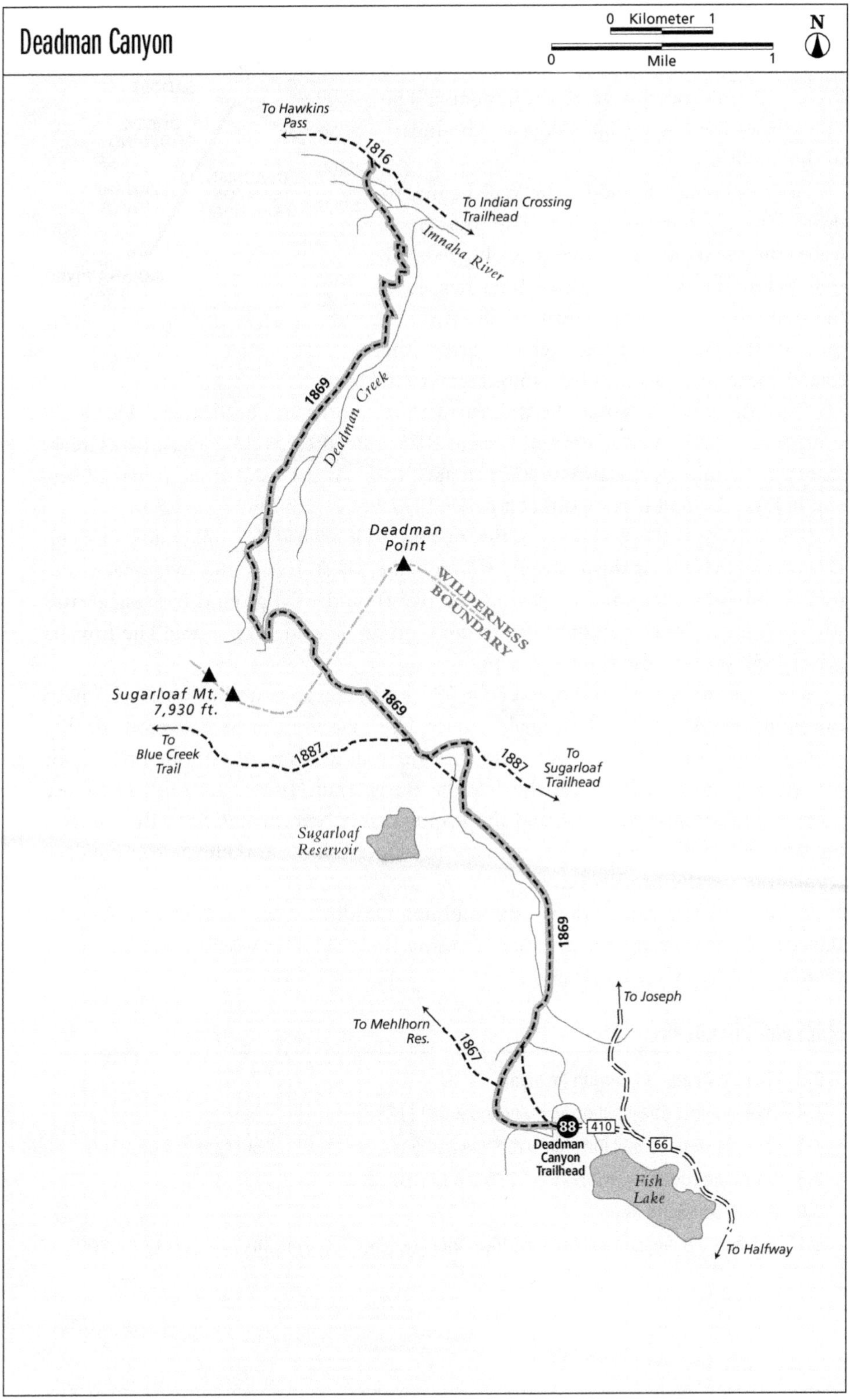
Deadman Canyon
0 Kilometer 1
0 Mile 1
N
To Hawkins Pass
1816
To Indian Crossing Trailhead
Imnaha River
1869
Deadman Creek
Deadman Point
WILDERNESS BOUNDARY
Sugarloaf Mt. 7,930 ft.
1869
To Blue Creek Trail
1887
1887
To Sugarloaf Trailhead
Sugarloaf Reservoir
1869
To Joseph
To Mehlhorn Res.
1867
88
410
66
Deadman Canyon Trailhead
Fish Lake
To Halfway

open meadows to the saddle between Deadman Point and Sugarloaf Mountain. This saddle (7,460 ft.) is 0.2 mile northwest of the junction. The trail crosses the Eagle Cap Wilderness boundary in the saddle.

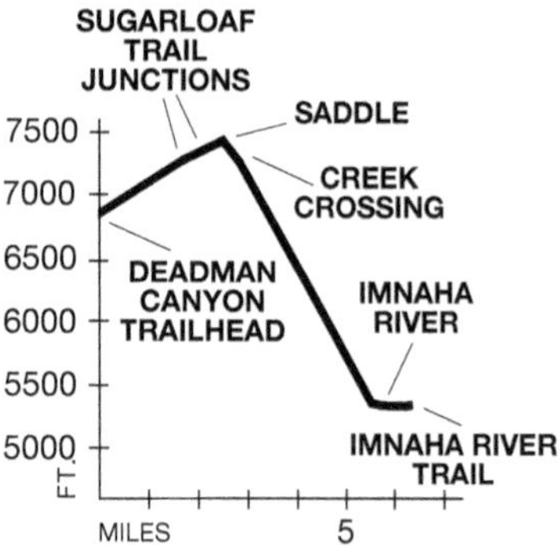

After crossing the saddle the trail begins to drop through burned timber. The trail soon leaves the burn area. It crosses a small creek 0.2 mile below the saddle. A few yards farther along the trail crosses Deadman Creek (7,280 ft.). The forks of the creeks run together just below the trail. A meadow and a possible campsite are to the left.

After the creek crossing, the trail turns to the north and heads down Deadman Canyon. It crosses a couple more streams 0.75 mile after crossing Deadman Creek. Another 0.8 mile down there is an open area, with a good view of the Imnaha Canyon below. The trail may be difficult to see here, but it soon shows up again.

The trail begins a mile-long series of nine switchbacks 1.9 miles after crossing Deadman Creek, as it drops steeply through the forest. Below the switchbacks the trail becomes less steep and soon heads left (west) on the flat ground, crossing a small stream. A short distance farther, a campsite is on the left side of the trail. The Imnaha River is 50 yards to the right at this point.

The trail heads west and upriver for 300 yards, crossing another small stream, to the point where it fords the Imnaha River. This crossing can be dangerous during times of high water. After crossing the river the trail heads northeast, then north, for 0.1 mile to the junction with the Imnaha River Trail (1816; 5,310 ft.). There are good campsites near the river, and the fishing can be excellent. Check the Oregon Department of Fish and Wildlife regulations before fishing, as there are some special regulations for the Imnaha River.

A one-way trip can be done by combining Deadman Canyon Trail with Imnaha River Trail and coming out at Indian Crossing Trailhead. This would necessitate a car shuttle to Indian Crossing Trailhead.

Miles and Directions

0.0 Start at Deadman Canyon Trailhead.

1.8 Pass the first trail junction with Sugarloaf Trail (1887).

2.1 Pass the second trail junction with Sugarloaf Trail. (GPS: N45 04.560'/W117 06.970')

2.6 Cross the saddle. (GPS: N45 04.775'/W117 07.335')

6.0 Ford the Imnaha River.

6.1 Arrive at the junction with Imnaha River Trail (1816). (GPS: N45 06.741'/W117 07.200')

89 Twin Lakes

This day hike or backpack leads from the Twin Lakes Trailhead and Campground to the Imnaha River. This area was burned in the Twin Lakes Fire of September 1994. The flowers and views are great along the upper part of this trail. (Trail 1874)

Distance: 3.1 miles one way
Hiking time: 1.5–2.5 hours
Difficulty: Moderate to strenuous, with bushwacking and route-finding skills required
Trail maintenance: Seldom
Best season: Mid-June through early Nov
Traffic and other trail users: Light foot traffic
Canine compatibility: Dogs permitted without leashes, but must be kept away from the stock of other parties
Fees and permits: Eagle Cap Wilderness Permit
Maximum elevation: 6,490 feet
Map: USGS Deadman Point OR
Trail contact: USDA Forest Service Wallowa Mountains Office, 201 E 2nd St./ PO Box 905, Joseph, OR 97846; (541) 426-5546, (541) 426-4978; www.fs.usda.gov/wallowa-whitman; or USDA Forest Service Pine Field Office, 38470 Pine Town Ln., Halfway, OR 97834; (541) 742-7511. Office closed Dec 21 through Apr 30; contact Baker City office at (541) 523-6391.

Finding the trailhead: Twin Lakes Trail begins at Twin Lakes Trailhead and Campground. To reach the trailhead from Halfway, take OR 86 east for 9 miles. Turn left (north) on FR 39 and go 14 miles to FR 66. Turn left (west) and follow FR 66 12 miles to Twin Lakes Campground and Trailhead. From Joseph take the Imnaha Highway east for 8 miles to the junction with the Wallowa Mountain Loop Road (FR 39). Turn right on FR 39, drive south for 40 miles to the junction with FR 66, and turn right.
GPS: N45 04.795'/W117 03.360'

The Hike

The area around the trailhead and along most of this trail was burned in the September 1994 Twin Lakes Fire. The trail heads northwest from the trailhead (6,480 ft.). After a short distance it crosses the creek that connects the lakes. There is another creek crossing 0.2 mile farther along. Just past this second creek crossing is the Eagle Cap Wilderness boundary. Soon after passing the wilderness boundary, the trail starts to descend through the now completely burned forest into the Imnaha River Canyon.

The trail descends for 200 yards, then follows a bench to the right (east) for 125 yards before bearing to the left (northeast) and dropping steeply again. The trail descends for 0.8 mile more, then crosses a creek (5,820 ft.). After crossing the creek the trail bears left and heads northwest.

The trail comes to an open bench area 0.1 mile after the creek crossing. There is a campsite on the bench, if you don't mind camping among the burnt snags. The elevation is 5,760 feet. There is a rock outcropping on the right side of the trail on

Blue Hole.

this bench; the top of the outcropping provides a good viewpoint overlooking the Imnaha Canyon.

The trail drops off the bench and descends fairly steeply for 0.4 mile to the northwest. Then it flattens out and heads west, finally reaching an area that was not

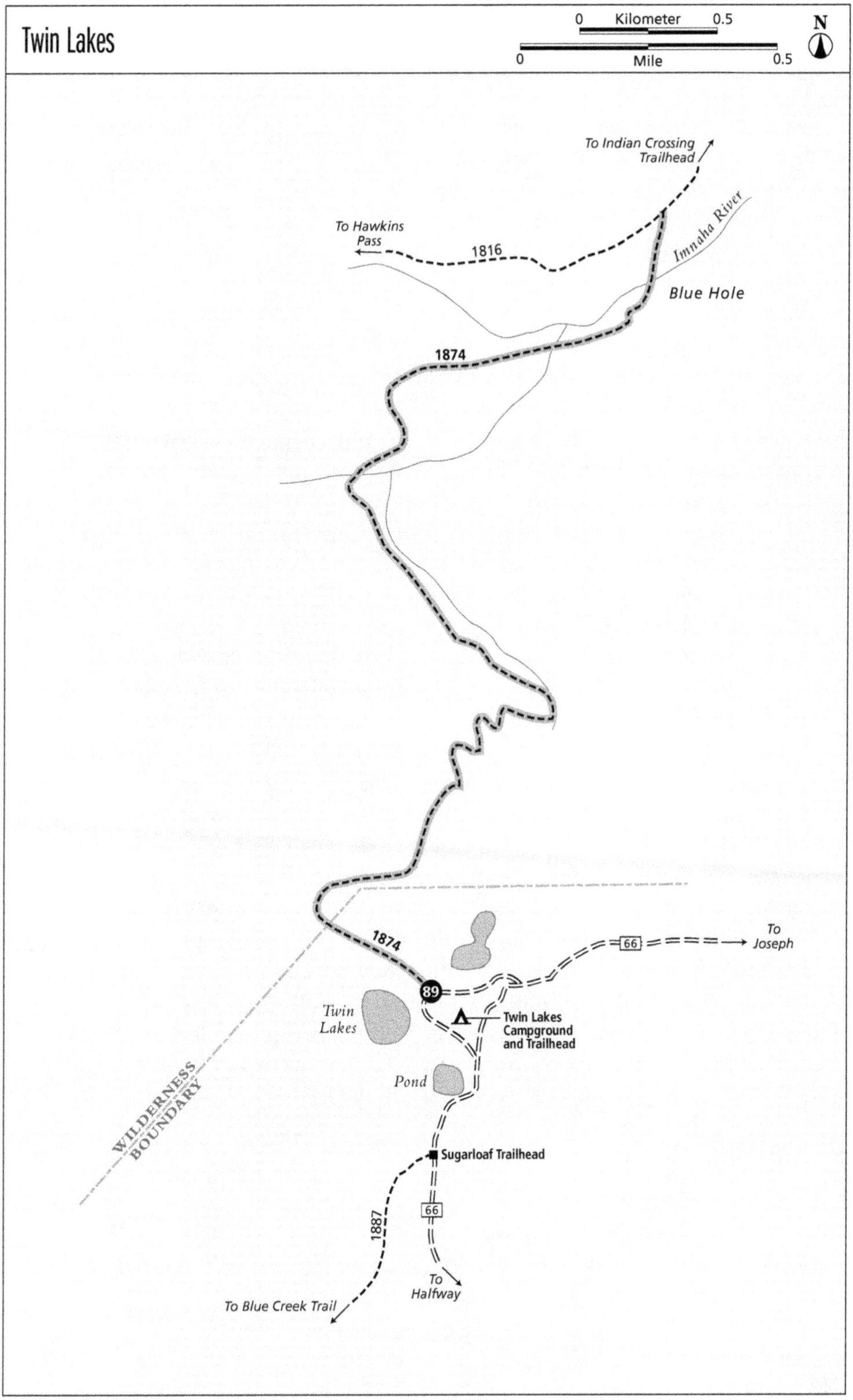

Twin Lakes
0 Kilometer 0.5
0 Mile 0.5
N
To Indian Crossing Trailhead
To Hawkins Pass
1816
Imnaha River
Blue Hole
1874
1874
66
To Joseph
89
Twin Lakes
Twin Lakes Campground and Trailhead
Pond
WILDERNESS BOUNDARY
Sugarloaf Trailhead
66
1887
To Halfway
To Blue Creek Trail

completely burned in the forest fire. It doesn't flatten out for long, and soon drops to a creek crossing.

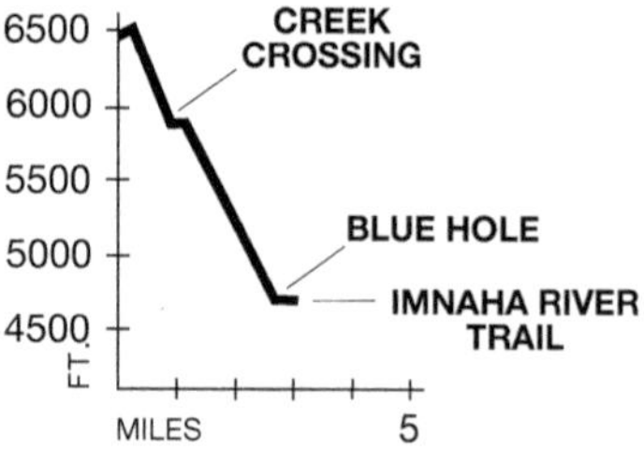

After crossing the creek the trail heads west-southwest through a meadow. Smooth, glacier-carved rock outcroppings are on the right side of the trail. The trail winds its way down through these outcroppings and crosses another stream 0.25 mile past the last stream crossing.

After the stream crossing the track goes between and over more rock outcroppings. It soon drops steeply for a short distance, then heads east again, crossing atop a small beaver dam (Thick alders may impede this crossing.) Soon the route crosses another small creek. A little farther along, the trail descends steeply for a short distance to another, larger beaver dam. The trail goes through the pond behind the dam, but it may be easier to walk across the top of the dam. The trail descends a shallow draw, heading northeast, below this beaver dam; however, it may be easier to take an alternate but slightly less brushy route for the next 75 yards or so. To do this, continue straight ahead (east) for about 20 yards after crossing the dam. Then turn left (northeast) and make your way through the brush for about 25 yards. Turn slightly left again and descend back to the trail.

Turn right on the trail and soon cross another small creek. A short distance farther the course crosses an opening in the brush. One hundred feet to the left (north) at the opening is a viewpoint overlooking a gorge with the Imnaha River flowing through it. Continue east on the sometimes brush-choked route, and in a little less than 0.2 mile you reach the point where the trail crosses the Imnaha River.

The crossing is at a place called Blue Hole (4,720 ft.). This crossing can be dangerous during high water. It is usually a safe but wet waist-deep crossing in August, September, and October, but in June and July it may be much deeper and very swift. Be careful. There is a good but heavily used campsite just across the Imnaha River, on the north side. The junction with Imnaha River Trail is 0.2 mile past the crossing.

The return trip may be made by the same trail, or a one-way trip can be made by heading east for 2 miles on Imnaha River Trail to Indian Crossing Trailhead. A car shuttle can be made by going north on FR 39 to Upper Imnaha River Road (FR 3960), then turning left and following it 10 miles to Indian Crossing Trailhead. FR 39 is the Wallowa Mountain Loop Road, running from Halfway to Joseph.

Miles and Directions

0.0 Start at the Twin Lakes Trailhead.

2.9 Cross the Imnaha River at Blue Hole.

3.1 Arrive at the junction with Imnaha River Trail (1816). (GPS: N45 06.062'/W117 02.826')

90 South Fork Imnaha River

This backpack route goes along the South Fork Imnaha River, from West Fork Wallowa River Trail over Hawkins Pass to the junction with North Fork Imnaha River Trail. It makes a great multiday trip through the north-central and eastern parts of the Wallowa Mountains. Access to Cliff Creek, Blue Creek, Boner Flat, North Fork Imnaha River, Lick Creek, Deadman Canyon, and Imnaha River Trails can be had from this trail. (Trails 1820 and 1816)

Distance: 12.6 miles one way
Hiking time: 5–7 hours
Difficulty: Moderate
Trail maintenance: Infrequent
Best season: July through Sept
Traffic and other trail users: Moderate foot and horse traffic
Canine compatibility: Dogs permitted without leashes, but must be kept away from the stock of other parties
Fees and permits: Eagle Cap Wilderness Permit
Maximum elevation: 8,330 feet
Maps: USGS Eagle Cap OR, Krag Peak OR, Cornucopia OR, and Deadman Point OR; Geo Graphics Wallowa Mountains Eagle Cap Wilderness
Trail contact: USDA Forest Service Wallowa Mountains Office, 201 E 2nd St./ PO Box 905, Joseph, OR 97846; (541) 426-5546, (541) 426-4978; www.fs.usda.gov/wallowa-whitman

Finding the trail: This trail begins as Hawkins Pass Trail (1820) at its junction with West Fork Wallowa River Trail (1806). Trail 1806 goes on up to Glacier Lake. From Joseph drive south on OR 82 for 7 miles, passing Wallowa Lake, to the Wallowa Lake Trailhead (4,650 ft.). Hike south from the trailhead on the West Fork Wallowa River Trail for 9.3 miles to the junction with Trail 1806. Bear left at the junction, staying on Trail 1820 (now the Hawkins Pass Trail).
GPS: Wallowa Lake Trailhead: N45 16.049'/W117 12.754'

The Hike

Hawkins Pass Trail, which is also the South Fork Imnaha River Trail, turns left (southwest) off West Fork Wallowa River Trail at the junction (7,140 ft.) just west of Frazier Lake. The trail crosses a stream 0.25 mile from the junction. This is the outlet stream of Glacier Lake, part of the headwaters of the Wallowa River. After crossing the stream the trail climbs a ridge between the stream and the outlet stream of Little Frazier Lake. The outlet stream from Little Frazier Lake is another part of the headwaters of the Wallowa River. After climbing the ridge for 300 yards, the trail crosses the Little Frazier Lake outlet stream. Another 0.3 mile and five switchbacks farther is Little Frazier Lake (7,430 ft.).

The trail goes around the left (east) side of the lake. The waterfall across the lake is the outlet from Prospect Lake. The trail climbs above the south side of Little Frazier Lake for 0.5 mile, then makes a switchback to the left. It makes seven more switchbacks in the next 0.3 mile. Here there is a hand-built rock wall about 75 yards to the right of the trail. This is part of the mining operations that took place in this area. A small stream enters the trail, runs down it for a short distance, then runs off the other side. The trail makes six more switchbacks climbing the last 0.4 mile to Hawkins Pass (8,330 ft.).

There has been a lot of mining activity at Hawkins Pass. There is evidence of this to the right, up the hill from the trail. This area is very interesting geologically. There are many types of rock strata, ranging in color from white to black. To the south and southeast, at the head of the South Fork Imnaha Canyon, there is a huge limestone wall. Eagle Cap can be seen to the northwest. This area is private land, so please respect it. No permission is necessary to cross this private land on the trail.

After going through Hawkins Pass, where the trail number changes to 1816, the trail starts to descend into the glacial valley at the head of the South Fork Imnaha River. This is one of the most spectacular valleys in the Wallowa Mountains. Flowers carpet the area in summer. After going 150 yards, there is a switchback to the right. Descend five more switchbacks in the next 0.7 mile. In that 0.7 mile the trail drops 720 vertical feet. An older trail heads down here. It is shorter and cuts off some switchbacks, but it is also steeper. For your knees and for the environment, it is better to use the main trail.

After the last switchback the trail heads down the valley. There is a spring to the left of the trail 300 yards past the last switchback. The trail goes past the first grove of trees since Hawkins Pass, 150 yards past the spring. It crosses the South Fork Imnaha River about 0.4 mile after going past this first grove of trees. There is no bridge at this crossing (7,100 ft.). You are now 3.5 miles from the junction with West Fork Wallowa River Trail.

Beyond the river crossing the trail may be difficult to see for a short distance in a lush, grassy area. Actually, a lot of the "grass" is not grass; it is wild onion. This area may be quite wet. The trail goes along about 50 yards to the left (east) of the river. A campsite is to the right of the trail 0.3 mile beyond the river crossing. In this area the trail alternates, going through groves of trees and flower-covered meadows. Soon it gradually makes its turn to the east. It crosses a couple of streams and comes into a large open area 1.25 miles past the campsite. To the left is a huge, exposed limestone slope. This is the south side of 9,518-foot-high Cusick Mountain.

In the next 1.5 miles the trail crosses three streams before coming to the junction with Cliff Creek Trail (1885; 6,100 ft.). Cliff Creek Trail turns off to the right (south). See Cliff Creek (hike 80). This junction is 7.2 miles from the junction with West Fork Wallowa River Trail.

There is a small stream crossing 0.5 mile past the Cliff Creek Trail junction. A campsite is in the trees, to the right of the trail, 0.3 mile beyond the stream crossing. There is an unmarked trail junction 75 yards past the campsite. The unmarked trail is an alternate to Cliff Creek Trail, and it joins Cliff Creek Trail on its way south. Between this junction and the Blue Creek Trail (1865) junction, 0.6 mile farther

Author near Hawkins Pass. GARY FLETCHER PHOTO

along, there are three small stream crossings, which may be dry in late summer. Sego lilies are common here in the open areas. There are also some very large tamarack (western larch) trees in this area.

After the Blue Creek Trail junction the trail continues for 1.9 miles to the unmarked junction with Boner Flat Trail (1801). There are several small stream crossings between the trail junctions. Boner Flat Trail is very difficult to spot from South Fork Imnaha River Trail. It heads up to the left (north) through an open grassy area, but there may be no sign of it on the ground. A sign marking the route is on a tree 50 yards off South Fork Imnaha River Trail, but this sign is almost impossible to see from South Fork Imnaha River Trail. See Boner Flat (hike 93). The elevation at this junction is 5,680 feet.

After passing the Boner Flat Trail junction, South Fork Imnaha River Trail heads down the river. It crosses several more small streams in the 2.1 miles from the Boner Flat Trail junction to the bridge over the North Fork Imnaha River. Just past the bridge is the junction with North Fork Imnaha Trail (1814; 5,400 ft.). This junction is 12.6 miles from the junction with West Fork Wallowa River Trail. Some very large tamarack trees grow in this area. From here to Indian Crossing Trailhead, Trail 1816 is Imnaha River Trail. See more about this trail in Imnaha River (hike 98).

The junction with Lick Creek Trail (1809) is 600 yards past the North Fork Imnaha River Trail junction. Lick Creek Trail turns off to the left. There is a sign at this junction. The junction with Deadman Canyon Trail (1869) is 150 yards past the Lick Creek Trail junction. This trail turns off to the right. There is a good campsite

South Fork Imnaha River

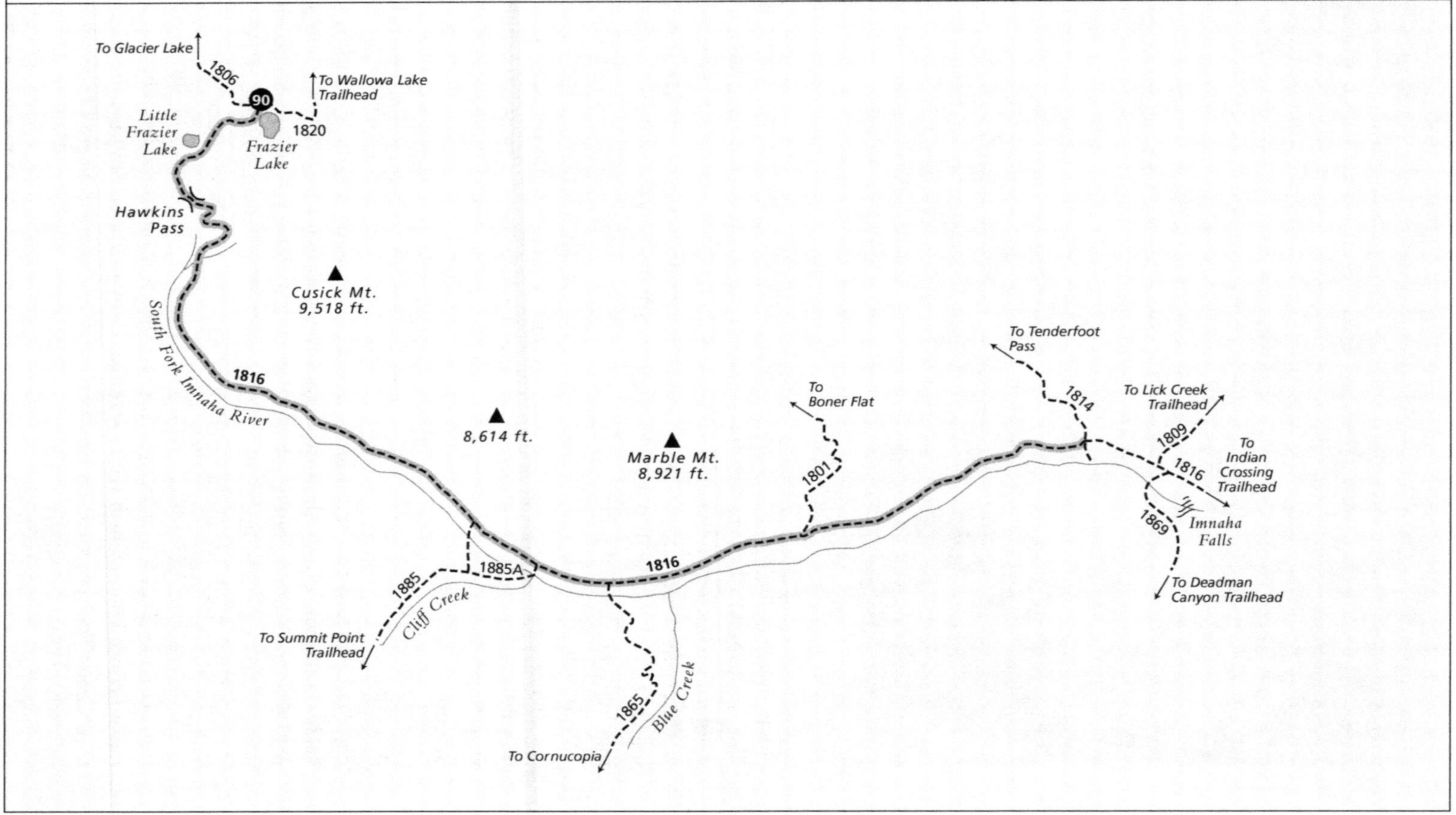

0 Kilometers 2
0 Miles 2
N
To Glacier Lake
1806
90
To Wallowa Lake Trailhead
1820
Little Frazier Lake
Frazier Lake
Hawkins Pass
Cusick Mt. 9,518 ft.
South Fork Imnaha River
1816
8,614 ft.
Marble Mt. 8,921 ft.
To Boner Flat
1801
To Tenderfoot Pass
1814
To Lick Creek Trailhead
1809
1816
To Indian Crossing Trailhead
Imnaha Falls
1869
To Deadman Canyon Trailhead
1885A
1885
Cliff Creek
To Summit Point Trailhead
1816
1865
Blue Creek
To Cornucopia

here. The trail crosses a small stream 350 yards past Deadman Canyon Trail, and another small stream 275 yards farther. A path drops off to the right 350 yards past the second stream. This path goes 100 yards to Imnaha Falls.

The area around the Deadman Canyon Trail junction is a great place to camp and explore the many trails that come together in this area. You can also reach the area in a popular day hike from Indian Crossing Trailhead. A one-way trip can be done from Wallowa Lake Trailhead to Indian Crossing; this involves a 53-mile car shuttle and 29.8 miles on the trail. Allow at least two days to make this one-way trip, if the whole party is in excellent shape. A better schedule would be three days, with a camp at Frazier Lake the first night and one around the junction with Cliff Creek Trail the second night.

Miles and Directions

0.0 From the junction with West Fork Wallowa River Trail (1806), bear left on the Hawkins Pass Trail (1820).

0.7 Arrive at Little Frazier Lake. (GPS: N45 09.115'/W117 15.985')

2.1 Cross Hawkins Pass. (GPS: N45 08.725'/W117 15.987')

7.2 Pass the junction with Cliff Creek Trail (1885). (GPS: N45 06.555'/W117 13.651')

8.0 Pass the junction with Cliff Creek Alternate Trail (1885A).

8.6 Pass the junction with Blue Creek Trail (1865). (GPS: N45 06.010'/W117 12.197')

10.2 Pass the junction with Boner Flat Trail (1801). (GPS: N45 06.338'/W117 10.359')

12.6 Arrive at the junction with North Fork Imnaha River Trail (1814); Trail 1816 becomes Imnaha River Trail. (GPS: N45 06.933'/W117 07.700')

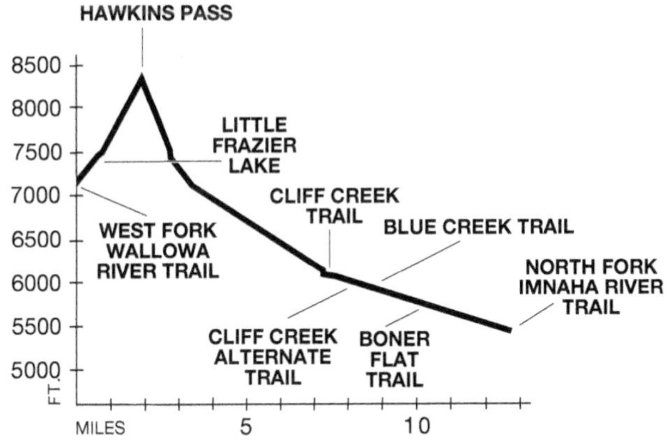

91 North Fork Imnaha River

This backpack route leads from the open tundra of Tenderfoot Pass down to the North Fork Imnaha River. Then the route continues down the beautiful North Fork Imnaha River Canyon to a junction with the Imnaha River Trail. The North Fork Imnaha River Trail accesses Polaris Pass, Tenderfoot Wagon Road, Middle Fork Imnaha River, and Boner Flats Trails. (Trail 1814)

Distance: 8.1 miles one way
Hiking time: 3–5 hours
Difficulty: Moderate
Trail maintenance: Infrequent
Best season: July through Sept
Traffic and other trail users: Light to moderate foot and horse traffic
Canine compatibility: Dogs permitted without leashes, but must be kept away from the stock of other parties
Fees and permits: Eagle Cap Wilderness Permit
Maximum elevation: 8,500 feet
Maps: USGS Aneroid Mountain OR and Cornucopia OR; Geo Graphics Wallowa Mountains Eagle Cap Wilderness
Trail contact: USDA Forest Service Wallowa Mountains Office, 201 E 2nd St./ PO Box 905, Joseph, OR 97846; (541) 426-5546, (541) 426-4978; www.fs.usda.gov/wallowa-whitman

Finding the trail: North Fork Imnaha River Trail is a continuation of the East Fork Wallowa River Trail (1804), which begins at Wallowa Lake Trailhead. To reach Wallowa Lake Trailhead take OR 82 for 7 miles south from Joseph, passing Wallowa Lake, to the Wallowa Lake Trailhead (4,650 ft.). Hike south from the trailhead on the East Fork Wallowa River Trail for 8.5 miles, passing Aneroid Lake along the way, to Tenderfoot Pass and the start of the North Fork Imnaha River Trail.
GPS: Wallowa Lake Trailhead: N45 16.049'/W117 12.754'; Tenderfoot Pass junction: N45 11.387'/W117 12.316'

The Hike

From Tenderfoot Pass (8,500 ft.) the trail drops to the south for 0.3 mile to the junction with Polaris Pass Trail (1831; 8,210 ft.). The junction with Trail 1814A is 250 yards past the Polaris Pass Trail junction. Trail 1814A, which bears to the right, is an alternate trail for descending into the North Fork Imnaha River Canyon. The alternate trail is a bit shorter than the main trail; however, it misses the junction with Tenderfoot Wagon Road Trail and is somewhat steeper than the main trail.

After passing the junction with Trail 1814A, the trail heads on down at a moderate grade through mostly open country. There are lots of flowers in this area, including asters, whitetops, and many others. There is also some sage on these open, south-facing slopes. The trail crosses two streams in the 1.3 miles from the junction with Trail 1814A to the junction with Tenderfoot Wagon Road Trail (1819). See Tenderfoot Wagon Road (hike 95). The altitude at the wagon road junction is 7,570 feet. North Fork Imnaha River Trail turns to the right (southwest) and heads down the wagon road.

North Fork Imnaha River Canyon from near Tenderfoot Pass. GARY FLETCHER PHOTO

After going down the wagon road for 300 yards, the trail makes a switchback to the left in the bottom of a streambed. The trail goes down the streambed for a few feet. At certain times this streambed is a regular flower garden. After leaving the streambed, the trail goes 400 yards, then makes a switchback to the right. After making the switchback, it crosses one more stream in the 400 yards to the second junction with Trail 1814A (7,000 ft.). This is the lower end of the alternate trail. Just past the junction the trail makes a switchback to the left and heads down the bottom of the North Fork Imnaha River Canyon.

From here down to the junction with the Middle Fork Imnaha River Trail, there are many good campsites. However, it is a good idea to camp back away from the river in this area because this river does flash flood occasionally.

After going down the canyon for 1.9 miles and crossing numerous small streams, the trail fords the cold waters of the North Fork Imnaha River (6,400 ft.). Most maps show the junction with Boner Flat and Middle Fork Imnaha River Trails to be just below this crossing. However, the Middle Fork trail from here to the Middle Fork Imnaha River is difficult to find. It is better to go on down North Fork trail approximately 1.1 miles to the marked junction.

After going down along the right (west) side of the river for 400 yards, the trail crosses the North Fork Imnaha River again. The trail heads on down the left (east) side of the river for 0.9 mile to the junction with Middle Fork Imnaha River Trail (6,010 ft.). It crosses three small streams before reaching the junction. The junction is

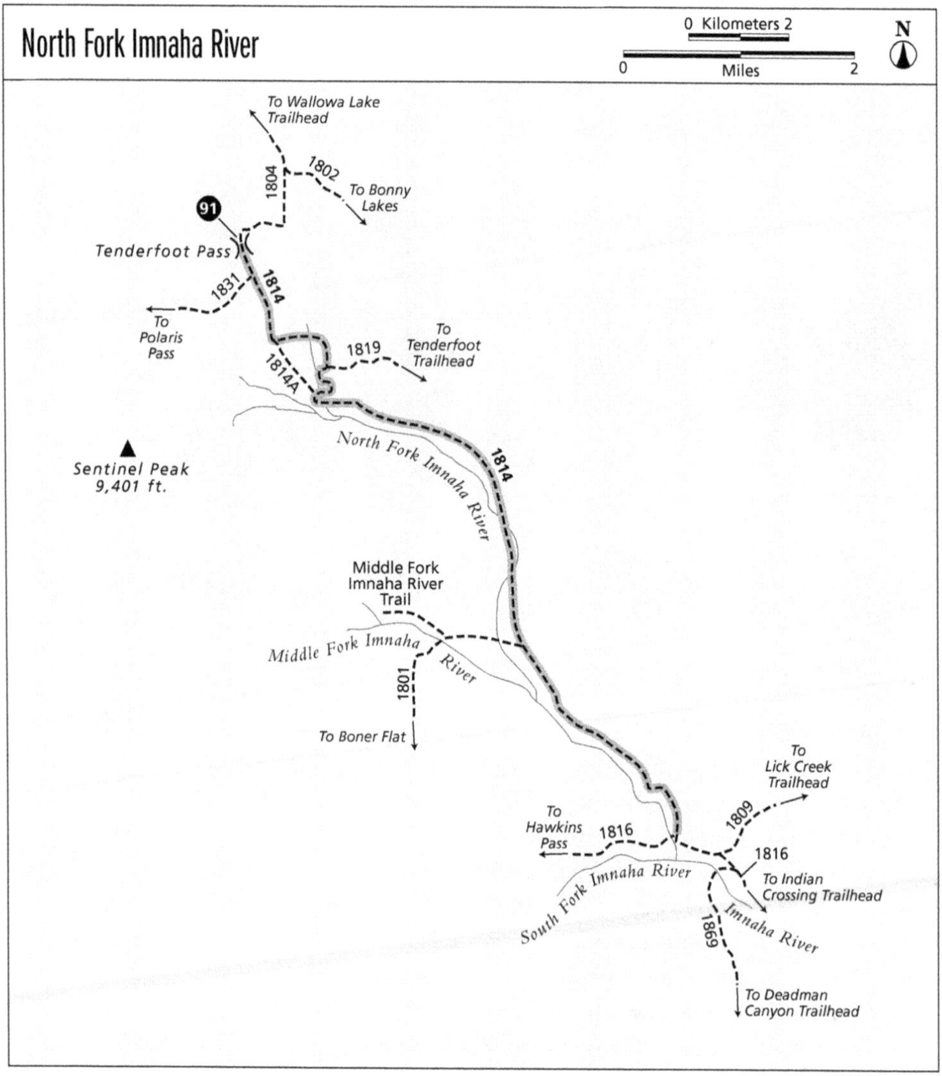

marked with a sign on a tamarack tree on the left (east) side of the trail. This junction is 5.5 miles from Tenderfoot Pass.

The trail crosses a stream 350 yards past the junction with Middle Fork Imnaha River Trail. There is a campsite on the right 0.25 mile past the stream crossing. The trail crosses another stream 0.5 mile past the campsite. After going 0.3 mile past this stream crossing, it begins to climb away from the river. The trail climbs for 350 yards, then drops for 300 more yards to a switchback to the right. After the switchback the trail continues to descend, crossing a couple of streambeds as it drops to the river level again.

Half a mile past the switchback the trail climbs again for a short distance and makes a switchback to the right. In another 75 yards the trail begins to drop again.

It drops at a moderate grade for 600 yards to the junction with the Imnaha River Trail (1816; 5,400 ft.). Some of the trail in the last 600 yards before Trail 1816 may be badly eroded—nearly washed away. This junction is 8.1 miles from Tenderfoot Pass.

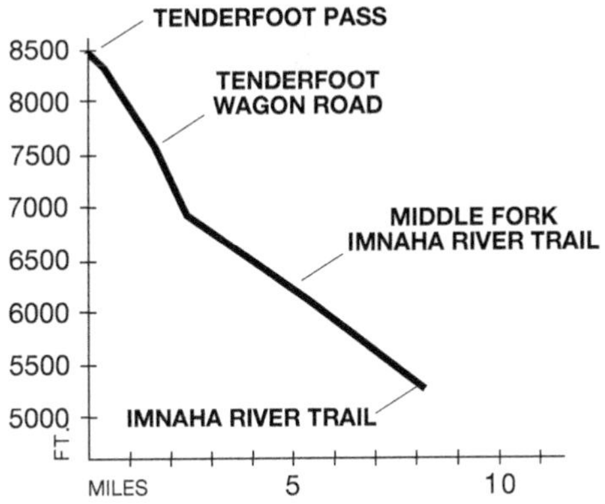

Many wonderful campsites are to be found along the Imnaha River, and fishing can be very good. Check for the special regulations on the bull trout (Dolly Varden), which inhabit these waters.

From the junction with Imnaha River Trail, you can head on down the Imnaha River to the east for 6.8 miles to Indian Crossing Trailhead. This requires a car shuttle. For the more ambitious hiker, a loop trip can be made by going up South Fork Imnaha River Trail, over Hawkins Pass, and back down West Fork Trail. Allow one and a half days to get to Frazier Lake and another half day to get back to Wallowa Lake Trailhead.

Miles and Directions

0.0 From Tenderfoot Pass, follow the North Fork Imnaha River Trail (1814) south.

0.3 Pass the junction with Polaris Pass Trail (1831).

1.8 Pass the junction with Tenderfoot Wagon Road Trail (1819). (GPS: N45 10.428'/W117 11.260')

5.5 Pass the junction with Middle Fork Imnaha River Trail. (GPS: N45 08.190'/W117 09.165')

8.1 Arrive at the junction with Imnaha River Trail (1816). (GPS: N45 06.933'/W117 07.700')

92 Middle Fork Imnaha River

This side trail from North Fork Imnaha River Trail leads to a campsite on the Middle Fork Imnaha River Trail, which is not maintained. However, the trail does connect with Boner Flat Trail and gets enough use to be fairly easy to follow up to the junction.

Distance: 1.7 miles one way
Hiking time: 1 hour
Difficulty: Easy, but the path fades out above Boner Flat Trail.
Trail maintenance: Rare or none
Best season: June through Nov
Traffic and other trail users: Generally light, with most of its use by horse traffic during fall hunting seasons
Canine compatibility: Dogs permitted without leashes, but must be kept away from the stock of other parties
Fees and permits: Northwest Forest Pass and Eagle Cap Wilderness Permit
Maximum elevation: 6,300 feet
Map: Green Trails #475sx: Wallowa Mountains Eagle Cap Wilderness shows this old trail as a route; USGS Aneroid Mountain OR covers the area but does not show this trail. Some of the older forest service and Eagle Cap Wilderness maps show the trail, but they are hard to find anymore.
Trail contact: USDA Forest Service Wallowa Mountains Office, 201 E 2nd St./ PO Box 905, Joseph, OR 97846; (541) 426-5546, (541) 426-4978; www.fs.usda.gov/wallowa-whitman. Further information may be very limited.

Finding the trail: There are several ways to access the Middle Fork Imnaha River Trail. You can hike there from Wallowa Lake via the East Fork Wallowa River (1804) and North Fork Imnaha River (1814) Trails, from Lick Creek Trailhead over the Lick Creek Trail (1809), but the best way to get there (slightly longer than Lick Creek, but much easier) is from Indian Crossing Trailhead on the Imnaha River and North Fork Imnaha River Trails. To reach the trailhead, take Imnaha Highway (OR 350) for 8 miles east from Joseph. Turn right on Wallowa Mountain Loop Road (FR 39) and follow it for 32 miles to the Upper Imnaha River Road (FR 3960). Turn right and follow FR 3960 for 9.5 miles to its end at Indian Crossing Campground and Trailhead. Hike west from the trailhead on the Imnaha River Trail (1816) for 6.8 miles to the junction with the North Fork Imnaha River Trail. Turn right on the North Fork Imnaha River Trail and go 2.7 miles to the junction with the Middle Fork Imnaha River Trail (6,010 ft.), where this hike begins.
GPS: Indian Crossing Trailhead: N45 06.730'/W117 00.939'; Middle Fork trail junction: N45 08.190'/W117 09.165'

The Hike

Middle Fork Imnaha River Trail turns west off the North Fork Imnaha River Trail. After heading west a few feet, it fords the cold, rushing waters of the North Fork Imnaha River. An unmarked trail turns to the right (north) 0.75 mile after crossing the river. The unmarked trail contours around to the north and joins the North Fork

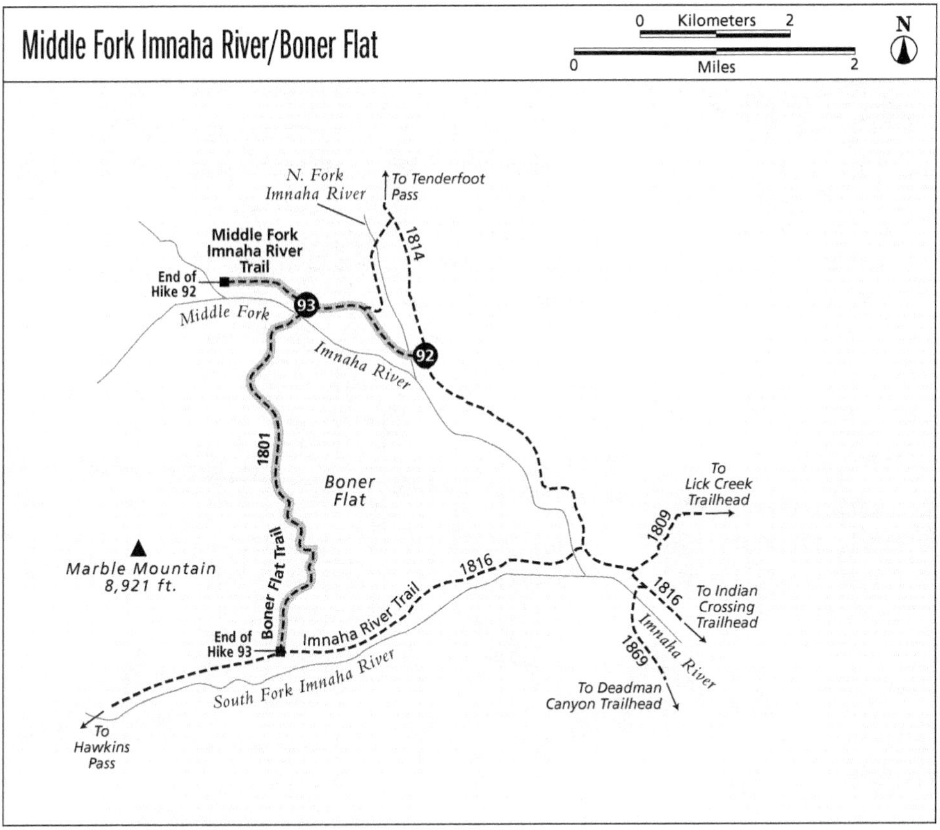

trail about 1 mile upriver from the junction. Middle Fork Imnaha River Trail heads west from the junction.

There is a metal trail sign on a tree on the left side of the trail 350 yards past the unmarked trail junction. The sign says Middle Fork Imnaha River Trail. Boner Flat Trail (1801) turns to the left a short distance past the sign. See Boner Flat (hike 93). The elevation at this junction is 6,180 feet.

Past the Boner Flat Trail junction, Middle Fork Imnaha River Trail becomes difficult to see as it heads up the right side of the river. The trail is generally within 20 yards of the river in this area. After 500 or 600 yards the trail disappears completely in an open area. Across the open area is a well-used campsite. This campsite (6,300 ft.) is about 1.7 miles from North Fork Imnaha River Trail.

The trail becomes just a route past the campsite. It is generally not visible on the ground and is not shown on newer maps. The Middle Fork Imnaha River forks 200 yards southwest of the campsite. This campsite makes a good base camp from which to explore the upper part of the Middle Fork Imnaha River drainage. There are fish to be caught in the Middle Fork.

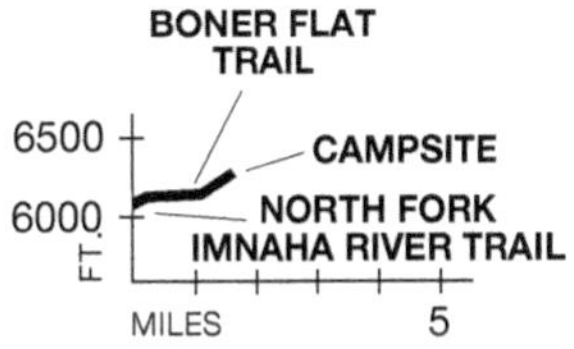

Return by the same trail, or make a loop trip, requiring some route finding, over Boner Flat Trail and back down South Fork Imnaha River Trail.

Miles and Directions

0.0 From the junction with North Fork Imnaha River Trail (1814), head west on the Middle Fork Imnaha River Trail.

0.7 Pass the junction with the unmarked trail.

1.0 Pass the junction with Boner Flat Trail (1801). (GPS: N45 08.416'/W117 10.123')

1.7 Arrive at the campsite; the trail disappears.

93 Boner Flat

This trail climbs from the Middle Fork Imnaha River Trail, up and over the ridgetop meadows of Boner Flat, where the views are great. It then descends steeply into the South Fork Imnaha River Canyon and the South Fork Imnaha River Trail. (Trail 1801)

See map page 331.
Distance: 4 miles one way
Hiking time: 2-3 hours
Difficulty: Strenuous, with trail-finding skills required
Trail maintenance: Seldom to none
Best season: Mid-June through Oct
Traffic and other trail users: Light foot and horse traffic
Canine compatibility: Dogs permitted without leashes, but must be kept away from the stock of other parties
Fees and permits: Northwest Forest Pass and Eagle Cap Wilderness Permit
Maximum elevation: 7,510 feet
Maps: USGS Aneroid Mountain OR and Cornucopia OR; Geo Graphics Wallowa Mountains Eagle Cap Wilderness. Green Trails #475sx: Wallowa Mountains Eagle Cap Wilderness shows this trail, but the northern part is shown as a route. Middle Fork Imnaha River Trail is not shown on many newer maps, including USGS quads. Refer to the map in this description for route finding.
Trail contact: USDA Forest Service Wallowa Mountains Office, 201 E 2nd St./ PO Box 905, Joseph, OR 97846; (541) 426-5546, (541) 426-4978; www.fs.usda.gov/wallowa-whitman

Finding the trail: There are several ways to access the Boner Flat Trail. You can hike there from Wallowa Lake via the East Fork Wallowa River (1804), North Fork Imnaha River (1814), and Middle Fork Imnaha River Trails, from Lick Creek Trailhead over the Lick Creek Trail (1809), but the best way to get there (slightly longer than Lick Creek, but much easier) is from Indian Crossing Trailhead on the Imnaha River and North Fork Imnaha River Trails. To reach the trailhead, take the Imnaha Highway (OR 350) for 8 miles east from Joseph. Turn right on Wallowa Mountain Loop Road (FR 39) and follow it for 32 miles to the Upper Imnaha River Road (FR 3960). Turn right and follow FR 3960 for 9.5 miles to its end at Indian Crossing Campground and Trailhead. Hike west from the trailhead on the Imnaha River Trail (1816) for 6.8 miles to the junction with the North Fork Imnaha River Trail. Turn right on the North Fork Imnaha River Trail and go 2.7 miles to the junction with the Middle Fork Imnaha River Trail. Turn left on the Middle Fork Imnaha Trail and go 1 mile to the junction with the Boner Flat Trail (6,180 ft.), where this hike description starts.
GPS: Indian Crossing Trailhead: N45 06.730'/W117 00.939'; Boner Flat Trail junction: N45 08.416'/W117 10.123'

The Hike

Boner Flat Trail turns left off the Middle Fork Imnaha River Trail. It crosses a meadow, then crosses the Middle Fork Imnaha River. After crossing the river the trail heads south and up. It is difficult to see in some of the open areas, so watch for blazes on the trees.

The trail climbs steeply 0.4 mile to a small stream crossing (6,540 ft.). It crosses the same stream again 0.3 mile farther along. Between the stream crossings the trail goes almost straight up the hillside for a short distance. It is hard to see the trail in this area.

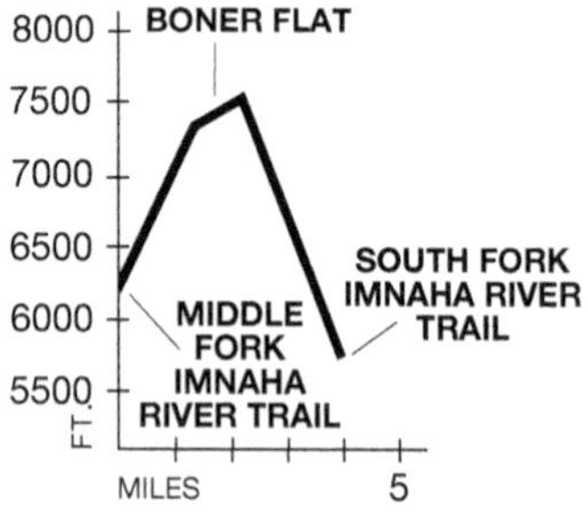

After crossing the stream the second time, the trail turns to the left. It flattens out a bit for a short distance, then starts to climb again. The trail climbs for 0.25 mile, then makes a series of eight switchbacks in the next 0.4 mile. Above the switchbacks the grade moderates and the country opens up.

The trail now goes through more rolling country. This area of large, sloping meadows spotted with wildflowers and groves of subalpine timber is known as Boner Flat. It is about 0.9 mile from the top of the switchbacks across the meadow to the summit (7,510 ft.). Before the summit the trail is deeply eroded in places. In other places it is difficult to see. It heads generally south. Watch for blazes on the trees. Mule deer and elk are often seen on Boner Flat. Boner Flat is not a good place to be in a thunderstorm, as happened to me.

After passing the summit, the trail heads down to the southeast for a short distance. It then turns to the south-southwest. The trail makes three switchbacks 0.25 mile below the summit. After passing the switchbacks it winds down steeply for 0.25 mile to another short series of switchbacks. After these switchbacks the grade moderates again and the trail heads southwest. A couple hundred yards past the switchbacks the trail crosses a small stream. It then goes down a small ridge for 300 yards and turns to the left (east) for 125 more yards before heading down another series of switchbacks. The trail makes five switchbacks, then crosses the same stream again.

After crossing the stream the trail enters an open area and becomes difficult to see. Follow the blazes. It goes down along the left (east) edge of the open area, passing a very large tamarack tree. There is a blaze on a small fir tree 40 yards to the right of the tamarack tree. There is another blaze on a small lodgepole pine on the right side of the opening 125 yards below the small fir. Thirty yards past the lodgepole is another blaze on a larger fir. This tree also has a sign on it, which points back up the hill to Boner Flat.

South and down 50 yards is the junction with South Fork Imnaha River Trail (1816; 5,680 ft.). The junction is not marked, and Boner Flat Trail is not visible on the ground at the junction. The junction with South Fork Imnaha River Trail is 4 miles from the junction with Middle Fork Imnaha River Trail.

Boner Flat Trail is very difficult to find when hiking along Imnaha River Trail. I walked past it twice before I found it. The forest service maps are not too good in this area. If you are going to go up Boner Flat Trail from the south, I suggest you get a USGS map or, better yet, take someone along that knows exactly where it leaves Imnaha River Trail. The USGS map you need for this end of the trail is the

Cornucopia quad. The other end of the trail is covered by the Aneroid Mountain quad.

This trail can be done as part of a loop hike from a base camp on the Imnaha River near Imnaha Falls. This loop is hiked by going up North Fork Imnaha River Trail to Middle Fork Imnaha River Trail, then taking Middle Fork Imnaha River Trail to Boner Flat Trail, following Boner Flat Trail to South Fork Imnaha River Trail, and taking South Fork Imnaha River Trail back to the campsite. This loop makes a long day hike of about 13 miles. There are lots of campsites along Imnaha River Trail near its junction with North Fork Imnaha River Trail. Imnaha Falls is 0.9 mile downriver (east) of the junction.

Miles and Directions

0.0 From the junction with Middle Fork Imnaha River Trail, go south on the Boner Flat Trail (1801).

2.2 Reach the summit on the south side of Boner Flat.

4.0 Arrive at the junction with South Fork Imnaha River Trail (1816). (GPS: N45 06.338'/W117 10.359')

94 Lick Creek

This day hike or backpack trip travels from Lick Creek Trailhead to the Imnaha River near Imnaha Falls. Recently burned areas along this trail have improved the views. (Trail 1809)

Distance: 5 miles one way
Hiking time: 2-3 hours
Difficulty: Moderate
Trail maintenance: Infrequent
Traffic and other trail users: Light foot and horse
Canine compatibility: Dogs permitted without leashes, but must be kept away from the stock of other parties
Fees and permits: Eagle Cap Wilderness Permit
Maximum elevation: 7,020 feet
Maps: USGS Lick Creek OR and Deadman Point OR; Geo Graphics Wallowa Mountains Eagle Cap Wilderness
Trail contact: USDA Forest Service Wallowa Mountains Office, 201 E 2nd St./ PO Box 905, Joseph, OR 97846; (541) 426-5546, (541) 426-4978; www.fs.usda.gov/wallowa-whitman

Finding the trailhead: Lick Creek Trail starts at Lick Creek Trailhead, 25 miles southeast of Joseph. To get to the trailhead, take the Imnaha Highway east from Joseph. After going 8 miles, turn right on Wallowa Mountain Loop Road (FR 39). Follow Wallowa Mountain Loop Road 15.75 miles to Lick Creek Campground. At the entrance to the campground, turn right (south) off the Loop Road onto FR 3925; the campground is to the left, across FR 39 from FR 3925. Go 0.15 mile on FR 3925, then turn right on FR 015. Follow FR 015 for 2.2 miles to the trailhead (6,080 ft.). The area around the trailhead was near the edge of the 1994 Twin Lakes Fire. There were a few spot fires next to the road, but the major part of the burn was to the south.
GPS: N45 08.049'/W117 03.321'

The Hike

The route begins at the Lick Creek Trailhead. At first the trail is an old roadbed. It traverses around a hillside to the west for 0.25 mile to Quartz Creek. At the crossing (6,140 ft.) the trail leaves the roadbed, and just after crossing the creek the trail turns to the left. The roadbed goes on up along Quartz Creek to the Zollman and Wells Mine, which is about 500 feet from the trail. There is a trail sign just past the crossing, pointing out Lick Creek Trail (1809).

The trail crosses another creek 300 yards farther along. Just after this crossing there is a burn area on the right side of the trail. The trail climbs up to and crosses an old roadbed (6,420 ft.) 0.25 mile after the creek crossing. The burned area is passed before the roadbed. Watch for Brown's peonies along the trail in this area.

After crossing the roadbed the areas burned by spot fires get smaller and farther apart, and are completely gone by the time the trail crosses another creek (6,710 ft.) 0.8 mile after crossing the roadbed. Just after this creek crossing the trail is built up

Red Mountain from Imnaha Divide.

with log sides, which makes crossing a wet area easier. The trail crosses a couple of streams in the next 0.5 mile. It then crosses Lick Creek (6,650 ft.). There is no bridge at this crossing. It is easier to cross Lick Creek a couple hundred feet upstream from the trail.

A short distance after crossing Lick Creek, the trail enters Eagle Cap Wilderness. There is a sign marking the boundary (6,680 ft.). After entering Eagle Cap Wilderness, the trail continues to climb gradually for another 0.6 mile to the top of Imnaha Divide. Imnaha Divide is the ridge between the Imnaha River and Sheep Creek drainages. The elevation where the trail crosses the divide is 7,020 feet. There are some good campsites on the top of the divide, but no water.

After crossing the divide the trail starts to switchback its way down toward the Imnaha River. Just over 1.5 miles below the divide, it crosses a creek. After the creek crossing there are some good viewpoints looking into the upper Imnaha River Canyon. The trail continues to descend, crossing four more small streams in the next 0.75 mile. It then makes some switchbacks and comes to the junction with Imnaha River Trail (1816; 5,340 ft.). The distance from Lick Creek Trailhead to the junction with the Imnaha River

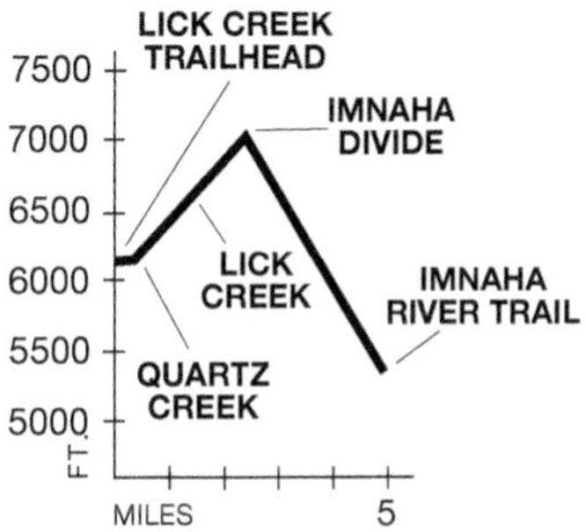

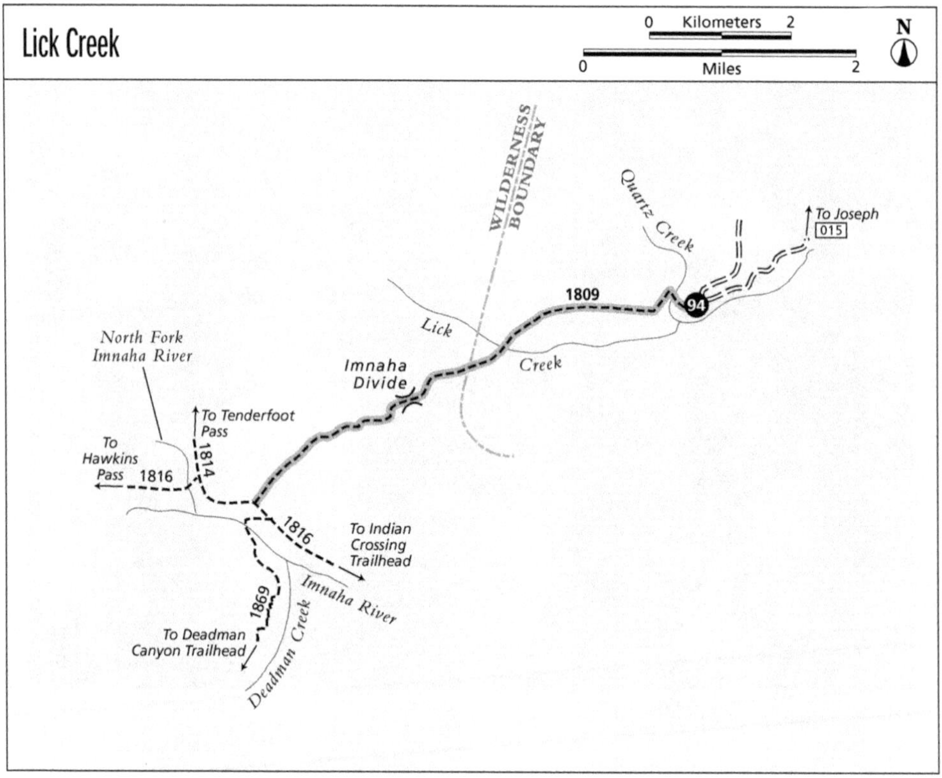

Trail is 5 miles. This junction is quite close to the junctions with Deadman Canyon Trail and North Fork Imnaha River Trail, and not far upstream from Imnaha Falls.

The area around the junction with Imnaha River Trail was also hit by some spot fires from the Twin Lakes Fire, but most of the damage from the fire was to the east and south. There are many good campsites along the Imnaha River. Fishing can be very good, but be sure to check the current angling regulations for special rules.

A one-way trip can be made by combining Lick Creek Trail and Imnaha River Trail. This combination would involve a 20-mile car shuttle to Indian Crossing Trailhead.

Miles and Directions

0.0 Begin at Lick Creek Trailhead.

0.2 Cross Quartz Creek.

0.5 Cross roadbed.

1.8 Cross Lick Creek.

1.9 Pass the Eagle Cap Wilderness boundary.

2.5 Cross Imnaha Divide. (GPS: N45 07.624'/W117 05.620')

5.0 Arrive at the junction with Imnaha River Trail (1816). (GPS: N45 06.820'/W117 07.270')

95 Tenderfoot Wagon Road

Tenderfoot Wagon Road Trail is a backpacking route from Salt Creek Summit Sno-Park and Trailhead to North Fork Imnaha River Trail. From the trailhead to just past the Tenderfoot Trailhead connecting trail junction, the trail goes through the burn area of the 1989 Canal Fire. This route follows the historic Tenderfoot Wagon Road, which was built in the first decade of the twentieth century. The wagon road was built as an access route to the Tenderfoot Mine and townsite. It was soon discovered that the mine had been salted, and the only real mining that had been done was from the pockets of the investors from the East. Burned areas along this trail have improved the views. (Trail 1819)

Distance: 11.2 miles one way
Hiking time: 4–7 hours
Difficulty: Easy, except for a short stretch just before reaching Imnaha Divide, where it is fairly steep
Trail maintenance: Infrequent
Best season: June through Oct up to the junction with Big Sheep Cut-Off Trail; July through mid-Oct past the junction. For skiing, Dec to Apr up to Bonny Lakes Trail.
Traffic and other trail users: Light foot and horse traffic from Salt Creek Pass to Tenderfoot Trailhead connecting trail; moderate to Bonny Lakes Trail; light past Bonny Lakes Trail. Horse traffic is heavier during fall hunting seasons, and the part of the trail between Salt Creek Summit and the trail to the Nordic ski shelters is quite heavily used by skiers in the winter. This trail is also occasionally used by mountain bikers from Salt Creek Summit Trailhead to Tenderfoot Trailhead.
Canine compatibility: Dogs permitted without leashes, but must be kept away from the stock of other parties
Fees and permits: Northwest Forest Pass and Eagle Cap Wilderness Permit. A Sno-park pass is required Nov 30 to Apr 1.
Maximum elevation: 8,100 feet
Maps: USGS Lick Creek OR and Aneroid Mountain OR; Green Trails #475sx: Wallowa Mountains Eagle Cap Wilderness; Geo Graphics Wallowa Mountains Eagle Cap Wilderness. The part of the trail between Salt Creek Summit and the Tenderfoot Trailhead connecting trail is not shown on the USGS maps.
Trail contact: USDA Forest Service Wallowa Mountains Office, 201 E 2nd St./PO Box 905, Joseph, OR 97846; (541) 426-5546, (541) 426-4978; www.fs.usda.gov/wallowa-whitman. For skiing and use of the ski shelters, contact Wing Ridge Ski Tours, 500 N River St., Enterprise, OR 97828; (541) 398-1980 or (888) 812-4707, ext. 3; www.facebook.com/Wing-Ridge-Ski-Tours-239313479446588.

Finding the trailhead: The trail begins at Salt Creek Summit Sno-Park and Trailhead. To reach Salt Creek Summit Sno-Park and Trailhead, take Imnaha Highway (OR 350; also known as Little Sheep Creek Highway and Hells Canyon Scenic Byway) for 8 miles east from Joseph. Turn right on FR 39 (Wallowa Mountain Loop Road) and follow it 10 miles south to Salt Creek Summit. The parking area is a short distance to the left (east) of FR 39 at the summit.
GPS: N45 12.506'/W117 04.410'

To reach Tenderfoot Trailhead, drive a couple of miles on FR 39 past Salt Creek Summit, then turn right (southwest) on FR 100. Follow FR 100 to its end at the trailhead, approximately 4 miles. From the trailhead a short connecting trail crosses Big Sheep Creek and joins Tenderfoot Wagon Road Trail. **GPS:** N45 10.651'/W 117 06.211'

The Hike

For the first 0.3 mile, Tenderfoot Wagon Road Trail and Wing Ridge Trail (1828) follow the same route. From Salt Creek Summit Trailhead (6,100 ft.), cross the canal bridge and follow Wing Ridge Trail 0.3 mile to its junction with Tenderfoot Wagon Road Trail. See Wing Ridge (hike 97). The wagon road goes straight ahead (south) at the junction, and Wing Ridge Trail turns to the right.

Soon the trail crosses the bridge over Salt Creek. Just after crossing the bridge the trail is elevated on two boardwalks to cross a wet area. The trail then climbs slightly around the point of a small ridge. From the ridge there is a good view of the Seven Devils Mountains to the east, across Hells Canyon in Idaho.

The trail crosses a couple more small creeks, one of them on another bridge, then begins to climb steadily but gently, reaching 6,430 feet at about 3 miles from the trailhead. For a short distance near the high point, the trail goes through green timber that was missed by the fire.

At 3.3 miles the Big Sheep Cut-Off Trail turns to the left (south), drops a couple hundred feet in switchbacks, crosses Big Sheep Creek on two wooden bridges, and goes to some Nordic ski shelters. These shelters, which are about 0.5 mile off Tenderfoot Wagon Road Trail, are mostly dismantled in summer. The shelters are next to Big Sheep Creek Road, which is the access road to Tenderfoot Trailhead. At the junction, Tenderfoot Wagon Road Trail heads straight ahead, to the west-northwest. Big Sheep Cut-Off Trail is marked with blue diamonds, but from here on the wagon road is not.

The junction (6,500 ft.) with the short connecting trail to Tenderfoot Trailhead is 0.8 mile past the trail to the Nordic shelters trail junction. The trail to Tenderfoot Trailhead turns to the left (south). The unmarked Wing Ridge Trail (1828) junction is 0.9 mile farther. The junction with McCully Basin Trail (1812; 6,750 ft.) is 0.1 mile farther, after crossing the North Fork Big Sheep Creek. Both Wing Ridge and McCully Basin Trails turn to the right (north). See Wing Ridge (hike 97) and McCully Basin (hike 1). The junction with Bonny Lakes Trail (1802; 7,200 ft.) is 1.1 miles beyond the McCully Basin Trail junction. Bonny Lakes Trail bears to the right (west).

From the Bonny Lakes Trail junction the wagon road heads southwest. It quickly starts to climb out of the Middle Fork Big Sheep Creek Valley. The trail goes by a melt pond 0.9 mile after leaving the junction. This pond may dry up in late summer. The trail heads up a streambed 300 yards after passing the pond. After going up the streambed a few yards, it climbs out on the right side. The trail reaches the ridgeline (7,900 ft.) of Imnaha Divide 0.6 mile after leaving the streambed. This ridgeline divides the drainages of Big Sheep Creek and the North Fork Imnaha River. Evidence of the old

Tenderfoot Wagon Road/Wing Ridge

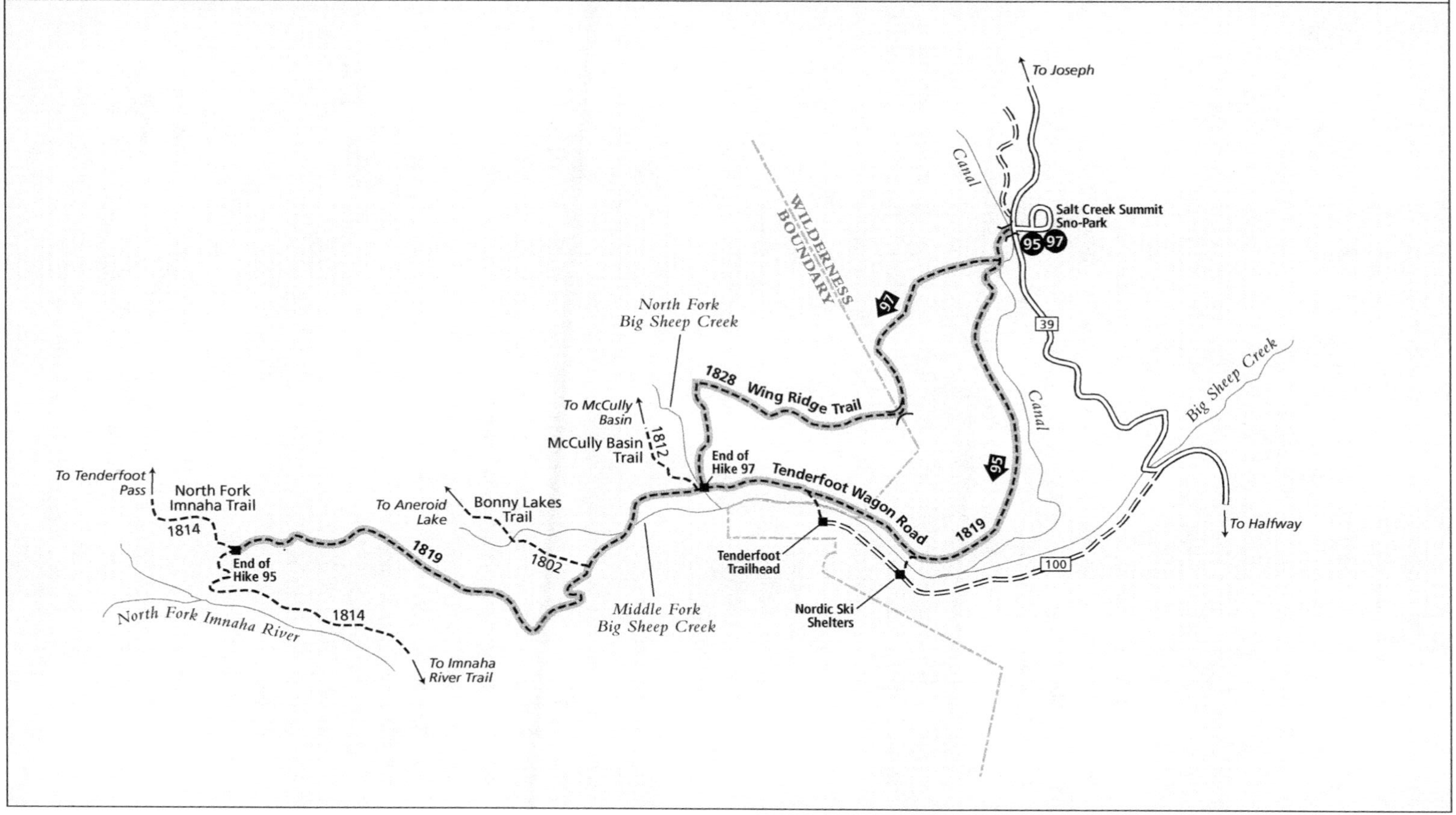

wagon road is not always easy to see between Bonny Lakes Trail junction and the top of the ridge, but it becomes quite obvious from here on.

At the top of the ridge the trail turns right. It heads up the ridgeline, climbing approximately 100 feet in 0.5 mile. After going up the ridge, the trail begins a traverse on the left side of the ridge. This traverse climbs slightly to 8,080 feet, then descends back to 8,000 feet and climbs again to 8,100 feet. The traverse is 1.5 miles long and goes along a fairly open south-facing slope. The open area along the traverse makes for a good view of the North Fork Imnaha River Canyon and the high peaks above its headwaters. There are some very large whitebark pines along this traverse.

Just past where the trail starts to head down at the end of the traverse, an unmarked path turns off to the right. This path, known as the Hawkey Cut-Off, is a way to connect to Tenderfoot Pass without dropping down into the North Fork Imnaha River Canyon. It is not a maintained trail and may be hard to follow. It should not be used by horses because of the damage they cause to this alpine terrain.

Tenderfoot Wagon Road Trail descends for 1.25 more miles to the junction with North Fork River Imnaha Trail (1814; 7,570 ft.), 11.2 miles from Salt Creek Summit Trailhead. At this junction the wagon road becomes North Fork Imnaha River Trail. See North Fork Imnaha River (hike 91). The old Tenderfoot townsite—the reason the wagon road was built—is a couple of switchbacks down North Fork Imnaha River Trail, next to the river.

Several one-way hikes are possible by connecting wagon road with other trails. All of them except Wing Ridge require a car shuttle. You can also end your hike at Tenderfoot Trailhead.

Miles and Directions

0.0 Start at the Salt Creek Summit Sno-Park and Trailhead.

0.3 Pass the junction with Wing Ridge Trail (1828). (GPS: N45 12.274'/W117 04.533')

3.3 Pass the junction with Big Sheep Cut-Off Trail. (GPS: N45 10.472'/W117 05.398')

4.1 Pass the junction with the connecting trail to the Tenderfoot Trailhead.

5.0 Pass the second junction with Wing Ridge Trail. (GPS: N45 10.847'/W117 07.190')

5.1 Pass the junction with McCully Basin Trail (1812). (GPS: N45 10.852'/W117 07.266')

6.2 Pass the junction with Bonny Lakes Trail (1802). (GPS: N45 10.321'/W117 08.220')

7.9 Cross the top of Imnaha Divide.

11.2 Arrive at the junction with North Fork Imnaha River Trail (1814). (GPS: N45 10.428'/W117 11.260')

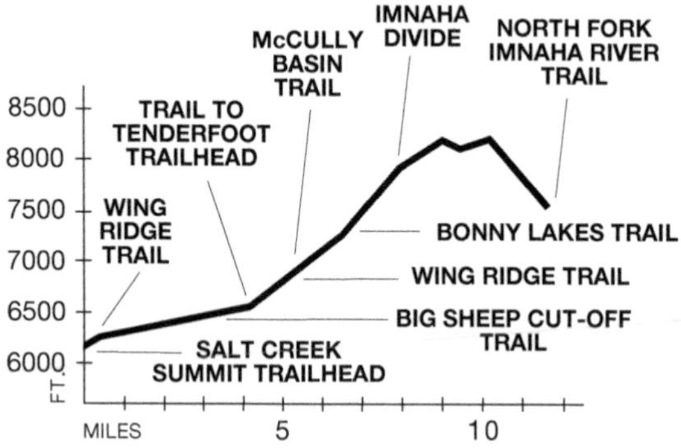

96 Bonny Lakes

This backpack route or day hike runs from Tenderfoot Wagon Road Trail to East Fork Wallowa River Trail. (Trail 1802)

Distance: 5.5 miles one way; 7.8 miles one way from Tenderfoot Trailhead
Hiking time: 2–2.5 hours; 3–3.5 hours from Tenderfoot Trailhead
Difficulty: Moderate
Trail maintenance: Infrequent
Best season: July through mid-Oct; Jan through Apr for skiing
Traffic and other trail users: Moderate foot and horse traffic; heavier during fall hunting seasons. This trail has light cross-country ski traffic in winter. In winter, skiing is done from Salt Creek Summit Sno-Park via Tenderfoot Wagon Road or from Wallowa Lake Trailhead via East Fork Wallowa River Trail.
Canine compatibility: Dogs permitted without leashes, but must be kept away from the stock of other parties
Fees and permits: Eagle Cap Wilderness Permit
Maximum elevation: 8,420 feet
Map: USGS Aneroid Mountain OR
Trail contact: USDA Forest Service Wallowa Mountains Office, 201 E 2nd St./PO Box 905, Joseph, OR 97846; (541) 426-5546, (541) 426-4978; www.fs.usda.gov/wallowa-whitman. For winter ski information or use of the Nordic shelter, contact Wing Ridge Ski Tours, 500 N River St., Enterprise, OR 97828; (541) 398-1980 or (888) 812-4707, ext. 3; www.facebook.com/Wing-Ridge-Ski-Tours-239313479446588.

Finding the trail: To reach Tenderfoot Trailhead take Imnaha Highway (OR 350; also known as Little Sheep Creek Highway and Hells Canyon Scenic Byway) for 8 miles east from Joseph. Turn right on FR 39 (Wallowa Mountain Loop Road) and follow it 10 miles south to Salt Creek Summit. Drive a couple of miles farther on FR 39 past Salt Creek Summit, then turn right (southwest) on FR 100. Follow FR 100 to its end at the trailhead, approximately 4 miles. From the trailhead (6,440 ft.), a short connecting trail crosses Big Sheep Creek and joins Tenderfoot Wagon Road Trail (1819). Bear left on the wagon road following the well-used route west. (The junction with the wagon road is not marked and may be vague here.) In 2.2 miles you reach the junction with the Bonny Lakes Trail (1802; 7,200 ft.).
GPS: Tenderfoot Trailhead: N45 10.651'/W117 06.211'; Bonny Lakes Trail junction: N45 10.321'/W117 08.220'

The Hike

Bonny Lakes Trail heads to the right (west) off Tenderfoot Wagon Road Trail. The trail crosses a creek 0.75 mile (7,310 ft.) after leaving the wagon road trail. After going 0.3 mile farther there is another creek crossing (7,440 ft.). Bonny Lakes (7,800 ft.) are 0.9 mile past the second creek crossing. The trail goes between the lakes, but only the one to the left can be seen from the trail. There are campsites at Bonny Lakes, but the mosquitoes may be bad in July and August.

After passing Bonny Lakes the trail climbs through thinning timber for 2 miles to Dollar Pass. This pass (8,420 ft.) is on the ridge dividing the Big Sheep Creek and the

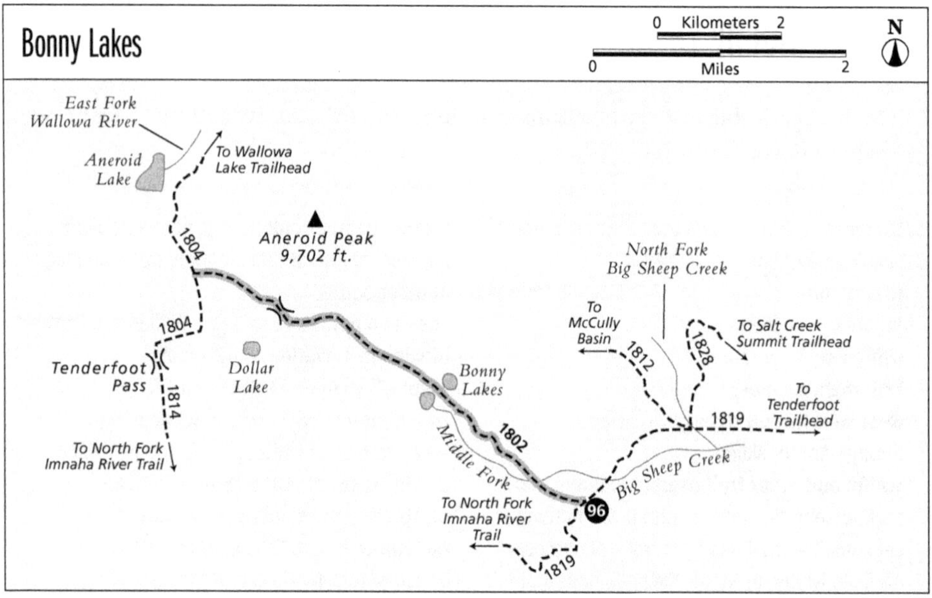

East Fork Wallowa River drainages. To the north of the pass, the dark brown 9,702-foot summit of Aneroid Mountain reaches well above timberline. To the south are Dollar Lake (8,450 ft.) and Dollar Mountain. To reach the alpine tarn called Dollar Lake, follow the faint trail along the ridgetop to the left (south).

Trail 1802 continues west over the pass and drops straight down a small valley. The trail is very faint in this area, but there are cairns to follow. It soon becomes easier to find as it drops down to the junction with East Fork Wallowa River Trail (1814; 7,820 ft.), 5.5 miles from Tenderfoot Wagon Road Trail.

At the junction, Tenderfoot Pass is to the left (south) 1.5 miles; Aneroid Lake is to the right (north) 1 mile. See East Fork Wallowa River (hike 2). From the junction a return trip requiring a car shuttle can be made to Wallowa Lake Trailhead, which is 7 miles from the junction via Aneroid Lake.

Caution: In winter there is avalanche danger along this trail.

Miles and Directions

0.0 At the junction with Tenderfoot Wagon Road Trail (1819), go right (west) on the Bonny Lakes Trail (1802).

2.0 Arrive at Bonny Lakes. (GPS: N45 10.995'/W117 09.583')

4.0 Pass the junction with the path to Dollar Lake and cross the pass.

5.5 Arrive at the junction with East Fork Wallowa River Trail (1804). (GPS: N45 11.898'/W117 11.839')

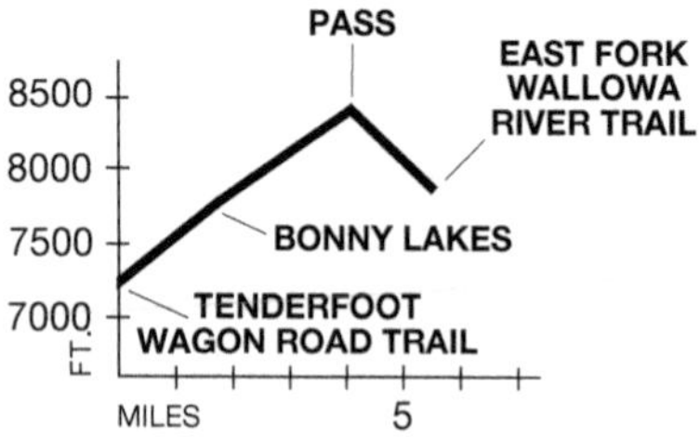

97 Wing Ridge

This day hike leads from Salt Creek Summit Trailhead over Wing Ridge to Tenderfoot Wagon Road Trail. This trail can be used as a more scenic, and also far more strenuous, alternate to Tenderfoot Wagon Road Trail. (Trail 1828)

See map page 341.
Distance: 4.7 miles one way
Hiking time: 2–4 hours
Difficulty: Moderate to strenuous
Trail maintenance: Infrequent
Traffic and other trail users: Light foot and horse traffic during summer, moderate during fall hunting seasons. The part of this trail near Salt Creek Summit Sno-Park and Trailhead is used heavily during winter by cross-country skiers.
Canine compatibility: Dogs permitted without leashes, but must be kept away from the stock of other parties
Fees and permits: Northwest Forest Pass and Eagle Cap Wilderness Permit
Maximum elevation: 7,585 feet
Map: USGS Lick Creek OR
Trail contact: USDA Forest Service Wallowa Mountains Office, 201 E 2nd St./ PO Box 905, Joseph, OR 97846; (541) 426-5546, (541) 426-4978; www.fs.usda.gov/wallowa-whitman. For winter skiing information contact Wing Ridge Ski Tours, 500 N River St., Enterprise, OR 97828; (541) 398-1980 or (888) 812-4707, ext. 3; www.facebook.com/Wing-Ridge-Ski-Tours-239313479446588.

Finding the trailhead: To reach Salt Creek Summit Sno-Park and Trailhead, take Imnaha Highway (OR 350, also known as Little Sheep Creek Highway and Hells Canyon Scenic Byway) for 8 miles east from Joseph. Turn right on FR 39 (Wallowa Mountain Loop Road) and follow it 10 miles south to Salt Creek Summit. The parking area is a short distance to the left (east) of FR 39 at the summit.
GPS: N45 12.506' / W117 04.410'

The Hike

The first 3 miles of this trail goes through an area burned by the 1989 Canal Fire, which is now mostly covered with young lodgepole pine timber. From Salt Creek Summit (6,100 ft.) go west across FR 39 and the canal bridge. After crossing the bridge, bear left and climb past the cross-country ski trails, which are marked with blue diamonds, as is Wing Ridge Trail at this point. At 0.3 mile the trail crosses the top of a small rise, then drops slightly. A short distance farther is the junction with Tenderfoot Wagon Road Trail (1819). Turn right (west) at the junction.

Past the junction the trail begins to climb steeply, passing two more cross-country ski trails. At 1.2 miles the trail enters an unburned area and crosses Salt Creek (6,690 ft.). A short distance farther (6,850 ft.), the trail enters the burned area again, turns right, and goes 200 vertical feet up a steep, open ridge. Just below the top of the open area the trail turns left and the grade moderates. Soon it turns steeply uphill again,

Wing Ridge Trail.

climbing to 7,220 feet. Watch for blazes on the trees, because the trail is faint on the ground. There is a stock driveway sign on a burnt tree at the top of this open area. The blazes and stock driveway signs may be difficult to spot in this burned area.

Soon the trail turns left and enters an area of small, partially burned trees. It then continues up to the ridgetop and enters a semi-open area (7,350 ft.). In the open area there is a good view of the Seven Devils Mountains to the east. The trail crosses the Eagle Cap Wilderness boundary, then makes a switchback as it climbs the last few feet to the pass over Wing Ridge (7,490 ft.). The pass is 2.5 miles from Salt Creek Summit Trailhead.

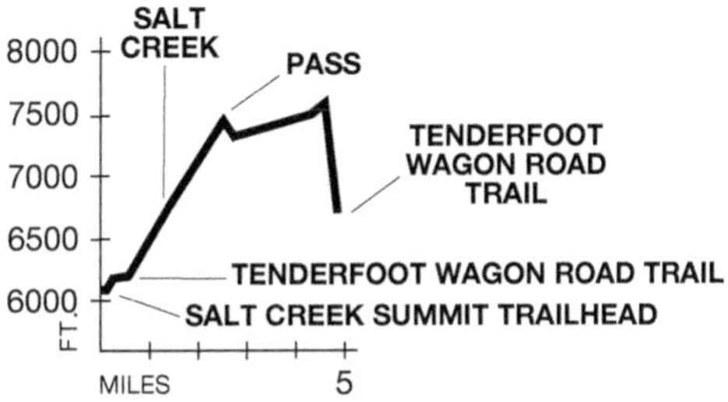

Beyond the pass the trail comes into an area that was only partially burned and becomes difficult to see. It crosses Wing Ridge, then descends slightly for 0.1 mile to the west. At this point (7,340 ft.) the trail appears to turn steeply downhill to the left into some small timber. However, here you must contour on the level to the right (west) for a short distance. Soon the trail shows up again. This is the easiest place to lose the route. If you descend below this point, it will be difficult to find the trail again. An altimeter can be a real help here.

A couple hundred feet farther, the trail climbs slightly again to a gully crossing. Just before the gully, some logs have been sawed off, clearing the trail and marking it. The trail goes 5 feet straight up the gully, then climbs out on the other side. Past the gully the trail climbs slightly around a small ridge (7,425 ft.), and then flattens out for a period. Watch for the yellow rectangular stock driveway signs. They are difficult to spot, but they mark the trail in this area.

The trail crosses an open, sage-covered hillside, then enters scattered timber again. It then drops slightly into another gully with a small stream. Just before the gully is a yellow stock driveway sign (7,520 ft.). After crossing the stream the trail leaves the partly burned area for good. It climbs slightly through a rocky area where it may be difficult to spot for a few yards. At 4.2 miles the trail rounds another small ridge (7,510 ft.).

The trail continues to contour along, crossing a couple more gullies to a small stream (7,585 ft.). This is the highest point on this trail. This stream is a little odd, as it is not in a gully but rather on a flat slope.

After crossing the stream the trail turns left and goes downhill to the south. It passes a campsite (7,530 ft.) and then continues downhill. The trail soon bears right and crosses a small gully. A short distance beyond the gully, the trail goes straight down a poorly defined ridge. It makes a right switchback in an open area (7,350 ft.), then drops straight down the ridge to the junction with Tenderfoot Wagon Road Trail (1819; 6,750 ft.). This junction is 4.7 miles from Salt Creek Summit Trailhead.

This trail requires considerable route finding on its southwestern end. The return trip can be made by turning left (east) on Tenderfoot Wagon Road Trail and following it back to Salt Creek Summit Trailhead for a 9-mile loop trip. The wagon road is slightly longer than going back over Wing Ridge, but it is nearly flat and usually takes less time to cover.

Miles and Directions

0.0 Start at the Salt Creek Summit Snow-Park and Trailhead.

0.3 Pass the junction with Tenderfoot Wagon Road Trail (1819). (GPS: N45 12.274'/W117 04.533')

1.2 Cross Salt Creek.

2.5 Cross the pass over Wing Ridge. (GPS: N45 11.263'/W117 05.430')

4.7 Arrive at the junction with Tenderfoot Wagon Road Trail. (GPS: N45 10.847'/W117 07.190')

98 Imnaha River

This day hike or backpacking trail leads from Indian Crossing Trailhead to the junction with North Fork Imnaha River Trail, along the scenic Imnaha River. Observe the recovering forest along the canyon, and allow enough time to visit Blue Hole and Imnaha Falls. Both of these spots offer good swimming holes on a hot day, and both have good fishing when it's cooler. (Trail 1816)

Distance: 6.8 miles one way
Hiking time: 2.5–4 hours
Difficulty: Easy
Trail maintenance: Yearly
Best season: May through Oct
Traffic and other trail users: Heavy foot and moderate horse traffic
Canine compatibility: Dogs permitted without leashes, but must be kept away from the stock of other parties
Fees and permits: Northwest Forest Pass and Eagle Cap Wilderness Permit
Maximum elevation: 5,400 feet
Map: USGS Deadman Point OR
Trail contact: USDA Forest Service Wallowa Mountains Office, 201 E 2nd St./PO Box 905, Joseph, OR 97846; (541) 426-5546, (541) 426-4978; www.fs.usda.gov/wallowa-whitman

Finding the trailhead: The trail begins at Indian Crossing Trailhead, at the upper end of the Imnaha River Road (4,550 ft.). To reach the trailhead take Imnaha Highway (OR 350) for 8 miles east from Joseph. Turn right on Wallowa Mountain Loop Road (FR 39) and follow it for 32 miles to the Upper Imnaha River Road (FR 3960). Turn right and follow FR 3960 for 9.5 miles to its end at Indian Crossing Campground and Trailhead. There are stock facilities and restrooms at the trailhead.
GPS: N45 06.730'/W117 00.939'

The Hike

The trail heads upriver (west) from the parking area. Just after leaving the parking lot there is a fenced area and some small buildings on the right side of the trail. A trail junction (4,650 ft.) is at 0.7 mile; the trail to the right goes back to the pack station, so bear left and head on up the Imnaha River Trail. Just after passing the junction, the trail enters the burned area of the 1994 Twin Lakes Fire. At first the burn was not too hot, and most of the larger trees, especially the big ponderosa pines, survived, but a little farther along the trail the fire became hotter and killed nearly everything. The beginnings of a new forest are evident, as there are many small pine trees, and flowers cover the more open areas.

The Eagle Cap Wilderness boundary (4,710 ft.) is at 1.5 miles. Up to this point the trail appears to have been a road at one time. The trail crosses Quartz Creek 0.1 mile farther, and at 1.8 miles makes another creek crossing. There is a short wooden bridge at 2 miles, and a few yards farther is the Twin Lakes Trail (1874) junction

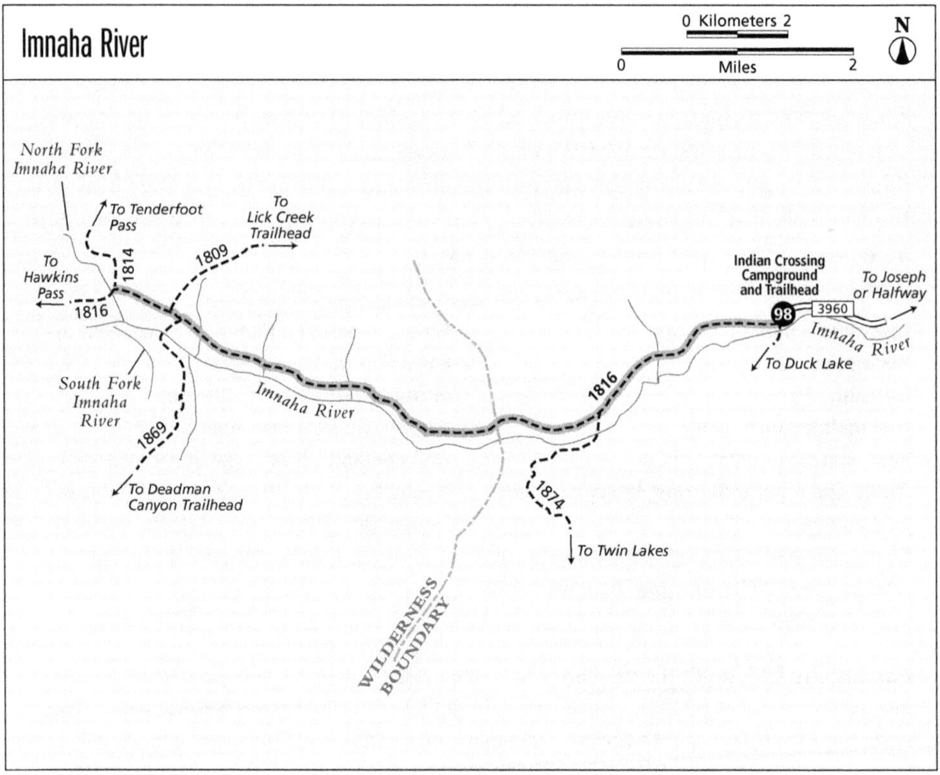

(4,740 ft.). Imnaha River Trail continues straight ahead. To the left a short distance is Blue Hole. There are nice campsites next to the river at Blue Hole.

After passing the Twin Lakes Trail junction, the forest is more lightly burned. The trail climbs up a gully for 0.3 mile. At the top of the gully (4,970 ft.) the trail begins a traverse along a talus slope. To the left and below the trail, the Imnaha River boils through a steep canyon. After crossing the 0.25-mile-wide talus slope, the trail climbs three switchbacks to the top of a small rise, then drops slightly, making two more switchbacks.

The trail then crosses three small streams in 0.8 mile to the top of the next outcropping. From the top of the outcropping, the patchwork pattern of the Twin Lakes Fire can be seen to the south across the Imnaha River, and the high peaks of the upper Imnaha drainage come into view to the west. After passing the outcropping the trail drops slightly, then climbs gently for 1.1 miles, crossing nine small streams to the top of another rocky outcropping (5,290 ft.) with a viewpoint overlooking the Imnaha River Canyon. There is a well-used campsite below the trail to the left 0.4 mile past this outcropping.

The unmarked junction with the path to Imnaha Falls is 0.3 mile after passing the campsite. The falls can be seen a short distance before the path through the trees to the left of the trail. The path goes 100 yards to Imnaha Falls. A beautiful little gorge and swimming hole are below the falls. There are strong currents in the pool, so be very careful if you decide to swim.

For the next 0.25 mile above Imnaha Falls, the fire burned most of the trees on the left side of the trail between the trail and the river. The path crosses a couple of small streams, then leaves the burn area. The junction with Deadman Canyon Trail (5,310 ft.) is 0.5 mile past the path to the falls. Deadman Canyon Trail (1869) turns to the left (south) and crosses the Imnaha River. See Deadman Canyon (hike 88). A campsite is a few yards to the left of the Imnaha River Trail, next to Deadman Canyon Trail.

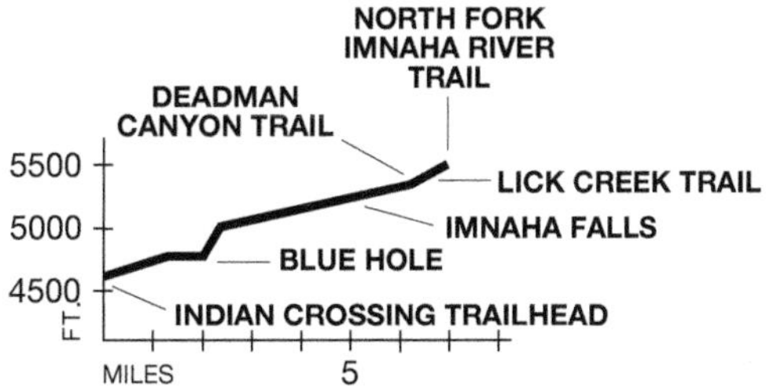

The junction with Lick Creek Trail (1809) is 150 yards past the junction with Deadman Canyon Trail. Lick Creek Trail turns to the right (north). The junction with North Fork Imnaha River Trail (1814) is 600 yards past the junction with Lick Creek Trail.

North Fork Imnaha River Trail junction (5,400 ft.) is 6.8 miles from Indian Crossing Trailhead. The area between Imnaha Falls and the junction with North Fork Imnaha River Trail is excellent for camping and exploring the surrounding territory. Several loops are possible by combining this trail with the other trails mentioned above.

Miles and Directions

0.0 Begin at the Indian Crossing Campground and Trailhead.

0.7 Pass the junction with the trail to the pack station.

1.5 Pass the Eagle Cap Wilderness boundary.

2.0 Pass the junction with Twin Lakes Trail (1874). (GPS: N45 06.062'/W117 02.826')

5.7 Reach Imnaha Falls.

6.1 Pass the junction with Deadman Canyon Trail (1869). (GPS: N45 06.760'/W117 07.150')

6.2 Pass the junction with Lick Creek Trail (1809).

6.8 Arrive at the junction with North Fork Imnaha River Trail (1814); Trail 1816 becomes South Fork Imnaha River Trail. (GPS: N45 06.933'/W117 07.700')

Climbs

Overview—Climb Section

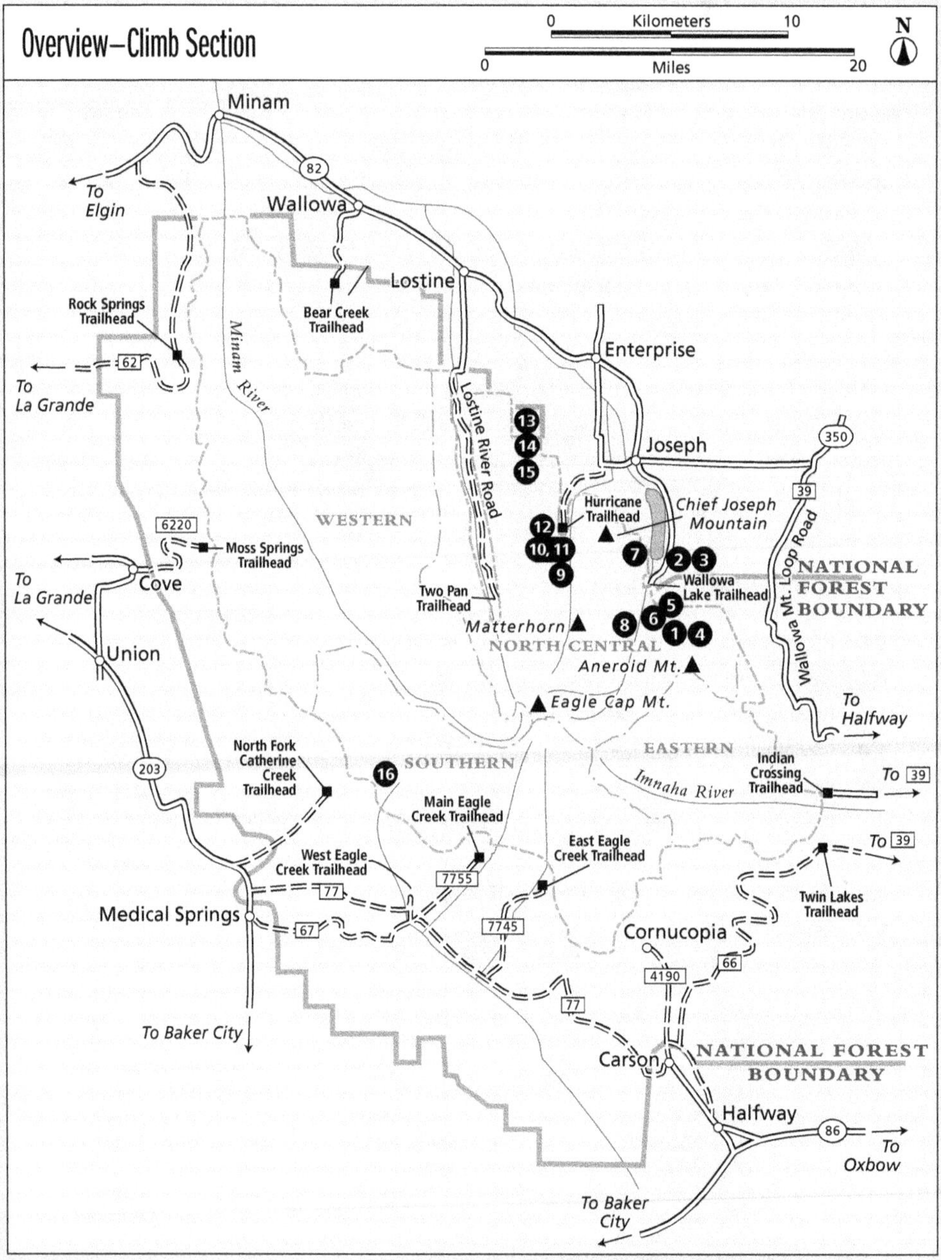

Climb 1 **Aneroid Mountain**

A moderate scramble leads up Aneroid Mountain from East Fork Wallowa River Trail. From Aneroid Mountain, the fourth-highest peak in the Wallowas, the view is absolutely superb in all directions. In summer (August) flowers cover the alpine terrain. Just below the summit on the south side of the peak are a scattering of scruffy whitebark pines. These little trees are living at the highest elevation of any trees in Oregon.

Distance: 2.5 miles from East Fork Wallowa River Trail
Hiking time: 3–5 hours from East Fork Wallowa River Trail
Difficulty: Moderate by climbing standards; strenuous when considered as a hike
Best season: July through Sept
Traffic and other trail users: Light foot traffic; no horses after leaving the East Fork Wallowa River Trail
Canine compatibility: Dogs permitted without leashes, but must be kept away from the stock of other parties
Fees and permits: Eagle Cap Wilderness Permit
Maximum elevation: 9,702 feet
Map: USGS Aneroid Mountain OR
Trail contact: USDA Forest Service Wallowa Mountains Office, 201 E 2nd St./ PO Box 905, Joseph, OR 97846; (541) 426-5546, (541) 426-4978; www.fs.usda.gov/wallowa-whitman

Finding the route: Drive south from Joseph on OR 351 for 7 miles, passing Wallowa Lake, to the Wallowa Lake Trailhead (GPS: N45 16.049'/W117 12.754'). Then hike south on the East Fork Wallowa River Trail (1804) for 4.4 miles. Turn left (east) off the trail in a meadow 0.25 mile south of the point where the divided inbound and outbound trails join back together. The elevation where the route leaves the trail is 7,120 feet.
GPS: N45 13.474'/W117 11.588'

The Route

Go east off the trail on flat ground through the timber for a short distance. Then head up a ridge, which will be to your right. Climb directly up the ridge to timberline (8,650 ft.). The ridge becomes less well defined as you ascend. This is where Hidden Peak climbers head straight up. See Hidden Peak from East Fork Wallowa River (climb 4). At timberline, angle to the right and continue to climb slightly to the saddle on the ridge between Hidden Peak and Aneroid Mountain. The elevation at the saddle is approximately 8,850 feet. Go south on the ridge for 1 mile. Then scramble the last few feet to the summit of Aneroid Mountain (9,702 ft.).

From the top of Aneroid Mountain, Aneroid Lake is below to the west. McCully Basin is to the east, and Bonny Lakes are to the southeast. There is beautiful alpine country in all directions. Carry all the water you will need, as there may be none above the East Fork Wallowa River.

Aneroid Mountain/ Hidden Peak from East Fork Wallowa River

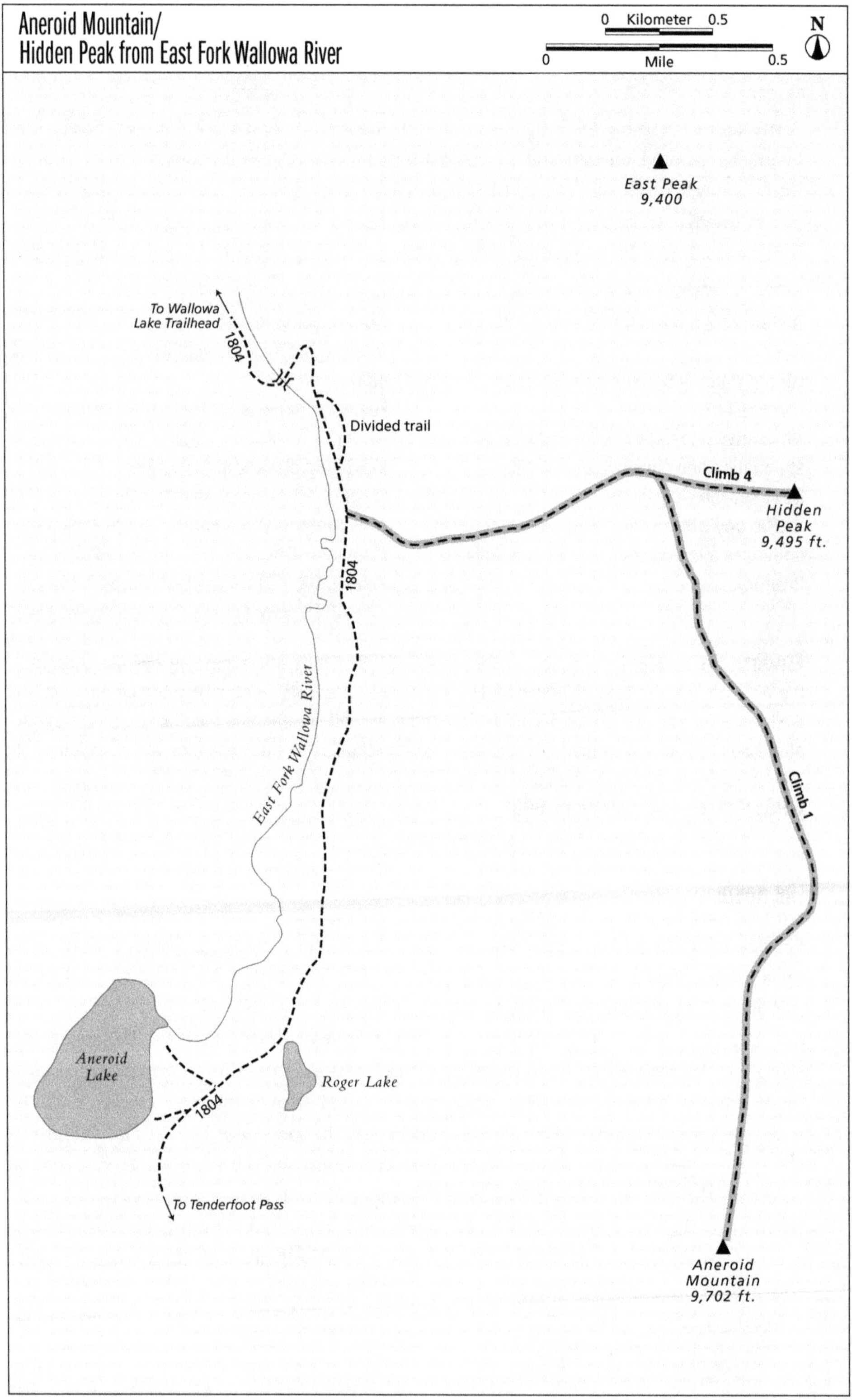

Camp near the summit of Aneroid Mountain.

The descent can be made by the same route or by taking a 3-mile longer but easier route down the south ridge of Aneroid Mountain to Bonny Lakes Trail (1802). Bonny Lakes Trail is reached near Dollar Lake (8,020 ft.). See Bonny Lakes (hike 96). Upon reaching Bonny Lakes Trail, turn right (west) and follow it to East Fork Wallowa River Trail. Turn right on East Fork Wallowa Trail and follow it for 7 miles, passing Aneroid Lake, to Wallowa Lake Trailhead.

Climb 2 East Peak from Mount Howard

This mostly uphill hike and scramble leads from the top of the Mount Howard Gondola to the summit of East Peak. This route traverses subalpine country all the way. It has wonderful views, and lots of flowers in the summer.

Distance: 2 miles one way
Hiking time: 1.5–3 hours
Difficulty: Easy by climbing standards; strenuous when considered as a hike
Best season: July through mid-Sept
Traffic and other trail users: Heavy foot traffic on the nature trails near the gondola, moderate past the gondola. No horses.
Canine compatibility: Dogs are not permitted on the Mount Howard Gondola.
Fees and permits: Fee to ride the gondola; Eagle Cap Wilderness Permit also required
Maximum elevation: 9,400 feet
Maps: USGS Joseph OR and Aneroid Mountain OR
Trail contact: USDA Forest Service Wallowa Mountains Office, 201 E 2nd St. / PO Box 905, Joseph, OR 97846; (541) 426-5546, (541) 426-4978; www.fs.usda.gov/wallowa-whitman

Finding the route: From Joseph drive 6.5 miles south on OR 351 to the parking area for the Mount Howard Gondola (aka Wallowa Lake Tram). The bottom terminal of the Mount Howard Gondola is located on the left (east) side of the highway, in the resort area at the head of Wallowa Lake. Take the gondola to the upper terminal, where this hike begins.
GPS: Top of gondola/trailhead: N45 15.770' / W117 10.788'

The Route

From the top terminal of the gondola (8,150 ft.), follow the nature trail east for 0.1 mile to the ridgeline (GPS: N45 15.714'/W117 10.654'). The view from here is wonderful, with the Wallowa Mountains to the south and west, and the Seven Devils Mountains in the distance to the east.

From the ridgeline continue east a short distance to the point where the path turns to your right (south). Follow the path south to the saddle dividing Royal Purple Creek, which flows to the west, and upper Prairie Creek, which drains to the east (GPS: N45 15.481' / W117 10.654'). (These coordinates could be very handy when returning in a whiteout.) Nature trails can and should be followed to this point, if the ground is not covered with snow. Alpine vegetation is fragile and this is a high-use area, so please use the trails. Two latrines are located in the saddle.

From the saddle follow the trail south, climbing an ascending traverse around the right (west) side of the first small peak on the ridge to another saddle (8,400 ft.). After passing this saddle the trail climbs 200 vertical feet to the south, then goes around the left (east) side of the next peak on the ridge. Just past this peak the trail comes close to another saddle but does not quite reach it. This is the point where the East Peak and Hidden Peak routes separate.

East Peak from Mount Howard/ Hidden Peak from Mount Howard

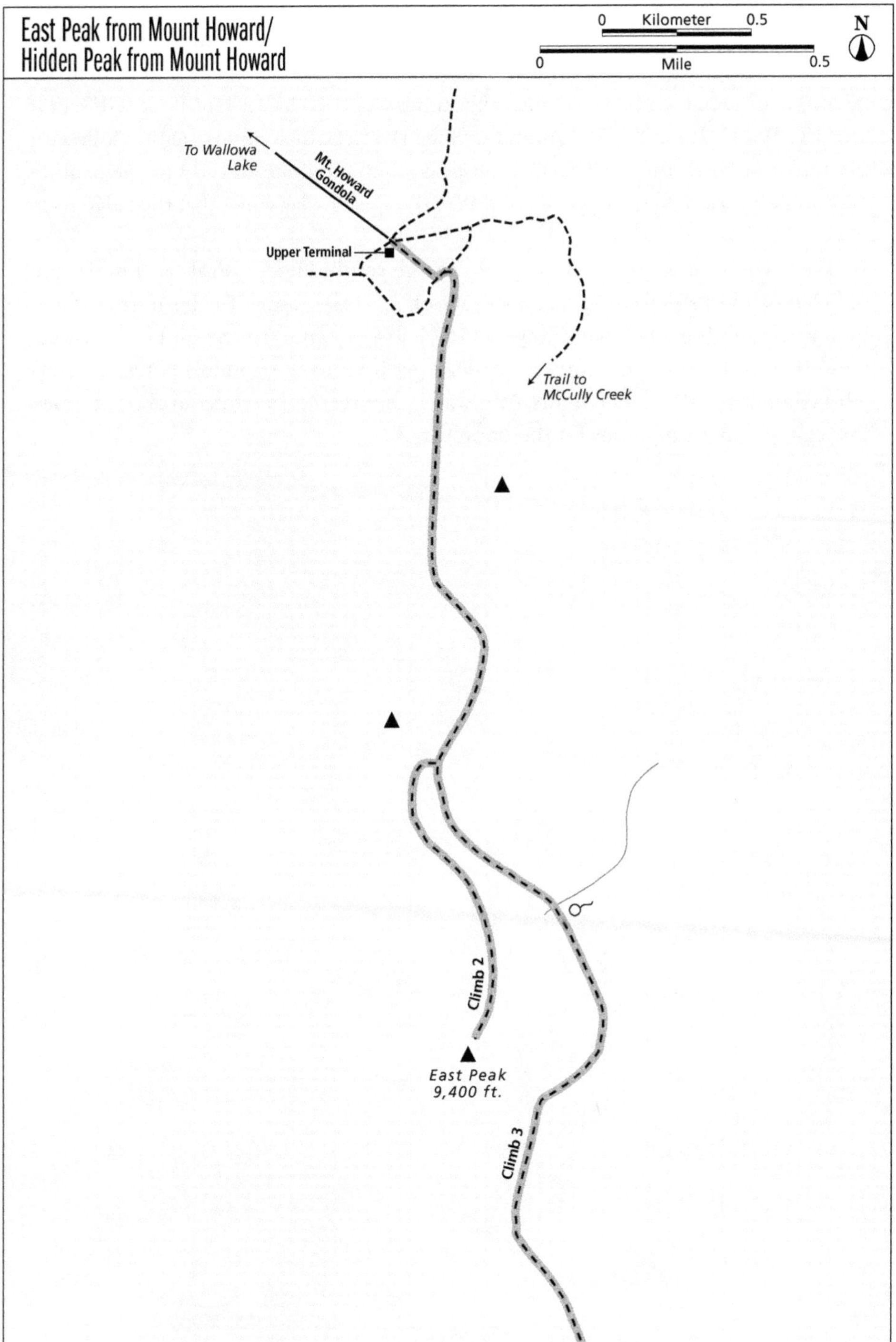

From the point where the trail is closest to this saddle, climb west (straight up) to the ridgeline (8,680 ft.) (GPS: N45 14.735'/W117 10.794'), then turn left (south) and scramble up the ridge to the summit of 9,400-foot East Peak (GPS: N45 14.212'/W117 10.632'). The summit of East Peak can also be reached by following the trail around to the left (east) of the peak, then climbing directly to the summit. This route is not difficult, but does not offer the spectacular views that the ridge route does.

From the summit the view is great. To the south, Hidden Peak is close by, and 9,702-foot-high Aneroid Mountain is about 2.5 miles away. To the northeast you look across the Imnaha River Canyon and Hells Canyon to the Seven Devils Mountains. Be sure to watch the time so you can get back to the gondola before it closes. This climb may take several hours. Also watch the weather; a whiteout above timberline can be quite dangerous for the unprepared.

Climb 3 Hidden Peak from Mount Howard

This hike and scramble leads from the top terminal of the Mount Howard Gondola to the summit of Hidden Peak.

See map page 357.
Distance: 2.5 miles one way
Hiking time: 2–3 hours
Difficulty: Easy to moderate
Best season: July through mid-Sept
Traffic and other trail users: Heavy foot traffic on the nature trails on Mount Howard, light to moderate after passing the first saddle. No horses.
Canine compatibility: Dogs are not permitted on the Mount Howard Gondola.
Fees and permits: Fee to ride the gondola. You also need an Eagle Cap Wilderness Permit.
Maximum elevation: 9,495 feet
Maps: USGS Joseph OR and Aneroid Mountain OR
Trail contact: USDA Forest Service Wallowa Mountains Office, 201 E 2nd St. / PO Box 905, Joseph, OR 97846; (541) 426-5546, (541) 426-4978; www.fs.usda.gov/wallowa-whitman

Finding the route: Drive south from Joseph on OR 351 for 6.5 miles to the Mount Howard Gondola parking area. The parking area is on the left (east) side of the road in the resort area at the head of Wallowa Lake. Ride the gondola (aka Wallowa Lake Tram) to the upper terminal, which is your trailhead.
GPS: N45 15.770' / W117 10.766'

The Route

From the top of the Mount Howard Gondola, follow the nature trail for 0.1 mile east to the ridgeline. Cross the ridge and descend easterly on a poorer trail. The track soon turns right and contours around the sidehill for about 0.2 mile to Royal Purple Saddle (the saddle just south of the very summit of Mount Howard). From the saddle continue south, climbing rather steeply in places. The route contours around the east side of East Peak about 1.8 miles from the top of the gondola. By now you have climbed to nearly 9,000 feet elevation. The last part of the traverse around East Peak is on a steep sidehill, and the route is a little vague. Continuing south, head for the saddle between East Peak and Hidden Peak (9,010 ft.). From the saddle, climb southeast directly to the summit of Hidden Peak (9,495 ft.).

Climb 4 Hidden Peak from East Fork Wallowa River

Climb to the timberline above the East Fork Wallowa River. Then make a short scramble from timberline to the summit of Hidden Peak. Take time to enjoy the view while you are on the summit. If you are here in early summer, there may be thousands of ladybugs on and under the rocks near the summit.

See map page 354.
Distance: 1.3 miles from the East Fork Wallowa River Trail; 5.7 miles from the Wallowa Lake Trailhead
Hiking time: 2–4 hours from the East Fork Wallowa River Trail; 3–5 hours from Wallowa Lake Trailhead
Difficulty: Easy by climbing standards; strenuous when considered as a hike
Best season: July through Sept
Traffic and other trail users: Light foot traffic. No horses after leaving the East Fork Wallowa River Trail.
Canine compatibility: Dogs permitted without leashes, but must be kept away from the stock of other parties
Fees and permits: Eagle Cap Wilderness Permit
Maximum elevation: 9,495 feet
Map: USGS Aneroid Mountain OR
Trail contact: USDA Forest Service Wallowa Mountains Office, 201 E 2nd St./ PO Box 905, Joseph, OR 97846; (541) 426-5546, (541) 426-4978; www.fs.usda.gov/wallowa-whitman. Further information may be limited.

Finding the route: Drive 7 miles south from Joseph on OR 351 to the Wallowa Lake Trailhead (GPS: N45 16.049'/W117 12.754'), which is at the end of the road. From the Wallowa Lake Trailhead take East Fork Wallowa River Trail (1804) for 4.4 miles south. Turn left and leave the trail at 7,120 feet elevation.
GPS: N45 13.474'/W117 11.588'

The Route

From the East Fork Wallowa River Trail head east through the timber, then climb a ridge, which will be to your right. The ridge becomes less well defined as you go up. Continue up the ridge to timberline (8,650 ft.). From timberline climb straight up to the summit (9,495 ft.), which is directly above and to the east (GPS: N45 13.569'/W117 10.287').

Climb 5 Bonneville Mountain (East Side)

Bonneville Mountain is the pyramid-shaped peak directly south of Wallowa Lake. It is the first major peak on the ridge dividing the East and West Forks of the Wallowa River. The east-side route is a steep scramble, with some moderate rock climbing from the East Fork Wallowa River Trail to the summit.

Distance: 2 miles from East Fork Wallowa River Trail; 4.3 miles from Wallowa Lake Trailhead
Hiking time: 3–6 hours from East Fork Wallowa River Trail; 4–7 hours from Wallowa Lake Trailhead
Difficulty: Strenuous; route-finding and some rock climbing skills required
Best season: July through Sept
Traffic and other trail users: Very light foot traffic only after leaving the East Fork Wallowa River Trail
Canine compatibility: Dogs permitted without leashes, but must be kept away from the stock of other parties. However, dogs will have a very difficult time climbing the nearly vertical terrain near the summit.
Fees and permits: Eagle Cap Wilderness Permit
Maximum elevation: 8,860 feet
Map: USGS Aneroid Mountain OR. Most maps incorrectly show one of the subpeaks north of the true summit as the top of Bonneville Mountain.
Trail contact: USDA Forest Service Wallowa Mountains Office, 201 E 2nd St./ PO Box 905, Joseph, OR 97846; (541) 426-5546, (541) 426-4978; www.fs.usda.gov/wallowa-whitman. Further information may be very limited.

Finding the route: Drive south from Joseph on OR 351 for 7 miles to the road's end at the Wallowa Lake Trailhead. The east-side route on Bonneville Mountain leaves the East Fork Wallowa River Trail (1804) 2.3 miles above (south of) the Wallowa Lake Trailhead. The spot to leave the trail is 0.3 mile above (south of) the Pacific Power and Light Company intake dam and 70 yards below (north of) the Eagle Cap Wilderness boundary sign (5,920 ft.).
GPS: Wallowa Lake Trailhead: N45 16.049'/W117 12.754'; Bonneville climb leaves trail: N45 15.088'/W117 12.068'

The Route

The route turns off the trail to the right (west) in a semi-open area. Climb the low ridge between the obvious gullies. Continue to climb, on game trails when available, to a saddle on the north ridge of Bonneville Mountain. Just below the saddle, traverse left (south) to reach its lowest point (7,320 ft.).

From the saddle climb up the ridge to the south to a false summit (7,970 ft.), which is actually the second peak on the ridge as you come up from Wallowa Lake. From here the light gray summit of the 9,834.8-foot Matterhorn is in view to the west. To the southwest is Eagle Cap, and Mount Howard is to the northeast.

From the false summit follow the ridge on the south to the next subpeak (8,320 ft.), then traverse to the right of the ridge, dropping slightly to the second gully. This gully originates in the notch between the twin summits of Bonneville Mountain.

Bonneville Mountain (East Side)/Bonneville Mountain (West Side)

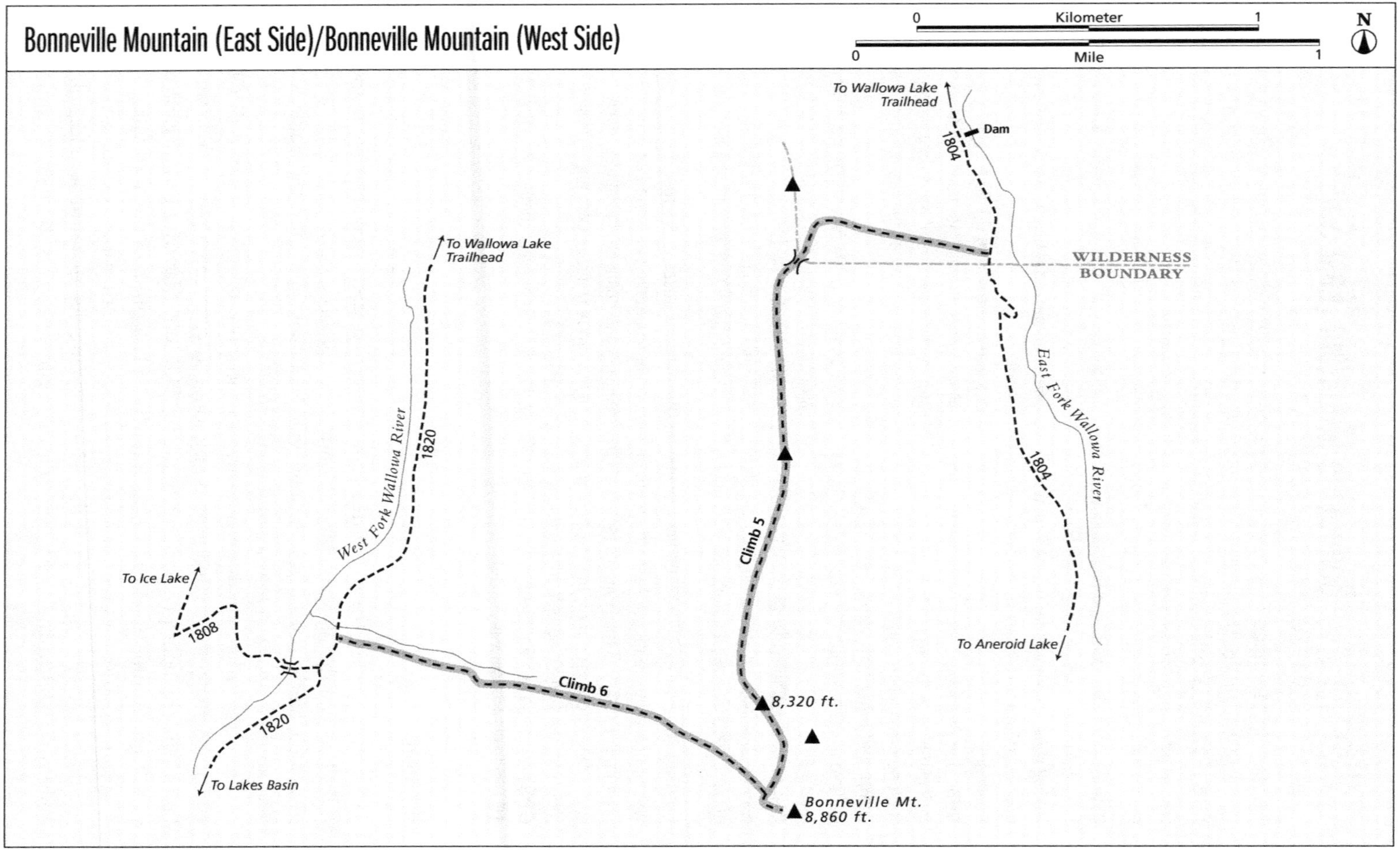

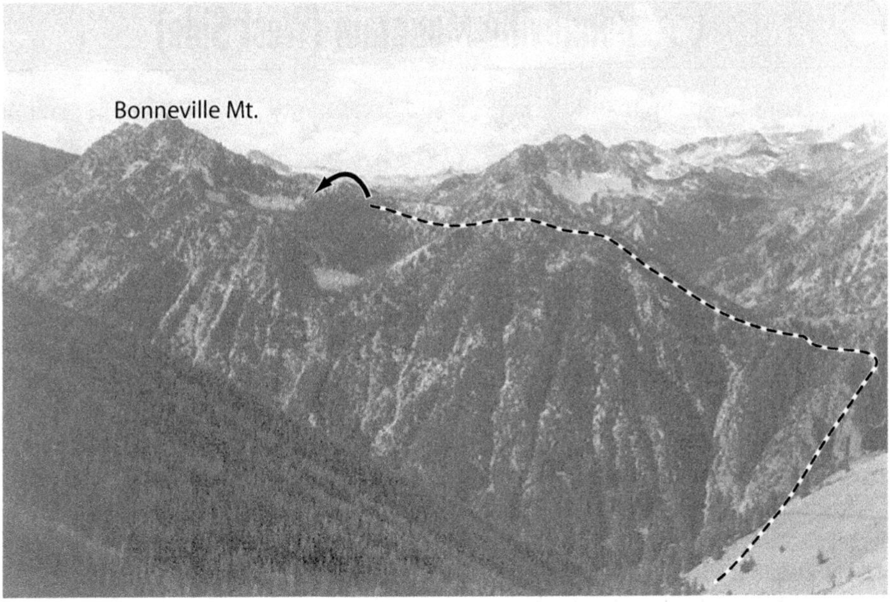

Bonneville Mountain, east side.

Turn left (east) and climb up the gully over the boulders and ledges. Stay generally to the right (south) of the bottom of the gully. Watch and listen for possible rockfall.

Just below the notch at the top of the gully is a large boulder. At the boulder traverse right 75 feet to a smaller gully. Turn left and climb straight up the gully to the ridgeline. At the ridgeline scramble right a few feet to the summit of Bonneville Mountain (8,860 ft.; GPS: N45 13.949' /W117 12.600'). The summit block of Bonneville Mountain has a distinctly castle-like appearance, with rock pillars.

Climbing Bonneville Mountain requires considerable route finding and some moderately steep rock climbing. A rope may be necessary for inexperienced climbers. There is considerable rockfall danger in some spots. No water is available on the east-side route after leaving the East Fork Wallowa River. The easiest way to descend is to retrace the route back down to the East Fork Wallowa River Trail.

Climb 6 Bonneville Mountain (West Side)

A fairly long, steep climb leads from the West Fork Wallowa River Trail to the summit of Bonneville Mountain.

See map page 362.
Distance: 1.5 miles from West Fork Wallowa River Trail
Hiking time: 3–6 hours from West Fork Wallowa River Trail
Difficulty: Strenuous, with considerable rockfall danger
Best season: July through Sept
Traffic and other trail users: Very light foot traffic only after leaving the West Fork Wallowa River Trail
Canine compatibility: Dogs permitted without leashes, but must be kept away from the stock of other parties. However, dogs will have a very difficult time climbing the nearly vertical terrain near the summit.
Fees and permits: Eagle Cap Wilderness Permit
Maximum elevation: 8,860 feet
Map: USGS Aneroid Mountain
Trail contact: USDA Forest Service Wallowa Mountains Office, 201 E 2nd St./ PO Box 905, Joseph, OR 97846; (541) 426-5546, (541) 426-4978; www.fs.usda.gov/wallowa-whitman. Further information may be very limited.

Finding the route: From Joseph drive 7 miles south on OR 351, passing Wallowa Lake, to the road's end at Wallowa Lake Trailhead. To climb Bonneville Mountain from the west side, take the West Fork Wallowa River Trail for 2.5 miles south to an open area, just before the Ice Lake Trail junction.
GPS: Wallowa Lake Trailhead: N45 16.049' / W117 12.745'; Bonneville climb junction: N45 14.263' / W117 13.791'

The Route

Turn off West Fork Wallowa River Trail and climb the gentle open slope to the left (east) to a point where two gullies can be seen ahead. The two gullies run nearly parallel. Climb up the left gully all the way, nearly 3,000 vertical feet, to the large boulder just below the notch. Some rockfall is possible in the gully, so watch and listen for it. At the boulder, traverse right 75 feet to a smaller gully. Turn left and climb straight up the gully to the ridgeline. At the ridgeline scramble right a few feet to the summit of Bonneville Mountain (8,860 ft.; GPS: N45 13.949' / W117 12.600').

The easiest way to descend is via the east-side route. To descend via the east-side route, descend the gully you climbed up to well below the large boulder, then traverse right across the talus to the ridgeline well to the north of the peak. Follow the ridgeline north to the saddle at 7,320 feet elevation. From the saddle descend to the east nearly straight down, but allowing for outcrops and cliffs, to the East Fork Wallowa River Trail. At the trail turn left and hike back to the Wallowa Lake Trailhead.

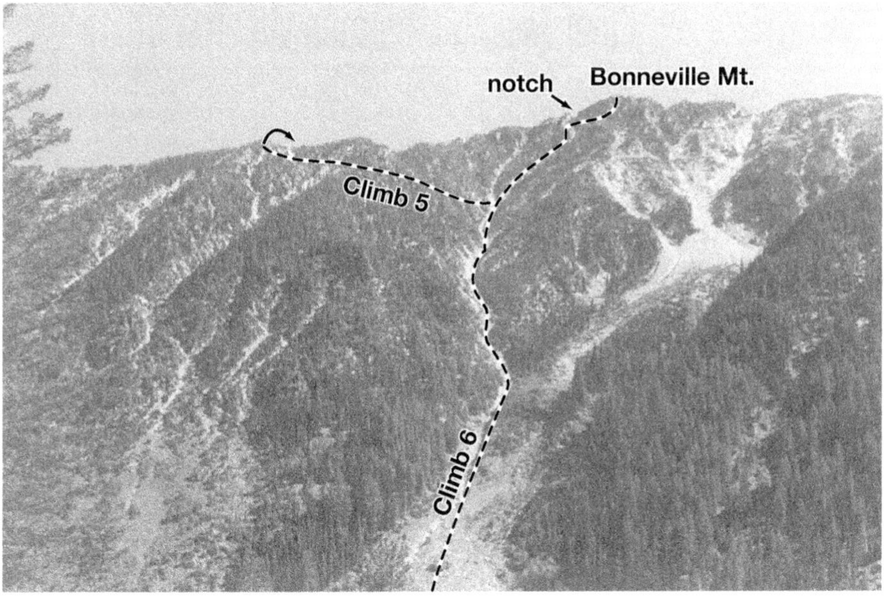

Bonneville Mountain, west side.

This route is more difficult than the east-side route. It takes a fair amount of rock climbing to get up the gully, and in some places it is quite exposed. There is considerable rockfall danger in some spots. A climbing rope may be necessary for less experienced climbers. Water is not available after entering the gully.

Climb 7 **Chief Joseph Mountain via First Chute**

First Chute route is the easiest way to the summit of Chief Joseph Mountain from the resort area at the head of Wallowa Lake.

Distance: 2 miles from the Chief Joseph Mountain Trail
Hiking time: 4–8 hours from Wallowa Lake Trailhead; 3–6 hours from Chief Joseph Mountain Trail
Difficulty: Moderate to strenuous
Best season: Late July through early Oct; June through early Oct if you take the alternate route from the marina parking area at Wallowa Lake
Traffic and other trail users: Heavy foot and horse traffic on Chief Joseph Mountain Trail; light foot traffic on the route
Canine compatibility: Dogs permitted without leashes, but must be kept away from the stock of other parties
Fees and permits: Eagle Cap Wilderness Permit
Maximum elevation: 9,617 feet
Maps: USGS Chief Joseph Mountain OR and Joseph OR
Trail contact: USDA Forest Service Wallowa Mountains Office, 201 E 2nd St./ PO Box 905, Joseph, OR 97846; (541) 426-5546, (541) 426-4978; www.fs.usda.gov/wallowa-whitman

Finding the route: Drive south from Joseph on OR 351 for 7 miles to the Wallowa Lake Trailhead, which is at the end of the road. From the trailhead hike south on the West Fork Wallowa River Trail (1820) for 0.3 mile to the junction with the Chief Joseph Mountain Trail (1803). Turn right and follow Chief Joseph Mountain Trail for 4.4 miles to a switchback at 6,380 feet elevation. Just beyond the switchback turn left (west).
GPS: Wallowa Lake Trailhead: N45 16.049'/W117 12.754'; First Chute route leaves trail: N45 17.068'/W117 13.886'

Early in the season (June–July) the B C Creek crossing 1.5 miles up the Chief Joseph Trail from Wallowa Lake Trailhead is usually unsafe. At this time of year it is better to park in the marina parking lot at the head of Wallowa Lake. From the southwest corner of the parking area, take the nature trail south for 0.1 mile to a junction and a signboard, where you can get your wilderness permit. Turn right at the trail junction and climb the steep path for 1 mile to an unsigned junction with the Chief Joseph Mountain Trail. This puts you 1.2 miles above the B C Creek crossing. Turn right on Chief Joseph Mountain Trail and follow it to the point where the First Chute route leaves it.

It is also possible to continue on the steep (now steeper) path for another 0.5 mile to another unsigned junction with Chief Joseph Mountain Trail. If you do this, turn left on Chief Joseph Mountain Trail and contour around the slope to the southwest and west for about 0.3 mile, to the point where the First Chute route leaves the trail.

The Route

Go straight up the high valley for 400 yards. Look to the left at the face of Chief Joseph Mountain. The first open avalanche chute on the southeast end of the face marks the route.

Chief Joseph Mountain via First Chute

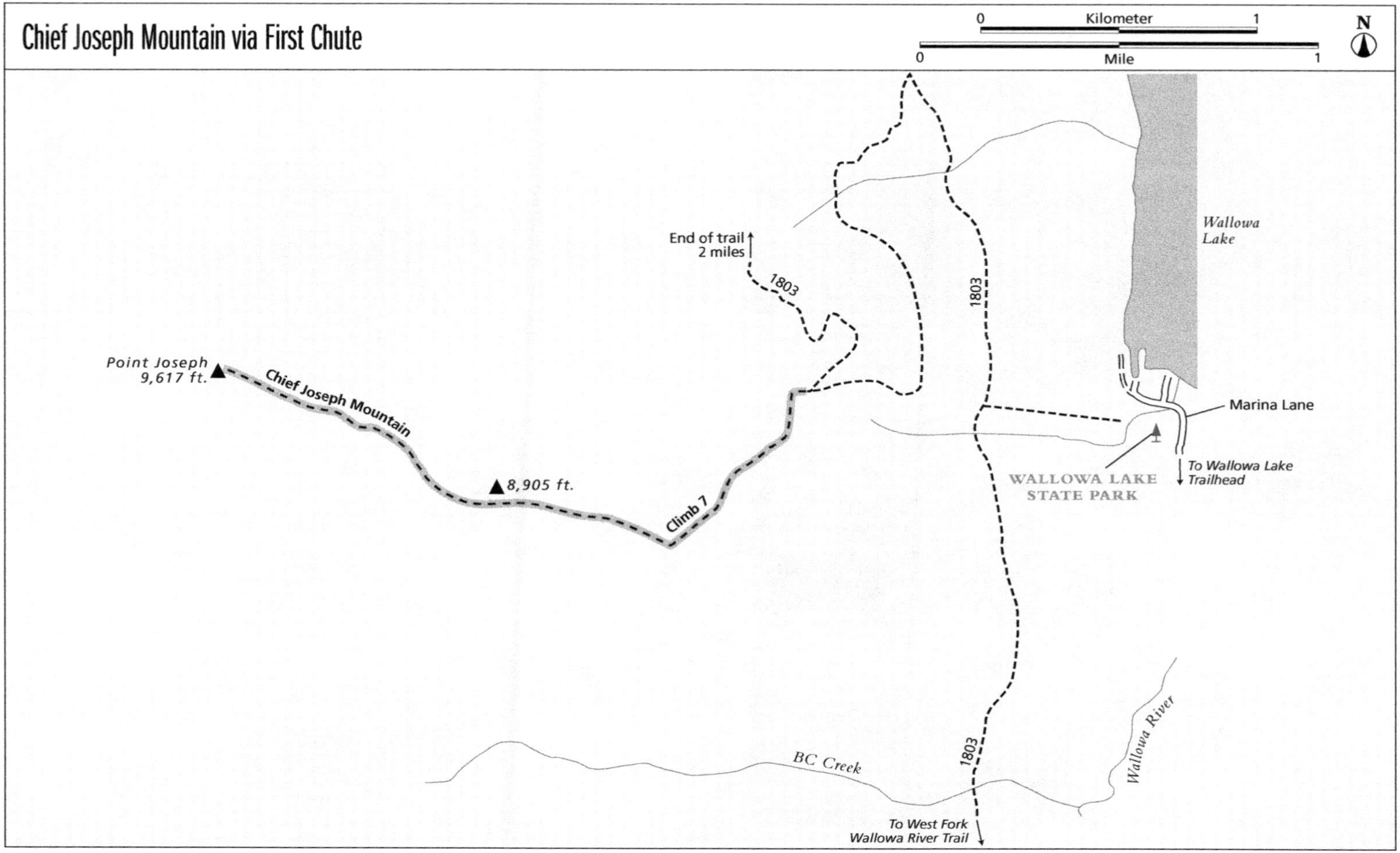

Chief Joseph Mountain.

To the left of the chute is timbered hillside, and to the right is a rock ridge with scattered trees. Make your way through the trees and bushes to the base of the chute. Climb up along the left side of the chute through the timber to the top of the main ridge, at slightly over 8,000 feet (GPS: N45 16.702' / W117 14.290'). Follow the faint trail in a northwesterly direction along the main ridge, passing around the left side of a rock outcropping to the summit (9,617 ft.; GPS: N45 17.140' / W117 15.705'). The summit is about 1 mile and 1,600 vertical feet above the point where the route first reached the main ridge.

This is probably the easiest and quickest route to the summit from the Wallowa Lake resort area. Early in the season, when there is snow, there may be avalanche danger in the chute. Water will be difficult to find, so carry what you will need. Watch for mountain goats near the summit. They are usually seen on the ridge just past (northwest of) the summit or in the cliffs below to the northeast.

Return via the same route.

Climb 8 **Matterhorn from Ice Lake**

This moderately steep hike leads from Ice Lake to the Summit of the Matterhorn.

Distance: Approximately 2 miles
Hiking time: 1.5–4 hours from Ice Lake
Difficulty: Moderate
Best season: July through Sept
Traffic and other trail users: Moderate to heavy foot traffic
Canine compatibility: Dogs permitted without leashes, but must be kept away from the stock of other parties
Fees and permits: Eagle Cap Wilderness Permit
Maximum elevation: 9,835 feet
Map: USGS Eagle Cap OR
Trail contact: USDA Forest Service Wallowa Mountains Office, 201 E 2nd St./ PO Box 905, Joseph, OR 97846; (541) 426-5546, (541) 426-4978; www.fs.usda.gov/wallowa-whitman

Finding the route: Drive south from Joseph on OR 351 for 7 miles to the Wallowa Lake Trailhead, passing Wallowa Lake along the way. The Wallowa Lake Trailhead is at the end of the road. From Wallowa Lake Trailhead, take West Fork Wallowa River Trail (1820) for 2.6 miles to the junction with Ice Lake Trail. Take Ice Lake Trail (1808) for 5.1 miles to Ice Lake.
GPS: Wallowa Lake Trailhead: N45 16.049'/W117 12.254'; Ice Lake Trail junction: N45 14.333'/W117 13.809'

The Route

To climb the Matterhorn, follow the trail around the north side of Ice Lake to the northwest corner (7,849 ft.). Climb to the northwest on a poorly defined trail. Soon the trail turns to the west and is marked with cairns. Climb steadily up a small ridge until you are a couple of hundred feet below the summit. Turn left and do an ascending traverse to the summit of Matterhorn (GPS: N45 13.657'/W117 17.929').

There is a vague path all the way to the top; look some distance ahead for the faint trail and the cairns marking it. Route finding could be difficult during times of poor visibility. The return trip is best made by retracing the same route.

Matterhorn, at 9,834.8 feet, is the second-highest peak in the Wallowa Mountains. The Matterhorn and Sacajawea peaks were resurveyed in the fall of 2013 by Eric Stahlke, using sophisticated GPS equipment. This should end the long-standing question of which is higher. The entire summit area and the Matterhorn are white limestone, which is part of the Martin Bridge Formation. This makes the Matterhorn a very distinct peak, especially when viewed from the west. The west face is a 3,500-foot wall of this white limestone. It is interesting to note that this limestone is the compressed skeletal remains of tiny marine animals, probably coral, which were deposited on the ocean floor many millions of years ago.

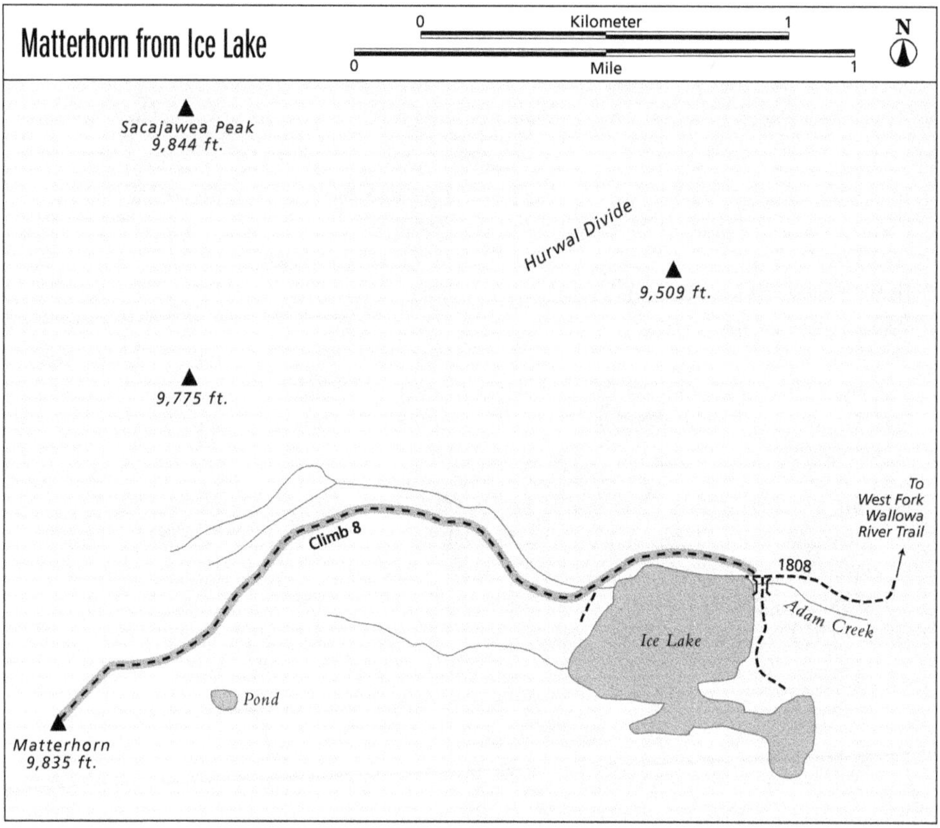

Just below the summit, to the northeast, is good evidence of recent glacial action in the form of a well-defined cirque and moraines. Mountain goats are common in this area. Watch for them on the ridge to the north of the route and near the summit.

Navigation above Ice Lake can be difficult during times of poor visibility, and thunderstorms are common most of the summer, so keep an eye on the changing weather.

Climb 9 Sacajawea Peak via Thorp Creek Basin

This fairly steep hike climbs from Hurricane Creek Trail to the summit of Sacajawea Peak. Sacajawea was surveyed in the fall of 2013 by Eric Stahlke, using up-to-date GPS equipment, and was found to be the highest peak in the Wallowa Mountains.

Distance: 5 miles one way from Hurricane Creek Trail
Hiking time: 4–8 hours from Hurricane Creek Trail
Difficulty: Moderately strenuous
Best season: July through Sept
Traffic and other trail users: Heavy foot and horse traffic on Hurricane Creek Trail; light stock traffic on Thorp Creek Trail, only foot traffic above there
Canine compatibility: Dogs permitted without leashes, but must be kept away from the stock of other parties
Fees and permits: Northwest Forest Pass and Eagle Cap Wilderness Permit
Maximum elevation: 9,843.7 feet
Maps: USGS Chief Joseph Mountain OR and Eagle Cap OR. The Chief Joseph Mountain quad shows Thorp Creek Trail. Most other maps do not.
Trail contact: USDA Forest Service Wallowa Mountains Office, 201 E 2nd St./PO Box 905, Joseph, OR 97846; (541) 426-5546, (541) 426-4978; www.fs.usda.gov/wallowa-whitman

Finding the route: Drive south from Enterprise on Hurricane Creek Road for 5 miles to the Hurricane Creek Grange Hall. Bear right (nearly straight ahead) here, leaving the pavement, and continue south on Hurricane Creek Road. The road soon becomes paved again as you enter the national forest. You reach the Hurricane Creek Trailhead at the end of the road 3 miles from the grange hall. Hike south on Hurricane Creek Trail for 1.8 miles to the unmarked junction with Thorp Creek Trail. Thorp Creek Trail, the route to the summit, leaves Hurricane Creek Trail 0.25 mile south of Deadman Creek. Although Thorp Creek Trail is not marked, it usually has had enough use to be fairly obvious.
GPS: Hurricane Creek Trailhead: N45 18.673'/W117 18.438'; Thorp Creek Trail junction: N45 17.192'/W117 18.436'

The Route

Thorp Creek Trail turns left off Hurricane Creek Trail and goes 0.25 mile southeast, where it crosses Hurricane Creek (5,420 ft.). A few yards upstream from the crossing, logs can be used to cross the creek dry-footed.

After crossing Hurricane Creek the trail goes east for a short distance and enters an open, grassy area. It then climbs gradually to the southeast through the open area. The trail soon enters the timber again and crosses Twin Creek (5,650 ft.). After crossing Twin Creek the trail climbs steeply, via switchbacks, to the top of the ridge overlooking Thorp Creek (6,170 ft.). At this point the north face of Sacajawea Peak is in full view, to the south across the Thorp Creek Canyon. The trail continues to climb, generally following the ridgetop, to 7,450 feet, then traverses to the south-southeast

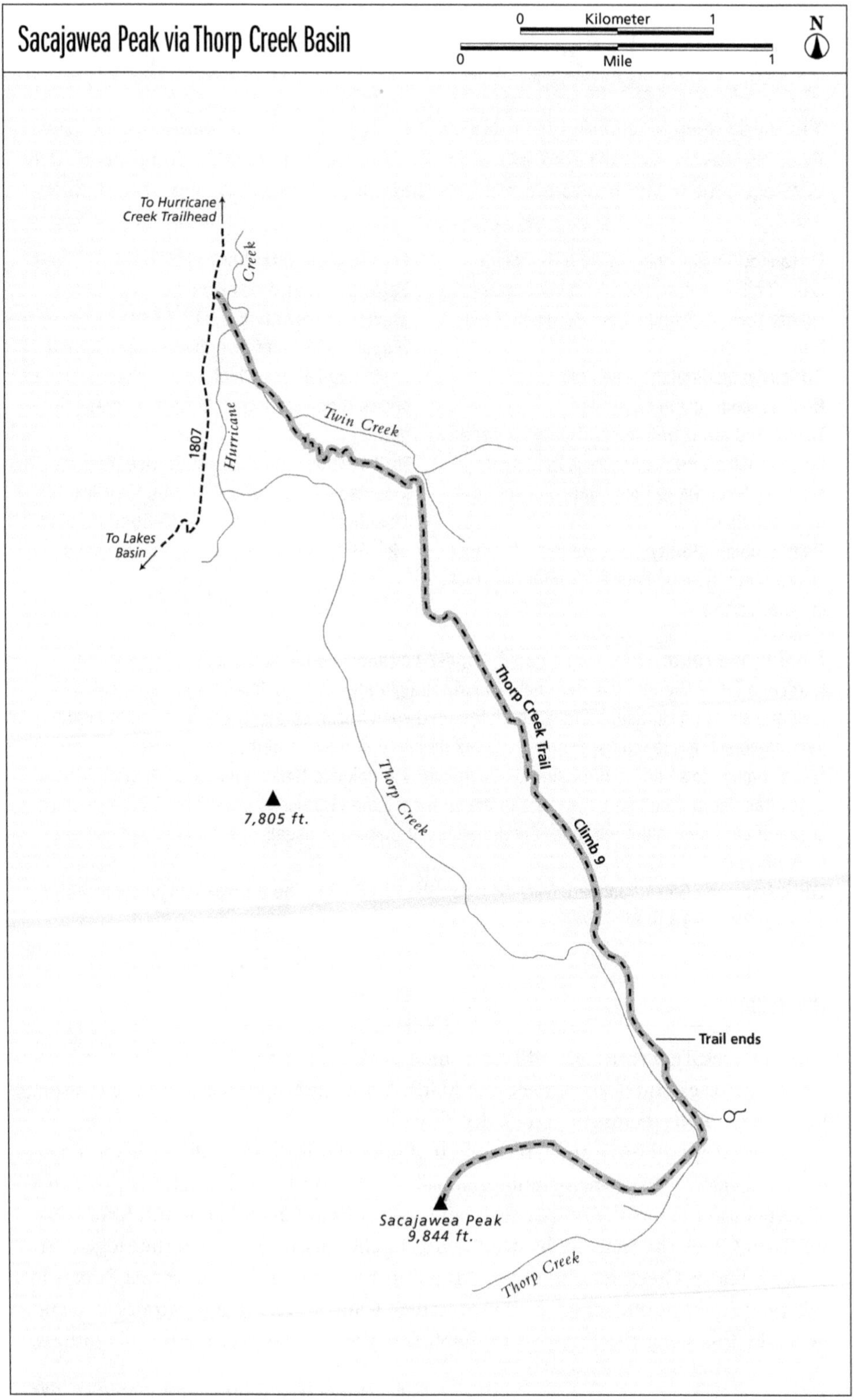

Sacajawea Peak via Thorp Creek Basin
0
Kilometer
1
0
Mile
1
N
To Hurricane Creek Trailhead
Creek
Hurricane
1807
Twin Creek
To Lakes Basin
Thorp Creek Trail
Thorp Creek
7,805 ft.
Climb 9
Trail ends
Sacajawea Peak 9,844 ft.
Thorp Creek

Signing the summit register on Sacajawea Peak. Gary Fletcher photo

into the beautiful alpine upper Thorp Creek Valley. The trail ends 3.5 miles from the Hurricane Creek Trail junction.

To continue to the summit of Sacajawea Peak, follow the creek up the valley. Then bear to the right (south), passing a large spring (7,800 ft.). Head on up the creekbed to the south, to what appears from below to be a saddle. It is really a point where the creekbed flattens out (8,000 ft.; GPS: N45 14.660' / W117 16.731'). At this point turn right (west) and climb the prominent ridge to the west. To your right and below is the north face of Sacajawea Peak, and to your left is the basin at the head of Thorp Creek. When you reach the false summit, traverse left (south) to the summit of Sacajawea Peak (9,843.7 ft.; GPS: N45 14.710' / W117 17.576'), the highest peak in the Wallowa Mountains and number six in Oregon.

The total distance from Hurricane Creek Trail to the summit of Sacajawea Peak is about 5 miles, with a 4,424-foot elevation gain. The route is steep but not technically difficult. There are plenty of good campsites in the upper Thorp Creek Valley.

Watch for mountain goats above timberline on Sacajawea Peak, especially in the huge basin on the west side. Return by the same route, or follow the ridge south for 2 miles to the Matterhorn and descend via Ice Lake to Wallowa Lake Trailhead. Descending via Ice Lake requires a car shuttle to Wallowa Lake Trailhead.

Climb 10 Twin Peaks via Legore Mine (North Ridge)

This is the easiest route up Twin Peaks, but it still requires a steep, exposed, Class 4 rock climb to reach the very summit. The views are wonderful all the way, and the chance of spotting mountain goats and bighorn sheep is excellent.

Distance: 1.3 miles one way from Falls Creek Trail; 4.9 miles one way from Hurricane Creek Trailhead
Hiking time: 1–3 hours from Falls Creek Trail
Difficulty: Moderate climb except for the pinnacle, which is a short but exposed Class 4. Very strenuous when considered as a hike.
Best season: July through mid-Oct
Traffic and other trail users: Generally light traffic on Falls Creek Trail; very light after leaving the trail
Canine compatibility: Dogs are permitted, but because of wildlife viewing opportunities and steep rock at the summit, they are not recommended.
Fees and permits: Northwest Forest Pass and Eagle Cap Wilderness Permit
Maximum elevation: 9,665 feet
Map: USGS Chief Joseph Mountain OR; Green Trails #475sx: Wallowa Mountains Eagle Cap Wilderness
Trail contacts: USDA Forest Service Wallowa Mountains Office, 201 E 2nd St. / PO Box 905, Joseph, OR 97846; (541) 426-5546, (541) 426-4978; www.fs.usda.gov/wallowa-whitman. Don't expect a lot of additional information.

Finding the route: Drive south from Enterprise on Hurricane Creek Road for 5 miles to the Hurricane Creek Grange Hall. Turn right (also on Hurricane Creek Road) and continue south for about another 3 miles to the road's end at the Hurricane Creek Trailhead (5,025 ft.). Hike south on Hurricane Creek Trail (1807) for 0.1 mile to the junction with the Falls Creek Trail (1807A). Turn right (west) on Falls Creek Trail and follow it for 3.2 mostly steep miles to the Legore Mine and remains of the Legore cabin at 7,950 feet elevation. The trail becomes vague as you pass the old cabin. Continue west-northwest and soon pick it up again. The vague trail climbs to a saddle, then continues west-northwest through a small valley with a stream. Then the course climbs a talus slope of granite boulders. At the top of the talus slope (8,620 ft.) the route enters a beautiful timberline basin. This spot, 3.6 miles from Hurricane Creek Trailhead, is the point where the North Ridge route to the summit of Twin Peaks (as well as the route to Sawtooth Peak) leaves the Falls Creek Trail.
GPS: Hurricane Creek Trailhead: N45 18.673' /W117 18.438'; leave Falls Creek Trail: N45 18.900'/ W117 20.704'

The Route

Hike west-southwest across the basin, allowing for a patch of small alpine trees as you go. Mountain goats and bighorn sheep are often seen here. At the far (west) side of the basin, climb the scree slope (snow in early season) to the low point on the ridgeline (9,000 ft.; GPS: N45 18.803'/ W117 21.111'). Turn left (south) and scramble uphill for about 0.15 mile, gaining approximately 100 feet of elevation.

Pinnacle at the summit of Twin Peaks.

The route bears right slightly, leaving the ridgeline to traverse its west slope, heading generally south along a faint game (mountain goat) trail. Along this traverse are a couple of tricky spots where you must cross steeply sloping areas of slippery-when-wet, volcanic mud. A fall in these spots could easily cause an injury. The mountain goats don't seem to have any trouble here, but we humans don't seem to have the

Twin Peaks Climbs/Sawtooth Peak

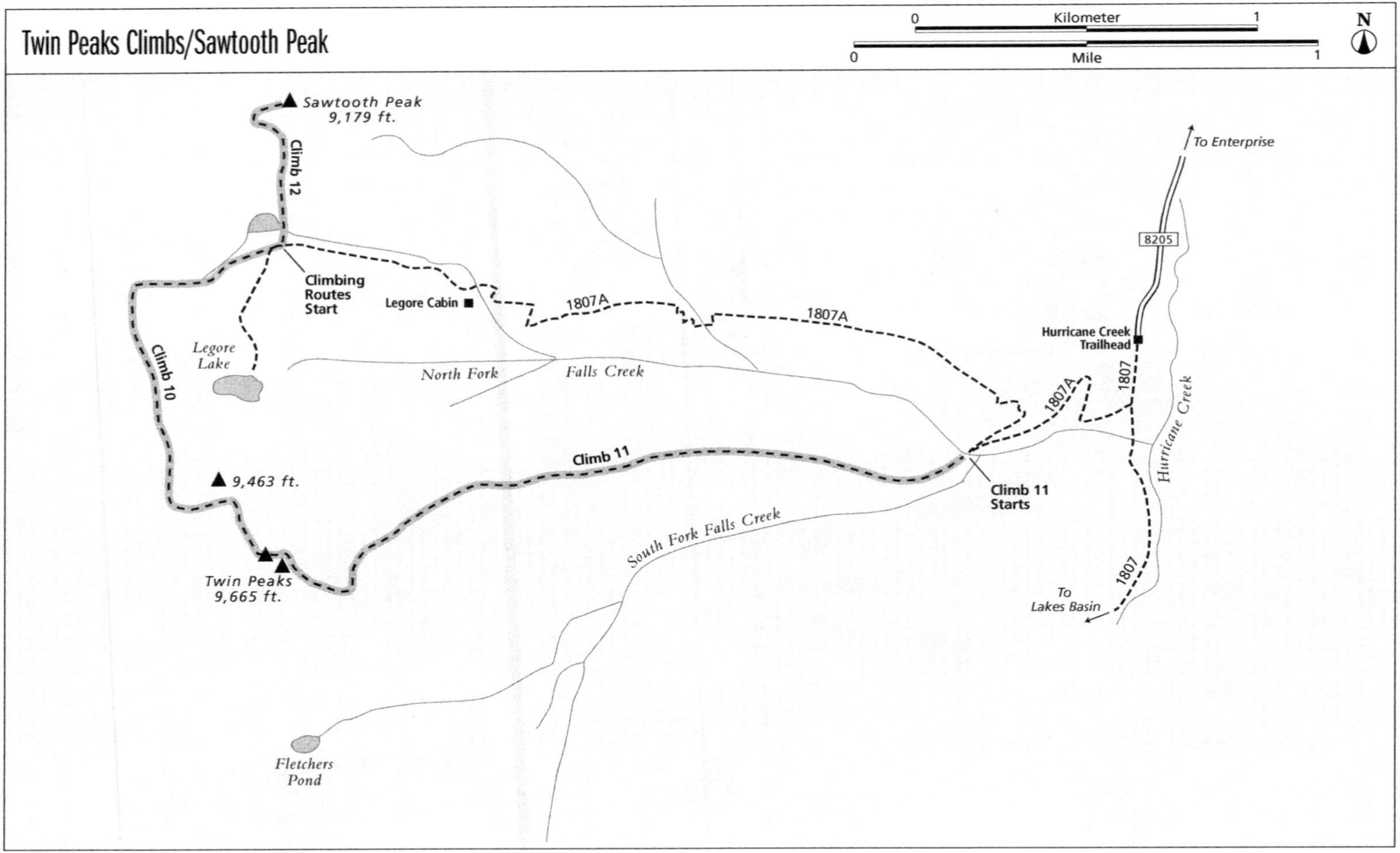

same good traction on this mud slope. Scattered whitebark pines dot the area, and far below to the right is sparkling Frances Lake. Alpine flowers are excellent here and along the ridge above in mid-July. The route follows this faint path, climbing very slightly, for about 0.5 mile.

Turn left here, leaving the path (GPS: N45 18.329'/ W117 20.959'), and climb east and very slightly north for 0.2 mile back to the ridgeline at nearly 9,500 feet elevation. On the ridgeline (GPS: N45 18.357'/ W117 20.804') turn right and climb southeast for another 0.2 mile to the base of the pinnacle. Mountain goats are often seen along this ridgeline.

Unless you are a technical rock climber, this should be your high point. The pinnacle at the top of Twin Peaks is a short but steep and exposed climb that can be dangerous. The route up the pinnacle first climbs a ledge southwest for a short distance, then turns right and heads up a shallow gully for a few feet to the knife-edge summit. Be sure that you are up to it if you try to climb the pinnacle.

Return as you came or, if time allows, make the side trip to Sawtooth Peak along the ridgeline to the northeast. You can descend from Sawtooth Peak back to the Falls Creek Trail. See Sawtooth Peak (climb 12) for information about this descent route.

Climb 11 **Twin Peaks via Falls Creek Ridge**

A steep route climbs from Falls Creek Trail to the summit of Twin Peaks, with a short, steep, exposed scramble at the top.

See map page 376.
Distance: 3 miles one way from Falls Creek Trail; 3.8 miles from Hurricane Creek Trailhead
Hiking time: 3–7 hours from Falls Creek Trail
Difficulty: Strenuous
Best season: Mid-June through Sept
Traffic and other trail users: Light foot and stock traffic on Falls Creek Trail; very light foot traffic after leaving the trail
Canine compatibility: Because of steep terrain, dogs are not advised on this route.
Fees and permits: Northwest Forest Pass and Eagle Cap Wilderness Permit
Maximum elevation: 9,665 feet
Map: USGS Chief Joseph Mountain OR
Trail contact: USDA Forest Service Wallowa Mountains Office, 201 E 2nd St./ PO Box 905, Joseph, OR 97846; (541) 426-5546, (541) 426-4978; www.fs.usda.gov/wallowa-whitman. Further information may be limited.

Finding the route: Drive south from Enterprise on Hurricane Creek Road for 5 miles to the Hurricane Creek Grange Hall. Turn right at the grange hall, leaving the pavement for about a mile, and continue south on Hurricane Creek Road 2 more miles to its end at the Hurricane Creek Trailhead. Hike south on the Hurricane Creek Trail (1807) for 0.1 mile to the junction with Falls Creek Trail (1807A). Turn right on Falls Creek Trail and hike 0.75 mile west. Falls Creek Trail makes a switchback at this point, and a rough, hard-to-spot path goes down to the North Fork of Falls Creek (5,570 ft.).
GPS: Hurricane Creek Trailhead: N45 18.673'/W117 18.438'; Falls Creek Trail junction: N45 18.596'/W117 18.412'; leave Falls Creek Trail: N45 18.537'/W117 18.921'

The Route

Drop down to the left off Falls Creek Trail and cross the North Fork Falls Creek just above the point where the North and South Forks Falls Creek join.

After crossing the creek, follow a game trail south for a short distance through a wooded area, then turn right and climb straight up a rockslide. Climb the band of moderate rock at the top of the rockslide (6,000 ft.). Above the rock band head up the prominent ridge, which divides the forks of Falls Creek. At 7,700 feet is another steep rock band. Climb this rock band and continue up the ridge to 9,110 feet. Here the ridge gets much steeper. Traverse to the left to a rib. Turn right on the rib and climb straight up to the south summit of Twin Peaks (9,646 ft.).

From the south summit traverse north, going around the smaller pinnacle between the summits on the right (east) side, to the base of the summit pinnacle. Go around the summit pinnacle on the right (east) to the north side. Then climb southwest up a

Twin Peaks via Falls Creek Ridge.

ledge to a gully. Turn right and climb the gully to the summit of Twin Peaks (9,665 ft.; GPS: N45 18.270' /W117 20.692').

Twin Peaks is one of the most prominent summits on Hurricane Divide, or in the Wallowa Mountains for that matter. It can be seen from most of the summits in the western part of the range. The summit pinnacle of Twin Peaks is composed of volcanic rock that sits uncomfortably on a softer layer of volcanic ash. The south peak slid away early in the last century. Its remains are now a jumble of boulders at the foot of Frances Lake, far below to the southwest. The present summit, which is North Twin Peak, has also partly slid away in the last few years, lowering the summit elevation by several feet.

The alpine area around Twin Peaks is a good place to observe both mountain goats and bighorn sheep, which are fairly common in this area. The view from the summit is excellent, with Frances Lake below and other high peaks in all directions.

The pinnacle of Twin Peaks is among the most difficult of the major Wallowa Mountain peaks to climb. A rope will be wanted by all but experienced and daring climbers. There may be no water available after crossing the North Fork Falls Creek.

Return as you came, or an alternate descent can be made by following the ridge north of Twin Peaks for 0.3 mile, then turning right (northeast) and dropping down the ridge just south of Legore Lake, the highest lake in the Wallowas. Then Falls Creek Trail can be followed back to Hurricane Creek Trail and Hurricane Creek Trailhead. This also makes a good ascent route. Campsites are available at Legore Lake.

Climb 12 **Sawtooth Peak**

Hike and scramble from the Falls Creek Trail, through spectacular alpine country, to the summit of Sawtooth Peak, often with mountain goats and bighorn sheep watching your progress.

See map page 376.
Distance: 0.7 mile one way from Falls Creek Trail; 4.4 miles one way from Hurricane Creek Trailhead
Hiking time: 1 hour from Falls Creek Trail
Difficulty: Easy to moderate if classified as a climb; strenuous as a hike
Best season: Mid-June through early Oct
Traffic and other trail users: Light foot traffic
Canine compatibility: Dogs are permitted without a leash as long as they are under the owner's voice control. Please don't let your dog chase the bighorn sheep or mountain goats (or any wildlife); it is illegal and can also be very dangerous for your dog and the wildlife.
Fees and permits: Northwest Forest Pass and Eagle Cap Wilderness Permit
Maximum elevation: 9,179 feet
Map: USGS Chief Joseph Mountain OR; Green Trails #475sx: Wallowa Mountains Eagle Cap Wilderness
Trail contact: USDA Forest Service Wallowa Mountains Office, 201 E 2nd St./ PO Box 905, Joseph, OR 97846; (541) 426-5546, (541) 426-4978; www.fs.usda.gov/wallowa-whitman

Finding the route: Drive south from Enterprise on Hurricane Creek Road for 5 miles to the Hurricane Creek Grange Hall. Turn right (also on Hurricane Creek Road) and continue south for about another 3 miles to the road's end at the Hurricane Creek Trailhead (5,025 ft.). Hike south on Hurricane Creek Trail (1807) for 0.1 mile to the junction with the Falls Creek Trail (1807A). Turn right (west) on Falls Creek Trail and follow it for 3.2 mostly steep miles to the Legore Mine and remains of the Legore cabin (7,950 ft.). The trail becomes vague as you pass the old cabin. Continue west-northwest and soon pick it up again. The route climbs to a saddle, then continues west-northwest through a small valley with a stream. Then the course climbs a talus slope of granite boulders. At the top of the talus slope (8,620 ft.) the route enters a beautiful timberline basin. This spot, 3.6 miles from Hurricane Creek Trailhead, is the point where the route to Sawtooth Peak leaves Falls Creek Trail.
GPS: Hurricane Creek Trailhead: N45 18.673' / W117 18.438'; leave Falls Creek Trail: N45 18.900'/ W117 20.704'

The Route

Leaving the Falls Creek Trail, the route heads north first, crossing the creek then staying on the gentle slope just right (east) of a swampy area. (This wet area is shown as a lake on some maps.) The route climbs gently for about 300 yards, rising to about 8,800 feet elevation. Then the course begins to climb more steeply, still heading north. A couple hundred yards farther, at a little over 8,900 feet, the route bears left to head northwest, on now steeper ground, for another 100 yards or so. Head west then northwest for a short distance to the ridgeline (9,040 ft.; GPS: N45 19.140'/ W117

Sawtooth Peak.

20.740'). Turn right on the ridgeline and head northeast, climbing through the boulders to the summit of Sawtooth Peak (9,179 ft.; GPS: N45 19.167'/ W117 20.680').

Take a few minutes (or hours) taking in the fabulous view from the summit before you descend as you came. Be sure to keep an eye out for mountain goats and bighorn sheep all along this route, as they are very common here.

Climb 13 Ruby Peak from the Gap

Scramble up the northwest ridge of Ruby Peak from Murray Saddle. Although this is not the easiest route to the summit of Ruby Peak, it is the most popular.

Distance: A little over 1 mile from Murray Saddle
Hiking time: 1.5–3 hours from Murray Saddle
Difficulty: Moderate if classified as a climb; strenuous as a hike
Best season: Mid-June through Sept
Traffic and other trail users: Light foot traffic only above Murray Saddle
Canine compatibility: Dogs permitted without leashes, but must be kept away from the stock of other parties. However, dogs will have a very difficult time climbing the nearly vertical terrain near the summit.
Fees and permits: Eagle Cap Wilderness Permit
Maximum elevation: 8,884 feet
Map: USGS Chief Joseph Mountain OR
Trail contact: USDA Forest Service Wallowa Mountains Office, 201 E 2nd St./PO Box 905, Joseph, OR 97846; (541) 426-5546, (541) 426-4978; www.fs.usda.gov/wallowa-whitman

Finding the route: From OR 82 in Enterprise take Hurricane Creek Road south for 2 blocks, then turn right on Fish Hatchery Road. Follow Fish Hatchery Road west for 1.2 miles to the junction with Alder Slope Road. Turn left on Alder Slope Road and drive south for 1.7 miles to the junction with Black Marble Lane. Turn right (really straight ahead) on Black Marble Lane and follow it for 1.8 miles to the junction with Lime Quarry Road. Turn left on Lime Quarry Road and go 2.1 miles to a wide spot in the road, where a couple of vehicles can park on the right. This is the trailhead for the Bill George Trail (5,580 ft.). Hike the Bill George Trail up the small draw to the right (west), then to the south for 2.5 miles to Murray Saddle (aka the Gap). The route to the summit of Ruby Peak begins at Murray Saddle.
GPS: Bill George Trailhead: N45 22.677'/W117 21.090'; Murray Saddle: N45 22.094'/W117 21.963'

The Route

Head left (southeast) at the saddle, cross the ditch, and climb on the right side of the ridgeline, following the faint bighorn sheep path. The route works its way up through rock outcroppings to the bottom of a large rock band. This band blocks the ridgeline route to all but technical rock climbers.

Traverse to the right at the bottom of the rock band for 400 yards. Here a break in the band makes for a fairly easy scramble back to the ridgeline. After regaining the ridge, follow it to the southeast to the summit (8,884 ft.; GPS: N45 21.196'/W117 21.275').

Just before reaching the summit, the route is to the right of and slightly below the ridgeline. Watch for bighorn sheep on this route. There is no water after leaving the Gap.

Ruby Peak from the Gap/Ruby Peak via Silver Creek/ Ruby Peak via South Ridge

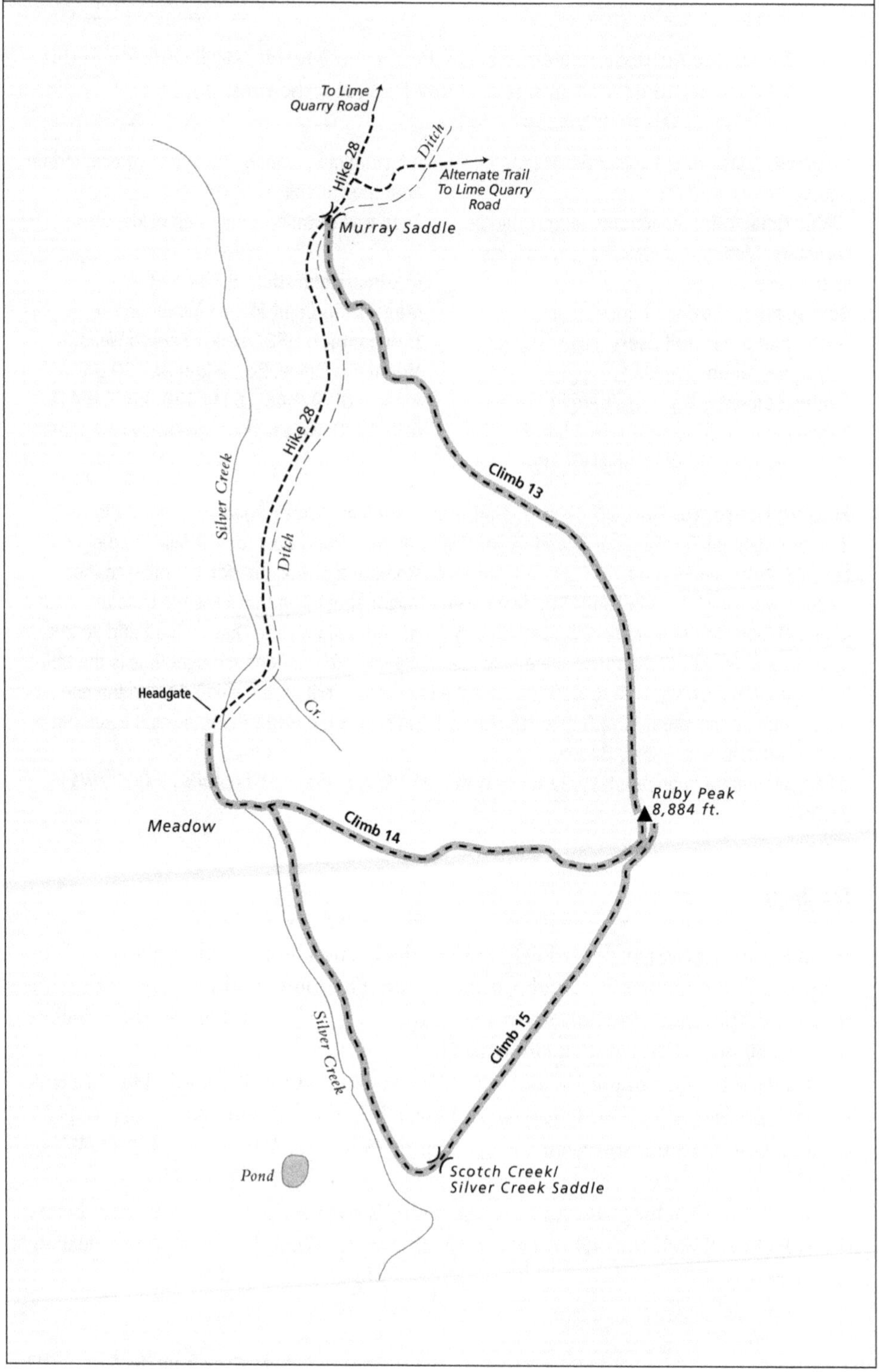

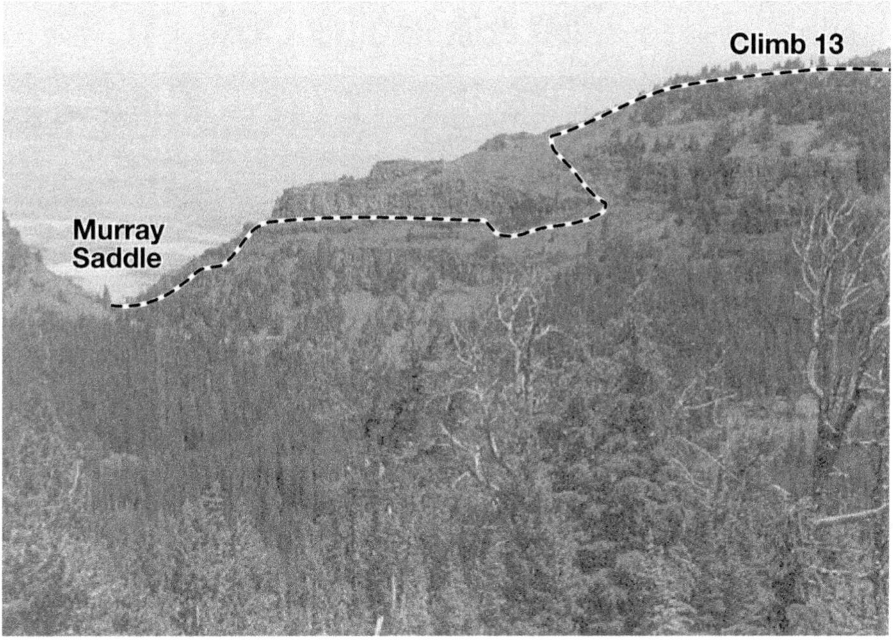

Northwest ridge of Ruby Peak.

The easiest return route is via South Ridge. To descend the South Ridge (really south-southwest), traverse around the rock outcropping on the left side. Then regain the ridgeline and follow it to the saddle between the Silver Creek and Scotch Creek drainages (GPS: N45 20.669' /W117 21.719'). There are game trails most of the way down this ridge. Turn right in the saddle and descend along Silver Creek, heading north-northwest for about 1.5 miles to where the creek intersects the Silver Creek Ditch. Then follow the Silver Creek Ditch north for 1 mile to Murray Saddle. From the saddle return to the trailhead as you came.

Climb 14 **Ruby Peak via Silver Creek**

A steep but short scramble leads from Silver Creek Ditch to the summit of Ruby Peak.

See map page 384.
Distance: 0.75 mile one way from Silver Creek Ditch
Hiking time: 1.5–3 hours from Silver Creek Ditch
Difficulty: Moderate to strenuous
Best season: Mid-June through Oct
Traffic and other trail users: Light foot and stock traffic to the upper end of Silver Creek Ditch; light foot traffic past there
Canine compatibility: Dogs permitted without leashes, but must be kept away from the stock of other parties
Fees and permits: Eagle Cap Wilderness Permit
Maximum elevation: 8,884 feet
Map: USGS Chief Joseph Mountain OR
Trail contact: USDA Forest Service Wallowa Mountains Office, 201 E 2nd St./ PO Box 905, Joseph, OR 97846; (541) 426-5546, (541) 426-4978; www.fs.usda.gov/wallowa-whitman. Further information may be limited.

Finding the route: From OR 82 in Enterprise take Hurricane Creek Road south for 2 blocks, then turn right on Fish Hatchery Road. Follow Fish Hatchery Road west for 1.2 miles to the junction with Alder Slope Road. Turn left on Alder Slope Road and drive south for 1.7 miles to the junction with Black Marble Lane. Turn right (really straight ahead) on Black Marble Lane and follow it for 1.8 miles to the junction with Lime Quarry Road. Turn left on Lime Quarry Road and go 2.1 miles to a wide spot in the road, where a couple of vehicles can park on the right. This is the trailhead for the Bill George Trail (5,580 ft.). Hike the Bill George Trail up the small draw to the right (west), then to the south for 2.5 miles to Murray Saddle (aka the Gap). From the saddle hike 1 mile south along the Silver Creek Ditch to its upper end, where this route begins (7,320 ft.).
GPS: Bill George Trailhead: N45 22.677' / W117 21.090'; south end of Silver Creek Ditch: N45 21.487' / W117 22.108'

The Route

The route leaves Silver Creek Ditch at the headgate, where the ditch gets its water out of Silver Creek, and goes up the right side of Silver Creek. The route enters a meadow 0.25 mile after leaving the ditch. There is a good campsite in the trees next to the meadow (7,400 ft.; GPS: N45 21.402' / W117 22.102'). At the meadow cross Silver Creek and head east up through the timber. The route climbs over a couple of benches to the open scree slope leading to the summit of Ruby Peak (8,884 ft.; GPS: N45 21.196' / W117 21.275').

This route to the summit of Ruby Peak requires some navigational skills. It will be necessary to work around a few rock outcroppings near the summit. There is a fairly steep scree slope for the last 800 vertical feet, which can be a problem for the inexperienced off-trail hiker. An easier but slightly longer descent can be made

Ruby Peak.

by using South Ridge route. To descend the South Ridge (really south-southwest), traverse around the rock outcropping on the left side. Then regain the ridgeline and follow it to the saddle between the Silver Creek and Scotch Creek drainages (GPS: N45 20.669' / W117 21.719'). There are game trails most of the way down this ridge. Turn right in the saddle and descend along Silver Creek, heading north-northwest for about 1.5 miles to where the creek intersects the Silver Creek Ditch. Then follow the Silver Creek Ditch north for 1 mile to Murray Saddle. From the saddle return to the trailhead as you came.

Climb 15 **Ruby Peak via South Ridge**

This off-trail hike climbs from the upper end of Silver Creek Ditch to the summit of Ruby Peak. This is the easiest, but also the longest, route to the summit.

See map page 384.

Distance: 2 miles one way from upper end of Silver Creek Ditch
Hiking time: 1.5–3 hours from upper end of Silver Creek Ditch
Difficulty: Easy to moderate if classified as a climb; strenuous as a hike
Best season: Mid-June through Oct
Traffic and other trail users: Light foot and stock traffic to the meadows above the upper end of Silver Creek Ditch; light foot traffic above there
Canine compatibility: Dogs permitted without leashes, but must be kept away from the stock of other parties. This is the best way to take your dog to the summit of Ruby Peak.
Fees and permits: Eagle Cap Wilderness Permit
Maximum elevation: 8,884 feet
Map: USGS Chief Joseph Mountain OR
Trail contact: USDA Forest Service Wallowa Mountains Office, 201 E 2nd St./PO Box 905, Joseph, OR 97846; (541) 426-5546, (541) 426-4978; www.fs.usda.gov/wallowa-whitman. Further information will probably be limited.

Finding the route: From OR 82 in Enterprise take Hurricane Creek Road south for 2 blocks, then turn right on Fish Hatchery Road. Follow Fish Hatchery Road west for 1.2 miles to the junction with Alder Slope Road. Turn left on Alder Slope Road and drive south for 1.7 miles to the junction with Black Marble Lane. Turn right (really straight ahead) on Black Marble Lane and follow it for 1.8 miles to the junction with Lime Quarry Road. Turn left on Lime Quarry Road and go 2.1 miles to a wide spot in the road, where a couple of vehicles can park on the right. This is the trailhead for the Bill George Trail (5,580 ft.). Hike the Bill George Trail up the small draw to the right (west), then to the south for 2.5 miles to Murray Saddle (aka the Gap). From the saddle follow the Silver Creek Ditch for 1 mile to its upper end, where the ditch takes its water out of Silver Creek.
GPS: Bill George Trailhead: N45 22.677'/W117 21.090'; route leaves Silver Creek Ditch: N45 21.487'/W117 22.108'

The Route

From the end of the ditch, follow Silver Creek upstream on a faint path on the right side of the creek. Go past the meadow 0.25 mile above the end of the ditch. Continue on up Silver Creek and pass through another meadow.

Above the second meadow climb steeply, following the main fork of Silver Creek to the southeast to a large, open timberline basin (8,200 ft.). A small side stream, sometimes dry, enters Silver Creek from the west as you climb above the meadow and before you reach the timberline basin. A short distance up this side stream is a pond with a few fairly good campsites near it. As soon as you enter the basin, bear left (east) and climb over a small rise for 0.1 mile to the saddle between Silver Creek drainage and Scotch Creek drainage.

At the saddle (GPS: N45 20.669' /W117 21.719') turn left and follow a faint along the right side of the ridge to the northeast to the summit (8,884 ft; GPS: 1 21.196' /W117 21.275'). It will be necessary to traverse along the right side of t ridgeline to avoid climbing over some rock outcroppings. This is the easiest route t follow when climbing or descending Ruby Peak.

The path from the Silver Creek and Scotch Creek saddle to the summit is a main route that bighorn sheep use when they travel from their winter range on lower Sheep Ridge to their higher summer range. The whole Wallowa Valley can be seen from the summit, as can the north end of Wallowa Lake.

Return via the same route.

…16 China Cap

…e leads from China Ridge Trail to the summit of China Cap.

…nce: 0.5 mile one way from China Ridge …il
Hiking time: About 45 minutes from China Ridge Trail
Difficulty: Easy to moderate
Best season: July through Sept
Traffic and other trail users: Moderate foot and horse traffic on the trails; light foot traffic on the route to the summit
Canine compatibility: Dogs permitted without leashes, but must be kept away from the stock of other parties
Fees and permits: Eagle Cap Wilderness Permit
Maximum elevation: 8,656 feet
Map: USGS China Cap OR
Trail contact: USDA Forest Service Wallowa Mountains Office, 201 E 2nd St./ PO Box 905, Joseph, OR 97846; (541) 426-5546, (541) 426-4978; www.fs.usda.gov/wallowa-whitman; or USDA Forest Service Pine Field Office, 38470 Pine Town Ln., Halfway, OR 97834; (541) 742-7511. Office closed Dec 21 through Apr 30; contact Baker City office at (541) 523-6391.

Finding the route: From Union drive 11.5 miles southeast on OR 203 to the junction with FR 7785. Turn left on FR 7785 and go 4 miles to the junction with FR 7787. Turn right on FR 7787 and drive 3.7 miles, then turn left onto the Buck Creek Trailhead access road. Go 0.3 mile to Buck Creek Trailhead. From the trailhead follow Elk Creek Trail (1944) for 3.8 miles to the junction with China Ridge Trail (1906). Turn left on China Ridge Trail and hike 0.7 mile to a saddle. The route up the west ridge of China Cap leaves China Ridge Trail in this saddle 0.5 mile northwest of the peak. Turn right off the trail at the Eagle Cap Wilderness boundary sign in the saddle (7,830 ft.).
GPS: Buck Creek Trailhead: N45 08.919'/W117 34.340'; leave China Ridge Trail: N45 09.434'/W117 31.095'

The Route

From the saddle the route heads up the ridge to the east, staying just to the right of the ridgeline, or by climbing the path just to the left of the ridge for 200 yards, then crossing the ridgeline. After climbing a couple hundred yards, a path traverses slightly to the right. Take this path for 200 yards, then climb to the left, back to the ridge. Turn right on the ridge and head up just to the right of the ridgeline.

There are high cliffs on the other (north) side of the ridge. Traverse on the right side just below the rock outcroppings. Turn left and climb up through the break in the outcropping on a grassy slope. Once on the ridgeline again, turn right and climb through a few small whitebark pines to the summit of China Cap (8,656 ft.; GPS: N45 09.349'/W117 30.595').

This is a 30- to 45-minute climb from the saddle. From the summit the higher peaks of the north-central Wallowa Mountains come into view to the east and

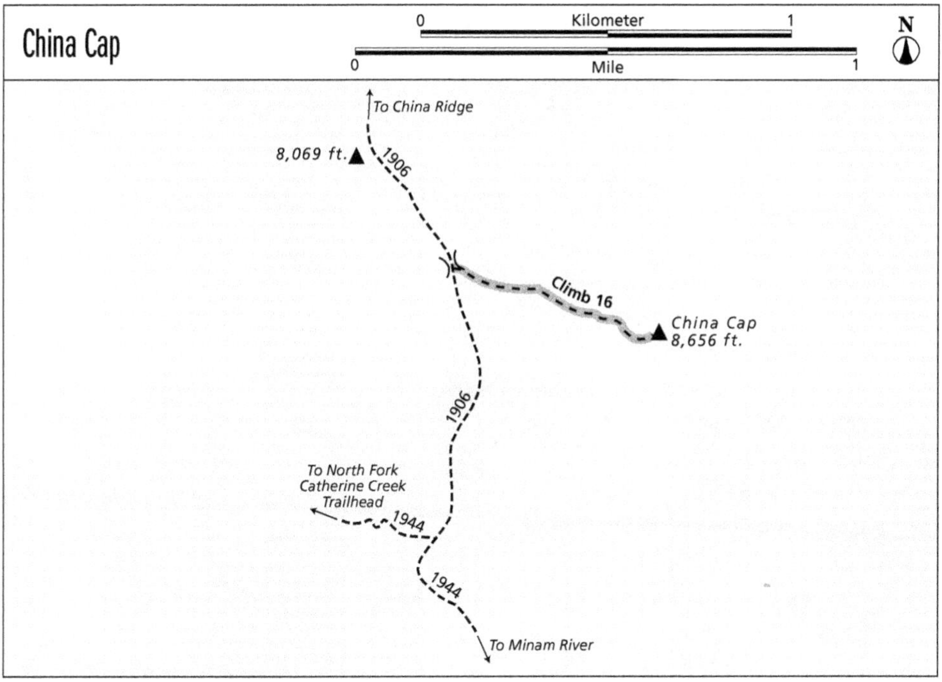

northeast. There are many peaks in view, but Twin Peaks to the northeast and Aneroid Mountain to the east stand out and are easy to identify.

Return by the same route.

Appendix A: For More Information

USDA Forest Service
Wallowa Mountains Office
201 E 2nd St./PO Box 905
Joseph, OR 97846
(541) 426-5546; (541) 426-4978
www.fs.usda.gov/wallowa-whitman

USDA Forest Service
Pine Ranger Station, Pine Ranger District
General Delivery
Halfway, OR 97834
(541) 742-7511
www.fs.usda.gov/wallowa-whitman

For flights to the Horse Ranch or Minam Lodge
Spence Air Service
PO Box 217
Enterprise, OR 97828
(541) 426-3288

To help with trail maintenance
Wallowa Mountains Hells Canyon Trail Association (WMHCTA)
401 NE First St., Ste. A
Enterprise, OR 97828
www.wmhcta.org
E-mail: info@wmhcta.org
Or visit on Facebook.

Wing Ridge Ski Tours
500 N River St.
Enterprise, OR 97828
(541) 398-1980; (888) 812-4707, ext. 3
www.facebook.com/Wing-Ridge-Ski-Tours-239313479446588

Appendix B: Glossary

Blaze: A mark on a tree formed by cutting away a small section of bark with a hatchet or ax. There may be one or two marks. Blazes can usually be seen some distance ahead.

Braided trail: A section of trail formed by two or more interconnecting paths. Not to be confused with cattle trails, which do not necessarily return to the main trail.

Cairn: A stack or pile of rocks that marks the trail or route.

Cirque: A glacier-carved bowl in a mountain, usually at the head of a valley, canyon, or gully.

Clear-cut: An area that has been logged of all its timber.

Complete burn: An area where all the trees were killed by a forest fire.

Gully: A trench in the ground, smaller than a canyon. It may be steep and may or may not have a stream in it.

Jeep road: A road that is impassable for most two-wheel-drive vehicles. Roads may be blocked and closed to motor vehicles.

Notch: Naturally carved-out sections of a ridge, much smaller than a saddle, with rock outcroppings on both sides.

Outcropping: Bedrock protruding through the surface of the ground.

Partial burn: An area where a forest fire killed some, but not all, of the trees.

Pika: A small mammal that lives in steep, rocky areas or talus slopes. Pikas are related to rabbits and do not hibernate.

Red digger: A species of ground squirrel.

Ridgeline: The top of a ridge; may slope steeply.

Saddle: The low point of a ridge, usually gently sloping. Much larger than a notch.

Scree: Loose rock on a slope. Rocks in a scree slope are smaller than the rocks on a talus slope. May be tiring to climb.

Semi-switchback: A tight corner (120 degrees or less) in a trail.

Small stream: A stream 2 feet wide or less; smaller than a creek or stream. May dry up in late summer or fall.

Spur ridge: A smaller ridge protruding off the main ridge. May be quite steep.

Switchback: A tight corner (more than 120 degrees) in a trail where the trail turns back on itself as it traverses a hill. Allows hikers to negotiate steep slopes.

Talus slope: A slope covered with large rocks or boulders.

Tiny stream: A stream less than 1 foot wide. Usually dry in fall.

Traverse: The crossing of a slope, climbing or descending, but usually in a nearly straight line. This term is also used to describe a route or trail that follows a fairly flat ridgeline.

Hike/Climb Index

Hikes

Climbs

About the Author

A native Oregonian, Fred Barstad developed a keen interest in the remote high country of his state when he was young. As a teenager in the 1960s, Barstad roamed the Cascade Range in search of lakes to fish and peaks to climb. This search soon became an addiction for "bagging peaks." Barstad has climbed all the major Cascade peaks in Oregon, many of them several times, including sixty-three climbs to the summit of Mount Hood.

Barstad eventually developed a desire to climb mountains outside of Oregon, which took him to Mount Rainier in Washington, 20,320-foot-high Mount McKinley in Alaska, Aconcagua in Argentina, and Popocatépetl and Citlaltépetl in Mexico.

Ever since he saw the Wallowa Mountains on a family vacation in 1961, Barstad has spent many years exploring, hunting, and fishing the canyons and peaks of this range. In 1987 he moved to Enterprise, Oregon, and began exploring the vast wild area of Eagle Cap Wilderness. He soon recognized a need for a guidebook to this spectacular area and eventually sold his business interest in the Wallowa Lake Marina to devote all of his attention to writing hiking books.

Barstad has hiked all the trails and routes featured in this book, nearly 1,500 miles' worth. He hopes that *Hiking Oregon's Eagle Cap Wilderness* will promote more interest in helping to preserve its pristine quality.

CPSIA information can be obtained
at www.ICGtesting.com
Printed in the USA
BVHW041357220221
600435BV00011B/2

9 781493 043767